Lecture Notes in Artificial Intelligence   5603

Edited by R. Goebel, J. Siekmann, and W. Wahlster

Subseries of Lecture Notes in Computer Science

T0238835

Zygmunt Vetulani   Hans Uszkoreit (Eds.)

Human Language Technology

Challenges of the Information Society

Third Language and Technology Conference, LTC 2007
Poznań, Poland, October 5-7, 2007
Revised Selected Papers

 Springer

Series Editors

Randy Goebel, University of Alberta, Edmonton, Canada
Jörg Siekmann, University of Saarland, Saarbrücken, Germany
Wolfgang Wahlster, DFKI and University of Saarland, Saarbrücken, Germany

Volume Editors

Zygmunt Vetulani
Adam Mickiewicz University Poznań
Faculty of Mathematics and Computer Science
Umultowska 87
61614 Poznań, Poland
E-mail: vetulani@amu.edu.pl

Hans Uszkoreit
German Research Center for Artificial Intelligence (DFKI)
Language Technology Lab
Campus D 3 1, Stuhlsatzenhausweg 3
66123 Saarbrücken, Germany
E-mail: uszkoreit@dfki.de

Library of Congress Control Number: 2009933613

CR Subject Classification (1998): H.2.5, I.2.1, I.2.7, H.5.2, F.4.2, I.5, I.2

LNCS Sublibrary: SL 7 – Artificial Intelligence

ISSN   0302-9743
ISBN-10   3-642-04234-1 Springer Berlin Heidelberg New York
ISBN-13   978-3-642-04234-8 Springer Berlin Heidelberg New York

springer.com

© Springer-Verlag Berlin Heidelberg 2009
Printed in Germany

Typesetting: Camera-ready by author, data conversion by Scientific Publishing Services, Chennai, India
Printed on acid-free paper   SPIN: 1274607   06/3180   5 4 3 2 1 0

Preface

Half a century ago not many people had realized that a new epoch in the history of homo sapiens had just started. The term "Information Society Age" seems an appropriate name for this epoch.

Communication was without a doubt a lever of the conquest of the human race over the rest of the animate world. There is little doubt that the human race began when our predecessors started to communicate with each other using language. This highly abstract means of communication was probably one of the major factors contributing to the evolutionary success of the human race within the animal world. Physically weak and imperfect, humans started to dominate the rest of the world through the creation of communication-based societies where individuals communicated initially to satisfy immediate needs, and then to create, accumulate and process knowledge for future use.

The crucial step in the history of humanity was the invention of writing. It is worth noting that writing is a human invention, not a phenomenon resulting from natural evolution. Humans invented writing as a technique for recording speech as well as for storing and facilitating the dissemination of knowledge across the world. Humans continue to be born illiterate, and therefore teaching and conscious supervised learning is necessary to maintain this basic social skill. The invention of writing and the resulting writing-based civilizations based on know-how accumulation stimulated the development of ever more sophisticated technologies created in tune with the laws of nature and based on ever better understanding of these laws. It must be recognized, however, that many of these inventions were accidental and there is no evidence that they were in any way necessary (i.e., they might simply not have happened). The development of technologies and the production of artifacts now seems be beyond the control of any individual, group or organization. This remark is especially valid for the so-called intelligent technologies characteristic of the current epoch which merits the name Information Society Age.

The incipient Information Society is a novel kind of social structure where humans will be surrounded by a new generation of information-rich artifacts and technologies designed to collaborate with human users. Their main role will be to augment the cognitive capabilities of their owners by extending their information resources, memories, knowledge and perception. A central component of this augmented cognition is the preprocessing of huge volumes of information with the goal of exploiting it effectively for improved decision making. Although the new technologies may not be able to fully simulate human intelligence in the foreseeable future, they will certainly exceed human performance in many essential tasks just as they are already outperforming people in memory, search and numeric calculation. Artifacts made by humans "in their own image" will be intended to communicate with them.

This emerging Information Society will probably be characterized by the use of Human Language Technologies which contribute to a world where humans need to communicate not only with each other but also with the artificially created interactive and autonomous technological environment—collaborative, but possibly also hostile.

The history of human civilization tells us that humanity evolves in ways which are barely under control and which are difficult to anticipate. This development is stimulated by the human need to rise to ever greater challenges. We claim that proper development of Human Language Technologies is one of such challenges and we hope that picking up the gauntlet will result in a better, cleverer and happier world.

Human Language Technologies are already in daily use in many areas of human life. Machine translation assists Web users and human translators. Spell and grammar checkers help people to write well-formed texts. Automated telephone dialogues enable information access and transactions outside of business hours. Powerful search engines facilitate the gathering of information from the WWW. The users of these technologies still complain about ridiculous translation errors, communication deadlocks with automated call center agents and incorrect warnings of their grammar checkers.

However, the technologies keep improving at a fast pace. New exciting application areas are explored such as the analysis of opinions in Web fora and discussion groups, the automatic construction of multiple choice questions for educational testing and voice interfaces to all kinds of machinery. We may now already safely predict that in the future every new technology that is put in service will have to master human language—the most powerful and most natural communication medium of mankind.

However, during its evolution and steady adaptation to the needs of its users human language has developed properties that make it well suited for human use but especially unsuited for processing on today's digital computers. The logical complexity of human language, its omnipresent ambiguity, its vagueness and its intricate interplay of regularities and exceptions are serious obstacles to a straightforward formal modeling of the human language proficiency. Do we have to understand all the hidden regularities behind this central cognitive faculty or can we build systems that can learn these principles without understanding any of them such as toddlers, when they acquire their language through interaction?

To make the task even harder, our race does not have only one language. How can we blame technology for not mastering our language if we ourselves cannot speak and understand most of the 2,000 plus languages of the world? The multilingual global society poses another grand challenge to human language technologies. If we want to preserve the multicultural setup of our globalizing world, all surviving languages need to be supported by information technology.

Another central challenge is the different modalities of language (speech, writing, signing) and the integration of language with other media of communication such as gestures, facial expressions, pictures and films. Each of the media and modi requires different techniques for encoding and processing that need to interact with the processing of language.

A last challenge to be mentioned here is the combination of human language technologies with a new generation of knowledge technologies, which are nowadays often called semantic technologies. The technological avant-garde of the World-Wide Web has gathered behind the powerful vision of a Semantic Web, a Web 3.0 that does connect the contents of the global information infrastructure by their shape or by stipulated hyperlinks but by their true meanings. The resulting Web could answer difficult questions and permit services based on complex inferences. To this end, powerful Web-suited knowledge representation languages have been designed. Language technology is expected to play an essential role in upgrading today's Web to version 3.0 by extracting the knowledge from texts into some structured representation suited for transformation into the Semantic Web languages.

This brief description of the main challenges for Human Language Technologies shows the complexity and diversity of the field. None of the practitioners and users of human language can keep up with the wide scope of developments in the field. This book is a snapshot of this dynamic evolution. It assembles recent results in a variety of subfields that have been selected for wider publication.

In the volume the reader will find 40 papers which are the extended and updated versions of selected papers presented at the Third Language and Technology Conference. The selection was made from the 105 high-quality technical contributions (written by 275 authors) accepted on the basis of anonymous peer reviewing for conference presentation by the international jury. The editors basically followed the ranking established on the ground of reviewers' assessments. We are conscious of the sometimes subjective character of our decisions. We are also conscious that in some cases very interesting and promising papers were left out of the selection, especially where they referred to on-going projects or contributed interesting but partial or over-technical solutions. These 40 selected papers represent the considerable effort of 106 authors from Australia, Estonia, France, Germany, Italy, Japan, Mexico, Poland, Portugal, Romania, Slovenia, Spain, Sweden, Tunisia, Turkey, UK and USA.

For the convenience of the reader we have "structured" this book into thematic chapters. Assigning papers to chapters was a difficult task, as in most cases they addressed more than one thematic issue, so some of our decisions may look arbitrary. This is due to the obvious fact that language processing shares one common feature with language itself: it is complex and multidimensional. In particular there is no natural ordering of the thematic chapters we have proposed except perhaps the order in which a humans appear to process language production in a linguistic communication act, i.e., starting with (spoken) speech analysis, through morphology etc. To follow this natural order we start the volume with the Speech Processing chapter. Within chapters the papers are presented in alphabetical order with respect to the first author name.

Contributions have been grouped into eight chapters. These are:

1. Speech Processing (6)
2. Computational Morphology (3)
3. Parsing and Generation (9)
4. Computational Semantics (5)
5. Digital Language Resources (6)
6. WordNet (3)
7. Information Retrieval/Extraction (5)
8. Machine Translation (3)

The first chapter, Speech Processing, starts with a paper that discusses a solution to the practical problem of automatically detecting the start and end points of broadcast news (Amaral, Trancoso). It is followed by a contribution describing a method of speech feature extraction using morphological signal processing (Drgas, Dabrowski). Next comes an article contributing to the development of a spoken language interface (European Portuguese) for mobile devices (Freitas, Calado, Barros, Sales Dias). The next paper is about a bilingual—Spanish, Valentian—speech recognition system (Luján-Mares, Martínez-Hinarejos, Alabau). The fifth paper in this chapter is a presentation of a project aiming at an annotated speech corpus of spoken dialogues for Polish (Mykowiecka, Marasek, Marciniak, Rabiega-Wiśniewska, Gubrynowicz). The chapter closes with a report on the spoken corpus research resulting with triphone statistics for Polish (Ziółko, Gałka, Manandhar, Wilson, Ziółko).

In the Computational Morphology chapter, the reader will find three papers. The first one is a description of a morphological generator for Romanian word forms out of lemmas and morpho-lexical descriptions, initially designed to serve MT purposes (Irimia). The next paper in this chapter presents a set of tools for the morphological pre-processing of Polish texts in order to obtain "a reasonable input" for further processing (e.g., parsing) (Sagot). Although for most of highly inflected Indo European languages the problem of the formal description of their morphology have been solved and resources and tools exist, the next paper, the last one in this part, presents an alternative approach consisting in application of relational data-base methodology (Woliński).

The Parsing and Generation chapter is dominated by contributions to parsing. It opens with a proposal to use the idea of spreadsheets to represent parse tree forests in a human-readable form (Bień). The next contribution shows how to use a robust deep parser to solve named entity metonymy (Brun, Ehrmann, Jacquet). It is followed by a contribution presenting an application of shallow parsing used as a morphological disambiguation engine (Buczyński, Przepiórkowski). The fourth contribution proposes an object-oriented technique of text generation aimed at NLG designers who are not specialists in computational linguistics (Cullen, O'Neill, Hanna). The fifth paper is a contribution to the study of the relationship between the analogies of form between chunks and corresponding analogies of meanings (for Japanese) (Lepage, Migeot, Guillerm). Another application of shallow parsing as a disfluency detector in transcribed

Estonian speech is described in the next paper (Müürisep, Nigol). The next paper is again an application of a parser, this time to perform lexical corrections (Nicolas, Sagot, Molinero, Farré, de la Clergerie). This is followed by a presentation of two parsers based on recursive transition nets with a string output together with a scrupulous efficiency considerations (Sastre-Martínez, Forcada). Finally the reader will find a description of a deep parser for Polish based on Syntactical Groups Grammar (Suszczańska, Szmal, Simiński).

The first of the five papers in the Computational Semantics chapter is about using supervised learning techniques to augment a semantically complex lexicon of texts with sentimental valence (Argamon, Bloom, Esuli, Sebastiani). The second one deals with the problem of the evaluation of text readability, i.e., automatic identification of easy-to-read fragments in a text corpus, which seems to have important practical potential (vor der Brück, Hartrumpf). Another application with a possible practical importance is the tagger for temporal expressions described in the next paper (Mazur, Dale). The data mining techniques of detecting the sequential structure of texts for text segmentation purposes are described in the fourth paper in this section (Recanati, Rogovski, Bennani). The last paper describes a machine learning-based algorithm of anaphora resolution for Turkish (Yıldırım, Kılıçaslan, Yıldız).

We have included six papers in the Digital Language Resources chapter. These are contributions concerning tools, methodology and resources. The chapter starts with the proposal of a graphical tool to query highly formalized lexical resources observing the LFM standard (Ben Abderrahmen, Gargouri, Jmaiel). The next paper is about the acquisition of new terminology with special attention to parallel corpora as a source (Dura, Gawronska). The third contribution in this chapter presents a system for a text corpus construction using the Internet (Kulików). The fourth paper is about the methodology of building an important grammatical resource for English, namely a lexicon-grammar of predicative nouns (Malik, Royauté). (This is one of the rare examples of an important research topic on a language where English so far has been less profoundly investigated than some other languages—e.g., French.) A large-scale terminological lexicon in biology supporting text mining and information extraction application is presented in the fifth paper (Quochi, Del Gratta, Sassolini, Bartolini, Monachini, Calzolari). The chapter closes with a contribution on extracting Romanian verbo-nominal collocations from large tagged and annotated corpora (Todirascu, Gledhill, Stefanescu).

The WordNet-related chapter has three contributions. The first is about extending English WordNet with morphosemantic links to aid automatic reasoning with Wordnet (Fellbaum, Osherson, Clark). The remaining two contributions in this chapter are about two different approaches for constructing wordnets. In the first, the author proposes a method for the automatic construction of a wordnet for Slovenian through the use of a multilingual parallel corpus (the Orwell Corpus) and several wordnets (Fišer). The second paper presents a completely different approach: an algorithm for the manual construction of a wordnet (designed and first used for Polish but in fact language-independent for a large class of Indo European languages) using classical monolingual dictionaries (Vetulani, Walkowska, Obrębski, Marciniak, Konieczka, Rzepecki).

The Information Retrieval and/or Extraction chapter opens with a paper on the identification of knowledge about terms in specialized texts using definition extraction techniques (Alarcón, Sierra, Bach) . The next paper describes a hybrid method for extracting pairs of similar terms from Japanese documents (Fukumoto, Suzuki). The next three papers are contributions to name identification in texts, which appears to be an important issue in the IR/IE field. The first focuses on the problem of proper name search on a noisy and difficult data set (Miller, Arehart), the second considers string distance measures for name lemmatization (Piskorski, Sydow, Wieloch), whereas the third is about the identification of co-reference of person names, which may be useful for people search tasks (Popescu, Magnini).

Finally, we have included three papers·in the Machine Translation chapter. The first one is a contribution to the problem, often marginalized, of hapaxes in text alignment (Lardilleux, Lepage). The second is about a statistical machine translation from Slovenian to English (Maučec, Brest). In the last paper the authors propose a method of translation of English nominal compounds into Polish and Internet-based validation of translation output (Stępień, Podlejski).

July 2009   Zygmunt Vetulani
                                                             Hans Uszkoreit

Committee Listings

Organizing Committee

Zygmunt Vetulani - Conference Chair
Filip Graliński
Paweł Konieczka
Maciej Lison
Jacek Marciniak
Tomasz Obrębski
Jędrzej Osiński
Justyna Walkowska
   (All at the Adam Mickiewicz University, Poznań, Poland)

Program Committee

Victoria Arranz
Anja Belz
Janusz S. Bień
Christian Boitet
Leonard Bolc
Nicoletta Calzolari
Nick Campbell
Julie Carson-Berndsen
Khalid Choukri
Adam Dąbrowski
Grażyna Demenko
Elżbieta Dura
Katarzyna
   Dziubalska-Kołaczyk
Tomaz Erjavec
Cedrick Fairon
Christiane Fellbaum
Maria Gavrilidou
Aleksander Gerd

Dafydd Gibbon
Stefan Grocholewski
Franz Guenthner
Roland Hausser
Wacław Iszkowski
Margaret King
Orest Kossak
Eric Laporte
Gerard Ligozat
Natalia Loukachevitch
Wiesław Lubaszewski
Bente Maegaard
Joseph Mariani
Jacek Martinek
Václav Matousek
Keith J. Miller
Nicholas Ostler
Karel Pala
Pavel S. Pankov

Marcin Paprzycki
Patrick Paroubek
Emil Pływaczewski
Adam Przepiórkowski
Reinhard Rapp
Mike Rosner
Justus Roux
Vasile Rus
Frédérique Ségond
Włodzimierz Sobkowiak
Marek Świdziński
Ryszard Tadeusiewicz
Dan Tufiş
Hans Uszkoreit
Zygmunt Vetulani
Piek Vossen
Tom Wachtel
Jan Węglarz
Richard Zuber

Table of Contents

III   Parsing and Generation

IV   Computational Semantics

V Digital Language Resources

VI WordNet

VII   Information Retrieval/Extraction

VIII   Machine Translation

Exploring the Structure of Broadcast News for Topic Segmentation

Rui Amaral[1,2,3] and Isabel Trancoso[1,3]

[1] Instituto Superior Técnico
[2] Instituto Politécnico de Setúbal
[3] L^2F - Spoken Language Systems Lab, INESC-ID
Portugal
ramaral@est.ips.pt, Isabel.Trancoso@inesc-id.pt

Abstract. This paper describes our on-going work toward the improvement of Broadcast News story segmentation module. We have tried to improve our baseline algorithm by further exploring the typical structure of a broadcast news show, first by training a CART and then by integrating it in a 2-stage algorithm that is able to deal with shows with double anchors. In order to deal with shows with a thematic anchor, a more complex approach is adopted including a topic classification stage. The automatic segmentation is currently being compared with the manual segmentation done by a professional media watch company. The results are very promising so far, specially taking into account that no video information is used.

Keywords: Topic segmentation.

1 Introduction

Topic segmentation is one of the main blocks of the prototype system for Broadcast News (BN) processing developed at the Spoken language Systems Lab of INESC-ID. This system integrates several core technologies, in a pipeline architecture (Fig. 1):

- jingle detection (JD) for excluding areas with publicity;
- audio pre-processing (APP) which aims at speech/non-speech classification, gender and background conditions classification, speaker clustering, and anchor identification;
- automatic speech recognition (ASR) that converts the segments classified as speech into text;
- punctuation and capitalization (Pu/Ca);
- topic segmentation (TS) which splits the broadcast news show into constituent stories and topic indexation (TI) which assigns one or multiple topics to each story;
- summarization (Su), which assigns a short summary to each story.

Z. Vetulani and H. Uszkoreit (Eds.): LTC 2007, LNAI 5603, pp. 1–12, 2009.

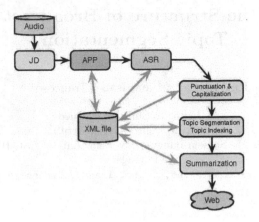

Fig. 1. Broadcast News processing system architecture

The first modules of this system were optimized for on-line performance, given their deployment in the fully automatic subtitling system that is running on the main news shows of the public TV channel in Portugal (RTP), since early March[1]. The topic related modules, on the other hand, are running off-line, exploiting cues that are computed over the whole BN show.

Except for jingle detection, all the components of this pipeline structure produce information that is stored in an XML (Extendible MarkUp Language) file. At the end, this file contains not only the transcribed text, but also additional information such as the segments duration, the acoustic background classification (e.g. clean/music/noise), the speaker gender, the identification of the speaker cluster, the start and end of each story and the corresponding topics.

Story or topic segmentation is just one of many types of segmentation that can be performed in spoken language documents [2]. Whereas audio pre-processing or audio diarization aims to segment an audio recording into acoustically homogeneous regions, given only features extracted from the audio signal, structural segmentation include tasks that also represent linguistic structure, for which algorithms combine both acoustic and linguistic cues. Sentence segmentation has been one of the most researched tasks within structural segmentation, but topic segmentation may be also a very useful task.

The major contributions to the area of topic segmentation come from two evaluation programs: Topic Detection and Tracking (TDT) and TREC Video Retrieval (TRECVID), where TREC stands for The Text Retrieval Conference (TREC), both co-sponsored by NIST and the U.S. Department of Defense. The work described in this paper is closer to the goals of the TRECVID campaigns, in the sense that it examines story segmentation in an archival setting, allowing the use of global off-line information.

The majority of approaches for story segmentation [3] explore lexical features such as word similarity [4], cue phrases [5], cosine similarity of lexical windows [6] [7], and adaptive language modeling [8]. Many of these approaches do not exploit acoustic features, considering that each word boundary is a candidate for a story boundary. This is not the case of [4], which only considers candidates at prosodic phrase boundaries, and [9], which considers candidates at pauses of duration greater than 650 ms. Other approaches consider candidate story boundaries at sentence boundaries [10] [11]. This type of approach thus implicitly involves both acoustic and linguistic features.

The application of story segmentation to the Broadcast News domain has mostly been reported for English corpora, but more recently also for Mandarin [12] [13] [3], and for Arabic [14] [3].

Our previous work in topic segmentation for European Portuguese was based on exploring simple heuristics derived exclusively from acoustic features. These heuristics failed in more complex scenarios and motivated us to further explore the typical structure of a BN show, which is commonly found among several TV stations in Portugal. One of the first tasks was thus to extend our original BN corpus which was restricted to several types of BN shows from a single station to include shows from other stations. This extended corpus is briefly described in Section 2. The next Section is devoted to the presentation of our segmentation methods, starting by the baseline approach, the CART approach and the multi-stage one. Section 4 presents the results for the different approaches, compares the performance of the TS method when the APP and ASR modules are replaced by manual labels and evaluates the contribution of non-news information to the TS task. The integration of the topic segmentation module in an off-line BN processing system is illustrated in Section 5. The final Section concludes and presents directions for future research, emphasizing our promising results in a media monitor task and discussing how video-derived cues can potentially contribute towards improving topic segmentation.

2   The European Portuguese BN Corpus

Our original European Portuguese Broadcast News corpus, collected in close co-operation with RTP (the public TV station in Portugal), involves different types of news shows, national and regional, from morning to late evening, including both normal broadcasts and specific ones dedicated to sports and financial news. The part of this corpus which is relevant for the current work is divided into 2 main subsets:

- SR (Speech Recognition) - The SR corpus contains around 57h of manually transcribed news shows, collected during a period of 3 months, with the primary goal of training acoustic models and adapting the language models of our large vocabulary speech recognition component of our system. The corpus is subdivided into training (51h) and development (6h) sets. This corpus was also topic labeled manually. Only a subset of 33 shows was used for the current work.
- JE (Joint Evaluation) - The JE corpus contains around 13h, corresponding to two weeks. It was fully manually transcribed, both in terms of orthographic

and topic labels. Half of the 14 shows were presented by a single anchor. The other half also included a thematic anchor for sports.

The JE corpus contains a much higher percentage of spontaneous speech and a higher percentage of speech under degraded acoustical conditions than our SR training corpus. A potential justification for this fact was that it was recorded during the outbreak of a major war.

As described above, this corpus was recently complemented with extra BN shows from other TV stations in order to test the performance of our method in different scenarios, namely in terms of the presence of a single anchor, double anchor, special anchor for a given theme (e.g. sports), presence of a local comentator, etc.. This extra BN corpus (EB) contains around 4h and was also fully manually transcribed. Table 1 lists the number of BN shows and stories in each subset of the full corpus which falls within a given category: 1A (single anchor), 2A (double anchor) and TA (thematic anchor). One of the 2A shows also includes the commentator. Note that, on average, one TA show has 30 stories where 28 are presented by the anchor and only 2 are presented by the thematic anchor.

Table 1. Number of shows (and stories) in each of the three subsets, for the three types of anchor - single, double and thematic

	1A	2A	3A
SR	15 (924)	- -	18 (36)
JE	7 (196)	- -	7 (14)
EB	1 (30)	2 (60)	- -

3   Topic Segmentation Algorithms

The goal of TS module is to split the broadcast news show into the constituent stories. This may be done taking into account the characteristic structure of broadcast news shows [15]. They typically consist of a sequence of segments that can either be stories or fillers (i.e. headlines / teasers). The fact that all stories start with a segment spoken by the anchor, and are typically further developed by out-of-studio reports and/or interviews is the most important heuristic that can be exploited in this context. Hence, the simplest TS algorithm is the one that starts by defining potential story boundaries in every transition non-anchor/ anchor.

Anchor detection could be done by speaker identification, but in order to give the algorithm the potential to process BN shows with previously unknown anchors, the detection was done by finding the speaker with the largest number of turns. This heuristic may be further refined by finding the speaker with the largest number of terms of duration larger than a given threshold, and which also is detected throughout the duration of the show, and not only during a relative short period.

This baseline algorithm has several pitfalls. It fails to detect a boundary between two stories when the first story is all spoken by the anchor and produce false boundaries in every anchor intervention after the story introduction. The considerable amount of miss and false alarm problems led us into further explore the typical structure of a BN show, by adding further heuristics, such as eliminating stories that are too short to put a label on. Rather than hand-tuning these heuristics, we decided to train a CART (Classification and Regression Tree)[16] with potential characteristics for each segment boundary such as: the number of turns of the speaker in the whole show; the total amount of time for that speaker in the whole show; the segment duration (close to a sentence-like unit); the speaker gender; the acoustic background condition; the presence or absence of speech in the segment; the time interval until the next speaker; and the insertion of the segment within an interview region (i.e. with alternating speakers). Each feature vector has these characteristics for the present segment as well as for the previous one.

Figure 2 depicts the characteristics automatically selected by the CART in our development corpus. It is interesting to notice how the CART manages to discard potential story boundaries in non-anchor/anchor transitions in interviews, for instance, by discarding short segments by the anchor.

3.1 Two-Stage Approach

The CART approach performs reasonably well for BN shows with a simple structure, i.e. single anchor, but fails with more complex structures, involving 2 anchors, for instance, leading us to adopt a two-stage approach: in a first stage of re-clustering, if the BN show is labeled as having two anchors, the two speaker ids with the most frequent turns are clustered into a single anchor label. This stage works as a pre-processing stage, which is then followed by the CART stage.

3.2 Three-Stage Approach

The CART approach also fails in the presence of a thematic anchor for a certain period of the BN show. In order to deal with this complex structure, a multi-stage approach was adopted, where topic segmentation is interleaved with topic indexation.

The first stage uses a simple rule to identify potential story boundaries in every non-speech/anchor transitions. The second stage applies the topic indexation module to isolate the portion of the BN show corresponding to the given theme (sports). This stage allows potential story boundaries to appear within the given theme, instead of creating one huge story, with all sports events grouped together.

After these initial two stages which create potential story boundaries, a third stage of boundary removal is applied. This final stage uses the same type of rules adopted by the CART to remove boundaries inside interview segments, or boundaries which would create a too short introduction by the anchor, or boundaries that would create a too short story. The relatively short number

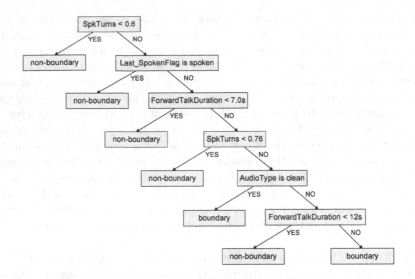

Fig. 2. Diagram of the CART tree. SpkTurns = number of turns of the speaker in the whole show; LastSpokenFlag = presence or absence of speech in the segment; ForwardTalkDuration = time interval until the next speaker; AudioType = acoustic background condition.

of stories introduced by the thematic anchor prevented us from training a new CART that would learn these rules automatically.

The analysis of the behavior of this multi-stage approach also indicated that whereas the sports news needed to be split into constituent stories, for other topics, the opposite problem occurred. In fact, false alarms were very frequent for the weather forecast topic, which was typically split into multiple stories, due to the relatively long pauses made by the anchor between the forecasts for each part of the country. In order to deal with this problem, the topic indexation stage was used to detect weather forecast stories. When two or more adjacent weather forecast stories are detected, they are merged into a single one.

4   Results

The evaluation of the topic segmentation was done using the standard measures Recall (% of detected boundaries), Precision (% of marks which are genuine boundaries) and F-measure (defined as $2RP/(R + P)$). Table 2 shows the TS results. Every time a story boundary was inserted in the beginning of a filler segment, this was counted as a false alarm. These results together with the field trials we have conducted [17], show that we have a boundary deletion problem when a story is finished back in the studio. In those situations, the TS algorithm frequently produces a false boundary and if the next story boundary is to close to this one, the later will be deleted. A boundary deletion can also occur if the anchor presence is detected inside a filler segment. Since the filler segments are very short, a false boundary produced inside the filler segment will be to close to the next story boundary. When this happens, the story boundary is deleted (19% of the program events are fillers). The false alarm problems are mainly due to the anchor interventions during the development of a story by a reporter or during an interview.

Table 2. Topic segmentation results for manually annotated data

Approach	%Recall	%Precision	F-measure	Corpus
Baseline	58.8	47.3	0.52	JE
CART	79.6	69.8	0.74	JE
2-Stage	81.2	91.6	0.85	EB
3-Stage	88.8	56.9	0.69	JE

The comparison of the segmentation results achieved for the JE corpus shows that the CART performance is better than the 3-stage algorithm. In fact, the increase in the recall score attained with the 3-stage algorithm is achieved by finding new story boundaries introduced by the thematic anchor, but at the cost of generating some false alarms which consequently lowers the precision value. For the EB corpus, the CART with the pre-processing stage achieved very good results which indicates that the shows in the EB corpus have a similar structure.

4.1 Dependence on Previous APP and ASR Stages

The experiments described above were done using manually annotated data. When this manual annotation is replaced by our automatic audio pre-processing stage, we achieve comparable results. In fact, the F-measure for the baseline approach is even higher with the APP module (0.57), whereas for the 3-stage approach, we obtain almost the same (0.68). We were expecting a larger degradation, given that the approaches were trained with manually annotated data.

The most relevant role of our APP module in terms of topic segmentation is speaker clustering. The diarization error rate is 26.1%, a fairly good value if we take into account the very high number of speakers in a typical show of the JE corpus (close to 80), and the fact that we are using a low latency method that does not perform any global optimization on all the speakers of each show [18]. The current algorithm still produces more than one cluster per speaker sometimes, specially when the background conditions differ for the same speaker. This never compromises the anchor detection, as the speaker with the higher number of turns. However, some of the segments spoken by the anchor may be attributed to a different cluster. When this happens at the beginning of a story we have a miss, but when this happens in the middle of a story (for instance in a sequence involving anchor - journalist 1 - anchor - journalist 2) this clustering error will avoid a false alarm.

Despite the different corpus, a close look at the best results achieved in TRECVID story segmentation task (F=0.7) [19] show our good results, specially considering the lack of video information in our approach.

The automatic identification of the type of BN show (single anchor, double anchor or thematic anchor) was not yet dealt with. In fact, so far, Portuguese TV channels have adopted a very regular pattern for each show. This is the type of problem, however, where video information can play a very important role.

4.2   Impact of Non-news Information

The type of features used in the CART makes our automatic topic segmentation module very dependent on the good performance of the audio-preprocessing module, and mainly on its ability to correctly identify the anchor. On-going work in terms of APP improvement thus has a great influence on the TS module. One of the most recent improvements of the APP module concerns the inclusion of a non-news detector which marks the jingles that characterize the start and end of the BN show, the jingles that delimit publicity segments, and also headlines/teasers.

Recently our APP module started to include additional information on the XML file indicating non-news segments inside the broadcast news program. The non-news segments correspond to fillers, jingles delimiting publicity segments, and also headlines/teasers. That information was used in the TS task to define another story boundary detection rule, since after the filler there is a story boundary defining the beginning of a new report. A preliminary experiment was done using the non-news information in the story segmentation of three automatically annotated broadcast news programs (3h). Table 3 shows the results.

Table 3. Topic segmentation results using non-news information

Approach	%Recall	%Precision	F-measure
CART	98.9	71.7	0.83
3-Stage	96.8	73.9	0.84

The comparison of the results in table 3 with the ones presented in table 2 shows that the use of non-news information in the story segmentation increases the recall and precision value. The use of non-news information avoids the false boundaries inside fillers with the consequent boundary deletion after the fillers, and avoids also the boundary deletion after the jingle of the program start and after the advertising in the middle of the program. The performance achieved with both approaches is comparable, because there is no thematic anchor in the three programs used in the evaluation.

A close inspection of the results shows that the main problem is still the false alarm rate due to the anchor interventions in the program, whose talk duration is long enough to be a story introduction, and do not occur at story boundaries. The most frequent false alarms occur at the end of a story. In fact, the anchor frequently finishes a story by a short comment or a short acknowledgment of the reporter. These ending segments by the anchor are typically merged with the introduction of the following story, thus creating both a false alarm (when the ending segment starts) and a boundary deletion (when the new story starts).

5 Integration in the BN Processing System

The earlier version of the BN processing system at our lab was designed as a media watch application. This version was capable of continuously monitoring a TV channel, and searching inside its news shows for stories that match the profile of a given user, to whom email alerts were subsequently sent. This alert message enabled a user to follow the links to the video clips referring to the selected stories [20].

The current version aimed at a more generic use. The broadcast news processing chain was originally developed for European Portuguese, but was already ported to other varieties of Portuguese (Brazilian and African). The on-line modules which were optimized for the subtitling aplication are also available for European Spanish and for English.

A significant part of the topic segmentation system is language independent. By removing the part that is dependent on the topic indexation (not yet trained for these two languages), the segmentation module could be used for all languages. Figure 3 illustrates the off-line Broadcast News processing chain. The

Fig. 3. Off-line usage of the Broadcast News processing system

user can select one of multiple topics (in the example, Sports is selected), see the first keyframes of several stories on the selected topic, together with the first sentence that serves as a short summary of the story, and click in one of the stories if he/she desires to see and hear the complete video of that story. The integration of all modules in the current application was the work of Hugo Meinedo.

6   Conclusions and Future Work

This paper presented our on-going work toward the improvement of the story segmentation module of our alert system. We have tried to improve our baseline algorithm by further exploring the typical structure of a broadcast news show, first by training a CART and then by integrating it in a 2-stage algorithm that is able to deal with shows with double anchors. In order to deal with shows with a thematic anchor, a more complex approach was adopted including a topic classification stage.

The recent cooperation with a media watch company allowed us to assess the precision of our topic segmentation module as compared to manual labeling. This assessment was formally performed for only 6 BN shows, yielding very promising results. We obtained a recall of 88.0% and a precision of 81.7%.

In another paper [21], we explored the automatic transcriptions of the BN shows in order to decrease the number of the cases of false alarms/missed boundaries at the end of stories, by merging short segments by the anchor with either their left or right neighbors. By training a CART where linguistic derived features are used in conjunction with acoustic-derived ones, significant improvements were obtained in terms of recall (91.2%) and precision (83.0%).

The fact that the manual mark is inserted by looking at the video and audio signals simultaneously justifies a small delay in the automatic story labels which only use the audio signal, as the anchor is typically visible for 1 or 2s before he/she actually starts speaking. In fact, some of the stories were correctly detected although their automatic boundaries were delayed by an average of 2s, which exceeds the test window of plus or minus 1s used to evaluate the number of hits. If the duration of this test window is increased to 2s, the recall becomes 97.0% and the precision 88.2%.

The correction of this short delay is just one of the several ways in which the integration of video and audio derived cues could benefit topic segmentation. In fact, the fusion of our topic segmentation boundaries with the ones provided by a shot segmentation module may contribute towards a higher precision of the automatically computed boundaries. This integration is currently being addressed in the framework of the VIDI-Video European project.

Another potential advantage concerns the strong dependence of our topic segmentation module on the results provided by the audio pre-processing module. Although this module is quite robust, its errors, namely in terms of anchor identification, significantly contribute to the overall miss and false alarms. In terms of video shot representation, semantic concepts such as single news anchor, double news-anchor, news studio, etc. may contribute towards making the overall anchor detection more robust and hence improve topic segmentation.

Another potentially important video semantic concept is weather news, although for this particular topic, the performance of the topic indexation module is the best of all topics.

When debating whether to merge a short story featuring the anchor with its left or right neighbors, the detection of a split screen might also be useful. In fact, it is fairly common, nowadays, to end a story by showing both the anchor and the reporter in a split screen, while the first one is thanking the latter.

These are the type of video derived cues we are currently studying for the potential integration with our audio-based topic segmentation module.

Whereas video-based cues can be important for audio-based segmentation, the opposite can be also true. In fact, the speaker diarization results of our APP module have already been successfully applied by another partner (CERTH, Greece) in the VIDI-VIDEO consortium to shot regrouping, thus improving the results of shot representation.

Acknowledgments. The present work is part of Rui Amaral's PhD thesis, initially sponsored by a FCT scholarship. This work was partially funded buthe European VIDI-VIDEO project. The authors would like to acknowledge the continuing support of their colleagues Hugo Meinedo and João Neto.

References

1. Neto, J., Meinedo, H., Viveiros, M., Cassaca, R., Martins, C., Caseiro, D.: Broadcast news subtitling system in Portuguese. In: Proc. ICASSP 2008, Las Vegas, March, pp. 1561–1564 (2008)
2. Ostendorf, M., Favre, B., Grishman, R., Hakkani-Tüur, D., Harper, M., Hillard, D., Hirschberg, J., Ji, H., Kahn, J., Liu, Y., Maskey, S., Matusov, E., Ney, H., Rosenberg, A., Shriberg, E., Wang, W., Woofers, C.: Speech segmentation and spoken document processing. IEEE Signal Processing Magazine 25(3), 59–69 (2008)
3. Rosenberg, A., Sharifi, M., Hirschberg, J.: Varying input segmentation for story boundary detection in english, arabic, and mandarin broadcast news. In: Proc. Interspeech 2008, Antwerp, Belgium, September 2007, pp. 2589–2592 (2007)
4. Kozima, H.: Text segmentation based on similarity between words. In: 31st Annual Meeting of the ACL, Columbus, Ohio, USA, June 1993, pp. 286–288 (1993)
5. Passonneau, R., Litman, D.: Discourse segmentation by human and automated means. Comput. Linguist. 23(1), 103–139 (1997)
6. Hearst, M.: Segmenting text into multi-paragraph subtopic passages. Computational Linguistics 23(1), 33–64 (1997)
7. Galley, M., McKeown, K., Fosler-Lussier, E., Jing, H.: Discourse segmentation of multi-party conversation. In: 41st Annual Meeting of ACL, Sapporo, Japan, July 2003, pp. 562–569 (2003)
8. Beeferman, D., Berger, A., Laffert, J.: Statistical models for text segmentation. Machine Learning 31(1-3), 177–210 (1999)
9. Shriberg, E., Stolcke, A., Hakkani-Tür, D.: Prosody based automatic segmentation of speech into sentences and topics. Speech Communication 32(1-2), 127–154 (2000)

10. Rosenberg, A., Hirschberg, J.: Story segmentation of broadcast news in english, mandarin and arabic. In: HLT/NAACL 2006, New York, USA, June 2006, pp. 125–128 (2006)

11. Tür, G., Hakkani-Tür, D., Stolcke, A., Shriberg, E.: Integrating prosodic and lexical cues for automatic topic segmentation. Computational Linguistics 27, 31–57 (2001)

12. Wayne, C.L.: Multilingual topic detection and tracking: Successful research enabled by corpora and evaluation. In: LREC 2000, Athens, Greece, May 2000, pp. 1487–1494 (2000)

13. Levow, G.A.: Assessing prosodic and text features for segmentation of mandarin broadcast news. In: HLT/NAACL 2004, Boston, Massachusetts, USA, May 2004, pp. 28–32 (2004)

14. Palmer, D., Reichman, M., Yaich, E.: Feature selection for trainable multilingual broadcast news segmentation. In: HLT/NAACL 2004, Boston, Massachusetts, USA, May 2004, pp. 89–92 (2004)

15. Barzilay, R., Collins, M., Hirschberg, J., Whittaker, S.: The rules behind roles: Identifying speaker role in radio broadcast. In: Proc. AAAI 2000, Austin, USA, July 2000, pp. 679–684 (2000)

16. Breiman, L., Friedman, J., Olshen, R., Stone, C.: Classification and Regression Trees, Wadsworth, NY (1983)

17. Trancoso, I., Neto, J., Meinedo, H., Amaral, R.: Evaluation of an alert system for selective dissemination of broadcast news. In: Proc. Eurospeech 2003, Geneva, Switzerland, September 2003, pp. 1257–1260 (2003)

18. Amaral, R., Meinedo, H., Caseiro, D., Trancoso, I., Neto, J.: Automatic vs. manual topic segmentation and indexation in broadcast news. In: Proc. IV Jornadas en Tecnologia del Habla, Zaragoza, Spain, November 2006, pp. 123–128 (2006)

19. Smeaton, A., Over, P., Kraaij, W.: Trecvid: evaluating the effectiveness of information retrieval tasks on digital video. In: MULTIMEDIA 2004: Proceedings of the 12th annual ACM international conference on Multimedia, pp. 652–655. ACM Press, New York (2004)

20. Meinedo, H., Neto, J.: Automatic speech annotation and transcription in a broadcast news task. In: Proc. MSDR 2003, Hong Kong, April 2003, pp. 95–100 (2003)

21. Amaral, R., Trancoso, I.: Topic segmentation and indexation in a media watch system. In: Proc. Interspeech 2008, Brisbane, Australia, September 2008, pp. 2183–2186 (2008)

Application of Slope Filtering to Robust Spectral Envelope Extraction for Speech/Speaker Recognition

Szymon Drgas and Adam Dabrowski

Chair of Control and Systems Engineering,
Poznan University of Technology,
ul. Piotrowo 3a, Poznan, Poland
{Szymon.Drgas,Adam.Dabrowski}@put.poznan.pl

Abstract. This paper describes a method for speech feature extraction using morphological signal processing based on the so-called "slope transformation". The proposed approach has been used to extract the signal upper spectral envelope. Results of experiments of the automatic speech recognition (ASR) and automatic speaker identification (ASI), which were undertaken to check the performance of the presented method, have shown some evident improvements of the effectiveness of recognition of isolated words, especially for women voices. The benefits of using slope transformation was also observed in speaker identification experiment.

Keywords: automatic speech recognition, slope filtering.

1 Introduction

During last years speech technology has evolved rapidly. The solutions for automatic speech, speaker or language recognition can be applied in such domains as telecommunication, education or human-computer interfaces. Although the existing algorithms for automatic extraction of information achieve acceptable performance for speech recorded in laboratory conditions, they typically fail in presence of noise and distortions. Thus, more robust algorithms must be developed to make possible real-world application of speech technologies.

Feature extraction is one of the main components of automatic speaker and speech recognition systems. The aim of extraction of particular features of speech in information extraction systems is to get an appropriate parametric speech signal representation dependent only on characteristics relevant to the given task. It is often based on source-filter model of speech, in which it is assumed that the excitation is produced in glottis and next it is independently filtered by the vocal tract. The nature of excitation depends on position, size, mass of vocal folds. It can also be influenced by constrictions in the vocal tract. The resonance characteristics of the vocal tract depend on the size and shape of vocal tract that are speaker dependent features, and therefore this information is useful in speaker recognition systems. The shape of vocal tract is changing during speech

Z. Vetulani and H. Uszkoreit (Eds.): LTC 2007, LNAI 5603, pp. 13–23, 2009.
© Springer-Verlag Berlin Heidelberg 2009

due to movement of articulators. Thus it carries a phonetic-information that is important in automatic speech recognition.

In the vocoder model, the excitation signal is filtered by the transfer function that models the vocal tract. Feature extraction methods are based on the extraction of the spectral envelope. It has been proven that the upper envelope is that carrying the relevant information about resonance characteristics of the vocal tract [2].

One of the most commonly accepted and widely used methods for the speech signal parameterization in speech/speaker recognition systems is the method based on mel-frequency cepstral coefficients (MFCC's) [1,2,5,8].

Cepstral analysis can be interpreted as smoothing the spectrum. This method is very effective but nevertheless it has some disadvantages. It is, e.g., sensitive to noise [6,8]. In case of voiced phonemes the extracted spectral envelope is an averaged upper and lower envelope while the lower envelope dependency makes MFCC method less robust to noise for voiced sounds.

MFCCs depend also on the fundamental frequency F0, if it is higher than 150 Hz. For voices with high F0, MFCCs carry harmonic structure information. It is also well known, that MFCCs are often applied in automatic speaker recognition systems. It can by said that this parameterization method is not optimal for the speaker independent ASR because it carries speaker dependent information.

Gu and Rose proposed another feature extraction method referred to as the PHCC (perceptual harmonic cepstral coefficients) [6]. The signal in each frame is classified as voiced, unvoiced, or transitional. In this method, in case of voiced phonemes, the fundamental frequency is estimated. Next the HWS (harmonic weighted spectrum) is calculated. In case of voiced speech the frequency bins with harmonics are amplified, while for transitional speech frames are multiplied with smaller factor. The frames with unvoiced signal remain unchanged. This selective amplification makes cepstrum coefficients less sensitive to lower envelope. The fundamental frequency is estimated using the spectro-temporal autocorrelation (STA) function that is computationally complex. Moreover STA is elusive and corrections of F0 have to be made by peak picking algorithm [6]. Experiments showed that the PHCC performance in noise was better than that of MFCC. However, necessity of the STA computation and peak picking make this method computationally inefficient. Another approach to upper envelope extraction was proposed by Yapanel and Hansen [11]. It was based on the minimum variance distortionless response and outperformed MFCC.

2   Envelope Extraction by Means of Slope Filtering

In general, an envelope of the signal is the absolute value of the analytic extension of this signal. Direct use of this definition to recognition of speech is, however, problematic because of the presence of irrelevant high frequency content in the envelope. Filtering, signal transformations, and morphological signal analysis are means to reduce the high frequency envelope content. An appropriate morphological approach seems to be a transformation of the signal into the slope domain, i.e., the so-called Legendre or "slope" transformation [7]. This transformation was already successfully used to detect endpoints of isolated words [8] and to denoise the speech [9]. A slope of the tangent line to the function s in time t can be calculated as:

$$\alpha = s'(t), \tag{1}$$

where $s'(t)$ denotes the derivative. Legendre transform is defined as:

$$S_L(\alpha) = s(t) - \alpha t \tag{2}$$

and by this means the signal $s(t)$ is transformed into α (slope) domain. We can eliminate time and then we get the following expression:

$$S_L(\alpha) = s((s')^{-1}(\alpha)) - \alpha[(s')^{-1}(\alpha)]. \tag{3}$$

In order to assure uniqueness of the function specified in the slope domain, a pair of slope transforms must be defined:

− for concave functions

$$S(\alpha) = \vee_t s(t) - \alpha(t), \tag{4}$$

− and for convex functions

$$S(\alpha) = \wedge_t s(t) - \alpha(t), \tag{5}$$

where $\vee$ denotes supremum and $\wedge$ denotes infimum. The respective definitions of the inverse slope transforms are:

$$s(t) = \wedge_\alpha S(\alpha) + \alpha t \tag{6}$$

and

$$s(t) = \vee_\alpha S(\alpha) + \alpha t. \tag{7}$$

Similarly to the Fourier transformation there is a possibility to define the generalized convolution of two waveforms and to show the result in the slope domain. According to (6) the convolution is then defined as:

$$\wedge_\alpha s(\tau) + f(t - \tau) \rightarrow S(\alpha) + F(\alpha). \tag{8}$$

The slope filtering of the signal $s(t)$ using the filter $g(t)$ can be defined as

$$s_f(t) = \wedge_\tau s(\tau) + g(t - \tau) \tag{9}$$

or

$$s_f(t) = \vee_\tau s(\tau) + g(t - \tau). \tag{10}$$

Application of the slope filtering to the envelope extraction consists in removing such signal components, which go beyond the specified slope region. There are two features of the slope filtering that are beneficial for ASR: first, the slope filtering saves extremal values of the signal; second, the slope filter does not cause any signal delay, similarly as it does a linear zero phase filter.

In this paper a modified MFCC method is proposed.The modification consists in applying slope transformation after FFT and before mel-scale filtering (see 1). In result it makes it possible to extract the spectral envelope in a computationally efficient and thus fast way.

3   Feature Extraction Method by Means of Slope Filtering

Block diagram of the proposed feature extraction method is depicted in Fig. 1.

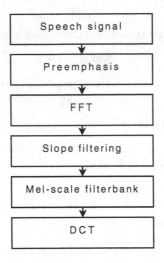

Fig. 1. Block diagram representing steps of the proposed feature extraction method

Speech signal is first processed using the preemphasis first-order filter with the following transfer function

$$H(z) = 1 - az^{-1} \tag{11}$$

Coefficient a, which describes selectivity of the high pass preemphasis filter, is usually set value from the range 0.95-0.98. This filter is used in order to equalize the spectrum of the speech signal.

Then the signal is divided into frames. These frames do overlap. The length of frames is chosen to assure quasi-stationarity of the signal in each frame (20-25 ms).

Next the Hamming window is used and FFT is computed in each frame. Absolute values of the spectrum are squared according to

$$S(f) = |F\{s(t)\}|^2 \tag{12}$$

where F denotes the Fourier transform. Power spectrum is processed with the slope filter described with

$$g(f) = \begin{cases} \alpha_1 f, f \geq 0 \\ \alpha_2 f, f < 0 \end{cases} \tag{13}$$

The operation of the spectral envelope extraction can be expressed as

$$\widetilde{S}(f) = \wedge_\phi S(\phi) + g(f - \phi) \tag{14}$$

The effect of this morphological processing is shown in figure 2. The power spectrum of a vowel (the fundamental frequency of about 150 Hz) is shown with the continuous line. This spectrum was morphologically filtered using slope filter with cutoff slope 0.5. The result of this operation is shown at the figure 2 by the dashed line. It can be noticed that by this means the deepness of spectral valleys are reduced while peaks related to harmonics are preserved.

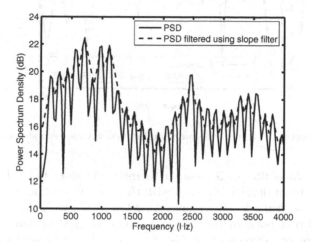

Fig. 2. Power spectrum filtered

After this nonlinear filtering the spectrum is multiplied by the bank of the triangle-shaped mel-scale filters. These filters are used in order to simulate the human perception of the pitch. Values that are result of multiplication for each filter are summed.

In the last step the discrete cosine transform of the type III is computed. This operation can be expressed with

$$X_K = \frac{1}{2}x_0 + \sum x_n cos[\frac{\pi}{N}n(k + \frac{1}{2})] \tag{15}$$

Finally the computed coefficients are liftered - multiplied by the liftering function $u(n)$

$$u(n) = 1 + \frac{L}{2}sin(\frac{\pi n}{L}) \tag{16}$$

In the case of voiced speech sounds, the additive noise disrupts mainly the spectral valleys between the harmonics. This can be noticed in figure 3. The original spectrum of the vowel is marked with the continuous line, while the spectrum of the vowel mixed with the speech shaped noise is denoted with dashed line. In order to emphasize the effect, only low frequency range is shown (up to 1500 Hz).

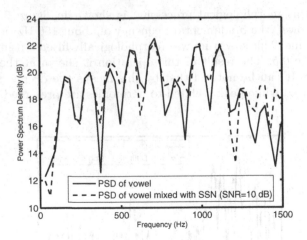

Fig. 3. Power spectra of clean vowel and signal mixed with speech shaped noise (SSN)

The effect of slope filtering is shown in figure 4. The slope filtered (cutoff slope 0.5) power spectrum density is shown with the continuous line, while the slope filtered power spectrum density of noisy vowel is shown with the dashed line. It can be noticed that both curves are quite similar after slope filtering. There is a smaller difference between estimates of clean and noisy signal spectra. Thus sloped filtered spectra seem to be less sensitive to additive noise for voiced speech sounds. For higher frequencies (above 1500 Hz) local SNR is much lower and the filtering does not bring any benefit. The lack of improvement can be observed for unvoiced speech sounds.

4   Experiment

The proposed feature extraction algorithm was implemented in the MATLAB computing environment. Two experiments were carried out to test robustness of the proposed method. Isolated word recognition (IWR) experiment was undertaken to check the performance of the proposed method in automatic speech recognition system. In the second experiment the accuracy of speaker recognition system was examined.

4.1   Automatic Speech Recognition Experiment

The speech samples used in the experiment were a set of 195 polish names taken from the Corpora database [5]. The recognition task was speaker independent. Each word was uttered once by 24 men and 12 women. Speech recognizer accuracy was checked for men and for women voices separately. In the first experiment, which concerned men voices, we used 12 utterances for training and 12 others for the test. In the second experiment 6 utterances with women voices were used for the training and 6 others for the test.

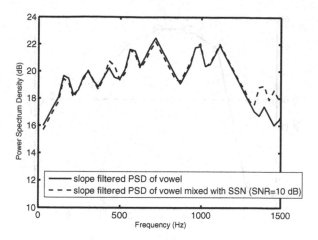

Fig. 4. Power spectra of clean vowel and signal mixed with speech shaped noise (SSN)

Speech signal was filtered with the preemphasis filter (11). The preemphasis coefficient value was 0.97. The signal was divided into frames. Each frame was 25 ms long. The frame step was 10 ms. Mel-frequency filters spanned 20-4000 Hz frequency range divided into passbands of 20 mel-spaced filters. The mel integration windows had peaks normalized to 1. Cepstral coefficients were obtained by means of the DCT type III.

In preliminary experiments various slope filters were used and ASR system performance was tested for small set of words (Polish numbers). The results of this part of the study are depicted in Fig. 5. The dashed line indicates results obtained for MFCC coefficients.

Cepstral coefficients were liftered. The liftering coefficient was equal to 22. There was a hidden Markov model (HMM) with 10 states used for each word. This number of states gave the best results in the preeliminary experiment. Feature vector consisted of 12 parameters plus the first and the second derivative. The standard HTK software [10] package supplemented with the authors' interface written in Matlab was used to perform experiments. A topology of the HMM according to the Bakis model [1] was used. In the training phase the initial values were estimated with HInit and the values were three times reestimated with HRest tool. HMM's with one mixture continuous density were used. Diagonal covariance matrices were applied to describe observations of the probability distribution. The accuracy was measured for 5 signal-to-noise ratios (SNR's) - 20, 15, 10, 5, and 0 dB. White Gaussian noise was added. Cutoff slope was 0.5. It gave the maximum performance for relatively small data sets (Polish numbers).

4.2   Automatic Speaker Recognition

In order to realize speaker identification, the recognition system was implemented using Gaussian mixture models (GMM). Speaker was parameterized by means of

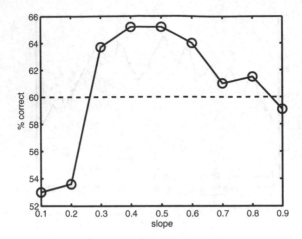

Fig. 5. Relation between slope and recognizer accuracy

the tested methods. The processing was similar to that in the automatic speech recognition experiment, but the number of mel-filters was changed to 30 and number of cepstral coefficients was set to 20. After the feature extraction stage GMM modeling was undertaken. The process was performed by expectation-maximization (EM) algorithm [3]. In identification experiments TIMIT database was used [4]. It was recorded in laboratory conditions i.e. with negligible level of noise and distortions. The TIMIT database contains utterances of 630 speakers: 70% males and 30% females from 10 regions of United States. 30 seconds of speech were recorded for each speaker in a form of 10 utterances.

Recordings from the TIMIT database are sampled with the rate 16000 samples/s. These files were downsampled to the rate of 8000 samples/s. To train speaker models sentences SA1-2, SI1-2 and SX1-2 were used while in test sentences SX4 and SX5 were chosen.

In order to model voices of speakers, GMMs with 28 components were applied. Covariance matrices were diagonal. At the beginning the parameters had random values. By means of vector quantization, initial values of means of components were estimated. In the next step EM algorithm was applied to estimate GMM parameters. The maximum number of iterations was 100. The variance floor was 0.01 and the minimum weight was set to 0.05.

5   Results and Discussion

5.1   Automatic Speech Recognition

The results of experiments are shown in Fig. 6 and in Fig. 7. The curves shown in these figures illustrate dependence of the percentage of the correctly recognized words on the SNR. Effectiveness of the classical MFCC feature extraction method is compared with that of the proposed modified feature extraction

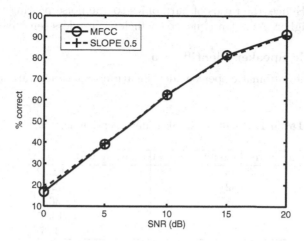

Fig. 6. Results of experiments for men voices

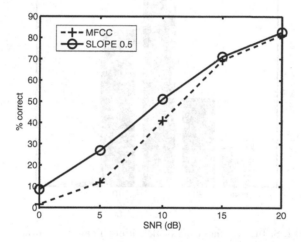

Fig. 7. Results of experiments for women voices

method. Circles are used to depict the classical MFCC method while crosses indicate the proposed modified MFCC method (i.e., that with the additional envelope extraction by means of the slope filtering). It can be noticed that for men voices the maximal difference between both methods is about 1.7 percent only, i.e., it is almost negligible. In the case of women voices, however the difference is growing for small SNR's. The maximal difference (the percentage of the correctly recognized words that our method outstrips the classical method) is larger than 10 percent. We think that this improvement is a consequence of the fact that for women voices the fundamental frequencies are higher than those for men voices, thus the distances in the spectral domain between the harmonics are also higher. Hence, the ratios of harmonics to the noise passing through the filters are also higher. As a consequence coefficients are less sensitive to noise.

5.2   Automatic Speaker Identification

The results of the automatic speaker identification experiment are summarized in table 1.

Table 1. Results of speaker identification accuracy

SNR (dB)	accuracy with slope filtering (%)	accuracy without slope filtering (%)
inf	93.33	91.82
20	65.32	62.54
15	42.38	36.5
10	18.09	13.17
5	3.33	3.17

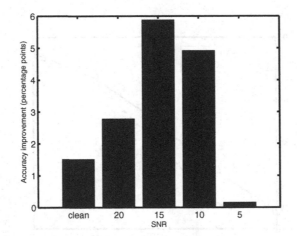

Fig. 8. Improvement of speaker identification accuracy

Performance of the MFCC-based automatic speaker identification system is compared with the system in which the proposed feature extraction method is employed. For clean test samples the performance is above 91%. However, when speech shaped noise is added, the performance decreased drammaticaly. For 5 dB SNR fewer then 5% of trials were classified correctly for both feature extraction methods. When slope transform was used, the accuracy improvement was observed for noisy samples (see fig. 8). The highest benefit was obtained for 15 dB SNR (about 6 percentage points). For 10 dB SNR the improvement due to slope transform was also significant (about 5 percentage points). For SNR values lower than 10 dB improvement decreases and is below 1 percentage point. Thus, in case of moderate SNR the proposed method significantly improves accuracy of the automatic speaker recognition system.

6 Conclusions

The described feature extraction method, which uses the considered nonlinear morphological slope filtering, offers substantially better performance of automatic speech recognition for voices with relatively high fundamental frequency. These are, e.g., women and children voices.

For voices with low fundamental frequency, i.e., for men voices, the ASR performance remains practically unchanged. However, for voices with high F0 and in low SNR conditions, accuracy can increase by about 10 percentage points.

The slope filtering of the spectral envelope can substantially improve performance of automatic speaker recognition systems. The significant increase of accuracy can be obtained for moderate SNRs.

It should be stressed that in the proposed method it is not necessary to estimate the fundamental frequency F0. In other approaches the fundamental frequency is usually estimated using the spectro-temporal autocorrelation function, which is quite complex, computationally inefficient, and needs corrections of F0 with the peak picking algorithm.

In result, the proposed approach is much faster. Furthermore, it is robust to such effects as noise and distortion in speech including also speech prosody, speaker accent, emotion, and the utterance speed.

References

1. Bakis, R.: Continuous speech recognition via centisecond acoustic states. Acoustical Society of America Journal 59, 97-+ (1976)
2. Davis, S., Mermelstein, P.: Comparison of parametric representations for monosyllabic word recognition in continuously spoken sentences. IEEE Transactions on Acoustics, Speech, and Signal Processing [see also IEEE Transactions on Signal Processing] 28(4), 357–366 (1980)
3. Dempster, A., Laird, N., Rubin, D.: Maximum likelihood from incomplete data via the em algorithm. Journal of the Royal Statistical Society 39(1), 1–38 (1977)
4. Garofolo, J.S., et al: TIMIT Acoustic-Phonetic Continuous Speech Corpus. Linguistic Data Consortium, Philadelphia (1993)
5. Grocholewski, S.: Statystyczne podstawy systemu ARM dla języka polskiego. Wyd. Politechniki Poznańskiej (2001)
6. Gu, L., Rose, K.: Perceptual harmonic cepstral coefficients for speech recognition in noisy environment. In: Proc. ICASSP (2001)
7. Maragos, P.: Slope transforms: theory and application to nonlinear signal processing. IEEE Transactions on Signal Processing 43(4), 864–877 (1995)
8. Marciniak, T., Rochowniak, R., Dabrowski, A.: Detection of endpoints of isolated words using slope transformation. In: Proc. MIXDES, pp. 655–659 (2006)
9. Meyer, A.: Zastosowanie transformacji zafalowaniowej do odszumiania sygnaw audio i poprawy zrozumiaoci mowy. PhD thesis, Poznan University of Technology (2005)
10. Odell, J., Ollason, D., Woodland, P., Young, S., Jansen, J.: The HTK Book for HTK V2.0. Cambridge University Press, Cambridge (1995)
11. Yapanel, U.H., Hansen, J.H.L.: A new perceptually motivated mvdr-based acoustic front-end (pmvdr) for robust automatic speech recognition. Speech Communication 50(2), 142–152 (2008)

Spoken Language Interface for Mobile Devices

João Freitas[1], António Calado[1], Maria João Barros[2], and Miguel Sales Dias[1]

[1] MLDC, Microsoft Language Development Center, Edifício Qualidade C1-C2 Av. Prof.
Doutor Aníbal Cavaco Silva Tagus Park 2744-010 Porto Salvo, Portugal
[2] Eurescom GmbH, Wieblinger Weg 19/4, 69123 Heidelberg, Germany
i-joaof@microsoft.com, i-antonc@microsoft.com,
barros@eurescom.eu, Miguel.Dias@microsoft.com

Abstract. In this paper, we present a set of optimizations for a spoken language interface for mobile devices that can improve the recognition accuracy and user interaction experience. A comparison between a speech and a graphical interface, when used to accomplish the same task, is provided. The implications of developing a spoken language interface and integrating speech recognition and text-to-speech modules for European Portuguese in a mobile device, are also discussed. The paper focuses in the speech recognition module and in an algorithm for name matching optimization that provides the user with a more comfortable interaction with the device. Usability evaluation trials have shown that spoken language interfaces can provide an easier and more efficient use of the device, especially within a community of users less experienced in handling mobile devices.

Keywords: language interface, speech interface, human-computer interface, mobility, user experience, usability evaluation.

1 Introduction

Spoken language interfaces impose a well know challenge to application developers: speech recognition is not perfect. We this in mind, software engineers should fully understand the strengths and weaknesses of the underlying speech technologies and identify the appropriate methodology and context, to use speech technology effectively. The process of integrating spoken language technologies in mobile applications as a Human-Computer Interface (or HCI) modality is highly dependent on the nature of the service provided by such technologies. In any case, any new HCI design should make the interaction between the user and the device easier. A well-designed HCI requires the consideration of the application user group, while making sure that the interface matches the way users expect it to behave [1]. The mobile environment adds challenges to the development of speech applications, due to the hardware limitations, e.g. in memory and in performance, and the conditions imposed by the different usage scenarios, e.g. background noise so common on mobility and the problem of device positioning towards the user. Nevertheless, the integration of spoken language technologies in mobile devices is gaining momentum. Common scenarios "busy hands, busy eyes" of the mobile world, e.g. driving, are classic examples of the

Z. Vetulani and H. Uszkoreit (Eds.): LTC 2007, LNAI 5603, pp. 24–35, 2009.

need of integrating speech applications in the mobility world. The trend leads to a presence of automatic systems in our daily lives and in many situations the space for a large keyboard or a mouse is inexistent, e.g. wearable computers. Speech is a solution and can be adopted as a command and control modality in parallel with others, or as a primary interface modality for multimodal interfaces. The combination of speech with other interaction modalities is generally more effective than a unimodal speech interface, due the inexistence of a 100% accurate method to perform speech recognition [1], [2], which resides in the probabilistic nature of current technologies.

Speech applications face yet another challenge: users want to interact with the application in their native language and want to use their own pronunciation. The localization of speech, that is, the provision of speech recognition and synthesis (spoken language interface) for a new language, includes a complex set of engineering and computational linguistics procedures and modules, which vary if we are considering recognition or synthesis. Some are of linguistic nature (pronunciation lexicons, phone sets, annotated and orthographically transcribed speech corpus, etc.) and some of a more mathematical/stochastically/algorithmic nature (acoustic models, language models, prosody models, grapheme-phoneme mappings, etc.). The example for mobile application presented in this paper, has a spoken language interface for European Portuguese (EP), designed for Pocket PC, which allows the user to place phone calls to any contact in the contact list. The purpose of this work is to demonstrate that a well designed speech HCI, in comparison with a graphical HCI, makes the usage of mobile devices easier, for a diversity of users including those with no experience in mobility. The application accommodates the user through a name matching algorithm and a well designed grammar, with the intention of simplifying the recognition problem. It is shown that by modelling the grammar, the application developer can improve the recognition accuracy and still implement a comfortable spoken language interface. This paper is organized as follows. Section 2 describes the basic components used in the development of speech applications. Section 3 details the development of a speech application, along with a name matching algorithm and grammar design considerations. In section 4, tests results are presented and discussed. Section 5 presents a usability evaluation trial and its results. Finally, in Section 6, the work conclusions are summarized.

2   Speech Applications

There are four classes of applications requiring different user interfaces: Desktop, Telephony, Home and Mobility. Desktop speech applications include widely used computing environments, such as Microsoft Windows and Microsoft Office. Telephony applications require server-side speech applications, such as Microsoft Speech Server and Microsoft Exchange. Home user interfaces are usually localized in the TV, living room or kitchen and speech introduces a great benefit since home appliances don't have a keyboard or a mouse and the traditional graphical user interface application can't be directly extended for this category. In the mobile case, Smartphone, PDA and automotive are the most important mobile scenarios due to the physical size and the hands-busy and eyes-busy constraints [1]. All classes of speech applications have several development stages in common, as depicted in figure 1.

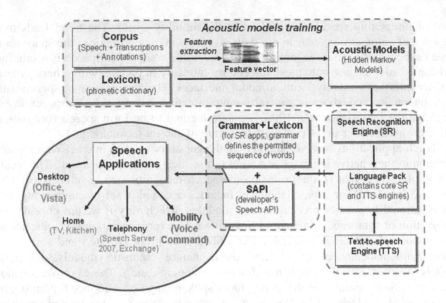

Fig. 1. Components of speech applications

The used speech recognition technology is based on statistical data-driven models of time-series known as Hidden Markov Models (HMM's) [3]. Each HMM in a speech recognition system models the time-based acoustic information of a specific speech segment within a language, which needs to be trained with real speech recorded for the language and acoustic environment in question, for example, EP telephony speech. These speech segments become representations of the speech units and can be of different sizes, e.g. whole sentences, whole words or even sub-word phonetic units like phones, diphones, triphones, syllables, etc.

2.1 Speech Recognition Engine

The application is responsible for loading the SR engine and for requesting actions/information from it. It communicates with the engine via a Speech API (SAPI) interface [4]. The SAPI abstracts the developer from the low level details of the SR engine. Nonetheless, it's essential that the developer is aware of the potential, functionality and technique performed by the SR engine, in order to model and optimize the target application. Usually, speech recognition engines for mobile devices present lower performance when compared to desktop engines. Optimizations, like fixed point calculations, lead to less recognition accuracy. Due to this, applications should perform a compensating effort in terms of recognition, e.g. minimize the number of grammar items, take in consideration the speech corpus used to train the acoustic models and model the application flow to avoid errors. In section 3 several optimization examples are presented.

2.2 Grammars

Speech applications are often built with a command and control application in mind. Section 3 shows an example that uses SAPI command and control features to implement its functionalities. Command and control features are implemented through context-free grammars (CFGs). This kind of grammar defines a set of imbricated production rules. These rules are able to generate a set of words and combinations of these words that can be used to build all types of allowed sentences. The result of a grammar production can be seen as a list of valid words/sentences that can be pronounced by the user, when interacting with the application via speech, which is passed on to the SR engine. Speech applications use grammars to improve recognition accuracy by restricting and indicating to the engine which words/sentences should be expected. The valid sentences need to be carefully chosen, considering users profile and the application nature. However, other approaches to SR without using CFG do exist [5], [6].

3   Example Application Development

In this section, the stages of development of an application that allows a user to place a phone call to a contact, in a Pocket PC device, are described. The intention is to present its architecture and the relevant design decisions, considering the language, mobile environment and speech recognition procedure. The example application was referenced as "Pocket Reco" and it is a C++ application developed for Pocket PC devices, interacting with the user through a spoken language interface in EP and influenced by applications such as Microsoft Voice Command [7], Cyberon Voice Commander [8] and Voice Signal [9]. The application allows the user to place phone calls to any contact in the MS Windows contact list and to consult his/her agenda. It was developed using Microsoft Visual Studio 2005 and MS Windows Mobile 5.0 Pocket PC SDK [10]. The application is localized for EP, in a context where the amount of applications with spoken language interfaces in EP, that exist in the market, is reduced. If we consider only the mobility world, that number decreases even more. It's important that Portuguese users have the possibility to use speech recognition and speech synthesis applications in European Portuguese, especially those with special needs, such as with vision impairments, which depend on this type of applications to use a mobile device.

3.1 System Description

When the user initiates the application Pocket Reco, by pressing a button or by running the executable file, the speech recognition and text-to-speech modules are initiated. To notify the user, an icon is loaded to the notifications tray and a spoken message is synthesized. At this point the application expects the user to input a speech command. If no expected command is recognized there is a predefined timeout. Once the speech command is recognized, a set of actions associated with the command are executed. When these actions are finished, the application ends, unloading all resources. The user can input commands to make phone calls or check the calendar. When the user chooses to make a phone call by saying the respective command followed by the contact name, it may be the case that the contact has more than one phone number (mobile, home, work, etc). In this situation the user is notified to choose between the available numbers by saying the respective command.

3.2 Architecture

Pocket Reco contains a SR and a TTS module, which communicate with the respective engines through SAPI. SAPI communicates with the engines through a device driver interface [4]. Both SR and TTS engines contain a SAPI interface layer, allowing the use of SAPI runtime. Figure 2 illustrates the interaction of the application with the engines, through SAPI.

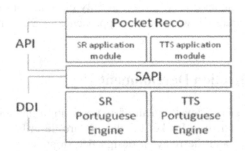

Fig. 2. Diagram of the speech architecture

3.3 CFG Grammar

The application uses a CFG grammar to parse the recognizer output. The grammar is composed by dynamic and static rules. The dynamic rules are empty when the application starts and their contents are updated in runtime. The separation between static and dynamic rule contents allows the application to start and load the static content, without loading the SAPI grammar compiler, thus preventing additional delays in the start-up sequence. When the application loads the dynamic content it forces SAPI to initialize the backend grammar compiler [4].

In Pocket Reco there is a distinction between static rule content and dynamic rule content, in order to develop a well-designed grammar and to improve initial SAPI grammar compiler performance. The dynamic content is, in this case, the list of contacts names, as these can only be accessed at runtime. The static rules that use the contact names will reference the respective dynamic rule.

3.4 Name Matching Algorithm

A spoken language interface with command and control modality, like Pocket Reco, should supply natural and simple voice commands. This way, the user will not need to memorize the commands and the required words will be spoken naturally. The speech command responsible for placing a phone call to a contact in the contact list is composed by a static part, such as "Chama" ("Call"), that resides in the grammar file, and a dynamic part composed by the contact name. If we consider a user with a large contact list he/she might not remember exactly the contact's name. In a different scenario, one can consider the case of persons with many names (six and seven names occur frequently within European Portuguese full names), which might be called by their first, their last, their middle or any combinations of these names and more. For example, if we download a contact list from an Exchange server with a contact named João Paulo de Oliveira Esperança Gonçalves, he might be known as "João Paulo" by user "A" and "João Esperança" by user "B". Considering the functionality provided by Pocket Reco to make a phone call to a contact in the contact list, the correspondent command is dependent on the contact name. The developed name matching algorithm allows the user to say the contact name in any form he/she is used to. Instead of residing in the grammar only the first and last name of each contact, all different names from the contact list are placed into the CFG grammar in separate phrases, without repetitions. This will allow the recognizer to accept any combination of names, e.g. "Chama João Paulo Gonçalves", "Chama João Gonçalves", etc. After the recognition stage, the spoken contact name must be analysed. The application will access the contact list, which is, in this particular case, residing in memory (loaded when the application starts), and search, through this list, the contact that has the highest number of matches with the spoken name. With the proposed algorithm there is the chance of name ambiguities. When this happens, the algorithm either chooses the first name occurrence or gives the user the possibility of solving the ambiguity, which is the most correct approach. This can be achieved by giving the user the contacts possibilities and respective full names (through TTS), asking him to choose the desired contact. The disadvantage of providing flexibility to the user's interface with this algorithm is the increased number of items in the grammar, leading to an increase of the word error rate in the recognition process. There must be a compromise between application flexibility and recognition accuracy, depending of the application user's group and the recognition engine.

3.5 Locale Culture

The application localization is an important factor in the application design. It is necessary to understand the locale specific issues relative to the application. In the specific case of EP, it was necessary to identify the naming procedures executed by EP speakers, or in other words, checking the common way of placing a phone call. For example, in EP it is common to say "Chama" or "Liga" followed by the person name and less common to say "Efectuar chamada". The inclusion of the most common words in the grammar to describe an action leads to a more natural user interaction.

4 Experimental Results

In this section, a subjective usability evaluation experiment that compares the accomplishment of a task through the use of a graphical interface and of a speech interface is presented. This set of subjective usability tests compares the usage of a graphical interface with the usage of a speech interface while performing a common task in mobile devices.

The tests were applied to a universe of 30 unpaid adult persons, 16 male and 14 female, from the Portuguese academia. Two groups, each with 15 subjects, were considered: one group had prior experience with speech interfaces in mobility; the other group presented no previous experience with speech interfaces and the experience with mobile devices is resumed to cell phones. Both groups covered all the considered ranges of ages as shown in the table 1. Each person performed two tasks, calling to a predefined contact number that resided in a contact list with 20 contacts, through the graphical HCI and the same task through the speech HCI, e.g. "Call to Pedro Silva mobile phone". The usability experiment collected the time duration of the task as a metric that relates to its difficulty. Each subject received a script with clear instructions on how to perform both tasks. The tasks were executed by each subject in a random order, under the same conditions, with Pocket Reco running on a Pocket PC (HTC P3600 - 400MHz, 128MB ROM, 64MB SDRAM), in the following environments: Office, Home, Party (Crowded room) and Car.

Both groups presented similar average value of recognition accuracy - around 84% - with an advantage of 0,5% for the subjects with previous experience on speech applications in mobile devices. Table 2 shows the average time (in seconds) taken to accomplish the proposed tasks.

Table 1. Subjects distribution

Age	Subjects	
	With experience	*Without experience*
< 24	4	4
24-29	6	2
30-35	3	3
> 36	2	6
Total	15	15

Table 2. Time taken to perform the tasks

	GUI (seconds)	Speech (seconds)
With mobility experience	15,0	12,2
Without mobility experience	26,5	14,9
Both groups	20,8	13,6

In the presented results there is a clear advantage in the time metric (34,6% lower), for actions executed with the help of the speech interface. Nonetheless, some of the subjects (especially those with no experience) had to execute more than one attempt, due to recognition errors, to accomplish the task using the speech interface. The recognition errors happened due to background noise and the way subjects interacted with the speech interface, such as bad positioning of the device, covering the microphone and uttering words unclearly, often using abbreviations.

5 Usability Evaluation

In this section, we present the results of a wider usability evaluation test. The goal of this second set of experiments was to assess the usefulness of a speech interface in comparison with the mobile device Graphical User Interface (GUI) provided by Windows Mobile, using a localized EP version of Voice Command [7] and, this time, cover the majority of the basic functionalities provided by a Pocket PC. To determine the usability of a speech interface, an evaluation methodology was adopted and a usability test was developed. The device used was the same HTC P3600 that was used for the previous tests, however, the amount of stock data increased from 20 to 300 contacts and 50 new music files where inserted in the device storage card. The tests were conducted at home and office environments. In the home environment the tests took place under a common living room scenario (television on, though relatively quiet). In the office environment the tests took place in a room with an average 4 to 5 people talking/working.

5.1 Methodology

The usability testing experiment was designed to assess the usefulness of Voice User Interface (VUI) interaction compared to traditional GUI interaction. For this, the time taken and efficiency of the subjects when accomplishing two groups of tasks commonly available in a mobile device was evaluated. The tasks are described in table 3. Nowadays, there are many actions and services provided by a Pocket PC or a Smartphone; so we selected a first group of tasks that are the primary reason or essential when using a device and, consequently, more common amongst users. A second group of tasks was also selected and represents actions that are not so popular, but depending on the user, they can be more or less used. The tasks were designed with the intent of being the most global and representative of a group of services.

Table 3. Tasks performed in the usability evaluation test

Common tasks	Other tasks
1. Placing a phone call	5. Lookup contact information
2. Checking calendar	6. Open an application
3. Verifying device status	7. Play media
4. Change profile or sound options	8. Manipulate media

These sets of tasks are performed using both interfaces alternately (e.g. the subject performs the tasks with the VUI and then performs the same tasks using the GUI; the next subject first performs the tasks with GUI and then performs the same tasks with the VUI). By alternating the interface order independence is gained, breaking any kind of relation between the interfaces that may affect test results. The tests, regarding each interface, are preceded by a four minutes session for interface adaptation. The adaptation is divided in a two minutes explanation and followed by a two minutes training session, so that the subject is able to adapt himself/herself to the device. Each subject also receives a two pages user guide and a half page quick user guide, about each interface, explaining how to use the device. The tutorial about the user interfaces include the tasks mentioned in table 3. The tutorials are as clear and equivalent as possible. Each testing session took about 15-25 minutes, depending on the subject feedback.

5.2 Subject Profiles

The usability experiment was run on 35 unpaid subjects with ages between 23 and 65. There were 26 male and 9 female subjects with a variety of business occupations (IT engineers, Senior Consultants, Retired, Students, etc). In order to obtain a reference profile the subjects were asked to fill a questionnaire about their previous experience on speech interfaces, use of stylus (on mobile devices) and mobile devices in general. The results reveal that the majority of the subjects had low experience with speech interfaces and in a scale of 0 to 3 (0 – None, 1 – Low, 2 – Medium, 3 - High) presented an 1, 2 average value; a medium experience in the use of stylus, with an 1,8 average on the same scale and high experience with mobile devices, presenting an 2,7 average (again same scale of 0 to 3). These results are presented in the graphic of fig. 3 below and were gathered through a questionnaire filled before executing the tasks.

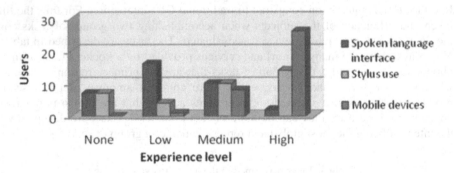

Fig. 3. Subjects experience profile

5.3 Evaluation Results and Analysis

All subjects were successful in completing the experiments with both interfaces, showing different degrees of efficiency and taking different durations to fulfil the tasks. During the experiments we became aware of some problems that rose while using the system and received valuable feedback which is described below. It was also performed an analysis on: the time that the subjects spent to perform the experiment; the number of attempts when performing a task; why subjects failed to use the VUI on a first attempt; the questionnaires filled after the usability test.

When analysing the times taken in the several tasks, there is a clear advantage of the VUI placing a call to a determined contact, checking a contact card and playing a group of songs (fig. 4). VUI's advantage in such tasks is explained by the task complexity. All of these tasks have in common the fact that they require a set of actions, such as menu navigation, scrolling, etc, to be executed with success. The VUI gives a way of accessing all of these services through a single action, as simple as issuing a voice command. The inverse situation can be noticed when checking tomorrow's appointments or passing to the next song. To execute these tasks both interfaces only need a single action, so it is natural to have a balance in terms of time when executing them. Despite the time needed to accomplish a task, it will be shown that the subject not always prefer the fastest way to perform the task.

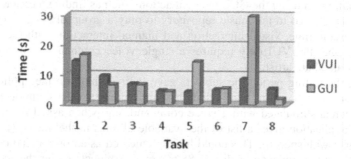

Fig. 4. Time taken in accomplishing the tasks (VUI and GUI)

When using the VUI, recognition errors are expected to occur, especially considering that the majority of the subjects reported a low experience level with speech interfaces. The main reasons for recognition errors in these tests were: The spoken command is not included in the grammar; the command sentence was spoken in an incorrect order (e.g. in the grammar is available the command sentence "Que horas são?" and the user says "São que horas?"); covering the microphone with the hand that holds the device when uttering the voice command; bad interaction with the push-to-talk (PTT) button, such as saying the command without pushing the button; taking more time than usual to input the command (after pressing the PTT button); push the PTT button and not wait for the noise or visual signal from the application to input the voice command; and talking before introducing the speech command (when the application is waiting for a command).

Regarding the number of attempts taken to accomplish the tasks, it was registered that the number of attempts decreases during the test execution, except for task number five. The decrease in the number of attempts can be justified by the quick adaptation of the subjects to the VUI, since the tasks where independent. This was also visible during the tests. The exception verified, for task number five (lookup for contact information), is due to the lack of synonyms in the application grammar to perform this particular action.

5.4 Subject Feedback

The subjects provided valuable feedback during and after the experiment, mostly regarding the VUI interface. Right after the testing session, the subjects were asked to fill a short questionnaire that allowed extracting the opinions and preferences of the subjects, when asked to compare both interfaces and about the VUI.

From section 5.2 can be concluded that the subjects are more familiar with the GUI, as opposed to VUI. Ideally, the subjects had equal familiarity with both modalities so that we could make a more precise comparison based on it. Despite that, there are still some interesting conclusions that one can extract. When analysing the provided feedback, a clear preference for the VUI in accomplishing the tasks is observed, despite the time taken to accomplish the task. The tasks one and seven reveal that interaction via VUI is overwhelming, when compared to the GUI. This is justified by the fact that, when using the GUI, inherent actions such as finding a contact to place a call, or having to go to the music repository to play a group of songs requires additional attention, time, visual interaction and manual interaction with the device. On the other hand, the VUI only requires a single voice command to index a contact number or an album artist.

During the testing period the subjects gave their opinion on the application, presenting a set of suggestions that include having a more stronger component of visual feedback when stimulated with a voice command, e.g. when asked for available albums the application gives a list of the available albums in the device (on which we can navigate with speech). This could be implemented as an option. To conclude the analysis about the subject's feedback, 88,6% of the subjects prefer the VUI interface when asked to choose between the two interfaces, and only 11,4% prefer the GUI interface. Nonetheless, 21% of the subjects mentioned that their option on which interface to use depends on the situation and location. These subjects commonly choose the GUI interface for public places such as shopping malls, and the VUI for "busy hands, busy eyes" scenarios such as, automotive and sports.

6 Summary

The known disadvantage of speech HCI, including its applicability in mobility, is that speech recognition is not 100% accurate, due to its probabilistic nature. This fact may lead to recognition errors which the application must handle and try to resolve, for example, by asking for confirmation on a given voice command to avoid false-positive results. In some use cases, with noisy environments or less experienced users, several attempts may be needed to successfully accomplish the task. In speech recognition for mobility, the optimizations performed over the models and SR engine often decrease the components performance. If that happens, the application implementation can compensate this decrease in quality. The grammar is an application component that the developer can design carefully to optimize the recognition.

In this paper we have described a set of optimizations to improve recognition accuracy and user interaction experience, in the framework of a spoken language interface in a mobile device. In order to complement the approach it was developed an example application that places a phone call to a contact, through a spoken language interface. The application interacts with the SR engine through SAPI and implements a name matching algorithm to improve the user experience. It was also presented the results of a usability evaluation trial, to demonstrate the advantage of using a speech HCI versus a graphical HCI. In this work, it was shown that the set of words chosen to be recognized will influence the application performance. This choice of words is influenced by the acoustic models, the quality of the speech recognition engine and language specifications. The developer has the responsibility to balance the application according to its usage scenario and needs to adapt the application to the user group. In this paper we presented an application that takes into account all these considerations, discussing the advantages and drawbacks of the various design choices. The name matching algorithm here presented is an example which trades recognition accuracy for a more intuitive and natural interface. The executed tests have shown that we can manipulate the grammar to improve the performance of the algorithm. The conducted subjective usability tests demonstrated that users with no experience in speech applications and mobile devices can easily learn how to execute a simple call action in the device, through a spoken language interface. The presented results showed that the time to accomplish a simple task, like placing a phone call, is 34,6% lower when using a speech interface as a replacement for a graphical interface. The time difference between the two types of interfaces decreases drastically according to the level of the user expertise with speech applications in mobile devices. The conclusions also showed that complex tasks, such as playing a group of songs, are easier to accomplish with a VUI (Voice User Interface). A quick adaptation by the users to the spoken language interface, during the conducted usability tests, was verified, resulting in lesser attempts to accomplish a task.

Acknowledgements

The authors would like to thank to the Microsoft Language Development Center members, in Microsoft Portugal, and to all the persons that participated in the usability experiments.

References

1. Huang, X., Acero, A., Hon, H.-W.: Spoken Language Processing - A Guide to Theory, Algorithms, and System Development. Prentice Hall, New York (2001)
2. Acero, A.: Building Voice User Interfaces. MSDN Magazine, February edn. (2006)
3. Rabiner, L.R.: A tutorial on hidden Markov models and selected applications in speech recognition. IEEE 77(2), 257–286 (1989)
4. Microsoft Speech SDK,
   http://msdn.microsoft.com/library/aa914072.aspx
5. Acero, A.: Acoustical and Environmental Robustness in Automatic Speech Recognition. The Springer International Series in Engineering and Computer Science, vol. 201 (1993)
6. Stern, R., Acero, A., Liu, F., Ohshima, Y.: Signal Processing for Robust Speech Recognition. In: Automatic Speech and Speaker Recognition, Advanced Topics. Kluwer Academic Publishers, Dordrecht (1996)
7. Microsoft Voice Command,
   http://www.microsoft.com/windowsmobile/en-us/
   downloads/microsoft/about-voice-command.mspx
8. Cyberon Voice Commander, http://www.cyberon.com.tw
9. Voice Signal, http://www.voicesignal.com
10. MSDN Windows Mobile 5.0 SDK Documentation,
   http://msdn.microsoft.com/en-us/library/ms376766.aspx

A Study on Bilingual Speech Recognition
Involving a Minority Language*

Míriam Luján-Mares, Carlos-D. Martínez-Hinarejos, and Vicente Alabau

Institut Tecnològic d'Informàtica
Universitat Politècnica de València
Camí de Vera, s/n. 46071 València, Spain
{mlujan,cmartine,valabau}@dsic.upv.es

Abstract. Multilingual Automatic Speech Recognition (ASR) systems are of great interest in multilingual environments. We have studied the case of the *Comunitat Valenciana* because the two official languages are *Spanish* and *Valencian*. These two languages share most of their phonemes and their syntax and vocabulary are also quite similar since they have influenced each other for many years. In this work, we present the design of the language and the acoustic models for this bilingual situation. Acoustic models can be separate for each language or shared by both of them, and they can be obtained directly from a training corpus or by adapting a previous set of acoustic models. Language models can be separate for each language (monolingual recognition) or mixed for both languages (bilingual recognition). We performed experiments with a small corpus to determine which option was better for this case.

Keywords: multilingual speech recognition, language identification, language adaptation.

1 Introduction

Automatic Speech Recognition (ASR) is one of the most interesting applications of natural language technologies and signal processing [1]. ASR has improved, but recognition performance is still low under adverse circumstances. Nevertheless, there are currently some commercial products or applications with ASR [1], which demonstrates interest in these systems.

In multilingual environments, it is useful to have a multilingual ASR system [2]. In order to build a classical ASR system, it is necessary to train language and acoustic models. Language models are task-dependent and language-dependent. For this reason, a multilingual ASR system must include several language models, one for each language that the system must deal with.

* Work partially supported by VIDI-UPV under PAID06 program by the EC (FEDER) and the Spanish MEC under grant TIN2006-15694-CO2-01 and by the Spanish research programme Consolider Ingenio 2010: MIPRCV (CSD2007-00018).

Z. Vetulani and H. Uszkoreit (Eds.): LTC 2007, LNAI 5603, pp. 36–49, 2009.
© Springer-Verlag Berlin Heidelberg 2009

Acoustic models are also language-dependent because each language defines its own phonemes differently from other languages. In addition, the articulation of shared phonemes may differ in each language. Some work has already been done to find more robust acoustical units for this situation [3]. Therefore, in multilingual systems there is a new difficulty: the system has to determine which language is being spoken.

This can be done before the recognition process, with the aim of using the correct language and acoustic models. However, it can be done after a parallel recognition process in all the languages supported by the ASR system. In this last case, the recognition process can provide important information to obtain a more accurate detection of the language.

Another important problem is that languages are usually influenced by other languages, and, in multilingual environments, the influence of the speaker's mother tongue can produce an inappropriate pronunciation of the other languages that are present in the environments (e.g., the perception distortion of a native Dutch speaker is equivalent to a reduction of the signal-to-noise ratio of 3-4 dB for non-native Dutch speakers [4]).

In this work, we study the multilingual environment that is actually present in the *Comunitat Valenciana*. In this community, two languages are spoken, Spanish and Valencian. Valencian is a dialect of *Catalan* that is spoken in the *Comunitat Valenciana*. The Valencian dialect has special phonetic features with respect to standard Catalan. This is due to its dialectal variance and the great influence that Spanish has had on it. This influence has been much greater on Valencian than on other Catalan dialects. According to [5], the total number of people who are able to speak Catalan is 7,200,000, and the number of people who understand it is over 9,800,000. The Valencian dialect is spoken by 27.35% of all Catalan speakers.

Due to immigration and the linguistic repression of Valencian during the Franco period (1939-1977), at the present time, native Valencian speakers are also good Spanish speakers. However, most non-native Valencian speakers are not competent Valencian speakers. Also, the great influence of the Spanish language on the Valencian dialect has modified Valencian phonetics in the average speaker. Thus, Spanish and Valencian have a set of similar phonemes, and most acoustic models could be shared by both languages.

Our objective is to compare the different variants in order to build a multilingual system and to choose the best alternative for this pair of languages. We have studied different alternatives for language and acoustic models. We used separate language and a mixed language model. Separate language models can be used when automatic language identification is done before recognition and the corresponding monolingual system is used. The mixed language model is used when automatic language identification is done after recognition and a multilingual system is used. We used different sets of acoustic models: separate, mixed and adapted acoustic models. Separate acoustic models are used in monolingual systems. Mixed acoustic models are used in monolingual and multilingual systems.

Table 1. Corpus statistics

		Spanish	Valencian
	Sentences	240	240
Training	Running words	2887	2692
	Length	1 h 33 m	1 h 29 m
	Vocabulary	131	131
	Sentences	60	60
Test	Running words	705	681
	Length	23m	21m

Adapted acoustic models are obtained with different adaptation techniques and used in the monolingual and multilingual case.

This work is organized as follows. In Section 2, we describe the corpus that was used for the experiments. In Section 3, we explain the design of the language and the acoustic models. In Section 4, we describe the MLLR adaptation technique. In Section 5, we detail the different experiments carried out. In Section 6, we present our conclusions and future work.

2 Corpus

To perform the experiments, we employed a corpus about an Information System task. The corpus was acquired from the telephone line. The corpus is made up of approximately 4 hours of recording (2 hours for each language). It contains a set of 120 sentences (60 for each language) for each of the 20 speakers. Some example sentences can be found in Figure 1. Half of the speakers (10) were native Spanish speakers and the other half (10) were native Valencian speakers. All the speakers were university students and recorded sentences in the two languages. Table 1 summarizes the statistics of the corpus. The distribution of men and women was equal. The complete description of the corpus can be found in [6].

There were no out-of-vocabulary (OOV) words in the Spanish test corpus, and only 2 OOV words were observed in the Valencian test corpus. Due to the small size of the speech corpus, both in signal and vocabulary, we can expect low perplexity language models but badly estimated acoustic models.

3 Language and Acoustic Modelling

3.1 Language Models

Language models define what type of sentences are allowed by a system. Therefore, our language models must accept all the sentences of the training corpus.

In our case, all the sentences of the corpus have a common structure: greeting, question, information, title, person, and farewell. Some examples of sentences are shown in Figure 1. A sentence is not required to have all the fields. In accordance with this idea, we constructed an automaton using blocks (each block modelled one field) as language model. We developed three language models:

Spanish

  – Por favor, quiero saber el e-mail de Francisco Casacuberta, adiós.
  – Hola, cuál es el horario de consultas de Enrique Vidal, muchas gracias.

Valencian

  – Per favor, vull saber l'e-mail de Francisco Casacuberta, adeu.
  – Hola, quin és l'horari de consultes d'Enrique Vidal, moltes gràcies.

English

  – Please, I want to know Francisco Casacuberta's e-mail, goodbye.
  – Hello, what are the Enrique Vidal's office hours?, thank you very much.

Fig. 1. A selection of sentences of the corpus. The English sentences are provided for a better understanding of the examples.

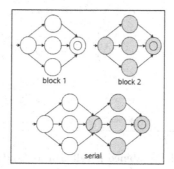

Fig. 2. Illustration of the serialization process

  – Two separate language models: an automaton was built for each language using the acceptor automaton (in the corresponding language) of each block. It was made by joining the acceptor automata in a series. For every two consecutive automata, we merged the final states of the first acceptor automaton with the initial states of the second one. Figure 3.1 shows an example of the serialization process.
  – A mixed language model: a single automaton was built for the two languages. This automaton was built by joining the two separate language automata. We joined the acceptor automata in parallel by merging the initial states and the final states of each language for each block. Figure 3 shows an example of the parallelization process. The acceptor automata were also joined in a series. Therefore, a sentence can start in a block in Spanish (for example, the greeting block) and continue in a block in Valencian. Therefore, if the sentence was actually in Valencian, the system can recognize the sentence as Valencian and answer the question in Valencian. Figure 3.1 shows an example of the parallelization process for the joint automata.

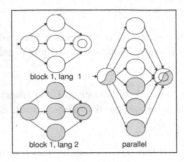

Fig. 3. Illustration of the parallelization process

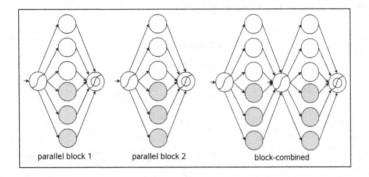

Fig. 4. Illustration of the combined parallelization and serialization process

We computed the perplexity of these language models with the following results: Spanish only 5.98, Valencian only 6.46, and mixed language 8.42. Note that the perplexity of the models is very low. This is in accordance with the size of the speech corpus, which is also small.

Another option is to use two monolingual systems with two parallel recognitions. This option has several disadvantages: more time is needed to obtain two recognitions, and it is not possible to share information between the monolingual systems.

3.2 Acoustic Models

Each acoustic model is associated to a phoneme (i.e., monophones) in order to make a comparison of the features of an acoustic sequence with the acoustic models. The acoustic models were hidden Markov models (HMM) that were trained using the HTK toolkit [7]. The HMMs followed a three-state, left-to-right topology without skips. We tested models from one Gaussian per state up to 128 Gaussians per state. Each gaussian modeled a 33-component feature vector (10 cepstral coefficients plus energy with the first and second derivatives).

We used different sets of acoustic models to perform the experiments:

- Spanish acoustic models only: these models were obtained for the Spanish phone set that corresponds to the phonetical scheme that we used. We automatically made transcriptions following the rules described in [8] for the SAMPA phonetic alphabet [9]. This set was trained with the Spanish utterances only.

- Valencian acoustic models only: these acoustic models share phonemes with Spanish acoustic models, but they also have different phonemes that only appear in Valencian. However, in Valencian, there are no rules to help us transcribe the sentences automatically. Therefore, each word in the vocabulary was transcribed with known phonetic variations. This set was trained with the Valencian utterances only.

- Mixed Spanish and Valencian acoustic models: in order to obtain these acoustic models, we used all the training sentences that were available (both in Spanish and Valencian). The mixed acoustic models were obtained using all the phonemes of Spanish and Valencian because almost all the phonemes are shared by the two languages. The same acoustic model was used for each shared phoneme in Spanish and Valencian. Training was performed with Spanish and Valencian information.

- Adapted acoustic models: To obtain reliable acoustic models, they must be trained with huge amounts of training data. It was easy to find large Spanish corpora, but for this study we did not have a large Valencian corpus available. However, since Valencian is phonetically very similar to Spanish, we were able to use the small amount of training material available in Valencian to adapt acoustic models that were trained from a large Spanish corpus. We used the *Senglar* corpus, which has been successfully used in other tasks [10]. The recording conditions for the *Senglar* corpus were different from those of our corpus. For this reason, we obtained adapted acoustic models (separate and mixed) from *Senglar* acoustic models for both Spanish and Valencian so that they could be used in our task.

Adapted acoustic models were obtained with the MLLR (Maximum Likelihood Linear Regression) technique [11] estimating a global adaptation matrix for each language. We used our training corpus as adaptation material to obtain the adapted acoustic models. This technique has been used before for multilingual speech recognition. The quantity of signal we used to adapt the models is similar to the quantity of signal used in a previous work [12]. Details on the MLLR technique are given in the next section.

4 The MLLR Adaptation Technique

The aim of speaker adaptation techniques is to obtain a speaker-dependent recognition system by using a combination of general speech knowledge from well-trained hidden Markov models and speaker-specific information from a new speaker's data. Speaker adaptation is applied to a speech recognition system in order to obtain a speaker-dependent system with a better performance than the original system for a specific speaker.

MLLR is a technique to adapt a set of speaker-independent acoustic models to a speaker by using small amounts of adaptation material. This technique can also be used in language adaptation by using adaptation material in the language being adapted to.

The MLLR approach requires an initial independent continuous density HMM system. MLLR takes some adaptation data from a speaker to adapt the acoustic models. MLLR updates the model mean parameters to maximize the likelihood of the adaptation data. The means are updated using a transformation matrix, which is estimated from the adaptation data. We applied the formulation presented in [11] to language adaptation: we took some adaptation data from a language to adapt the acoustic models using MLLR in the same way as in speaker adaptation.

The theory is based on the concept of regression classes. A regression class is a set of mixture components that share the same transformation matrix, which is estimated from the adaptation data. When all the models are in the same regression class, it is a global regression class. However, any set of regression classes can be manually or automatically defined over the gaussians of the HMM. There is no method to analytically determine the optimal number and composition of regression classes [11].

To perform the adaptation of the means, we computed a transformation matrix W for each regression class. This matrix is applied to the extended mean vector of all the mixtures pertaining to the regression class to obtain an adapted mean vector. Given a state q in a HMM, for the ith gaussian of the output distribution, we denote its mean vector as $\boldsymbol{\mu}_{qi}$. The adapted mean vector $\widehat{\boldsymbol{\mu}}_{qi}$ is obtained by:

$$\widehat{\boldsymbol{\mu}}_{qi} = W \cdot \boldsymbol{\xi}_{qi}$$

where $\boldsymbol{\xi}_{qi}$ is the extended mean vector defined as:

$$\boldsymbol{\xi}_{qi} = [w, \mu_{qi}^1, \ldots, \mu_{qi}^n]' = [w : \boldsymbol{\mu}_{qi}]$$

where n is the number of features, $\boldsymbol{\mu}_{qi}$ is the original mean vector and w is an offset term.

If we have a set of adaptation data denoted by the sequence of acoustic feature vectors $X = x_1 x_2 \ldots x_T, x_t \in \mathbb{R}^n, t = 1, \ldots, T$, we can estimate the adaptation matrix $\widehat{W}$ using the maximum likelihood approach as:

$$\widehat{W} = \max_{W} p_{\boldsymbol{\theta}}(X)$$

where $\boldsymbol{\theta}$ defines the parameters of the adapted model.

To compute the transformation matrix, we can use several variants: without the same covariances of the distributions (with a full or a diagonal matrix) or with the same covariances of the distributions. Details on the estimation of these variants can be consulted in [11]. The following formulation assumes only one adaptation sample, but it can be easily extended for n adaptation samples.

4.1 Full Matrix

Given a state q in a HMM, for the ith gaussian of the output distribution, we denote its mean vector as $\boldsymbol{\mu}_{qi}$ and its covariance matrix as $\boldsymbol{\Sigma}_{qi}$.

To compute a full matrix, it is necessary to compute an auxiliary tridimensional matrix $\boldsymbol{G}$. In this case, $\widehat{\boldsymbol{W}}$ must be calculated by rows because $\boldsymbol{G}$ is a tridimensional matrix. We calculate the row k of $\widehat{\boldsymbol{W}}$ as:

$$\widehat{\boldsymbol{w}}'_k = \boldsymbol{G}^{(k)-1}\boldsymbol{z}'_k$$

where

$$\boldsymbol{z} = \sum_t \sum_q \sum_i (\gamma_{qi}(t))\boldsymbol{\Sigma}_{qi}^{-1}\boldsymbol{x}_t\boldsymbol{\xi}'_{qi}$$

$\gamma_{qi}(t)$ is defined as the posteriori probability of occupying state q at time t given that the observation sequence $\boldsymbol{x}_t$ is generated by the ith gaussian.

The row k of $\boldsymbol{G}$ is defined as:

$$\boldsymbol{G}^{(k)}_{jq} = \sum_{q,i} v^{(qi)}_{ii} d^{(qi)}_{jq}$$

where

$$\boldsymbol{D}^{(qi)} = \boldsymbol{\xi}_{qi}\boldsymbol{\xi}'_{qi}$$

and

$$\boldsymbol{V}^{(qi)} = \sum_t \gamma_{qi}(t)\boldsymbol{\Sigma}^{(-1)}_{qi}$$

4.2 Diagonal Matrix

To compute a $\widehat{\boldsymbol{W}}$ transformation matrix, we define a diagonal matrix:

$$\boldsymbol{W} = \begin{bmatrix} w_{1,1} & w_{1,2} & 0 & \cdots & 0 \\ w_{2,1} & 0 & w_{2,3} & \ddots & \vdots \\ \vdots & \vdots & \ddots & \ddots & 0 \\ w_{n,1} & 0 & \cdots & 0 & w_{n,n+1} \end{bmatrix}$$

For non-zero elements of this matrix, we rewrote the matrix to a transformation vector $\boldsymbol{w}$ as:

$$\boldsymbol{w} = \begin{bmatrix} w_{1,1} \\ \vdots \\ w_{n,1} \\ w_{1,2} \\ \vdots \\ w_{n,n+1} \end{bmatrix}$$

We defined a matrix $\boldsymbol{D_{qi}}$ made up of the elements of the extended mean vector $\boldsymbol{\xi}_{qi}$ as:

$$\boldsymbol{D_{qi}} = \begin{bmatrix} w & 0 & \cdots & 0 & \mu_{qi1} & 0 & \cdots & 0 \\ 0 & w & \ddots & \vdots & 0 & \mu_{qi2} & \ddots & \vdots \\ \vdots & \ddots & \ddots & 0 & \vdots & \ddots & \ddots & 0 \\ 0 & \cdots & 0 & w & 0 & \cdots & 0 & \mu_{qin} \end{bmatrix}$$

Then, $\widehat{w}$ can be calculated as:

$$\widehat{w} = \left[\sum_t \sum_q \sum_i (\gamma_{qi}(t)) \boldsymbol{D}'_{qi} \boldsymbol{\Sigma}_{qi}^{-1} \boldsymbol{x}_t \right]^{-1} \left[\sum_t \sum_q \sum_i (\gamma_{qi}(t)) \boldsymbol{D}'_{qi} \boldsymbol{\Sigma}_{qi}^{-1} \boldsymbol{D}_{qi} \right]$$

4.3 Mean Square

We can consider that all covariances of the distributions are the same. We can follow the Viterbi approximation, where each speech frame is assigned to exactly one distribution. Therefore, the adaptation matrix can be computed by:

$$\widehat{\boldsymbol{W}} = \left(\sum_t \boldsymbol{x}_t \boldsymbol{\mu}'_{qi} \right) \left(\sum_t \boldsymbol{\mu}_{qi} \boldsymbol{\mu}'_{qi} \right)^{-1}$$

The sequence of $\boldsymbol{\mu}_{qi}$ is usually defined by a Viterbi alignment of the samples.

5   Experiments

In this section, we explain the experiments that we carried out within this experimental framework. A first attempt to do this was made in a previous study [6], but the results were not conclusive. In this work, we have performed a more exhaustive experimentation. The aim of the experiments was to find the option that obtains the best results for the test set and to study the behaviour of a multilingual Spanish-Valencian system.

In order to analyze the results, we used different evaluation measures:

- *Word Error Rate (WER)*: This measure computes the edit distance between a reference sentence and the recognized sentence.
- *Semantic Word Error Rate (SemWER)*: The task of the corpus has fields that refer to the required information (for example, e-mail and name). These fields are the semantic fields. Therefore, we computed the edit distance between the fields of the reference sentence and the fields of the recognized sentence.

- *Language Identification Rate (LIR)*: In multilingual environments, the speaker's language must be known in case the system has to answer the speaker in that language. For this reason, when both languages could be decoded, we computed the percentage of sentences in which the speaker's language was correctly identified.

The WER in an experiment is computed by taking into account all the speakers in the test database. However, we need to know who is committing the errors in each language in order to determine the influence of the mother language. Therefore, we obtained the errors for the speaker's mother tongue, and we indicated these results as *Native Speaker*. Thus, we knew if all the speakers of the corpus could speak the two languages of the system equally well.

Since we must compare the different variants in order to build a multilingual system, several experiments were performed: with non-adapted/adapted acoustic models and monolingual/bilingual systems. We tried adapted acoustic models because we only had a small quantity of signal for training acoustic models and adaptation techniques could be beneficial.

5.1 Monolingual Recognition with Non-adapted Acoustic Models

First, we performed the easiest experiments using separate language models with non-adapted acoustic models. These experiments assume perfect language identification before the recognition process.

Table 2 shows the best results obtained for the separate language models with non-adapted acoustic models. It can be observed that the results with separate acoustic models for Spanish were better than for Valencian for both WER and SemWER. These results can be explained by the higher variability in Valencian pronunciations since proper names can be said in either Spanish or Valencian. Also, each person pronounces them in a different way. Another reason could be the quality of the transcriptions of the Valencian sentences that were used in the training process, which were not as accurate as the Spanish transcriptions. With mixed acoustic models, the Spanish WER was better than the WER for the separate acoustic models. However, the Valencian WER was the worst of all. To explain these results, we computed the WER for each group of people, according to the speaker's mother tongue. Table 2 shows that those speakers whose mother tongue was Valencian spoke both languages better than those whose mother tongue was Spanish. Furthermore, the Spanish speakers spoke

Table 2. Results for separate language models with non-adapted acoustic models

Acoustic models	Not mixed			Mixed		
Language models	Spanish	Valencian	Mean	Spanish	Valencian	Mean
WER	3.5%	5.4%	4.4%	3.1%	6.2%	4.6%
SemWER	1.7%	3.8%	2.7%	1.7%	3.6%	2.6%
Native Spanish	4.7%	7.3%	6.0%	4.4%	8.1%	6.2%
Speaker Valencian	2.2%	3.4%	2.8%	1.9%	4.4%	3.1%

Table 3. WER results of experiments with the three variants of MLLR. The best results are in boldface.

WER	Spanish	Valencian
Baseline	11.0%	16.5%
Full Matrix	6.0%	10.4%
Diagonal Matrix	7.3%	11.4%
Mean Square	**5.4%**	**9.8%**

Valencian very badly, whereas the Valencian speakers spoke Spanish very well. The reason for this is that today in the *Comunitat Valenciana*, it is mandatory to learn both Spanish and Valencian. However, a few years ago it was only mandatory to learn Spanish. Therefore, in general, the people of the *Comunitat Valenciana* currently speak better Spanish than Valencian.

5.2 Monolingual Recognition with Adapted Acoustic Models

Second, we performed the experiments using separate language models with adapted acoustic models. In this case, perfect language identification is also assumed.

To obtain baseline results for the adapted acoustic models, we performed experiments for Spanish and Valencian with *Senglar* acoustic models without adaptation. *Senglar* Valencian models were built by cloning the most similar Spanish model for each Valencian phoneme. The best results that we obtained were 11.0% WER and 7.9% SemWER for Spanish, and 16.5% WER and 18.9% SemWER for Valencian. These were the worst results for this work because these acoustic models were not adapted for our task.

We implemented the three variants of MLLR presented above: full matrix, diagonal matrix and mean square. The adaptation data was small, so we adapted the acoustic models with only one regression class and, therefore, we only computed one transformation matrix.

Full matrix and diagonal matrix were calculated with one iteration of Expectation-Maximization because more iterations provided worse results. In general, when the initial models provide good Gaussian frame alignments, only a single iteration of EM is required to estimate the transformation matrix [13].

Table 3 shows the best results obtained in the experiments. Under the same conditions, another standard MLLR tool (HTK) provided similar results for the full matrix case (6.0% in Spanish, 11.0% in Valencian) [7]. As the results show, for the task under consideration, it is best to use Mean Square because the WER improved by 5.6 points in Spanish (from 11.0% to 5.4%) and by 6.7 points in Valencian (from 16.5% to 9.8%). Mean Square obtains the best results because the difference between the *Senglar* acoustic models and the adaptation data is large enough to make the different covariances a source of errors when computing the

Table 4. Results for separate language models with adapted acoustic models

Acoustic models	Not mixed			Mixed		
Language models	Spanish	Valencian	Mean	Spanish	Valencian	Mean
WER	5.5%	9.7%	7.6%	5.4%	9.8%	7.6%
SemWER	2.2%	7.8%	5.0%	2.0%	8.2%	5.1%
Native Spanish	7.2%	12.5%	9.8%	7.1%	12.8%	9.9%
Speaker Valencian	3.7%	6.7%	5.2%	3.7%	6.7%	5.2%

state occupancy $(\gamma_{qi}(t))$. The difference between a full matrix and a diagonal matrix is small, but the results are better with a full matrix than with a diagonal matrix.

Table 4 shows the best results for separate language models with adapted acoustic models using the variant Mean Square of MLLR. The results were very bad because of the way the acoustic models were obtained. However, the behaviour was similar to the behaviour shown in Table 2. The explanation for these results is the same as the explanation for the results in Table 2.

5.3 Bilingual Recognition

Finally we tested two experiments: mixed language models with non-adapted and adapted acoustic models. This is a parallel recognition process, without previous language identification.

Table 5 shows the results for the mixed language models. Since a multilingual recognition is possible in this case, LIR must be calculated. To determine the language of the sentences, we counted the number of words in each language in the recognised sentence. The language that had the highest number of words in this count was designated as the language of the sentence; e.g., "bona nit quería el correo electrónico de carlos hinarejos gracias", is a sentence that has two words in Valencian ("bona" and "nit"), four words in Spanish ("quería", "correo", "electrónico" and "gracias") and the others words ("el", "de", "carlos" and "hinarejos") are present in the two languages (therefore these words do not count for LIR's calculation).

The results (with non-adapted acoustic models) for mixed language models were worse than for mixed acoustic models and separate language models (Table

Table 5. Results for mixed language models. Native speaker WER is presented as Spanish/Valencian WER.

Mixed acoustic models	Not adapted	Adapted
WER	7.4%	11.8%
SemWER	3.0%	5.2%
LIR	98.1%	97.1%
Native Spanish	9.1%/10.5%	15.1%/14.8%
Speaker Valencian	3.6%/6.4%	7.2%/10.3%

2). Therefore, for the non-adapted acoustic models, the best option is separate language models and mixed acoustic models. Mixed language models produce more errors because the perplexity is higher (8.42) than the perplexity for separate language models (5.98-6.46).

The results (with adapted acoustic models) for mixed language models were worse than for mixed acoustic models and separate language models (Table 4). As Table 5 shows, the WER is the worst, but the SemWER is equal to the average shown in Table 4 (5.1%). This might be explained by the difference in the recording conditions of the *Senglar* corpus and the recording conditions of our corpus. Thus, in spite of the adaptation, the original acoustic models had more influence than our adaptation data. Also, the results for Valencian were worse because Valencian is different from the language used in the *Senglar* acoustic models (Spanish). LIR was very good, and this is positive because, in a multilingual ASR system, it is very important for the system to guess what language is being spoken (e.g., in order to answer in the same language that is being spoken).

Native Speaker in Table 5 is presented as Spanish/Valencian WER. The results show the same tendency as in the other tables, i.e., Spanish speakers spoke both Spanish and Valencian worse than Valencian speakers.

6   Conclusions and Future Work

This article presents an initial work on bilingual Spanish-Valencian speech recognition. The results obtained are very promising. We have obtained a system with a good WER and a better SemWER. The results show that the minority language obtained worse results than the major language. This is reasonable because the average speaker is usually more competent in the major language. The use of mixed acoustic models seem to be favorable because we obtained better overall results. The results for mixed language models were worse than for separate language models. Therefore, the best option is separate language models.

Moreover, we have implemented three variants of MLLR for language adaptation in order to choose the best alternative for our system, which deals with two languages: Spanish and Valencian. Our proposal is to employ language adaptation in these languages. We used acoustic models (trained with a large corpus in Spanish) and our training corpus as adaptation material to obtain the adapted acoustic models. The results show that, in this case, it is better to use Mean Square. The results with language adaptation are better than with *Senglar* acoustic models without adapting. In conclusion, we think that MLLR is a good option for language adaptation, but the adaptation of acoustic models is highly dependent on the original acoustic models. Thus, the original acoustic models must be reasonably appropriate.

Nevertheless, these conclusions should be confirmed with a larger corpus and a more realistic task. In future work, we plan to adapt our acoustic models with more appropriate initial acoustic models, i.e., a set of Spanish acoustic models that is closer to our conditions. It would be interesting to obtain the adapted

Valencian acoustic models from a set of standard Catalan acoustic models [14]. Moreover, we plan to test different quantities of regression classes and other adaptation techniques such as MAP [15].

References

1. Wald, M.: Using Automatic Speech Recognition to enhance education for all students: turning a vision into reality. In: ASEE/IEEE Frontiers in Education Conference, Session S3G, October 2004, pp. 22–25 (2004)
2. Uebler, U.: Multilingual speech recognition in seven languages. Speech Communication 35, 53–69 (2001)
3. Eklund, R., Lindström, A.: Xenophones: An investigation of phone set expansion in Swedish and implications for speech recognition and speech synthesis. Speech Communication 35, 81–102 (2001)
4. van Wijngaarden, S.J.: Intelligibility of native and non-native Dutch speech. Speech Communication 35, 103–113 (2001)
5. Vilajoana, J., Pons, D.: Catalan, language of Europe. Generalitat de Catalunya (2001)
6. Alabau, V., Martínez, C.D.: Bilingual speech corpus in two phonetically similar languages. In: Proc. of LREC 2006, pp. 1624–1627 (2006)
7. Young, S., Evermann, G., Hain, T., Kershaw, D., Moore, G., Odell, J., Ollason, D., Povey, D., Valtchev, V., Woodland, P.: The HTK Book. v3.2, CUED, UK (July 2004)
8. Quilis, A.: Tratado de fonología y fonética españolas, 2nd edn., Madrid, Gredos (1999)
9. UCL, SAMPA computer readable phonetic alphabet (1993)
10. Casacuberta, F., Ney, H., Och, F.J., Vidal, E., Vilar, J.M., Barrachina, S., García-Varea, I., Mart'inez, C., Llorens, D., Molau, S., Nevado, F., Pastor, M., Picó, D., Sanchis, A.: Some approaches to statistical and finite-state speech-to-speech translation. Computer Speech and Language 18, 25–47 (2004)
11. Leggetter, C.J., Woodland, P.C.: Maximum Likelihood Linear Regression for Speaker Adaptation of continuous density hidden Markov models. Computer Speech and Language 9, 171–185 (1995)
12. Schultz, T., Waibel, A.: Language-independent and language-adaptive acoustic modeling for speech recognition. Speech Communication 35, 31–51 (2001)
13. Woodland, P.C.: Speaker Adaptation for Continuous Density HMMs: A Review. In: ITRW on Adaptation Methods for Speech Recognition, pp. 11–19 (2001)
14. Moreno, A., Febrer, A., Márquez, L.: Generation of Language Resources for the Development of Speech Tecnologies in Catalan. In: Proc. of LREC 2006, pp. 1632–1635 (2006)
15. Gauvain, J., Lee, C.: MAP Estimation of Continuous Density HMM: Theory and Applications. In: Proc. DARPA Speech and Natural Language Workshop, February 1992, pp. 185–190 (1992)

Annotated Corpus of Polish Spoken Dialogues

Agnieszka Mykowiecka[1,2], Krzysztof Marasek[2], Małgorzata Marciniak[1],
Joanna Rabiega-Wiśniewska[1], and Ryszard Gubrynowicz[2]

[1] Institute of Computer Science, Polish Academy of Sciences
J.K. Ordona 21, 01-237 Warsaw, Poland
{Agnieszka.Mykowiecka,Malgorzata.Marciniak,
Joanna.Rabiega}@ipipan.waw.pl
[2] Polish Japanese Institute of Information Technology
Koszykowa 86, 02-008 Warsaw, Poland
{kmarasek,rgubryn}@pjwstk.edu.pl

Abstract. The paper presents a corpus of Polish spoken dialogues being
a result of the LUNA (spoken **L**anguage **UN**derstanding in multilingu**A**l
communication systems) project. We describe the process of collecting
the corpus and its annotation on several levels, from transcription of
dialogues and their morphosyntactic analysis, to semantic annotation
on concepts and predicates. Annotation on the morphosyntactic and semantic levels was done automatically and then manually corrected. At
the concept level, the annotation scheme comprises about 200 concepts
from an ontology designed specially for the project. The set of frames
for predicate level annotation was defined as a FrameNet-like resource.

Keywords: annotated corpora, Polish spoken dialogues, city public
transportation.

1 Introduction

The main goal of the LUNA project is to create a robust and effective spoken language understanding (SLU) module for French, Italian and Polish, which can be
used to improve the speech-enabled telecom services in multilingual context. The
SLU methods try to tackle the problem of enabling human-machine dialogues
by adding higher level models and descriptors to the proposals given by a speech
recognizer. It is expected that usage of semantic models will improve the quality
of the dialogue system as well as increase the acceptance of human-computer
interaction. The project focuses on five main scientific problems:

- language modeling for speech understanding,
- semantic modeling for speech understanding,
- automatic learning of semantic annotation rules,
- robustness issues for SLU,
- multilingual portability of SLU components.

To achieve the goals mentioned above, annotated corpora are required. As semantically annotated data did not exist for all chosen languages, their creation

Z. Vetulani and H. Uszkoreit (Eds.): LTC 2007, LNAI 5603, pp. 50–62, 2009.

was one of the important project aims, and several spoken dialogues corpora for French, Italian and Polish were created. The data were annotated on several levels up to semantic constituents and are used to train and validate models and methods of SLU.

The French data were prepared by France Telecom which enlarged and developed two corpora of human/machine dialogues concerning stock exchange and customer support service. The project uses semantic annotation, taking advantage of the MEDIA project experience [1]. Italian partners collected and annotated dialogues in the computer help-desk domain. The Polish corpus contains dialogues concerning public transportation. It was constructed in the following stages which will be described in the subsequent parts of the paper:

- data recording and manual transcription,
- automatic creation of files with information about speakers' turns,
- automatic morphological analysis followed by manual disambiguation,
- automatic annotation of elementary syntactic chunks borders,
- automatic annotation at the level of domain attributes,
- manual verification and correction of the attribute-values annotation,
- automatic annotation at the predicate level (in progress).

2   Collection Procedure

The corpus of dialogues was collected at the Warsaw Transport Authority (WTA) information center known as ZTM Service Center. Its telephone number is posted on all city transportation line stops in the city and within the vehicles. The telephone information service (dial 94-84) is available 24 hours a day, 7 days per week. Operators provide information on tram and bus connections, schedules, routes, fares etc. The call center is used also by the WTA to collect the citizens' opinions on recent changes in the schedules and routes of certain bus lines, and complaints about drivers, late arrivals, etc.

During the data collection period one of the project members conducted on-site observations of call center agents to obtain a better understanding of the work-flow, group dynamics and interaction between call center agents. The center is staffed daily by two to four persons who typically answer 200-300 calls per day with an average call duration of 1-2 minutes. Prior to the connection to the operator the caller is forewarned that the conversation is to be recorded. If this is not accepted by the caller they can hang up. Following the privacy laws, during the conversation no personal data are requested and the calling number identification (CNID/CLIP) is not stored.

A technical problem we had to solve was that the call center did not accept any interference into their LAN and PBX structures. For these reasons we decided to apply an external device that allowed for automatic and independent recording of phone calls on multiple analogue phone lines. The device applied (FonTel phone call recorder) supported 4 analog lines and was connected to a PC through an audio card and RS232 control ports. The software detected the beginning and the end of each call and recorded it to an uncompressed audio file (riff-wav format, sampling frequency 16 kHz, 16 bits). The exact date, time and line name of the dialogue recording was used as a file name.

The full recorded corpus consists of around 12 000 calls made to a transportation information center during late March to mid-May 2007. Before further processing, registered calls were classified according to a dialogue topic. Some calls were irrelevant to the call-center competence and they are not further processed (about 10%). For the purpose of later processing in the LUNA project 501 dialogues were selected and divided into five classes:

- information requests on the itinerary between given points in the city,
- timetable for a given stop and given line and the travel time from a given stop to a destination,
- information on line routes, type of bus, tram (e.g. wheelchairs access),
- information on stops (the nearest from a given point in the city, stops for a given line, transfer stops, etc.),
- information on fare reductions and fare-free transportation for specified groups of citizens (children, youth, seniors, disabled persons, etc.).

It should be stressed, however, that many calls could not be easily categorized into one of the presented classes. Quite often, a caller moved from one topic to another, asking for more information. Statistics over the selected dialogues are summarized in Table 1.

Table 1. Quantitative characteristics of the selected groups of dialogues

Category	Number of calls	Percentage of dialogues	Average dialogues duration [s] (user's part)	Average number of user's turns per call	Average number of user's words per call
Transportation routes	93	18,6%	81	14	98
Itinerary	140	28%	97	16	96
Schedule	112	22,4%	63	11	61
Stops	55	11%	68	11	86
Reduced and free-fares	101	20%	48	8	61
All corpus	501	100%	73	12	80

3   Segmentation and Transcription

The recordings were converted into plain texts applying Transcriber [2]. Every conversation was divided into turns referring to the caller and the operator, respectively. The transcription output is an XML file which includes the dialogue text and some meta-data referring to articulation distortions, speaker and non-speaker noises, and time-stamps of the beginning and the end of each turn.

Transliteration and acoustic annotation of corpora was time consuming due to the following problems:

- Noisy recordings: most of them were made in adverse acoustic conditions. Many calls were made while driving or waiting on the street, thus a lot of external noises, wind noises, etc. disturbed speech.
- Low quality of speech transmission: many calls were made over GSM whilst moving or using low quality microphones; overall low level of speech signal.
- Disfluencies, hesitations, repetitions, grammatical and pronunciation errors, mistakes and corrections, jargon, false starts and disruptions, word and phrase fragments, pauses, indeed all possible spontaneous speech effects were observed.
- Long pauses and long speeches, quite often not at all relevant to the main topic of the dialogue.
- Strong emotions (quite often negative) of the speaker influencing her/his articulation.

As the aim of this annotation level was to gain natural, uninterpreted utterances, an annotator manually transcribed segmented turns. To make further processing easier and the form of a transcribed file more uniform within the project, the following conventions were adopted:

- It was agreed to capitalize proper names and acronyms following the standards of each language, e.g. *Galeria Mokotów, Bitwy Warszawskiej.*
- Spellings were transcribed using capital letters separated by spaces and tagged with the symbol *pron=SPELLED*. The same approach was used to transcribe acronyms that are spelled, e.g. *[pron=SPELLED-] A W F [-pron=SPELLED]*.
- Syllabification, used in Polish especially for proper names, was introduced by the symbol *pron=SYL* e.g. *Bank [pron=SYL-] Narodowy [-pron=SYL]*.
- Acronyms pronounced as words were written in capitals without dots or spaces between letters, e.g. *PEKAES*. If an acronym undergoes inflection, an inflection suffix is added to the basis in small letters, e.g. *KRUSu, KRUSem*.
- Foreign words or acronyms were transcribed in their original orthographic form and tagged with a symbol *lang=* and the name of the language, e.g. *[lang=French-] Carrefour [-lang=French]*. In Polish such words can be also inflected. In such cases the inflection suffix appears directly after the closing tag *lang=*, e.g. *[lang=English-] Marriott [-lang=English]a*.
- Only the actually spoken part of a word should be transcribed. Truncation was marked with the symbol *[lex=~]*, e.g. *centra[lex=~]*. However, we distinguished an exception. When a truncation may cause a lack of results at higher levels of annotation, and at the same time, the word can be reconstructed unequivocally, the missing parts are added between tags *[lex=~]*, e.g. *czy[lex=~-]l[-lex=~]i*.
- In case of mispronunciation, the correct form was transcribed with an indication that it had been mispronounced, e.g. *[pron=*-] Placu [-pron=*] Narutowicza*.
- Text that could not be recognized, was represented by the symbol *pron=***.

- The tag *lex=filler* was used to represent pauses, hesitations and articulatory noises as breath, laugh, cough, etc. In order to capture significant non-verbal answers as confirmation, which could be helpful at other levels of annotation, we distinguished a subtype of fillers marked with the tag *lex=filler+*.
- Noises were divided into two types: non human noises and human noises in the background. They are annotated with tags *noise* and *babble*. Silence was annotated only if it lasted more than 1 second – as *silence*.
- Numbers were transcribed as words following the standards of each language.
- In general, the transcription did not include punctuation marks. The only exception is the question mark *[lex=?]*, which was used to mark rising intonation of questions.

A sample of transcribed conversation concerning the user's question referring to the city communication network is presented in Fig. 1.

[babble-] ewentualnie [-babble] może pan [lex=filler] dojechać do
alternatively you may go to

Dworc[lex=~-]a[-lex=~] Centralnego i tam przesiąść się [babble-] w dziesiątkę
Main Railway Station and there switch to nine

albo dwadzieścia cztery [-babble]
or twenty four

Fig. 1. Sample of the transcribed text

4 Morphosyntactic Annotation

After transcription, the set of dialogues was annotated with morphosyntactic tags. The annotation was done in two steps.

The POS tags were added to each word to identify its morphological characteristics. As the project concerns three different languages, the partners adopted the EAGLES recommendations for the morphosyntactic annotation of text corpora [3]. For each language, a core set of tags consistent with this standard was defined. To perform automatic analysis of words in the dialogues, from several programs available for Polish [4], we chose the AMOR analyser [5]. It was easy to extend it with the domain vocabulary and proper names. The most important changes made in the lexicon, such as introducing of several POS classes for proper names, marking names not recognized by an operator with the tag [PropName], and adding regular colloquial expressions to the lexicon, are presented in [6]. The manually disambiguated results of the morphological analysis are stored in an XML file in format presented in Fig. 2.

Morphologically annotated texts of dialogues are segmented into elementary syntactic chunks. The aim of syntactic description is to group the words into basic nominal phrases and verbal groups. As no chunker suitable for the analysis of

```
<w id="100" word="ewentualnie" lemma="ewentualnie" POS="ADV"
     morph="pos" />
<w id="101" word="może" lemma="móc" POS="VV"
     morph="3.sg.gender.pres.ind.imperf" />
<w id="102" word="pan" lemma="pan" POS="Nc" morph="nom.sg.m1" />
<w id="103" word="dojechać" lemma="dojechać" POS="VV"
     morph="inf.perf" />
<w id="104" word="do" lemma="do" POS="PreP" morph="-" />
<w id="105" word="Dworca" lemma="Dworzec" POS="Np"
     morph="gen.sg.m3"/>
<w id="106" word="Centralnego" lemma="Centralny" POS="ADJp"
     morph="gen.sg.masc/neut" />
<w id="107" word="i" lemma="i" POS="CC" morph="-" />
<w id="108" word="tam" lemma="tam" POS="PART" morph="-" />
<w id="109" word="przesiąść" lemma="przesiąść" POS="VV"
     morph="inf.perf"/>
<w id="110" word="się" lemma="się" POS="PART" morph="-" />
<w id="111" word="w" lemma="w" POS="PreP" morph="-" />
<w id="112" word="dziewiątkę" lemma="dziewiątka" POS="Nc"
     morph="acc.sg.fem" />
<w id="113" word="albo" lemma="albo" POS="CC" morph="-" />
<w id="114" word="dwadzieścia" lemma="dwadzieścia" POS="NUM"
     morph="acc.nm1" />
<w id="115" word="cztery" lemma="cztery" POS="NUM" morph="acc.nm1" />
```

Fig. 2. Example of the morphological annotation

Polish spoken texts exists, a program used in the project was designed especially for the purpose. It uses morphological description of words, and information about turns in order to find phrases within an utterance of one speaker.

The chunker recognizes compound verbal phrases (VP): *[będzie jechał]*[1] *'[will go]'*, but does not create one chunk when an infinitive is a complement of a verb: *[chcę] [jechać] '[want] [to go]'*. In this example, there are two chunks VP and VP_INF, each is composed of one word. In the case of nominal phrases we distinguish the following subtypes:

- NP_PRON for pronominals (*ja 'I', on 'he'*),
- PN for proper names[2] (*Złote Tarasy, Praga Południe*),
- NP for nominal phrases that consist of nouns and adjectives (*[ostatni przystanek] '[the last stop]'*),
- NUM for numeral phrases (*dwadzieścia dwa 'twenty two'*).

Nominal phrases do not include prepositional modifiers, so the following expression *[przystanek autobusowy] [na] [żądanie] '[the bus stop] [on] [request]'* consists of three chunks: NP, PP, NP.

---

[1] Square brackets indicate chunks.

[2] The problem of proper name processing in the dialogues is described in [7].

For NP and VP groups, the chunker indicates the main word i.e., the word semantically most significant. For nominal phrases the main word coincides with the head of the phrase, e.g. for *[ostatni przystanek]* *'[the last stop]'* it is *przystanek 'stop'*. In the verbal phrase *[będzie jechał]* *'[will go]'* the main word is *jechał 'go'*.

The parser uses some domain knowledge, which helps for example to recognize transportation line numbers. The following phrase: *autobusy pięćset dwadzieścia dwa sto siedemdziesiąt cztery 'buses five hundred twenty two one hundred seventy four'* can be theoretically divided in many ways, but we know that all buses in Warsaw have three-digit numbers thus we can recognize the numeral phrases properly as: *[pięćset dwadzieścia dwa]* *'[five hundred twenty two]'* and *[sto siedemdziesiąt cztery]* *'[one hundred seventy four]'*.

We also tuned our chunker on the basis of analysed data. For example, we blocked the possibility of creating chunks longer than one word with the nouns: *pan, pana_{gen} 'Mr'*, and *pani 'Ms'*. This was done because of the problems caused by the, often occurring, courtesy expression *proszę pana* ('please Sir') for which the noun *pana* was incorrectly connected with nouns and adjectives following it.

The automatic chunker is not perfect, but sometimes it is not easy to divide phrases properly. The following phrases have the same grammatical construction ([noun, adjective, adjective] agreeing in case, number, and gender) but they should be divided into chunks differently: *[bilet sieciowy imienny] jest...* — *'[personal network ticket] is...'* and *[wózek dziecięcy] [przewożony] jest...* — *'[baby carriage] [transported] is...'*. That is why, results of automatic chunking have to be manually corrected.

Syntactic segmentation for the fragment of the dialogue presented in Fig. 1 is shown in Fig. 3.

5   Concept Level Annotation

The first semantic level of dialogues' annotation concerns assigning attributes' names to sequences of words which realize them. Contrary to the previous levels, there are no standard sets of attributes which can be chosen for describing a particular domain. So, the appropriate model has to be defined within the project. To do this, we used a widely accepted method of representing semantics by defining domain ontologies. Although their universality can be questioned, and the reuse of resources is not easy, see [8], it is still the best existing solution for achieving portability. For the purpose of describing Warsaw public transportation, we decided to develop a new ontology using OWL-DL standard. Our *CityTransport* ontology contain about 200 concepts which cover:

- different transportation means (buses, trams, local trains and metro), their routes, and route features,
- town topology in the aspects needed for traveling (stops, important buildings, streets' names),
- trips' plans using one or more transport means.

> *ewentualnie może pan dojechać do Dworca Centralnego i tam przesiąść się*
> *w dziewiątkę albo dwadzieścia cztery*
>
> *<chunk id="89" span="word_ 100" cat="ADV" />*
> *<chunk id="90" span="word_ 101" cat="VP" main="word_ 101" />*
> *<chunk id="91" span="word_ 102" cat="PP" />*
> *<chunk id="92" span="word_ 103" cat="VP_INF" />*
> *<chunk id="93" span="word_ 104" cat="PP" />*
> *<chunk id="94" span="word_ 105..word_ 106" cat="PN" />*
> *<chunk id="95" span="word_ 107" cat="CC" />*
> *<chunk id="96" span="word_ 108" cat="PART" />*
> *<chunk id="97" span="word_ 109" cat="VP_INF" />*
> *<chunk id="98" span="word_ 110" cat="PART" />*
> *<chunk id="99" span="word_ 111" cat="PP" />*
> *<chunk id="100" span="word_ 112" cat="NP" main="word_ 112" />*
> *<chunk id="101" span="word_ 113" cat="CC" />*
> *<chunk id="102" span="word_ 114..word_ 115" cat="NUM" />*

Fig. 3. Example of the syntactic annotation

Fig. 4 shows a fragment of the classes tree defined in our ontology which includes description of places in a town. Apart from the typology, an ontology allows for describing class properties. We can define types of values and cardinality. For example, for every identified place we define its name, address and a set of public transportation stops which are nearby.

Concept level annotation uses names and values from the ontology (properties defined within the ontology are not visible within the annotation). Fig. 5 shows annotation for the example given in Fig. 1.

Semantic annotation of the data was done in two stages. In the first one, the dialogues were annotated automatically by a set of 950 rules. Next, the results were manually checked and corrected by a human expert. As our dialogues concern traveling within a city, they contain a lot of proper names. In most cases, it is impossible to recognize the type of an object without the context. Words introducing their type, e.g. *street* or *bus stop* are used rather rarely. To recognize these names properly, we created a lexicon which contains street names, town districts, important buildings, parks and some other types of names together with their classification. The biggest group contains street names – there are 3883 one-word and 100 multi-word names. This lexicon allows us to perform the lemmatization of proper names. In Polish, lemmatized form of multi-word names usually does not consist of the lemmas of their elements. The description of the lemmatization process is given in [7].

Rules for attribute-value annotation are regular expressions which can use information from lower annotation levels – words, lemmas, morphological tags, turns and chunks borders, as well as recognized proper names. The rules were created on the basis of manual analysis of a subset of dialogues (in total, on various stages of rules creation 142 dialogues were inspected) and converted into

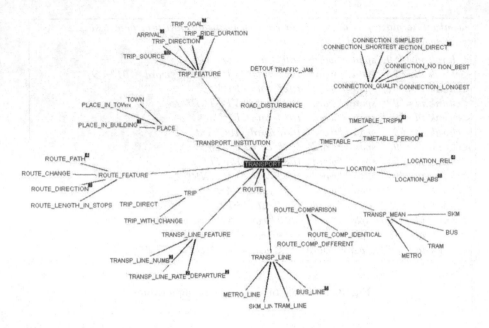

Fig. 4. Fragment of the ontology

*ewentualnie może pan dojechać do Dworca Centralnego i tam przesiąść się
w dziewiątkę albo dwadzieścia cztery*

$<c$ $id="40"$ $span="word\_103"$ $attribute="Action"$ $value="Approach"$ $/>$
$<c$ $id="41"$ $span="word\_104..word\_106"$ $attribute="GOAL\_RS"$
$\quad value="Dworzec Centralny"$ $/>$
$<c$ $id="42"$ $span="word\_108"$ $attribute="LOCATION\_REL"$ $value="There"$ $/>$
$<c$ $id="43"$ $span="word\_109..word\_111"$ $attribute="TRSPM\_CHANGE"$
$\quad value="TO"$ $/>$
$<c$ $id="44"$ $span="word\_112"$ $attribute="TRAM"$ $value="dziewiątka"$ $/>$
$<c$ $id="45"$ $span="word\_113"$ $attribute="Conj"$ $value="Alternative"$ $/>$
$<c$ $id="46"$ $span="word\_114..word\_115"$ $attribute="TRAM"$
$\quad value="dwadzieścia cztery"$ $/>$

Fig. 5. Attribute level annotation example

scripts which were then used to annotate the data. The rules were organized
in three subsets which were applied sequentially to the results of the previous
set. Before the final annotation of the corpus, several correction steps were conducted, each based on the verification of a test set of over 20 dialogues. To
control the results of the introduced changes, a special program for comparing
two annotation sets was created. A thorough description of the method and its
evaluation is presented in [9]. The final set of rules were applied to the rest of the

Table 2. The most frequent concepts

	number		number
BUS	1467	QUESTION_CONFIRMATION	572
LOCATION_RELATIVE	1277	LOCATION_STREET	463
AT_HOUR	782	STREET	459
STOP_DESCRIPTION	641	SOURCE_STREET	402
GOAL_STREET	601	MEANS_OF_TRANSPORT	379

corpus. Then, all dialogues were manually corrected. Most frequently occurring concepts in the corpus are listed in Tab. 2.

6 Predicate Level Annotation

The next level of semantic annotation is the predicate structure level at which we represent relations between already recognized concepts. These relations are imposed by the verbs used within an utterance. In the LUNA project partners agreed to follow function-argument structures proposed by Jackendoff [10] and applied in the Berkeley FrameNet project [11,12,13,14]. A frame describes a common or abstract situation involving roles called frame elements [12]. In practice, it means that a frame is built by a word whose complements or adjuncts constitute frame elements. Every language can be characterized by a lexicon containing possible configurations of frame elements for predicative words. Unfortunately, for Polish this data have not been created yet. According to our knowledge, the only project concerning Polish is the RAMKI project, which at the moment covers only a small part of the semantic domain of our corpus (http://www.ramki.uw.edu.pl/). Therefore, to perform predicate level annotation we had to define a set of frames necessary for describing Polish verbs important in the transportation domain. The set, named VFrames, was created manually based on the corresponding frames for English. In order to build this set we selected all important verbs from the corpus and, for each sense of every verb, defined a separate frame.

Every frame is described as a set of patterns containing lists of frame elements names. We took into account only frame realizations which were found in the corpus. In Tab. 3 we present a few patterns for the verb *jechać 'to go (by bus)'*. These patterns contain the lemma of the verb, frame name SELF_MOTION and pairs of a frame element and an attribute which realizes it, e.g. frame element SELF_MOVER is covered by the concept BUS. While defining a frame for Polish, we tried to keep to the source frame definition from the FrameNet, but we limited our description to frame elements actually found in the dialogues. Consequently, some frames describing generic knowledge as motion or spatial relations match those from the FrameNet. Other frames specific to the application or language are defined according to the Berkeley FrameNet paradigm [12]. Tab. 4 shows the size of our frame set and the FrameNet. It also presents the comparison of one frame description in the VFrames and FrameNet.

Table 3. Example of frame patterns for verb *jechać*

Verb	Frame	Frame elements
jechać	SELF_MOTION	SOURCE (SOURCE_STR) GOAL (GOAL_STR) DURATION (RIDE_DURATION)
jechać	SELF_MOTION	SELF_MOVER (BUS) SOURCE (SOURCE_RS) GOAL (GOAL_DIRECTION_TD)
jechać	SELF_MOTION	DIRECTION (ROUTE_DIR) PATH (PATH_STR) GOAL (GOAL_DIRECTION_BLD)
jechać	SELF_MOTION	PATH (PATH_STR) TIME (TIME_REL)
jechać	SELF_MOTION	PATH (PATH_STR) DIRECTION (ROUTE_DIR)

Table 4. Comparison of SELF_MOTION frame in VFrames and FrameNet

	VFrames	FrameNet
Frames	19	951
FEs	27	> 9,000
Frame FEs	SELF_MOTION Area, Direction, Distance, Goal, Path, Place, Self_mover, Duration, Source, Time	SELF_MOTION Area, Direction, Goal, Path, Source, Self_mover, Coordinated_event, Time, Cotheme, Depictive, Distance, Duration, External_cause, Internal_cause, Means, Path_shape, Place, Purpose, Manner, Reason, Result, Speed

To apply the frame description to the dialogue corpus annotation we have developed a program that seeks occurrences of a given verb and for each of them tries to find an appropriate frame in the VFrames. Once the script finds a verb, it checks the list of frame patterns and matches frame elements to a set of

```
dojechać do Dworca Centralnego i tam przesiąść się w dziewiątkę albo
    dwadzieścia cztery
<Set id='2' span='word_103' frame='ARRIVING' main='dojechać'>
    <Frame fe='1' span='word_104..word_106' c_id='41' slot='GOAL' />
</Set>
<Set id='3' span='word_109' frame='CAUSE_CHANGE' main='przesiąść'>
    <Frame fe='1' span='word_108' c_id='42' slot='PLACE' />
    <Frame fe='2' span='word_112' c_id='44' slot='FINAL_CATEGORY' />
    <Frame fe='3' span='word_114..word_115' c_id='46'
        slot='FINAL_CATEGORY' />
</Set>
```

Fig. 6. Predicate level annotation example

concepts recognized within the utterance. Each frame hypothesis is put into a file containing results. When more than one frame matches the data, the results are disambiguated manually.

Fig. 6 presents the result of automatic frame annotation for part of the example given in Fig. 1. In this example the verbs *dojechać 'to arrive'* and *przesiąść się 'to switch (a tram)'* constitute two frames ARRIVING and CAUSE_CHANGE, respectively. The first frame is realized only by one component GOAL matching the previously annotated concept GOAL_RS (c_id=41). For the second frame three frame elements were found: PLACE, FINAL_CATEGORY, FINAL_CATEGORY, which relate to concepts: LOCATION_REL (c_id=42), TRAM (c_id=44), TRAM (c_id=46).

7 Summary

The result of the project is the first corpus of Polish spoken dialogues annotated with morphological, syntactic and semantic information. Tab. 5 shows the overall statistics of the collected data. So far, only a few Polish speech corpora have been collected at all. One of the first research done on speech data was undertaken in the seventies by K. Pisarkowa and concerned Polish syntax of a telephone conversation [15]. Although the linguist had recorded the dialogues for the study, that corpus is not available. SpeechDat Polish [16] is the only widely distributed Polish speech database collected over telephone lines, but it does not contain dialogues nor spontaneous speech.

Table 5. Corpus statistics

	number		number
dialogues	501	chunks	71885
turns	13191	concepts	26594
word forms	19847	concept types	180
different lemmas	2759	predicate frames types	19

The collected corpus will be available for research purposes and it can be used to test various linguistic and application oriented hypotheses. A collection of real dialogues is a source of great value for studying human-human interaction and spontaneous speech phenomena. The corpus will also be used in research aimed at developing dialogue systems with high level of user acceptance.

Acknowledgements. This work is supported by LUNA – STREP project in the EU's 6th Framework Programme (IST 033549) which started in 2006.

The authors would like to thank Warsaw Transport Authority (ZTM Warszawa) and its call center employees for their support and cooperation.

References

1. Bonneau-Maynard, H., et al.: Semantic Annotation of the MEDIA Corpus for Spoken Dialog. In: ISCA Interspeech, Lisbon, pp. 3457–3460 (2005)
2. Barras, C., Geoffrois, E., Wu, Z., Liberman, M.: Transcriber: a Free Tool for Segmenting, Labeling and Transcribing Speech. In: LREC 1998, pp. 1373–1376 (1998)
3. Leech, G., Wilson, A.: EAGLES. Recommendations for the Morphosyntactic Annotation of Corpora, EAG-TCWG-MAC/R. Technical report, ILC-CNR, Pisa (1996)
4. Hajnicz, E., Kupść, A.: Przeglad analizatorów morfologicznych dla jêzyka polskiego. Raport IPI PAN, Warszawa (2001)
5. Rabiega-Wiśniewska, J., Rudolf, M.: Towards a Bi-Modular Automatic Analyzer of Large Polish Corpora. In: Kosta, R., Blaszczak, J., Frasek, J., Geist, L., Żygis, M. (eds.) Investigations into Formal Slavic Linguistics. Contributions of the Fourth European Conference on Formal Description of Slavic Languages – FDSL IV, pp. 363–372. Peter Lang (2003)
6. Mykowiecka, A., Marasek, K., Marciniak, M., Rabiega-Winiewska, J., Gubrynowicz, R.: On Construction of Polish Spoken Dialogs Corpus. In: Proceedings of the Sixth International Language Resources and Evaluation (LREC 2008). 2nd Linguistic Annotation Workshop (LAW II), Marrakech, Morocco, pp. 52–55 (2008)
7. Marciniak, M., Rabiega-Winiewska, J., Mykowiecka, A.: Proper Names in Dialogs from the Warsaw Transportation Call Center. In: Intelligent Information Systems XVI 2008. EXIT (2008)
8. Paslaru-Bontas, E.: A Contextual Approach to Ontology Reuse Methodology, Methods and Tools for the Semantic Web. PhD thesis, Fachbereich Mathematik u. Informatik, Freie Universität Berlin (2007)
9. Mykowiecka, A., Marciniak, M., Głowińska, K.: Semantic Annotation of Polish Dialogue Corpus. In: Sojka, P., Horák, A., Kopeček, I., Pala, K. (eds.) TSD 2008. LNCS (LNAI), vol. 5246, pp. 625–632. Springer, Heidelberg (2008)
10. Jackendoff, R.: Semantic structures. The MIT Press, Cambridge (1990)
11. Fillmore, C.J.: Frame Semantics. In: Linguistics in the Morning Calm, Seoul, pp. 111–137. Hanshin Publishing Co (1982)
12. Lowe, J.B., Baker, C.F., Fillmore, C.J.: A Frame-Semantic Approach to Semantic Annotation. In: Proceedings of the SIGLEX Workshop on Tagging Text with Lexical Semantics: Why, What, and How?, April 4-5, Washington, D.C., USA in conjunction with ANLP-1997 (1997)
13. Fillmore, C.R., Johnson, C.J., Petruck, M.R.: Background to Framenet. International Journal of Lexicography 16.3, 235–250 (2003)
14. Meurs, M.J., Duvert, F., Bechet, F., Lefevre, F., De Mori, R.: Semantic Frame Annotation on the French MEDIA corpus. In: Proceedings of the Sixth International Language Resources and Evaluation (LREC 2008), Marrakech, Morocco (2008)
15. Pisarkowa, K.: Składnia rozmowy telefonicznej. Wydawnictwo PAN (1975)
16. Heuvel, H., et al: SpeechDat-E: Five Eastern European Speech Databases for Voice-Operated Teleservices Ccompleted. In: Dalsgaard, P. (ed.) Eurospeech 2001 Scandinavia, 7th European Conference on Speech Communication and Technology, Aalborg, Denmark (2001)

Triphone Statistics for Polish Language

Bartosz Ziółko[1], Jakub Gałka[1], Suresh Manandhar[2], Richard C. Wilson[2], and Mariusz Ziółko[1]

[1] Department of Electronics, AGH University of Science and Technology
al.Mickiewicza 30, 30-059 Kraków, Poland
[2] Department of Computer Science, University of York
Heslington, YO10 5DD, York, UK
{bziolko,jgalka,ziolko}@agh.edu.pl,
{suresh,wilson}@cs.york.ac.uk
http://www.dsp.agh.edu.pl
http://www.cs.york.ac.uk

Abstract. The Polish text corpus was analysed to find information about phoneme statistics. We were especially interested in triphones as they are commonly used in many speech processing applications like HTK speech recogniser. An attempt to create the full list of triphones for Polish language is presented. A vast amount of phonetically transcribed text was analysed to obtain the frequency of triphone occurrences. A distibution of frequency of triphones occuring and other phenomena are presented. The standard phonetic alphabet for Polish and methods of providing phonetic transcriptions are described.

Keywords: Polish, phoneme statistics, speech processing.

1 Introduction

There is much statistical research at the word and sentence level for different languages [1,3]. On the other hand similar research on phonemes is rare [6,15,10]. The frequency of phonetic unit presence is an interesting topic itself and can find use in many applications in speech processing, for example speech recognition. It is very difficult to provide proper acoustic data for all possible triphones, but there are methods to synthesise no-recorded ones using data for other triphones and phonological similarities between different phonemes [16]. This means that the list of possible triphones has to be provided for a given language. The triphone statistics can be also used to generate hypotheses used in recognition of out-of-dictionary words.

This paper describes several issues related to phoneme, diphone and triphone statistics and is divided as follows. Section 2 provides information about general scheme of our data acquisition method and standards we used. Section 3 describes the technically most difficult step which is changing the text corpus into a phonetic transcription. Section 4 contains a description of data we used and our results. Phenomena we uncovered are described as well. We sum up the paper with conclusions.

Z. Vetulani and H. Uszkoreit (Eds.): LTC 2007, LNAI 5603, pp. 63–73, 2009.

Table 1. Phoneme transcription in Polish - SAMPA [5]

SAMPA	example	transcr.	occurr.	%
#		#	23,810,956	16.086,7
a	pat	pat	13,311,163	8.993
e	test	test	11,871,405	8.020,3
o	pot	pot	10,566,010	7.138,4
s	syk	sIk	5,716,058	3.861,8
t	test	test	5,703,429	3.853,2
r	ryk	rIk	5,171,698	3.494
p	pik	pik	5,150,964	3.48
v	wilk	vilk	5,025,050	3.394,9
j	jak	jak	4,996,475	3.375,6
i	PIT	pit	4,994,743	3.374,4
I	typ	tIp	4,974,567	3.360,8
n	nasz	naS	4,602,314	3.109,3
l	luk	luk	4,399,366	2.972,2
u	puk	puk	4,355,825	2.942,8
k	kit	kit	4,020,161	2.716
z	zbir	zbir	3,602,857	2.434,1
m	mysz	mIS	3,525,813	2.382
d	dym	dIm	3,267,009	2.207,2
n'	koń	kon'	3,182,940	2.150,4
f	fan	fan	2,030,717	1.372
ts	cyk	tsIk	1,984,311	1.340,6
g	gen	gen	1,949,890	1.317,3
S	szyk	SIk	1,739,146	1.175
b	bit	bit	1,668,103	1.127
x	hymn	xImn	1,339,311	0.904,84
tS	czyn	tSIn	1,285,310	0.868,36
dz	dzwoń	dzvon'	692,334	0.467,74
ts'	ćma	ts'ma	690,294	0.466,36
dz'	dźwig	dz'vik	589,266	0.398,11
Z	żyto	ZIto	536,786	0.362,65
s'	świt	s'vit	531,402	0.359,02
o~	wąs	vo~s	306,665	0.207,18
N	pęk	peNk	184,884	0.124,91
w	łyk	wIk	144,166	0.097,399
z'	źle	z'le	66,518	0.044,94
dZ	dżem	dZem	27,621	0.018,661
e~	gęś	ge~s'	1,011	0.000,683
w~	ciąża	ts'ow~Za	sampa extension	
j~	więź	vjej~s'	sampa extension	
c	kiedy	cjedy	sampa extension	
J	giełda	Jjewda	sampa extension	

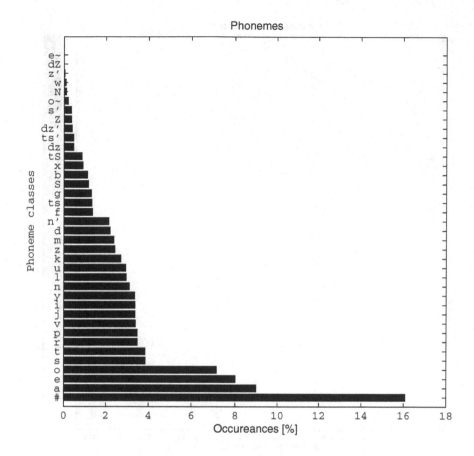

Fig. 1. Phonemes in Polish

2 Statistics Extraction Scheme

Obtaining of phonetic information from an orthographic text-data is not straight-forward [8,12]. Transcription of text into phonetic data has to be applied first [11]. We used PolPhone [5] software for this aim, which is described in the next section. The SAMPA extended phonetic alphabet was applied with 39 symbols and pronunciation rules typical for cities Kraków and Poznań. We altered the PolPhone phonetic alphabet (Table 1) to a 37 symbol version which is used in the largest corpus of spoken Polish [7] and currently recognised as a SAMPA standard. We reduced the number of symbols by changing phoneme c to k and phoneme J to g. We also replaced $w\sim$ to $o\sim$ and $j\sim$ to $e\sim$. These changes were done to work on an offical standard version of SAMPA, which is frequently used, i.e. in the audio corpus with transcription [7], rather than an extended SAMPA used in PolPhone, which is going to be suggested as a new standard. For pro-gramming reasons we used our own single letter only symbols corresponding to

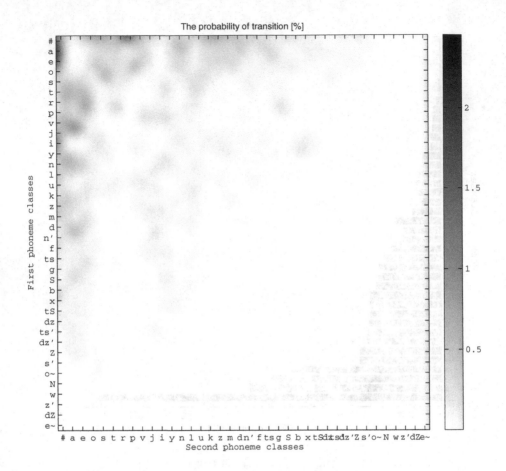

Fig. 2. Diphone probabilities in Polish

SAMPA symbols instead of typical ones to distinguish phonemes easier while analysing received phonetic transcriptions. Statistics can be now simply calculated by counting number of occurrences of each phoneme, phoneme pair, and phoneme triple in analysed text, where each phoneme is just one symbol. The analysis of the whole corpus took 3 weeks using PolPhone and scripts written in Matlab.

3   Text to Phonetic Data Transcriptions

Two main approaches are used for the automatic transcription of texts into phonemic form. The classical approach is based on phonetic grammatical rules specified by human [14] or automatic machine learning process [4]. A second

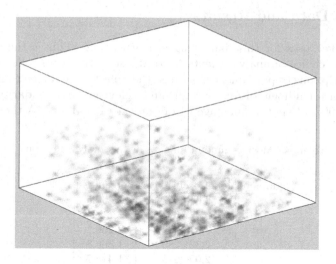

Fig. 3. Triphone probabilities in Polish

solution utilises graphemic-phonetic dictionaries. In practice both mentioned methods are used in order to cover both typical and exceptional transcriptions. Polish phonetic transcription rules are relatively easy to formalise because of their regularity.

The necessity of investigating large text corpus pointed to the use of the high-performance Polish phonetic transcription system PolPhone [9,5]. In this system strings of Polish characters are converted into their phonetic SAMPA representation. Extended SAMPA (Table 1) is used, to deal with all nuances of Polish phonetic system. The transcription process is performed by a table-based system, which implements the rules of transcription. A matrix $T[1..m][1..n]$ is a *transcription table* and its cells meet a set of requirements [5]. The first element ($T[1][1]$) of each table contains currently processed character of the input string. For every character (or character substring) one table is defined. The first column of each table ($T[i][1]$, where i=1,...,m) contains all possible character strings that could preceed currently transcribed character. The first row ($T[1][j]$, where $j = 1, ..., m$) contains all possible character strings that can follow a currently transcribed character. All possible phonetic transcription results (SAMPA symbols) are stored in the remaining cells of the tables ($T[2..n][2..m]$). A particular element $T[i][j]$ is chosen as a transcription result if $T[i][1]$ matches the substring proceeding $T[1][1]$ and $T[1][j]$ matches the substring following $T[1][1]$. This basic scheme is extended to cover overlapping phonetic contexts. When more then one result is possible, then longer context is chosen for transcription, which increases its accuracy. Exceptions are handled by additional tables in the similar manner.

Specific transcription rules were designed by a human expert in an iterative process of testing and updating rules. Text corpora used in design process consisted of various sample texts (newspaper articles) and a few thousand words and phrases including special cases and exceptions.

4   Input Data and Results

One of the key uses for this data is speech processing. This is the reason for quite specific choice of analysed texts. Data for statistics were collected mainly from transcriptions of parliament meetings, the Select Committee to investigate corruption in amendment of Act on Radio and Television and Solidarity meetings (more than 90% of spoken language), from literature and an MA thesis.

Table 2. Most common diphones in the analysed corpus

diphone	no. of occurrences	percentage
e#	3,640,557	2.460,5
#p	3,379,372	2.284
a#	3,353,504	2.266,5
je	2,321,280	1.568,8
o#	2,094,619	1.415,7
i#	1,987,880	1.343,5
po	1,717,235	1.160,6
#z	1,700,044	1.149
st	1,614,996	1.091,5
y#	1,583,405	1.070,2
#s	1,572,893	1.063
ov	1,535,630	1.0379
#v	1,448,739	0.979,14
n'e	1,443,190	0.975,39
na	1,390,834	0.94
ra	1,306,527	0.883,02
#o	1,236,294	0.835,56
ja	1,236,189	0.835,49
#t	1,208,541	0.816,8
ro	1,195,087	0.807,71
ta	1,128,953	0.763,01
al	1,120,931	0.757,59
os	1,078,738	0.729,07
va	1,043,964	0.705,57
u#	1,033,050	0.698,19
#d	1,019,796	0.689,23
pr	999,628	0.675,6
#m	963,911	0.651,46
m#	959,333	0.648,37

Total number of 148,016,538 phonemes were analysed. They are grouped in 38 categories (including space). Their distribution is presented in Table 1 and in Fig. 1. 1,095 different diphones (Fig. 2 and Table 2) and 14,970 different triphones (Fig. 3) were found. It has to be mentioned that all combinations like *#*, where * is any phoneme and # is space, were removed as we do not treat these triples as triphones. The reason for it is that first phoneme * and the second one are actually in 2 different words and we are interested in triphone statistics inside words. The list of most common triphones is presented in Table 3. This list seems to be not fully representable because of text choice, specifically vast amount of parliament transcriptions, which caused probably some anomalies. I.e. the most common triphone #po and another on the list pos are probably related to corpus topic - poseł means MP in Polish. The word poseł appeared 141,904 in just its basic form, which is 11% of total appearence of #po and 42% of pos. Polish is a morphologically rich language so there are other cases of this word, including plural forms, all of them starting with pos. Assuming 38 different phonemes (including space) and subtracting mentioned *#* combinations there are 53,503 possible triples. We found 14,970 different triphones which gives a conclusion that almost 28% of possible combinations were actually found as triphones. An average length of words in phonemes can be estimated as 6.22 due to space (noted as #) frequency 16.09.

Fig. 2 shows some symmetry. Of course, the probability of diphone $\alpha\beta$ is usually different than probability of $\beta\alpha$. Some symmetry results from the fact that high values of α probability and β probability gives usually high probability of product $\alpha\beta$ and $\beta\alpha$ as well. Similar effects can be observed for triphones. Data presented in this paper illustrate the well-known fact that probabilities of triphones (presented in Table 3) cannot be calculated from the diphone probabilities (some of them are presented in Table 2). The reason for this is that the conditional probabilities have to be known.

Besides the frequency of triphones occurring, we are also interested in distributions of different frequencies, which is presented in logarithmic scale in Fig. 4. We expected to receive a very different distribution as very large amount of text was analysed. We hoped to have very few triphones with occurrences smaller than 3 and deduce that they are not real triphones but errors due to foreign names etc. in the corpus. Still even though we added extra text to the corpus several times the distribution did not change much at all. We noted around 1600 triphones which occurred just once, 800 with occurrence 2, 500 with 3, 300 to 400 for 4 to 6 occurrences, 200 for 7 to 9, and up to 100 for 10 or more, every time after we analysed extra text. Such phenomena is nothing unexpected in natural language processing on a level of words or above, where amount of analysed text do not change statistics (considering reasonable large amounts). Still in case of triphones the number of possibilities is much smaller and limited to mentioned 53503. The open question is if we would find distribution we expected if we analysed much bigger corpus or there is no limit in number of triphones lower than number of possible combinations. Every time we analysed extra text we found some new triphones. The new trigrams come from unusual Polish word combinations, slang and other variations of dictionary words, onomatopoeic words, foreign words, errors in phonisation and typos in the text corpus. It is difficult to predict if one can reach a situation new triphones do not appear and distribution of occurrences is changing as a result of more data being analysed. Still it is possible that the large number of triphones with very small occurrence are non-Polish triphones which should be excluded. In our further works we assume

Table 3. Most common triphones in the analysed corpus

triphone	no. of occurrences	percentage
#po	1,273,417	1.026,1
n'e#	925,893	0.746,09
#na	699,608	0.563,75
#pS	660,062	0.531,88
je#	659,674	0.531,57
na#	655,722	0.528,38
#pr	627,962	0.506,02
Ix#	613,589	0.494,43
ej#	602,920	0.485,84
#za	598,060	0.481,92
n'a#	574,708	0.46,31
ova	561,910	0.452,79
ego	558,788	0.450,27
sta	554,876	0.447,12
#do	551,423	0.444,34
go#	551,042	0.444,03
pSe	522,611	0.421,12
pra	492,128	0.396,56
#pa	481,772	0.388,21
#i#	478,500	0.385,58
vje	468,848	0.377,8
#n'e	430,178	0.346,64
#je	421,223	0.339,42
#f#	416,467	0.335,59
#v#	412,967	0.332,77
#vy	407,092	0.328,04
pro	390,429	0.314,61
#sp	357,008	0.287,68
#ko	342,254	0.275,79
#te	341,900	0.275,5
an'e	338,530	0.272,79
pos	337,190	0.271,71
ze#	335,941	0.270,7
ym#	332,437	0.267,88
em#	328,629	0.264,81
rav	318,232	0.256,43
#ze	310,008	0.249,81
ne#	309,151	0.249,12
nyx	307,657	0.247,91
kje	304,426	0.245,31
do#	296,635	0.239,03
ja#	294,220	0.237,08
#st	291,797	0.235,13

Table 4. Most common triphones in the analysed corpus (2nd part)

triphone	no. of occurrences	percentage
s'e#	285,355	0.229,94
#o#	283,500	0.228,45
ki#	282,413	0.227,57
#ro	282,059	0.227,28
to#	272,585	0.219,65
an'a	270,668	0.218,11
mje	266,812	0.215
ktu	265,128	0.213,64
#s'e	257,323	0.207,35
#to	256,113	0.206,38
la#	254,175	0.204,82
#ja	246,452	0.198,59
uv#	244,102	0.196,7
#ma	243,374	0.196,11
pov	242,231	0.195,19
ny#	239310	0.19284
ka#	234660	0.18909

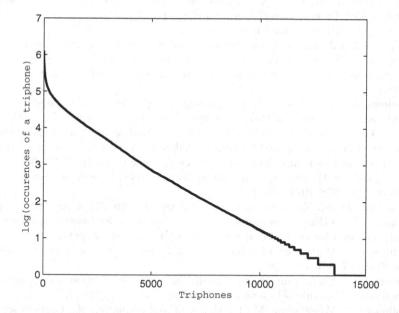

Fig. 4. Distribution of frequency of occurring phonemes in logarithmic scale

that from statistical point of view it is not important, especially when smoothing operation is applied in order to eliminate disturbances caused by lack of text data [13,2].

5   Conclusions

The statistics of phonemes, diphones and triphones were collected for Polish using a large corpus of mainly spoken formal language. The paper presents summarisation of the data and focus on interesting phenomena in the statistics. Triphone statistics play an important role in speech recognition systems. They are used to improve the proper transcription of the analysed speech segments. 28% of possible triples were detected as triphones, but many of them appeared very rarely. A majority of rare triphones came from foreign or twisted words. The statistics are available on request by an email.

Acknowledgements

We would like to thank Institute of Linguistics, Adam Mickiewicz University for providing PolPhone - a software tool to make a phonetic transcription for Polish.

References

1. Agirre, E., Ansa, O., Martínez, D., Hovy, E.: Enriching wordnet concepts with topic signatures. In: SIGLEX Workshop on WordNet and Other Lexical Resources: Applications, Extensions and Customizations (2001)
2. Altwarg, R.: Language models in speech recognition, http://www.shlrc.mq.edu.au/masters/students/raltwarg/lmtoc.htm
3. Bellegarda, J.R.: Large vocabulary speech recognition with multispan statistical language models. IEEE Transactions on Speech and Audio Processing 8(1), 76–84 (2000)
4. Daelemans, W., van den Bosch, A.: Language-independent data-oriented grapheme-to-phoneme conversion. In: Progress in Speech Synthesis. Springer, New York (1997)
5. Demenko, G., Wypych, M., Baranowska, E.: Implementation of grapheme-to-phoneme rules and extended SAMPA alphabet in Polish text-to-speech synthesis. In: Speech and Language Technology, PTFon, Poznań, vol. 7(17) (2003)
6. Denes, P.B.: Statistics of spoken English. The Journal of the Acoustical Society of America 34, 1978–1979 (1962)
7. Grocholewski, S.: Założenia akustycznej bazy danych dla języka polskiego na nośniku cd rom (Eng. Assumptions of acoustic database for Polish language). Mat. I KK: Głosowa komunikacja człowiek-komputer, 177–180. Wrocław (1995)
8. Holmes, J.N., Mattingley, I.G., Shearme, J.N.: Speech synthesis by rule. Language and Speech 7, 127–143 (1964)
9. Jassem, K.: A phonemic transcription and syllable division rule engine. In: Onomastica-Copernicus Research Colloquium. Edinburgh (1996)
10. Kollmeier, B., Wesselkamp, M.: Development and evaluation of a German sentence test for objective and subjective speech intelligibility assessment. The Journal of the Acoustical Society of America 102, 2412–2421 (1997)
11. Oliver, D.: Polish Text to Speech Synthesis, MSc. Thesis in Speech and Language Processing. Edinburgh University (1998)
12. Ostaszewska, D., Tambor, J.: Fonetyka i fonologia współczesnego języka Polskiego (Eng. Phonetics and phonology of modern Polish language). PWN (2000)

13. Rabiner, L.R.: A tutorial on hidden Markov models and selected applications in speech recognition. Proceedings of the IEEE 77(2), 257–286 (1989)
14. Steffen-Batóg, M., Nowakowski, P.: An algorithm for phonetic transcription of ortographic texts in Polish. Studia Phonetica Posnaniensia 3 (1993)
15. Yannakoudakis, E.J., Hutton, P.J.: An assessment of n-phoneme statistics in phoneme guessing algorithms which aim to incorporate phonotactic constraints. Speech Communication 11, 581–602 (1992)
16. Young, S., Evermann, G., Gales, M., Hain, T., Kershaw, D., Moore, G., Odell, J., Ollason, D., Povey, D., Valtchev, V., Woodland, P.: HTK Book. Cambridge University Engineering Department, UK (2005)

ROG – A Paradigmatic Morphological Generator for Romanian

Elena Irimia

Research Institute for Artificial Intelligence
Calea 13 Septembrie, No. 13, Bucharest 050711, Romania
elena@racai.ro

Abstract. We describe here the process of implementing a morphological generator for Romanian, together with references to the resources and previous work that made this achievement possible. The generator receives a lemma and a morpho-lexical description of the intended word-form and it is supposed to generate that very word-form. It uses a paradigmatic description of Romanian morphology and a large dictionary of lemmas associated with their inflectional paradigms. The work is motivated by an ongoing example-based machine translation system and by its utility in extending the lexical resources created in our group. The generation process distinguishes two major situations, depending on the lemma being recorded or not into the generator's dictionary. In the first case, the generated inflected form is guaranteed to be a real word of Romanian language while in the second case the inflected form might be a potential but not extant word of Romanian.

Keywords: paradigmatic morphology, morphological generator.

1 Introduction

The empirical corpus-based paradigm in Machine Translation, originating in the IBM's Peter Brown statistical approach in 1988 [1], has as first underlying issue the acquisition of large repositories of parallel corpora. Some of the important aspects to deal with (both in SMT and EBMT) are the size of the example databases and the data sparseness. Translation models, be they based on words or phrases, tend to be extremely large when one or both of the languages concerned are highly inflectional. There are various ways to avoid overgrowing of the bilingual data structures used by the translation models. Among them, lemmatization of the translation equivalents and generalization of certain constituents (in case of phrase–based translation models) are very effective. Additionally, by these generalizations, data sparseness is diminished and the linguistic coverage is increased. Obviously, there is a price to be paid and this is represented by what we call the morpho-lexical properties transfer between source and target translation equivalents followed by a generation of the inflected form in the target language. In this paper we will consider English as a source language and dwell on the morpho-lexical generation in Romanian as a target language.

In our approach the input text is tokenized into lexical items (words or expressions), tagged and lemmatized. Lemmatization is a post-processing phase of the

Z. Vetulani and H. Uszkoreit (Eds.): LTC 2007, LNAI 5603, pp. 74–84, 2009.

tiered tagging [2] both for Romanian and English (for the newest implementation, TTL, see [3]).

This normalized text is subject to a rough translation, using a standard noisy-channel model. The translation model is based on lemmas [4] and therefore the target text is produced in a lemmatized form. The morpho-lexical descriptors (MSDs) of the lexical tokens in the source language, as assigned by the source language tagger, are aligned with equivalent morpho-lexical descriptors (MSDs) for the lexical tokens in target language. In [4], this alignment is called POS-affinity. The MSDs are compliant with the Multext-East V3 specifications [5] as used by our SMT project.

Once we obtained the lexical tokens (via MT model) and their MSDs (via POS affinity model) for the target language, the generation phase is required to produce the inflected form of every token in accordance with its transferred MSD. In the rest of this paper we will address this very issue.

The paper is organized as follows:

- in section 2 we give a brief account of the paradigmatic morphology model of Romanian on which we built our morphological generator;
- in section 3 we describe ROG, the proper generator;
- in section 4 we discuss the use of ROG in improving the language model of Romanian and draw some conclusions.

2 The Development of the Paradigmatic Morphology Theory

The paradigmatic morphology of Romanian [6, 7] has been developed for several years in different formats and variants, starting with a flat (theory neutral) attribute-value representation (FAVR) and having the most complete version implemented in the LISP-based ELU linguistic programming environment [8]. This unification-based implementation of the paradigmatic morphology (which we will name ROPMORPH), together with lexical repositories containing associating paradigms and lexical roots for almost 35.000 of Romanian lemmas are the resources which we built on our application's development.

In the context of this theory, a word is regarded as an entity made of two fundamental units: a *root* and an *ending* (built of one or more desinences and/or suffixes). The root carries context-free information, while the ending is a bearer of contextual information. When the inflection of a word involves modification of the root (root alternation), some contextual information (consisting of restrictions on its use in conjunction with the specified endings) can be associated with the root.

The information associated with the root is stored in a dictionary (lexical repository) entry corresponding to the lemma of the corresponding root. Such an entry has the following structure:

pos
@lemma
root_1 root_2 ... root_k associated_paradigm1
root_k+1 ...root_j associated_paradigm2
...

Fig. 1. The structure of an entry in the dictionary

The information associated with the ending is stored in ROPMORPH, the file containing a complete inventory of the Romanian paradigms for verbs, nouns, pronouns and adjectives. A paradigm is a collection of endings, each of them associated with the morphological information characterizing an occurrence formed from a root and the respective ending. An entry in this file has the structure shown in Fig. 4, in the next section.

By combining the information supplied in the dictionary with the one in ROPMORPH, we can identify all the legal endings (and the associated root restrictions) that can be concatenated with the root or roots of a specific lemma, to obtain correct inflected forms.

During the implementation of ROG we derived from ROPMORPH a resource of great use for dealing with unknown words: a list of all the Romanian suffixes (ROMSFX), together with their corresponding associated paradigms and MSD-tags. In the following figure you can see the suffixes list for the nominal masculine 1 paradigm:

u	Ncms-n	$nommasc1	i	Ncmp-n	$nommasc1
ul	Ncmsry	$nommasc1	ii	Ncmpry	$nommasc1
ule	Ncmsvy	$nommasc1	ii	Ncmpvy	$nommasc1
ului	Ncmsoy	$nommasc1	ilor	Ncmpoy	$nommasc1
ul	Ncmsvy	$nommasc1	ilor	Ncmpvy	$nommasc1

Fig. 2. The nominative masculine 1 paradigm. The first column lists the suffixes while the second column contains the MSD-tags.

The MSD-tag set has specific position for a specific feature. For a noun, the predefined order of the features is: type, gender, number, case, definiteness, clitic. In the figure above, the second column contains the MSD tags: the tag Ncms-n corresponds to the common with masculine gender, with singular number and undefined. The word-form is the same for any case (direct, oblique, vocative) and this information is represented by "-" in the case position. The interpretation is similar for the other MSD-tags in Figure 2.

Additionally, we used a very large word-form lexicon containing more than 800,000 manually validated lexical entries, each containing a word-form occurrence, its lemma and the appropriate MSD tag. This lexical resource, referred to in the following as tbl.wordform.ro, has the following structure:

<tbl.wordform.ro>::= <entry>+
<entry>::= <word-form><tab><lemma><tab><MSD>

Fig. 3. The structure of tbl.wordform.ro

3   The Description of ROG

ROG is a .Net (C#) application which, having as input data the lemma of a word and the MSD tag corresponding to the word-form that we wish to generate, can produce a correct inflected form. In the paradigmatic morphology theory's context, this implies the necessity of a correct identification of the paradigm corresponding to the lemma – from 167 paradigms for the noun and 72 paradigms for the verb documented in the complete description of the Romanian morphology. The input data is insufficient for this choice problem. Therefore, we are appealing to the resources described in the previous section. The application has three modules, corresponding to the three following cases for the input lemma:

- the lemma is in the lexical repositories, annotated with the morphological root(s) and the morphological paradigm (the paradigmatic dictionary);
- the lemma is not in the paradigmatic dictionary but, together with some (possibly not all) of its inflected forms, it is to be found in the word-form lexicon tbl.wordform.ro
- the lemma is neither in the paradigmatic dictionary nor in the tbl.wordform.ro lexicon.

3.1 The Generation Module

The first step in the generation process is looking up the lemma in the lexical repositories and extracting from there the possible roots and the possible paradigms. In Romanian, the root changing phenomenon is frequent: many nouns have two possible roots, one for singular, other for plural (ex.: romanian *"fereastra/ferestre"*, english "window/windows"); several adjectives have root variations depending on the number and gender of the noun they modify; the number of roots for a verb can vary from one to seven, depending on various features (especially tense). The following cases and examples can offer a closer look at some of these situations and also to some cases when the paradigm associated to a specific lemma is not unique:

1. A specific noun can be associated with its correspondent simple paradigm and also to some diminutive and augmentative paradigms.
   Example 1:
   n   @copil (English: child)
   copi $nommasc7
   copil $nomdimmasc2 (produces "copilaş", English : little child)
   copil $nomaugmmasc1 (produces : "copiloi", English: big child)
   copil $nomaugmmasc3 (produces : "copilandru", English: big child)

2. An adjective is associated with one masculine noun paradigm and one feminine noun paradigm.
   Example 2:
   adj   @frumos (English: beautiful)
   frumos   frumoş $nommasc8
   frumoas $nomfem1

3. A verb can be associated with its correspondent verbal paradigm and to some nominal or adjectival paradigms that transform the verb either in a noun or in an adjective by suffixation.

```
<PARADIGM PARADIGM="nommasc1" GEN="masculine" INTENSIFY="none">
 <TYPE TYPE="{proper common}">
  <NUM NUM="singular">
   <ENCL ENCL="no">
    <CASE CASE="{nominative genitive dative accusative vocative}">
     <TERM TERM="u" ALT = "1"/>
    </CASE>
   </ENCL>
   <ENCL ENCL="yes">
    <CASE CASE="{nominative accusative}">
     <TERM TERM="ul" ALT = "1"/>
    </CASE>
    <CASE CASE="{genitive dative}">
     <TERM TERM="ului" ALT = "1"/>
    </CASE>
    <CASE CASE="vocative">
     <HUM HUM="imperson">
      <TERM TERM="ul" ALT = "1"/>
     </HUM>
     <HUM HUM="person">
      <TERM TERM="ule" ALT = "1"/>
     </HUM>
    </CASE>
   </ENCL>
  </NUM>
  <NUM NUM="plural">
   <ENCL ENCL="no">
    <CASE CASE="{nominative genitive dative accusative vocative}">
     <TERM TERM="i" ALT = "2"/>
    </CASE>
   </ENCL>
   <ENCL ENCL="yes">
    <CASE CASE="{nominative accusative}">
     <TERM TERM="ii" ALT = "2"/>
    </CASE>
    <CASE CASE="{genitive dative}">
     <TERM TERM="ilor" ALT = "2"/>
    </CASE>
    <CASE CASE="vocative">
     <HUM HUM="imperson">
      <TERM TERM="ii" ALT = "2"/>
     </HUM>
      <HUM HUM="person">
       <TERM TERM="ilor" ALT = "2"/>
      </HUM>
    </CASE>
   </ENCL>
  </NUM>
 </TYPE>
</PARADIGM>
```

Fig. 4. An entry in the ROPMORPH file

Example 3:
v   @*consulta*   *(English: to consult)*
consult   consulţ $verb1
n   @*consulta*
consult $verbsuf15
(produces the noun " consultant", English: consultant)
consult $verbsuf4
(produces the noun " consultare", English: consulting)

After extracting the list of roots and (sub-)paradigms, the module looks in the file that describes completely the Romanian morphology (ROPMORPH). Any entry in this file has a structure similar with the one in the following example (naturally, the structure for a verb or a pronoun will have attributes and values specific to their grammatical category):

One may notice that an entry has the form of a tree and specifies all the necessary grammatical information for identifying the POS-tag of a word-form (we will use the MSD-tag set) if we follow a tree branch; the leaves contain information about the ending that should be concatenated to the word's root to obtain a specific inflected form. The ALT attribute specifies the alternate root: the numerical value represents the position of the root in the list of all possible roots for a lemma and a POS-tag.

Fig.4. has to be interpreted as following: the first paradigm for the masculine noun receives additional termination (TERM = "u") for both the proper and common types, for the singular number and the undefined form (ENCL = "no") – in Romanian, nouns can be marked for definiteness with the enclitic definite article – in all the cases: nominative, genitive, dative, accusative and vocative. In case of root alternation, the root chosen for the features described is the first in the list of the possible roots (Alt = "1"). The interpretation is similar for the defined (enclitic) form, with different terminations corresponding to different cases.

Exploiting the structure of such an entry, we can easily generate the family of all the inflected forms for a lemma (provided this lemma is in the dictionary, where we can identify its roots and paradigms). Also, we consider important that this family can be annotated with the corresponding MSD-tags, allowing us to subsequently extract only the inflected form associated to the MSD received as input data.

For the paradigm presented in Fig. 4 and the entry in the lexical repository corresponding to the lemma "maestru" (en "master"):

n   @*maestru*
maestr $nommasc1
maeştr $nommasc1,

the generator will produce the following forms:

maestru Ncms-n	*maeştri Ncmp-n*
maestrul Ncmsry	*maeştrii Ncmpry*
maestrului Ncmsoy	*maeştrilor Ncmpoy*
maestrul Ncmsvy	*maeştrilor Ncmpvy*
maestrule Ncmsvy	

3.2 The Module for Paradigm Identification

The real difficult problem to be solved is the situation when the lemma cannot be found in the dictionary. For enriching this resource, we developed a module that identifies roots and associated paradigms for new words, having as input data as many inflected forms as we can extract from tbl.wordform.ro (all the forms that this data-base contains, annotated with lemmas and MSD-tags, have been manually validated). If the process of identification is successful we can also enrich tbl.wordform.ro with new inflected forms.

The description of the identification algorithm

Input data:

$$
L_1 \longrightarrow \begin{array}{ccc} w_1 & l & POS \\ w_2 & l & POS \\ \vdots & \vdots & POS \\ w_n & l & POS \end{array} \tag{1}
$$

L_1: the list of word-forms for a given lemma l (extracted from tbl.worform.ro) and a specific part of speech POS (POS values can be "noun", "verb", "adjective"); the algorithms works without MSD-tags information, to have the possibility of processing other lexical databases than tbl.worform.ro.

$$
L_2 \longrightarrow \begin{array}{ccc} s_1 & M_1 & p_1 \\ \vdots & \vdots & \vdots \\ s_k & M_k & p_k \end{array} \tag{2}
$$

L_2: a list of all the possible suffixes in Romanian (s), together with their associated MSD-tags (M) and paradigms (p) – the file ROMSFX (see Figure 1).

Output data:

$$
\begin{array}{ccc} w_1 & M_1 & p \\ \vdots & \vdots & \vdots \\ w_n & M_n & p \end{array} \tag{3}
$$

Output: the list of the input word-forms associated with their MSD tags and with a set of possible paradigms P. P is a subset of $\{p_1, \ldots, p_k\}$ and is common to all the word-forms in $\{w_1, \cdots, w_n\}$.

The description of the identification process:

Step 1. For each w_i in L_1, find the set S_i of all the t triplets (s_j, p_j, M_j), where s_j is a suffix of w_i and the triplet is from L_2

At this stage, we extract, for every inflected form in the list L_l, the set of all paradigms to which the form, by its suffix, can be associated.

Step 2. For identifying the **root(s)** of the set $\{w_1, \cdots, w_n\}$ we follow the next procedure:

    I.   For each w_i, compute the set $R_{w_i} = \{w_i - s_1 = r_1, \cdots, w_i - s_t = r_t\}$. This means that for each inflected form, we extract a list of roots by eliminating the suffix specific to every applicable paradigm.

    II. Compute $R = \bigcap_{i=1}^{n} R_{w_i}$, for finding the set of roots common to all the lists constructed at the previous step.

    III. If $|R| > 1$ (the intersection has more than one element), it is very possible to have encountered a derivative word (i.e. nouns formed by the suffixation of the verb, augmentative or diminutive words). These kinds of words have particular paradigms documented in the paradigmatic morphology and so they can be correctly characterized by two different roots and two different paradigms. For the lexical suffixes that change the grammar category of the word (privi+tor+ul), as suggested before, the selected root is the one with the category compliant with the category of the set $\{w_1, \cdots, w_n\}$ and, therefore, no ambiguity is present. For the preserving category lexical suffixes (such as augmentatives or diminutives), in principle, there might be considered two legal roots. For instance, the word copilaşul (the small child) may have the following two correct interpretations: i) copil+aş+ul – $nomdimmasc2 or ii) copilaş+ul – $nommasc8. However, for the sake of morpho-syntactic tagging, as the grammatical suffix carries contextual relevant information (e.g. gender), the selected root will always be considered at the grammatical suffix boundary[1]. If $|R| = 1$, the element of the set R is identified as the root of the word family correspondent to the current lemma. If $|R| = 0$, we analyze again all the R_{w_i} and extract a list of roots $(r_1, ..., r_m)$ that are elements of different R_{w_i} but share the same paradigmatic information p. This is a clear case of root alternation and can be completely solved for nouns and adjectives (in which case the list of roots is limited to two elements) but, usually, is much more difficult to deal with it for irregular verbs, which present more than two alternate roots (the likelihood that all relevant forms of the verb, containing the alternate roots, co-occur in tbl.wordform.ro is very low).

---

[1] For instance, the word *căsoiului* (of the big house) could be arguably interpreted as *casa* (feminine noun) + *oi* (augmentative) + *ului* (masculine, oblique case, definite form). Any modifier of the word *căsoiului* should have the masculine gender, in spite of the semantic gender of the word (which is feminine).

Step 3. During the process of root(s) identification, the paradigmatic information p is maintained and sometimes used (in case of root alternation). When the process is finished, every root in the R set is associated with the correct paradigm p. If the number of available word-forms is not enough to uniquely identify the correct paradigm, we have to deal with a set of possible paradigms *PAR*. In this case, we generate all the possible word-forms for all the paradigms in *PAR* and use an in house library that extracts information from the Google™ search engine to count, for every word-form, the number of occurrences on the web. Discarding word-forms which appear less then 10 times, every set of words with the same identifier $p_i \in PAR$ is scored with respect to the sum of the web occurrences of its word-forms and the highest scored paradigm p is chosen.

Once the paradigm and the root identified, we can generate the forms that are missing from the table, together with their MSDs, using the first module of the application. In more complicated cases of root alternation, the user also has the possibility to study the results, choose the proper roots and the proper paradigms and then update the dictionary.

Example 4:
For the input line
muezin n
the module identifies in tbl.wordform.ro the following 4 forms:
muezin, muezini, muezinilor, muezinului. (en. muezzin / muezzins)

The structure containing all the (s, M, p) compatible with the four forms has the following dimension:

Word-form	Number of pairs (paradigm, MSD)
muezin	*19*
muezini	*32*
muezinilor	*24*
muezinului	*17*

The root R, identified in the step 2 of the process, is *"muezin"* and the corresponding paradigm is   *$nommasc8*.
The result of the generation step is the following:

Word-form	Associated MSD	Word-form	Associated MSD
muezin	*Ncms-n*	*muezini*	*Ncmprn*
muezinul	*Ncmsry*	*muezinii*	*Ncmpry*
muezinului	*Ncmsoy*	*muezinilor*	*Ncmpoy*
muezinule	*Ncmsvy*	*muezinilor*	*Ncmpvy*

3.3 The Module for Paradigm Guessing

For the ultimate situation in which the lemma is not to be found in the extended dictionary or in tbl.wordform.ro, we conceived a procedure to predict a root and a paradigm for the new word, based on the similarities between the unknown lemma ending and the endings for the lemmas in the dictionary. We used a simple pattern-matching technique, seeking for the longest common ending substring (obviously, the searching is made only in the subset of words having the same grammatical category as the lemma's). For instance, searching for lemmas having the same ending as the word *fanzin* (inexistent in the ROG dictionary), one gets the following results:

bazin	noun	*zin*	*$nomneu1*
magazin	noun	*zin*	*$nomneu1*
mezin	noun	*zin*	*$nommasc8*
muezin	noun	*zin*	*$nommasc8*
sarazin	noun	*zin*	*$nommasc8*

Thus, *fanzin* may be inflected according to two paradigms$_2$: $nomneu1 or $nommasc8. All the found examples show regular behavior, with the root identical to the lemma form. Hence, we set *fanzin* as root and generate the whole set of word-forms for $nomneu1 and $nommasc8 respectively. After the possible word-forms have been generated according to the two paradigms, we apply the Google filtering method from the previous section to select only one paradigm. Thus, for this example, given the much more Google evidence, the winning model will be the $nomneu1 paradigm.

Then, the module for generation can be used to produce all the inflected forms of the lemma. Finally, the word-form needed in the machine translation process is selected and the new word-forms and lemmas are introduced in the lexical resources.

4 Conclusions

We are convinced that we developed a very useful (crucial for language generation process of such a strong inflected language as Romanian) tool, both to enrich the lexical resources available at ICIA and to be integrated in the future machine-translation system that represents one of our team's ambitious goals. We also think that this application can be successfully integrated in a question-answering system for Romanian (another ongoing project, which will develop in a web-service offering to the user the facility to find answers about Romanian legislation). The application usefulness was already proved by extending tbl.wordform.ro with 240.464 new word-forms, from which 9149 are corresponding to new lemmas.

For the first module, the error rate is minimal: the cause for an error stands basically in the resources (it can be a dictionary error or an error in ROPMORH) – most of these errors have been corrected in the process of testing the application. For the modules implying Google searching, the performance is depending on the correctness of the information encountered on the Internet and sensitive to misspell.

References

1. Brown, P., Cocke, J., Della Pietra, S., Della Pietra, V., Jelinek, F., Mercer, R.: A statistical approach to French/English translation. In: Second International Conference on Theoretical and Methodological Issues in Machine Translation of Natural Languages, p. 16. Carnegie Mellon University, Center for Machine Translation, Pittsburgh (1988)

2. Tufis, D.: Tiered tagging and combined language models classifiers. In: Matoušek, V., Mautner, P., Ocelíková, J., Sojka, P. (eds.) TSD 1999. LNCS (LNAI), vol. 1692, pp. 28–33. Springer, Heidelberg (1999)
3. Ion, R.: Methods for Word Sense Disambiguation; Applications for English and Romanian. Phd Thesis, Romanian Academy (2007)
4. Tufi , D., Ion, R., Ceau u, A.l., tef nescu, D.: Improved Lexical Alignment by Combining Multiple Reified Alignments. In: Proceedings of the 11th Conference of the European Chapter of the Association for Computational Linguistics (EACL 2006), Trento, Italy, pp. 153–160 (2006)
5. Erjavec, T.: MULTEXT-East Version 3: Multilingual Morphosyntactic Specifications, Lexicons and Corpora. In: Proceedings of the Fourth International Conference on Language Resources and Evaluation, LREC 2004, ELRA, Paris, pp. 1535–1538 (2004)
6. Tufi , D.: It Would Be Much Easier If WENT Were GOED. In: Somers, H., Wood, M.M. (eds.) Proceedings of the 4th European Conference of the Association for Computational Linguistics, Manchester (1989)
7. Tufi , D.: Paradigmatic Morphology Learning. In: Miklosko, J. (ed.) Computers and Artificial Intelligence. VEDA Publishing House, Bratislava (1990)
8. Estival, D., Tufis, D., Popescu, O.: Devélopment d'outils et des données linguistiques pour le traîtement du langage naturel. Rapport Final – Projet EST (7RUPJO38421) ISSCO, Geneve (1994)

Building a Morphosyntactic Lexicon
and a Pre-syntactic Processing Chain for Polish

Benoît Sagot

ALPAGE* — INRIA Paris-Rocquencourt & Université Paris 7
Domaine de Voluceau, Rocquencourt, B.P. 105, 78153 Le Chesnay cedex, France
and
Instytut Podstaw Informatyki Polskiej Akademii Nauk (IPI PAN)
ul. J.K. Ordona 21, 01-237 Warszawa, Poland
benoit.sagot@inria.fr

Abstract. This paper introduces a new set of tools and resources for
Polish which cover all the steps required to transform a raw unrestricted
text into a reasonable input for a parser. This includes (1) a large-
coverage morphological lexicon, developed thanks to the IPI PAN corpus as well as a lexical acquisition techique, and (2) multiple tools for
spelling correction, segmentation, tokenization and named entity recognition. This processing chain is also able to deal with the XCES format
both as input and output, hence allowing to improve XCES corpora such
as the IPI PAN corpus itself. This allows us to give a brief qualitative
evaluation of the lexicon and of the processing chain.

Keywords: Morphosyntactic lexicon, pre-syntactic processing, tokenization, spelling correction, named entites recognition, Polish language.

1 Introduction

In recent years, a considerable effort has been made towards efficient and robust
surface processing of large corpora for various tasks such as information extraction and retrieval, linguistic information acquisition, grammar induction, and
others. However, this effort has been mostly focused on a few major languages,
notably English. Less effort has been made on most other languages.

This paper concentrates on Polish, one of the Slavonic languages for which
resources and tools do exist, although much less than for, e.g., Czech. Indeed,
[1] introduces a rule-based named-entity recognition system for Polish built on
top of the NLP plateform SProUT [2]. As regards linguistic resources, which are
needed for the construction and/or acquisition of linguistic processing chains,
[3] presents the results of projects POLEX, CEGLEX and GRAMLEX, which
consitute, among others, a morphological resource for Polish. But this resource
is not freely available. On the contrary, the IPI PAN corpus of Polish [4], which
is morphologically annotated, is publicly available.

---

* The work described in this paper has been carried out when the author was a member
of the SIGNES team of INRIA, during a 3-month stay at IPI PAN in 2007.

Z. Vetulani and H. Uszkoreit (Eds.): LTC 2007, LNAI 5603, pp. 85–95, 2009.
© Springer-Verlag Berlin Heidelberg 2009

Therefore, this corpus is a valuable starting point for developing NLP tools and resources for Polish. This paper describes the two first steps of a long-term program, namely the development of a morphlogical lexicon and of a pre-parsing processing chain. The following step, the development of a phrase-level parser, is ongoing. It should be followed by a syntactic lexicon (which is to be acquired thanks to results provided by the phrase-level parser, thanks to techniques already presented in [5]) and, finally, a deep parser.

The work presented here can be considered as the application and adaptation to Polish of a set of tools that have been initially developed for French. We first discuss the construction of a baseline morphological lexicon for Polish from the IPI PAN data, then techniques to improve this lexicon, and finally the development of a robust pre-parsing processing chain, SxPipe-pl. We sketch how these results already enabled us to improve the IPI PAN corpus, which could lead in a near future to a new version of the corpus.

2   A Baseline Polish Morphological Lexicon

2.1   Lexical Framework

An NLP lexicon has to represent several kinds of information: morphological, syntactic, and possibly semantic. However, there are different ways to model such a rich information, and in particular different levels of information factorization. We call **extensional lexicon** a resource that associates with each *form* a detailed structure that represents all this information. Such a lexicon is typically used by parsers. We call **intensional lexicon** a resource that factorizes the information, by associating with each *lemma* a morphological class and deep syntactic information. In [6], the authors sketch a framework named Alexina that implements this two-level vision of lexical information, and introduce the Le*fff*, a large-coverage syntacic lexicon for French which relies on (an more recent version of) this framework.

An intensional entry, i.e., an entry of the intensional lexicon, is defined as a triple of the form *(lemma, morphological class, deep syntactic information)*. An extensional entry, i.e., an entry of the extensional lexicon, is a triple of the form *(inflected form, category, surface syntactic information)*, where the syntactic structure includes the lemma, morphological information, the sub-categorization frame (when relevant), and other syntactic features. However, since we do not consider syntactic information in this paper, both the intensional and the extensional lexicons are simplified: the *compilation* process which transforms an intensional lexicon into its extensional counterpart is mostly an *inflection* process. Moreover, both lexicons are simplified: an intensional entry becomes a couple *(lemma, morphological class)* and an extensional entry a triple *(form, lemma, (morphological) tag)*. We call *morphological lexicon* a set of such simplified extensional entries which only represent morphological information. The inflection process relies on a formalized morphological description of the language, i.e., a definition of all morphological classes.

In the remainder of this section, we show how we extracted directly from the IPI PAN corpus a baseline morphological description of Polish. In Section 3, we show how we extended this baseline, thanks, in particular, to an automatic lexical information acquisition technique.

2.2   Extracting a Morphological Lexicon from the IPI PAN Corpus

When starting from a morphosyntactically annotated corpus, the most direct way to build a lexicon is to extract directly the triples *(form, lemma, tag)* that are attested in the corpus. This can be seen as a simplified version of an extensional lexicon. It is simplified because the syntactic information is virtually absent, and because for a given lemma, only the forms that are attested in the corpus are present in the lexicon. Although this step could seem trivial, is does raise several problems.

Our work is based on the IPI PAN corpus [4]. The IPI PAN corpus is a large (over 250 million words) morphosyntactically annotated and publicly available corpus of Polish. It has been developed for several years by the Linguistic Engineering Group at the Instytut Podstaw Informatyki (IPI) of the Polska Akademia Nauk (PAN). The morphosyntactic annotation has been obtained automatically, thanks to a morphological analyser named Morfeusz [7, ch. 4][1] and a disambiguator that has been trained on a manually annotated subset of the corpus [8]. It is encoded in a specific variant of the XCES format [9].

Table 1. Example of a token in the IPI PAN corpus (XCES format)

```
<tok>
<orth>Chciał</orth>
<lex disamb="1"><base>chcieć</base><ctag>praet:sg:m1:imperf</ctag></lex>
<lex><base>chcieć</base><ctag>praet:sg:m2:imperf</ctag></lex>
<lex><base>chcieć</base><ctag>praet:sg:m3:imperf</ctag></lex>
</tok>
```

It seems easy to extract a morphological lexicon from such a corpus, excluding of course unknown words (tokens tagged **ign**). For example, from the token of Table 1, one wordform can be infered (*chciał*) for which three (morphological) entries can be extracted: *(chciał, chcieć, praet:sg:m1:imperf)*, *(chciał, chcieć, praet:sg:m2:imperf)* and *(chciał, chcieć, praet:sg:m3:imperf)*.

However the IPI PAN corpus suffers from a light over-simplification of its annotation: all lemmas are lowercase, including proper nouns and other lemmas that should be capitalized. For example, in the corpus, the form *Warszawa*

---

[1] Cf. http://nlp.ipipan.waw.pl/~wolinski/morfeusz/. It is important to state here the fact that the lexicon on which Morfeusz is based is *not* publicly available. If it were, the work of this section would be strongly simplified, since only capitalization and unknown word problems would remain.

has *warszawa* as a lemma (i.e., as `base` attribute of the `lex` element). To (imperfectly) solve this problem, we developed simple heuristics to identify proper nouns at a lemma level. It is important to be able to identify those words which are both a proper noun and a common noun (`subst`) or an adjective (`adj`) (cf. Łódź, the city, vs. łódź, *boat*).[2] Results are satisfying, although specific problems remain for words that frequently occur in capitalized phrases (*Atlantycki*, *Demokratyczny*).

At this point, we have a baseline morphological Polish lexicon. It is a starting point both in terms of quality and coverage. It contains 865,673 entries representing 233,099 different wordforms (e.g., we have seen that the wordform *chciał* corresponds to 3 different entries). The aim of the next section is to go beyond this baseline.

3   Improving the Baseline Lexicon

In order to improve the quality and coverage of this baseline lexicon, we decided to extend it thanks to an automatic acquisition technique, as sketched below. This technique relies on the availability of a morphological description of the language. Therefore, we first describe the morphological formalism and the (partial) morphological description of Polish that we used. We show how this description allows us to detect annotation errors in the corpus as well as extending the baseline lexicon.

3.1   Morphological Formalism

A morphological description of a language should have four main goals: optimal factorization of the information, readability and maintainability, coverage and accuracy, and ability to be used by a morphological compiler to generate automatically both an inflection tool (from a lemma to its forms) and a (non-deterministic) lemmatization tool (from a form to all its possible lemmas, restricted or not to lemmas which are known in a lexicon).

As part of the lexical framework described in [6], such a formalism and the associated morphological compiler have been already developed and applied to French as well as Slovak [10]. The formalism, which shares some ideas with the DATR formalism [11], relies on the following scheme:

- A set of morphological (inflection) classes which can inherit (partly or completely) from one another,
- Each class contains a set of forms represented as suffixes that are to be added to the stem,

---

[2] We used approximately the following heuristics: (1) Any lemma which is not a `subst` or an `adj` is not a proper noun (2) Any lemma whose corresponding raw tokens (its `orth` elements) start with a capital letter more that 50% of all cases exists as a proper noun, (3) Any lemma whose corresponding raw tokens (its `orth` elements) start with a capital letter more that 99% of all cases is only a proper noun.

- Forms can be controlled by tests over the stem (a given rule can apply only if a given regular expression matches the stem and/or if another one does not match the stem, and so on),
- Forms can be controlled by "variants" of the classes (e.g., one or more form can be selected by one or more flag which complements the name of the class),
- "Collision patterns" allow to link the surface form to the sequence *stem_ suffix*.

To illustrate this, Table 2 show examples of collision patterns in our morphological description of Polish described below (3.2). Table 3 shows an extract of the inflection class for m1 (personal-masculine) substantives.

Table 2. Morphological formalism: example of "letter" classes and of collision patterns. In a collision pattern, the underscore sign denotes the boundary between the stem and the suffix. A rule is applied from the "source" to the "target" when inflecting, and from the "target" to the "source" when lemmatizing.

```
<letterclass name="hard"
             letters="b p f w m n ł t d r s z ch h"/>
...
<collision source="r_'" target="rz_"/>
<collision source="[:soft:]_y" target="[:soft:]_i"/>
<collision source="[:kg:]_e" target="[:kg:]_ie" final="+"/>
...
```

3.2 Description of Polish Nouns and Adjectives

In order to prepare the construction of an intensional lexicon of Polish and to expand the lexicon so as to lower the percentage of unknown words (`ign` tokens), we developed a morphological description of Polish in the formalism sketched above. Its main linguistic basis is [12]. Currently, our morphological description covers adjectives and common nouns:

- 1 class for adjectives, plus 2 other classes (comparatives and superlatives) that exactly inherit from the standard class and are here for technical reasons[3]
- 10 classes for substantives: *m1*, *m1a* for *m1* substantives in *-a*, *m2* which inherits from *m1* and redefines pl:nom, pl:voc and pl:acc, *m3* which inherits from *m2* and redefines sg:acc and sg:gen, class *n* (neutral), class *num* for neutrals in *-um* (inherits from class *n*, all singular forms in *-um*, pl:gen in *-ów*), classes *nen* and *net* respectively for types *ramię/ramiona* and *cielę/cielęta*, class *fv* for feminine substantives in *-a* or *-i* and class *fc* for feminine substantives with a zero ending for sg:nom.

---

[3] They assign tags in `-comp` or `-sup` instead of `-pos`, so as to match the IPI PAN corpus tagset.

Table 3. Example of a morphological class

```
<class name="subst-m1" tag_suffix=":m1" stems="...*">
    <form suffix="" tag="sg:nom"/>
    <form like="sg:gen" tag="sg:acc"/>
    <form suffix="a" tag="sg:gen" except="(wol|bawol)"/>
    <form suffix="u" tag="sg:gen" stems="(wol|bawol)"/>
    <alt>
        <form suffix="owi" tag="sg:dat" var="Dowi"/>
        <form suffix="u" tag="sg:dat" var="Du"/>
    </alt>
    <form suffix="em" tag="sg:inst"/>
    <form suffix="'e" tag="sg:loc" stems="..*[:hard:]"
                    except="(syn|dom|pan)"/>
    <form suffix="u" tag="sg:loc" except="..*[:hard:]"/>
    <form suffix="u" tag="sg:loc"
                    stems="(syn|dom|pan|bor)"/>
...
```

3.3   Detecting Annotation Errors in the Corpus

Our morphological description of Polish is currently limited to nouns and adjectives. Its precision and coverage already enables us to detect some errors in the annotated corpus. Indeed, any nominal or adjectival form which is in the morphological lexicon (i.e., which was found in the corpus) must be analysable by the ambiguous lemmatizer with the appropriate category, tag and lemma.

Indeed, we were able to discover some errors, including systematic ones, in the IPI PAN corpus. Of course, these errors are reproduced as such in the baseline lexicon, from which they had to be removed. Some of them come from the automatic annotation tool, `Morfeusz`, and/or its underlying lexical database,[4] whereas others come from tokenization and related problems, as we shall see in Section 4.

3.4   Automatic Extension of the Lexicon

In [10], the author describes a technique to acquire automatically lexical information from a raw corpus and a morphological description of the language. It has been applied to French verbs and to all open categories of Slovak. The availability of the morphological description of Polish allowed us to use this technique to extend automatically (with manual validation) our Polish lexicon so as

---

[4] A few examples: (1) sg:acc (and sg:gen) of m1, except *wół* and *bawół*, is in -*a*; however, many m1 forms ending in -u are tagged as sg:acc and sg:gen in the corpus (*aptekarzu, energetyku, kierowniku, laiku,...*); (2) pl:acc for m1 is identical to pl:nom; however, a huge amount of m1 in -*a* (*archiwista, finansista,...*) have forms in -*y* that are tagged as pl:acc (*archiwisty, finansisty,* whereas pl:acc forms are *archiwistów, finansistów*); (3) Some relatively frequent isolated problems.

to minimize as much as possible the amount of unknown words in the IPI PAN corpus (ign tokens).

The idea underlying this automatic lexical acquisition technique is the following: First, we use the ambiguous lemmatizer generated from the morphological description: we build all hypothetical lemmas that have at least one inflected form attested in the corpus. Then, we inflect these lemmas and rank them according to their likelihood given the corpus (fix-point algorithm); Many kinds of information are taken into account (derivational morphology, prefixes, frequency of tags depending on the category,...). Afterwards, manual validation is performed on the best-ranked hypothetical lemmas, thanks to an easy-to-use web interface. Finally, the whole process is launched anew, and benefits from the manual validation step (this loop is repeated as many times as necessary). For details, see [10].

Thanks to Radoslaw Moszczynski and Adam Przepiórkowski, who performed the manual validation, a few hours proved enough to acquire 1,460 validated lemmas (only nouns, adjectives and adverbs derived from adjectives). Moreover, a quick study of unkown words in the corpus allowed to add manually 46 lemmas and 186 so-called "manual forms", mostly abbreviations of (forms of) already existing lemmas.

Let us consider all ign tokens of the *law* sub-corpus of the IPI PAN corpus, on which we performed this automatic lexical acquisition process (over 3 million ign tokens out of 75 million tokens). As we will see in the next section, an appropriate pre-processing step can eliminate, among others, several tokenization and "named-entity" problems. We apply a simplified version of this pre-processing step, *without* spelling error correction and built *before* this lexicon extension process, so as to eliminate problems that are not linked with the incompleteness of the lexicon. We also eliminate all ign tokens which contain a capital letter. The result includes a lot of spelling errors, hence the following result is underestimated: the 1,460 validated lemmas, acquired and validated in only a few hours, cover almost 56% of the remaining occurrences of unknown words, which is a very satisfying result.

The resulting lexicon has 929,184 entries for 243,330 different wordforms. It is freely available under the Cecill-C (LGPL-compatible) license on the web site of the Alexina framework.[5]

4   Pre-parsing Processing: A Polish SxPipe

Current parsers, both shallow and deep, are able to deal with large corpora. However, parsers often rely on lexicons and grammars designed to deal with "correct" language, which differs significantly from what can be found in real-life corpora. Hence pre-parsing processing methods are required to turn real-life corpora into acceptable parser inputs. This pre-parsing step is not as basic as it could seem, in particular because it has to be very robust and non-deterministic.

---

[5] http://alexina.gforge.inria.fr/

This is the goal achieved by the pre-parsing processing chain SxPipe [13,14], developed initially for French.

We decided to develop a Polish version of SxPipe for two different reasons: first, many errors in the IPI PAN corpus do come from an imperfect pre-processing; second, a Polish SxPipe is a necessary step before developing a Polish parser, which is one of our future objectives.

4.1   SxPipe

In [13,14], the authors present SxPipe, a set of tools which performs several tasks, which can be grouped into three categories:

- "named entities" (n.e.) recognition: pre-tokenization n.e. (URLs, emails, dates, addresses, numbers,...), lexicon-aware n.e. (phrases in foreign languages,...), and multi-words n.e. (numbers in full text, proper nouns...);
- tokenization and segmentation in sentences;
- (possibly) non-deterministic spelling error correction and multi-words identification (incl. re-accentuation and re-capitalization) with TEXT2DAG.

TEXT2DAG relies on an efficient spelling correction module, named SxSpell. Ontop of this module, TEXT2DAG performs sophisticated non-deterministic heuristics to segment and/or re-glue tokens into forms and to identify multi-token forms ("compound words"). Of course, both tasks strongly interact (in a quite complicated way) with the spelling correction proper.

4.2   A Polish Version of SxPipe

Some of SxPipe modules are partly language-dependent. E.g., most "named entities" recognition tools had to be adapted and extended, because there are language-specific ways to say most things covered by named entities (addresses, dates, times...). Spelling correction rules used by SxSpell are partly encoding-specific (s vs. $ś$,...) and partly language-specific ($ż$ vs. rz,...). However, once these adaptations are done, tokenization, spelling and multi-token identification tools just needed to be linked with the Polish (morphological) lexicon.

Moreover, SxPipe has been extended so as to deal, in input and output, with the XCES format used in the IPI PAN corpus, which includes all meta-textual information (XML content), morphological information on tokens (both ambiguous morphogical analysis and morphological disambiguation), token-boundary information (presence or not of a white space between two tokens), and others. All this information had to be preserved throughout the processing chain and restored in the output (when no correction applied), which was not possible in the previous version of SxPipe. On the other hand, some components used in the original French SxPipe have been adapted but are not used in the default configuration of SxPipe-pl, because they introduce information which has proven irrelevant for improving the IPI PAN corpus (e.g., sequences of the form *acronym (acronym expansion)*, and others).

This work resulted in an XCES-compatible SxPipe available for three different languages: SxPipe for French, SxPipe-pl for Polish, and a very preliminary

Table 4. Sequence of components used by SxPipe-pl in its default configuration

(conversion from XCES to internal format)
e-mail addresses recognition
URLs recognition
dates recognition
phone numbers recognition
times recognition
postal adresses recognition
smileys, other special punctuation and oral transcripts marks recognition
numerical prefixes recognition
numbers and (numerical/symbolic) list markers recognition
(embedded n.e. removal)
tokenization and segmentation
TEXT2DAG: non-deterministic multi-word identification, tokenization correction and spelling error correction
recognition of numbers in full text
proper nouns identification
(conversion from internal format to XCES)

SxPipe-sk for Slovak. Since then, other versions of SxPipe have been developed for English, Spanish and Italian. All these tools are freely available.[6] The list of modules used in SxPipe-pl is shown in Table 4.

4.3 Tokenization, Spelling, and Named Entities Problems in the Corpus

As said above, the IPI PAN corpus contains a non-negligible proportion of unknown words, i.e., `ign` tokens — e.g., in the 75-million-token *law* sub-corpus, 3 million (4%) of tokens are `ign`. Some of these tokens are really words that are unknown from `Morfeusz`, and which have to be added to the lexicon, as previously described.

However, in order to identify these "real" unknown words as well as directly improve the corpus, all other sources of problems in the original corpus have to be identified. Hence the use of SxPipe-pl, whose impact on 430,924 tokens of the *law* subcorpus is summed up in Table 5.[7]

The most frequent problems in the corpus that are detected and solved by SxPipe-pl are the following:

---

[6] http://gforge.inria.fr/projects/lingwb/

[7] Precision and recall measurements still need to be performed. Manual obervation of the results lead to the following conclusion: all modules but the spelling correction module have extremely high precision and recall. The spelling correction module introduces a bit of noise because it sometimes manages to correct tokens which are unknown but correct.

Table 5. SxPipe-pl on 430,924 tokens of the *law* subcorpus: a few figures (note that multi-word units and named entities involve several tokens, hence the discrepancy between the number of `ign` token in the original corpus and the sum of all situations found in the processed corpus)

Token kind	#tok	wrt all	wrt `ign`
`ign` tokens	17,913	**4.2%**	*100%*

(a) Original corpus

automatically acquired words	453	0.1%	2.5%
manually added words	293	0.1%	1.6%
multi-word units	447	0.1%	2.5%
dates and times	850	0.2%	4.7%
numbers and numeric prefixes	4,474	1.0%	25.0%
list markers	256	0.1%	1.4%
"special double-quote"	1,404	0.3%	7.8%
productive prefixes	35	0.0%	0.2%
spelling errors	812	0.2%	4.5%
unknown proper nouns (capitalized words)	4,144	1.0%	23.1%
other (remaining) unknown tokens	413	**0.1%**	2.3%

(b) Corpus processed by SxPipe-pl

- The "special double-quote"[8] tokenization-based errors;
- "Named entities", especially numbers and proper nouns (tokens starting with a capital letter);
- Productive prefixes (e.g., wielko-, post-, agro-, anty-,...);
- Spelling errors (e.g.: *aberacji* (*aberracji*), *abmasadora* (*ambasadora*), *abowiem* (*albowiem*), *abp* (*aby*), *abrbitralności* (*arbitralności*), *absolutniej* (*absolutnej*)...).

Of course, the last important source of `ign` tokens in the original IPI PAN corpus are abbreviations (manually added in the lexicon) and "real" unknown words (e.g.: *abolicjonistycznej, abonamencka, aborcyjna, abortera, absolutoryjny*...). We have previously shown how to extend the lexicon so as to decrease the importance of this problem.[9]

---

[8] There are two different Unicode double-quote-like characters; only the usual one was recognized by the original tokenizer, hence many erroneous `ign` tokens such as ˝*aby*.

[9] A non-trivial problem remains: the corpus is a sequence of tokens with associated morphological interpretations, whereas SxPipe's output is a graph of forms (defined as atomic units for a subsequent parser), with associated token-level anchors. But tokens and forms do not always correspond directly. Cf. for example *piątek 10.5.90 r.* — considered by SxPipe-pl as one (special) form, namely _ *DATE* —, *po prostu, bez mała, niespełna, naprawdę, szliśmy, dwakroć*,... We solved this problem by introducing special XML elements to identify complex forms (`<sw>`, i.e., "syntactic words"). The description of the underlying mechanism and linguistic decisions is beyond the scope of this paper.

5   Conclusions and Perspectives

We have introduced the morphological lexicon for Polish we have developed, based on the IPI PAN corpus annotations and extended thanks to an automatic lexical acquisition technique. We also introduced SxPipe-pl, a full-featured pre-syntactic processing chain for Polish.

Our long-term objective is to develop a phrase-level LFG grammar and the associated parser (which will take as input the output of SxPipe-pl), so as to enable the automatic acquisition of syntactic information from the output of this parser (sub-categorization frames,...), using techniques evoked in [5]. This will lead to a full syntactic lexicon of Polish, which is a necessary step before the development of a robust large-coverage (LFG) parser for Polish.

References

1. Piskorski, J.: Automatic named-entity recognition for Polish. In: International Workshop on Intelligent Media Technology for Communicative Intelligence, Warsaw, Poland (2004)
2. Drożdżyński, W., Krieger, H.-U., Piskorski, J., Schäfer, U., Xu, F.: Shallow processing with unification and typed feature structures — foundations and applications. Künstliche Intelligenz 1, 17–23 (2004)
3. Vetulani, Z.: Electronic Language Resources for Polish: POLEX, CEGLEX and GRAMLEX. In: Second International Conference on Linguistic Ressources and Evaluation (LREC 2000), Athens (2000)
4. Przepiórkowski, A.: Korpus IPI PAN: Wersja wstępna / The IPI PAN Corpus: Preliminary version. IPI/PAN, Warsaw (2004)
5. Fast, J., Przepiórkowski, A.: Automatic extraction of Polish verb subcategorization: An evaluation of common statistics. In: Proceedings of LTC 2005, Poznań, Poland, pp. 191–195 (2005)
6. Sagot, B., Clément, L., de La Clergerie, E., Boullier, P.: The lefff 2 syntactic lexicon for French: architecture, acquisition, use. In: Proceedings of LREC 2006, Genova, Italy (2006)
7. Woliński, M.: Komputerowa weryfikacja gramatyki Świdzińskiego. PhD thesis, Instytut Podstaw Informatyki Polskiej Akademii Nauk, IPI PAN (2004)
8. Piasecki, M., Godlewski, G.: Reductionistic, tree and rule based tagger for Polish. In: Kłopotek, M.A., Wierzchoń, S.T., Trojanowski, K. (eds.) Intelligent Information Processing and Web Mining. Advances in Soft Computing. Springer, Berlin (2006)
9. Ide, N., Bonhomme, P., Romary, L.: XCES: An XML-based encoding standard for linguistic corpora. In: Proceedings of LREC 2000, Paris (2000)
10. Sagot, B.: Automatic acquisition of a Slovak lexicon from a raw corpus. In: Matoušek, V., Mautner, P., Pavelka, T. (eds.) TSD 2005. LNCS (LNAI), vol. 3658, pp. 156–163. Springer, Heidelberg (2005)
11. Evans, R., Gazdar, G.: The DATR Papers: February 1990. Technical Report CSRP 139, University of Sussex, Brighton (1990)
12. Grappin, H.: Grammaire de la langue polonaise. Institut d'études slaves, Paris (1985)
13. Sagot, B., Boullier, P.: From raw corpus to word lattices: robust pre-parsing processing. Archives of Control Sciences 15(4), 653–662 (2005)
14. Sagot, B., Boullier, P.: SxPipe 2: architecture pour le traitement pré-syntaxique de corpus bruts. Traitement Automatique des Langues 49 (2008) (to appear)

A Relational Model of Polish Inflection
in *Grammatical Dictionary of Polish*

Marcin Woliński

Institute of Computer Science
Polish Academy of Sciences
ul. Ordona 21, 01-237 Warszawa, Poland
wolinski@ipipan.waw.pl

Abstract. The subject of this article is a description of Polish inflection in the form of a relational database. The description has been developed for a grammatical dictionary of Polish that aims at complete inflectional characterisation of all Polish lexemes.

We show some complexities of the Polish inflectional system for various grammatical classes. Then we present a relatively compact relational model which can be used to describe Polish inflection in a uniform way.

Keywords: Polish morphology, inflection, relational modelling.

1 Introduction

Grammatical Dictionary of Polish [1, henceforth: SGJP] aims at providing a description of Polish inflection as complete as possible. Although the dictionary is large (about 180,000 lexemes, 3,600,000 orthographic words), it does not of course include all Polish words, as new words continuously enter the language. It is hoped, however, that the dictionary includes all reasonably frequent words and all possible inflectional patterns for all inflecting lexemes of Polish.

The idea of SGJP was conceived by Saloni under the influence of Zalizniak's grammatical dictionary of Russian [2]. SGJP is based on numerous earlier works: Tokarski's and Saloni's work on Polish inflectional suffixes [3], Saloni's description of Polish verbs [4,5], Gruszczyński's description of Polish nouns [6], Wołosz's morphological data [7] and some other.

The scope of the dictionary is complete morphological characterisation and basic syntactic characterisation of Polish words. For each lexeme all its inflected forms are given with values of all morphological categories (categories for which given lexeme inflects). Moreover values of some syntactic features are provided: gender for nouns, aspect for verbs, required case for prepositions. The dictionary also contains some links between lexemes, e.g., between elements of aspectual pairs for verbs, between a verb and its nominal derivatives (gerund and participles), between adjectives and adverbs derived from them, between positive, comparative, and superlative adjectives.

In SGJP the inflection is described according to theoretical decisions set in the above-mentioned linguistic works. Since we do not concentrate on phonological

Z. Vetulani and H. Uszkoreit (Eds.): LTC 2007, LNAI 5603, pp. 96–106, 2009.

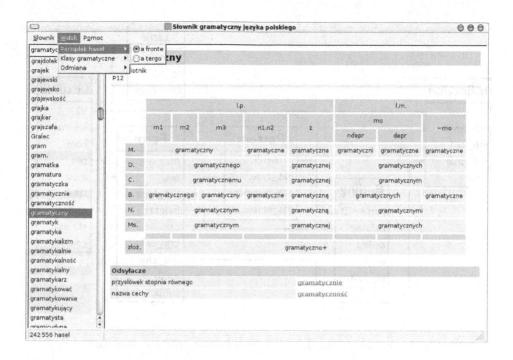

Fig. 1. The interface of *Grammatical Dictionary of Polish*

issues and our approach is paradigm-centric, the commonly used two-level morphology model [8] seems not appropriate. The model used by Wołosz [7] (which
derives from Prószéky's ideas, cf. [9]) is based on similar assumptions as SGJP,
but its drawback is complexity. To verify the description of any given lemma in
this model one needs to understand quite complex system of constraints placed
on word formation. The description used in SGJP, however, should be easy
to use for involved linguists (including students, not necessarily with a formal
background). One of the design goals is also to minimise the number of needed
inflectional patterns. On the other hand, the description does not have to directly lead to fast tools for analysis or synthesis. The data can be converted to
a finite state transducer afterwards (this is what we actually do).

Due to the large amount of data involved SGJP is being worked on using
relational database machinery. A question arises whether it is possible to model
the inflection according to the set rules within the relational model. Such a
possibility would mean the whole work on the dictionary could be done with
database tools alone. Otherwise the database would be merely a means of storage
while some other facilities would be needed, e.g., to generate all inflected forms
from dictionary data.

In the following, we give an affirmative answer to this question and present a
relational model of SGJP (we assume some basic knowledge of relational modelling from the reader).

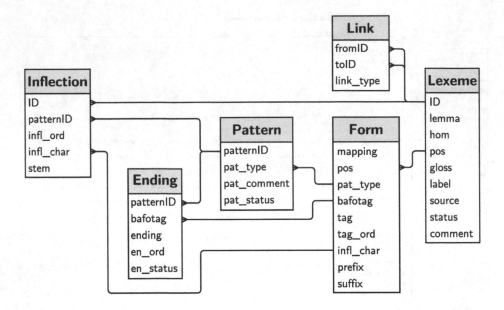

Fig. 2. The schema of the dictionary database (slightly simplified)

2   The Model

For the user, SGJP has the form of a dedicated interface program (cf. Fig. 1).
The data in the backend is represented as a relational database—the program
communicates with the database in SQL. In this section we will briefly present
the schema of this database.

The central entity is Lexeme (cf. Fig. 2). It is the basic unit of description in
the dictionary.[1] Its attributes include a numerical ID (which is the primary key),
the lemma (base form) and a homonym number hom (these two attributes form
an alternate key). Other attributes are the grammatical class (part of speech)
pos and several attributes needed to present the entry to the user: labels, glosses,
comments, source, and so on. Although the attributes are quite numerous, the
most important for the present article are the ID and pos.

In the works of Tokarski, Saloni, and Gruszczyński inflection is described by
means of inflectional patterns. Consider all inflected forms of a Polish lexeme. In
majority of cases, all the forms share a common first part (and in the remaining
cases we assume this part to be empty). We shall call this common part a *stem*

---

[1] Lexeme is not identical with an entry in the list of entries of the dictionary. A
Lexeme may be represented by several entries. In one of the user-selectable views of
the interface all inflected forms are used as entries.

and the rest of each form an *ending*.[2] To describe inflection of a lexeme we have to state its stem and the inflectional pattern containing all respective endings.

Inflectional patterns are modelled here with entities Pattern and Ending. Patterns are identified with patternIDs and classified with the attribute pat_type, whose role will be explained in section 4. For each instance of Pattern we have several instances of Ending with the respective endings as the value of the attribute ending.

For the sake of compactness Endings describe only what we call *basic inflected forms*. Other inflected forms are generated from the basic ones in a way which does not depend on the lexeme's inflectional pattern, but depends on the grammatical class, and so will be discussed for each class separately in the following sections. The mapping between basic inflected forms and the remaining ones is provided by the entity Form.

Sometimes it is necessary to assign more than one Pattern to a Lexeme. For that reason patternID is not an attribute of Lexeme. A separate entity Inflection models the many-to-many relationship between Lexemes and Patterns.

Entity Link is used to represent the links between Lexemes mentioned in the introduction. The attribute link_type describes type of the relation modelled by the given Link.

3   Adjectives

We start with presentation of adjectives since they provide the simplest example of distinction between basic inflected forms and inflected forms.

Adjectives in SGJP are described according to the principles set in the work of Tokarski [3]. A typical Polish adjective can be realised (represented) in texts by any of 11 shapes (orthographic words). However, if we try to attach the values of case, number, and gender to these shapes we end up with $7 \times 2 \times 9 = 126$ combinations.[3]

To make this plethora of forms manageable, inflectional patterns for adjectives describe only 11 basic inflected forms whose basic form tag bafotag is a number from 1 to 11. So for each adjectival Pattern the entity Ending has 11 instances.[4]

These basic forms are mapped to actual inflected forms by the instances of the entity Form. For example, the basic form with bafotag of 2 (e.g., *białego*) can be interpreted as genitive singular of any masculine or neuter gender or accusative singular of masculine personal or masculine animal genders, cf. Table 1. This mapping is universal to all adjectival patterns.

---

[2] Quite commonly these parts are not what could be called a stem or an ending from the morphological point of view.

[3] A rather detailed system of 9 genders for Polish is used in SGJP. It includes masculine personal m1 (e.g., *profesor*), animal m2 (*pies*), inanimate m3 (*stół*); neuter n1 (*dziecko*), n2 (*okno*); feminine f (*wanna*); plurale tantum p1 (*państwo*), p2 (*drzwi*), and p3 (*spodnie*); cf. [10,11].

[4] In fact up to 4 more basic forms are used to account for some additional forms present only for some adjectives.

Table 1. Instances of the entity Form for adjectival forms with basic form tag 2

pos	bafotag	tag
adj	2	sg:gen:m1
adj	2	sg:gen:m2
adj	2	sg:gen:m3
adj	2	sg:gen:n1
adj	2	sg:gen:n2
adj	2	sg:acc:m1
adj	2	sg:acc:m2

Some additional flexibility is present in this scheme thanks to the use of the mapping attribute of Form. This attribute selects which of the various presentations of forms is delivered to the user. This applies to lexemes of all grammatical classes. We use three mappings in SGJP. The one presented above is used to show all inflected forms to the user. In fact, the tags used in this mapping are different than those shown in the table above since, e.g., the inflection tables for adjectives are presented in a slightly compacted form and do not have 126 cells (as can be seen in Fig. 1). The second mapping includes only basic inflected forms, so it shows the real representation of inflectional patterns to the user. The third one is used to generate all forms necessary for searching in the dictionary. This includes some forms which are not normally displayed, but to which the program should react when typed in the search window (e.g., negated gerunds). An additional mapping is used to convert the dictionary to the form used by the morphological analyser *Morfeusz* [12].

The key point of these remarks is that providing another view of data is rather trivial since the interface of SGJP is driven by the contents of the table Form.

4   Nouns

Inflection of Polish nouns is described in SGJP in a more complicated way. Inflectional patterns for nouns constructed according to the simple stem-ending rule would be very numerous. However, some of them differ in a very regular manner. For example we can find triples of nouns of all masculine genders which differ only in forms of the accusative case and presence of a special form of nominative plural for masculine personal nouns. This applies for example to nouns *płetwonurek* m1, *skowronek* m2, and *nagłówek* m3. The following rule works for all masculine Polish nouns: accusative singular is equal to genitive for gender m1 and m2, and to nominative for m3; accusative plural is equal to genitive for gender m1 and to nominative for m2 and m3. It makes sense to have only one inflectional pattern for these lexemes [13,14]. For that reason accusative forms are not included in the set of basic inflected forms for nouns. The right form of accusative is created depending on the value of infl_char attribute, which for nouns carries the value of gender.

Table 2. Accusative singular Forms of nouns are generated from basic forms with different bafotags depending on pattern type (pat_type) and gender (infl_char)

pos	pat_type	infl_char	bafotag	tag
subst	m	m1	sg:gen	sg:acc
subst	m	m2	sg:gen	sg:acc
subst	m	m3	sg:nom	sg:acc
subst	f	any	sg:acc	sg:acc
subst	n	m1	sg:gen	sg:acc
subst	n	m2	sg:gen	sg:acc
subst	n	m3	sg:nom	sg:acc
subst	n	n1	sg:nom	sg:acc
subst	n	n2	sg:nom	sg:acc
subst	0	any	lemma	sg:acc

The next complication is introduced by masculine personal nouns, which have two possible forms of nominative plural differentiated with the value of depreciativity [15]. For example nominative plural of the noun *płetwonurek* has a neutral variant *płetwonurkowie* and a stylistically marked (depreciative) variant *płetwonurki*. The only possible form for gender m2 and m3 has the same ending as the depreciative form for m1. For that reason we have two basic inflected forms for nominative plural. Both are used for masculine personal nouns, and only the second for the remaining masculine genders.

Unfortunately the above remarks do not apply to feminine nouns. Those have a specific form of singular accusative which has to be noted explicitly. Moreover, in Polish we have some masculine nouns which inflect in a way so similar to feminine nouns that it makes sense to have a common pattern for the two (e.g., *poeta* m1 'poet' inflects almost exactly in the same way as *kobieta* f 'woman'). Moreover for some feminine nouns we need to account for two regular variants of genitive plural (e.g., *funkcji/funkcyj*).

Yet another set of basic inflected forms is needed for neuter nouns, since for them accusative and vocative is always equal to nominative in both numbers. Also there exist masculine (personal) nouns which inflect similarly to neuter nouns (e.g., the p2 *plurale tantum* noun *mistrzostwa* has the same forms as *dynamo* n2 in plural).

To account for these phenomena we introduce types of inflectional patterns differentiated with the attribute pat_type of Pattern. This attribute together with the gender contained in the infl_char of a given Inflection selects the right instance of Form. Three pattern types have been introduced for masculine, feminine, and neuter type of inflection (not gender). One more type is used for "noninflecting" nouns, which have just one shape used for all grammatical forms. As an example, the Table 2 lists instances of Form for singular accusative forms of various pattern types. The complete list of basic inflected forms for nouns

Table 3. The sets of basic inflected forms (bafotags) used for various pattern types pat_type

pat_type	m	f	n
bafotags	sg:nom	sg:nom	sg:nom
	sg:gen	sg:gen	sg:gen
	sg:dat	sg:dat	sg:dat
		sg:acc	
	sg:inst	sg:inst	sg:inst
	sg:loc		sg:loc
	sg:voc	sg:voc	
	pl:nom:m1	pl:nom:m1	pl:nom
	pl:nom:m2	pl:nom:m2	
	pl:gen	pl:gen:funi	pl:gen:m
		pl:gen:fnuni	pl:gen:n
		pl:gen:m	
	pl:dat	pl:dat	pl:dat
	pl:inst	pl:inst	pl:inst
	pl:loc	pl:loc	pl:loc

(or more precisely their bafotags) used for various types of inflection pat_type is presented in Table 3.

A word of explanation is due as for why infl_char is an attribute of Inflection and not of Lexeme. There are nouns in Polish whose gender is not stable. For example the noun *człowieczysko* can be reasonably included both in the m1 and n2 class. Similarly *cabernet* can be m2, m3, or n2. In this case we choose to have one Lexeme with multiple Inflections differing in gender. Of course for regular homonyms (e.g., *bokser* m1 'boxer (athlete)', m2 'bulldog', and m3 'type of engine') SGJP has separate Lexemes.

5 Verbs

The main feature which determines the set of forms of a typical Polish verb is its aspect. Present tense in indicative mood, adverbial simultaneous participle, and adjectival active participle are specific to imperfective verbs. Perfective verbs form simple future tense and adverbial anterior participle. For that reason in our model aspect is kept in the infl_char attribute for verbs.

Verbal forms are very numerous (and, not like in the case of adjectives, this means numerous different orthographic words). Fortunately they can be easily derived from twelve basic inflected forms [16]. For example the basic form denoted with bafotag of 10 is used to create the impersonal past form (e.g., *wiedzion-o*) and all forms of the passive adjectival participle except for m1 nominative plural (e.g., *wiedzion-y*, *wiedzion-e*, *wiedzion-a*, ..., *wiedzion-ych*). We construct verbal forms from the stem specific to a Lexeme, ending specific to the

Table 4. Verbal Forms generated from basic inflected form 10: finite impersonal past form, affirmative and negated forms of passive adjectival participle

pos	infl_char	bafotag	tag	prefix	suffix
v	any	10	imps		*o*
v	any	10	ppas:sg:nom:m1:aff		*y*
v	any	10	ppas:sg:nom:m2:aff		*y*
v	any	10	ppas:sg:nom:m3:aff		*y*
v	any	10	ppas:sg:nom:n1:aff		*e*
v	any	10	ppas:sg:nom:n2:aff		*e*
v	any	10	ppas:sg:nom:f:aff		*a*
			. . .		
v	any	10	ppas:pl:loc:p3:aff		*ych*
v	any	10	ppas:sg:nom:m1:neg	*nie*	*y*
v	any	10	ppas:sg:nom:m2:neg	*nie*	*y*
v	any	10	ppas:sg:nom:m3:neg	*nie*	*y*
v	any	10	ppas:sg:nom:n1:neg	*nie*	*e*
v	any	10	ppas:sg:nom:n2:neg	*nie*	*e*
v	any	10	ppas:sg:nom:f:neg	*nie*	*a*
			. . .		
v	any	10	ppas:pl:loc:p3:neg	*nie*	*ych*

basic inflected form, and suffix[5] characteristic for a Form. For the verb *wieść* ('to lead') used above the stem is *wi-*, the ending 10 is *-edzion-*, and the suffixes are marked in the above examples.

Some verbal forms, namely the negated gerunds and adjectival participles, are formed by prepending the prefix *nie* to the affirmative forms. For that purpose we use the attribute prefix of Form. The prefix and suffix is empty for other classes except for superlative degree of adjectives which is formed with prefix *naj*.

The Table 4 presents examples of Forms derived from basic inflected form 10.

The class of verbs includes some lexemes with very non-typical inflection. These include verbs like *powinien* ('ought to') which has very limited set of forms as well as pseudo-verbs which do not inflect for person (*braknie* ('it lacks'), *warto* 'it is worth'). For these groups separate pattern types have been introduced.

6   Other Grammatical Classes

The class of numerals is very small, only 92 Lexemes in SGJP, but very irregular. It includes numerals which do not inflect at all (e.g., *pół*), those which inflect only for gender (e.g., *półtora*), those inflecting for gender and case, and finally those

---

[5] The terms *prefix* and *suffix* are used here in the technical (and not linguistic) meaning of an arbitrary first (respectively last) part of a string.

which inflect for gender, case, and the category of accomodability which specifies whether given form agrees with the noun (e.g., in the phrase *dwaj chłopcy* 'two boys') or requires the noun to be in genitive (*dwóch chłopców*, 'two boys', both examples are nominative) [17].

Inflectional patterns for numerals of each of these four groups belong to a separate pattern type in our description.

Lexemes traditionally described as nominal, adjectival, adverbial, and numeral pronouns are treated in SGJP as regular nouns, adjectives, adverbs, and numerals [18]. The class of pronouns is limited to personal pronouns (including the reflective pronoun *się*). These lexemes cannot be treated as nouns since they have no value of gender assigned. Moreover some of them have special forms depending on whether they appear on an accented position in the sentence (e.g., *ciebie* vs. *cię*) or whether they appear after a preposition (e.g., *jego* vs. *niego*). We need three separate pattern types to describe Polish personal pronouns.

The dictionary lists as well non-inflecting lexemes, which is rather trivial. An interesting point is however that some prepositions have two forms depending on phonological features of the following word (e.g., *w* and *we*). We obviously use a dedicated inflectional pattern for these lexemes.

Table 5. The number of inflectional patterns needed for respective grammatical classes in SGJP

adjectives	71
nouns	744
verbs	214
numerals	45
pronouns	6

7 Conclusion

It may seem that with the given simple construction of inflectional patterns the description of inflection is almost trivial. However, numerous issues which need to be taken into the account show that this is not the case.

In general, an inflected form in our model consists of four parts: prefix, stem, ending, and suffix controlled by several entities of the model. Each of these parts can be empty. However, since the mapping from Endings to Forms is universal, this complexity does not influence the process of adding new lexemes or verifying the existing description. These tasks can be successfully performed on the limited set of basic inflected forms, which are built only from a stem and an ending.

The Table 5 presents numbers of Patterns needed for various grammatical classes in the dictionary. Without the mechanism of reusing nominal patterns for various genders, we would need 1086 nominal patterns to describe all lexemes currently present in our database (46% more patterns). If verbs of different aspect were to require separate patterns, 384 verbal ones would be needed (79% more).

Due to irregularities in Polish inflection there exist numerous Patterns which are needed for only one Lexeme.

The presented model covers all inflectional phenomena accounted for in SGJP. The model features a rather dense net of relations but still it is rather compact and manageable. In particular it provides a unified method of generating forms of a lexeme of any grammatical class although the inflectional patterns for particular classes are constructed in a substantially different way.

References

1. Saloni, Z., Gruszczyński, W., Woliński, M., Wołosz, R.: Słownik gramatyczny języka polskiego. Wiedza Powszechna, Warszawa (2007)
2. Zalizniak, A.: Grammaticheskij slovar' russkogo yazyka, 1st edn. Russkij yazyk, Moscow (1977)
3. Tokarski, J.: Schematyczny indeks a tergo polskich form wyrazowych. In: Saloni, Z. (ed.). Wydawnictwo Naukowe PWN, Warszawa (1993)
4. Saloni, Z.: Czasownik polski. Odmiana, słownik. Wiedza Powszechna, Warszawa (2001)
5. Saloni, Z., Woliński, M.: A computerized description of Polish conjugation. In: Kosta, P., Błaszczak, J., Frasek, J., Geist, L., Żygis, M. (eds.) Investigations into Formal Slavic Linguistics (Contributions of the Fourth European Conference on Formal Description on Slavic Languages), pp. 373–384 (2003)
6. Gruszczyński, W.: Fleksja rzeczowników pospolitych we współczesnej polszczyźnie pisanej. vol. 122 of Prace językoznawcze. Zakład Narodowy im. Ossolińskich, Wrocław (1989)
7. Wołosz, R.: Efektywna metoda analizy i syntezy morfologicznej w języku polskim. Akademicka Oficyna Wydawnicza EXIT (2005)
8. Koskenniemi, K.: Two-Level Morphology: A General Computational Model for Word Form Recognition and Production. vol. 11 of Publication. Helsinki University, Helsinki (1983)
9. Prószéky, G., Tihanyi, L.: Humor: High-speed unification morphology and its applications for agglutinative languages. La tribune des industries de la langue 10(28-29) (1995), OFIL, Paris
10. Mańczak, W.: Ile rodzajów jest w polskim? Język Polski XXXVI(2), 116–121 (1956)
11. Saloni, Z.: Kategoria rodzaju we współczesnym języku polskim. In: Kategorie gramatyczne grup imiennych we współczesnym języku polskim, pp. 41–75. Ossolineum, Wrocław (1976)
12. Woliński, M.: Morfeusz — a practical tool for the morphological analysis of Polish. In: Kłopotek, M., Wierzchoń, S., Trojanowski, K. (eds.) Intelligent Information Processing and Web Mining, IIS:IIPWM 2006 Proceedings, pp. 503–512. Springer, Heidelberg (2006)
13. Gruszczyński, W.: Rzeczowniki w słowniku gramatycznym współczesnego języka polskiego. In: Gruszczyński, W., Andrejewicz, U., Bańko, M., Kopcińska, D. (eds.) Nie bez znaczenia... Prace ofiarowane Profesorowi Zygmuntowi Saloniemu z okazji jubileuszu 15000 dni pracy naukowej, Białystok, pp. 99–116 (2001)

14. Gruszczyński, W., Saloni, Z.: Notowanie informacji o odmianie rzeczowników w projektowanym Słowniku gramatycznym języka polskiego. In: Bobrowski, I., Kowalik, K. (eds.) Od fonemu do zdania. Prace dedykowane Profesorowi Romanowi Laskowskiemu, Kraków, pp. 203–213 (2006)
15. Saloni, Z.: O tzw. formach nieosobowych [rzeczowników] męskoosobowych we współczesnej polszczyźnie. Biuletyn Polskiego Towarzystwa Językoznawczego XLI, 155–166 (1988)
16. Saloni, Z.: Wstęp do koniugacji polskiej. Wydawnictwo Uniwersytetu Warmińsko-Mazurskiego, Olsztyn (2000)
17. Saloni, Z.: Kategorie gramatyczne liczebników we współczesnym języku polskim. In: Studia gramatyczne I, Wrocław, pp. 145–173 (1977)
18. Saloni, Z.: Klasyfikacja gramatyczna leksemów polskich. Język Polski LIV, fasc. 1, 3–13, fasc. 2, 93–101 (1974)

Syntactic Spreadsheets:
In Search for a Human-Readable Representation
of Parse Tree Forests

Janusz S. Bień

Formal Linguistics Department, The University of Warsaw
Browarna 8/10, 00-311 Warszawa, Poland
jsbien@uw.edu.pl

Abstract. The paper presents an example of a representation of parse
tree forests advocated by the author. Although motivated by the need
to analyse the forests generated by Świdziński's grammar, the representation can be used for any grammar handled by Woliński's Birnam
parser, and the basic ideas can be applied to any Immediate Constituent
grammar. Syntactic spreadsheets can serve several purposes. They can
be simply included in printed publications or dynamically displayed by
an appropriate viewer. Unfortunately the implementation of the idea is
not easy and therefore it is still in progress.

Keywords: parsing, parse trees, tree forests, visualization, Birnam
parser.

1 Introduction

At present computationally useful syntactic description of Polish is limited to
the surface level. Ambiguity is an intrinsic feature of surface grammars, so parse
tree forests need to be handled in a convenient way. An idea to use 'syntactic
spreadsheets' for this purpose has been proposed by the present author in a
paper in Polish [2]. Similar diagrams have been used to represent single trees
at least since Charles Hockett's *A Course in Modern Linguistics*, first published
in 1964 (cf., for example, the Polish translation [5, pp. 175-184]), so the main
novelty of the proposal lies in applying them to whole forests. To the best of my
knowledge, existing tools with similar purpose operate only on single trees. An
example of such a tool is the *Linguistic User Interface* (http://wiki.delph-in.
net/moin/LkbLui) developed in the DELPH-IN project. Although the problem
is recognised

> Grammars often produce numerous tree structures for any input parsing
> or generation request.

the user is just offered many windows with a single tree in each of them (http://
wiki.delph-in.net/moin/LuiTree).

The ultimate goal is to create a forest browser which will allow to dynamically
change the arrangement and granularity (the amount and kind of details) of the

Z. Vetulani and H. Uszkoreit (Eds.): LTC 2007, LNAI 5603, pp. 107–117, 2009.

display. It should also allow to dynamically highlight interesting parts of the forest. As the forest doesn't need to be complete, such a browser can be used also as a debugging tool for new grammars.

For the time being, however, the goal is much more modest: to create tools for including syntactic spreadsheets in research publications typeset with the current version of LaTeX, i.e. PDFeLaTeX 2_ε and XeLaTeX. The tools should allow the user to introduce — by hand, if necessary — corrections, additions and modifications. As a side effect, electronic spreadsheets with hyperlinks can be created without the size limits of paper.

2   Preliminaries

As the primary motivation is the need to analyse forests generated by Świgra (*ŚWIdzińskiego GRAmatyka*), which is the implementation [11] of Świdziński's formal grammar of Polish [9], we will illustrate the idea of syntactic spreadsheets with a Świgra forest.

We will use the notable example designed by Marcin Woliński and discussed e.g. in [10, p. 40], as it demonstrates in particular the ambiguity of input segmentation:

(1)   *Miałem miał.*

The example sentence is assigned with 4 parse trees. Its primary reading is

(2)   *I had [some] coal dust.*

The interesting thing is that two perfectly legal parse trees are assigned to this reading. The trees differ only in the segmentation of words into morphological units:

(3)   *Miałem miał.*
       I had   [some] coal dust.
(4)   *Miał   + em miał.*
       [some] coal dust   I   had.

There is also a second elliptic reading which results in the third parse tree:

(5)   *Miałem   miał.*
       [some] coal dust$_{Instr}$ he had.
       [With some] coal dust he had.

The sentence is quite correct as an answer to an appropriate question, e.g.

(6)   *Czym miał posypaną podłogę?*
       What had he covered his floor with?

The fourth parse tree is just an artifact of Świdziński's grammar.

The current way of presenting the results of Świgra employs hyperlinked PDF documents described in [13]; this is just a modification of the tree representation

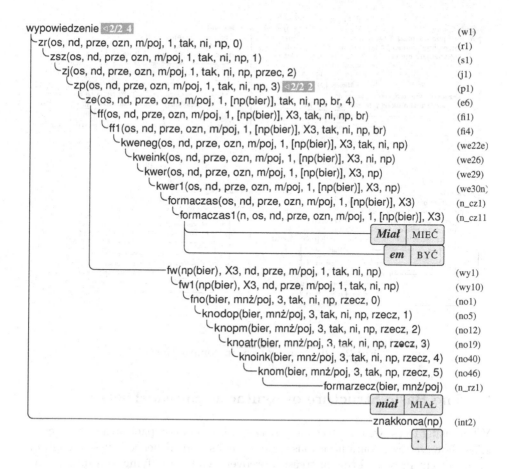

Fig. 1. One of 4 parsing trees in full form

designed by Woliński over 10 years ago for the AMOS parser [1]. As the full versions of trees use a lot of space but contain too many uninteresting details, by 1999 the compact form was introduced for use with the AS parser [3]. In the compact form every path without branches is represented as a dotted line and the intermediate nodes are omitted, while real arcs are represented by continuous lines.

To make the paper self-contained, we present in Figure 2 the compact form of all the trees for the sentence under consideration, and in Figure 1 the full form of one of them. More examples of compact trees can be found at Woliński's site (http://nlp.ipipan.waw.pl/~wolinski), while both full and compact trees are provided at http://fleksem.klf.uw.edu.pl/~jsbien/synspread/; as the address suggests, in due time the trees will be supplemented or replaced by the respective syntactic spreadsheets (depending on the availability of the server disk storage, trees and spreadsheets will be provided either as PDF files or their LATEX source).

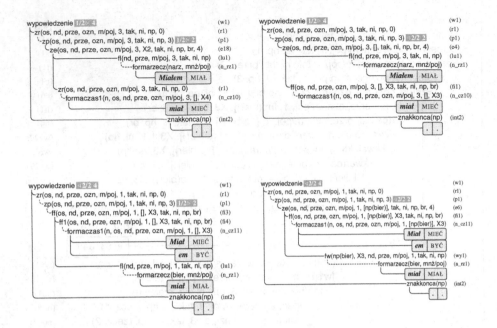

Fig. 2. All 4 parsing trees in compact form

3   The Basic Structure of Syntactic Spreadsheets

When using trees, we have to choose between full and compact forms. A spreadsheet however can contain various types of cells and, if needed, it can contain data present in both forms of trees. Moreover, while modifying a grammar, for easy comparison we can mix parse forests from several grammars in a single spreadsheet.

The spreadsheet is obviously a table. The number of columns is the length of the longest path, measured in some segmentation units, from the beginning to the end of the sentence. In the full version of the spreadsheet the segmentation units are those of the morphological analyzer. As demonstrated by our example, morphological segmentation in Polish can be ambiguous.

In our sample spreadsheet on Figure 3 there are three kinds of cells:

1. auxiliary,
2. terminal,
3. main (nonterminal).

Auxiliary nodes are used in the sample only for row identifiers (T.1, M.1 etc.), but can be used also to provide headers and footers with column identification (by numbers or by appropriate substrings of the input).

The purpose of the terminal cells is obvious, as well as their primary content: form, lemma, tags.

T.1	T-1 2/4 *miał* MIEĆ: praet sg:[m1, m2|m3]:imperf	T-2 2/4 *em* BYĆ: agit sg:pri:imperf:wok	T-3 2/4 *miał* MIAŁ: subst sg:[nom|acc]:m3	T-4 4/4 . .: interp	T.1
T.2	T-5 2/4 *miałem* MIAŁ: subst sg:inst:m3	T-6 2/4 *miał* MIEĆ: praet sg:[m1, m2|m3]:imperf			T.2
M.1	M-1 2/4 ⇑[T-5]⇑ trees: 1, 2 *formarzecz*	M-2 2/4 ⇑[T-6]⇑ trees: 1, 2 *formaczas1*			M.1
M.2	M-3 2/4 ⇑[T-1][T-2]⇑ trees: 3, 4 *formaczas1*	M-4 2/4 ⇑[T-3]⇑ trees: 3, 4 *formarzecz*	M-5 4/4 ⇑[T-4]⇑ trees: 1, 2, 3, 4 *znakkonca*		M.2
M.3	M-6 2/4 ⇑[M-1]⇑ trees: 1, 2 *fl*	M-7 1/4 ⇑[M-2]⇑ trees: 1 *zr*			M.3
M.4		M-8 1/4 ⇑[M-2]⇑ trees: 2 *ff*			M.4
M.5	M-9 1/4 ⇑[M-3]⇑ trees: 3 *ff1*	M-10 1/4 ⇑[M-4]⇑ trees: 3 *fl*			M.5
M.6	M-11 1/4 ⇑[M-3]⇑ trees: 4 *ff*	M-12 1/4 ⇑[M-4]⇑ trees: 4 *fw*			M.6
M.7	M-13 1/4 ⇑[M-6][M-7]⇑ trees: 1 *ze*				M.7
M.8	M-14 1/4 ⇑[M-6][M-8]⇑ trees: 2 *ze*				M.8
M.9	M-15 1/4 ⇑[M-9][M-10]⇑ trees: 3 *ff*				M.9
M.10	M-16 1/4 ⇑[M-11][M-12]⇑ trees: 4 *ze*				M.10
M.11 a b	M-17 4/4 a ⇑[M-13]⇑[M-14]⇑ trees: 1, 2 b ⇑[M-15]⇑[M-16]⇑ trees: 3, 4 *zp*				M.11 a b
M.12 a b	M-18 4/4 a ⇑[M-17a]⇑ trees: 1, 2 b ⇑[M-17b]⇑ trees: 3, 4 *zr*				M.12 a b
M.13	M-19 4/4 ⇑[M-18][M-5]⇑ trees: 1, 2, 3, 4 *wypowiedzenie*				M.13

Fig. 3. Parse forest in compact form with the tree number 4 highlighted

All other cells in the sample are the cells of main nonterminal nodes; by main nonterminal node we understand the nodes which are present in Woliński's compact form of the trees. In general, the spreadsheet can contain all nonterminal nodes, instead of main nodes, or in addition to them.

The top row of every non-auxiliary cell contains tree information: the cell identifier (e.g., T-1 or M-1), the number of trees in which the cell node occurs, and the total number of trees in the forest (redundant but convenient).

The crucial parts of the nonterminal cell are the component subrows. In the sample they contain in turn just 2 subsubrows: the component list and the list of relevant trees.

The component subsubrow may consist of a single (hyper)link to the appropriate cell, as in, e.g., M-1. In general, it consists of a list of (hyper)links to the appropriate cells, as in, e.g., M-3 and M-13. To save space, whenever possible such rows are collapsed into one. This is exemplified in rows M.11a and M.11b — each of them is to be interpreted as two subsubrows. Hence M-13 and M-14 are separate alternative components of M.11a.

At present the second subsubrow of the components subrow is just a list of the numbers of trees in which the nodes in question occur. It is planned that in the electronic version of the spreadsheet the numbers will be hyperlinks to the trees in Woliński's format (kept in separate files).

The components rows account for links downwards in the trees and the spreadsheet table. If needed, upwards links can be also provided. Upwards links can be provided also for terminal cells.

In the general case, the node label is actually a quite complicated Prolog term. In our sample the labels are represented only by their main functors. In the future the amount of displayed information about the label will be controlled by the user.

A specific tree can be highlighted by changing, e.g., the background of appropriate cells. In our sample spreadsheet we used this method to highlight tree number 4 (the same which is shown on Figure 1). As you can see, the tree is composed of all the cells of rows T1, M.2, M.6, M.10, subrows M.11b and M.12b, and the row M.13 (containin the single cell representing the root of the tree).

4   More Examples

It should be stressed that the applications of syntactic spreadsheets are not limited to successful parses of single sentences. They can be used also to present the forests created during incomplete or unsuccessful parsing processes, so they can be used also as a debugging tool. Moreover, they can be used for units larger than a single sentence. Although the arrangement of the cells is important for clarity, the links between cells are specified explicitly, so in principle spreadsheets can show also the structure of sentences with non-standard word order and discontinuous constituents.

In the general case the sheet can be quite large and may require splitting into several pages. A technique analogical to that used for geographical maps and plans seems to be fully applicable also to syntactic spreadsheets.

For long sentences and large spreadsheets it seems useful to create partial spreadsheets representing only the top parts of the forest trees; in such a case the number of columns will be smaller as some columns will represent several consecutive morphological segments (words and punctuation marks).

We present now some sample spreadsheets used in [4] to ilustrate the parsing results for some computer messages. The spreadsheets has been more or less simplified for printing purposes. The more detailed versions, which are also more readable thanks to the use of color, are available at `http://fleksem.klf.uw.edu.pl/~jsbien/synspread/samples`.

Figure 4 demonstrates using a simplified fragment of a spreadsheet for texts larger than a single sentence. The text in the example consists of two sentences (*wypowiedzenie* literary means 'utterance'), the segmentation has been done by the parser; the spreadsheet shows the morphological ambiguities, but the strictly syntactic parts contains only the tips of the forest.

T-1 *trwa* TRWAĆ: fin	T-2 *pobieranie* POBIERANIE: subst	T-3 *.* .: interp	T-4 *czy* CZY: qub	T-5 *zapisać* ZAPISAĆ: inf	T-6 *zmiany* ZMIANA: subst	T-7 *?* ?: interp
	T-8 *pobieranie* POBIERAĆ: ger				T-9 *zmiany* ZMIANA: subst	
wypowiedzenie				*wypowiedzenie*		
trwa pobieranie.				*czy zapisać zmiany?*		

Fig. 4. Segmentation into sentences

Figure 5 shows rather a drastically simplified fragment of a spreadsheet for an unsuccessful parse result, which however provides useful information about recognized sub-sentence components; you can see that the culprit is the *mailman* placeholder for date, which has to be incorporated into the grammar.

T-1 *ostatni* OSTATNI: adj	T-2 *zwrot* ZWROT: subst	T-3 *otrzymano* OTRZYMAĆ: imps	T-4 *z* Z: prep	T-5 *twojego* TWÓJ: adj	T-6 *adresu* ADRES: subst	T-7 *dnia* DZIEŃ: subst	T-8 *%(date)s* %(DATE)S: [date]
zd							*mailman*
ostatni zwrot otrzymano z twojego adresu dnia							*%(date)s*

Fig. 5. Segmentation into sub-sentence units

Figure 6 demonstrates a case when parsing was bound to fail because the input string is not a complete sentence. The morphological analysis is highly ambiguous, so we see 4 possible syntactic interpretations of *lata*: genitive singular and nominative plural of LATO ('summer'), a form of ROK ('year') and a form of LATAĆ ('to fly'). Moreover the text contains also the *evolution* placeholder for a number. To the fragment *lata temu* ('years ago') 5 different syntactic structures

T.1	T-1	T-2	T-3	T.1
	%d %D: %d 0	*lata* LATAĆ: fin sg:ter:imperf	*temu* TEN: padj sg:dat:[m1, m2, m3, n1|n2]:pos	
T.2		T-4 *lata* LATO: subst sg:gen:[n1|n2]		T.2
T.3		T-5 *lata* LATO: subst pl:[nom, acc|voc]:[n1|n2]		T.3
T.4		T-6 *lata* ROK: subst pl:[nom|acc]:m3		T.4
	evolution	*fl*		
		fpt		
		fw		
		fzd		
		zd		
	%d	*lata temu*		

Fig. 6. Parsing incomplete sentence

are assigned represented by non-terminals *fl*, *fpt*, *fw*, *fzd*, *zd*; their meaning is specific to a variant of Świdziński's grammar (described in [8]), so there is no need to explain this here.

It should be noted that syntactic spreadsheets can incorporate also quite sophisticated methods of beautifying parse trees. As it was already pointed in [11, p. 36], in Świdziński's grammar the number of parse trees of sentences containing coordination of more than two components can be described as Catalan numbers, which depend in almost exponential way on the number of components. In consequence it would be very useful to collapse such segments of the tree forest into a single 'Catalan cell'. Similar ideas, but applied to single trees, has been advocated in [6].

5   Spreadsheet Cells

In [2] I proposed to include in spreadsheet cells full information about their respective nodes, but it no longer seems practical to me. In particular, it seems there is no reason to print the node labels in exactly the same form as in the tree format. We plan, however, to include this information in a processed form. The idea is to display below the main functor only those of its arguments which have the same value for all component subrows, and in the subrows to highlight only the specific information. So cell M-12 of the spreadsheet presented in Figure 3 (highlighting the tree number 4) may look as in Figure 7. Please compare this notation with the second top row of the parsing trees in Figure 2 (the letter O is the abbreviation of *osoba* meaning *person*). The tree rows are labelled with the appropriate symbol of the grammar rule used (in this case r1), such information can be of course provided also in the spreadsheet cells.

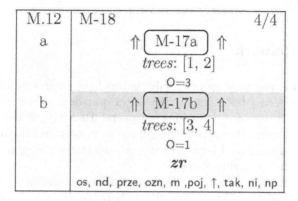

Fig. 7. A sample cell

6   Technical Considerations

The first approach assumed that the input to the spreadsheet generator is just the output of Woliński's Birnam parser [12]. It turned out, however, that recovering all the needed data from Birnam's output is quite difficult. As a consequence, a fork of Birnam is used now, which provides much more information in the output.

The additional information helps to determine the number of columns, which is not trivial because of a peculiarity of Świgra. The original grammar by Świdziński assumes the existence of the 'virtual comma' which has an empty realization. Because such rules are not allowed in bottom-up parsing, the commas are added to the input in appropriate places. As a consequence, counting the length of the longest path from the beginning to the end of a sentence is not sufficient, as unused virtual commas should not be included in the spreadsheet.

The spreadsheet is typeset as a longtable, using \cellcolor from the colortbl package for background and \colorbox from the color package for foreground elements [7]. Some details are still to be worked out (e.g., at present some vertical rules vanish when a cell is highlighted), but for the time being we consider the output to be satisfactory. For black and white printing the use of color is switched off by means of replacing the respective commands by dummy ones.

As every spreadsheet row consists of several lines, the data belonging to a single cell must be split into several parts, which makes the LaTeX source difficult to read and edit, even if supplemented by comments. Therefore, we introduced an intermediate forest representation in Prolog, which is used to generate the LaTeX source. The source of some sample spreadsheets described in the present paper is available for inspection at `http://fleksem.klf.uw.edu.pl/~jsbien/synspread/samples`.

It seems that the generated PDF files put a heavy strain on the previewers, as some of them display some spreadsheets in a distorted way. The matter is still to be investigated.

7   Closing Remarks

A grammar and a parser are worth only as much as their results. In the case of language engineering tasks the output of the parser is processed further and is read by humans only for debugging purposes. However, if we aim at a linguistically sound description of a language, the grammar and the parser' output have to be easily readable. I hope to have demonstrated the great potential of syntactic spreadsheets in this respect.

Implementing the ideas appeared to be more difficult than expected. Therefore at the moment of writing (December 2008) there exists only a quick and dirty program to convert the output of Birnam's fork to the tentative intermediate representation. A program to convert the intermediate representation to LaTeX is still under development.

Work on the spreadsheet generation tool is going to be continued, hopefully with a help of a student, and in due time the results will be made available under the terms of the GPL, probably at `http://fleksem.klf.uw.edu.pl/~jsbien/synspread/`

References

1. Bień, J.S.: Komputerowa weryfikacja formalnej gramatyki Świdzińskiego. Biuletyn PTJ, LII:147–164 (1997)
2. Bień, J.S.: Wizualizacja wyników analizy syntaktycznej. Poradnik Językowy, 9:24–29 (2006)
3. Bień, J.S., Szafran, K., Woliński, M.: Experimental parsers of Polish. In: 3. Europäische Konferenz Formale Beschreibung, slavischer Sprachen, Leipzig 1999. Linguistische ArbeitsBerichte. Institut für Linguistik, Universität Leipzig (2000)
4. Bień, J.S., Bilińska, J.A., Moszczyński, R.: Towards linguistic analysis of computer messages in Polish and English. In: Studia Kognitywne 8, pp. 288–302. Slawistyczny Ośrodek Wydawniczy, Warszawa (2008), `http://bc.klf.uw.edu.pl/32/`
5. Hockett, C.F.: Kurs językoznawstwa współczesnego. PWN (1968)

6. Kovář, V., A, H.: Reducing the Number of Resulting Parsing Trees for the Czech Language Using the Beautified Chart Method. In: 3rd Language & Technology Conference: Human Language Technologies as a Challenge for Computer Science and Linguistics, October 5-7, 2007, pp. 433–437. Poznań, Poland (2007)
7. Mittelbach, F., Goosens, M., Braams, J., Carliste, D., Rowley, C.: The LaTeX Companion, 2nd edn. Addison-Wesley Publishing Company, Reading (2004)
8. Ogrodniczuk, M.: Weryfikacja korpusu wypowiedników polskich (z wykorzystaniem gramatyki formalnej Świdzińskiego). PhD thesis, Uniwersytet Warszawski (2006), http://bc.klf.uw.edu.pl/30/
9. Świdziński, M.: Gramatyka formalna języka polskiego. In: Rozprawy Uniwersytetu Warszawskiego, Wydawnictwa Uniwersytetu Warszawskiego, Warszawa (1992)
10. Woliński, M.: System znaczników morfosyntaktycznych w korpusie IPI PAN. Polonica XXII–XXIII, 39–55 (2003)
11. Woliński, Marcin, Komputerowa weryfikacja gramatyki Świdzińskiego. Ph.D. thesis, Instytut Podstaw Informatyki PAN, Warszawa. (2004), http://www.ipipan.waw.pl/~wolinski/publ/mw-phd.pdf
12. Woliński, M.: An efficient implementation of a large grammar of Polish. In: Vetulani, Z. (ed.) Human Language Technologies as a Challenge for Computer Science and Linguistics. 2nd Language & Technology Conference, Poznań, April 21–23 (2005)
13. Woliński, M.: Jak się nie zgubić w lesie, czyli o wynikach analizy składniowej według gramatyki Świdzińskiego. Poradnik Językowy 9, 102–114 (2006)

A Hybrid System for Named Entity Metonymy Resolution

Caroline Brun, Maud Ehrmann, and Guillaume Jacquet

Xerox Research Centre Europe,
6, Chemin de Maupertuis, 38240 Meylan, France
{Caroline.Brun,Maud.Ehrmann,Guillaume.Jacquet}@xrce.xerox.com
http://www.xrce.xerox.com

Abstract. This paper is an extended version of [1], describing our participation to the Metonymy Resolution (task #8) at SemEval 2007. In order to perform named entity metonymy resolution on location names and company names, as required for this task, we developed a hybrid system based on the use of a robust parser that extracts deep syntactic relations combined with a non supervised distributional approach, also relying on the relations extracted by the parser.

Keywords: named entities, named entity metonymy, hybrid method.

1 Introduction

Named entity recognition appears to be an essential task of natural language processing. Appeared during the 90's along with the MUC conferences, this task is indeed fundamental for a wide variety of applications, such as information extraction in general, question answering, machine translation, etc. Consequently, a large range of methods and systems have been developed, obtaining very satisfying performances. Following this success, research about named entities moves towards new perspectives, such as fine grained categorization, normalization and disambiguation. Like other kinds of lexical units, named entities are subject to semantic shift or superposition, and among these phenomena, to metonymic shifts.

Metonymy is a figure of speech in which a thing or a concept is not called by its own name but by the name of something intimately associated to that thing or concept, and named entities can have metonymic usage, such as in the following examples:

It is time to acknowledge the consequences of Iraq.
England won a world cup with a goal that never crossed the line.

In the first sentence *Iraq* refers to the event that happens in the country (*i.e.* the war), while in the second example *England* refers to the national football team of England and not to the country itself. This use of country names as event happening there or sport team representing the country can be found quite

Z. Vetulani and H. Uszkoreit (Eds.): LTC 2007, LNAI 5603, pp. 118–130, 2009.

regularly: it is therefore possible to exhibit productive and regular metonymic patterns for named entities. Moreover, studies conducted by K. Markert, U. Hann, and M. Nissim ([2] and [3]), show that 17% of named entity's uses were metonymic, in a corpus made of 27 German magazines, as well as 20% of country name's uses and 30% of organization name's uses.

Named entity metonymy is a regular and productive phenomenon, which is a real issue for natural language processing. The remaining of the paper describes the work that has been performed on that research topic in the framework the SemEval 2007 competition.

2   Metonymy Resolution at SemEval

SemEval 2007[1] proposed 18 different tasks dealing with various semantic phenomena, from preposition disambiguation to temporal analysis (TempEval), including personal names disambiguation (Web People Search). The metonymy resolution task, introduced by K. Markert and M. Nissim, aimed at resolving metonymy for named entities in English, more precisely for location and organization names. As stated in the metonymy resolution task guidelines [4], "metonymy is a form of figurative speech, in which one expression is used to refer to the standard referent of a related on". The following examples illustrate the phenomenon, on the two defined semantic classes:

> He was shocked by Vietnam.
> The BMW slowed down.

In (1), *Vietnam*, the name of a location, refers to the war that happened here, therefore to an event. In (2), *BMW*, the name of a company, stands for the vehicle manufactured by this company. As said in the introduction, such phenomenon can apply in a regular way, therefore, given a semantic class (*e.g.* location), one can specify several regular metonymic shifts (*e.g.* place-for-event) that instances of the class are likely to undergo.

Participants to this task had to automatically classified preselected names of country and names of organization as having a literal or a metonymic reading, within a four-sentence context. Once stated this first alternative (literal or metonymic), also defined as the "coarse grained" annotation, annotation could be specified with, firstly, the use of a mixed reading as a third choice ("medium annotation") and, secondly, the use of predefined metonymic patterns (such as place-for-people or org-for-index), along with the possibility of an innovative reading ("fine-grained annotation"). Table 1 summarizes these annotation levels. Participants were free to submit to one or more level, and for one or two semantic classes.

The scope of each metonymic pattern was specified in guidelines described in [5]. To complete the task, participants were given trial and test corpora, both

---

[1] The semantic evaluation campaign that succeeded the SensEval ones ; information could be found at http://nlp.cs.swarthmore.edu/semeval/index.php

Table 1. Granularity levels and annotation categories for ORGANISATION and LOCATION classes

Categorie : ORGANISATION	*coarse*	*medium*	*fine*
	literal	literal	literal
		mixed	mixed
	non-literal	metonymic	othermet
			object-for-name
			object-for-representation
			organisation-for-members
			organisation-for-event
			organisation-for-product
			organisation-for-facility
			organisation-for-index
Categorie : LOCATION	*coarse*	*medium*	*fine*
	literal	literal	literal
		mixed	mixed
	non-literal	metonymic	othermet
			object-for-name
			object-for-representation
			place-for-people
			place-for-event
			place-for-product

containing about 950 entities of each classes. Within these corpora, metonymic patterns showed heterogeneous distribution, revealing the organization class as "metonymically" richer than the location one, thus more difficult to treat. Given these annotation categories, we tried to perfect a system able to properly annotate metonymic shifts.

3 Description of Our System

The system we develop addresses the task of Named Entity Metonymy resolution by combining a purely symbolic approach based on robust deep parsing and lexical semantic information, with a distributional method using syntactic context similarities calculated on large corpora.

3.1 Robust and Deep Parsing with XIP

As a fundamental component of the system we designed for named entity metonymy resolution, we use the Xerox Incremental Parser (XIP, see [6]) in order to perform robust and deep syntactic analysis. Deep syntactic analysis consists here in the construction of a set of syntactic relations[2] from an input text. These relations link lexical units of the input text and/or more complex

---

[2] Inspired from dependency grammars, see [7] and [8].

syntactic domains that are constructed during the processing (mainly chunks, see [1]). These relations are labeled with deep syntactic functions. More precisely, a predicate (verbal or nominal) is linked with what we call its deep subject (SUBJ-N), its deep object (OBJ-N), and modifiers.

In addition, the parser calculates more sophisticated and complex relations using derivational morphologic properties, deep syntactic properties (subject and object of infinitives in the context of control verbs), and some limited lexical semantic coding (Levin's verb class alternations, see [9], and some elements of the Framenet[3] classification, [10]). These deep syntactic relations correspond roughly to the agent-experiencer roles that are subsumed by the SUBJ-N relation and to the patient-theme role subsumed by the OBJ-N relation, see [11] and [12]. Not only verbs bear these relations but also deverbal nouns with their corresponding arguments. Here is an example of an output (chunk tree and deep syntactic relations):

> Lebanon still wanted to see the implementation of a UN resolution.

```
TOP { NP{Lebanon} FV {still wanted}} IV{to see} NP{the implementation} PP{of
NP{a UN resolution}}.
```

MOD_PRE (wanted,still)	EXPERIENCER-PRE (wanted,Lebanon)
MOD_PRE (resolution,UN)	EXPERIENCER (see,Lebanon)
MOD_POST (implementation,resolution)	CONTENT (see,implementation)
COUNTRY (Lebanon)	EMBED_INFINIT(see,wanted)
ORGANISATION(UN)	OBJ-N(implement,resolution)

3.2   Adaptation to the Task

The parser described in previous section includes a module for "standard" Named Entity recognition, but needs to be adapted in order to handle Named Entity metonymy. Following the guidelines of the SemEval task #8, we performed a corpus study on the trial data in order to detect lexical and syntactic regularities triggering a metonymy, for both location names and organization names. For example, we examined the subject relation between organizations or locations and verbs and we then classify the verbs accordingly. From this study, we draw hypothesis like "if a location name is the subject of a verb referring to an economic action, like import, provide, refund, repay, etc., then it is a place for people". We adapted our parser by adding dedicated lexicons that encode, in the format of "semantic features", the information collected from the corpus and developed rules modifying the interpretation of the entity, for example, the hypothesis mentioned above permits to develop the following rule:

> if (LOCATION(#1) & SUBJ-N (#2[v_econ],#1))
> LOC-FOR-PEOPLE (#1)[4]

---

[3] http://framenet.icsi.berkeley.edu/

[4] Which read as "if the parser has detected a location name (#1), which is the subject of a verb (#2) bearing the feature v-econ, then create a PLACE-FOR-PEOPLE unary predicate on #1".

We focus our study on syntactico-semantic relations like subject, object, experiencer, content, modifiers (nominal and prepositional) and attributes. We also capitalize on the already-encoded lexical information attached to verbs by the parser, like communication verbs like say, deny, comment, or categories belonging to the FrameNet Experiencer subject frame, *i.e.* verbs like *feel, sense, see.* This information was very useful since experiencers denote persons, therefore all organizations or locations having an experiencer role can be considered as organization-for-members or place-for-people. Here is an example of output, when applying the modified parser on the following sentence (only dependencies are shown):

It was the largest Fiat everyone had ever seen.

ORG_FOR_PRODUCT (**Fiat**)   MOD_PRE (**seen,ever**)
SUBJ-N_PRE (**was,It**)   ATTRIB(**It,Fiat**)
EXPERIENCER_PRE(**seen,everyone**) QUALIF(**Fiat,largest**)

In this example, the relation QUALIF(**Fiat,largest**) triggers the metonymical interpretation of *Fiat*, as org-for-product.

The availability of Great Britain players has boosted the medal hopes of Glasgow Western.

PLACE_FOR_PEOPLE (**Great Britain**) MOD_PRE (**Western,Glasgow**)
PREP_OF (**availability,players**)   SUBJ-N_PRE(**boosted,availability**)
PREP_OF (**hopes,Western**)   OBJ-N(**boosted,hopes**)
MOD_PRE (**players,Great Britain**) LOCATION(**Glasgow**)
MOD_PRE(**hopes,medal**)

In this example, the relation MOD_PRE[5](**players,Great Britain**) triggers the metonymical interpretation of *Great Britain* as place-for-people, because *players* refers to a sport team designated by the name of the country.

In order to widen the lexical coverage of our system, we decided to use the whole BNC corpus[6] to collect lexical information. We parse the corpora and then extract all previously mentioned relations involving a named entity of type location or organization along with their frequencies. For example the relation PREP-OF(**invasion,COUNTRY**) appears 469 times in the BNC, the relation SUBJ(**COMPANY,decides**) appears 420 times, etc. We then filter manually the most frequent relations in order to decide if such a context is triggering a metonymy or not, and to which class it belongs. Once the words of the context are classified, they are integrated in our semantic lexicons.

This first development step is the starting point of our methodology, which is completed by a non-supervised distributional approach described in the next section.

---

[5] Modifier relation where the modifier is placed before the modified element.
[6] From which trial and test corpora were extracted for the SemEval Campaign; see http::/www.natcorp.ox.ac.uk

3.3   Hybridizing with a Distributional Method

The distributional approach proposes to establish a distance between words depending on there syntactic distribution. The distributional hypothesis is that words that appear in similar contexts are semantically similar, [6]. In other words, the more two words have the same distribution, *i.e.* are found in the same syntactic contexts, the more they are semantically close. We propose to apply this principle for metonymy resolution. Traditionally, the distributional approach allows to group words like *USA, Britain, France, Germany* because there are in the same syntactical contexts:

(1) Someone live in Germany.
(2) Someone works in Germany.
(3) Germany declares something.
(4) Germany signs something.

The metonymy resolution task implies to distinguish the literal cases, (1) & (2), from the metonymic ones, (3) & (4). Our method establishes these distinctions using the syntactic context distribution (instead of using words distribution): we group contexts occurring with the same words: the syntactic contexts *live in* and *work in* are occurring with *Germany, France, country, city, place*, when syntactic contexts subject-of-declare and subject-of-sign are occurring with *Germany, France, someone, government, president.*

For each Named Entity annotation, the hybrid method consists in using symbolic annotation if there is (1.2), else using distributional annotation (1.3) as presented below.

We constructed a distributional space with the 100M-word BNC. We prepared the corpus by lemmatizing and then parsing with the same robust parser than for the symbolic approach (XIP, see section 3.1). It allows us to identify triple instances. Each triple have the form w1.R.w2 where w1 and w2 are lexical units and R is a syntactic relation, [13] [14].

Our approach can be distinguished from classical distributional approach by different points. First, we use triple occurrences to build a distributional space (one triple implies two contexts and two lexical units), but we use the transpose of the classical space: each point of this space is a syntactical context (with the form R.w.), each dimension is a lexical units, and each value is the frequency of corresponding triple occurrences. Second, our lexical units are words but also complex nominal groups or verbal groups. Third, contexts can be simple contexts or composed contexts (for our application, one context can be composed by two simple contexts).

We illustrate these three points on the phrase *provide Albania with food aid*, for which the XIP parser gives the following triples (where we can see that *food aid* is considered as a lexical unit):

```
IND-OBJ-N(VERB :provide,NOUN :Albania)
PREP_WITH(VERB :provide,NOUN :aid)
PREP_WITH(VERB :provide,NOUN :food aid)
```

From these triples, we create the following lexical units and contexts (in the context 1.VERB :provide.IND-OBJ-N, "1" means that the verb *provide* is the governor of the relation IND-OBJ-N) :

Lexical units	Simple contexts	Composed contexts
VERB :provide	1.VERB :provide.IND-OBJ-N	1.VERB :provide.IND-OBJ-N + 2.NOUN : aid.PREP_WITH
NOUN :Albania	1.VERB :provide.PREP_WITH	1.VERB :provide.IND-OBJ-N + 2.NOUN :aid.PREP_WITH
NOUN :aid	2.NOUN :Albania.IND-OBJ-N	1.VERB :provide.IND-OBJ-N + 2.NOUN :food aid.PREP_WITH
NOUN :food aid	2.NOUN :aid.PREP_WITH	1.VERB :provide.PREP_WITH + 2.NOUN :Albania.IND-OBJ-N
	2.NOUN :food aid.PREP_WITH	

We use a heuristic to control the high productivity of these lexical units and contexts. Each lexical unit and each context should appear more than 100 times in the corpus. From the 100M-word BNC we obtained 60.849 lexical units and 140.634 contexts. Then, our distributional space has 140.634 units and 60.849 dimensions.

Using the global space to compute distances between each context appear to be too consuming and would induce artificial ambiguity [15]. If any named entity can be used in a metonymic reading, in a given corpus each named entity has not the same distribution of metonymic readings. The country *Vietnam* is more frequently used as an event than *France* or *Germany*, so, knowing that a context is employed with *Vietnam* allow to reduce the metonymic ambiguity.

For this, we construct a singular sub-space according to the context and to the lexical unit (the ambiguous named entity that the symbolic component didn't manage to annotate): given a couple made up of a context i and a lexical unit j we construct a sub-space as follow: the sub-space of contexts (points) corresponds to the list of contexts occurring with the lexical unit i and the sub-space of lexical units (dimensions) corresponds to the list of lexical units occurring with at least one context of the sub-space context. For the context sub-space construction, if there is more than k contexts, we take only the k more frequents, and for the lexical unit sub-space construction, if there is more than n lexical unit, we take only the n more frequents (relative frequency) with the sub-contexts list (for this application, $k = 100$ and $n = 1,000$).

We reduce dimensions of this sub-space to 10 dimensions with a PCA (Principal Components Analysis). In this new reduced space ($k*10$), we compute the closest context of the context i with the Euclidian distance.

At this point, we use the results of the symbolic approach described before as starter. We assign to each context of the Sub_contexts list the annotation, if there is, assigned by the symbolic component. Then, for each annotation (literal, place-for-people, place-for-event, etc.), we compute a score corresponding to the inverse of the sum of the distances of each context bearing this annotation ; this corresponds to the following formula (where $annot_i$ is the annotation for which we calculate the score and C_j is the contexts bearing this annotation):

$$score_{annot_i} = \sum_{C_j} \frac{1}{d(C_j)} \tag{1}$$

We illustrate this process with the sentence *provide Albania with food aid*. The unit *Albania* is found in 384 different contexts ($|Sub\_contexts| = 384$) and 54183 lexical units are occurring with at least one context of the Sub_contexts list ($|Sub\_dimension| = 54183$). After reducing dimension with PCA, we obtain a list of contexts (Table 2) ordered by closeness with the context 1.VERB :provide. IND-OBJ-N.

Table 2. List of the closenest contexts of the context VERB :provide.IND-OBJ-N

Context	Distance	Annotation
VERB :provide.IND-OBJ-N	0.00	
VERB :allow.OBJ-N	0.76	LOC-FOR-PEOPLE
VERB :include.OBJ-N	0.96	
ADJ :new.MOD_PRE	1.02	
VERB :be.SUBJ-N	1.43	
VERB :supply.SUBJ-N_PRE	1.47	LITERAL
VERB :become.SUBJ-N_PRE	1.64	
VERB :come.SUBJ-N_PRE	1.69	
VERB :support.SUBJ-N_PRE	1.70	LOC-FOR-PEOPLE
...	...	...

According to the annotation assigned by the symbolic component to ones of the contexts closed to the context 1.VERB :provide.IND-OBJ-N, we can compute the score (Table 3) and annotate the entity *Albania* with a place-for-people metonymic reading. If we can't choose only one annotation (all scores = 0 or equality between two annotations) we do not annotate. Before presenting the results obtained by this system during the SemEval evaluation, let's briefly consider related work.

Table 3. Annotation scores for each context

Annotation	Score
LOC-FOR-PEOPLE	3.11
LITERAL	1.23
LOC-FOR-EVENT	0.00
...	...

4   Related Work

Beyond "classical" research on metonymy (mainly focusing on common nouns), identification and resolution of metonymic readings of proper names emerged as an important challenge in computational linguistic during the last few years. Actually, this task did benefit from works of analysis and definition of what it really consists in, and from various experiments showing its difficulty but also its feasibility. Concerning the analysis of the task, K. Market and M. Nissim gave an important contribution with corpus studies for location and organization names ([16] and [3]) that enabled them to, firstly, specify reliable frameworks for metonymy annotation and, secondly, to redefine proper names metonymy resolution as a classification task [17]) similar to word sense disambiguation, with the difference that the objects of disambiguation are semantic classes and not yet individual words. They experimented with word sense disambiguation methods for metonymy resolution, taking into consideration features that were not used until then and that they found relevant [18]. They experimented, with promising results, supervised machine learning algorithms (using decision list classifier) on location and organization names [19]. These works emphasize the role of context, and the importance of grammatical features, and show its possible generalization using context similarity (via a thesaurus based on similarity between words). Other works on proper names metonymy resolution are also based on machine learning techniques: Peirsman carried out comparative experiments for location names with supervised algorithms (based on Schtze's approach) and non-supervised ones (Memory-based learning), investigating the relevance of various features [20]. Less complex than Market and Nissim's approach, these methods produced state-of-the-art results. Using a different annotation framework, T.Poibeau also sets out to resolve metonymic readings of French location named entities using probability levels that compute the discriminative power of various features [21].

5   Evaluation

In this section, we present results obtained with our hybrid system during the Semeval2007 evaluation. We present also how each component of our system, symbolic and distributional, contribute in the results.

5.1   Results and Comments

The results obtained on the test corpora are significantly above the baseline[7] for both location and organization names (Table 4). Table 5 and 6 describe results obtained in each specific reading. For the LOCATION annotations, we obtained good precision for the readings place-for-people, place-for-event but also for object-for-name which is rare in the training corpus but quite easy to recognize with the information given in the guideline for this reading. The other readings are too rare or too difficult to recognize (i.e. mixed and othermet), then they are not covered by our system. For the ORGANISATION annotations, we have the same distinction between some well recognized readings (organisation-for-members, organisation-for-product and object-for-name) and some other ignored readings.

---

[7] For this task, the baseline corresponds to the results obtained by assigning the literal annotation to each occurrence to annotate.

Table 4. Global results

Annotation levels	Samples nb.	Accuracy	Coverage	Baseline acc.	Baseline cov.
LOCATION-coarse	908	0.851	1	0.794	1
LOCATION-medium	908	0.848	1	0.794	1
LOCATION-fine	908	0.841	1	0.794	1
ORGANISATION-coarse	842	0.732	1	0.618	1
ORGANISATION-medium	842	0.711	1	0.618	1
ORGANISATION-fine	842	0.700	1	0.618	1

Table 5. Results for the LOCATION class

Scores LOCATION-fine	Occurrences nb.	Precision	Recall	F-measure
literal	721	0.867	0.960	0.911
place-for-people	141	0.651	0.490	0.559
place-for-event	10	0.5	0.1	0.166
place-for-product	1	-	0	0
object-for-name	4	1	0.5	0.666
object-for-representation	0	-	-	-
othermet	11	-	0	0
mixed	20	-	0	0

Table 6. Results for the ORGANISATION class

Scores ORGANISATION-fine	Occurrences nb.	Precision	Recall	F-measure
literal	520	0.730	0.906	0.808
organisation-for-members	161	0.622	0.522	0.568
organisation-for-event	1	-	0	0
organisation-for-product	67	0.550	0.418	0.475
organisation-for-facility	16	0.5	0.125	0.2
organisation-for-index	3	-	0	0
object-for-name	6	1	0.666	0.8
othermet	8	-	0	0
mixed	60	-	0	0

The identified errors are of different nature:

– Parsing errors: as our system makes use of a robust parser, the quality of the results depends of the quality of the syntactic analysis. For example in the sentence "Many galleries in the States, England and France declined the invitation", because the treatment of the coordination is not correct, France is calculated as subject of declined, a context triggering a place-for-people interpretation, which is wrong here.

- Mixed cases: these phenomena, while relatively frequent in the corpora, are not properly treated by our system at the moment.
- Uncovered contexts: some of the syntactico-semantic contexts triggering a metonymy are not covered by the system at the moment, neither by the symbolic component nor by the distributional analysis.

Despite to these errors, our system was 2nd on location names and 3rd on organization names in the Semeval competition. It was the only system using an unsupervised component. Moreover, organizers of the competition gave to each participant some hand written syntactic dependencies for each Named Entity to annotate. Our system was the only which didn't use this hand written information, but a parser instead. Despite to this, the differences with the best system are sometimes due to only one or two annotations.

5.2 Contribution of Each Component

In order to study the contribution of our two components, symbolic and distributional, we split our system and evaluated each module on the Semeval test corpus. Results are described in the table 5. Preliminary comment: in this table, results obtained by our hybrid system are better than the one obtained during the Semeval competition. This is due to improvements of the symbolic component between 2007 and today. Consequently, these results are interesting to study the contribution of our two components but they can't be compared with the results obtained by the other systems during the 2007 competition.

In table 7, the contribution of the distributional component is not so impressive: the improvement of precision with the hybrid system is weak (0.4 to 1 point) compare to the symbolic component. Even if we would have expected a better improvement from the distributional component, these results reveal interesting

Table 7. Contribution of each component

System / Task	Baseline	Symbolic syst.	Distributional syst.	Hybrid syst.
Precision per granularity level on LOCATION class				
LOCATION-coarse	0.794	0.863	0.814	0.867
LOCATION-medium	0.794	0.860	0.813	0.863
LOCATION-fine	0.794	0.855	0.812	0.859
Precision per granularity level on ORGANISATION class				
ORGANISATION-coarse	0.618	0.710	0.635	0.732
ORGANISATION-medium	0.618	0.699	0.626	0.711
ORGANISATION-fine	0.618	0.690	0.618	0.700

details. Results obtained by the distributional component are a bit better than the baseline but far behind the symbolic component.

Even if we would have expected a better improvement from the distributional component, these results reveal interesting details. Results obtained by the distributional component are a bit better than the baseline but far behind the symbolic component. At the ORGANISATION-fine level, the distributional component is even equal to the baseline, however, it give 1 point better for the precision in the hybrid system. As a consequence, we can say that the distributional component is not enough alone for this task, but it allows annotating some named entities missed by the symbolic component. Recently, we developed another hybrid system for Named Entity annotation and disambiguation where we replace the context distance computing by a clique-based clustering approach [22]. We plan to apply this approach to Named Entity metonymy resolution.

6 Conclusion

This paper describes a system combining a symbolic and a non-supervised distributional approach, developed for solving location and organization names metonymy. Results obtained by the system in the framework of the SemEval 2007 task#8 are reported. The competition enables us to work deeply on the metonymy phenomenon, which is of great interest for NLP applications, in particular information extraction, question answering, but can also improves NLP components such as coreference resolution components. Further work could be done according to two directions. At the level of the task, it would be worthwhile to follow up the named entity metonymy study carried out by M. Nissim and K. Markert with the re-examination of some metonymic patterns which are, contrary to frequent and consensual patterns (place-for-people, org-for-members), rare and difficult to annotate (object-for-name, mixed and object-for-representation). At the level of our system, the results obtained are quite encouraging and, consequently, we plan to pursue this research work in order to improve the system on the already-covered phenomenon as well as on different names entities. Currently, we are also working on the improvement of the distributional component.

References

1. Brun, C., Ehrmann, M., Jacquet, G.: XRCE-M: A hybrid system for named entity metonymy resolution. In: 4th International Workshop on Semantic Evaluations, Prague (June 2007)
2. Markert, K., Hahn, U.: Understanding metonymies in discourse. Artificial Intelligence 135(1/2), 145–198 (2002)
3. Markert, K., Nissim, M.: Metonymic proper names : a corpus based account. In: Stefanowitsch, A., Gries, S. (eds.) Corpus-based approaches to Metaphor and Metonymy, pp. 152–174. Mouton de Gruyter, Berlin (2006)

4. Markert, K., Nissim, M.: Semeval-2007 task 08: Metonymy resolution at semeval-2007. In: 4th International Workshop on Semantic Evaluations, Prague, ACL-SemEval (Juin 2007)
5. Markert, K., Nissim, M.: Metonymy Resolution at SemEval i : Guidelines for Participants. Technical report, SemEval (2007)
6. Aït-Mokhtar, S., Chanod, J.P., Roux, C.: Robustness beyond shallowness: incremental dependency parsing. NLE Journal (2002)
7. Mel'cuk, I.: Dependency Syntax. State University of New York Press (1988)
8. Tesnière, L.: Eléments de Syntaxe Structurale. Klincksiek (1959)
9. Levin, B.: English Verb Classes and Alternations - A Preliminary Investigation. The University of Chicago Press (1993)
10. Ruppenhofer, J., Ellsworth, M., Petruck, M., Johnson, C., Scheffczyk, J.: Framenet II: Extended theory and practice. Technical report, University of Berkeley (2006), Disponible sur : http://framenet.icsi.berkeley.edu/
11. Hagège, C., Roux, C.: Entre syntaxe et smantique : Normalisation de la sortie de l'analyse syntaxique en vue de l'amlioration de l'extraction d'information partir de textes. In: TALN 2003, Batz-sur-Mer (Juin 2003)
12. Brun, C., Hagège, C.: Normalization and paraphrasing using symbolic methods. In: Proceeding of the Second International Workshop on Paraphrasing, ACL (2003)
13. Kilgarriff, A., Rychly, P., Smrz, P., Tugwell, D.: The sketch engine. In: Proceeding of EURALEX, Lorient, France (2004)
14. Lin, D.: Automatic retrieval and clustering of similar words. In: Proceeding of COLING-ACL, Montreal, Quebec, Canada (1998)
15. Jacquet, G., Venant, F.: Construction automatique de classes de sélection distributionnelle. In: Actes de la 10ème conférence annuelle sur le Traitement Automatique des Langues (TALN 2003), Dourdan, France (2003)
16. Markert, K., Nissim, M.: Toward a corpus annotated for metonymies : the case of location names. In: Proceedings of the 3rd International Conference on Language Resources and Evaluations, Las Palmas, Iles Canaries (2002)
17. Markert, K., Nissim, M.: Metonymy Resolution as a Classification Task. In: Proceedings of the 2002 Conference on Empirical Methods in Natural Language Processing, Philadelphia, Penn (2002)
18. Nissim, M., Markert, K.: Syntactic features and word similarity for supervised metonymy resolution. In: Proceedings of the 41st Annual Meeting of the Association of Computational Linguistics (ACL-2003), Sapporo, Japon (2003)
19. Nissim, M., Markert, K.: Learning to buy a Renault and to talk to a BMW: A supervised approache to conventional metonymy. In: Proceedings of the 6th International Workshop on Computational Semantics, Tilburg (2005)
20. Peirsman, Y.: What's in a name? Computational approaches to metonymical location names. In: Proceedings of the Workshop on Making Sense of Sense: Bringing Psycholinguistics and Computational Linguistics Together, Trento, Italie (2006)
21. Poibeau, T.: Dealing with metonymic readings of named entities. In: Proceedings of the 28th Annual Conference of the Cognitive Science Society, Canada (2006)
22. Ah-Pine, J., Jacquet, G.: Clique-based clustering for improving named entity recognition systems. In: Proceedings of EACL, Athens, Greece (to appear, 2009)

Spejd: A Shallow Processing and Morphological Disambiguation Tool

Aleksander Buczyński and Adam Przepiórkowski

Polish Academy of Sciences, Institute of Computer Science
ul. Ordona 21, 01-237 Warsaw, Poland
{adamp,olekb}@ipipan.waw.pl
http://www.ipipan.waw.pl

Abstract. This article presents a formalism and a beta version of a new tool for simultaneous morphosyntactic disambiguation and shallow parsing. Unlike in the case of other shallow parsing formalisms, the rules of the grammar allow for explicit morphosyntactic disambiguation statements, independently of structure-building statements, which facilitates the task of the shallow parsing of morphosyntactically ambiguous or erroneously disambiguated input.

Keywords: morphosyntactic disambiguation, partial parsing, shallow parsing, constituency parsing, syntactic words, syntactic groups, spejd, poliqarp.

1 Introduction

Two observations motivate the work described here. First, morphosyntactic disambiguation and shallow parsing inform each other and should be performed in parallel, rather than in sequence. Second, morphosyntactic disambiguation and shallow parsing rules often implicitly encode the same linguistic intuitions, so a formalism is needed which would allow to encode disambiguation and structure-building instructions in a single rule.

The aim of this paper is to present a new formalism and tool, Spejd,[1] abbreviated to "♠" (the Unicode character 0x2660). The formalism is essentially a cascade of regular grammars, where (currently) each regular grammar is expressed by a — perhaps very complex — single rule. The rules specify both morphosyntactic disambiguation/correction operations and structure-building operations, but, unlike in pure unification-based formalisms, these two types of operations

---

[1] *Spejd* stands for the Polish *Składniowy Parser (Ewidentnie Jednocześnie Dezambiguator)*, the English *Shallow Parsing and Eminently Judicious Disambiguation*, the German *Syntaktisches Parsing Entwicklungsystem Jedoch mit Disambiguierung*, and the French *Super Parseur Et Jolie Désambiguïsation*. Originally the system was called *Shallow Parsing And Disambiguation Engine* and abbreviated to *SPADE*. However, to avoid confusion with the other SPADE parsing system (*Sentence-level PArsing for DiscoursE*, http://www.isi.edu/licensed-sw/spade/), it was renamed to Spejd.

Z. Vetulani and H. Uszkoreit (Eds.): LTC 2007, LNAI 5603, pp. 131–141, 2009.

are decoupled, i.e., a rule may be adorned with instructions to the effect that
a structure is built even when the relevant unification fails.

After a brief presentation of some related work in §2, we present the formalism
in §3 and its implementation in §4, with §5 concluding the paper.

2   Background and Related Work

Syntactic parsers differ in whether they assume morphosyntactically disambiguated or non-disambiguated input: deep parsing systems based on unification
usually allow for ambiguous input, while shallow (or partial) parsers usually expect fully disambiguated input. Some partial parsing systems (e.g., [11], [7], [1],
[15]) allow for the interweaving of disambiguation and parsing.

[6] present a unified formalism for disambiguation and *dependency* parsing.
Since dependency parsing in that approach is fully *reductionistic*, i.e., it assumes
that all words have all their possible syntactic roles assigned in the lexicon and
it simply rejects some of these roles, that formalism is basically a pure disambiguation formalism. In contrast, the formalism described below is *constructive*:
it groups constituents into larger constituents.

Previous work that comes closest to our aims is reported in [9,10] and [8],
where INTEX local grammars [16], normally used for disambiguation, are the
basis for a system that recognises various kinds of noun phrases and handles
agreement within them. However, it is not clear whether these extensions lead
to a lean formalism comparable to the formalism presented below.

3   Formalism

3.1   The Basic Format

In the simplest case, each rule consists of up to 4 parts marked as Left, Match,
Right and Eval:

```
Left:  ;
Match: [pos~~"prep"] [base~"co|kto"];
Right: ;
Eval:  unify(case,1,2); group(PG,1,2);
```

The rule means:

1. find a sequence of two tokens[2] such that the first token is an unambiguous
   preposition ([pos~~prep]), and the second token is a form of the lexeme CO
   'what' or KTO 'who' ([base~"co|kto"]);

---

[2] A terminological note is in order, although its full meaning will become clear only
later: by *segment* we understand the smallest interpreted unit, i.e., a sequence of
characters together with their morphosyntactic interpretations (lemma, grammatical
class, grammatical categories); *syntactic word* is a non-empty sequence of segments
and/or syntactic words marked by the action **word**; *token* is a segment or a syntactic
word; *syntactic group* (in short: *group*) is a non-empty sequence of tokens and/or
syntactic groups, marked as an entity by the action **group**; *syntactic entity* is a token
or a syntactic group.

2. if there exist interpretations of these two tokens with the same value of case, reject all interpretations of these two tokens which do not agree in case (cf. `unify(case,1,2)`);

3. if the above unification did not fail, mark thus identified sequence as a syntactic group (`group`) of type `PG` (prepositional group), whose syntactic head is the first token (1) and whose semantic head is the second token (2; cf. `group(PG,1,2)`).

`Left` and `Right` parts of a rule, specifying the context of the match, may be empty; in such a case they may be omitted.

Note that, unlike in typical unification-based formalisms, unification and grouping are decoupled here. In particular, it is possible to reverse the order of `group` and `unify` in the rule above: in this case the rule will always mark the match as a group and only subsequently unify case values, if possible. This feature of the formalism is useful, e.g., for dealing with systematic deficiencies of the morphological analyser used.

3.2 Matching (Left, Match, Right)

The contents of parts `Left`, `Match` and `Right` have the same syntax and semantics. Each of them may contain a sequence of the following specifications:

1. **token specification**, e.g., `[pos~~"prep"]` or `[base~"co|kto"]`; these specifications are compatible with segment specifications of the Poliqarp [5] corpus search engine as specified in [12]; in particular, a specification like `[pos~~"subst"]` says that *all* morphosyntactic interpretations of a given token are nominal (substantive), while `[pos~"subst"]` means that there *exists* a nominal interpretation of a given token;

2. **group specification**, extending the Poliqarp query language as proposed in [13], e.g., `[semh=[pos~~"subst"]]` specifies a syntactic group whose semantic head is a token whose all interpretations are nominal;

3. one of the **following specifications**: ns: no space; sb: sentence beginning; se: sentence end;

4. an **alternative** of such sequences in parentheses, e.g., `([pos~~"subst"] | [synh=[pos~~"subst"]] se)`.

Additionally, each such specification may be modified with one of the three **regular expression quantifiers**: ?, * and +.

An example of a possible value of `Left`, `Match` or `Right` might be:

```
[pos~~"adv"] (
     [pos~~"prep"] [pos~"subst"] ns? [pos~"interp"]? se |
     [synh=[pos~~"prep"]]
)
```

The meaning of this specification is: find an adverb followed by a prepositional group, where the prepositional group is specified as either a sequence of an unambiguous preposition and a possible noun at the end of a sentence, or an already recognised prepositional group.

3.3 Conditions and Actions (Eval)

The Eval part contains a sequence of Prolog-like predicates evaluating to true or false; if a predicate evaluates to false, further predicates are not evaluated and the rule is aborted. Almost all predicates have side effects, or actions. In fact, many of them always evaluate to true, and they are 'evaluated' solely for their side effects. In the following, we will refer to those predicates which may have side effects as *actions*, and to those which may evaluate to false as *conditions*.

There are two types of actions: morphosyntactic and syntactic. While morphosyntactic actions delete some interpretations of specified tokens, syntactic actions group entities into syntactic words (consecutive segments which syntactically behave like single words, e.g., multi-segment named entities, etc.) or syntactic groups.

Natural numbers in predicates refer to tokens matched by the specifications in Left, Match and Right. These specifications are numbered from 1, counting from the first specification in Left to the last specification in Right. For example, in the following rule, there should be case agreement between the adjective specified in the left context and the adjective and the noun specified in the right context (cf. unify(case,1,4,5)), as well as case agreement (possibly of a different case) between the adjective and noun in the match (cf. unify(case,2,3)).

```
Left:   [pos~~"adj"];
Match:  [pos~~"adj"][pos~~"subst"];
Right:  [pos~~"adj"][pos~~"subst"];
Eval:   unify(case,2,3); unify(case,1,4,5);
```

The exact repertoire of predicates still evolves, but currently the following are defined:

agree(<cat> ...,<tok>,...) — a condition checking if the grammatical categories (<cat> ...) of tokens specified by subsequent numbers (<tok>,...) agree. It takes a variable number of arguments: the initial arguments, such as case or gender, specify the grammatical categories that should *simultaneously* agree, so the condition agree(case gender,1,2) is stronger than the sequence of conditions: agree(case,1,2), agree(gender,1,2). Subsequent arguments of agree are natural numbers referring to entity specifications that should be taken into account when checking agreement.

unify(<cat> ...,<tok>,...) — a condition (and, simultaneously, an action) which checks agreement, just as agree, but also deletes interpretations that do not agree.

delete(<cond>,<tok>,...) — delete all interpretations of specified tokens matching the specified condition (for example delete(case~"gen|acc",1)).

leave(<cond>,<tok>,...) — leave only the interpretations matching the specified condition.

add(<tag>,<base>,<tok>) — add to the specified token the interpretation <tag> with the base form <base>.

word(<tag>,<base>) — create a new syntactic word comprising of all tokens matched by the Match specification, and assign it the given tag and base form.

In both cases, `<tag>` may be a simple complete tag, e.g., `conj` for a conjunction or `adj:pl:acc:f:sup` for a superlative degree feminine accusative plural form of an adjective, but it may also be a specification of a number of tags. For example, `add(subst:number*:gen:m3, procent, 1)` will add 2 (one for each number) nominal genitive inanimate masculine interpretations to the token referred by 1, in both cases with the base form PROCENT 'per cent'. Moreover, the sequence `<tag>,<base>` may be repeated any number of times, so, e.g., the abbreviation *fr.* may be turned into a syntactic word representing any of the 2×7 number/case values of the noun FRANK 'franc' (the currency), or any of the $2 \times 7 \times 5$ number/case/gender values of the (positive degree) adjective FRANCUSKI 'French':

```
Match: [orth~"fr"] ns [orth~"\."];
Eval:  word(subst:number*:case*:m3,frank;
            adj:number*:case*:gender*:pos,francuski);
```

`<base>` is a sequence of static strings and references to tokens' base or orthographic forms. The base form of a new syntactic word is created by evaluating and concatenating all elements of the sequence, for example the action `word(qub, "po " 2.orth)` creates a new base form by concatenating PO, space and the orthographic form of the second token.

   `word(<tok>, <tag_fragment>,<base>)` — create a new syntactic word comprising of all tokens matched by the `Match` specification, by copying all interpretations of the token `<tok>`, adding or replacing `<tag_fragment>` (for example a negation marker) in each interpretation of that token, and possibly modyfying the respective base forms. The original interpretations are not modified, if both `<base>` and `<tag_fragment>` are empty, as in the following rule, which turns the three tokens of *„Rzeczpospolita”* (i.e., *„*, *Rzeczpospolita* and *”*) into a single word with exactly the same interpretations (and base form) as *Rzeczpospolita* (the name of a Polish newspaper):

```
Match: [orth~",,"] ns? [] ns? [orth~"''"];
Eval:  word(3,,);
```

The orthographic form of the newly created syntactic word is always a simple concatenation of all orthographic forms of all tokens immediately contained in that syntactic word, taking into account information about space or its lack between consecutive tokens.

   `group(<type>,<synh>,<semh>)` — create a new syntactic group with syntactic head and semantic head specified by numbers. The `<type>` is the categorial type of the group (e.g., PG), while `<synh>` and `<semh>` are references to appropriate token specifications in the `Match` part. For example, the following rule may be used to create a numeral group, syntactically headed by the numeral and semantically headed by the noun:[3]

---

[3] A rationale for distinguishing these two kinds of heads is given in [13].

```
Left:   [pos~~"prep"];
Match:  [pos~~"num"] [pos~~"adj"]*
        [pos~~"subst"];
Eval:   group(NumG,2,4);
```

Of course, rules should be constructed in such a way that references <synh> and <semh> refer to specifications of single entities, e.g., [case~~"nom"] or ([pos~~"subst"] | [synh=[pos~~"subst"]]) but not, say, [case~~"nom"]+

In all these predicates, a reference to a token specification takes into account all tokens matched by that specification, so, e.g., in case 1 refers to the specification [pos~~adj]*, the action unify(case,1) means that all the adjectives matched must be rid of all interpretations whose case is not shared by all of them.

Moreover, the numbers in all predicates are interpreted as referring to tokens; when a reference is made to a syntactic group, the action is performed on the syntactic head of that group. For example, assuming that the following rule finds a sequence of a nominal segment, a multi-segment syntactic word and a nominal group, the action unify(case,1) will result in the unification of case values of the first segment, the syntactic word as a whole and the syntactic head of the group.

```
Match:  ([pos~~"subst"]|[synh=[pos~~"subst"]])+;
Eval:   unify(case,1);
```

The only exception to this rule is the semantic head parameter in the group action; when it references a syntactic group, the semantic, not syntactic, head is inherited.

4 Implementation

Since the formalism described above is novel and to some extent still evolving, its implementation had to be not only reasonably fast, but also easy to modify and maintain. This section briefly presents such an implementation.

The implementation has been released under the GNU General Public License (version 3). The release address is http://nlp.ipipan.waw.pl/Spejd/.

4.1 Input and Output

The parser implementing the specification above currently takes as input the version of the XML Corpus Encoding Standard assumed in the IPI PAN Corpus of Polish (http://korpus.pl/; [12]). Rules may modify the input in two possible ways. First, morphosyntactic actions may reject certain interpretations of certain tokens; such rejected interpretations are marked by the attribute disamb_sh="0" added to <lex> elements representing these interpretations. Second, syntactic actions modify the input by adding <syntok> and <group> elements, marking syntactic words and groups.

For example, the rule given at the top of §3.1 above may be applied to the following input sequence (slightly simplified in irrelevant aspects; e.g., the token *co* actually has 3 more interpretations, apart from the two given below) of two tokens *Po co* 'why, what for', lit. 'for what', where *Po* is a preposition which either combines with an accusative argument or with a locative argument, while *co* is ambiguous between, *inter alia*, a nominative/accusative noun:

```
<tok id="tA5">
 <orth>Po</orth>
 <lex><base>po</base>
       <ctag>prep:acc</ctag></lex>
 <lex><base>po</base>
       <ctag>prep:loc</ctag></lex>
</tok>
<tok id="tA6">
 <lex><base>co</base>
       <ctag>subst:sg:nom:n</ctag></lex>
 <lex><base>co</base>
       <ctag>subst:sg:acc:n</ctag></lex>
</tok>
```

The result should have the following effect (bits added by the rule are *emphasised*):

```
<group type="PG"
        synh="tA5" semh="tA6">
<tok id="tA5">
 <orth>Po</orth>
 <lex><base>po</base>
     <ctag>prep:acc</ctag></lex>
 <lex disamb_sh="0"><base>po</base>
       <ctag>prep:loc</ctag></lex>
</tok>
<tok id="tA6">
 <lex disamb_sh="0"><base>co</base>
       <ctag>subst:sg:nom:n</ctag>
 </lex>
 <lex><base>co</base>
       <ctag>subst:sg:acc:n</ctag></lex>
</tok>
</group>
```

4.2 Algorithm Overview

During the initialisation phase, the parser loads the external tagset specification and the rules, and converts the latter to a set of compiled regular expressions and actions/conditions. Then, input files are parsed one by one (for each input file a corresponding output file containing parsing results is created).

To reduce memory usage, parsing is done by chunks defined in the input files, such as sentences or paragraphs. In the remainder of the paper we assume the chunks are sentences.

The parser concurrently maintains two representations for each sentence: 1) an object-oriented syntactic entity tree, used for easy manipulation of entities (for example, for disabling certain interpretations or creating new syntactic words) and preserving all necessary information to generate the final output; 2) a compact string for quick regexp matching, containing only the information important for the rules which have not been applied yet.

Tree Representation. The entity tree is initialised as a flat (one level deep) tree with all leaves (segments and possibly special entities, like no space, sentence beginning, sentence end) connected directly to the root. Application of a syntactic action means inserting a new node (syntacting word or group) to the tree, between the root and some of the existing nodes. As the parsing proceeds, the tree changes its shape: it becomes deeper and narrower.

Morphosyntactic actions do not change the shape of the tree, but also reduce the string representation length by deleting from that string certain interpretations. The interpretations are preserved in the tree to produce the final output, but are not relevant to further stages of parsing.

String Representation. The string representation is a compromise between XML and binary representation, designed for easy, fast and precise matching, with the use of existing regular expression libraries.[4] The representation describes the top level of the current state of the sentence tree, including only the information that may be used by rule matching. For each child of the tree root, the following information is preserved in the string: type (token / group / special) and identifier (for finding the entity in the tree in case an action should be applied to it). The ensuing part of the string depends on the type of the child: for a token, it is orthographic forms and a list of interpretations; for a group — number of heads of the group and lists of interpretations for the syntactic and semantic head.

Because the tagset used in the IPI PAN Corpus is intended to be human-readable, the morphosyntactic tags are fairly descriptive and, as a result, they are rather long. To facilitate and speed up pattern matching, each tag is converted to a relatively short string of fixed width. In the string, each character corresponds to one morphological category from the tagset (first part of speech, then number, case, gender, etc.) as, for example, in the Czech positional tag

---

[4] Two alternatives to this approach were considered: 1) building a custom finite state automata on binary representation: our previous experience shows that while this may lead to an extremely fast search engine, it is at the same time costly to maintain; 2) operating directly on XML files: the strings to search would be longer, and matching would be more complex (especially for requirements including negation); a prototype of this kind was written in Perl and parsing times were not acceptable.

system [4]. The characters — upper- and lowercase letters, or 0 (zero) for categories non-applicable to a given part of speech — are assigned automatically, on the basis of the external tagset definition read at initialisation. A few possible correspondences are presented in Table 1.

Table 1. Examples of tag conversion between human-readable and inner positional tagset

IPI PAN tag	fixed length tag
`adj:pl:acc:f:sup`	`UBDD0C0000000`
`conj`	`B000000000000`
`fin:pl:sec:imperf`	`bB00B0A000000`
`subst:pl:nom:m1`	`NBAA000000000`

Matching (Left, Match, Right). The conversion from the `Left`, `Match` and `Right` parts of the rule to a regular expression over the string representation is fairly straightforward. Two exceptions — regular expressions as morphosyntactic category values and the distinction between existential and universal quantification over interpretations — are described in more detail below.

First, the rule might be looking for a token whose grammatical category is described by a regular expresion. For example, `[gender~~"m."]` should match personal masculine (also called virile; `m1`), animal masculine (`m2`), and inanimate masculine (`m3`) tokens; `[pos~~"ppron[123]+|siebie"]` should match all pronouns (`ppron12`, i.e., first or second person personal pronouns, `ppron3`, i.e., third person personal pronouns, or forms of the reflexive/reciprocal pronoun SIEBIE, which happens to have a separate grammatical class in the IPI PAN Corpus, called `siebie`); `[pos!~~"adj.*"]` should match all segments except for (various classes of) adjectives; etc. Because morphosyntactic tags are converted to fixed length representations, the regular expressions also have to be converted before compilation.

To this end, the regular expression is matched against all possible values of the given category. Since, after conversion, every value is represented as a single character, the resulting regexp can use square bracket notation for character classes to represent the range of possible values.

The conversion can be done only for attributes with values from a well-defined, finite set. Since we do not want to assume that we know all the text to parse before the compilation of the rules, we assume that the dictionary is infinite. The assumption makes it difficult to convert requirements with negated `orth` or `base` (for example `[orth!~"[Nn]ie"]`). As for now, such requirements are not included in the compiled regular expression, but instead handled by special predicates in the `Eval` part.

Second, a segment may have many interpretations and sometimes a rule may apply only when all the interpretations meet the specified condition (for example `[pos~~"subst"]`), while in other cases one matching interpretation should be enough to trigger the rule (`[pos~"subst"]`).

In the string interpretation, < and > were chosen as convenient separators of interpretations and entities, because they should not appear in the input data (they have to be escaped in XML). In particular, each representation of a fixed length tag is preceded by <. Assuming that tags representing a nominal (`subst`) are translated into fixed length string starting with an N, the universal specification [pos~~"subst"] will be translated into the regular expression (<N[^<>]+)+, while the existential specification [pos~"subst"] will be translated into (<[^<>]+)*(<N[^<>]+)(<[^<>]+)*.

Of course, a combination of existential and universal requirements is a valid requirement as well, for example: [pos~~"subst" case~"gen|acc"] (all interpretations noun, at least one of them in genitive or accusative case) should translate to: (<N[^<>]+)*(<N.[BD][^<>]+)(<N[^<>]+) (if genitive and accusative translate to B and D).

Conditions and Actions (Eval). As described in §3.3, when a match is found, the parser evaluates a sequence of predicates connected to the given rule. Each predicate may be a condition with no side effects involved, a morphosyntactic action or a syntactic action. The parser executes the sequence until it encounters a predicate which evaluates to false (for example, unification of cases fails).

The actions affect both the tree and the string representation of the parsed sentence. The tree is updated instantly (the cost of update is constant or linear with respect to match length), but the string update (cost linear to sentence length) is delayed until it is really needed (at most once per rule).

4.3 Efficiency

The system has been implemented in Java. So far, it has been tested in two practical applications: valence acquisition from the morphosyntactically annotated IPI PAN Corpus of Polish [14] and sentiment analysis of product reviews [2] [3].

When given a set of over 90 rules of varying complexity, ♠ processed a 12MB XML file containing over 56 thousand words in about 42 seconds, which gives the average of about 1340 words per second (as measured on a contemporary Intel Core2Duo T7200 laptop). In the process, almost 6800 syntactic words and over 5600 syntactic groups were marked. While parsing times increase with the size of the grammar, they are still acceptable.

5   Conclusion

The system presented, ♠, is perhaps unique in allowing the grammar developer to encode morphosyntactic disambiguation and shallow parsing instructions in the same unified formalism, possibly in the same rule. The formalism is more flexible than either the usual shallow parsing formalisms, which assume disambiguated input, or the usual unification-based formalisms, which couple disambiguation (via unification) with structure building. While the rule sets so far have been prepared for parsing of Polish, ♠ is fully language-independent and we hope it will also be useful in the processing of other languages.

References

1. Aït-Mokhtar, S., Chanod, J.-P., Roux, C.: Robustness beyond shallowness: incremental deep parsing. Natural Language Engineering 8, 121–144 (2002)
2. Buczyński, A., Wawer, A.: Automated classification of product review sentiments using bag of words and Sentipejd. In: Kłopotek, M.A., Przepiórkowski, A., Wierzchoń, S.T., Trojanowski, K. (eds.) Intelligent Information Systems, Institute of Computer Science, Polish Academy of Sciences, Warsaw (2008)
3. Buczyński, A., Wawer, A.: Shallow parsing in sentiment analysis of product reviews. In: Proceedings of the Partial Parsing workshop at LREC 2008, pp. 14–18 (2008)
4. Hajič, J., Hladká, B.: Probabilistic and rule-based tagger of an inflective language - a comparison. In: Proceedings of the ANLP 1997, Washington, DC (1997)
5. Janus, D., Przepiórkowski, A.: Poliqarp: An open source corpus indexer and search engine with syntactic extensions. In: Proceedings of ACL 2007 Demo Session (2007)
6. Karlsson, F., Voutilainen, A., Heikkilä, J., Anttila, A.: Constraint Grammar: A Language-Independent System for Parsing Unrestricted Text. Mouton de Gruyter, Berlin (1995)
7. Marimon, M., Porta, J.: PoS disambiguation and partial parsing bidirectional interaction. In: Proceedings of the Third International Conference on Language Resources and Evaluation, LREC 2000. ELRA, Athens (2000)
8. Nenadić, G.: Local grammars and parsing coordination of nouns in Serbo-Croatian. In: Proceedings of Text, Dialogue and Speech (TSD) 2000. Springer, Heidelberg (2000)
9. Nenadić, G., Vitas, D.: Formal model of noun phrases in Serbo-Croatian. BULAG, 23. Presses de l'Université de Franche-Comté, Besançon, France (1998)
10. Nenadić, G., Vitas, D.: Using local grammars for agreement modeling in highly inflective languages. In: Proceedings of Text, Dialogue and Speech, TSD (1998)
11. Neumann, G., Braun, C., Piskorski, J.: A divide-and-conquer strategy for shallow parsing of German free texts. In: Proceedings of ANLP-2000, Seattle, Washington (2000)
12. Przepiórkowski, A.: The IPI PAN Corpus: Preliminary version. Institute of Computer Science, Polish Academy of Sciences, Warsaw (2004)
13. Przepiórkowski, A.: On heads and coordination in valence acquisition. In: Gelbukh, A. (ed.) CICLing 2007. LNCS, vol. 4394, pp. 50–61. Springer, Heidelberg (2007)
14. Przepiórkowski, A.: Powierzchniowe przetwarzanie języka polskiego. Akademicka Oficyna Wydawnicza EXIT. Warsaw (2008)
15. Schiehlen, M.: Experiments in German noun chunking. In: Proceedings of the 19th International Conference on Computational Linguistics (COLING 2002), Taipei (2002)
16. Silberztein, M.: INTEX: a corpus processing system. In: Fifteenth International Conference on Computational Linguistics (COLING 1994), Kyoto, Japan (1994)

Flexible Natural Language Generation in Multiple Contexts

Caroline Cullen, Ian O'Neill, and Philip Hanna

The Institute of Electronics, Communications and Information Technology (ECIT),
Queen's University Belfast, Northern Ireland
{ccullen09,i.oneill,p.hanna}@qub.ac.uk

Abstract. We present a practical approach to Natural Language Generation
(NLG) for spoken dialogue systems. The approach is based on small template
fragments (mini-templates). The system's object architecture facilitates generation of phrases across pre-defined business domains and registers, as well as
into different languages. The architecture simplifies NLG in well-understood
application contexts, while providing the flexibility for a developer and for the
system, to vary linguistic output according to dialogue context, including any
intended affective impact. Mini-templates are used with a suite of domain term
objects, resulting in an NLG system (MINTGEN – MINi-Template GENerator)
whose extensibility and ease of maintenance is enhanced by the sparsity of information devoted to individual domains. The system also avoids the need for
specialist linguistic competence on the part of the system maintainer.

Keywords: Natural Language Generation, Spoken Dialogue Systems,
Object-Orientation.

1 Introduction

Natural Language Generation (NLG) is concerned with the mapping between the
semantic representation of a phrase and its corresponding natural language expression. The NLG component in a multi-domain spoken dialogue system must supply
information to the user using the phrasing most appropriate to each of the system's
domains. It must also present information in a manner appropriate to the context,
taking into consideration the user's experience of working with the system, and the
'personality' that the system wants to adopt.

By abstracting similar concepts between domains and identifying modifications between domains, we created an ordered hierarchy of mini-templates and sparse domain-
specific terms that forms the basis of an intuitive object-based toolkit. The toolkit is
designed to enhance system usability for developers and end-users alike. Such an approach to NLG, where an output can be closely specified and can draw on ready-made
object components, provides a practical solution for application developers who wish
to create naturalistic output, but who are not specialist computational linguists and may
be unfamiliar with conversational usage in the target application domains. Specialist
terminology obtained from domain experts is stored in such a way that, for a given
dialogue context, an automated Dialogue Manager can access the appropriate term, at

Z. Vetulani and H. Uszkoreit (Eds.): LTC 2007, LNAI 5603, pp. 142–153, 2009.

the correct level of specialisation. In due course we aim to develop an easily navigated GUI which will support NLG system maintenance by non-specialist developers.

This ability to dynamically match NLG capabilities to context becomes a more pressing requirement as speech-based dialogue systems attempt to emulate more closely human-to-human communications. The NLG component must be able to 'change tone', not only as the context changes in a discourse, but also as the relationship with the user evolves, within and between dialogue sessions - cf. GRETA [1] and the broad research into affect in computing being conducted by the EU network of excellence HUMAINE [2].

2 MINTGEN in Context

We have developed a test-bed application, MINTGEN (MINi-Template GENerator) which attempts to address the disadvantages of a number of established approaches to NLG:

1. *Canned Text* produces very natural utterances by printing a string of words 'as is'. These hand-crafted phrases are easy to create, but are inflexible.
2. *Template* or *Frame-Based* approaches slot data into specific locations in a message template. However, it is not easy to re-use templates across domains and applications and they are difficult to maintain as even a slight change to the output requires a large amount of recoding.
3. *Phrase-Based* approaches typically use phrase structure grammar rules to produce "generalized templates" at the sentence level and at the discourse level, resulting in a linguistic phrase-based NLG system which is generally quite adaptable. However, sensitivity towards the grammatical features of the target language is required.
4. *Feature-Based* approaches specify each sentence as a unique set of features e.g. question/imperative/ statement, positive/negative resulting in a system that is easily expanded by the addition of new features. However, the fine-grained linguistic detail required makes such a system difficult to maintain [3].

3 MINTGEN's Approach to NLG

The first three of the existing NLG approaches listed above would not, if used in isolation, provide the flexibility or the fluency required by an NLG module that is intended to cross between domains, registers and languages in real-time. The fourth and (to some extent) the third approach, while highly effective, are beyond the reach of most software engineers who, while sensitive to issues of natural language usage, are not a specialist in computational linguistics. Without the available services of such specialist staff, maintainability and extensibility of the system are problematic.

Register, *domain* and *language* were selected as vehicles through which to investigate our practical object-based approach to NLG. We provide hierarchies of generic and domain-, register- and language-specific components for the NLG task – the more specialized components making use of existing generic functionality wherever possible. This middle-ground approach uses easily configurable components, sparsely populated tables and mini-templates that are small enough to be rearranged so that they can generate from the numerous semantic constructs that the Dialogue Manager (DM) may present. This form of generation avoids the need for a highly abstracted linguistic representation such as the Sentence Planning Language (SPF) [4].

Elements of the approaches outlined in Section 2 benefit the implemented NLG module: since the object-based generation module comprises a hierarchical, extensible set of components tailored to known domains, any new element to be added is typically a further specialization of an existing element in the basic 'toolkit'.

3.1 Multi-context Capabilities

MINTGEN was designed to work flexibly in a variety of application contexts which include changes in domain, register and language, examples of which are given in Section 4.5. With the possible exception of language, these changes are likely to occur dynamically mid-dialogue. MINTGEN is not designed as a translating tool, although it could be manipulated for that purpose.

MINTGEN is intended to work with an updated version of the *Queen's Communicator* (QC) [5], but will work with any dialogue system whose Dialogue Manager conforms to the NLG's input specification. The QC already encompasses three application domains: Accommodation, Theatre and Cinema booking.

MINTGEN is a *cross-domain* system. By decomposing a domain into speech acts (e.g. requesting information, providing information etc.) and related domain terms (pertaining to hotel, airplane, cinema etc.), commonality and differences between domains are apparent, thus indicating which utterances are generic and which are domain-specific. Items within domains are grouped together by their characteristics in order to take advantage of their common attributes so that duplicate information is not repeated.

MINTGEN is capable of *multi-register* generation. As Poggi et al. [1] remark, "Words have formal and informal variants, connotations, positive or negative, tender or insulting nuances". As an exploration of how register is incorporated into the NLG input constructs and the subsequent effect on the generated phrase, normal, formal and informal registers are considered in the current implementation. We have made provision for the use of APML [6] to tag utterances that are intended to convey particular affective or emotional colouring.

Finally MINTGEN also has a *multi-lingual* capability. We currently generate from the abstracted semantic constructs used by the system's DM into two target languages: English and Irish, whose sentence structure and vocabulary are markedly different from each other [7] – a good test of the abstracted representations.

4   System Architecture

4.1 Description of Mini-templates

When the conversational context changes, the NLG component has to provide the building blocks to cope with the change. Templates are broken down into fine-grained structures or 'mini-templates'. These mini-templates are references to phrasal fragments consisting of one or more words and come from either the Domain Terms Class hierarchy (4.2) where they realise a concept associated with the domain or the Speech Act hierarchy (4.4) in which case they are classified as being a phrase, statement, verb or question. See 4.5 for an example of the mini-templates selected by the sentence planning part of the module and a step through of how they are realised based on the request from the Dialogue Manager.

By providing slots for specific data input from the user, these reusable mini-templates provide a more adaptable and precise sentence than would be possible with conventional larger templates. If a new form of utterance is to be added, the system is extended with new mini-templates.

The template required to present n options to a user, and to ask them to choose one, is defined by the generic mini-templates [QuestionDesire] from the Speech Act hierarchy and [DomainVerb] from the Domain Terms Class hierarchy, taking the form:

```
{QDesire.register}{domain.Verb}O_1...O_n
```

where each option (O_x) enters the NLG module as an input parameter passed from the DM. If, for example, the choice is between some hotels, then the options will be hotel names and specialized domain terms relating to hotels (e.g. 'stay at' being the verb for the hotel domain) will be used in the mini-templates. This eventually results in a generated phrase such as: 'Do you want to stay at The Europa, The Hilton or The Ramada?'

4.2 Domain Terms Class Hierarchy

For the cross-domain NLG task, we have identified five domains in the context of a notional City Information Service. The domains in this instance are Accommodation, Transport, Entertainment, Places to Visit and Places to Eat. Inheritance enables us to capture cross-domain similarities, and divide high-level domains into more specialized sub-domains, as shown in the inheritance fragment in Figure 1. Each of these domains and sub-domains comprises sets of domain terms, in the appropriate language and register, which can be used with the corresponding domain-specific mini-templates.

A top-level Domain Terms class encapsulates the high level terminology necessary to describe concepts – e.g. cost, start time, end time, duration, location, number, name, etc. – within each of the modelled domains.

Similarly, properties of the Transport Class, a subclass of Domain Terms, are inherited by each more specialized Transport class. However, some of the properties are overridden. Consider the generic, top-level concept of cost. This becomes cost/stay when in the Accommodation domain, or cost/journey in the Transport domain. Cost/stay can be further specialized to the domain-specific concept of price/night for a Hotel or price/week for an Apartment. This hierarchy of Domain Terms classes along with their associated properties and inheritance relationships determines the structure of the Domain Terms Store (DTS - See 4.5.f) The DTS contains the lexical information that enables the system to realize utterances in each of its domains. The DTS is stored as a database with each domain being a record which comprises its superdomain (the domain one level hierarchically above) and the potential to represent all generally applicable concepts. A blank entry denotes that the value is the same as that of its superdomain, which itself is also a record.

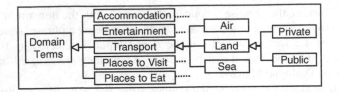

Fig. 1. Domain Terms Class Hierarchy

This lack of certain entries results in sparse database tables, a distinct advantage for system maintenance. A measure of this 'sparsity' has been taken (See 4.3). Domain-specific tables with additional concepts also exist and a similar process is in operation.

4.3 Domain Terms Store Sparsity

There are 9 main concepts in the Domain Terms Store which are applicable to all domains. There are 54 records in the store representing all of the domains and super-domains. This would result in 486 concept values in a densely populated store. However, by taking advantage of the repeated entries in the store which indicate the generic concepts that are inheritable down through the domains, we created a sparsely populated store, where values only need to be introduced at the level at which they are specialized – i.e. the presence of a value denotes that the corresponding value from its superdomain is overwritten. Table 1 lists for each of the 9 concepts the number of values which are present in the sparse store (maximum of 54), the number of those values that are unique and a percentage measurement of how populated the sparse store is in comparison to the densely populated one.

For the English Domain Term Store, there are 146 values represented out of a potential 486. This represents a 30% populated table i.e. - 70% of the values are inherited and thus do not need to be duplicated. Since the concept of location is almost always unique (41 times out of 54), if it is ignored, the sparsity improves, as there are 105 values out of a potential 432, resulting in a density of 24%, a great reduction in the information required.

Table 1. Number of Concept Values in Sparse Table

Concept	No. of Values	No. of Unique Values	Sparsity (No.Values/54)
People	10	6	19%
Start Time	14	8	26%
End Time	12	8	22%
Location	41	39	76%
Duration Concept	19	15	35%
Duration Unit	10	5	19%
Cost Concept	20	15	37%
Cost Unit	10	9	19%
Domain Verb	10	10	19%
TOTAL	146	115	30 %

This sparse approach to representing concepts that apply to the Domain Terms means that if a new domain is added to the system, it needs to know what its super-domain is (i.e. the category into which it falls and whose properties it shares with other members of that domain). The new domain automatically inherits these properties unless the developer specifically overrides them. This shows the commonality between the domains and demonstrates that an object-based approach using generic objects is an appropriate model for the NLG module.

4.4 Speech Act Definition and Hierarchy

The speech act hierarchy defines the interface for the NLG module by describing the semantic input constructs. It defines the range of utterances that the system is expected to realize.

The NLG system makes use of three main *Speech Acts* that are basic to the City Information task:

- *Statements*: conversational system utterances not requiring a response e.g. greeting, thanks, goodbye ...
- *Information Request*: the system elicits information from the user e.g. desire, number, location, duration ...
- *Information Provision*: the system provides the user with information e.g. existence, distance, closing time ...

The speech act hierarchy is refined to a level of specialization that corresponds with the top-level concepts in the Domain Terms hierarchy. Once the speech act is formulated, the appropriate specialized term is selected from the Domain Terms hierarchy – e.g. a 'start-time' Information Request causes a phrase to be generated that asks about arrival time in the Accommodation domain, departure time in the Transport domain and opening time in the Entertainment domain. See Figure 2 for a snapshot of the speech act hierarchy.

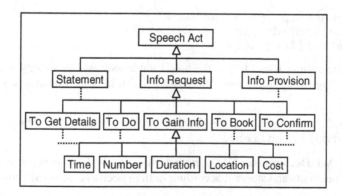

Fig. 2. Speech Act Hierarchy

The speech act hierarchy influences the basic structure of the Template Object Store (TOS – see 4.5.d) by providing a framework around which various generalised and more specific mini-templates can be defined. Sibling templates in alternative registers and languages are also stored in the TOS. The Sentence Planner (4.5.c) selects the appropriate templates from the TOS according to the speech act, domain, register and language specified by the DM.

4.5 Components

The language generation module itself consists of seven units which are supported by two stores of information. This section outlines realisation of the module output for a given Dialogue Manager request.

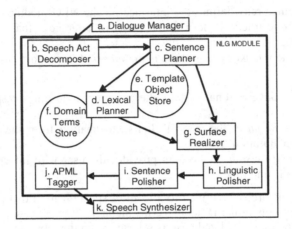

Fig. 3. Components of NLG System

a. **Dialogue Manager (DM)** – decides on abstracted semantic input constructs and passes them on to the NLG module in the form of:

```
[speechAct][purpose][actName]
[specialism][domain][parameters]
[register][language]
```

e.g. if the system wants to ask the how long a user wishes to stay at a hotel in a normal English register, the DM passes the following constructs to the NLG module:

DM: [info_request][gain_info][duration][-][hotel]
[-][normal][•nglish]

b. **Speech Act Decomposer (D)** – extracts the required information from the DM input constructs and stores it according to the specification in (a) above.

c. **Sentence Planner (SP)** – decides on the mini-templates (represented by entries within { }) that are to be selected from the TOS and the order in which they will be realised, e.g. For the DM's request in *a* above the SP decides that the following sequence of generic mini-templates is sufficient to realize the speech act:

```
SP:Eng[{Qnumber.register}{domain.durationUnit(plural)}
{Qdesire.register}{domain.domainVerb(infinitive)}
{domain.definite}]
```
SP passes any parameters to the SR along with the mini- template sequence. Any components that the SR cannot realize are passed first to the LP by the SP.

d. **Lexical Planner (LP)** – decides upon and retrieves the actual words to be generated from the DTS and TOS e.g.
   ```
   LP retrieves {Qnumber.english.normal} and
   {Qdesire.english.normal} from the TOS, and
   {hotel.english.durationUnit(plural)} and
   {hotel.english.domainVerb (infinitive)} from the DTS.
   ```

e. **Template Object Store (TOS)** – a collection of speech act objects in the form of mini-templates arranged in hierarchical structure to support the SP.
   ```
   TOS stores {how many} and {do you want} for the English, normal ver
   ```
   sions of {Qnumber} and {Qdesire}.

f. **Domain Terms Store (DTS)** – a collection of instantiated domain objects with the appropriately refined terms for each domain member. The DTS supports the Sentence Planner, Lexical Planner and the Surface Realizer. For

   ```
   {hotel.english.durationUnit(plural)} and
   {hotel.english.domainVerb (infinitive)},
   ```

   the DTS returns {night} and {stay at} respectively. It is the LIP that later deals with the plural and infinitive versions of these phrases.

g. **Surface Realizer (SR)** – realizes NL form of templates and words by combining output from SP and LP
   ```
   SR: How many night (plural) do you want
   stay at (infinitive) hotel (definite)?
   ```

h. **Linguistic Polisher (LIP)** – deals with language specific elements e.g. plurals, agreements, masc./fem. Etc., so {night (plural)} becomes 'nights', {stay at (infinitive)} becomes 'to stay at'
   and {hotel (definite)} becomes 'the hotel',
   thus resulting in the desired sentence:
   ```
   LIP: How many nights do you want to stay at the hotel?
   ```

i. **Sentence Polisher (SEP)** – searches for and rectifies any grammatical issues which affect the whole sentence e.g. certain word combinations. SEP does not detect any further polishing to be done with this particular sentence.

j. **APML Tagger** – has the ability to apply affective mark-up to the sentence to be uttered based on speech acts and concepts in the input specification. After several misunderstood repetitions, the APML tagging can change to emphasise an element.

k. **Speech Synthesizer** – takes the well-formed sentence output from the NLG module and the APML tagging along with any other realisation mark-up and voices the utterance.

In order to demonstrate the multi-context capabilities of MINTGEN, Table 2 parts (i) to (iv) in the Appendix to this paper give examples of the output of each system component – from the DM's request constructs through to full sentence realization. Changing just one of the DM's request constructs (e.g. the construct representing register or language or domain) significantly alters the resulting generation, thus demonstrating the multi-register, multi-lingual and cross-domain capabilities of the system.

5 Conclusion

The NLG module MINTGEN as described in this paper has been designed and implemented using an object-based approach. Examining the commonality and differences in the objects included in the system has allowed us to take advantage of object-orientation to develop a sparse repository of well-defined components, representing terms specific to each domain and terms required for more general speech acts. Identifying commonality amongst terms relating to domains has led to a 70% reduction in the number of values required by the system (Table 1). By standardising the descriptors for the semantic input constructs, we have removed part of the complexity of NLG. Already, using easily changed descriptor values, the NLG module can output in different registers and languages and across different domains (Table 2). This flexibility of output was a primary motivation of our research.

A recently conducted evaluation of the system, involving non-specialist end users and developer users, has proved very encouraging. We hope to collate and publish our results in the near future. Evaluation of the system has focussed on real-world usability, and two aspects of this in particular. Firstly, in the case of non-specialist end users, we have assessed the perceived appropriateness and quality of the words used in the system utterances. Secondly, in order to explore issues of maintainability and extensibility, we have tested the ability of novice developers to work with our utterance descriptors, including their ability to introduce new types of utterance, which, while exploiting some existing domain terms, involve the creation of new mini-templates.

Taking into account the results of evaluation and testing of the current MINTGEN system, future plans include a broadening of the system's vocabulary alongside an optimized range of mini-templates and Domain Terms objects for selected application domains.

Object-orientation is a well-established software design technique. However, the degree to which it may assist development of a cross-domain, multi-register, multi-lingual NLG system is, we believe, worthy of on-going investigation.

References

1. Poggi, I., et al.: Greta. A Believable Embodied Conversational Agent. In: Intelligent Information Presentation. Kluwer Academic, Dordrecht (2003)
2. HUMAINE website, http://emotion-research.net/
3. Cole, R.A., et al.: Survey of the State of the Art in Human Language Technology. In: Language Generation, Ch. 4, CSLU, Oregon (1995)
4. Kasper, R.T.: A Flexible Interface for Linking Applications to Penman's Sentence Generator. In: Proceedings of the DARPA Speech and Natural Language Workshop, Philadelphia (1989)
5. O'Neill, I.M., et al.: The Queen's Communicator: An Object-Oriented Dialogue Manager. In: Proceedings of Eurospeech 2003, Geneva, pp. 593–596 (2003)
6. De Carolis, B., et al.: APML, A Mark-Up Language for Believable Behaviour Generation. In: Proceedings of AAMAS Workshop, Bologna (2002)
7. Carnie, A.: Flat Structure, Phrasal Variability and Non-Verbal Predication in Irish. In: Celtic Linguistics, Galway (2005)

Appendix: Tables of Sample Outputs from the System Components

Table 2(i). English *normal* generation for 'How many nights do you want to stay at the hotel?' This table corresponds to the DM request processing that was examined step-by-step in Section 4.5

DM	`[info_request][gain_info][duration][-]` `[hotel][-][normal][•nglish]`
SP	`Eng[{Qnumber.register}{domain.durationUnit` `(plural)}{Qdesire.register}{domain.domain` `Verb(infinitive)}{domain.definite}]`
LP	`EngNorm[{QNumber}{hotel.durationUnit` `(plural)}{QDesire}{hotel.domainVerb` `(infinitive)}{hotel.definite}}]`
TOS	`{how many} for {QNumber.english.normal}` `{do you want} for {QDesire.english.normal}`
DTS	`{night} for {hotel.english.durationUnit}` `{stay at} for {hotel.english.normal.` `domainVerb}`
SR	`{how many}{night (plural)}{do you` `want}{stay at (infinitive)}{hotel` `(definite)}`
LIP	`{nights} for {night (plural)}{to stay at}` `for {stay at (infinitive)}{the hotel} for` `{hotel (definite)}`
SEP	–
NLG	`how many nights do you want to stay at the` `hotel`

Table 2(ii). English *formal* generation of the 'hotel' request – a *register* change from the request in the previous table

DM	[info_request][gain_info][duration] [-][hotel][-]**[formal]**[english]
SP	Eng[{QNumber.register}{domain.durationUnit (plural)}{QDesire.register}{domain.domain Verb(infinitive)}{domain.definite}]
LP	EngForm[{QNumber}{hotel.durationUnit(plural)} {QDesire}{hotel.domainVerb(infinitive)} {hotel.definite}}]
TOS	{for how many}for{QNumber.english.formal} {does one wish}for{QDesire.english. formal}
DTS	{night} for{hotel.english.durationUnit} {be accommodated at} for {hotel.english.formal.domainVerb}
SR	{for how many}{night (plural)}{does one wish}{be accommodated at (infinitive)}{hotel (definite)}
LIP	{nights} for {night (plural)}{to be accommodated at} for {be accommodated at (infinitive)}{the hotel} for {hotel (definite)}
SEP	–
NLG	for how many nights does one wish to be accommodated at the hotel

Table 2(iii). *Irish* normal generation of the 'hotel' request – a *language* change

DM	[info_request][gain_info][duration][-] [hotel][-][normal]**[irish]**
SP	Ir[{QNumber.register}{domain.durationUnit} {Qdesire.register}{domain.domainVerb (infinitive)}{domain.verbLinkWord} {domain.definite}]
LP	IrishNorm[{Qnumber}{hotel.durationUnit} {Qdesire}{hotel.domainVerb(infinitive)} {hotel.verbLinkWord}{hotel.definite}}]
TOS	{cé mhéad} for {Qnumber.irish.normal} {ar mhaith leat} for {Qdesire.irish.normal}
DTS	{oíche} for {hotel.irish.durationUnit} {stop} for {hotel.irish.normal.domainVerb} {i} for {hotel.irish.normal.verbLinkWord}

Table 2(iii). (*Continued*)

SR	{cé mhéad}{oíche}{ar mhaith leat}{stop (infinitive)}{i}{ostán(definite)}
LIP	{stopadh} for {stop (infinitive)} {an ostán} for { ostán (definite)}
SEP	{san} for {i}{an}
NLG	Cé mhéad oíche ar mhaith leat stopadh san ostán

Table 2(iv). English normal generation for a '*car*' request, which other than the domain change from hotel to car, is equivalent to the initial 'hotel' request

DM	[info_request][gain_info][duration][-] **[car]**[-][normal][English]
SP	Eng[{QNumber.register}{domain.durationUnit (pl)}{QDesire.register}{domain.domainVerb (infinitive)}{domain.definite}]
LP	EngNorm[{QNumber}{car.durationUnit(plural)} {QDesire}{car.domainVerb(infinitive)} {car.definite}}]
TOS	{how many} for {QNumber.english.normal} {do you want} for {QDesire.english.normal}
DTS	{day} for {car.english.durationUnit} {hire} for {car.english.normal.domainVerb}
SR	{how many}{day (plural)}{do you want} {hire(infinitive)}{car(definite)}
LIP	{days} for {day (plural)}{to hire} for {hire (infinitive)}{the car} for {car (definite)}
SEP	-
NLG	how many days do you want to hire the car

A Measure of the Number of True Analogies between Chunks in Japanese

Yves Lepage, Julien Migeot, and Erwan Guillerm

GREYC, University of Caen Basse-Normandie, France
Yves.Lepage@info.unicaen.fr
http://users.info.unicaen.fr/~ylepage/

Abstract. This study relates to the assessment of the argument of the poverty of the stimulus in that we conducted a measure of the number of true proportional analogies between chunks in a language with case markers, Japanese. On a bicorpus of 20,000 sentences, we show that at least 96% of the analogies of form between chunks are also analogies of meaning, thus reporting the presence of at least two million true analogies between chunks in this corpus. As the number of analogies between chunks overwhelmingly surpasses the number of analogies between sentences by three orders of magnitude for this size of corpora, we conclude that proportional analogy is an efficient and undeniable structuring device between Japanese chunks.

Keywords: Chunks, Japanese language, true analogies, structure of language.

1 Introduction

Proportional analogy is a general relationship between four objects, four pieces of language in this study, A, B, C and D, that states that 'A is to B as C is to D'. The standard notation is $A : B :: C : D$. For instance, one can write the following proportional analogies between words (1), sentences (2) or chunks (3):

$$\text{unrelated : relate :: unmodulated : modulate} \tag{1}$$

$$\begin{array}{l}\text{Do you like . Do you go to .. Do \quad you \quad like . Do you go to classi-}\\ \text{music? \qquad . concerts often? .. classical music? . cal concerts often?}\end{array} \tag{2}$$

$$\text{my room key : the room key :: my first visit : the first visit} \tag{3}$$

The three previous analogies are valid in form and in meaning. For this reason, they are called true analogies. But it is not always the case that analogies of form are also analogies of meaning, nor that some solutions of formal analogies conform to the rules of the language considered:

$$\text{walk : I walked :: go : *I goed} \tag{4}$$

$$\text{sketch : sketches :: part of speech : *part of speeches [1]} \tag{5}$$

___
[1] Sometimes heard at international conferences on natural language processing!

Z. Vetulani and H. Uszkoreit (Eds.): LTC 2007, LNAI 5603, pp. 154–164, 2009.

Recently, a number of works in natural language processing make use of proportional analogies. Turney and Littman [1] show the use of different machine techniques to answer SAT tests (analogical puzzles on words) with scores comparable to those of a human being; Turney [2] extends and simplifies the previous techniques to propose a uniform approach to synonyms, antonyms, and word associations, through analogies, an approach that could extend to hypernyms/hyponyms, holonyms, *etc.*; Stroppa and Yvon [3] show the application of analogy to morphological analysis in three different languages with results comparable or higher to that of another proposed technique; Claveau and L'Homme [4] show how to guess the meaning of unknown terms using analogical proportions; Lepage and Denoual [5] use proportional analogies to translate sentences in a system that compares well with state-of-the-art machine translation systems; Langlais and Patry [6] propose to specialize the previous technique to translate unknown words.

In linguistics, proportional analogy depreciated at the birth of historical linguistics in the 19th century when phonetic laws were considered the only scientific objects worth studying. In this respect, Anttila's book entitled *Analogy* [7] is a virulent defense of the notion with linguistic change as its main perspective. Still, until now, some linguists doubt the value of analogy because of the controversial argument of the poverty of the stimulus which claims that there would be no inductive device like analogy in language acquisition because (1) young children produce sentential structures they have never heard before and (2) young children never produce some ungrammatical structures.

The purpose of this paper is to make an experimental contribution to the discussion of the argument of the poverty of the stimulus, by inspecting the reality of true analogies in syntax. Hence, we shall question the reality, estimate the amount and assess the truth of analogies between chunks. This obviously relates to the usefulness of analogy in terms of linguistic performance, and in terms of language acquisition.

The rest of the article is organised as follows. Section 2 briefly sets the scene for the argument of the poverty of the stimulus to justify the purpose of the measure conducted here. Section 3 illustrates the notion of true analogy by examples. Section 4 describes the experimental protocol used and gives details about a formal definition of analogy, the method used for chunking and, statistical tests. The results are summarized and analyzed in Sections 5 and 6.

2   The Argument of the Poverty of the Stimulus

The argument of the poverty of the stimulus is a controversial argument in the study of language and mind (see volume 19 of the Linguistic Review: [8], [9], [10]). It assumes that the information in the environment would not be rich enough to allow a human learner to attain adult competence in his/her native language. More precisely, the argument is based on the controversed fact that young children would produce some sentential structures they would have never heard before. In addition, according to the proponents of the argument of the poverty of the stimulus, if some sentential structures would be derived by an induction device like analogy, then, children would also derive ungrammatical structures which, accordingly to the proponents of this argument, they never utter.

A representative example of such a structure is auxiliary fronting in interrogative sentences that involve a relative clause. Positing analogy as the induction device in language acquisition would imply that children would indifferently produce the following sentence:

Is the student who is in the garden hungry?

the structure of which they have never heard before, but also the following sentence that they, supposedly, never produce:

*Is the student who in the garden is hungry?

The two previous sentences would be possible utterances because both sentences are valid formal solutions to the following analogical equation built from sentences that children may well have heard before:

$$\frac{\text{The student in the}}{\text{garden is hungry.}} : \frac{\text{Is the student in the}}{\text{garden hungry?}} :: \frac{\text{The student who is in}}{\text{the garden is hungry.}} : x$$

Against the hypothesis that children would have never heard the structure in question, Pullum and Scholtz [8] showed that this structure does actually appear in books for children and in the CHILDES corpus and support some of their claims with counting from corpora. Legate and Yang [9] however disagree with the significance of these countings, to which Scholtz and Pullum [10] answer that in matter of analogy, rare events do count, and that the set of examples should be extended to consider all sentences involving relative clauses. The debate is still open.

Also, the argument partly relies on the assumption that children would learn exclusively by positive examples, an hypothesis objected by Chouinard and Clark in [11], where it is shown that children between the age of two and three and a half do produce ungrammatical sentences, that adults do correct them, and that children do repeat the corrected utterances in 50 to 60% of the cases, which indicates that children understand correction, and consequently, that they can memorize pairs of negative and positive examples.

Despite all these pieces of evidence, Pullum, a defender of analogy, still acknowledges the fact that analogy cannot overlook some grammatical boundaries without the risk of producing meaningless utterances, as shown with his example [12]:

white skirt : green blouse

::

| Often commentators who are white skirt the problem of institutional racism. | : | *Often commentators who are green blouse the problem of institutional racism. |

3   Goal of the Study and True Analogies

The purpose of this study is to give support to the proponents of analogy in syntax, by testing the reality of proportional analogies between the most elementary grammatical units, i.e., chunks, in a given language. The way we achieved this is by gathering all possible analogies of form between chunks extracted from a corpus and by estimating the number of true analogies.

True analogies are proportional analogies which are valid on the level of form and that are meaningful. They are best illustrated in declension and conjugation where they explain paradigms. For instance:

> to walk : I walked :: to laugh : I laughed

Conversely, misleading analogies of form which are not analogies of meaning have been illustrated by Chomsky's famous example in syntax:[2]

$$
\frac{\text{Abby is baking}}{\text{vegan pies.}} : \text{Abby is baking.} :: \frac{\text{Abby is too tasteful}}{\text{to pour gravy on vegan pies.}} : \frac{\text{Abby is too tasteful}}{\text{to pour gravy on.}}
$$

Analogies of meaning which are not supported by an analogy of form are illustrated with the following example:[3]

> I drink. : I'd like to drink. :: I can swim. : I'd like to be able to swim.

4   Experimental Protocol

As a logical consequence of what has been said above, a counting of true analogies between chunks on a real corpus can adopt the following steps where all steps can be performed automatically, except for Step 4 where human intervention is required.

1. chunk the texts;
2. gather, by machine, all analogies of form;
3. sample the set of analogies of form if it is too big;
4. filter, with the help of a human annotator, the analogies of form contained in the sample that are true analogies;
5. apply a statistical test to estimate the proportion of true analogies on the entire collection of all analogies of form.

---

[2] *Noam Chomsky, Conference at the university of Michigan,* 1998, a report by Aaron Stark. In the third sentence, gravy is poured on the vegan pies whereas it is poured on Abby in the fourth sentence. Hence, the difference in structure between sentences 3 and 4 is not parallel to the one between 1 and 2.

[3] The sentence '*I'd like to can swim.' is ungrammatical.

The data used are from the machine evaluation campaign IWSLT 2005 [13]. They consist in 20,000 sentences in Japanese. Some statistics on sizes in characters and words are to be found in Table 1.

4.1 Step 1. Chunking

Chunking is the process by which a sentence is divided into chunks. There exists a standard chunker for Japanese, YamCha [14], but already chunked training data are required in order to feed a training phase. Firstly, we did not have any extra data at our disposal, and, secondly, part of our interest in this study resided in testing another standard approach to chunking for languages like Japanese. Indeed, Japanese is a language with cases markers, a closed set of words (or morphemes) appearing at the end of chunks (called *bunsetsus* in Japanese grammar). For instance, in the following transcribed Japanese excerpt from our data (translation: 'usually on business, seldom for pleasure'), the words in uppercase are such case markers.

> [*taitei shigoto DE*] [*metta NI*] [*asobi DE WA*]
> [often FOR work] [seldomLY] [FOR pleasure]

To determine the markers we finally used, we started with 16 well identified nominal case markers (9), verbal endings (5) and punctuations (2). The most productive ones in terms of number of analogies were automatically selected using a hill-climbing method on a sampling of 3,500 sentences from our data. The 11 most productive markers for which we observed significant increase until a plateau are, in this order, the two punctuation marks, 8 nominal case markers and only one verbal ending[4].

4.2 Step 2. Gathering Analogies of Form

The next problem is to extract all possible analogies between the elements of a corpus, be the elements sentences or chunks. From the program point of view, the elements are just strings of characters, whatever the character set, the Latin alphabet or the Japanese kanji-kana character set.

To leave out trivial cases of analogies, the implemented program inspects only analogies of the type $A : B :: C : D$ where the character strings A, B, C and D are all different.

The formalization of proportional analogies of form adopted here follows the simpler proposal in [15] rather than the more complex form of [16] or other proposals in terms of automata like [3]. From the programming point of view, this formalization reduces to the counting of number of symbol occurrences and the computation of edit distances. Precisely:

---

[4] The punctuations are the symbols corresponding to fullstop and comma. The next nominal case markers are *no* (genitive), *de* (instrumental or location), *e* (direction), *ni* (dative or location), *wo* (accusative, i.e., object), *wa* (topic), *ga* (subject), *kara* (origin). The verbal ending is, surprisingly, the past ending *-masita*.

$$A : B :: C : D \; \Rightarrow \; \begin{cases} \mid A \mid_a - \mid B \mid_a = \mid C \mid_a - \mid D \mid_a, \forall a \\ \\ \mathrm{dist}(A, B) = \mathrm{dist}(A, C) \end{cases}$$

where $\mid A \mid_a$ stands for the number of occurrences of character a in string A and $\mathrm{dist}(A, B)$ is the edit distance between strings A and B with only insertion and deletion as edit operations. As B and C may be exchanged in an analogy, the constraint on edit distance has also to be verified for $A : C :: B : D$, i.e. $\mathrm{dist}(A, C) = \mathrm{dist}(B, D)$. There is no need to verify the first constraint as, trivially, $|A|_a - |B|_a = |C|_a - |D|_a \Leftrightarrow |A|_a - |C|_a = |B|_a - |D|_a$.

A naïve approach of the computation of all possible analogies between the N elements of a corpus would examine all possible 4-tuples and would thus be in $O(N^4)$, an asymptotic behaviour that is simple unaffordable for the size of the corpus we work with: nearly a hundred thousand chunks.

The above formalization allows us to exploit the sparseness of the search space by first looking for those 4-tuples (A, B, C, D) such that $|A|_a - |B|_a = |C|_a - |D|_a$, as it is tantamount to look inside different sets of pairs (A, B) such that $|A|_a - |B|_a = n_a$ for all possible values of vectors (n_a) where a scans the character set. By sorting the vectors in lexicographic order and in decreasing order of the numerical values, one may incrementally inspect relevant pairs only. For these relevant pairs with the same vector value, one can, in the last instance, evaluate the truth of $\mathrm{dist}(A, B) = \mathrm{dist}(C, D)$ and then $\mathrm{dist}(A, C) = \mathrm{dist}(B, D)$.

The use of bit representation techniques, even for distance computation as proposed by Allison and Dix in [17], yields tractable computational times. We were able to gather all analogies from more than thirty thousand chunks in less than five hours on a 2.16 GHz processor (the size of the search space being theoretically of 10^{20}!).

4.3   Steps 3., 4. and 5. Sampling, Filtering and Testing

As the number of analogies of form automatically gathered is untractable by hand, we had to sample them. Each analogy in the sample was then presented to an annotator whose task was to estimate its validity in meaning so as to establish the truth of the analogy, i.e., its validity in form and meaning.

This task was carried out using a browser interface. Each analogy is presented to the annotator one after another and the annotator has to check a radio box to invalidate an analogy as being a true analogy before going to the next analogy of form. At the end of the task, a summary presents the annotator with a number of pieces of information: the p-value for the null-hypothesis, 5 examples of true analogies and 5 examples (if possible) of analogies of form that were not considered analogies on the level of meaning.

As there are only two issues in this experiment – an analogy may be true or false – we applied a binomial test to test a null hypothesis of 96% of the analogies being true analogies. This figure of 96% comes from Lepage [15] who reported it for a collection of 160,000 short sentences in Chinese, English and Japanese.

5   Results

5.1   Chunking

Coming back to chunking (Step 1), the total number of chunks that we observed is of around 5 chunks in average in the number of sentences considered for different number of sentences. On the whole, 99,719 chunks were obtained for 20,000 sentences in total. The figures for the number of different sentences and the number of different chunks are given in Table 1.

5.2   Counting Analogies of Form

As for gathering analogies of form (Step 2), the graph on the left of Fig. 1 plots the number of analogies between sentences against the number of sentences. Until 2,500 sentences, no analogies are found. After this value, the increase looks at least polynomial.

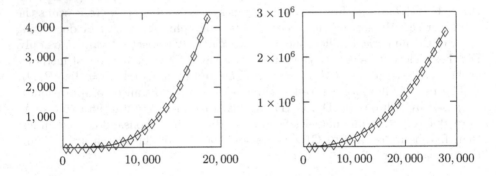

Fig. 1. Number of analogies (in ordinates) against the number of different sentences (on the left) or different chunks (on the right). Average figures obtained over thirty different samplings. Caution: the ordinate scale is a different order of magnitude in both graphs. The curve on the right grows thousand times faster that the one on the left. The number of analogies between different sentences can be aproximated as the number of sentences to the power of 3.60, times 1.93 ($y = 1.93 \times x^{3.60}$).

On the right of the same figure, the number of analogies between chunks has been plotted against the number of chunks (the chunks being gradually obtained from the sentences).

Notice that the ordinate scales of the two graphs in Fig. 1 differ by an order of 3 digits: 4,342 analogies only between 18,454 different sentences; 2,566,783 analogies between the 27,936 different chunks obtained from these very 18,454 different sentences.

The graph in Fig. 2 plots the number of analogies between different chunks in ordinates, against the number of analogies between different sentences in abscissae (the chunks coming only from the corresponding sentences). The graph is

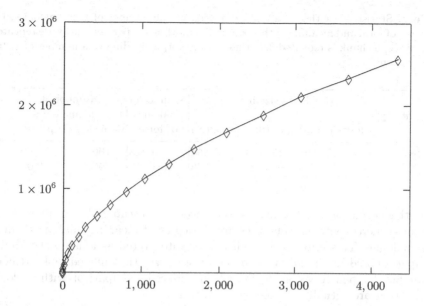

Fig. 2. Number of analogies between chunks in abscissae, number of analogies between sentences in ordinates. Caution: the ordinate scale is three orders of magnitude the scale of the abscissae. Average figures obtained over thirty different samplings.

delusive as it is drawn here: the number of analogies between chunks is roughly thousand times larger than the corresponding number of analogies between sentences. If the actual proportion between scales were respected, the graph would almost look like a vertical line.

To precisely characterize the increase, we could make the experimental number of analogies between chunks fit well with the number of analogies between sentences taken to the power of 0.575, times 20,555 ($y = 20,555 \times x^{0.575}$). This was obtained by linear regression.[5] A theoretical interpretation of this law is that the number of analogies between different sentences can be expected to exceed the number of analogies between different chunks only for more than one million different sentences. Exactly: the number of analogies between chunks equals the number of analogies between sentences for $20,555^{1/(1-0.575)} = 20,555^{1/0.425} = 20,555^{2.35} = 13,657,024,252$, which would correspond to roughly 1,140,892 different sentences according to the law given in the caption of Fig. 1.

5.3 Estimating the Percentage of True Analogies

The two final figures, that were the actual goal of this study, are the percentage of true analogies observed on a few samples of 100 analogies. They are given in the right column in Table 1.

---

[5] If y is the number of analogies between chunks and x the number of analogies between sentences, $y = b \times x^a \Rightarrow \log y = a \times \log x + \log b$. Linear regression can then be applied with $X = \log x$ and $Y = \log y$ to obtain a and $\log b$.

Table 1. Statistics for the data and estimation of the number of true analogies, i.e., analogies of form and meaning with a 96% null hypothesis. 1,646 sentences are repeated. On average, a chunk is repeated 3.76 times in the corpus leading to a number of 27,936 different chunks.

Data type	Data size in			Number of analogies of form	Number of true analogies	
	units (total)	words	units ($\neq$)		% observed	p-value
Sentences	20,000	173,091	18,454	4,428	100%	n.r.
Chunks	99,719	693,526	27,936	2,131,269	96%	0.005

On this corpus of 20,000 Japanese sentences, it is estimated that all analogies of form gathered between sentences are analogies of meaning, making them all true analogies. This important result can be interpreted as follows: the kind of examples quoted in Section 3 (Abby and the gravy) that indeed look artificial, may in fact happen very scarcely in real utterances in comparison with analogies of form that are actually analogies of meaning.

As for chunks, the null hypothesis of 96% true analogies has been verified. Only a few analogies of form have been judged invalid in meaning. As has already been mentioned, with our data, the number of analogies of form between chunks is enormous in comparison with the number of sentences, and the result of 96% true analogies should be considered bearing this explosion in mind. In absolute figures, our estimate of at least 96% of the analogies of form being true analogies yields an absolute figure of at least two million true analogies between chunks (precisely: $2,566,783 \times 96\% = 2,464,112$) for nearly thirty thousand chunks (precisely: 27,936). A possible interpretation is that, in average, each chunk takes part in 88 true analogies.

6   Analysis of the Results and Conclusion

In this paper, we addressed the problem of the reality, the amount and the truth of analogies between chunks contained in a Japanese corpus.

The amount of analogies gathered and the estimation of the number of true analogies obtained, i.e., analogies of form and meaning, establish in an undeniable manner the reality of proportional analogies.

As for the amount of analogies of form, we have shown on our data that their number between chunks is much higher than that between sentences. We obtained more than two million analogies of form between chunks extracted from a corpus of 20,000 short sentences, each sentence containing an average of five chunks. As for their truth, we estimated that more than 96% of the analogies of form are true analogies. These figures are in blatant contradiction with the opinion that analogies of form would almost necessarily lead to nonsense and would have weak connection with meaning.

The results obtained here are promising because they show that analogies can be exploited in natural language processing applications at a higher level than the ordinary level of words as in [3], or the level of terms as in [4]. On the other hand, our comparison of sentences with chunks has shown that, on our data, the number of analogies between chunks are a thousand times more numerous than analogies between those sentences containing these chunks. A supposition that can be laid is that chunks may be the most productive level for true proportional analogies.

The practical goal of this study is to increase the possibilities and the performance of a machine translation engine that uses analogy as its main operation[5]. It was observed that on a 500 sentences test set to translate the system could only translate half of the sentences by analogy, the other ones being translated by backing off on a translation memory behavior. The main reason is that the system used entire sentences to build analogies. An analysis of the results and preliminary experiments showed that the use of chunks could increase the possibilities, i.e., the number of test sentences translated, and the performance of the system as measured with objective measures like BLEU.

Future work should test whether analogy is a valid device to produce new chunks. The embodiement of the test will be a natural language processing application like the previously mentioned machine translation engine or translation memories where the production of new chunks is required for new data to be translated.

References

1. Turney, P.D., Littman, M.: Corpus-based learning of analogies and semantic relations. Machine Learning 60(1–3), 251–278 (2005)
2. Turney, P.D.: A uniform approach to analogies, synonyms, antonyms, and associations. In: Proceedings of the 22nd International Conference on Computational Linguistics (Coling 2008), Manchester, UK, August 2008, pp. 905–912. Coling 2008 Organizing Committee (2008)
3. Stroppa, N., Yvon, F.: An analogical learner for morphological analysis. In: Proceedings of the 9th Conference on Computational Natural Language Learning (CoNLL 2005), Ann Arbor, MI, June 2005, pp. 120–127 (2005)
4. Claveau, V., L'Homme, M.C.: Terminology by analogy-based machine learning. In: Proceedings of the 7th International Conference on Terminology and Knowledge Engineering (TKE 2005), Copenhagen (2005)
5. Lepage, Y., Denoual, E.: Purest ever example-based machine translation: detailed presentation and assessment. Machine Translation 19, 251–282 (2005), http://dx.doi.org/10.1007/s10590-006-9010-x
6. Langlais, P., Patry, A.: Translating unknown words by analogical learning. In: Proceedings of the 2007 Joint Conference on Empirical Methods in Natural Language Processing and Computational Natural Language Learning (EMNLP-CoNLL), pp. 877–886 (2006)
7. Anttila, R.: Analogy. In: Mouton – Trends in linguistics: state of the art reports 10, The Hague (1977)
8. Pullum, G.K., Scholtz, B.C.: Empirical assessment of stimulus poverty arguments. The Linguistic Review 19, 9–50 (2002)

9. Legate, J.A., Yang, C.D.: Empirical re-assessment of stimulus poverty arguments. The Linguistic Review 19, 151–162 (2002)
10. Scholtz, B.C., Pullum, G.K.: Searching for arguments to support linguistic nativism. The Linguistic Review 19, 185–224 (2002)
11. Chouinard, M.M., Clark, E.E.: Adult reformulations of child errors as negative evidence. Journal of Child Language 30, 637–669 (2003)
12. Pullum, G.K.: Generative grammar, pp. 340–343. The MIT Press, Cambridge (1999)
13. Eck, T., Hori, C.: Overview of the IWSLT 2005 evaluation campaign. In: Carnegie Mellon University (ed.) Proc. of the International Workshop on Spoken Language Translation, pp. 1–22 (2005)
14. Kudo, T., Matsumoto, Y.: Fast methods for kernel-based text analysis. In: Proceedings of ACL 2003, Sapporo, July 2003, pp. 24–31 (2003)
15. Lepage, Y.: Lower and higher estimates of the number of "true analogies" between sentences contained in a large multilingual corpus. In: Proceedings of COLING-2004, Geneva, August 2004, vol. 1, pp. 736–742 (2004)
16. Delhay, A., Miclet, L.: Analogical equations in sequences: Definition and resolution. In: Paliouras, G., Sakakibara, Y. (eds.) ICGI 2004. LNCS (LNAI), vol. 3264, pp. 127–138. Springer, Heidelberg (2004)
17. Allison, L., Dix, T.I.: A bit string longest common subsequence algorithm. Information Processing Letter 23, 305–310 (1986)

Shallow Parsing of Transcribed Speech of Estonian and Disfluency Detection*

Kaili Müürisep[1] and Helen Nigol[2]

[1] University of Tartu, Institute of Computer Science
J. Liivi 2, 50409 Tartu, Estonia
[2] University of Tartu, Institute of Estonian and General Linguistics
Ülikooli 18, 50090 Tartu, Estonia
{kaili.muurisep,helen.nigol}@ut.ee

Abstract. This paper introduces our strategy for adapting a rule based parser of written language to transcribed speech. Special attention has been paid to disfluencies (repairs, repetitions and false starts). A Constraint Grammar based parser was used for shallow syntactic analysis of spoken Estonian. The modification of grammar and additional methods improved the recall from 97.5% to 97.6% and precision from 91.6% to 91.8%. Also, the paper gives a detailed analysis of the types of errors made by the parser while analyzing the corpus of disfluencies.

Keywords: Parsing, Estonian language, spoken language.

1 Introduction

This paper introduces our strategy for adapting a rule based parser of written language to transcribed speech.

We use two types of corpora for our research: the Corpus of Spoken Estonian (1,065,000 words, 1,703 transcripts) contains 100,000 part-of-speech-tagged and manually morphologically disambiguated words [1], the Corpus of Estonian Dialects [2] has a similar size. Our goal is to provide syntactic annotation to the morphologically disambiguated part of the corpora.

Parsing of spontaneous speech is a serious challenge: spoken language has often different vocabulary, it is hard to determine where the sentence starts from and where it ends due to the lack of capitalized letters and punctuation marks. Spontaneous speech is also rich of disfluencies such as partial words, filled pauses (e.g., *uh*, *um*), repetitions, false starts and self-repairs. One type of disfluency that has proven particularly problematic for parsing is speech repairs: when a speaker amends what he is saying mid-sentence or "stretches of wording in which a speaker begins to realize one grammatical plan, but breaks off and either starts a fresh or continues in conformity to a different plan" [3].

---

* This study has been supported by the grant SF0180078s08 from Estonian Ministry of Education and Research.

Z. Vetulani and H. Uszkoreit (Eds.): LTC 2007, LNAI 5603, pp. 165–177, 2009.
© Springer-Verlag Berlin Heidelberg 2009

In this paper, we will focus on the parsing of non-fluent speech using a rule based parser.

The parser for written Estonian [4] is based on Constraint Grammar framework [5]. The CG parser consists of two modules: morphological disambiguator and syntactic parser. In this paper, we presume that the input (transcribed speech) is already morphologically unambiguous and the word forms have been normalized according to their orthographic forms.

The parser gives a shallow surface oriented description to the sentence where every word is annotated with the tag corresponding to its syntactic function (in addition to morphological description). The head and modifiers are not linked directly, only the tag of modifiers indicates the direction where the head may be found.

Figure 1 demonstrates the format and tag set of syntactically annotated sentence. The parser of written text analyzes 88 - 90% of words unambiguously and its error rate is 2% (if the input is morphologically disambiguated and unerroneous). The words which are hard to analyze remain with two or more tags.

```
vat  # so
    vat+0 //_B_ //    @B
see  # this
    see+0 //_P_ dem sg nom //    @SUBJ
on   # is
    ole+0 //_V_ main indic pres ps3 sg ps af #Intr //    @+FMV
hea  # good
    hea+0 //_A_ pos sg nom //    @AN>
pilt # picture
    pilt+0 //_S_ com sg nom //    @PRD
minu # my
    mina+0 //_P_ pers ps1 sg gen //    @NN>
arust # opinion
    aru+st //_S_ com sg el //    @ADVL
```

Fig. 1. Syntactically analyzed utterance 'In my opinion, this is a good picture'. (@SUBJ - subject, @PRD - predicative or complement of the subject, @+FMV - finite main verb, @ADVL - adverbial, @AN>, @NN> - attributes, @B - discourse particle).

The parser is rule based. The grammar consists of 1200 handcrafted rules, described thoroughly in [6]. The grammar rules try to avoid risks, they rather leave the word form ambiguous than remove the correct tag.

We have achieved promising results adapting this parser for spoken language in our previous experiment described in section 2. We have fixed the weakest point in our experiment, namely the limited size of the corpus. For our new experiments, we use different corpora for testing and training the parser and special corpora of disfluencies. The description of the corpora is given in section 3.

Finding the smallest appropriate syntactic unit for parsing is the key issue in automatic analysis of spoken language. The problems handling clause boundaries, false starts and overlaps are discussed in section 4.

The detection of self-repairs and repetitions is essential prior parsing since ungrammatical constructions disturb the analysis of correct parts of utterances. We give an overview of our methodology for discovering repairs and repetitions in section 5. Also, we describe the major error types that still occur in the parsed text and give a preliminary evaluation of the performance of disfluency detector in section 6.

2 Adaption of Existing Parser

The first experiment to adapt the parser of written language to spoken Estonian was made in 2005 [7]. This approach did not pay special attention to disfluencies. The end of dialogue turn was used as the delimiter of utterance. Two additional syntactic tags were added to the tag set of the parser: for discourse particles (based on their morphological information) and for words with unknown syntactic function. To adapt the parser for the spoken language, new rules for the sentence internal clause boundary detection were compiled and some of the syntactic constraints were reformulated, taking into account the specific features of the spoken language.

The outcome of the first experiment revealed that the adaptation of the written language parser for the spoken language is an easier task than initially expected. The efficient detection of clause boundaries became the key issue for successful automatic analysis, while syntactic constraints required only minimal modification. Quite surprisingly, the performance of the parser for the spoken language exceeded its original performance for the written language (which can be due to simpler and shorter clauses of spoken language). The output of the parser was compared with manually annotated corpus (2543 words) and the following results were achieved (the results for parsing the written language are in parentheses):

1. Recall (the ratio of the number of correctly assigned syntactic tags to the number of all correct tags): 97.3% (98.5%).
2. Precision (the ratio of the number of correctly assigned syntactic tags to the number of all assigned syntactic tags): 89.2% (87.5%).

The recall describes the correctness of the analysis and precision illustrates the level of noisiness.

The similar experiments using CG have been made by Eckhard Bick for parsing spoken Portuguese [8]. His parser achieved almost unambiguous output with correctness rate 95 - 96% (automatic morphological disambiguation included).

The grammar for spoken Estonian was easily convertible for the corpus of dialects. We had to modify rules for clause boundary detection again since the transcription of dialects does not contain mark-up of intonations and also the annotation of pauses differs. As the vocabulary of dialects is different, we had to add new entries to the lexical database of pronouns and adpositions.

3   Corpora

3.1   Overview of Corpora

We used morphologically disambiguated texts for the experiments described in this paper. The texts were normalized (vaguely articulated, colloquial or dialect specific words have the description of the corresponding word form in the written language) and provided with some transcription annotation (longer pauses, falling or rising intonation), only the corpus of dialects does not have intonation mark-up.

Our corpora contained both longer narrative dialogues and shorter dialogues where turns alternate swiftly. We used texts of face-to-face everyday conversations, institutional phone calls to travel agencies or information services, one short radio interview and interviews with informants of different dialects.

We divided the corpora into two parts: the training part was used to write new syntactic rules or modify them, the benchmark part was used only for assessment. Table 1 gives the overview of corpora types and sizes. The 'golden standard' of the training and benchmark corpora has been analyzed semiautomatically: the automatic syntactic analysis was corrected by a human expert.

Table 1. Types and sizes of corpora

Corpus	Training	Benchmark
Everyday conversation	8400	6280
Information dialogue	4900	5010
Interview	0	560
Disfluencies	4560	0
Dialects	3450	8280

3.2   The Corpus of Disfluencies

The corpus of disfluencies [9] was compiled from 13,000 words of information dialogues and was used for generating disfluency detection rules. First, it was annotated according to principles of the *Disfluency Annotation Stylebook for the Switchboard Corpus* [10]. During the annotation, the annotator detects the extent of the disfluency and annotates the reparandum and repair, as well as the editing phase. Different tags are used for marking the disfluency: repair - RP, repetition - RE, particle - D, filled pause - F, or non-analyzable unit - X. A false start is marked with '+/'. After the removal of the reparandum and the editing phase, the result should yield a syntactically well-formed utterance, e.g. consider the following example (1).

(1)   a. Original utterance:

meil lihtsalt sellist   nii-öelda süvenemiseks pole
we   simply this kind of so to say to indagate   do not have
eriti   aega
not much time

'simply we do not have such time to such so said to indagate'

b. Annotated utterance: meil lihtsalt [RP sellist + {D nii-öelda} süve-
nemiseks] pole eriti aega

c. Normalized utterance: meil lihtsalt süvenemiseks pole eriti aega
'we simply do not have the time to indagate'

The annotation scheme was applied to an information dialogue subcorpus of
Estonian, part of the Estonian Dialogue Corpus. In Table 2, the occurrence
times of disfluency types are presented.

Based on this corpus of disfluencies, two syntactically annotated corpora were
created. The first corpus was parsed in its original form; the second was parsed
after its normalization. In the first corpus, disfluencies have been annotated as
they were normal parts of the utterance and they had corresponding syntactic
tags. If it was impossible to determine the function of the word in the sentence,
special tag was used - @T (unknown syntactic function). Repetitions were considered as coordinated words.

In Table 3, the gained recall and precision with the preliminary version of the
parser for spoken Estonian [7] are presented. As the morphological disambiguation was made manually, the statistics shows only the syntax problems.

The results indicate a significant improvement in performance. For repairs,
the recall rate rose 0.7% and precision 1.9%. For repetitions, the recall/precision
rose slightly, 0.4% and 1.1% respectively. For false starts, the recall rate rose
1.5% and precision 3.8%. So the detection of disfluencies should improve the
overall performance of the rule-based parser.

Several experiments, for example, [11,12], have showed that parsing performance is increased when disfluencies are removed prior to data-driven parsing.
These results prove that this statement is valid also for rule based parsing.

Table 2. Occurrence of types of disfluencies

Disfluencies		Total
Repairs	Word fragments	53
	Substitutions	50
Repetitions		113
False starts		33
Total		249

Table 3. Results of the experiment (%)

Type of disfluency	Utterances	Recall	Precision
Repairs	original	95.5	85.4
	normalized	96.2	87.3
Repetitions	original	98.2	90.7
	normalized	98.6	91.8
False starts	original	97.4	90.0
	normalized	98.9	93.8

3.3   The Other Corpora

Everyday face-to-face dialogues are very heterogeneous. The situations vary from a chat of two female students to a discussion about a publication of a new popular scientific book by four editors in the cafeteria.

Information dialogues consist of phone calls to travel agencies and information desks. While the utterances of everyday conversations are quite long, the turns in information dialogues are shorter, containing sometimes only isolated phrases or feedback sounds.

The corpus of dialects contains texts from North-East, South, West and Central Estonia. The informants are typically elderly people who talk about the life style and traditions of their childhood. The texts were recorded mainly in 1960-1990. The morphological annotation of these texts had originally different scheme. For this reason, there are slight differencies in annotation principles. Also, the transcription of corpus lacks the annotation of intonation which would be a good lead for finding intrasentential clause boundaries. The questions and remarks of the interviewer have been commented out, only the marks of dialogue turns have been preserved. The dialogue turns are quite long, similar to monologues.

The short radio interview was included to the set of corpora in order to compare the results of parsing dialects and contemporary spoken language.

Table 4 presents the recall and precision of the parser on these corpora without disfluency detection.

Table 4. Recall and precision withoud dislfluency detection

Corpus	Type	Recall	Precision
Everyday conversation	training	97.44	89.50
	test	97.48	91.58
Information dialogues	training	97.00	87.39
	test	96.75	87.35
Interview	test	96.80	88.33
Dialects	training	96.70	87.56
	test	95.59	87.00

4   Clause Boundaries, False Starts and Overlaps

4.1   Intrasentential Clause Boundaries

The inner clause boundaries in the sentence of written language are detected using the conjunction words, punctuation marks and verbs. Parser assigns the tag CLB to the first word of the sentence internal clause. Since the usage of punctuation marks is different in the spoken language transcription, we had to remove original rules and write new ones which are less dependent on punctuation marks. Also the meaning of the clause is different in spoken language. A clause in our interpretation is something like a text chunk which may include a verb but this is not obligatory. For example, a dialog turn (2) is parsed as one unit but the presence of the clause boundary tag allows us write rules which check the context only inside the clause.

> (2)   A: mitte iga   liin see (CLB) sõltub   liinist
>   A: not   every line it   (CLB) depends on line
>
>   'Not every line. It depends on the line.'

False starts with or without a verb are considered as separate chunks but the verbless false starts are very hard to detect. As Estonian has a flexible word order (which is even more flexible in spoken language), we try to predict the border of the clauses by some most common word order patterns (noun in nominative - finite verb or noun in locative cases - finite verb, e.g. (3)). Also, relative pronouns and some proadverbs are potential starts of a clause. Unfortunately, these predictions sometimes lead to an erroneous analysis.

> (3)   mul   (CLB) on   kassetil   (CLB) oleks   ruumipuudus
>   I-SG-AD   be-SG3 tape-SG-AD   be-COND lack of space
>   tekkinud
>   arise-PCP
>
>   'I have — there would be no space on the tape'

A special attention has been paid to particles characterizing spoken language (*noh*, pause fillers *aa*, *ee*, *õõ*). These particles are used as delimiters if there are finite verbs in both left and right context.

As the corpus of dialects misses intonation mark-up, we had to rely more on using pauses as signals of possible clause boundaries. Experiments show that we can not trust shorter pauses and even longer pauses may occur inside a noun phrase. The use of pauses depends a lot on the speaker (or on the transcriber of the speech).

The rules for identification of clause boundaries consider also that direct speech may occur quite often in spoken language or there may be short embedded clauses inside the main clause starting with a second-person verb, e.g. (4).

(4)   aga selle taga   on saad aru   selline lähenemine
       but this behind is understand this   approach
       'this approach is used behind this as you understand'

The grammar for the spoken language consists of 35 clause boundary detection rules, some of them are designed for rather marginal occasions.

In spite of the fact that all the clause boundary detection rules were reformulated the erroneous clause boundaries remain the main source of errors: more than the third of errors in training corpus were caused by wrong or missing clause boundaries.

4.2 Overlaps

Overlaps occur when both speakers are talking at the same time. Overlaps break the utterance. If the overlap is short and lasts all the turn then it is possible to move the overlapping turn from the middle of the utterance to the next turn (see Example 5).

(5)   T: ma 'mõtsin   need on 'õutselt   'mugavad. [(0.8) et=nad]
          I   thought that these are extremely comfortable   that they

       L: [mh] [((naerab))]
          mh   (laugh)

       T: 'niigi   sobivad 'kätte. /.../
          anyway fit   to hand /.../

But sometimes such a short feedback utterance makes the speaker to change his/ her plans and the resulting utterance may not be well-formed (see Example 6).

(6)   M: /.../ ja   kui   me läksime olime   kui püksinööbid   ju
          /.../ and when we went   we were like buttons of trousers

       I: mhmh
          yes-like particle

       M: aint vaatamas
          only looking

       I: mhmh
          yes-like particle

       M: igasugu loomad
          different animals

An experiment to join the different parts of an utterance decreased the correctness of final analysis by 0.2-0.3% and we abandoned that idea.

5   Repetitions and Self-repairs

In order to detect repetitions and self-repairs, we use a grammar-external script which allows for defining patterns with the length of 5 words and also checking the word form, the base form and morphological information of each word.

We detect the following repetitions: a) a single word is repeated in the same form (*mis mis mis sa arvad*), b) a single word is repeated but the form alters (*meil meile meeldib*), c) there is an interrupted word or a particle between repetitions (*sinna ri- sinna rüütli kaubamajja*), or d) two words are repeated in the same form (*kui sa kui sa üles jõuad*). We have to be careful with some morphological categories – repetitions of verb *be* and numerals may occur in the normal sentence, so we had to consider the part-of-speech tags.

Repetitions of a single word usually do not cause parsing errors but if a subject or object is repeated then the principle of uniqueness has been violated (see Example 7).

(7)   noh [B] @B see [SUBJ] @NN> see [SUBJ] @SUBJ on [FMV] @FMV
       noh   this-SG-NOM   this-SG-NOM   be-SG-3PRS
       tähtis [PRD] @PRD
       important-SG-NOM

       'you know this this is important'

The parser removes the @SUBJ tag from any word if there is an unambiguous uncoordinated subject in the clause already. The first occurance of *see* has been analysed incorrectly.

The rule for repetitions of a single word in different forms appears to be the hardest issue.

(8)   noh erinevatel päevadel on võimalik siis mägi   mäge
       noh different   days   is possible then hill-NOM hill-PART
       valida
       to choose

       'so it is possible to choose a hill in different days'

Although we excluded pronouns and some combinations of cases (e.g, *samm sammult* /step by step/) from this rule, it can still produce errors (see 9).

(9)   siis pöörate alatskivile alatskivi loss   on seal
       then you turn to alatskivi alatskivi castle is there

       'then you turn to Alatskivi. There is a castle of Alatskivi.'

The detected repeated or repaired parts of the utterance have been commented out from the input text and restored with special tag @REP after parsing. This simplifies the check of contexts conditions of rules and the parser produces a less ambiguous output. The example in Figure 2 depicts detected self-repairs.

Table 5 presents the results gained for the corpus of disfluencies. The results of parsing of repetitions are as good as in the manually normalized corpus

```
väga [REP]                    # very
    väga+0 //_D_ // **CLB @REP
nor- [REP]                    # nor-
    nor //_T_ #- //    @REP
väga [ADVL]                       # very
    väga+0 //_D_ //   @ADVL
normaalne [PRD]                   # normal
    normaalne+0 //_A_ pos sg nom // @PRD
noh [B]                       # noh
    noh+0 //_B_ //     @B
väga [ADVL]                       # very
    väga+0 //_D_ //    @ADVL
naiss [T]                         # nice
    naiss //_T_ //     @T
```

Fig. 2. Example of analyzed utterance with self-repair

Table 5. Results with tagged repetitions and self repairs

	Recall	Precision
Repairs	96.1	86.3
Repetitions	98.6	92.1
False starts	98.1	91.1

(Table 3). Also, the detection of repetitions and repairs improved the results for the other corpora where these phenomena are not so dominant (Table 6).

The improvements were significant in the corpora where repetitions and repairs occured frequently (in every sentence). For the 'normal' corpora, the results are not so attractive. For everyday conversations, the precision and the recall improved slightly (0.10 % and 0.25% respectively). For information dialogues, the results were almost identical: recall improved only 0.02%. The disfluency detection in the corpus of dialects improved the results also by approximately 0.25%.

Table 6. Recall and precision after detection of disfluencies

Corpus	Type	Recall	Precision
Everyday conversation	training	97.46	89.66
	test	97.58	91.84
Information dialogues	training	97.06	87.63
	test	96.77	87.42
Interview	test	96.80	88.47
Dialects	training	96.78	88.08
	test	95.83	87.30

In one hand, the improvement is not remarkable but we also have to consider the fact that the resulting annotation is more informative. Also, the analysis of errors showed that if the utterance is not well-formed then it is really hard to perform its syntactic analysis correctly.

6   Error Types

The error types may vary quite a lot between text genres. A thorough comparison of errors in the analysis of everyday converstations and institutional calls revealed that one of the most dominant error cause is unfinished sentence or false start for the corpus of everyday conversations while ellipses are prevalent for information dialogues [13].

The closer look to error types in the corpus of self-repairs (see Table 7) shows that repairs and complicated phrases of repetitions are the reason for most of errors. The corpus consists of 2100 words and the parser made 82 errors during the analysis of the corpus.

Self-repairs are hard to detect and this error type is difficult to avoid. In some cases, the edited word and editing word have the same form (see Example 10) and it might be possible to refine our detector of disfluencies during further experiments.

(10)   see on siin selle kaubahalli uue kaubahalli kõrval
       this is here this shop   new shop   next to
       'it is here, next to the new shop'

The syntactic errors caused by false or undetected clause boundaries are also dominant. The situation where a turn of the dialog consists of a separate noun phrase and a clause with a verb is typical (see Example 2).

The utterances in spoken language are often unfinished or consist of unfinished phrases. Their automatic analysis is impossible in most of the cases.

If the pause fillers are special particles like *ee*, *noh*, *mmm*, they do not disturb the analysis of the sentence. Unfortunately, the demonstrative pronoun *see* (this) in nominative case is quite often used as a pause filler. It is very hard to detect

Table 7. Analysis of errors in the corpus of self-repairs

Type of errors	Count	%
self-repairs and repetitions	18	22.0
error in the clause boundary	15	18.3
regular syntactic errors	13	15.8
unfinished words, phrases, clauses	9	11.0
pause fillers	7	8.5
expressions of time	5	6.1
other	15	18.3

automatically, and it is a common error cause for incorrect analysis of subjects or objects (see Example 11).

(11) meil   on   olnud see   ee kapslid
      we-ADES have been this-NOM ee capsules-NOM

      'we have had these capsules'

Another prominent error class for the analysis of spoken language are the errors related to expressions of time. It is typical that the adverbial of the time is in nominative case in spoken language.

(12) kolmapäev   tuleb   tööle
      Wednesday-NOM come-SG3 work-ALLAT

      'he arrives to the office on Wednesday'

Also, the hours and minutes are expressed as a sequence of numbers; their analysis needs an extra work.

The 'regular syntactic errors' occur in a written text also. We should consider removing some heuristic rules which tend to cause errors in spoken language texts. Also, it might be beneficial to remove rules which declare only one possible uncoordinated subject for every clause, since we can not trust the clause boundary detection. Although this could yield more ambiguous output. This example illustrates how difficult it is to find a balance between recall and precision.

The script for disfluency detection added 272 @REP-tags to the test corpora of spoken language, two of them were wrong and one was missing. So, the precision and recall of the detector are higher than 99%, but we had not taken into account other types of disfluencies which have not been tagged in our syntactically annotated corpora. The words belonging to the edited phase of a disfluency have their most likely syntactic tag or the tag of unknown syntactic function.

7   Conclusions

The experiment for improving the efficiency of the parser demonstrates that the rule-based grammar composed originally for written unrestricted text is suitable for parsing spoken language – but one should pay a special attention to the detection of clause boundaries. Also, the automatic identification of disfluencies helps to improve the performance of the parser significantly.

We have found that repetitions can be analyzed as easily as in normalized corpus, almost half of false starts are well detectable and do not affect the analysis of the rest of the utterance. The hardest type of disfluencies is self-repairs – the improvements we observed had only a marginal nature.

For the future work, the next challenge is the adaptation of morphological disambiguator to spoken language.

Also, we need bigger annotated corpus, in order to analyze the syntactic phenomena of disfluencies. We plan to enhance the annotation scheme of our corpora with more exact disfluency information, similar to the works described in [14].

References

1. Hennoste, T., Lindström, L., Rääbis, A., Toomet, P., Vellerind, R.: Tartu University Corpus of Spoken Estonian. In: Seilenthal, T., Nurk, A., Palo, T. (eds.) Congressus Nonus Internationalis Fenno-Ugristarum. Pars IV, Dissertationes sectionum, Linguistica I, pp. 345–351 (2000)
2. Lindström, L., Pajusalu, K.: Corpus of Estonian Dialects and the Estonian Vowel System. Linguistica Uralica 4, 241–257 (2003)
3. Sampson, G.: Consistent Annotation of Speech-Repair Structures. In: Rubio, A. (ed.) Proc. of the First International Conference on Language Resources and Evaluation, vol. 2, Granada, Spain (1998)
4. Müürisep, K.: Parsing Estonian with Constraint Grammar. In: Online Proc. of NODALIDA 2001, Uppsala (2001)
5. Karlsson, F., Anttila, A., Heikkilä, J., Voutilainen, A.: Constraint Grammar: a Language-Independent System for Parsing Unrestricted Text. Mouton de Gruyter, Berlin (1995)
6. Müürisep, K.: Eesti keele arvutigrammatika: süntaks. Dissertationes Mathematicae Universitatis Tartuensis 22, Tartu (2000)
7. Müürisep, K., Uibo, H.: Shallow Parsing of Spoken Estonian Using Constraint Grammar. In: Henrichsen, P.J., Skadhauge, P.R. (eds.) Treebanking for Discourse and Speech. Proc. of NODALIDA 2005 Special Session. Copenhagen Studies in Language, vol. 32. Samfundslitteratur, pp. 105–118 (2006)
8. Bick, E.: Tagging Speech Data - Constraint Grammar Analysis of Spoken Portuguese. In: Proc. of the 17th Scandinavian Conference of Linguistics, Odense (1998)
9. Nigol, H.: Parsing Manually Detected and Normalized Disfluencies in Spoken Estonian. In: Proc. of NODALIDA 2007, Tartu (2007)
10. Meteer, M., Taylor, A., MacIntyre, R., Iver, R.: Dysfluency Annotation Stylebook for the Switchboard Corpus. LDC (1995)
11. Charniak, E., Johnson, M.: Edit Detection and Parsing for Transcribed Speech. In: Proc. of NAACL 2001, pp. 118–126 (2001)
12. Lease, M., Johnson, M.: Early Deletion of Fillers in Processing Conversational Speech. In: Proc. HLT–NAACL 2006, companion volume: short papers, pp. 73–76 (2006)
13. Müürisep, K., Nigol, H.: Where do parsing errors come from. In: Sojka, P., Horák, A., Kopeček, I., Pala, K. (eds.) TSD 2008. LNCS (LNAI), vol. 5246, pp. 161–168. Springer, Heidelberg (2008)
14. Bies, A., Strassel, S., Lee, H., Maeda, K., Kulick, S., Liu, Y., Harper, M., Lease, M.: Linguistic Resources for Speech Parsing. In: Fifth International Conference on Language Resources and Evaluation (LREC 2006), Genoa, Italy (2006)

Mining Parsing Results for Lexical Correction: Toward a Complete Correction Process of Wide-Coverage Lexicons

Lionel Nicolas[1], Benoît Sagot[2], Miguel A. Molinero[3],
Jacques Farré[1], and Éric de La Clergerie[2]

[1] Équipe RL, Laboratoire I3S, UNSA + CNRS, 06903 Sophia Antipolis, France
{lnicolas,jf}@i3s.unice.fr
[2] Projet ALPAGE, INRIA Rocquencourt + Paris 7, 78153 Le Chesnay, France
{benoit.sagot,Eric.De_La_Clergerie}@inria.fr
[3] Grupo LYS, Univ. de A Coruña, 15001 A Coruña, España
mmolinero@udc.es

Abstract. The coverage of a parser depends mostly on the quality of the underlying grammar and lexicon. The development of a lexicon both complete and accurate is an intricate and demanding task. We introduce a automatic process for detecting missing, incomplete and erroneous entries in a morphological and syntactic lexicon, and for suggesting corrections hypotheses for these entries. The detection of dubious lexical entries is tackled by two different techniques; the first one is based on a specific statistical model, the other one benefits from information provided by a part-of-speech tagger. The generation of correction hypotheses for dubious lexical entries is achieved by studying which modifications could improve the successful parse rate of sentences in which they occur. This process brings together various techniques based on taggers, parsers and statistical models. We report on its application for improving a large-coverage morphological and syntacic French lexicon, the Le*fff*.

Keywords: Lexical acquisition and correction, wide coverage lexicon, error mining, tagger, entropy classifier, syntactic parser.

1 Introduction

The manual development of a lexicon that is both accurate and wide coverage is a labour-intensive, complex and error prone task, requiring an important human expert work. Unless very important financial and human efforts are put in the balance, the lexicons usually do not achieve the expected objectives in terms of coverage or quality. However, this manual task can be improved through the use of tools which simplify the process and increase its relevance.

We present a set of techniques brought together in a chain of tools which detect missing, incomplete and erroneous entries in a lexicon and proposes relevant lexical corrections.

Z. Vetulani and H. Uszkoreit (Eds.): LTC 2007, LNAI 5603, pp. 178–191, 2009.

The methodology implemented in this chain can be summarized as follows:

1. Parse a high number of raw (non tagged) sentences considered as lexically and grammatically valid (law texts, newspapers, etc.) with a deep parser,[1] and spot those that are successfuly parsed and those which ones are not;[2]
2. For each non-parsable sentence, determine automatically, thanks to a statistical classifier, if the parsing failure is caused by a lack of coverage of the grammar or by incompleteness of the morphological and syntactic lexicon;
3. Detect automatically missing, incomplete or erroneous lexical entries. This is achieved by a statistical analysis of non-parsable sentences for which the lexicon has been identified during the previous step as the cause of the parsing failure;
4. Generate correction hypotheses by analyzing the expectations of the grammar about those detected entries when trying to parse the non-parsable sentences in which they occur.
5. Automatically evaluate and rank corrections hypotheses to prepare an easier manual validation.

Although our examples and results are related to French, this set of techniques is system independent, i.e., it can be easily adapted to most existing taggers, classifiers, lexicons and deep parsers, and thus to most electronically described languages.

This chain of tools is one of the starting points of the recently created Victoria project [3], which aims at developing efficiently large-coverage linguistic resources for Spanish and Galician languages, with inter-language links with French resources (incl. the Lefff syntactic lexicon, see section 8).

Please note that *some* results presented in section 8 were partly obtained with a previous version of the chain and its architectural model [1]. The differences between both models are presented in details in section 8.

This paper is organized as follows. We first detail step by step the process described above (Sect. 2, 3, 4, 5 and 6). Next, we compare our approach with previous related work (Sect. 7). We expose the practical context and the results we obtained in Sect. 8. Finally, we outline the planned improvements (Sect. 9) and conclude (Sect. 10).

2 Classifying Non-parsable Sentences

Let us suppose we have parsed a large corpus with a deep parser. Some sentences were successfully parsed, some were not. Sentences that were parsed are both

---

[1] In this paper, we consider only parsers that are able to exploit subcategorization information.
[2] These sentences need to be lexically and grammatically valid in order to ensure that a parsing failure is only due to shortcomings in the parser or of the resources it relies on.
[3] http://www.victoria-project.org (October 2008).

lexically and grammatically covered (even if the parses obtained do not match the actual meaning of the sentences). On the contrary, and in first approximation, the parsing failure of a given sentence can be caused either by a lack of grammatical coverage or by a lack of lexical coverage.

However, our focus is the improvement of the lexicon. Therefore, we need to apply first a method for determining whether the parser failed on a given sentence because of a problem in the grammar or in the lexicon.

Since syntactic structures are more frequent and less numerous than words, grammatical shortcomings tend to correspond to recurrent patterns in non-parsable sentences, contrarily to lexical shortcomings. Moreover, syntactic problems in lexical entries have no impact on a tagger. This means that we can train a statistical classifier to identify sentences that are non-parsable because of a shortcoming of the grammar; such a classifier needs to be trained with contextual information, e.g., the set of n-grams that constitute the sentence. We built these n-grams using the POS (*part-of-speech*) for open-class forms (i.e., verbs, nouns, etc.) and the form itself for closed-class ones (i.e., prepositions, determiners, etc.). The classifier we used is a maximum entropy classifier [2].

The POS information we used is obtained by two different means. For parsable sentences (i.e., sentences covered by the grammar), POS tags and forms are directly extracted from parsing outputs. Indeed, we are only interested in syntactic patterns covered by the grammar, even if ambiguous parse outputs are used as training. For non-parsable sentences, we simply used a POS tagger. Although taggers are not perfect, their errors are random enough not to blur the global coherence of the classifier's model.

When applied on non-parsable sentences, this classifier identifies two sets of sentences:

– sentences that are non-parsable because of shortcomings in the grammar;
– all other non-parsable sentences, i.e., sentences that are non-parsable because of shortcomings in the lexicon.

3   Detecting Lexical Shortcomings

The next step of our lexicon improvement process is to detect automatically missing, incomplete or erroneous lexical entries. To achieve this goal, we use two complementary techniques that identify dubious lexical forms and associate them with non-parsable sentences in which they appear, and in which it is suspected they caused the parsing failure.

3.1   Tagger-Based Approach for Detecting Shortcomings in Short-Range Lexical Information

We call short-range lexical information all information that can be determined by a tagger based on n-grams, such as the POS.

In order to detect problems in the lexicon that concern short-range lexical information, we use a specific POS tagger [3,4]. The idea is the following. Let us consider a sentence that is non-parsable because of a problem in the lexical entries for one of its form. A tagger might be able to guess for this form relevant short-range information which is missing or erroneous in the lexicon, based on the context in which it occurs. Comparing this "guessed" short-range information with the corresponding information in the lexicon might reveal relevant discrepancies. To achieve this, we apply a POS tagger to the sentence several times; each time, one of the forms that might be concerned by lexical shortcomings (usually, open-class forms) is considered as an unknown word, so as to bypass the tagger's internal lexicon. This allows the tagger to output tags that are compatible with the context of the form, including tags that might lack in the lexicon.

Of course, taggers do make errors. We reduce this problem by two different means. First, we take into account the precision rate $prec_t$ of the tagger for a tag t, as evaluated w.r.t. its training corpus. Second, we smooth the propositons of the tagger by averaging them on all sentences that are non-parsable because of a shortcoming in the lexicon. More precisely, we assign a global *short-range suspicion rate* $S_{sr}(w)$ to each relevant form w, defined as follows:

$$S_{sr}(w) = \frac{n_{wt} \cdot prec_t}{n_w} \cdot \log(n_{wt} \cdot prec_t). \tag{1}$$

where n_{wt} is the number of occurrences of the form w tagged as t, and n_w is the total number of occurrences of the form w in the non lexically parsable sentences.

3.2   Statistical Approach for Detecting Lexical Shortcomings

This lexical shortcomings detection technique, fully described in [5,6], relies on the following assumptions:

- The more often a lexical form appears in non-parsable sentences and not in parsable ones, the more likely its lexical entries are to be erroneous or incomplete [7];
- This suspicion rate $S(w)$ must be reinforced if the form w appears in non-parsable sentences along with other forms that appear in parsable ones.

This statistical computation quickly establishes a relevant list of lexical forms suspected to be incorrectly or incompletely described in the lexicon. The advantage of this technique over the previous one is that it is able to take into account all the syntactic information that is available in the lexicon, provided it is used by the tagger (e.g., subcategorization frames). However, it directly depends on the quality of the grammar used. Indeed, if a specific form is naturally tied with some syntactic construction that is badly covered by the grammar, this form will mostly be found in non-parsable sentences and will thus be unfairly suspected.

This problem can be overcome in at least two ways. First, we exclude from the statistical computation all sentences that are non-parsable because of short-comings of the grammar (as decided by the classifier defined in the previous section). Second, as already described in [5], we combine parsing results provided by various parsers that rely on different formalisms and grammars and thus, with different coverage lacks.

4   Generating Lexical Correction Hypotheses: Parsing Non-parsable Sentences

Depending on the quality of the lexicon and the grammar, the probability that both resources are simultaneously erroneous about how a specific form is used in a given sentence can be very low. If a lexically and grammatically valid sentence can not be parsed because of a suspected form, it implies that the lexicon and the grammar could not find an agreement about the role this form can have in a parse for this sentence. Since some suspected forms have been previously detected, we believe some parsing failures to be the consequence of lexical problems about those forms. In order to generate lexical corrections, we study the expectations of the grammar for every suspected form in its associated non-parsable sentences. In a metaphorical way, we could say that we "ask" the grammar its opinion about the suspected forms.

To fulfill this goal, we get as close as possible to the set of parses that the grammar would have allowed with an error-free lexicon. Since we believe the lexical information of a form to have restricted the way it could have been part of a successful parse and led the parsing to a failure, we decrease those lexical restrictions by underspecifying the lexical information of the suspected form. A full underspecification can be simulated in the following way: during the parsing process, each time a lexical information is checked about a suspected form, the lexicon is bypassed and all the constraints are considered satisfied, i.e., the form becomes whatever the grammar wants it to be. This operation is achieved by changing the suspected form in the associated sentences to underspecified ones called *wildcards*.

If the suspected form has been correctly suspected, and if indeed it is the unique cause of the parsing failure of some sentences, replacing it by a wildcard allows these sentences to become parsable. In these new parses, the suspected form (more precisely, the wildcard that replaces it) takes part to grammatical structures. These structures correspond to "instanciated" syntactic lexical entries, i.e., lexical entries that would allow the original form to take part in these structures. *Those instantiated lexical entries are the information used to build lexical corrections.*

As explained in [8], using totally underspecified wildcards introduces too large an ambiguity in the parsing process. This often has the consequence that no parse (and therefore no correction hypothesis) is obtained at all, because of time or memory constraints, or that too many parses (and therefore too many correction hypotheses) are produced. Therefore, we add lexical information to the wildcards to keep the introduced ambiguity below reasonable limits. Unlike other approaches [9,10] which generate all possible combinations of lexical information and test only the most probable, we choose to add only POS to the wildcards and to rely upon the parsers' ability to handle underspecified forms. The ambiguity introduced by our approach clearly generates a more important number of corrections hypotheses. However, as explained in section 5, this ambiguity can be handled, provided there are enough non-parsable sentences associated with a given suspected form.

In practice, the POS added to a wildcard depends on the kind of lexical shortcoming we are trying to solve, i.e., it is chosen according to the kind of detection technique that suspected the form. So far, we only used the tagger-based detection to validate new POS for a suspected form. Thus, when using this approach, we generate wildcards with the POS given by the tagger to the form. When using the statistical detection approach, we generate wildcards with the different POS present in the lexicon for the suspected form: we want to validate new syntactic structures for the form, without changing its POS.

5 Extracting and Ranking Corrections

The way correction hypotheses are extracted depends on how they are used. In a previous work [11], the corrections were extracted in the output format of the parser. Such an approach has three important drawbacks:

- One first need to understand the output format of the parser before being able to study the corrections hypotheses;
- Merging results produced by various parsers is difficult, although it is an efficient solution to tackle some limitations of the process (see Sect. 5.2);
- Some parts of the correction might use information that is not easy to relate with the format used by the lexicon (specific tagsets, under- or overspecified information w.r.t. the lexicon, etc.).

We thus developed for each parser a conversion module which extracts the instantiated lexical entry given to the wildcard in a parse and translate it from the output format of the parser to the format of the lexicon.

Natural languages are ambiguous, and so have to be the grammars that model them. Thus, the reader should note that even an inadequate wildcard might perfectly lead to new parses and thus provide irrelevant corrections. In order to take this problem into account and prepare an easier manual validation, the corrections hypotheses obtained for a given suspected form with a given wildcard are ranked according to the following ideas.

5.1 Baseline Ranking: Single Parser Mode

Within the scope of only one sentence, there is not enough information to rank corrections hypotheses. However, by considering simultaneously various sentences that contain the same suspected form, one can observe that erroneous correction hypotheses are randomly scattered. On the other hand, correction hypotheses that are proposed for various syntactically different sentences are more likely to be valid.

This is the basis of our baseline ranking metrics, that can be described as follows. Let us consider a given suspected form w. First, all correction hypotheses for w in a given sentence form a *group* of correction hypotheses. This group receives a weight according to its size: the more corrections it contains, the lower weight it has, since it is probably related to several *permissive* syntactic skeletons. Therefore, for each group, we compute a score $P = c^n$ with c being a numerical constant in $]0, 1[$ close to 1 (eg. 0.95) and n the size of the group. Each correction hypothesis σ in the group receives the weight $p_{g\sigma} = \frac{P}{n} = \frac{c^n}{n}$, which depends twice on the size n of group g.

We then sum up all the weights that a given correction hypothesis σ has received in all groups it appears in. This sum is its global *score* $s_\sigma = \Sigma_g p_{g\sigma}$. Thus, the best corrections are the ones that appear in many small groups.

5.2   Reducing Grammar Influence: Multi-parser Mode

As it is the case for the statistical detection technique, crossing the results obtained with different parsers allows to improve the ranking. Indeed, most erroneous corrections hypotheses depend on the grammar rules used to reparse the sentences. Since two parsers with two different grammars usually do not behave the same, erroneous corrections hypotheses are even more scattered. On the opposite, it is natural for grammars describing a same language to find an agreement about how a particular form can be used, which means that relevant corrections hypotheses usually remain stable. Corrections can then be considered less relevant if they are not proposed by all parsers. Consequently, we separately rank the corrections for each parser as described in section 5.1 and merge the results using an harmonic mean.

6   Manual Validation of the Corrections

Thanks to the previous steps, validating the corrections proposed by a given wildcard for a given suspected form is easy. Three situations might occur:

1. There are no corrections at all: the form has been unfairly suspected, the generation of wildcards has been inadequate or the suspected form is not the only reason for its associated parsing failures;
2. There are some relevant corrections: the form has been correctly detected, the generation of wildcards has been adequate and the form is the only reason for (some of) its associated parsing failures;
3. There are only irrelevant corrections: the ambiguity introduced by the wildcards on the suspected form has opened the path to irrelevant parses providing irrelevant corrections; if the grammar does not cover all the possible syntactic structures, there is absolutely no guarantee that we generate relevant corrections.

Consequently, if the aim of the correction process is to improve the quality of a lexicon and not just to increase the coverage of parsers that rely on it, such a process should always be semi-automatic (with manual validation) and not strictly automatic.

7   Related Work

To our knowledge, the first time that grammatical context was used to infer automatically lexical information was in 1990 [12]. In 2006 [9,10], error minning techniques like [7] started to be used to detect erroneous lexical forms. The detection technique described in [5,6] and the tagger-based detection technique have been used so far mostly by ourselves [11,1], with convincing results. The idea of a preliminary classification/filtering of non-parsable sentences to improve the detection techniques has also not been considered much so far (Sec. 2).

Wildcard generation started to be refined in [8]. Since then, wildcards have been partially underspecified and limited to open-class POS. In [10], the authors use an elegant technique based on a maximum entropy classifier to select the most adequate wildcards.

Ranking corrections is a task usually accomplished through the use of maximum entropy classifiers like in [9,10]. However, the evaluation of correction hypotheses based on all sentences associated with a given suspected form (see Sect 5.1), without generalizing to the POS of the form, has never been considered so far.

It is worth mentioning that all previous work on correction hypotheses generation has been achieved with HPSG parsers, and that no results have been presented until 2005. Since then, apart from [5], nobody reported on merging results provided by various parsers to increase the relevance of correction hypotheses.

In [9], the author presents his results for each POS. For POS with a complex syntactic behaviour (e.g., verbs), it clearly appears that it is impossible to apply such a set of techniques fully automatically without harming the quality of the lexicon. And the results would be even worse if applied to corpus with sentences that are not covered by the grammar.

8   Results and Discussion

We now detail the practical context in which we performed our experiments. We give some correction examples and explicit for each important element of our chain what is done, what is to be completed and which results could be achieved.

8.1   Practical Context

We use and improve a lexicon called the Lefff[4]. This wide-coverage morphological and syntactic French lexicon with more than 600 000 entries has been built partially automatically [13] and is under constant development.

In order to improve the quality of our correction hypotheses, we used two parsers based on two different grammars:

---

[4] Lexique des formes fléchies du français/Lexicon of inflected forms of French. See
http://alpage.inria.fr/~sagot/lefff-en.html

- The FRMG (*French Meta-Grammar*) grammar is generated in an hybrid TAG/TIG form from a more abstract meta-grammar with highly factorized trees [14], and compiled into a parser by the DYALOG system [15].
- The SxLFG-FR grammar [16] is an efficient deep non-probabilistic LFG grammar compiled into a parser by SxLFG, a SYNTAX-based system.

We used a French journalistic corpus from *Le monde diplomatique*. It contains 280 000 sentences of 25 tokens or less for a total of 4,3 million of words.

8.2 Examples of Corrections

Here are some examples of valid corrections found:

- *isralien* (*"Israeli"*), *portugais* (*"Portuguese"*), *parabolique* (*"parabolic"*), *pittoresque* (*"picturesque"*), *minutieux* (*"meticulous"*) were missing as adjectives;
- *politiques* (*"politic"*) was missing as a common noun;
- *revenir* (*"to come back"*) did not handle constructions like *to come back from* or *to come back in*
- *se partager* (*"to share"*) did not handle constructions like *to share (something) between.*
- *aimer* (*"to love"*) was described as expecting a mandatory direct object and a mandatory attribute.
- *livrer* (*"to deliver"*) did not handle constructions like *to deliver (something) to somebody.*

8.3 Classification of Non-parsable Sentences

For time reasons, results described in this section have been obtained thanks to a previous version of the classification technique: the POS and forms used for parsable sentences were not extracted from the parser outputs but built thanks to a tagger, just like for non-parsable sentence. Therefore, the model learned by the maximum entropy classifier is not optimal.

We chose to use 3-grams generated from the list of POS and forms for each sentence as well as a start-of-sentence element at its beginning and a end-of-sentence one at its end.

To evaluate the relevance of this technique, we kept 5% of all parsable sentences for evaluating the maximum entropy classifier. Let us recall that this classifier distinguishes sentences that are non-parsable because of shortcomings in the lexicon from all other sentences (parsable or non-parsable because of shortcomings in the grammar). We checked if this classifier was actually classifying parsable sentences in the second class, as they should be. Since there is no difference when generating the 3-grams of parsable and non-parsable sentences, the figures that we get are likely to be close to the actual precision rate of the classifier on non-parsable sentences. These figures are described in table 1.

Table 1. Precision of the non-parsable sentence classification

Session	0	1	2	3
Precision rate	92.7%	93.8%	94.1%	94.9

After 3 correction sessions, the maximum entropy classifier is tagging around 80% of the non-parsable sentences as non-parsable because of shortcomings in the grammar. This sharp contrasts with the figures of table 1 on parsable sentences is an additional clue that this classifier performs satisfyingly.

The precision rate of the classifier raises as expected after each correction session. Indeed, the quality of its training data is improved by each session; in the training data, as explained in section 2, all non-parsable sentences are tagged as non-parsable because of shortcomings in the grammar, even those that are in fact non-parsable because of shortcomings in the lexicon. By correcting lexical shortcomings, the number of parsable sentences increases and many sentences that were incorrectly tagged in the training data become tagged as parsable. Since the quality of the training data could be improved by constructing the n-grams for the parsable sentences from the parser outputs, we believe the precision might increase even higher.

In the end, the 5% error rate (which prevents us from taking into account a few sentences that are non-parsable because of shortcomings in the lexicon) is not a significant problem, given the positive impact of this filtering step on our detection techniques. In addition, since there is no reason for a particular form to be more frequent than average in these incorrectly classified sentences, this can be balanced simply by increasing the size of the corpus.

8.4   Lexical Shortcomings Detection Techniques

The tagger-based technique has evolved a lot recently. The first tests were conducted with a simple preliminary version. At that time, the technique was different on many points.

1. We were only looking for POS shortcomings.
2. We were opening the ambiguity for all open-class forms in a sentence at the same time, which brings unnecessary ambiguity. We now open the ambiguity for one form at a time.
3. We were applying the technique on the whole corpus, which brings a lot of false positives. Even if there might be true positives in the parsable sentences and in non grammatically parsable sentences, it is far more interesting to restrict the detection to the non lexically parsable sentences.
4. We were not considering the error rate associated with each guessed tag when ranking the suspects.

At that time, the results were less convincing as they are today, as far as quality is concerned. However, this beta version of the technique allowed us to correct

182 lemmas in the lexicon. We expect the results of the newly implemented version to be even better.

In practice, our tagger-based technique already exhibits many positive aspects. In particular, the set of sentences that are non parsable because of shortcomings in the lexicon for a given session is a subset of the corresponding set for the previous session. This means that this detection technique only needs to be applied once on a given corpus. We also noticed some drawbacks. First, it can only detect short range lexical shortcomings. Second, we get a non negligible amount of false positives.

The Statistical technique proved relevant from the very beginning and allowed us to correct 72 different lemmas. It detects all kinds of lexical shortcomings, and the ranking it computes is extremely consistent. On the other hand, the grammar must have large enough a coverage to provide a reasonable proportion of parsable sentences; the quality of the detection directly depends on that of the grammar. Moreover, during a session, some suspected forms can prevent other problematic forms from being detected; it is necessary to make several correction sessions for a same corpus until no fairly suspected form arises.

8.5   Correction Generation and Ranking

The overall accuracy of the correction hypotheses decreases after each correction session. Indeed, after each session, there are less and less lexical errors that need to be corrected: the quality of the lexicon reaches that of the grammar. Since we want to improve efficiently our lexicon, we demonstrate the relevance of the whole process by showing the increase of the parsing rate obtained during our experiments. One must keep in mind that the corrections are manually validated, i.e., the noticeable increases of parsing coverage (Figure 1) are mostly due to the improvement of the quality of the lexicon.

Table 2 lists the number of lexical forms updated at each session.

Table 2. Lexical forms updated at each session

Session	1	2	3	total
nc	30	99	1	130
adj	66	694	27	787
verbs	1183	0	385	1568
adv	1	7	0	8
total	1280	800	413	2493

For all sessions but the second one, all correction sessions are based on the non-parsable sentence classification, the statistical detection and the correction generation. The second session has been achieved only thanks to the tager-based detection technique for identifying POS shortcomings (Sect. 3.1). As expected,

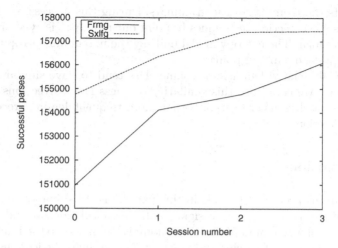

Fig. 1. Number of sentences successfully parsed after each session

we have been quickly limited by the quality of the grammars and the corpus. Indeed, the lexicon and the grammars have been developed together during the last few years, using this same corpus as a testing corpus. Therefore, on this corpus, there was not a huge gap between the coverage of our grammars and the coverage of our lexicon. Further correction and extension sessions only make sense after grammar improvements or if applied on new corpora.

However, the interaction between the grammar and the corpus can lead to complementary information: given a non-parsable sentence, if none of its suspected forms leads to a relevant correction, this sentence can be considered as lexically correct w.r.t. the current state of the grammar. This means that it exhibits shortcomings in the grammar, which can help improving it. Therefore, an iterative process which alternatively and incrementally improves both the lexicon and the grammar can be implemented. This is especially important given the fact that large scale French TreeBanks are rare.

To sum up our results, we have already detected and corrected 254 lemmas corresponding to 2493 forms. The coverage rate (percentage of sentences for which a full parse is found) has undergone an absolute increase of 3,41% (5141 sentences) for the FRMG parser and 1,73% (2677 sentences) for the SXLFG parser. Those results were achieved within only a few hours of manual work !

9   Future Improvements

We are planning the following improvements to continue our research:

- We shall complete the evaluation of all components of the new model and prove their relevance separately.
- In order to pursue the improvement of the lexicon, we will extend our grammars thanks to the corpus of non-parsable sentences which now globally

represents shortcomings of the grammars. During this process, we intend to develop some detection techniques to point out more precisely shortcomings in the grammar. The entropy model built by the maximum entropy classifier could be a good starting point.

– Semantically related lemmas of a same class tend to have similar syntactic behaviours. We could use this similarity to guess new corrections for some lemmas in a class where various other more frequent lemmas received the same correction.

10 Conclusion

In conclusion, the process described in this paper has three major advantages.

First, it does allow to improve significantly a morphological and syntactic lexicon within a short amount of time. We showed this thanks to the improvement of the parsing coverage of parsing systems that rely on such a lexicon, namely the Le*fff*. Moreover, our technique contributes to the improvement of deep parsing accuracy, which can be seen as a keystone for many avanced NPL applications.

Second, its iterative application on an input corpus eventualy turns this corpus into a global representation of the shortcomings of the grammar. Such a corpus could be an starting point for the development of a chain of tools dedicated to the improvement of deep grammars.

Third, an important advantage of our process is that it can be fed with raw text. This allows to use as an input any kind of text, including texts produced daily by journalistic sources as well as technical corpora. This is one of the techniques we are using to go on with the improvement the Le*fff*, in particular thanks to the 100 million words corpus of the French project Passage,[5] that combines fragments of the French Wikipedia, of the French wikisource, of the regional daily *L'Est Républicain*, of Europarl and of JRC Acquis.

Acknowledgments. The tagger-based detection technique could be achieved partially thanks to the support of Ministerio de Educación y Ciencia of Spain and FEDER (HUM2007-66607-C04-02), the Xunta de Galicia (IN-CITE08E1R104022ES, INCITE08PX IB302179PR, PGIDIT07SIN005206PR) and the "Galician Network for Language Processing and Information Retrieval" 2006-2009).

We would like also to thanks Olivier Lecarme, Carine Fédèle and Laurent Galluccio for their valuable comments.

References

1. Nicolas, L., Sagot, B., Molinero, M.A., Farré, J., Villemonte de La Clergerie, E.: Computer aided correction and extension of a syntactic wide-coverage lexicon. In: Proceedings of Coling 2008, Manchester (2008)

---

[5] http://atoll.inria.fr/passage/

2. Daumé III, H.: Notes on CG and LM-BFGS optimization of logistic regression. Paper available at, `http://pub.hal3.name/daume04cg-bfgs`, implementation available at, `http://hal3.name/megam/` (August 2004)
3. Molinero, M.A., Barcala, F.M., Otero, J., Graña, J.: Practical application of one-pass viterbi algorithm in tokenization and pos tagging. In: Proceedings of Recent Advances in Natural Language Processing (RANLP), pp. 35–40 (2007)
4. Graña, J.: Técnicas de Análisis Sintáctico Robusto para la Etiquetación del Lenguaje Natural (robust syntactic analysis methods for natural language tagging). Doctoral thesis, Universidad de A Coruña, Spain (2000)
5. Sagot, B., Villemonte de La Clergerie, É.: Error mining in parsing results. In: Proceedings of ACL/COLING 2006, Sydney, Australia, pp. 329–336. Association for Computational Linguistics (2006)
6. Sagot, B., de La Clergerie, E.: Fouille d'erreurs sur des sorties d'analyseurs syntaxiques. Traitement Automatique des Langues 49(1) (2008) (to appear)
7. Van Noord, G.: Error mining for wide-coverage grammar engineering. In: Proceedings of ACL 2004, Barcelona, Spain (2004)
8. Barg, P., Walther, M.: Processing unkonwn words in hpsg. In: Proceedings of the 36th Conference of the ACL and the 17th International Conference on Computational Linguistics (1998)
9. Van de Cruys, T.: Automatically extending the lexicon for parsing. In: Proceedings of the eleventh ESSLLI student session (2006)
10. Yi, Z., Kordoni, V.: Automated deep lexical acquisition for robust open texts processing. In: Proceedings of LREC- 2006 (2006)
11. Nicolas, L., Farré, J., Villemonte de La Clergerie, É.: Correction mining in parsing results. In: Proceedings of LTC 2007, Poznan, Poland (2007)
12. Erbach, G.: Syntactic processing of unknown words. In: IWBS Report 131 (1990)
13. Sagot, B., Clément, L., Villemonte de La Clergerie, É., Boullier, P.: The Lefff 2 syntactic lexicon for french: architecture, acquisition, use. In: Proceedings of LREC 2006 (2006)
14. Thomasset, F., Villemonte de La Clergerie, É.: Comment obtenir plus des méta-grammaires. In: Proceedings of TALN 2005 (2005)
15. Villemonte de La Clergerie, E.: DyALog: a tabular logic programming based environment for NLP. In: Proceedings of 2nd International Workshop on Constraint Solving and Language Processing (CSLP 2005), Barcelona, Spain (2005)
16. Boullier, P., Sagot, B.: Efficient parsing of large corpora with a deep LFG parser. In: Proceedings of LREC (2006)

Efficient Parsing Using Recursive Transition Networks with Output

Javier M. Sastre-Martínez[1,2] and Mikel L. Forcada[2]

[1] Laboratoire d'Informatique de l'Institut Gaspard Monge,
Université Paris-Est, F-77454 Marne-la-Vallée Cedex 2, France
[2] Grup Transducens,
Departament de Llenguatges i Sistemes Informàtics,
Universitat d'Alacant, E-03071 Alacant, Spain
javier.sastre@igm.univ-mlv.fr,
mlf@dlsi.ua.es

Abstract. We describe here two efficient parsing algorithms for natural language texts based on an extension of recursive transition networks (RTN) called recursive transition networks with string output (RTNSO). RTNSO-based grammars can be semiautomatically built from samples of a manually built syntactic lexicon. Efficient parsing algorithms are needed to minimize the temporal cost associated to the size of the resulting networks. We focus our algorithms on the RTNSO formalism due to its simplicity which facilitates the manual construction and maintenance of RTNSO-based linguistic data as well as their exploitation.

1 Introduction

This paper describes two efficient parsing algorithms for natural language texts which use recursive transition networks [1] (RTNs) generated from a large and manually built syntactic lexicon such as the one defined in [2], and discussed in section 1.1. Both algorithms are easily defined based on the formal definition of RTN with string output[1] (RTNSOs) given in section 2, which corresponds to a special type of pushdown letter transducer (a pushdown automaton with output), and the formal definition of the set of outputs (such as parses or translations) associated to an input string given in section 3. A first algorithm for the efficient computation of that set is given in section 4, paying special attention to null closure due to its crucial role in the algorithm. An explanation of how to modify the preceding algorithm in order to obtain a more complex but also more efficient Earley-like algorithm able to handle ε-moves with or without output is given in section 5. Further modifications of both algorithms, which use tries to represent the partial output sequences generated during the algorithm executions are given at the end of each algorithm section. Comparative results are given in section 6. Concluding remarks close the paper.

---

[1] The output may be the result of parsing in the form of a tagged version of the input.

Z. Vetulani and H. Uszkoreit (Eds.): LTC 2007, LNAI 5603, pp. 192–204, 2009.

1.1 Parsing with RTNs and Lexicon-Grammar

Lexicon-grammar is a systematic method for the analysis and the representation of the elementary sentence structures of a natural language [3] which has produced, over the last 30 years, a large and fine-grained linguistic resource[2] describing syntactic and semantic properties of simple sentences in French (among other languages) for 13375 simple verbs, 10325 predicative nouns (e.g.: *pride* as in *to be proud of*) and 39297 idiomatic expressions playing the role of predicative element (e.g.: *to wear the pants*). There exists a technique to semiautomatically build a RTN-based grammar from samples of the lexicon-grammar for automatic parsing [5]. Although the RTN formalism is not the most expressive, its simplicity has permitted its practical application to the analysis of specialized domain corpora [6] with RTN-based computer tools (INTEX [7], Unitex [8], Outilex [9]). However, the temporal cost of applying a large RTN to a large corpus may be too expensive. We expect to reduce it by employing efficient parsing algorithms.

2 Recursive Transition Networks with String Output

A non-deterministic RTNSO $R = (Q, \Sigma, \Gamma, \delta, Q_I, F)$ is a kind of finite state machine with a pushdown stack, where $Q = \{q_1, q_2, \ldots, q_{|Q|}\}$ is a finite set of states (which will also be used as the alphabet for the pushdown stack: the empty stack will be represented by λ), $\Sigma = \{\sigma_1, \sigma_2, \ldots, \sigma_{|\Sigma|}\}$ a finite input alphabet, $\Gamma = \{\gamma_1, \gamma_2, \ldots, \gamma_{|\Gamma|}\}$ a finite output alphabet, $Q_I \subseteq Q$ the set of initial states, $F \subseteq Q$ the set of acceptance states, and

$$\delta : Q \times (((\Sigma \cup \{\varepsilon\}) \times (\Gamma \cup \{\varepsilon\})) \cup Q) \to \mathcal{P}(Q) \tag{1}$$

a partial transition function where $\mathcal{P}(\cdot)$ is the set of all subsets of a given set. Transitions, also called moves, take the machine from a source state q_s to a target state q_t by performing an action; depending on this action, the possible types of *explicit* transitions, that is, those explicitly defined in δ, are

- *translating* transitions: $\delta(q_s, (\sigma, \gamma)) \to q_t$, read input symbol $\sigma \in \Sigma$ and write output symbol $\gamma \in \Gamma$,
- *inserting* transitions: $\delta(q_s, (\sigma, \varepsilon)) \to q_t$, read σ but do not write,
- *deleting* transitions: $\delta(q_s, (\varepsilon, \gamma)) \to q_t$, do not read but write γ,
- ε^2-*transition*: $\delta(q_s, (\varepsilon, \varepsilon)) \to q_t$, neither read nor write, and
- *call* transitions: $\delta(q_s, q_c) \to q_t$, perform a subroutine jump to state q_c, then bring the machine to target or return state q_t.

The precise behaviour of calls is governed by two kinds of *implicit* transitions (not explicitly defined in R), which are

- *push* transitions: for every call transition $\delta(q_s, q_c) \to q_t$, a push transition is implicitly assumed, which initializes the call by bringing the machine to call state q_c and pushing the return state q_t onto the stack, without reading or writing, and

---

[2] Accessible through the HOOP interface [4] at http://hoop.univ-mlv.fr

- *pop* transitions: for every acceptance state $q_f \in F$, a pop transition is implicitly assumed, which pops out the return state at the top of the stack (if the stack is not empty) and brings the machine from state q_f to the return state without reading or writing.

Apart from the explicit and implicit categories, we define the following categories of transitions depending on the input/output actions performed:

- *consuming* transitions: transitions that consume input, namely translating and deleting transitions,
- *generating* transitions: transitions that generate output, namely translating and inserting transitions, and
- *ε-transitions*: transitions that do not consume input; this category is subdivided into explicit ε-transitions, namely ε^2-transitions and inserting transitions, and implicit ε-transitions, namely push and pop transitions, where only the latter transitions are allowed to modify the stack.

As a general rule, loops consuming no input but generating output are not allowed: infinite length parses of natural language input sequences make no sense and make the corresponding parsing algorithms unfeasible because they may fall into infinite loops.

3   Language of Translations of a String

In this section we will formally derive the computation of the set of output translations associated to an input string, following a similar approach to that in [10].

During the application of a RTNSO, a triplet $(q, z, \pi) \in Q \times \Gamma^* \times Q^*$ represents the fact that a partial output (PO) z has been generated up to the point of reaching state q with a stack π of return states. We call (q, z, π) an *execution state* (ES) in contrast with simple states in Q, and we call $V \in \mathcal{P}(Q \times \Gamma^* \times Q^*)$ a set of ESs (SES). We define

$$\Delta : \mathcal{P}(Q \times \Gamma^* \times Q^*) \times \Sigma \to \mathcal{P}(Q \times \Gamma^* \times Q^*) \tag{2}$$

as the transition function for SES, so that, for a SES V and an input symbol σ, the resulting SES is

$$\Delta(V, \sigma) = \{(q_t, zg, \pi) : q_t \in \delta(q_s, (\sigma, g)) \wedge (q_s, z, \pi) \in V\}, \tag{3}$$

where q_s and q_t are states in Q, $z \in \Gamma^*$ is an output string, $\pi \in Q^*$ a stack, $\sigma \in \Sigma$ an input symbol, and $g \in \Gamma \cup \{\varepsilon\}$ an output symbol or an empty output. We define the ε-closure $C_\varepsilon(V)$ of a SES V,

$$C_\varepsilon : \mathcal{P}(Q \times \Gamma^* \times Q^*) \to \mathcal{P}(Q \times \Gamma^* \times Q^*), \tag{4}$$

as the smallest SES containing V and every ES directly or indirectly derivable from V through ε-transitions, that is, through zero, one or more transitions without consuming any input symbol, including push and pop transitions. Informally, elements are added to the ε-closure through three different kinds of ε-moves until no more elements are added:

- **explicit ε-transitions:** adding (q_t, zg, π) for each (q_s, z, π) in the ε-closure and for each $q_t \in Q$ and $g \in (\Gamma^* \cup \{\varepsilon\})$ such that $q_t \in \delta(q_s, (\varepsilon, g))$;
- **push transitions:** adding $(q_c, z, \pi q_t)$ for each (q_s, z, π) in the ε-closure and for each $q_c, q_t \in Q$ such that $q_t \in \delta(q_s, q_c)$;
- **pop transitions:** adding (q_r, z, π) for each $(q_f, z, \pi q_r)$ in the ε-closure such that $q_f \in F$;

An efficient way to compute the ε-closure will be described in section 4. We recursively define

$$\Delta^* : \mathcal{P}(Q \times \Gamma^* \times Q^*) \times \Sigma^* \to \mathcal{P}(Q \times \Gamma^* \times Q^*), \tag{5}$$

the extension of Δ to strings in Σ^*, as follows:

$$\Delta^*(V, \varepsilon) = C_\varepsilon(V) \tag{6}$$
$$\Delta^*(V, z\sigma) = C_\varepsilon(\Delta(\Delta^*(V, z), \sigma)) \tag{7}$$

We define the initial SES $X_I = Q_I \times \{\varepsilon\} \times \{\lambda\}$, that is, the set of ES in which the machine is in an initial state without neither having generated any output (no output has been generated yet) nor having any uncompleted calls (no call has been performed yet). We also define the acceptance SES $X_F = F \times \Gamma^* \times \{\lambda\}$, that is, the set of every ES in which the machine is in an acceptance state and has completed every call. Finally, we define $\tau(w)$, the language of translations of input string w, as the set of output strings of the acceptance ESs reached from the initial SES after consuming w:

$$\tau(w) = \{z \in \Gamma^* : (q_f, z, \lambda) \in \Delta^*(X_I, w) \cap X_F\}. \tag{8}$$

4   Processing an Input String

Based on the equations given in the previous section, we propose a breadth-first algorithm decomposed into algorithms 1 (*translate_string*), 2 (*translate_symbol*), and 3 (*closure*) to process an input string with a given (nondeterministic) RTNSO and to generate the set of corresponding output strings, where acceptance of the input is represented as a non-empty set of outputs and vice versa, and the RTNSO is considered as a global variable.

Algorithm 1 (*translate_string*) iteratively computes the Δ^* function of the initial SES for input string $w = \sigma_1 \ldots \sigma_l$, then extracts the output sequences of the acceptance ESs. It first initializes SES V to the ε-closure of the initial SES X_I. Let V_0 be equal to V at this initial stage and V_{i+1} the SES V computed during iteration i; at iteration i SES V_{i+1} is computed from the precedent SES V_i as the set of reachable ESs from V_i by consuming input σ_{i+1}, and then traversing zero, one or more ε-transitions, push and pop transitions included. We call V_i and V_{i+1} the source and the target SESs of iteration i. Iterations proceed for each input symbol, or are prematurely stopped if an empty source SES is reached, saving the computation of the remaining empty target SES $V_{i+1} \ldots V_l$. V_0 is empty iff there are no states in Q_I; V_i other than V_0 is empty iff input symbol σ_{i+1} cannot be consumed, that is, iff there is no transition $\delta(q_s, (\sigma_{i+1}, g)) \to q_t$ for any state q_s of the ESs in V_i. Once the computation of Δ^* is finished, a final loop fills a set of output strings T with every output of the acceptance ESs in the last computed SES. It is not necessary to verify whether the whole input was consumed because, otherwise, the last computed SES would be empty and therefore no outputs would be added to T.

Algorithm 2 (*translate_symbol*) computes the Δ function of a source SES V for a given input symbol σ, that is, the set of reachable ESs from V by consuming input symbol σ. It searches every transition $\delta(q_s, (\sigma, g)) \to q_t$ consuming σ and generating $g \in (\Gamma \cup \{\varepsilon\})$, for any source state q_s of the ESs (q_s, z, π) in V. For each transition found, ES (q_t, zg, π) is added to the target SES W.

Algorithm 3 (*closure*) efficiently computes the ε-closure of a source SES V, based on van Noord's *per subset* algorithm [11]. It first builds a queue E, which will contain every unexplored ES and enqueues every ES in V. Then iteratively computes the ε-closure by dequeuing at each iteration the next unexplored ES (q_s, z, π) and searching for every explicit or implicit ε-transition having q_s as source state. For each ε-transition found, the corresponding target ES is added to V. This addition operation returns a boolean indicating whether the ES was already in V or not. If the ES is new, the ES is also enqueued into E for further processing. Notice that checking whether an element belongs or not to a set before adding it to the set is required in order to avoid duplicates in the data structure representing the set, as for instance binary search trees. Since no ESs will be enqueued twice to E, enqueuing does not require a duplicity test.

Algorithm 1. translate_string$(\sigma_1 \ldots \sigma_l)$ ▷ τ, eq. (8)

Input: $\sigma_1 \sigma_2 \ldots \sigma_l$, an input string of length l
Output: T, the set of translations
1: $V \leftarrow$ closure(X_I) ▷ initial SES V_0
2: $i \leftarrow 0$
3: **while** $V \neq \emptyset \wedge i < l$ **do**   ▷ $V_{i+1} = C_\varepsilon(\Delta(V_i, \sigma_{i+1}))$
4:     $V \leftarrow$ closure(translate_symbol(V, σ_{i+1}))
5:     $i \leftarrow i + 1$
6: **end while**
7: $T \leftarrow \emptyset$
8: **for each** $(q_f, z, \lambda) \in V : q_f \in F$ **do**   ▷ return POs from ESs in $V_i \cap X_F$
9:     $T \leftarrow T \cup \{z\}$
10: **end for**

Algorithm 1 (*translate_string*) stores only two SESs at each iteration, the source and target SESs, and a queue for computing the ε-closure. The algorithm has two important limitations: (a) the impossibility of parsing with RTNSOs representing left-recursive grammars since the computation of the ε-closure would try to generate an ES with an infinite stack of return states, and (b) the fact that for a SES V_i having two ESs with different stacks and/or outputs from where a

---

Algorithm 2. translate_symbol(V, σ) $\triangleright \Delta(V, \sigma)$, eq. (3)

Input: V, the current SES σ, the current input symbol
Output: W, the SES reachable from V by consuming σ
1: $W \leftarrow \emptyset$
2: **for each** $(q_s, z, \pi) \in V$ **do**
3:      **for each** $(q_t, g) : q_t \in \delta(q_s, (\sigma, g))$ **do**
4:          $W \leftarrow W \cup \{(q_t, zg, \pi)\}$
5:      **end for**
6: **end for**

Algorithm 3. closure(V) $\triangleright C_\varepsilon(V)$

Input: V, the SES whose ε-closure is to be computed
Output: V after incrementing it with its ε-closure
1: $E \leftarrow V$ $\triangleright$ initial queue of unexplored ESs
2: **while** $E \neq \emptyset$ **do**
3:      $(q_s, z, \pi) \leftarrow \text{dequeue}(E)$
4:      **for each** $(q_t, g) : q_t \in \delta(q_s, (\varepsilon, g))$ **do** $\triangleright$ explicit ε-transitions
5:          **if** add($V, (q_t, zg, \pi)$) **then**
6:              enqueue($E, (q_t, zg, \pi)$)
7:          **end if**
8:      **end for**
9:      **for each** $q_t \in \delta(q_s, q_c)$ **do** $\triangleright$ push transitions
10:         **if** add($V, (q_c, z, \pi q_t)$) **then**
11:             enqueue($E, (q_c, z, \pi q_t)$)
12:         **end if**
13:     **end for**
14:     **if** $\pi = \pi' q_r \wedge q_s \in F \wedge \text{add}(V, (q_r, z, \pi'))$ **then** $\triangleright$ pop transition
15:         enqueue($E, (q_r, z, \pi')$)
16:     **end if**
17: **end while**

---

call to a same state q_c is performed, the computation of every ES derived from the call to q_c is performed twice although it could be factored out (for instance, for the RTNSO of Fig. 1 call to state q_0 is computed $\sum 2^{n+1}$ times for a string $a^n b^n$ when it could be computed $n + 1$ times by factoring out common calls). In section 5 we show how to modify this algorithm to avoid both limitations.

4.1   Trie-String Optimization

Retrieval trees [12], also called prefix trees or tries, can be defined as a deterministic finite state automata (FSA) having a tree structure, where the root is the initial state q_ε. Every state in a trie is reachable from q_ε by consuming a unique string, thus there is a bijective correspondence between strings and states: the empty string corresponds to state q_ε which is not reachable from any state, and string $\alpha\sigma$ corresponds to state $q_{\alpha\sigma}$ which is only reachable from state q_α by consuming symbol σ. One can take advantage of this property in order to optimize the management of the output strings of the presented breadth-first algorithm. The algorithm first builds a trie with $Q = \{q_\varepsilon\}$. The initial ESs annotate the pointer to the data structure representing q_ε instead of an effective sequence of zero output symbols. Whenever deriving a target ES it is necessary to copy the entire output string of the source ES, which in this case is reduced to copy a pointer instead of the potentially long sequence of symbols. As well, before adding an ES to a SES it is necessary to check whether the ES already belonged to the SES, which involves several sequence comparisons that are reduced to pointer comparisons. If the derivation needs to append an output symbol g to the source partial output (PO) z, it suffices to take the trie transition labeled with g from state q_z, whose pointer is already known, in order to retrieve the pointer to state q_{zg} which represents the target PO. Supposing that transitions are stored within the data structures of their source states as maps between symbols and target states, if the transition does not exist it suffices to add a new state q_{zg} to the trie as well as the correspondence $g \to q_{zg}$ to the transition map of state q_z. As the algorithm consumes input symbols, the trie is dynamically built in order to represent every PO, so independently of the length of the output strings we only require to copy and compare pointers instead of sequences. A second trie can manage the representation of stacks, which are sequences of states of the RTNSO. However, stacks not only grow but may also decrease when popping a state. If we store at each state $q_{\pi q_r}$ its incoming transition as well, it suffices to take this transition in order to retrieve the pointer to q_π which represents the popped stack. Once the algorithm execution finishes, the set of translations can be retrieved from the set of output pointers by following backwards the incoming transitions up to q_ε. This operation can be efficiently performed if we also store at each state its depth (number of incoming transitions up to reaching q_ε), which corresponds to the length of the associated string. This way a buffer of the exact string length can be created for each string and reversely filled as incoming transitions are taken.

5   Earley-Like RTNSO Processing

Finite-state automata can give a compact representation of a set of sequences by factoring out common prefixes and suffixes. RTNs can also factor infixes by defining only a subautomaton for each repeated set of infixes and by using transitions calling the initial state of the corresponding subautomaton each time any infix in the set is to be recognized. However, it is up to the parsing algorithm to detect that the same calling transition is made multiple times at an input point so that the called subautomaton is processed only once. Based on Earley's context-free grammar (CFG) parsing algorithm [13][3] and on the modification proposed in [15] for the correct and efficient management of ε-moves, we show here a modified and more efficient version of the algorithm in section 4 which is

---

[3] [1] mentions an adaptation of Earley's algorithm for RTNs in [14]. However we have not been able to obtain the latter paper.

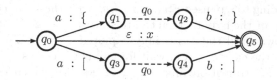

Fig. 1. Example of RTNSO. Labels of the form $x : y$ represent an input : output pair (e.g.: $a : \{$ for transition $\delta(q_0, (a, \{)) \to q_1$). Dashed transitions represent a call to the state specified by the label (e.g.: transition $\delta(q_1, q_0) \to q_2$).

able to process left-recursive RTNSOs, and which factors out the computation of the translations generated during the calls common to parallel explorations of the RTNSO, as in the RTNSO of Fig. 1.

We exchange the use of a stack of return states for a more complex representation of ESs, which mainly involves a modification of the ε-closure algorithm: when a call transition to a state q_c is found, we suppose that the call can be completed so we add to the current SES an hypothetical ES for the return state which remains *paused* until the hypothetical call is proved true, that is, no ESs are derived from the paused ESs until the call is completed; a single *active* (non-paused) ES is added for every call to state q_c in the current SES, from where acceptance states will be searched in order to complete the call. Each time a call is completed, every paused ES depending on the call is resumed. When parsing with left-recursive grammars, the algorithm does not explore the infinite sequences of recursive calls, as it does the breadth-first algorithm, but instead considers only the ones that can be completed for the given input string.

5.1 Language of Translations Using Earley-Like Processing

ESs, either paused or active, are represented as 5-tuples $(q_s, z, q_c, q_h, j) \in Q \times \Gamma^* \times (Q \cup \{\lambda\}) \times Q \times \mathbb{N}$, where

- q_s is the current (source) state,
- q_h is the state of the last unresolved call, that is, the state of the hypothetical call that will be proved true every time an acceptance state is reached from this ES,
- z is the output segment generated during the current call to q_h up to when state q_s was reached,
- q_c is the called state whose completion this ES depends on in order to be resumed, which determines whether the ES is paused ($q_c \in Q$) or active ($q_c = \lambda$, the *empty state*), and
- $(j, k) \in (\mathbb{N} \times \mathbb{N})$ is the input interval consumed during call to q_h up to reaching q_s, that is, the input interval PO z is the translation of, where k is not explicitly represented in the ES but given by the index of the SES this ES belongs to; indexes represent points between input symbols, 0 being the point just before the first input symbol σ_1 and $i > 0$ the point just after the recognition of input symbol σ_i.

The PO corresponding to a paused ES (q_s, z, q_c, q_h, j) is the set of concatenations of z with every output the hypothetical call to state q_c may generate. Since these outputs are unknown until the call is fully explored, paused ESs just annotate the dependence on the call to q_c and wait for call completions.

We extend the ES transition function Δ of eq. (3), which corresponds to Earley's "scanner", as follows:

$$\Delta : \mathcal{P}(Q \times \Gamma^* \times (Q \cup \{\lambda\}) \times Q \times \mathbb{N}) \times \Sigma \to \mathcal{P}(Q \times \Gamma^* \times (Q \cup \{\lambda\}) \times Q \times \mathbb{N}) \quad (9)$$

where

$$\Delta(V, \sigma) = \{(q_t, zg, \lambda, q_h, j) : q_t \in \delta(q_s, (\sigma, g)) \wedge (q_s, z, \lambda, q_h, j) \in V\} \quad (10)$$

Notice that the function only considers *active* ESs to derive new ESs.

Let $i, j, k \in \mathbb{N}$ such that $i \leq j \leq k$; we redefine the ε-closure in section 3 for Earley-like processing as follows:

- **explicit ε-transitions:** analogously to the preceding version, we add $(q_t, zg, \lambda, q_h, j)$ for each $(q_s, z, \lambda, q_h, j)$ in the ε-closure of V_k and for each q_t and $g \in (\Gamma \cup \{\varepsilon\})$ such that $q_t \in \delta(q_s, (\varepsilon, g))$;
- **push transitions:** analogously to Earley's "predictor", we add (q_t, z, q_c, q_h, j) and $(q_c, \varepsilon, \lambda, q_c, k)$ for each $(q_s, z, \lambda, q_h, j)$ in the ε-closure of V_k and for each q_c and q_t such that $q_t \in \delta(q_s, q_c)$; (q_t, z, q_c, q_h, j) is the paused ES waiting for the completion of call to q_c and $(q_c, \varepsilon, \lambda, q_c, k)$ is the active ES initiating the call;
- **pop transitions:** analogously to Earley's "completer", for each $(q_f, z_c, \lambda, q_c, j)$ such that $q_f \in F$ (the ESs completing call to q_c) and for each $(q_r, z_p, q_c, q_h, i) \in V_j$ (the paused ESs depending on call to q_c) we *retroactively* add $(q_r, z_p z_c, \lambda, q_h, i)$ to the ε-closure of V_k (we resume them with the concatenation of the *paused* and completed POs and *input* intervals represented by the indexes).

During the computation of a SES V_k, completing a call that has consumed at least one input symbol involves resuming a set of paused ESs that belong to SESs that have been computed before V_k. However, if the call is ε-*completed* (that is, completed without input consumption), paused ESs depending on this completion belong to V_k as well, so some of them may be added *after* the ε-completion has been processed. Therefore, the resumed ESs corresponding to these paused ESs will be missed as well as every complete translation of the input they may derive. When implementing the ε-closure algorithm, some kind of mechanism must be implemented so that ε-completions have a *retroactive* effect on paused ESs. Earley mentions this problem in [13] for the CFG case and Aycock et al. present an efficient solution in [15].

The extension of Δ to strings in Σ^* (eqs. 6 & 7) remains unchanged except for the use of the newly defined Δ and ε-closure.

We redefine the initial SES X_I as $Q_I \times \{\varepsilon\} \times \{\lambda\} \times Q_I \times \{0\}$, that is, the set of active ESs initiating the call to each initial state of the RTNSO, and the final

SES X_F as $F \times \Gamma^* \times \{\lambda\} \times Q_I \times \{0\}$, that is, the set of active ESs completing a call to an initial state which consumed the input sequence since the first symbol. Finally, the language of translations $\tau(w)$ stays the same except for the use of the redefined versions of initial and final SESs and function Δ^* for 5-tuples:

$$\tau(w) = \{z \in \Gamma^* : (q_t, z, \lambda, q_h, 0) \in \Delta^*(X_I, w) \cap X_F\}. \tag{11}$$

The adaptation of algorithms 1 (*translate_string*) and 2 (*translate_symbol*) is trivial and will not be given here. Algorithm 4 replaces algorithm 3 and is an almost straightforward implementation of the ε-closure for Earley-like processing. As stated before, ε-transitions may lead to analyses which may partially reject correct parses. Following the solution presented in [15], we have modified our ε-closure algorithm so that ε-completions are correctly handled. The algorithm first builds an empty set T we call the ε-translation set. Each time a call to a state q_h is completed, the algorithm checks whether the call consumed no input ($i = k$) and, if so, the output generated during the call is added to T as a possible ε-translation for call to state q_h. Each time a call to a state q_c is started, the algorithm checks if the call has been previously ε-completed and, if so, for each associated ε-translation in T the paused ES is *retroactively* resumed.

5.2   Trie-String Optimization for Earley-Like Parsing

The Earley-like algorithm no longer uses stacks, but the management of POs may be optimized by dynamically building a trie representing every PO generated during the algorithm execution, as for the breadth-first algorithm. However, completing a call involves the concatenation of the POs of two ESs, paused and completing, thus requiring to concatenate two strings both within the trie. This operation is more expensive than appending a simple sequence to a trie string, since trie strings can only be retrieved in reverse order; we must iterate twice over the completing string: one for building a reordered version and other for appending it to the state of the paused string. The grammar and input will determine the possitive or negative impact of this modification.

6   Empirical Tests

Both algorithms, their variants with trie-string management, and acceptor versions (suppressing output generation so only keeping string recognition) have been programmed using C++ and the Standard Template Library (STL). Execution times have measured for the RTNSO of Fig. 1 on a PC with a 2.0 GHz Pentium IV Centrino processor and 2 GB RAM (see Fig. 2(a) and 2(b)) running Debian GNU/Linux. As expected, our first algorithm has an exponential cost even for the acceptor version.   The original Earley's algorithm asymptotic cost is n^3, but it is usually better (even linear) for most natural language grammars and sentences. In our example, the cost of the acceptor-only Earley algorithm is linear (see Fig. 2(b)). However, incorporating output generation complicates the problem up to obtaining an exponential cost. An exponential number of steps

---

Algorithm 4. closure(V, k) $\triangleright C_\varepsilon(V_k)$

Input: V, the SES whose ε-closure is to be computed
       k, the current input position
Output: V after incrementing it with its ε-closure
1: $T \leftarrow \emptyset$ $\triangleright$ ε-translation set
2: $E \leftarrow V$ $\triangleright$ unexplored ES queue
3: **while** $E \neq \emptyset$ **do**
4:     $(q_s, z, \lambda, q_h, j) \leftarrow$ dequeue(E)
5:     **for each** $(q_t, g) : q_t \in \delta(q_s, (\varepsilon, g))$ **do** $\triangleright$ explicit ε-transitions
6:         **if** add($V, (q_t, zg, \lambda, q_h, j)$) **then**
7:             enqueue($E, (q_t, zg, \lambda, q_h, j)$)
8:         **end if**
9:     **end for**
10:    **for each** $q_t \in \delta(q_s, q_c)$ **do** $\triangleright$ push transitions
11:        **if** add($V, (q_t, z, q_c, q_h, j)$) **then** $\triangleright$ paused ES
12:           **if** $\{(g : (q_c, g) \in T\} \neq \emptyset$ **then** $\triangleright$ retroactive ε-completion
13:              **for each** $\{g : (q_c, g) \in T\}$ **do**
14:                 **if** add($V, (q_t, zg, \lambda, q_h, j)$) **then**
15:                     enqueue($E, (q_t, zg, \lambda, q_h, j)$)
16:                 **end if**
17:              **end for**
18:           **else if** add($V, (q_c, \varepsilon, \lambda, q_c, k)$) **then** $\triangleright$ active ES
19:              enqueue($E, (q_c, \varepsilon, \lambda, q_c, k)$)
20:           **end if**
21:        **end if**
22:    **end for**
23:    **if** $q_s \in F$ **then** $\triangleright$ pop transition
24:        **for each** $(q_r, z', q_h, q_h', i) \in V_j$ **do** $\triangleright$ for each paused ESs depending on q_h
25:           **if** $i = k$ **then** $\triangleright$ in case of ε-completion
26:              $T = T \cup \{(q_h, z)\}$ $\triangleright$ register ε-translation of q_h for retroactive
27:           **end if** $\triangleright$ ε-completions
28:           **if** add($V, (q_r, z'z, \lambda, q_h', i)$) **then** $\triangleright$ resumed ES
29:              enqueue($E, (q_r, z'z, \lambda, q_h', i)$)
30:           **end if**
31:        **end for**
32:    **end if**
33: **end while**

---

are saved due to the factoring of an exponential number of state calls; however, when we resume a set of paused ESs with every completion of their common calls, we are computing the concatenation of every paused PO with every completion PO. Earley's base algorithm is an acceptor only; it can be easily modified in order to also compute the set of parses for an accepted sequence, but if this set grows exponentially w.r.t. the input length the cost cannot be bound any longer to polynomial time. As be seen in Fig. 2(a), the breadth-first algorithm experiences an exponential speed up when incorporating trie-string management, as

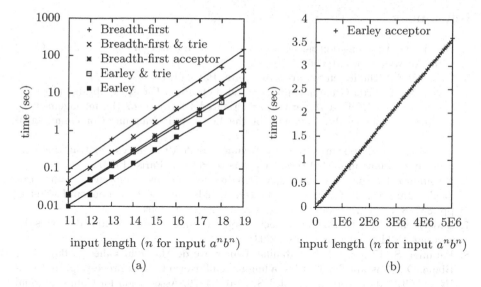

Fig. 2. Comparative graphics of execution times (in seconds) w.r.t. input length (n) of the different algorithms for the RTNSO of Fig. 1 and input $a^n b^n$. Notice the logarithmic scale of the vertical axis of graphic 2(a): all of its functions are exponential.

expected, but the Earley-like algorithm experiences an exponential slow down due to the concatenation of pairs of trie strings, as explained before.

7 Conclusion

We have first given here an efficient and simple parsing algorithm for natural language texts with RTNSOs with two limitations: left-recursive RTNSOs cannot be processed and infix calls are not factored. Based on Earley's parsing algorithm for context-free grammars, but taking into account ε-moves, we have shown how to modify the precedent algorithm in order to suppress both limitations. Moreover, we have shown a possible optimization of both algorithms involving tries for sequence representation. Finally, we have given comparative results which show that output generation, rather than being a simple issue, complicates algorithms up to obtaining exponential time costs in spite of the polynomial time of the acceptor-only Earley-like algorithm.

We are currently studying the use of an RTN-like structure to efficiently build and store the resulting set of outputs, to avoid the exponential complexity induced by the management of an exponentially growing set of outputs.

Acknowledgments. This work has been partially supported by the Spanish Government (grant number TIN2006–15071–C03–01), by the Universitat d'Alacant (grant number INV05-40), by the MENRT and by the CNRS. We thank Prof. E. Laporte for his useful comments.

References

1. Woods, W.A.: Transition network grammars for natural language analysis. Commun. ACM 13(10), 591–606 (1970)
2. Gross, M.: Méthodes en Syntaxe. Hermann, Paris (1975)
3. Gross, M.: Lexicon Grammar, pp. 244–258. Pergamon Press, Cambridge (1996)
4. Sastre, J.M.: HOOP: a Hyper-Object Oriented Platform for the management of linguistic databases. In: Commun. of the Lexis and Grammar Conference 2006 (2006)
5. Roche, E.: Analyse syntaxique transformationnelle du français par transducteurs et lexique-grammaire. PhD thesis, Université Paris 7, Paris (1993)
6. Nakamura, T.: Analyse automatique d'un discours spcialis au moyen de grammaires locales. In: Purnelle, G., Fairn, C., Dister, A. (eds.) JADT 2004, Louvain-la-Neuve, pp. 837–847. UCL Presses universitaires de Louvain (2004)
7. Silberztein, M.D.: Dictionnaires électroniques et analyse automatique de textes. Le systéme INTEX, Masson, Paris (1993)
8. Paumier, S.: Unitex 1.2 User Manual. Université de Marne-la-Vallée (2006)
9. Blanc, O., Constant, M.: Outilex, a linguistic platform for text processing. In: COLING/ACL 2006, Morristown, NJ, USA, pp. 73–76. Association for Computational Linguistics (2006)
10. Garrido-Alenda, A., Forcada, M.L., Carrasco, R.C.: Incremental construction and maintenance of morphological analysers based on augmented letter transducers. In: TMI 2002, pp. 53–62 (2002)
11. Van Noord, G.: Treatment of epsilon moves in subset construction. Comput. Linguist. 26(1), 61–76 (2000)
12. Fredkin, E.: Trie memory. Communications of the ACM 3(9), 490–499 (1960)
13. Earley, J.: An efficient context-free parsing algorithm. Commun. ACM 13(2), 94–102 (1970)
14. Woods, W.A.: Augmented transition networks for natural language analysis. Technical report CS-1, Comput. Lab., Harvard U., Cambridge, Mass. (1969)
15. Aycock, J., Horspool, N.: Practical Earley Parsing. The Computer Journal 45(6), 620–630 (2002)

The Deep Parser for Polish

Nina Suszczańska, Przemysław Szmal, and Krzysztof Simiński

Silesian University of Technology, Institute of Informatics
ul. Akademicka 16, 44-100 Gliwice, Poland
{Nina.Suszczanska,Przemyslaw.Szmal,Krzysztof.Siminski}@polsl.pl

Abstract. Although the first version of the Polsyn parser for the Polish language came into existence in 1997, there is no coherent description of it. This paper is an attempt to describe both the theoretical basis and the application of Polsyn. The parser is based on the Syntactical Groups Grammar for Polish (SGGP).

Keywords: NLP, Polish, SG-model of syntax, Syntactical Groups Systems formalism, SGGP grammar, deep parser.

1 Introduction

The syntactical analyser Polsyn for Polish language has been developed in the Institute of Informatics at the Silesian University of Technology. The first version of the parser was implemented in 1997. It had many shortcomings that in the course of time have been to some extent eliminated. The first application of the Polsyn parser was created in the framework of the research project TGT-1 [1]. Nowadays the parser is used in the Thetos [2], Polsumm [3] and Liana [4] projects. This paper describes the theoretical basis and the results produced by the parser.

The parser was developed on the basis of the Syntactical Groups Grammar for Polish (SGGP grammar, formerly the SG-grammar), the part of the SG-model of Polish syntax [5]. In the following sections the main features of the model will be described.

The SG-model is based on the SGS, Syntactical Groups Systems formalism [6] modified for natural language processing [7,8]. The basic element of the grammar is a syntactical group (SG). The productions constituting the SGGP describe not only the structure of SG but also the syntactical relations between SGs created when the production is applied. The SGGP grammar is defined as a finite set of productions $SG_L \rightarrow_{\omega,R} SG_R$, where SG_L and SG_R are syntactical groups. Each production is an instruction: "when the conditions ω are met put SG_R in place of SG_L and create the set R of relations". This dual form of production results from the nature of the SGGP formalism being a generalization of two known and distinctly different formalisms: constituency structure and dependency structure.

Each word is labeled with a number. Thus each sentence can be described as a finite set Z of integers representing the words. If a nonempty subset of the set Z meets the axioms of Gladky [6] it is called a syntactical group (SG). The

Z. Vetulani and H. Uszkoreit (Eds.): LTC 2007, LNAI 5603, pp. 205–217, 2009.

axioms define the general structure of SGs, relations between SGs, and general criteria of grouping.

The SGS formalism is the base for the computer SG-model for Polish syntax and the SGGP grammar. The grammar specifies the conditions of grouping the elements of Z into SGs and the syntactical relations between the elements of the SG. The advantage of the SGS formalism is the explicit pointing to the sets of words building SG and the capacity of determining the syntactical relations between groups. In compliance with the formalism each word is represented by a set of labels, the one of which is the number of the word in the text. Each SG is characterized by a finite set of labels (that are inherited or generated). The rules describing the SGs are a part of SGGP. A different order of applied grammar rules typically brings different results. The order of applying the grammar rules is also stated in SGGP.

2   SG-Model of Polish Language

Usually the model of language contains a grammar (and an alphabet V). In the SG-model the alphabet V has two elements: the alphabet V_G of syntactical groups and the alphabet V_R of relations. Because the natural language is too complicated to be described by a monolithic model, the proposed model is constructed from several joined models of various levels of language. In this section we describe the theoretical basis of our approach to syntax modeling aimed at the preparation of data to model the understanding of text. Thanks to SGS formalism the units of SG-model have a semantic nature that facilitates their following semantic interpretation. In the description of the SG-model the problems of semantic modeling will be mentioned only when it is necessary to understand the matter. This is why the term "SG-model" will be used instead of "SG-model of syntax".

2.1   The Syntactical Groups in the SG-Model

[9] presents three different kinds of definitions of syntactical groups:

1. The group is an abstract that is aimed to divide a sentence into positional syntactical parts. This approach enables the division of the sentence into the nominal and verbal phrases. A group may be empty and then the sentence is described by the remaining groups — the position of the lacking group in the sentence is preserved and filled with null value.
2. The group is a nonempty set of elements that are aggregated by nonpredicative relations. The two cases are considered: 1) only the subordinate relations are valid and 2) not only subordinate relations, but also relation that builds no tree (e.g. sequences) is valid.
3. The group is a nonempty set of elements that allows predicative and nonpredicative bonds between elements. The sentence is thus an example of the syntactical group [10].

Our approach to syntactical groups is compatible with the third of the above-mentioned definitions. *SG* has to meet the axioms of the SGS. Thus it is never empty — it contains at least one element. Distinct groups have no common elements. *SG* has no syntactical relations with itself. On the set of groups some operations have been defined including the natural ordering operation. In the *SG*-model of syntax, the groups of simple sentence compose a graph of a specific topology. The matter is discussed more precisely in [8,5].

There are five levels of syntax modeling. On each level there are several types of groups. Each group type of each level has its own rules of element grouping. The way the elements are gathered into *SG*s as well as the relationship of groups in the sentence are modeled in syntactical relations. In the SGGP the bonds are denoted with 35 syntactical relations [11].

During execution of the grouping operation an important role is played by selected *SG* attributes. The application of specific grammar productions is often directly dependent on the fact, if some conditions imposed on attributes of right-hand-side elements of those productions are met or not. The attribute system of the SGGP [12] contains elementary types of attribute values and sets of constants that are values of those types. The system also includes rules for construction of compound types, calculation of feature values, and type checking. To elaborate those rules we used elements of the categorial grammar theory [13]. The central part of the attribute system is the Feature Structure System (FSS). Its elements say what form and/or value may or should take the attributes associated with symbols that represent *SG*s detected in the grouping process and their components. The fundamental group of attributes of a given *SG* type are morpho-syntactic *SG* markers. The *SG* attribute set may be extended with syntactic relations in which given *SG* is involved, the number of component elements directly embedded in given *SG* and the list of those elements, the identifier of the variable used to represent the *SG*, *SG*s nesting depth in the *SG* corresponding to the whole sentence, the *SG*s logical model, etc. The structures of attributes that compose FSS are sets of pairs (*attrName* : *attrVal*), where *attrName* denotes a label used to identify the attribute category and *attrVal* - the value of the attribute (feature). The *attrVal* may be simple (scalar), in this capacity a number, identifier, or the dash sign "-" may be used.

2.2 Semantics of Groups and Relations

Our assumption is that the syntactical structure of the sentence depends on the information conveyed in it. The syntactical structure of the sentence is a hint for the algorithm of recognition of this information. This assumption facilitates the understanding of *SG*s structure and relations between them as the mechanisms of semantics of the language. Thus special attention is paid to the transformations of *SG*s and of their grammatical features. Semantically, the main representative of the syntactical group is the main word of its base group. Most often the subordinate group is semantically an attribute of the superior group. However semantic relation depends not only on the syntactical relation but also on the semantic features of both groups. The semantic interpretation of the syntactical structures is the task of the semantic analyser.

3 Multilevel SG-Syntax Model

The language is defined as a set of finite sequences composed of symbols of an alphabet, a finite set V. The generative grammar is defined as a set of rules that recursively determine the valid sequences of the language. In the SG-model (discussed below) there are five levels $(0-4)$ of formal languages that model the natural language.

The alphabet V_G^0 of the zero level contains lexical units – simple trivial groups, the words of the Polish language and separators $('.', ',', ';', '+', '-', '*', '/'$ etc.$)$ The elements of alphabet can aggregate and build up sequences, which we call compound trivial groups (CTG). Differently speaking, CTG is a fusion of words that occur in constant order and form.

$$CTG_i = \{x_{k_i}, x_{k_i+1}, \ldots, x_{k_i+l_i}\},$$

where $x_{k_i+t} \in V_G^0$, $0 \le t \le l_i$, $0 \le i \le n_0$, n_0 is the number of CTGs.
The set of valid sequences is composed of simple and compound trivial groups:

$$G^0 = \{CTG_1, CTG_2, \ldots, CTG_{n_0}\}.$$

It is finite and is stored in the dictionary. The grammar of the zero level is given in the dictionary. The alphabet V_R^0 is empty, since lexical unit aggregation does not cause relations to arise. The language L^0 of the zero level is composed of a finite number of nonempty sets – SGs of the zero level. The L^0 is described with a list of all trivial SGs (words, separators, compound trivial groups). The appropriate dictionaries have been prepared beforehand. The trivial SGs play a crucial role in the modeling process. The scope of the modeling language heavily depends on the dictionaries of the zero level. The dictionary V_G^0 in Polsyn is a set of several dictionaries — e.g. the $Morf$ dictionary contains more than 69000 words, and the beta version dictionary of CTGs – 147 entries.

Let's denote the set of elements of each trivial group as

$$X_i^0 = \{x_{k_i}, x_{k_i+1}, \ldots x_{k_i+l_i}\}, \quad 1 \le i \le n_0.$$

In accordance with the SGS, $X_i^0 \cap X_j^0 = \emptyset$ when $i \ne j$.

The alphabet V_G^1, the first element of the alphabet of the first level language L^1, is composed of groups of the zero level (G^0) and of the elements of V_G^0 that do not create the zero level groups (the elements that constitute G^0 i.e. $\bigcup_{i=1}^{n_0} X_i^0$ are excluded from the alphabet V_G^1):

$$V_G^1 = \left(V_G^0 \setminus \bigcup_{i=1}^{n_0} X_i^0\right) \cup G^0.$$

Alphabet V_R^1 contains m_1 first level relations:

$$V_R^1 = \{R_1^1, R_2^1, \ldots, R_{m_1}^1\}.$$

Now the alphabet V^1 of the first level can be expressed as:

$$V^1 = \langle V_G^1, V_R^1 \rangle.$$

The language L^1 is composed of a finite number of nonempty sets over the alphabet V^1 — the groups of the first level (SG^1). The grammar of the first level determines how the SG^1 are composed of the elements of V_G^1. Furthermore, only nonpredicative relations (both subordinate and nonsubordinate) are allowed between the components of the groups.Similarly as above,

$$SG_i^1 = X_i^1 = \{x_{k_i}, x_{k_i+1}, \ldots, x_{k_i+l_i}\},$$

where $x_{k_i+t} \in V_G^1$, $\quad 0 \le t \le l_i$, $\quad 0 \le i \le n_1$, $\quad n_1$ is the number of SG^1s and

$$G^1 = \{SG_1^1, SG_2^1, \ldots, SG_{n_1}^1\}.$$

The V_G^2, whose content can be described by the formula:

$$V_G^2 = \left(V_G^1 \setminus \bigcup_{i=1}^{n_1} X_i^1\right) \cup G^1,$$

is the first element of the alphabet of the second level language L^2. The alphabet V_R^2 is a sum of V_R^1 and the set of m_2 potential relations of the second level.

$$V_R^2 = V_R^1 \cup \{R_1^2, R_2^2, \ldots, R_{m_2}^2\},$$

$$V^2 = \langle V_G^2, V_R^2 \rangle.$$

The language L^2 is composed of a finite number of nonempty sets over the alphabet V^2, we call them second level syntactical groups (SG^2) . The grammar of the second level language determines the rules of composing the SG^2 of the V_G^2 elements. Between the components of the groups both the nonpredicative dependent syntactic relationships and predicative ones are allowed.

The elements of the second level language L^2 enable the creation of the alphabet V_G^3 of the next (third) level language L^3, analogously as in case of L^1 and L^2. The set V_G^3 is the first component of the third level language alphabet. On the third level $V_R^3 = V_R^2$. The language L^3 is composed of a finite number of nonempty sets over the alphabet V_G^3 – the third level groups (SG^3). The grammar of this level permits the both nonpredicative subordinate and predicative relations between the component parts of SG^3. The groups SG^3 are called coherent SGs and have a crucial role: only a coherent SG may have syntactical functions in the sentence.

The V_G^4 set is constructed similarly as the V_G^3 and is a part of the fourth level language L^4 alphabet. The language L^4 comprises a finite number of nonempty sets of SG^3; in our terminology SG^4 or simply sentences S. The grammar permits only predicative bonds between the elements of SG^4. The V_R^4 is the set of potential relations of the fourth level that are also called the function relations in the sentence.

The further level of modeling refers to the syntax of the text that is not discussed in this paper. The results of the research on this subject are presented in [14,5].

4   The Polsyn Parser

The parsing algorithm is a bottom-up one. The Polsyn parser builds more complicated structures beginning with trivial SGs and finishing with coherent SGs and sentences. The tokens are analysed from left to right (left-corner parsing). The problems of parsing occurring by bottom-up parsing are solved with the rules of applying the grammar productions on each level.

The parser is composed of several modules whose algorithms model all levels of the described model of syntax. The process of syntactical analysis is conducted in five stages. The stages are described below.

The task of the syntactical analysis program is to divide the sentence into component parts according to the rules of SGGP and to name the syntactical relations between them. The decomposition of compound sentences into simple ones is also its task.

There are more than 2000 rules of the grammar, the number of rules included in the parser nowadays exceeds 700. The lacking rules describe the passive constructions.

The way the Polsyn works will be exemplified using the sentence: *W lesie mieszkał szczwany wilk, który wielokrotnie obserwował dziewczynkę zza drzew, gdy biegła ścieżką do babci.* (In the forest lived a cunning wolf that many times observed the girl from behind the trees when she was running along the path to her grandma.)

4.1   Identification of Zero Level SGs

The zero level analysis works on the results of the morphological analysis (table 1). The list of tagged words of the analyzed text is the input set for the syntactical analysis. As it is mentioned in the section 3, the alphabet of the zero level is based on the dictionaries.

Usually each word is a separate trivial group. Some constant sequences of lexical units as abbreviations are added to the trivial groups. These CTGs are stored in a hash table. Nowadays the CTG dictionary contains abbreviations (e.g.: 'prof.', 'proc.', 'tzn.', 'p.n.e.', 'mjr', 'dr') and acronyms (e.g.: 'ONZ', 'USA', 'SOZ'). First the longest CTGs are searched up in the hash table, then shorter and shorter. (In the sentence *Widziałem dr. hab. Matianka.* 'I saw assisting professor Matianek.' the CTG 'dr. hab.' is extracted although the dictionary contains the CTG 'dr(.)'.)

Table 1. An excerpt of the result of the morphological analysis. Several dictionaries are used in the parser and the 'source' points to the appropiate ones. The part of speech (POS) and grammar features are encoded by numbers.

text	W	lesie	mieszkał	szczwany	...
lemma	w	las	mieszkać	szczwany	...
source	.&	.+	.+	.+	...
POS	7	1	4	21	...
features	—	161171	12312	111741	...

In the example there are no *CTG*s, therefore in the zero stage the parser tags each word with a separate *SG* label. Each word gets a unique identification integer number. The list of *SG*s for the example is shown the table 2. The word *biegła* is repeated because of homonymy (the word can be assigned to two infinitive lemmas *biec, biegnąć* and an adjective *biegły*).

Table 2. The list of zero level groups

id	word	lemma	id	word	lemma
1	W	w	12	drzew	drzewo
2	lesie	las	13	,	,
3	mieszkał	mieszkać	14	gdy	gdy
4	szczwany	szczwany	15	biegła	biec
5	wilk	wilk	16	biegła	biegły
6	,	,	17	biegła	biegnąć
7	który	który	18	ścieżką	ścieżka
8	wielokrotnie	wielokrotnie	19	do	do
9	obserwował	obserwować	20	babci	babcia
10	dziewczynkę	dziewczynka	21	.	.
11	zza	zza			

Special attention was paid to *CTG*s containing the full stop. In slightly more than 4/5 of cases the full stop in Polish text denotes the end of sentence. But in almost 1/5 of cases the full stop is an element of a *CTG* and does not denote the sentence boundary but an abbreviation, ellipsis of word(s), ellipsis of some letters of the word. The full stop is also used with ordinal numbers (*5.* – '5th'). This may sometimes cause an erroneous sentence boundary determination. The analysis is based on sentences, so incorrect sentence boundary detection can significantly garble the further analysis. In Polish, the *CTG*s — depending on their semantic role in the sentence — contain the full stop as an element or not; the sequence *dr hab.* has a different meaning from *dr. hab.* The *CTG*s analyser correctly treats these cases.

The additional difficulty is the differentiation of gender in Polish. The abbreviations may preserve the gender of the crucial word in the *CTG* or may get the new gender according to the morphological form of the abbreviation. Thus the abbreviation *ONZ* 'Organizacja Narodów Zjednoczonych, UN' may preserve the feminine gender (as the main word *Organizacja* is feminine) or may become masculine (the last syllable in pronunciation of the abbreviation *ONZ* is -*zet* that in Polish usually determines the masculine).

4.2   Identification of the First Level SG

The list of zero level groups is the input data for the stage of identification of first level *SG*s. The input data elements are gathered according to the rules of SGGP for the first level groups. Examples of first level groups types are listed in the Table 3.

Table 3. The first level groups types

GG	general group
ATG	attribute group
NaG	name group
NuG	numeral group
AdvG	adverbial group
CG	conjunction group
NG	noun group
PG	preposition group
VG	verb group
PM	punctuation mark

Each group type has its own grammar rules of the first level. As an example we will shortly discuss the ATG group. An ATG is composed of adjectives, ordinal numerals, pronouns and adjective participles, sometimes preceded by attribute operator [8]. More complicated ATGs are composed of serial constructions (of five kinds). The main element of the simple ATG represents the group, in more complicated — the last component of the serial. The grammatical features are inherited from the main element or are common features extracted from the serial. The ATGs with predicatives as main words and the ATGs with composed constructions (even sentences) are analysed on the further levels. The ATG is an element of NG or represents the NG in ellipses. The examples of the ATGs: *drugi, siódmy i dwudziesty* '[the] second, [the] seventh and [the] twentieth', *bardzo szybko* 'very quickly', *nie bardzo szybko* 'no so quickly'. The grammar of the first level uses not the words or lemmas but the morpho-syntactical features of the zero level groups. There are some exceptions when the words are used in the disambiguation filtering.

The results of the analysis of the first stage are shown in Table 4. Two two-element groups were built: NG7 and VG2, the representative of which are SG^0s ($id = 5$ and $id = 9$). The created relations are following: for the NG7 group:

$attr(4,5)$ – the SG^0 with $id = 4$ is an attribute of SG^0 with $id = 5$; for the
VG2: $mod(8,9)$ – the SG^0 with $id = 8$ may modify the meaning of the SG^0
with $id = 9$. The remaining groups contain only one element. The homonymy
phenomenon occurs in this text and is denoted with VG3 ($id = 15$) and NG9
($id = 16$). The SG^0 with $id = 17$ does not build the SG^1 and is not accepted
for further analysis.

Table 4. The list of zero, first, second and fourth level groups. The arrow ↓ denotes
that the group is not analysed in the following level. H1 and H2 are not groups, they
are the homonymy markers. The SG^0 groups #15 and #17 represent verbs (cf. table
2) and are marked as homonyms.

word	SG^0	SG^1	SG^2	SG^4
W	1	PG1		
lesie	2	NG1	PG4	
mieszkał	3	VG1	VG5	S2
szczwany	4			
wilk	5	NG7	NG11	
,	6	PM1	PM4	
który	7	NG8	NG12	
wielokrotnie	8			
obserwował	9	VG2	VG6	S3
dziewczynkę	10	NG3	NG13	
zza	11	PG2	PG5	
drzew	12	NG4		
,	13	PM2	PM5	
gdy	14	CG1	CG2	
		H1		
biegła	15	VG3	VG7	S1
biegła	16	NG9	NG15 ↓	
		H2		
biegła	17	↓		
ścieżką	18	NG5	NG16	
do	19	PG3	PG6	
babci	20	NG6		
.	21	PM3	PM6	

4.3   The Analysis of the Second Level

The list of first level groups SG^1 is the input data for second level analysis.
The grouping algorithms use the generative dictionary of Polish verbs [15]. The
examples of second level groups: *dom ojca siostry Jana* '[the] house of father
of John's sister', *demonstracja wynalazku kolegom* '[the] demonstration of [the]
contrivance to [the] colleagues'. As an example we will give a short description
of a noun SG creation.

A second-level NG creation process is based on broadly meant valency. All NG component elements group around so-called base group (NG_b), which in continuation of the analysis appears as a representative of the whole NG. Furthermore, for the NG_b a NG logical model is built, which is the base for other SGs to group around the NG_b. This is the way the NG arises, in which the NG_b is the main element. In the next phases the NG and neighboring SGs are subjected to different kind operations, according to the SGGP rules. In effect a NG arises with components, which collectively describe some notion. The SGGP rules define principles for evaluation of morpho-syntactical features of the NG and the syntactical relations that exist between its component elements. While building the NG, requirements of its NG_b against the semantic context are taken into consideration. It's relatively easy to obtain those requirements by using schemata collected in the Semsyn database.

Using Semsyn for purposes of noun group analysis is possible because for verbal nouns the morphologic analyzer provides two variants: a noun with a noun-lexeme and a noun with a verb-lexeme. With this verb we can turn to the database and obtain the list of its semantic surroundings schemas, and then transform the verb schemas into the noun ones. For example, schema for the verb *demonstrować* 'demonstrate' looks as follows:

$$NGn - NGacc + (NGd, "przed" \frown NGi, "wobec" \frown NGg)$$

and for the noun *demonstracja* 'demonstration' meant as *pokaz* 'outward expression or display':

$$-NGg + (NGd, "przed" \frown NGi, "wobec" \frown NGg)$$

Schema for the noun was obtained in effect of the verb schema's transformation. In the schemas, the '−' character represents the verb *demonstrować* or the noun *'demonstracja'*, respectively. NGn, NGg, NGd, Ngacc, NGi mean NGs − respectively − in nominative, genitive, dative, accusative, and instrumental.

4.4   The Analysis of the Third and Fourth Level

The list of second level groups is the input data for the analysis on the third level that is responsible for creation of SG^3s and appropriate syntactical relations. On this level the compound sentences are split into simple ones.

On this level backtrack algorithms are used what complicates and slows down the analysis. Sometimes after the list of SG^4 has been determined a need occurs to review the structure of certain SG^3s or to create new groups. An example for this situation is a participle group that is constructed of a noun group and a preposition. To reduce the time and memory complexity, the third and fourth level groups are created in the same stage of the analysis.

The Table 4 presents the results of this stage of the analysis. The analyzed sentence was split into three sentences. The new sentences are labeled with new *ids*, the previous *id* is assigned to the last component.

On the last stage, the analysis is applied to the sentences of the list of SG^4. The sentence's components that correspond to the SGGP of the fourth level are assigned syntactical roles. The sentences are labeled by the characteristics: *major, sentence, indicative, ellipsis, anaphora, nosubject, nopredicate* etc. The algorithm uses the semantic-syntactical dictionary of Polish verbs [16], [15]. The sentences of our example and their relations are presented in the table 5.

Table 5. The characteristics of sentences and their relations

S2:	PG4, VG5, NG11, PM4
	major, indicative, past tense
Rel S2:	#fun(sentence, S2), #predicate(VG5,S2), #subject(NG11, VG5), #adverbial group(PG4, VG5)
S3:	NG12, VG6, NG13, PG5, PM5
	major, indicative, past tense, ellipsis, no subject
Rel S3:	# fun(sentence, S3), #predicate(VG6, S3), #anaphore(S3, X), #object4(NG13, VG6), #adverbial group(PG5, VG6)
S1:	GSP2, VG7, NG16, PG6, PM6
	sentence, indicative, past tense, ellipsis, no subject
Rel S1:	#fun(sentence, S1), #predicate(VG7, S1), #anaphore(S1, X), #object5(NG16, VG7), #adverbial group(PG6, VG7)

5   Problems of Disambiguation in Polsyn

In most cases, the morphologic analysis provides ambiguous results. We can meet ambiguity of three basic types: ambiguity of morpho-syntactic features, lemmas, and analysis methods. Morphologic disambiguation consists in filtering ambiguous morphologic analysis results in order to select a single, proper morphologic interpretation. The task of disambiguation in the morphologic analyzer is in practice almost impossible to be done since the analyzer has no sufficient knowledge to unambiguously select a set of tags that describe individual morphological units. Moreover, as it can be observed in practice, disambiguation on the morphologic level may prove faulty – only some ambiguity types are worth solving. Ambiguous results are usually passed to the next processing levels, where – in a broader context, with higher-level knowledge at hand – it is easier to find and reject solutions which in given context are improper. In our parser almost all the weight of resolving the morpho-syntactic ambiguity is carried on the syntactic level. In our parser, mechanisms aimed to reduce the number of homonymic nodes have been applied. It happens however that it is impossible to solve the ambiguity on the syntactic level; in such case this task is done during the semantic analysis.

Mechanisms for ambiguity reduction use so called homonymic filters. There are a few dozen filters in our parser. The filtering algorithms are based on different approaches. Syntactic, semantic, pragmatic, and heuristic filters can be distinguished. Syntactic filters make use of grammar rules, semantic ones of lexical semantics. Pragmatic filters are based on limitations imposed on translated texts pragmatics. Filters used on different analysis levels differ each from other. One of the reasons for that is the fact that data, upon which filtering algorithms on different levels work, differ in format.

Principles of ambiguity reduction can be defined as follows. In the ideal case, from the set of tags in a homonymic node only one correct variant, consistent with grammar rules, has to be selected, all the rest can be rejected as incorrect. Unfortunately, such an ideal scenario happens very rarely. It turns out that usually there are more than one correct (i.e. consistent with the respective level grammar) variants. Moreover, on the lower level the knowledge about higher level grammar rules is inaccessible. As a matter of fact, some productions from higher levels are used, but they are the simplest ones and sometimes they are insufficient to get an unambiguous choice. Introduction of more complex rules would be too costly, the time of handling them would be comparable with the time of preliminary syntactic analysis, and even of the semantic one.

Disambiguation of syntactic analysis results is performed on the basis of rules. The rules have been implemented in the form of functions that filter tags assigned to syntax groups during the analysis process. Inspiration for writing the rules has issued from linguistic works, first of all [17]. In [18] we discussed the kinds of filters used to reduce ambiguity of this specific type, and also the results obtained after reduction is done.

6   Conclusions

In this paper we do not compare the Polsyn parser with other known parsers, as the analysers created by the teams of J. Bień, M. Świdziński or Z. Vetulani, or the parsers of T. Obrębski and the teams of other scientists.

The comparison of parsers is a thankless and almost impossible task. The scientists use different formalisms, grammars and algorithms and define various objectives. Our grammar is based on the model differing from the other ones. The solution closest to the ours is the one described in [19].

The parser is implemented in the C++ language. Recently the program has been optimized: the organization of the data access has been changed – in place of linear structures the associative queues have been used. Thus the computational complexity of most algorithms has been reduced from $O(n^3)$ down to $O(n \log n)$.

The processors for the syntactical analysis are parts of the Linguistic Analysis Server (LAS). The server is an Internet application available at the address http://las.aei.polsl.pl/las2/.

In construction of the natural language model it is impossible to guarantee the indefective splitting of the sentence into elements and the faultless choice of the basic constructions of the model. The SG-model is not an exception. In our work we limit ourselves only to the one model described in the paper.

References

1. Szmal, P.: Translation of Polish Texts into the Sign Language. Research Project no. 8 T11C 007 17 final report (in Polish), Politechnika Śląska, Gliwice (2001)
2. Szmal, P.: Computer Assistance to Hearing-impaired People by a Computer Generation of the Sign Language. Research project no. 4 T11C 024 24 final report (in Polish), Politechnika Śląska, Gliwice (2005)
3. Kulikow, S., Suszczańska, N.: A Polish Document Summarizer. In: 21st Iasted International Conference Applied Informatics – AI 2003, pp. 369–374, Innsbruck (2003)
4. Suszczańska, N.: The Liana System. In: Hnatkowska, B., Huzar, Z. (eds.) Inżynieria oprogramowania Metody wytwarzania i wybrane zastosowania (in Polish), pp. 146–159. PWN, Warsaw (2008)
5. Suszczańska, N.: GS–Grammar of Polish Syntax (in Polish). In: Conference "Speech Analysis, Synthesis and Recognition in Technology, Linguistics and Medicine", pp. 113–117. AGH, Kraków (2005)
6. Gladky, A.V.: Sintakticheskie struktury estestvennogo yazyka v avtomatizirovanykh sistemakh obshchenya (in Russian). Nauka, Moskva (1975)
7. Sushchanskaya, N.F.: Computer Grammar of Syntactical Groups. Cybernetics and Systems Analysis 35(6), 987–993 (1999)
8. Suszczańska, N.: GS–model of Polish Language Syntax (in Polish). Speech and Language Technology, 7 (2003)
9. Grzegorczykowa, R.: Wykłady z polskiej składni (in Polish). Wydawnictwo Naukowe PWN, Warsaw (2004)
10. Saloni, Z., Świdziński, M.: Składnia współczesnego języka polskiego (in Polish). Wydawnictwo Naukowe PWN, Warsaw (1998)
11. Suszczańska, N.: Automatic Identification of Relations Between Key Abstractions of the Domain Problem. In: V Conference Inżynieria Wiedzy i Systemy Ekspertowe (in Polish), pp. 319–326. Wrocław (2003)
12. Suszczańska, N., Szmal, P.: Categorial Grammar Elements in the Thetos Systems Parser. In: 2nd Language and Technology Conference, pp. 338–342. Poznań (2005)
13. Lambek, J.: Categorial and Categorical Grammars. In: Oehrle, R.T., Bach, E., Wheeler, D. (eds.) Categorial Grammars and Natural Language Structures, Studies in Linguistics and Philosophy, vol. 32, pp. 297–317. D. Reidel, Dordrecht (1988)
14. Kulikow, S., Romaniuk, J., Suszczańska, N.: A Syntactical Analysis of Anaphora in the Polsyn Parser. In: International IIS:IIPWM 2004 Conference, pp. 444–448, Zakopane (2004)
15. Grund, D.: Computer Implementation of Syntactic-generative Dictionary of Polish Verbs (in Polish). Studia Informatica 21(3(40), 243–256 (2000)
16. Polański, K.: Słownik syntaktyczno-generatywny czasownikow polskich (in Polish). Wydawnictwo Polskiej Akademii Nauk, Wrocław (1980)
17. Brill, E.: Transformation-based Error-driven Learning and Natural Language Processing: A Case Study of Part of Speech Tagging. Computational Linguistics 21(4), 543–565 (1995)
18. Suszczańska, N., Szmal, P.: Problems of Disambiguation in the Thetos-3 System. Accepted in Speech and Language Technology 11 (2008)
19. Vetulani, Z.: Komunikacja człowieka z maszyną. Komputerowe modelowanie kompetencji językowej (in Polish). Exit, Warsaw (2004)

Automatically Determining
Attitude Type and Force for Sentiment Analysis

Shlomo Argamon[1], Kenneth Bloom[1], Andrea Esuli[2], and Fabrizio Sebastiani[2]

[1] Linguistic Cognition Laboratory
Department of Computer Science
Illinois Institute of Technology
10 W. 31st Street – Chicago, IL 60616, USA
{argamon,kbloom1}@iit.edu
[2] Istituto di Scienza e Tecnologie dell'Informazione
Consiglio Nazionale delle Ricerche
Via G Moruzzi, 1 – 56124 Pisa, Italy
{andrea.esuli,fabrizio.sebastiani}@isti.cnr.it

Abstract. Recent work in sentiment analysis has begun to apply fine-grained semantic distinctions between expressions of attitude as features for textual analysis. Such methods, however, require the construction of large and complex lexicons, giving values for multiple sentiment-related attributes to many different lexical items. For example, a key attribute is what type of *attitude* is expressed by a lexical item; e.g., beautiful expresses appreciation of an object's quality, while evil expresses a negative judgment of social behavior. In this chapter we describe a method for the automatic determination of complex sentiment-related attributes such as *attitude type* and *force*, by applying supervised learning to Word-Net glosses. Experimental results show that the method achieves good effectiveness, and is therefore well-suited to contexts in which these lexicons need to be generated from scratch.

Keywords: Sentiment analysis, Lexicon learning, WordNet, Appraisal theory.

1 Introduction

Recent years have seen a growing interest in *non-topical text analysis*, in which characterizations are sought of the opinions, feelings, and attitudes expressed in a text, rather than just of the topics the text is about. A key type of non-topical text analysis is *sentiment analysis*, which includes several important applications such as *sentiment classification*, in which a document is labelled as a positive or negative evaluation of a target object (film, book, product, etc.), and *opinion mining*, in which text mining methods are used to find interesting and insightful correlations between writers' opinions. Immediate applications include market research, customer relationship management, and intelligence analysis.

Critical to sentiment analysis is identifying useful features for the semantic characterization of the text. At the lexical level, most work on sentiment analysis

Z. Vetulani and H. Uszkoreit (Eds.): LTC 2007, LNAI 5603, pp. 218–231, 2009.

has relied on either raw "bag-of-words" features from which standard text classifiers can be learned, or on "semantic orientation" lexicons [1], which classify words as positive or negative (possibly with a weight), as a basis for analysis. Recent work, however, has started to apply more complex semantic taxonomies to sentiment analysis, either by developing more complex lexicons [2,3] or by applying multiple text classifiers [4] using supervised learning.

Both approaches present practical difficulties—supervised learning requires extensive text annotation, while developing lexicons by hand is also very time-consuming. The purpose of this chapter is to explore the use of (semi-)supervised learning techniques to "bootstrap" semantically complex lexicons of terms with sentimental valence. Previous applications of such lexicons to sentiment analysis [2,3] have used the framework of Martin and White's [5] Appraisal Theory, developed for the manual analysis of evaluative language. This framework assigns several sentiment-related features to relevant lexical items, including *orientation* (Positive or Negative), *attitude type* (whether Affect, Appreciation of inherent qualities, or Judgment of social interactions), and *force* of opinion expressed (Low, Median, High, or Max). Such challenging multi-dimensional analysis can allow more subtle distinctions to be drawn than can just classifying terms as Positive or Negative.

Little research to date has applied such schemes in a computational context. Taboada and Grieve [2] used a small lexicon of adjectives manually classified for top-level attitude type, expanded by a technique based on pointwise mutual information (PMI) [1]. Their analysis showed that different types of review texts contain different amounts of each attitude type. Whitelaw et al. [3] and Bloom et al. [6] further showed how using attitude type, force and orientation, together with shallow parsing of evaluative adjective groups, can improve accuracy of sentiment-based text classification and also enables more detailed opinion mining than methods based only on classifying sentiment as Positive or Negative.

The current work explores how a lexicon such as that used in that work can be learned in a fully automatic fashion, concentrating on assigning the correct attitude type and force to lexical items. We examine here the extent to which such a semantically-complex lexicon for sentiment analysis can be learned automatically, starting from a core (manually-constructed) lexicon of adjectives and adverbs. We apply a variant of a technique [7] originally developed for classifying words as Positive or Negative based on dictionary glosses. Experiments show that this variant works well for detecting *attitude type* and *force*.

2   Appraisal Theory

Appraisal Theory is a linguistic approach to analyzing how subjective language is used to express various sorts of attitudes towards various targets [5]. Appraisal theory models appraisal as comprising three main linguistic systems: "Attitude", which distinguishes different kinds of attitudes that can be expressed (including attitude type and orientation); "Graduation", which enables strengthening or weakening such expression (including force and focus); and "Engagement",

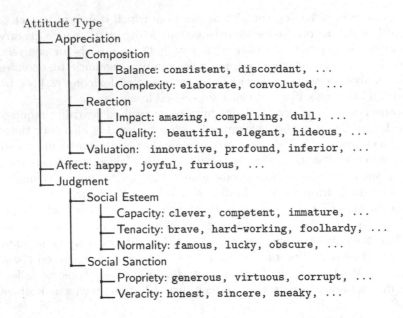

Fig. 1. Options in the attitude type taxonomy, with examples of appraisal adjectives from the base lexicon described in Section 4.1

which represents different possible degrees and kinds of commitment to the opinion expressed (including identification and relation of the speaker/writer to the source of an attributed evaluation). Previous application of Appraisal Theory to sentiment analysis [2,3,8] has focused on three key components:

Orientation determines whether the appraisal is Positive or Negative (this has also been termed "semantic orientation" or "polarity" in the sentiment analysis literature).

Attitude Type specifies the type of appraisal being expressed as one of Affect, Appreciation, or Judgment (with further sub-typing possible). Affect refers to a personal emotional state (e.g., happy, angry), and is the most explicitly subjective type of appraisal. The other two options differentiate between the Appreciation of 'intrinsic' object properties (e.g., slender, ugly) and social Judgment (e.g., heroic, idiotic). Figure 1 gives a detailed view of the attitude type taxonomy, together with illustrative adjectives.

Force describes the intensity of the appraisal being expressed. Force may be realized via modifiers such as very (increased force) or slightly (decreased force), or may be realized lexically in a head word, e.g., wonderful vs. great vs. good.

These semantic features are also related to other analyses of term "value" or "sentiment" in the literature. Osgood's [9] Theory of Semantic Differentiation delineated three dimensions of affective meaning: "evaluative", i.e., Orientation; "potency", referring to the strength of feeling expressed; and "activity", referring to how active or passive an evaluation is. This was the basis for Kamps and Marx's [10] analyses of affective meaning in WordNet. Mullen and Collier [11] estimated values for Osgood's three dimensions for adjectives in WordNet, by comparing path lengths to appropriate pairs of anchor words (such as good and bad) in WordNet's synonymy graph, using document-level averages of these values as input to SVMs for sentiment classification.

Also relevant is the Lasswell Value Dictionary, as applied in the General Inquirer [12]. It classifies words as relating to various basic "values", such as wealth, power, respect, rectitude, skill, enlightenment, affection, and wellbeing. Some have parallels in Appraisal Theory (for example "rectitude", which is similar to the attitude type of Social Sanction), while other Lasswell categories, such as "wealth" or "enlightenment" appear unrelated to any attitude type.

3   Methodology

3.1   Semi-supervised Learning of Orientation

The method we use in this chapter for determining the attitude type and force of terms is inspired to the method proposed by Esuli and Sebastiani [7] for determining orientation (called there "PN-polarity"). That method relies on training, in a semi-supervised way, a binary classifier that labels terms as either Positive or Negative. A *semi-supervised* method is a learning process whereby only a small subset $L \subset Tr$ of the training data Tr are manually labelled. In origin the training data in $U = Tr - L$ are instead unlabelled; it is the process itself that labels them, automatically, by using L (with the possible addition of other publicly available resources) as input. The method starts from two small seed (i.e. training) sets L_p and L_n of known Positive and Negative terms, respectively, and expands them into the two final training sets $Tr_p \supset L_p$ and $Tr_n \supset L_n$ by adding them new sets of terms U_p and U_n found by navigating the WordNet (2.0) graph along the synonymy and antonymy relations.

Note that when such expansion is used, nothing prevents a term from belonging *both* to Tr and Te. To see this, remember that the training set Tr is the union of a set L of manually labelled terms and a set U of automatically labelled ones. While, conforming to good machine learning practice, we do need to ensure that $L \cap Te = \emptyset$, there is nothing wrong if $U \cap Te \neq \emptyset$.

Perhaps more significant is the idea that terms are given vectorial representations based on their WordNet *glosses*. For each term t_i in $Tr \cup Te$ (Te being the test set, i.e. the set of terms to be classified), a textual representation of t_i is generated by collating all the glosses of t_i as found in WordNet. (In general, a term t_i may have more than one gloss, since it may have more than one sense.) Each such representation is converted into vectorial form by standard text indexing techniques.

In addition, *negation propagation* is performed on each gloss, by replacing all the terms that occur in the context of a negation with a synthetic term representing the negated term. For example, the vector for the gloss "*the act of moving hurriedly and in a careless manner*" (for the word "rushing"), will comprise elements for *act, moving, hurriedly, careless,* and *manner,* while that for the gloss "*not moving quickly*" (for the word "slow") will comprise elements for the synthetic features ¬*moving* and ¬*quickly.*

Once the vectorial representations for all terms in $Tr \cup Te$ have been generated, those for the terms in Tr are fed to a supervised learner, which thus generates a binary classifier. This latter, once fed with the vectorial representations of the terms in Te, classifies each of them as either Positive or Negative. Note that this method allows classification of *any* term, independent of its part-of-speech, provided there is a gloss for it in the lexical resource.

The basic idea is that terms of similar semantic types should tend to have "similar" glosses: for instance, the glosses of honest and intrepid will both contain positive expressions, while the glosses of disturbing and superfluous will both contain negative expressions.

In this chapter we adopt this gloss-based representation method using the above described vectorial representations to represent the terms of our lexicon.

3.2 Learning Attitude Type and Force

Force is the simpler case here—we are faced with four categories, with each term belonging to exactly one of the four. Since the categories (Low, Median, High, and Max) are ordered along a scale of value, deciding which one applies to a given term is an *ordinal regression* problem [13]. However, for the time being we (suboptimally) assume the problem is a 1-of-*n* *classification* problem (thereby disregarding the order among the categories), with *n*=4. We defer the use of ordinal regression for this problem to future work.

In determining attitude type, on the other hand, we are essentially faced with eleven binary distinctions, each consisting in determining whether or not the term belongs to any of the eleven fine-grained attitude types given in Figure 1. Note that a single term may be semantically ambiguous, and thus labeled by more than one attitude type (e.g., fair is labeled, in the base lexicon described in Section 4.1, with attitude types Quality, Propriety, and Veracity)[1]. This means this is an *at-least-1-of-n* task with $n = 11$, since we only work on terms that carry appraisal, and which thus belong to at least one of the attitude type classes. Since the eleven attitude types are leaves in a hierarchy, we may instead apply a hierarchical classification method, whereby the structure of the hierarchy is taken into account.

Thus, in determining attitude type we consider two alternative classification methods. The *flat* method simply ignores the fact that the categories are organized into a hierarchy and plainly generates eleven independent binary classifiers $\hat{\Phi}_1, \ldots, \hat{\Phi}_{11}$; each such classifier $\hat{\Phi}_i$ is generated by using all the terms in Tr_i as positive examples and all terms not belonging to Tr_i as negative examples.

The *hierarchical* method is similar, but generates binary classifiers $\hat{\Phi}_j$ for each leaf *and* for each internal node. For an internal node c_j, as the set of positive

---

[1] Out of 1855 terms in our lexicon, 192 have more than one attitude type assigned.

training examples, the union of the sets of positive training examples of its descendant categories is used. For each node c_j (be it internal or leaf), as the set of negative examples we use the union of the positive training examples of its sibling categories (minus possible positive training examples of c_j). Both choices follow consolidated practice in the field of hierarchical categorization [14]. At classification time, test terms are classified by the binary classifiers at internal nodes, and only the ones that are classified as belonging to the node percolate down to the lower levels of the tree. The hierarchical method has the potential advantage of using more specifically relevant negative examples for training.

To produce a vector for a given term, we collate all glosses for the term into a single document; note that only glosses of synsets having certain parts-of-speech are considered (see Section 4.3). From the resulting documents we then remove stop words, stem terms, and compute term weights by cosine-normalized $tf \cdot idf$, a standard method in information retrieval.

When performing training set expansion on seed sets $Tr^1 = \{Tr_1^1, \ldots, Tr_n^1\}$ and expand them into the final n training sets $Tr = Tr^K = \{Tr_1^K, \ldots, Tr_n^K\}$ after K iterations. For expansion, synonyms *and* antonyms of a training term are added to the training set of the same class, as antonyms will differ in *orientation* but neither in *attitude type* nor in *force* e.g., Balance includes both `consistent` and `discordant`, while Tenacity includes both `brave` and `foolhardy`. (This contrasts with expansion for binary *orientation* classification [7], where antonyms were added to the training set of the *opposite* class.)

4   Experiments

We examined the use of two base learners for this task: (i) multinomial Naive Bayes, using Andrew McCallum's Bow implementation[2], and (ii) (linear kernel) Support Vector Machines, using Thorsten Joachims' SVMlight implementation[3]. Note that we used the $tf \cdot idf$ weighted representations only when using the SVM learner, since Naive Bayes requires binary input. Actually, the use of *multinomial* Naive Bayes ensures that raw term frequencies are *de facto* taken into account.

We also compared three possible classification modes for combining binary classifiers for a multiple labeling problem: (i) m-of-n, which may assign zero, one, or several classes to the same test term; (ii) at-least-1-of-n, a variant of m-of-n which always assigns one class when m-of-n would assign no class; (iii) 1-of-n, which always assigns exactly one class. Note that the preferred approaches for classifying by attitude type and force are (ii) and (iii), respectively. However, we have run experiments in which we test each of (i)–(iii) on both attitude and force. There are several justifications for this; for instance, trying (i) on attitude type is justified by the fact that forcing at least one category assignment, as at-least-1-of-n does, promises to bring about higher recall but lower precision, and nothing guarantees that the balance will be favourable. Suboptimal as some

---

[2] http://www-2.cs.cmu.edu/~mccallum/bow/
[3] http://svmlight.joachims.org/

of these attempts may be a priori, they are legitimate provided that we use the correct evaluation measure for the task.

All experiments reported in this chapter were evaluated by running 10-fold cross validation on the eleven seed sets $Tr = \{Tr_1, \ldots, Tr_{11}\}$ for attitude type and on the four seed sets $Tr = \{Tr_1, \ldots, Tr_4\}$ for force. To guarantee that each category c_i is adequately represented both in the training and the testing sets, we use *stratified* cross-validation, where we split *each* set Tr_i into 10 roughly equal parts, each of which is used in turn as a test set.

4.1 The Lexicon

The lexicon[4] Tr has been constructed manually to give appraisal attribute values for a large number of evaluative adjectives and adverbs. Values for attitude type, orientation, and force are stored for each term. The lexicon was built starting with words and phrases given as examples for the different appraisal type values by Martin and White [5], finding more candidate terms and phrases using WordNet and two online thesauruses[5]. Candidates were then manually checked and assigned attribute values. Very infrequent terms were automatically discarded, thus reducing the amount of manual work required.

The attitude type dimension of the corpus is defined by eleven different leaf categories, described in Section 2, each one containing 189 terms on the average (the maximum is 284 for Affect, the minimum is 78 for Balance); every term is labelled by at least one and at most three categories (the average being 1.12). The hierarchy of the attitude taxonomy is displayed in Figure 1. Force comprises four values in the corpus: Low (e.g., adequate), Median (e.g., good), High (e.g., awesome), and Max (e.g., best). Most (1464) entries in the corpus have Median force, with 30 Low, 323 High, and 57 Max.

Note that while lexicon entries also include values for orientation, we only consider here classification by attitude and by force. For a thorough study of the problem of determining orientation by means of methods similar to the ones discussed here please refer to [7,15].

4.2 Evaluation Measures

For evaluation we use the well-known F_1 measure, defined as the harmonic mean of *precision* (π) and *recall* (ρ):

$$\pi = \frac{TP}{TP + FP} \tag{1}$$

$$\rho = \frac{TP}{TP + FN} \tag{2}$$

$$F_1 = \frac{2\pi\rho}{\pi + \rho} = \frac{2TP}{2TP + FP + FN} \tag{3}$$

---

[4] Available at: http://lingcog.iit.edu/arc/appraisal_lexicon_2007b.tar.gz
[5] http://m-w.com and http://thesaurus.com

Table 1. Summary of averaged cross-validation results for attitude type, showing microaveraged (π^μ, ρ^μ, F_1^μ) and macroaveraged (π^M, ρ^M, F_1^M) statistics. Each row shows the average over all runs (see text) for given values for certain independent variables (such as the learning algorithm, classification model, and so on), averaging over all others (indicated by –avg–). The baseline trivial acceptor result is reported for comparison. The fixed variable in each row and the highest value in each column for each set of comparable results are **boldfaced** for ease of reading.

Alg.	Model	Method	POS	π^μ	ρ^μ	F_1^μ	π^M	ρ^M	F_1^M
baseline	n/a	n/a	n/a	0.086	1.000	0.158	0.085	1.000	0.155
NB	–avg–	–avg–	–avg–	**0.320**	**0.397**	**0.332**	0.362	**0.376**	**0.305**
SVM	–avg–	–avg–	–avg–	0.254	0.237	0.223	**0.464**	0.233	0.186
–avg–	**flat**	–avg–	–avg–	**0.381**	**0.421**	**0.371**	0.389	**0.401**	**0.345**
–avg–	**hier**	–avg–	–avg–	0.192	0.213	0.184	**0.437**	0.208	0.147
–avg–	–avg–	**m-of-n**	–avg–	**0.334**	0.222	0.237	**0.509**	0.225	0.207
–avg–	–avg–	**at-least-1**	–avg–	0.243	**0.375**	0.285	0.388	**0.357**	0.253
–avg–	–avg–	**1-of-n**	–avg–	0.284	0.353	**0.310**	0.343	0.331	**0.277**
–avg–	–avg–	–avg–	**Adj,Adv**	0.286	**0.318**	0.277	0.411	0.305	0.245
–avg–	–avg–	–avg–	**Adj,Adv,V**	0.285	**0.318**	0.277	0.412	**0.306**	0.246
–avg–	–avg–	–avg–	**Adj,Adv,N**	**0.289**	0.317	**0.279**	**0.417**	0.303	**0.247**
–avg–	–avg–	–avg–	**Adj,Adv,V,N**	0.287	0.315	0.277	0.413	0.303	0.245

where TP stands for true positives, FP for false positives, and FN for false negatives. Note that F_1 is undefined when $TP + FP + FN = 0$. However, in our lexicon there is at least one positive example for each category, thus $TP + FN > 0$ and F_1 is always defined.

We compute both *microaveraged* F_1 (denoted by F_1^μ) and *macroaveraged* F_1 (F_1^M). F_1^μ is obtained by (i) computing the category-specific values $TP(c_i)$, $FP(c_i)$, and $FN(c_i)$, (ii) obtaining TP as the sum of the $TP(c_i)$'s (same for FP and FN), and then (iii) applying Equation 3. F_1^M is obtained by (i) computing the category-specific precision and recall scores $\pi(c_i)$ and $\rho(c_i)$, (ii) computing $F_1(c_i)$ values for the individual categories c_i, applying Equation 3, and (iii) computing F_1^M as the unweighted average of the category-specific values $F_1(c_i)$; macroaveraged precision and recall (π^M and ρ^M) are computed similarly.

4.3 Results

We ran evaluations for all combinations of learning algorithm (NB and SVM), classification model (flat and hierarchical), and classification method (*m-of-n*, at-least-1-of-*n*, and 1-of-*n*); we also considered the effect of using glosses from parts of speech other than adjectives and adverbs, to see how stable our method is in the face of the ambiguity introduced. For comparison we computed also F_1 as obtained by a trivial baseline consisting of a classifier which assigns every label to every document, which is the standard baseline classifier for the F_1 measure. Tables 1 through 4 summarize our results. We first note that in both cases we obtained substantial improvements in accuracy with respect to the baseline.

Table 2. Summary of best results for attitude type classification, showing, for each setting for each variable, the settings of the other variables that give the highest microaveraged F_1 value. In each row, the fixed variable value is given in boldface.

Alg.	Model	Method	POS	π^μ	ρ^μ	F_1^μ	π^M	ρ^M	F_1^M
NB	flat	1-of-n	Adj,Adv,N	**0.416**	**0.490**	**0.449**	0.429	**0.450**	**0.417**
SVM	flat	1-of-n	Adj,Adv,V	0.413	0.411	0.412	**0.430**	0.388	0.386
NB	**flat**	1-of-n	Adj,Adv,V,N	0.418	**0.483**	**0.448**	0.431	**0.442**	**0.413**
NB	**hier**	n-of-m	Adj,Adv	**0.482**	0.214	0.295	**0.521**	0.184	0.240
SVM	flat	**at-least-1**	Adj,Adv,V,N	0.404	0.409	0.406	0.410	0.382	0.379
NB	flat	**1-of-n**	Adj,Adv,N	**0.416**	**0.490**	**0.449**	**0.429**	0.450	**0.417**
NB	flat	**n-of-m**	Adj,Adv	0.338	0.484	0.398	0.306	**0.502**	0.380
NB	flat	1-of-n	**Adj,Adv**	0.408	0.489	0.444	0.419	0.450	**0.413**
SVM	flat	1-of-n	**Adj,Adv,N**	0.412	0.410	0.411	0.428	0.384	0.383
NB	flat	1-of-n	**Adj,Adv,V**	0.409	0.482	0.442	0.424	**0.444**	0.411
NB	flat	1-of-n	**Adj,Adv,V,N**	**0.418**	**0.483**	**0.448**	**0.431**	0.442	**0.413**

Table 3. Summary of averaged cross-validation results for force, as in Table 1. Note that only the flat classification model is applicable here.

Alg.	Method	POS	π^μ	ρ^μ	F_1^μ	π^M	ρ^M	F_1^M
baseline	n/a	n/a	0.201	1.000	0.334	0.158	1.000	0.239
NB	–avg–	–avg–	0.585	**0.732**	**0.634**	0.281	**0.614**	**0.352**
SVM	–avg–	–avg–	**0.586**	0.498	0.499	**0.662**	0.214	0.187
–avg–	**m-of-n**	–avg–	**0.755**	0.759	**0.757**	**0.501**	0.404	**0.305**
–avg–	**at-least-1**	–avg–	0.591	**0.806**	0.661	0.476	**0.487**	0.288
–avg–	**1-of-n**	–avg–	0.688	0.688	0.688	0.473	0.406	0.280
–avg–	–avg–	**Adj,Adv**	0.677	0.750	0.701	0.489	0.432	0.290
–avg–	–avg–	**Adj,Adv,V**	0.677	0.750	0.701	0.479	0.430	0.291
–avg–	–avg–	**Adj,Adv,N**	**0.680**	**0.753**	**0.704**	**0.490**	**0.434**	0.291
–avg–	–avg–	**Adj,Adv,V,N**	0.679	**0.753**	**0.704**	0.475	0.433	**0.292**

Attitude Type: Table 1 shows the overall effects of different values for each independent variable on attitude type classification, by averaging over results for the other variables. Table 2 shows the best results for various variable values—we repeatedly fixed the value of one variable and present the settings of the other variables that gave the highest microaveraged F_1. This was repeated for each value of each variable to give the results in the table.

For attitude type classification, when we consider the averaged results, we see that overall best results are achieved by Naive Bayes. When considering the best settings relative to other system variables in Table 2, we see a similar pattern, though the difference in F_1 performance is less. (Note that two specific sets of variable values, one using Naive Bayes and one using SVM, dominate the results in this table.)

Table 4. Summary of best individual results (for macroaveraged F_1) for force classification, arranged as in Table 2

Alg.	Method	POS	π^μ	ρ^μ	F_1^μ	π^M	ρ^M	F_1^M
NB	m-of-n	Adj,Adv,V	0.737	0.746	0.741	0.296	**0.549**	**0.384**
SVM	1-of-n	Adj,Adv,N	**0.771**	**0.770**	**0.771**	**0.715**	0.253	0.232
NB	**at-least-1**	Adj,Adv,N	0.414	0.844	0.555	0.286	**0.729**	0.350
NB	**1-of-n**	Adj,Adv,V,N	0.466	**0.880**	0.609	0.275	0.562	0.334
NB	**n-of-m**	Adj,Adv,V	**0.737**	0.746	**0.741**	**0.296**	0.549	**0.384**
NB	m-of-n	**Adj,Adv**	**0.740**	**0.751**	**0.746**	0.287	**0.562**	0.380
NB	m-of-n	**Adj,Adv,V**	0.737	0.746	0.741	**0.296**	0.549	**0.384**
NB	m-of-n	**Adj,Adv,N**	0.739	0.750	0.745	0.286	0.559	0.378
NB	m-of-n	**Adj,Adv,V,N**	0.736	0.747	0.741	0.286	0.560	0.379

Next, we find surprisingly that the flat classification model works noticeably better than the hierarchical model. This likely indicates that the shared semantics of siblings in the attitude type taxonomy is not well-represented in the WordNet glosses.

Regarding classification methods, when averaging over other variables, we see that while m-of-n and at-least-1-of-n achieve the highest precision and recall, respectively, the 1-of-n method achieves the best balance between the two, as measured by F_1. This may be explained by the relatively low average ambiguity (1.12 – defined as the average number of categories per term) of the lexicon, which makes this m-of-n task similar to an 1-of-n task. In practice, the higher recall method should probably be preferred, since incorrect category assignments could be weeded out at the text analysis stage. When considering the best individual runs, we see that the preferred classification method is nearly always 1-of-n as well.

Finally, we note that including glosses from parts-of-speech other than those in the lexicon did not appreciably change results.

Force: Table 3 shows the overall effects of different values for each independent variable on force classification, by averaging over results for the other variables. Table 4 shows the best results for macroaveraged F_1 for the various variable values, in the same format as in Table 2.

For force, when averaged over other variable settings, Naive Bayes achieves better recall and F_1, while SVMs achieve better precision under macroaveraging. The same pattern held for macroaveraged results for the best individual runs, though microaveraged results were similar for the two algorithms.

Also similar to the case of attitude type is that at-least-1-of-n classification increases recall at the expense of precision; 1-of-n, which is the a priori optimal method for force, achieves better (macroaveraged) F_1 than m-of-n, but the difference is small. When we consider the best individual runs for each method, we see at-least-1-of-n classification increases macroaveraged recall at the expense of

Table 5. 10-fold cross-validation results for attitude type classification using Naive Bayes with flat m-of-n categorization, under three different levels of expansion (K) of the training sets $(K = 0$ means no expansion)

K	π^μ	ρ^μ	F_1^μ	π^M	ρ^M	F_1^M
0	.338	.484	**.398**	.306	.502	**.380**
1	.316	.478	.380	.293	.495	.368
2	.305	.467	.369	.287	.480	.359

precision; 1-of-n, the *a priori* preferred method for force, gives slightly better microaveraged precision, but m-of-n gives the best F_1 by a slight margin.

As in the case of attitude type, the preferred classification method appears to be correlated with the choice of classification algorithm, with m-of-n working best with Naive Bayes and at-least-1-of-n working best with SVM.

For force, as for attitude type, we find that addition of glosses from other parts-of-speech did not appreciably affect results.

Significantly we find micro- and macroaveraged F_1 to be quite different for force, showing that the majority category, Median, comprising 78% of terms, is noticeably better classified than other classes, though results do indicate that minority classes are being identified with reasonable accuracy. Treatment of force in the future as an ordinal regression problem may help.

Expansion: Table 5 reports results for attitude type of applying expansion to the training sets, as described in Section 3.2. In contrast to previous results for orientation, expansion results in decreased effectiveness: the change in F_1^μ is -5.3% for $K = 1$ and -7.3% for $K = 2$. This is likely due to the fact that the seed sets of these experiments can be considered as already "expanded"; to see this, we need only to compare their size (average: 189 terms each) with the size of those used previously for orientation (maximum: 7 terms each). Expansion thus appears to add only "noise" to the training sets under these conditions. Future work will include exploration of the effect of expansion for different seed set sizes.

5   Previous Work

Most previous work dealing with the properties of terms from the standpoint of sentiment analysis has dealt with five main tasks:

1. Determining *orientation*: i.e., deciding if a given Subjective term (i.e. a term that carries evaluative connotation) is Positive or Negative.
2. Determining *subjectivity*: i.e., deciding whether a given term has a Subjective or an Objective (i.e. neutral, or factual) nature.
3. Determining the *strength* of term sentiment: i.e., attributing degrees of positivity or negativity.

4. Tackling Tasks 1–3 for term *senses*; i.e., properties such as Subjective, Positive, or Mildly Positive, are predicated of individual term senses, taking into account the fact that different senses of the same ambiguous term may have different sentiment-related properties.

5. Tackling Tasks 1–3 for *multiword terms*: i.e., properties such as Subjective, Positive, or Mildly Positive are predicated of complex expressions such as not entirely satisfactory.

The most influential technique for Task 1 is probably that of Turney [1], which determines the orientation of subjective terms by bootstrapping from two (a Positive and a Negative) small sets of "seed" terms. Their method computes the *pointwise mutual information* (PMI) of the target term t with each seed term t_i, as a measure of their semantic association. PMI is a real-valued function, and its scores can thus be used also for Task 3. Other efforts at solving Task 1 include use of rhetorical relationships between words [16,17], WordNet path lengths and synonym sets [18,19], and WordNet glosses [7,20].

Task 2 has received less attention than Task 1 in the research community. Esuli and Sebastiani [15] have shown it to be much more difficult than Task 1, by employing variants of the method by which they had obtained state-of-the-art effectiveness at Task 1 [7] and showing that much lower performance is obtained. Other methods that have been applied to this task are those of Andreevskaia and Bergler [20], who consider WordNet paths and glosses, Baroni and Vegnaduzzo [21], who use mutual information, Riloff et al. [22], who use bootstrapped information extraction patterns, and Wiebe [23], who combined supervised learning with distributional similarity measures.

Task 4 has been addressed by Esuli and Sebastiani [24] by applying a committee of independent classifiers to the classification of each of the WordNet synsets. The sum of the scores attributed by the individual classifiers is used for the final classification decision. The magnitude of this sum is used as an indication of the strength of association of the synset to either Positive, Negative, or Objective.

Comparatively little work has been done on Task 5. The most comprehensive approach to this task that we are aware of is that by Whitelaw et al. [3] as extended by Bloom et al. [6]. Their method uses a structured lexicon of appraisal adjectives and modifiers to perform chunking and analysis of multi-word adjectival groups expressing appraisal, such as not very friendly, analysed as having Positive orientation, Propriety attitude type, and Low force. The lexicon used in the experiments reported here is based on that developed in this work. Experimental results showed that using such "appraisal groups" as features for sentiment classification improved classification results. Other related work includes research on valence shifting [25,26] and contextual polarity [27].

6 Conclusion

We have shown how information contained in dictionary glosses can be exploited to automatically determine the type and force of attitudes expressed by terms.

These are challenging tasks, given that there are many classes (four levels of force and eleven of attitude type). We have used an adapted version of a method previously applied to the simpler task of recognizing *polarity* [7]. Though effectiveness values from experiments are not high in absolute value, the improvement with respect to the baseline is relevant, showing the feasibility of automatic construction of lexicons in which a variety of sentiment-related attributes are attributed to words for use in appraisal extraction and sentiment analysis. Future work will seek to improve the methods developed here by refining feature choice and processing from glosses, as well as incorporating other sources of information, such as collocations from large, general corpora.

Acknowledgments. The third and fourth authors were partially funded by the Project ONTOTEXT "From Text to Knowledge for the Semantic Web", funded by the Provincia Autonoma di Trento under the 2004–2006 "Fondo Unico per la Ricerca" funding scheme.

References

1. Turney, P.D., Littman, M.L.: Measuring praise and criticism: Inference of semantic orientation from association. ACM Transactions on Information Systems 21(4), 315–346 (2003)
2. Taboada, M., Grieve, J.: Analyzing appraisal automatically. In: Proceedings of the AAAI Spring Symposium on Exploring Attitude and Affect in Text: Theories and Applications (2004)
3. Whitelaw, C., Garg, N., Argamon, S.: Using appraisal groups for sentiment analysis. In: Proceedings of the 14th ACM International Conference on Information and Knowledge Management (CIKM 2005), Bremen, DE, pp. 625–631 (2005)
4. Wilson, T., Wiebe, J., Hwa, R.: Just how mad are you? Finding strong and weak opinion clauses. In: Proceedings of the 21st Conference of the American Association for Artificial Intelligence (AAAI 2004), San Jose, US, pp. 761–769 (2004)
5. Martin, J.R., White, P.R.: The Language of Evaluation: Appraisal in English. Palgrave, London (2005)
6. Bloom, K., Argamon, S., Garg, N.: Extracting appraisal expressions. In: Proceedings of NAACL-HLT 2007, pp. 308–315 (2007)
7. Esuli, A., Sebastiani, F.: Determining the semantic orientation of terms through gloss analysis. In: Proceedings of the 14th ACM International Conference on Information and Knowledge Management (CIKM 2005), Bremen, DE, pp. 617–624 (2005)
8. Argamon, S., Whitelaw, C., Chase, P., Hota, S., Garg, N., Levitan, S.: Stylistic Text Classification Using Functional Lexical Features. Journal of the American Society for Information Science and Technology 58(6), 802–822 (2007)
9. Osgood, C., Suci, G., Tannenbaum, P.: The measurement of meaning. University of Illinois Press, Urbana (1957)
10. Kamps, J., Marx, M.: Words with attitude. In: Proceedings of the 1st Global WordNet (GWC 2002) Conference, Mysore, IN, pp. 332–341 (2002)
11. Mullen, T., Collier, N.: Sentiment analysis using support vector machines with diverse information sources. In: Proceedings of the 9th Conference on Empirical Methods in Natural Language Processing (EMNLP 2004), Barcelona, ES, pp. 412–418 (2004)

12. Stone, P.J., Dunphy, D.C., Smith, M.S., Ogilvie, D.M.: The General Inquirer: A Computer Approach to Content Analysis. The MIT Press, Cambridge (1966)
13. Crammer, K., Singer, Y.: Pranking with ranking. In: Advances in Neural Information Processing Systems, vol. 14, pp. 641–647. MIT Press, Cambridge (2002)
14. Esuli, A., Fagni, T., Sebastiani, F.: Boosting multi-label hierarchical text categorization. Information Retrieval 11(4), 287–313 (2008)
15. Esuli, A., Sebastiani, F.: Determining term subjectivity and term orientation for opinion mining. In: Proceedings of the 11th Conference of the European Chapter of the Association for Computational Linguistics (EACL 2006), Trento, IT, pp. 193–200 (2006)
16. Hatzivassiloglou, V., McKeown, K.R.: Predicting the semantic orientation of adjectives. In: Proceedings of the 35th Annual Meeting of the Association for Computational Linguistics (ACL 1997), Madrid, ES, pp. 174–181 (1997)
17. Takamura, H., Inui, T., Okumura, M.: Extracting emotional polarity of words using spin model. In: Proceedings of the 43rd Annual Meeting of the Association for Computational Linguistics (ACL 2005), Ann Arbor, US, pp. 133–140 (2005)
18. Kamps, J., Marx, M., Mokken, R.J., De Rijke, M.: Using WordNet to measure semantic orientation of adjectives. In: Proceedings of the 4th International Conference on Language Resources and Evaluation (LREC 2004), Lisbon, PT, vol. IV, pp. 1115–1118 (2004)
19. Kim, S.M., Hovy, E.: Determining the sentiment of opinions. In: Proceedings of the 20th International Conference on Computational Linguistics (COLING 2004), Geneva, CH, pp. 1367–1373 (2004)
20. Andreevskaia, A., Bergler, S.: Mining WordNet for fuzzy sentiment: Sentiment tag extraction from WordNet glosses. In: Proceedings of the 11th Conference of the European Chapter of the Association for Computational Linguistics (EACL 2006), Trento, IT, pp. 209–216 (2006)
21. Baroni, M., Vegnaduzzo, S.: Identifying subjective adjectives through Web-based mutual information. In: Proceedings of the 7th Konferenz zur Verarbeitung Natürlicher Sprache (German Conference on Natural Language Processing) (KONVENS 2004), Vienna, AU, pp. 17–24 (2004)
22. Riloff, E., Wiebe, J., Wilson, T.: Learning subjective nouns using extraction pattern bootstrapping. In: Proceedings of the 7th Conference on Natural Language Learning (CONLL 2003), Edmonton, CA, pp. 25–32 (2003)
23. Wiebe, J.: Learning subjective adjectives from corpora. In: Proceedings of the 17th Conference of the American Association for Artificial Intelligence (AAAI 2000), Austin, US, pp. 735–740 (2000)
24. Esuli, A., Sebastiani, F.: SentiWordNet: A publicly available lexical resource for opinion mining. In: Proceedings of the 5th Conference on Language Resources and Evaluation (LREC 2006), Genova, IT, pp. 417–422 (2006)
25. Kennedy, A., Inkpen, D.: Sentiment classification of movie reviews using contextual valence shifters. Computational Intelligence 22, 110–125 (2006)
26. Miyoshi, T., Nakagami, Y.: Sentiment classification of customer reviews on electric products. In: Proceedings of the IEEE International Conference on Systems, Man and Cybernetics, pp. 2028–2033 (2007)
27. Wilson, T., Wiebe, J., Hoffmann, P.: Recognizing contextual polarity in phrase-level sentiment analysis. In: HLT 2005: Proceedings of the conference on Human Language Technology and Empirical Methods in Natural Language Processing, Morristown, NJ, USA, pp. 347–354. Association for Computational Linguistics (2005)

A Readability Checker
Based on Deep Semantic Indicators

Tim vor der Brück and Sven Hartrumpf

Intelligent Information and Communication Systems (IICS)
FernUniversität in Hagen
58084 Hagen, Germany
{tim.vorderbrueck,sven.hartrumpf}@fernuni-hagen.de

Abstract. One major reason that readability checkers are still far away from judging the understandability of texts consists in the fact that no semantic information is used. Syntactic, lexical, or morphological information can only give limited access for estimating the cognitive difficulties for a human being to comprehend a text. In this paper however, we present a readability checker which uses semantic information in addition. This information is represented as semantic networks and is derived by a deep syntactico-semantic analysis. We investigate in which situations a semantic readability indicator can lead to superior results in comparison with ordinary surface indicators like sentence length. Finally, we compute the weights of our semantic indicators in the readability function based on the user ratings collected in an online evaluation.

Keywords: readability, understandability, semantics, indicator weights, linear optimization, linear regression.

1 Introduction

Basically, a readability[1] checker has two major application areas. First, it can be used to automatically identify easy-to-read texts in a text corpus. In this case, it suffices to provide a global score which is usually calculated by a readability formula.

Second, a readability checker can be used to support authors to make their texts easy to read. In this case, more support is desirable than to compute only a global readability score. Instead, text passages which are difficult to read should be highlighted (e.g., the readability checker[2] of Rascu [1]). The calculation of a global score can here be useful too in order to give an estimation of the understandability of a text.

---

[1] In this paper, we use readability in the sense of understandability. We are aware that there exist other definitions where readability (or better: legibility) only relates to the form, but not to the contents of a text.

[2] Readability was not the only objective in this system. One further aspect was to ensure the fulfillment of certain formulation standards.

Z. Vetulani and H. Uszkoreit (Eds.): LTC 2007, LNAI 5603, pp. 232–244, 2009.
© Springer-Verlag Berlin Heidelberg 2009

In this paper, we will discuss both application areas. Therefore we describe how semantic information can improve both the calculation of a global readability score and the identification of difficult text passages. Readability checkers can compute a global score by applying a readability formula on several indicator values.

2   Related Work

There are various methods to derive a numerical representation of text readability. One of the most popular readability formulas was created in 1948: the so-called Flesch Reading Ease [2]. The formula employs the average sentence length[3] and the average number of syllables per word for judging readability. The sentence length is intended to roughly approximate sentence complexity, while the number of syllables approximates word frequency since usually long words are less used. Later on, this formula was adjusted to German [3]. Despite of its age, the Flesch formula is still widely used.

Also, the revised Dale-Chall readability index [4] mainly depends on surface-type indicators. Actually, it is based on sentence length and the occurrences of words in a given list of words which are assumed to be difficult to read.

Recently, several more sophisticated approaches which use advanced NLP technology were developed. They determine for instance the embedding depth of clauses, the usage of active/passive voice or text cohesion [5,6,7]. The method of [8] goes a step beyond pure analysis and also creates suggestions for possible improvements.

As far as we know, all of those approaches are based on surface or syntactic structures but not on a truly semantic representation, like a semantic network as described here, which represents the cognitive difficulties for text understanding more adequately.

3   Semantic Networks

Semantic networks (SNs) of the MultiNet (Multilayered Extended Semantic Networks) formalism [9] allow to homogeneously represent the semantics of single words, phrases, sentences, texts, or text collections. Such SNs are chosen as the semantic representation in our DeLite readability checker described in this paper.

An SN node represents a concept, while an SN arc expresses a relation between two concepts. In MultiNet, each node is semantically classified by a *sort* from a hierarchy of 45 sorts. Furthermore, a node has an inner structure (depending on its sort) containing *layer features* like CARD (cardinality) and REFER (referential determinacy). Fig. 2 and Fig. 3 show the graphical form of SNs. They were generated by the WOCADI parser [10], which is employed in DeLite.

---

[3] Throughout this work, sentence length is measured in words.

The WOCADI parser can construct SNs of the MultiNet formalism for German phrases, sentences, or texts. The text that is analyzed for readability is parsed sentence by sentence. During this process, SNs and syntactic dependency structures are built.

An important component of our deep syntactico-semantic analysis of natural language is HaGenLex, a semantically based computer lexicon [11]. This lexicon not only lists verb valencies, but also their syntactic and semantic types. Consider for example the German verb *essen* (*'eat'*). Sentences like *Die Birne isst den Apfel.* (*'The pear eats the apple.'*) are rejected because semantic selectional restrictions are violated. Besides this comprehensive lexicon with around 28,000 entries, we employ a flat lexicon, many name lexicons, and a sophisticated compound analysis to achieve the parser coverage required for applications like readability checkers.

Disambiguation is realized by specialized modules which work with symbolic rules and disambiguation statistics derived from annotated corpora. Currently, such modules exist for (intrasentential and intersentential) coreference resolution, the attachment of prepositional phrases, and the interpretation of prepositional phrases.

4   Conception of Our Readability Checker

Readability can be measured by way of numerous *readability criteria*. Each criterion (like semantic complexity) can be realized or approximated by one or more operable (i.e., implementable) *readability indicators* (like *Number of propositions per sentence*, *Maximum path length in the SN*, etc.). Note that an indicator can only be applied on a specific type of text segments which we call the *segment type*[4] of this indicator, e.g., the indicator *Number of propositions per sentence* can only be applied on an entire sentence, but not on single words. We differentiate between the segment types *word*, *phrase*, *sentence*, and *text*.

4.1   Calculating a Global Readability Score

In DeLite the calculation of the global readability score is done in several steps (see Fig. 1):

- Segmentation: In the first step, the entire document is segmented into words, phrases, and sentences based on the parser results.
- (Basic) Calculation: Indicator values are calculated for each segment the indicators are associated to, e.g., the indicator *Number of concepts in a compound* calculates one value for every word, the indicator *Sentence length* for every sentence.
- Aggregation: For each indicator, its values associated to text segments are averaged. This average is called the aggregated indicator value.

---

[4] In some rare cases the applicability is further restricted, e.g., the indicator *Number of reference candidates* is not applicable to all kinds of words, but only to pronouns.

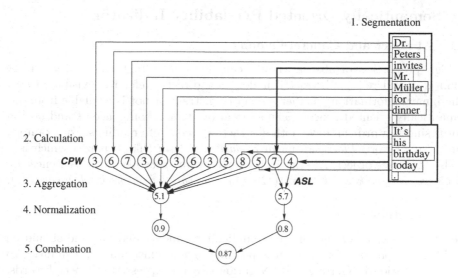

Fig. 1. Calculation of a global readability score with the two indicators *Number of characters per word (CPW)* and *Average sentence length (ASL)*

- Normalization: To combine indicators of different types their values have to be transformed to a common value range. In DeLite, the aggregated indicator values are all mapped to the interval from zero to one.
- Combination: In the last step, a global readability score is determined by calculating a weighted sum of all aggregated and normalized indicator values. All weights are non-negative and sum up to one.

4.2   Highlighting Text Segments

We compute an indicator value for each text segment this indicator is applicable to. If that value exceeds a certain threshold, the associated text segment is highlighted. For example, if the threshold for the indicator *Number of concept nodes in the SN* is 10, all sentences having 11 or more concept nodes will be highlighted.

We experienced that this approach did not suffice. Sometimes it is important for an exact understanding of the readability problem to highlight additional text segments. We call these text segments *supplementary highlight segments* in contrast to the *primary highlight segments* which directly refer to the found readability defect. (See Sect. 5.3 for an example.) Note that the segment type of a supplementary highlight segment does not have to match the segment type of the associated primary highlight segment.

In the following section, we describe some of the most important semantic readability indicators. For more motivation and references to the literature (e.g., from psycholinguistics) please see [12] and [13].

5   Semantically Oriented Readability Indicators

5.1   Abstract and Concrete Nouns

A high proportion of abstract nouns can deteriorate text readability [14]. A noun is considered as abstract if it does not directly refer to a visible object. The binary information whether a noun is abstract or not is available from our semantically oriented lexicon. The annotation is made on concepts and not on words since a word can have both abstract and concrete readings. For example, the German word *Platz* can mean *a place in a city* (like a plaza) which is a visible, concrete object. Alternatively, it can mean *space* like in the sentence: *Im Englisch-Kurs ist kein Platz frei.* (*'There is no space left in the English course.'*).

5.2   Negation

Negations can make a sentence more difficult to understand [14] and should be avoided if a positive formulation is possible. There exist many possibilities to convey negation in German [15]. Negation can be expressed by special words, e.g., *nicht* (*'not'*) and *niemals* (*'never'*), or prefixes, e.g., *unmöglich* (*'impossible'*) is the antonym of *möglich* (*'possible'*). While special words are quite easy to recognize, this is not the case for negation prefixes. First, such a prefix is not trivial to recognize, e.g., the German word *unterirdisch* does not contain the negation prefix *un*, but the prefix *unter* (*'under'*), which has a completely different meaning. Second, in some cases a word contains actually a negation prefix, but it is not used as a negation, e.g., the adjective *unheimlich* (*'weird'*) is not an antonym of *heimlich* (*'secret'*). However, if semantic information is available, this problem can be handled quite easily. Consider we have some word w which is the concatenation of the prefix *un* and a word v. We can infer that w is a negated adjective, if w is an antonym of v (which means that the lexicon contains an ANTO (antonymy) relation connecting v and w). Note that there exist several algorithms to extract semantic relations like ANTO by analyzing large text corpora. These methods would save the work to manually add ANTO relations to the lexicon; however, for cases like *unheimlich* and *heimlich* above, special treatment (or manual correction) is needed.

A special case of negations are *double negations*. A sentence contains a double negation if a similar (but not the same) semantics can be achieved by dropping two negations occurring in this sentence. This effect takes place if one negation is in the scope of another. Note that there are also sentences which contain triple or quadruple negations, e.g., the sentence *Ich glaube nicht, dass Peter nicht denkt, dass der Film nicht uninteressant ist.* (*'I do not believe that Peter does not think that the movie is not uninteresting.'*) contains a quadruple negation. In almost all cases, double negations are redundant and should be avoided. A double negation can relate to a sentence, to a phrase, or only to a word. Our readability checker can recognize several different kinds of double negations, e.g., a double negation occurs in a sentence if the sentence node is associated to the facticity (layer feature FACT) *nonreal* and is connected to the modality *non.0* by a MODL (modality) relation; see [9] for details on the semantic representation.

5.3   Indicators Concerning Anaphors

Several readability problems can concern anaphors. Consider the sentence: *Dr. Peters lädt Herrn Müller zum Essen ein, da heute sein Geburtstag ist.* (*'Dr. Peters invites Mr. Müller for dinner since it is his birthday today.'*). The possessive determiner *sein* (*'his'*) can either relate to the antecedent candidate *Dr. Peters* or to the antecedent candidate *Mr. Müller*. For a better understanding this sentence should be reformulated, e.g., by repeating either *Dr. Peters* or *Mr. Müller*. Thus we introduced a readability indicator counting the number of possible antecedents for each anaphor. In DeLite, the anaphor is marked as primary and the possible antecedents as supplementary highlight segments if this indicator value exceeds the associated threshold (e.g., 1).

Furthermore, an anaphoric reference can be difficult to resolve if the antecedent is too far away from the anaphor. The distance can be measured in words, sentences, or—more semantically and psycholinguistically motivated— by intervening entities (or discourse referents). Finally, we also use an indicator to check if there exists at least one antecedent for each anaphor.

5.4   Number of Propositions Per Sentence

A further measure for sentence complexity is the number of SN nodes which bear the semantic sort *si* (situation, like *to discuss*) or *abs* (abstract situation, for nominalized verbs like *discussion*) or one of their subsorts. Such nodes correspond to the propositions in a given sentence. This indicator is correlated to the sentence length since a long sentence usually contains also several propositions. However, this is not always the case. Consider for example the following long sentence: *Anwesend waren Dr. Schulz, Dr. Peters, Herr Werner, Frau Brand, Herr Mustermann, Herr Frank, Dr. Grainer, [...].* (*'Dr. Schulz, Dr. Peters, Mr. Werner, Mrs. Brand, Mr. Mustermann, Mr. Frank, Dr. Grainer, [...] were present.'*) which contains only a single proposition. Long item lists usually do not degrade readability [16]. Therefore in such situations the readability can more appropriately be judged by the indicator *Number of propositions per sentence* than by *Average sentence length*.

Also the opposite effect can be found: a quite short sentence can contain many propositions (for example expressed by participle constructions). The indicator *Average sentence length* would not be violated, while the sentence is definitely hard to read, e.g., *The man running downhill and meeting the colleague walking to the office fell over a dog chased by a boy.* This sentence contains five propositions and is definitely hard to understand.

5.5   Maximum Path Length

We measure the length of the longest path that the SN contains which is based on the assumption that information is often more difficult to understand if the constituents depend on each other and therefore a sequential interpretation is necessary. Consider for example the easy-to-read sentence *Ich besuche die Schwiegermutter, den Onkel, die Schwester und die Cousine.* (*'I visit the*

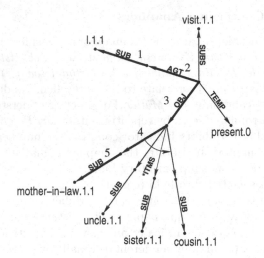

Fig. 2. Semantic network for the sentence *Ich besuche die Schwiegermutter, den Onkel, die Schwester und die Cousine.* (*'I visit the mother-in-law, the uncle, the sister, and the cousin.'*). One longest path, not taking into account the direction of arcs, is printed in bold face.

mother-in-law, the uncle, the sister, and the cousin.'). Since the constituents in the coordination do not depend on each other they can be interpreted in parallel which makes the sentence easy to understand. The length of the longest path in the SN is 5 which is still rather short (see Fig. 2). However, this is not the case for the following sentence where the constituents have to be interpreted sequentially: *Ich besuche die Schwiegermutter des Onkels der Schwester der Cousine.* (*'I visit the mother-in-law of the uncle of the cousin's sister.'*). Similar effects can be observed in connection with negations where the special phenomena of double negations can emerge (see Sect. 5.2). For this sentence, the length of the longest path is 7 (see Fig. 3). Thus, sequentially interpreted sentences usually lead to longer paths in the SN.

5.6   Semantic Network Quality

The case that the SN for some sentence could not be constructed or is assigned a low quality score is often caused by the fact that the associated sentence is syntactically or semantically complex or even incorrect. Thus we provide an indicator for this information. Note that this indicator is not purely semantic since the construction of the SN can fail if the syntactic structure of the sentence is invalid.

5.7   Passive Construction

The syntactic indicator *Passive* was enriched with semantic information leading to the new indicator *Passive with agent*. Usually sentence formulations in active

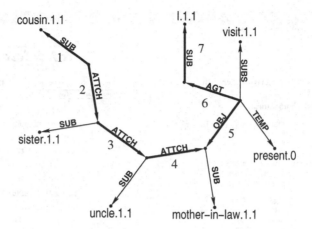

Fig. 3. Semantic network for the sentence *Ich besuche die Schwiegermutter des Onkels der Schwester der Cousine.* (*'I visit the mother-in-law of the uncle of the cousin's sister.'*). The longest path, not taking into account the direction of arcs, is printed in bold face.

voice are easier to understand than equivalent formulations in passive voice [14]. To convert a sentence into active voice the direct object and the subject have to change roles. We call the new subject the *semantic subject*. Passive constructions are very common in German. Thus we want to highlight a passive sentence (or reduce the readability score) only if it is obvious that an active formulation would be better.

There exist some exceptions to the rule that active formulations should be preferred. In some cases the semantic subject might not be known (or might be irrelevant), e.g., *Peter wurde rechtzeitig benachrichtigt.* (*'Peter was informed on time.'*). In this case, the impersonal pronoun *man* (*'one'*) can be inserted to convert the sentence into active: *Man benachrichtigte Peter rechtzeitig.* However, this formulation is usually not better than the original. Moreover, sometimes a passive formulation will be preferred if the semantic subject is neither a human being nor an animal. For example, the sentence *Peter wurde vom Blitz erschlagen.* (*'Peter was struck by a lightning.'*) need not be converted into *Der Blitz erschlug Peter.* (*'The lightning struck Peter.'*).

Since a complete linguistic treatment of all cases is not trivial we used a heuristic. We only penalized passive if the semantic subject is uttered and is connected to the sentence by the semantic relation AGT (agent). In this case, the semantic subject usually performs some sort of action and an active formulation should always be possible. This heuristic conforms to [17] who propose that an active formulation should be preferred if the sentence is agent-oriented.

5.8   Other Semantic Readability Indicators

We evaluated further semantic indicators. For instance, the inverse concept frequency is determined which is based on readings (as determined by word sense

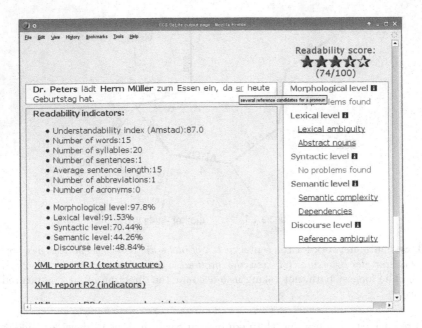

Fig. 4. Screenshot of DeLite's GUI in which a referential pronoun ambiguity is indicated for the sentence *Dr. Peters lädt Herrn Müller zum Essen ein, da er heute Geburtstag hat.* (*'Dr. Peters invites Mr. Müller for dinner, since it is his birthay today.'*; literally: *'..., since he has birthday today.'*).

disambiguation in the parser) instead of word forms. This indicator can detect cases where a reading is rare but the word (as a whole) is not rare.

We also introduced an indicator determining the average number of arcs the discourse entities of the SN were connected to (*Connectivity of discourse entities*), where the discourse entities are identified as SN nodes with the ontological sort *object* [9, p. 409–411]. For concessive and causal clauses, DeLite counts the causal and concessive relations in a chain.

6   User Interface

We provided a graphical user interface (GUI) for the readability checker DeLite [12] which displays a global readability score and highlights (by color) text passages that are difficult to read according to at least one indicator (see Fig. 4). If the user moves the mouse on such a text passage, the readability problem type will be described briefly. Supplementary highlight segments (if any) are printed in bold face if the user clicks on the colored text passage. In the upper right corner, a global readability score is provided which is calculated by a readability formula over all readability indicators.

7   Evaluation

We evaluated our algorithm as implemented in DeLite on a text corpus of 500 texts from the local administration domain. 315 users participated in the readability study, 43.1 % of them were female and 56.9 % male.

Almost 70 % of the participants were between 20 and 40 years old; the number of participants over 60 was very small (circa 3 %). The participants were mainly well-educated. 58 % of them owned a university or college degree. There is none who had no school graduation at all. The participants of the evaluation belonged to a large variety of professions, e.g., software developers, scientists, physicians, linguists, pharmacists, administrators, psychologists, and musicians. Each participant rated the readability of several texts on a 7-point Likert scale [18].

Table 1. Selected indicator weights; Sur=surface type indicator, Syn=syntactic indicator, Sem=semantic indicator

Indicator	Type	Weight (%)	
		Lin. regression	Lin. optimization
Average sentence length	Sur	34.1	35.0
Semantic network quality	Sem/Syn	20.3	27.6
Number of syllables per word	Sur	12.6	10.8
Number of words per NP	Syn	6.3	3.1
Inverse concept frequency	Sem	6.0	6.0
Word form frequency	Sur	5.9	1.4
Maximum path length in the SN	Sem	4.7	2.9
Conditional relations in a chain	Sem	1.3	2.1
Distance verb complement	Syn	0.9	0.8
Reference distance of a pronoun in words	Sem	0	1.2
3 other indicators	*All*	7.9	9.1
Number of characters per word	Sur	0	0
39 other indicators	*All*	0	0

We determined the weight of each indicator in our readability formula using both linear optimization [19] and linear regression with the Lagrange restriction [20] that indicator weights sum up to one (see Table 1). Both methods represent the readability score, as determined by the participants of the readability study, as a weighted sum of normalized indicators and estimated the weights in such a way that the mean absolute error (linear regression: mean squared error) is minimized [21]. Only 13 indicators (of 53 indicators) were assigned a weight greater than zero. The evaluation showed that deep semantic and syntactic indicators have quite comparable weights to traditional surface type indicators. The weights of the semantic indicators are expected to further improve if parser quality and coverage increases. Note that the weights should be seen with caution since changes in the parser can have a serious impact on them.

In a second experiment, we replaced the indicator *Abstract noun*, which was assigned a weight of zero, by a combination of the indicators *Abstract noun* and *Inverse concept frequency* in such a way that the indicator value is assigned to zero if the noun is concrete and to the inverse concept frequency otherwise. Afterwards, the weights were redetermined using the above-mentioned optimization algorithms. In this second experiment, the combined indicator was assigned the weight 9.7 % (7.8 % for linear optimization) while the weight of the now strongly correlated indicator *Inverse concept frequency* did not decrease.

Semantic indicators with the strongest correlation to the user ratings were *Semantic network quality*, *Inverse concept frequency*, *Maximum path length in the SN*, *Connectivity of discourse entities*, *Number of propositions per sentence*, and several anaphora related indicators. We noticed, however, that indicator correlation was not very reliable for estimating indicator importance in the readability function since, on the one hand, quite strongly correlated indicators can have a low weight if they are highly correlated to other indicators. On the other hand, indicators with rather weak correlation can have a considerable impact in the readability function if they are only weakly correlated to the other indicators.

Finally, the DeLite readability index was compared to a baseline: the Amstad readability index [3]. Applied on our test corpus this readability index reached a correlation with the user ratings of 0.187 which is far below the DeLite correlation of 0.509. However, this difference is mainly caused by the fact that the parameters of the Amstad readability index were derived by analyzing newspaper texts, which differ considerably from documents of local administration used here. Thus, we additionally determined a readability index resulting from employing a linear optimization only on the two indicators of the Amstad readability index, i.e., *Average sentence length* and *Number of syllables per word*. The correlation increased considerably to 0.458 but is still clearly outperformed by the DeLite index.

8   Conclusion and Future Work

We proposed a new kind of readability indicators which are semantic and predominantly operate directly on semantic representations (SNs). We further investigated indicator weights and correlations of indicators and user ratings. The evaluation showed that, although the SN could not be constructed for several sentences of our domain-specific corpus, semantic indicators can often yield scores that are more accurate than traditional, surface-oriented readability indicators. Therefore we expect that semantic readability indicators will play an important role for future readability checkers.

Acknowledgments

We wish to thank our colleagues Christian Eichhorn, Ingo Glöckner, Hermann Helbig, Johannes Leveling, and Rainer Osswald for their support. The research reported here was in part funded by the EU project Benchmarking Tools and Methods for the Web (BenToWeb, FP6-004275).

References

1. Rascu, E.: A controlled language approach to text optimization in technical documentation. In: Proceedings of KONVENS 2006, Konstanz, Germany, pp. 107–114 (2006)
2. Flesch, R.: A new readability yardstick. Journal of Applied Psychology 32, 221–233 (1948)
3. Amstad, T.: Wie verständlich sind unsere Zeitungen? PhD thesis, Universität Zürich, Zürich, Switzerland (1978)
4. Chall, J., Dale, E.: Readability Revisited: The New Dale-Chall Readability Formula. Brookline Books, Brookline, Massachusetts (1995)
5. McCarthy, P., Lightman, E., Dufty, D., McNamara, D.: Using Coh-Metrix to assess distributions of cohesion and difficulty: An investigation of the structure of high-school textbooks. In: Proceedings of the Annual Meeting of the Cognitive Science Society, Vancouver, Canada (2006)
6. Heilman, M.J., Collins-Thompson, K., Callan, J., Eskenazi, M.: Combining lexical and grammatical features to improve readability measures for first and second language texts. In: Proceedings of the Human Language Technology Conference, Rochester, New York (2007)
7. Segler, T.M.: Investigating the Selection of Example Sentences for Unknown Target Words in ICALL Reading Texts for L2 German. PhD thesis, School of Informatics, University of Edinburgh, Edinburgh, UK (2007)
8. Chandrasekar, R., Srinivas, B.: Automatic induction of rules for text simplification. Technical Report IRCS Report 96-30, University of Pennsylvania, Philadelphia, Pennsylvania (1996)
9. Helbig, H.: Knowledge Representation and the Semantics of Natural Language. Springer, Berlin (2006)
10. Hartrumpf, S.: Hybrid Disambiguation in Natural Language Analysis. Der Andere Verlag, Osnabrück (2003)
11. Hartrumpf, S., Helbig, H., Osswald, R.: The semantically based computer lexicon HaGenLex – Structure and technological environment. Traitement automatique des langues 44(2), 81–105 (2003)
12. Hartrumpf, S., Helbig, H., Leveling, J., Osswald, R.: An architecture for controlling simple language in web pages. eMinds: International Journal on Human-Computer Interaction 1(2), 93–112 (2006)
13. Jenge, C., Hartrumpf, S., Helbig, H., Nordbrock, G., Gappa, H.: Description of syntactic-semantic phenomena which can be automatically controlled by NLP techniques if set as criteria by certain guidelines. EU-Deliverable 6.1, FernUniversität in Hagen (2005)
14. Groeben, N.: Leserpsychologie: Textverständnis – Textverständlichkeit. Aschendorff, Münster (1982)
15. Drosdowski, G.: Duden - Grammatik der deutschen Gegenwartssprache. Dudenverlag, Mannheim (1995)
16. Langer, I., von Thun, F.S., Tausch, R.: Sich verständlich ausdrücken. Reinhardt, München (1981)

17. Helbig, G., Kempter, F.: Das Passiv. Zur Theorie und Praxis des Deutschunterrichts für Ausländer. Langenscheidt, Berlin (1997)
18. Likert, R.: A technique for the measurement of attitudes. Archives of Psychology 140, 1–55 (1932)
19. Bertsimas, D., Tsitsiklis, J.: Introduction to Linear Optimization., Athena Scientific, Belmont (1997)
20. Greene, W.: Econometric Analysis. Prentice Hall, Englewood Cliffs (1993)
21. vor der Brück, T., Leveling, J.: Parameter learning for a readability checking tool. In: Hinneburg, A. (ed.) Proceedings of the LWA 2007 (Lernen-Wissen-Adaption), Workshop KDML. Gesellschaft für Informatik, Halle/Saale, Germany (2007)

The DANTE Temporal Expression Tagger

Paweł Mazur[1,2] and Robert Dale[2]

[1] Institute of Applied Informatics, Wrocław University of Technology
Wyb. Wyspiańskiego 27, 50-370 Wrocław, Poland
Pawel.Mazur@pwr.wroc.pl
[2] Centre for Language Technology, Macquarie University,
NSW 2109, Sydney, Australia
{mpawel,rdale}@ics.mq.edu.au

Abstract. In this paper we present the DANTE system, a tagger for
temporal expressions in English documents. DANTE performs both
recognition and normalization of these expressions in accordance with
the TIMEX2 annotation standard. The system is built on modular principles, with a clear separation between the recognition and normalisation
components. The interface between these components is based on our
novel approach to representing the local semantics of temporal expressions. DANTE has been developed in two phases: first on the basis of
the TIMEX2 guidelines only, and then using the ACE 2005 development
data. The system has been evaluated on the ACE 2005 and ACE 2007
data. Although this is still work in progress, we already achieve highly
satisfactory results, both for the recognition of temporal expressions and
their interpretation.

Keywords: Temporal expression tagging, semantics, underspecification.

1   Introduction

The task of temporal expression recognition and normalisation involves identifying, within texts, expressions that refer to points or periods of time, and
re-expressing these temporal references in a standard format which (a) precisely
describes the semantics of the expressions, (b) disambiguates dates and times
from different time zones, and (c) makes it easier to determine the sequencing
of events described in these texts.

The time expression normalisation task is an interesting and challenging one
because, while some temporal references appear in well-defined formats, others
are expressed using a wide range of natural language constructions, and are
often ambiguous, requiring analysis of the surrounding text in order to arrive
at an interpretation. Of course, there are cases where information external to a
document—perhaps contained in another document, or best considered part of
world knowledge—is required in order to interpret a temporal expression; such
cases are not considered here.

Z. Vetulani and H. Uszkoreit (Eds.): LTC 2007, LNAI 5603, pp. 245–257, 2009.

There have always been sections of the linguistics, philosophy and natural language processing communities that have been interested in temporal referring expressions. However, interest in the recognition and interpretation of these expressions has grown significantly as a result of the DARPA-sponsored competitions in named entity recognition from the mid-1990s onwards. In contrast to earlier work in the area, these competitions and related exercises introduced a rigorous evaluation paradigm, whereby success or failure was measured in terms of the ability of software systems to replicate human 'gold standard' annotations of the scope and interpretation of temporal referring expressions.

Undoubtably, the key events and exercises that have played a role in this growth have been the Message Understanding Conferences (MUCs) in 1996 and 1998, and the workshops associated with the Automatic Content Extraction (ACE) program[1] in 2004, 2005 and 2007. While both MUC evaluations covered only recognition of two types of temporal expressions (dates and times), there has been a significant increase in the level of task difficulty in the ACE competitions. The fundamental move forward here was the addition of a normalisation task to the recognition task: annotations were provided for the interpretation of dates and times by using TIMEX2, a slightly modified version of ISO 8601, as the standard for the representation of normalized dates and times. The introduction of TIMEX2 also influenced the recognition task, as the range of temporal expressions to be recognised was broadened significantly as compared to the MUC-6 and MUC-7 task definitions.

Subsequently, the TIMEX2 standard has evolved through a number of versions, partially due to the wide interest it has received in the community, and the existence of the ACE program and similar competitions. This has also resulted in quite a large number of temporal expression taggers being constructed by the participants in these competitions. Details of the current, and most likely final, version of the TIMEX2 standard are provided in [1].

In this paper we present the DANTE (Detection And Normalisation of Temporal Expressions) system, which, as its name suggests, performs both recognition and normalisation of temporal expressions. Currently, the system works only for English texts; however, its extension to other languages is facilitated by its modular architecture, where some components are language independent. In January 2007, DANTE participated in the ACE Time Expression Recognition and Normalization (TERN) task.

The rest of this paper is organized as follows. First, in Section 2 we briefly introduce the TIMEX2 annotation schema. In Section 3 we describe related work, briefly presenting other existing temporal expression taggers. Then, in Section 4, we outline our model for the representation of temporal expressions. Section 5 presents the processing model we have adopted, and, in Section 6, DANTE's system architecture and development process is discussed. Section 7 provides information on DANTE's performance both in terms of recognition and normalisation results, and in terms of resource consumption and execution time. Conclusions and future work are discussed in Section 8.

---

[1] See http://www.nist.gov/speech/tests/ace

Table 1. Attributes in TIMEX2

Attribute	Description
VAL	Contains a normalized value in ISO-like format of the date or time of the annotated expression.
MOD	Captures temporal modifiers, using values such as BEFORE, AFTER, LESS_THAN, MORE_THAN, EQUAL_OR_LESS, START, MID, END or APPROX.
ANCHOR_VAL	Contains a normalized value in ISO-like format of an anchoring date or time.
ANCHOR_DIR	Captures the relative direction or orientation between VAL and ANCHOR_VAL attributes, as in WITHIN, STARTING, ENDING, AS_OF, BEFORE or AFTER. It is used to express information about *when* a duration is placed.
SET	Identifies expressions denoting sets of times; either takes the value YES or is empty.
COMMENT	Contains any comment that the annotator wants to add to the annotation; ignored from the point of view of automatic processing of the text.

2 The TIMEX2 Annotation Schema

The TIMEX2 schema provides an inline SGML tag, TIMEX2, for annotating temporal expressions. Annotations can be nested, as shown in Example (1).

(1)   I'm leaving on vacation <TIMEX2 VAL="1999-08-03">two weeks from <TIMEX2 VAL="1999-07-20">next Tuesday</TIMEX2></TIMEX2>.

There are six attributes defined in the schema for the tag; values of attributes express the semantics of an expression. A description of the attributes is given in Table 1. In this context, the recognition task is concerned with finding the boundaries of temporal expressions in texts, and the normalisation task involves determining the values of TIMEX2 attributes associated with this temporal expression.

3 Related Work

The earliest approaches, typical of work undertaken for MUC-6, were based on the construction of hand-crafted rules using a grammatical formalism that would match both fixed-format dates and times, and a range of expressions in natural language within the scope defined in the guidelines. For MUC-7, there were both solutions based on transducers, such as those described in [2] and [3], and also other techniques, such as Hidden Markov Models as used in IdentiFinder [4][2]. In both MUC competitions, the results achieved for TIMEX recognition by the best systems were high:

- at MUC-6, Recall of 93% and Precision of 96% were reported; and
- at MUC-7, Recall of 89% and Precision of 99% for dates, and Recall of 81% and Precision of 97% for times were reported [3].

---

[2] See also [5] for an extended description.

Table 2. The F-measure results for ATEL, Chronos and GUTime on ACE TERN 2004 data. ATEL and Chronos were evaluated on the ACE TERN 2004 evaluation data, while GUTime's performance was measured on the ACE TERN 2004 training corpus. All results cited here are from the original papers by the authors of the systems.

	Detection	Extent Recognition	VAL Attribute
ATEL	93.5	87.8	–
Chronos	92.6	83.9	87.2
GUTime	85	78	82

TempEx (see [6]) was the first TIMEX2 tagger developed. It is a relatively simple Perl tool that implements a few heuristics based on part-of-speech tags using finite state automata. It also performs limited normalisation of the expressions. The most recent version, from December 2001, implements the 2001 version of the TIMEX2 standard. There are certain classes of phrases that are not recognized by this tool: for example, *the last Monday of January*, *the end of 1999*, and *late yesterday morning*. This tool was provided to all participants of ACE TERN 2004 for use as an external source of text features; as such, it provides a reasonable baseline for performance on new data.

GUTime [7] was developed as an extension of TempEx for the purpose of constructing an automatic temporal annotation tool for TimeML (see [8]). TimeML is a sophisticated schema for the annotation of events; its complexity means that automatic tagging of events is best achieved via a cascade of modules that successively add more and more TimeML annotations to the document being processed. In this context, GUTime is the module responsible for the detection of temporal expressions and the introduction of the TIMEX3 tag into the annotations[3]. GUTime's coverage of temporal expressions is greater than that of TempEx. In addition, it also handles TIMEX3's functional approach to expressing values: that is, for relative expressions it first identifies what function is realised by an expression (for example, for *tomorrow* it would be PLUS ONE DAY), so that the actual value of that function (for example, *25th January 1996*) can be calculated at a later stage.

Chronos [9] is a more complex system designed to perform both recognition and normalisation of temporal expressions. Text processing in Chronos involves tokenization, statistical part-of-speech tagging and recognition of multiword elements based on a list of 5000 entries retrieved from WordNet. Then, the text is processed by a set of approximately 1000 basic rules that recognize temporal constructions and gather information about them that is expected to be useful in the process of normalization. This is followed by the application of composition rules, which resolve ambiguities when multiple tag placements are possible.

---

[3] TIMEX3 is part of the TimeML schema. It is very similar to TIMEX2, but provides a different approach to the annotation of sets and durations in time expressions and introduces the notion of temporal functions as means of providing the value of an expression.

The increasing availability of corpora annotated with temporal expressions[4] makes it possible to apply supervised machine learning techniques to the time expression recognition problem. Examples of such systems are ATEL [10], Timex-Tag[5] [11] and Alias-i's LingPipe[6]. ATEL and TimexTag are based on Support Vector Machine (SVM) classifiers, and LingPipe is constructed using a Hidden Markov Model (HMM). While ATEL only carries out the recognition of temporal expressions, TimexTag also performs interpretation, via 89 interpretation rules used by the interpreting SVM-based modules.

Table 2 presents the performance of a number of systems on the ACE 2004 TERN data. An annotation produced by a system counts as a correctly *detected* temporal expression if there is a gold standard annotation which which it overlaps by at least one character. A correctly *recognized* expression is one for which the extent produced by a system is exactly the same as in the gold standard. Evaluation of the VAL attribute involves checking that the correct value of this TIMEX2 attribute has been generated.

4   Representing Temporal Expressions

As is conventional in this area of research, we view the temporal world as consisting of two basic types of entities, these being **points in time** and **durations**; each of these has an internal hierarchical structure. We find attribute–value matrices to be a good means of clearly representing the semantics of temporal expressions. Figure 1 shows the representation of a reference to a specific point in time; in the ISO date and time format used in the TIMEX2 standard, this would be written as follows:

(2)   2006-05-13T15:00:00Z

Each atomic feature in the attribute–value structure thus corresponds to a specific position in the ISO format date–time string.

Of course, very few of the temporal expressions normally found in text are so fully specified. The attribute–value matrix representation we use makes it very easy to represent the content of underspecified temporal expressions. For example, the content of the temporal expression *13th May* in a sentence like *We will meet on 13th May* can be expressed as follows:

(3)
$$
\begin{bmatrix}
\text{point} \\
\text{timeanddate} \begin{bmatrix} \text{date} \begin{bmatrix} \text{day} & \begin{bmatrix} \text{daynum} & 13 \end{bmatrix} \\ \text{month} & 05 \end{bmatrix} \end{bmatrix}
\end{bmatrix}
$$

---

[4] See http://timexportal.wikidot.org for an extensive list of existing corpora with annotations of temporal expressions.

[5] See http://ilps.science.uva.nl/resources/timextag

[6] See http://www.alias-i.com/lingpipe

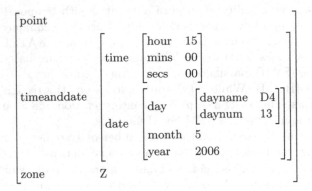

Fig. 1. The semantics of the expression *3pm Thursday 13th May 2006 GMT*

The values of the atomic elements in such an expression come from the lexicon, and the value of a composite structure is produced by unifying the values of its constituents. Here, the lexical entry for *13th* delivers the structure in Example (4a), and the lexical entry for *May* delivers the structure in Example (4b):

(4)   a. $\begin{bmatrix} \text{point} \\ \text{timeanddate} \begin{bmatrix} \text{date} \begin{bmatrix} \text{day} \begin{bmatrix} \text{daynum} & 13 \end{bmatrix} \end{bmatrix} \end{bmatrix} \end{bmatrix}$

       b. $\begin{bmatrix} \text{point} \\ \text{timeanddate} \begin{bmatrix} \text{date} \begin{bmatrix} \text{month} & 05 \end{bmatrix} \end{bmatrix} \end{bmatrix}$

When unified, these structures produce the representation shown in Example (3). Multiword sequences, such as idioms, that are best considered atomic and not compositional in their semantics can be assigned semantic representations directly in the lexicon.

5   The Processing Model

We take the view that an important step towards a truly broad-coverage yet semantically-well-founded approach is to recognize that there is a principled distinction to be made between the interpretation of the semantics of a temporal expression devoid of its context of use, and the fuller interpretation of that expression when the context is taken into account. The first of these, which we refer to here as the **local semantics** of a temporal expression, should be derivable in a compositional manner from the components of the expression itself; determining the value of the second, which we refer to as the **global semantics** of the expression, may require arbitrary inference and reasoning. Such a distinction is implicit in other accounts: Schilder's [12] use of lambda expressions allows representation

of partially specified temporal entities, and the temporary variables that Negri
and Marseglia [9] construct during the interpretation of a given temporal expression capture something of the same notion as our local semantics.

The above assumptions are reflected in our design, which comprises separate
and independent modules for the recognition and normalisation subtasks, with the
first being responsible for the computation of the local semantics, and the second
being responsible for determining the global semantics.

We assume a **granularity ordering** over what we might think of as the **defining attributes** in a temporal representation:

(5)   year > month > daynum > hour > minute > second

These are, of course, precisely the elements that are represented explicitly in an
ISO date–time expression.

Interpretation of a partially specified temporal expression then requires ensur-
ing that there is a value for every defining attribute that is of greater granularity
than the smallest granularity present in the partially specified representation. We
refer to this as the **Granularity Rule** in interpretation.

In the case of Example (3) above, the Granularity Rule tells us that in order to
compute the full semantic value of the expression we have to determine a value for
YEAR, but not for HOUR, MINS or SECS. This interpretation process may require
various forms of reasoning and inference, and is qualitatively different from the
computation of the local semantics.

6   System Architecture and Development

In our system, the stages of text processing are organized as a pipeline of processing resources, run using the architectural constructs provided in GATE [13].
The elements in our pipeline are a tokenizer, gazetteers, a sentence splitter, a POS
tagger, named entity recognition, temporal expression recognition, and temporal
expression interpretation[7].

6.1   Temporal Expression Recognition

The temporal expression recognizer is implemented using a JAPE grammar. The
grammar consists of five phases which are run over a document in sequence. Each
phase contains rules which match annotations introduced by earlier processing
components (for example, the tokenizer or POS tagger) and JAPE grammar
phases. There is also one initial additional phase which consists only of the expansion of macros used in the grammar rules. Altogether there are 81 macros and
252 rules; macro expansions are textually copied into the bodies of rules, and then
the rules are compiled into Java code. Some of the rules are *negative rules*; they

---

[7] We refer to this here as an "interpreter" since what is really happening in the "normalisation" process is in fact the interpretation of a temporal expression in the context
of the rest of the document.

do not generate any annotations and are used only to prevent the positive rules to match expressions which are not time-referring, but which are similar in their appearance.

JAPE rules are traditional pattern–action rules, where the left-hand side contains the pattern to be matched, and the right-hand side specifies the action to be taken when the pattern is matched. The pattern on the left-hand side is written using JAPE syntax, but the right-hand side can be implemented either in JAPE or directly in Java code. Our recognition rules use 33 gazetteers with a total of 1354 entries: these are strings used in the expression of dates and times, such as numbers written in words; the names of days, months and time zones; and the most common fractions (as used in, for example, *one third* or *1/2*).

The development of our temporal expression recognition module was carried out in a number of steps. The first of these took two and a half person months; the module was developed on the basis of the TIMEX2 guidelines and the examples contained therein. Then we tested DANTE on the ACE 2005 development data and identified frequently-occurring cases which were problematic for the system. Addressing these problems constituted a second stage of system development. Subsequent development has focussed on fixing bugs and other similar errors discovered as we have applied the system to an ever-wider range of document data sources; the system's grammatical coverage has remained relatively stable.

6.2 Local Semantics Encoding

Attribute-value matrices are relatively unwieldy in implementation as compared to the simple string structures used as values in the TIMEX standard; in particular, they are not usable as input to existing system evaluation tools. So, to enable easy evaluation of a system's ability to construct the intermediate semantic representations that correspond to our notion of local semantics, we would like to use a representation that is immediately usable by existing evaluation tools. To achieve this goal, we define a number of extensions to the standard TIMEX2 string representation for values of the VAL attribute; these extensions allow us to capture the range of distinctions we need to capture the different kinds of underspecification that are present only in our local semantics representation. Tables 6.3 and 6.3 present examples of string encodings of the local semantics of underspecified and relative temporal expressions. These type of strings are found in the output of the system's recognition module. See [14] and [15] for more details and examples of this representation.

6.3 Temporal Expression Interpretation

The interpreter module is a process that steps through a document sentence by sentence. Each temporal expression identified in the recognition stage is passed through the interpretation module, which transforms the local semantic representation into a document-internal semantic representation. The interpreter is fully

Table 3. Underspecified dates and times in ISO-like format

#	String	Representation	#	String	Representation
1	9 pm	xxxx-xx-xxT21	6	the nineteenth	xxxx-xx-19
2	11:59 pm	xxxx-xx-xxT23:59	7	January 3	xxxx-01-03
3	eleven in the morning	xxxx-xx-xxT11:00	8	November	xxxx-11
4	ten minutes to 3	xxxx-xx-xxt02:50	9	summer	xxxx-SU
5	15 minutes after the hour	xxxx-xx-xxtxx:15	10	the '60s	xx6

Table 4. Relative dates and times in ISO-like format

#	String	Representation	#	String	Representation
1	today	+0000-00-00	6	sixty seconds later	+0000-00-00T+00:00:60
2	tomorrow	+0000-00-01	7	five minutes ago	+0000-00-00T−00:05
3	yesterday	−0000-00-01	8	in six hours time	+0000-00-00T+06:00
4	last month	−0000-01	9	at 6 a.m. today	+0000-00-00T06:00
5	three years ago	−0003	10	last night	−0000-00-01TNI

implemented in Java and includes a library of functions for various calculations on dates and times. This module took approximately one and a half person months to develop.

In our current model, we assume that a document has a simple linear structure, and that any hierarchical structure in the document has no bearing on the interpretation of temporal expressions; for present purposes we also make the simplifying assumption that the **temporal focus** used to compute document-level values for temporal expressions does not advance during the processing of the document. Both assumptions may not always hold true, but are likely to work for the majority of cases we are dealing with.

Depending on the type of the temporal expression being interpreted (fully specified point in time, underspecified point in time, relative expression, duration, frequency and so on), different actions are taken. The two basic operations used in the interpretation are unification with some reference date and the addition or subtraction of a specified number of units to or from a reference date. The type of the temporal expression is also important for determining which TIMEX2 attributes other than VAL should be generated.

6.4   Cycle-Based Calendar Temporal Expression Interpretation

A distinctive class of relative temporal expressions are bare expressions based on calendar cycles—i.e., weekday names and month names—are used, as in the following example:

(6)   Jones met with Defense Minister Paulo Portas on *Tuesday* and will meet Foreign Minister Antonio Martins da Cruz before leaving Portugal *Wednesday*.

Here, the proper interpretation of the references to *Tuesday* and *Wednesday* requires at the least a correct syntactic analysis of the sentence, in order to locate the **controlling verb** for each weekday name. The tense of this verb can then be used to determine the direction—either in the past or in the future—in which we need to look to establish the fully specified date referred to. In the case of Example (6), this means determining that *Tuesday* is in the scope of the verb *met*, and that *Wednesday* is in the scope of the verb group *will meet*. It turns out, however, that there are cases where even the controlling verb does not provide sufficient information to determine the 'direction of offset'. But even in those cases where the tense of the verb *does* provide the relevant information, there are two problems. First, especially when the sentences considered are complex, there is a non-negligible likelihood that the analysis returned by a parser may not be correct, and this is especially the case when the sentences in question contain structures such as prepositional phrases: the attachment of these is notoriously a source of ambiguity, and they just happen to often be the hosts to temporal expressions. Second, even if a parser provides the correct analysis, parsing technology is still computationally expensive to use when processing very large bodies of text; if we are interested in time-stamping events described in significant volumes of data, we would prefer to have a faster, more heuristic-based approach.

In [16] we explored the development of a fast and high accuracy algorithm for the interpretation of weekday names, in particular with regard to determining the direction of offset to be used in the temporal interpretation of these expressions: in essence, how can we determine whether the day referred to is in the past or in the future? In that work, we described an approach, based on the algorithm presented by Baldwin in [17], that achieves 95.91% accuracy on a data set created from the ACE 2005 Training corpus, outperforming a range of other approaches we considered.

7   System Performance

7.1   Evaluation

The most significant evaluations of DANTE to date result from our participation in the ACE 2007 TERN task, and our subsequent re-evaluation of the system on the same data after further development on the ACE 2005 development data set.

In the ACE evaluations, a correctly recognized time expression is one which has a strictly accurate extent, and correct values for all the TIMEX2 attributes. An annotation generated by a system is classified as matched with an annotation from the gold standard if there is minimum 30% text span overlap between them

The ACE 2007 evaluation data included 2028 time expressions to be recognized and interpreted, spread across 254 documents from six different domains (see Table 5). As one might expect, documents were not equally distributed across the domains, both in terms of the number of documents and the total size. Across all domains, we currently achieve 74.19%, 77.66% and 75.89 for precision, recall and F-measure, respectively, for correct identification of extents of temporal expressions in text. Detailed results are shown in Table 5. The column titled

Table 5. The results of the DANTE system on the ACE 2007 evaluation data set

Domain	TIMEX2 in Gold Standard	Spurious	Missing	Error	ACE Value
Broadcast Conversations	142	33	29	48	43.8
Broadcast News	322	99	38	66	55.9
Newswire	894	125	110	221	63.0
Telephone Conversations	70	20	11	25	51.3
Usenet Newsgroups	167	20	22	42	65.5
Weblogs	433	66	58	137	57.9
Total	2028	363	268	537	59.1

'Spurious' indicates the numbers of false positive cases, i.e. when the system generated an annotation that is not present in the gold standard. The column titled 'Missing' presents the numbers of false negative cases, which are those cases when an annotation in the gold standard cannot be matched with any annotation in the system output. A matched annotation counts as an error if its textual extension or the value of any of the attributes is wrong. The ACE value score, which is shown in the last column, is an evaluation metric used in the ACE evaluations; it is defined to be 'the sum of the values of all of the system's output TIMEX2 tokens, normalized by the sum of the values of all of the reference TIMEX2 tokens. The value score attributed to each system token is based on its attributes and on how well it matches its corresponding reference token.' The attributes and the extent are weighted,[8] to allow for a difference in importance of the various attributes. The overall ACE TERN value for DANTE is 59.1 (out of 100), which indicates that DANTE's performance is in the range of state-of-the-art systems.

7.2   Resource Utilisation

The execution time for our text processing modules is presented in Table 6 as measured on a laptop with a 2GHz Intel Core Duo processor; however, only one core of the processor was used for processing documents. In characterising the processing cost, we do not take into account initialization of the system, the exporting of results into XML files, and the postprocessing required to meet the ACE formatting requirements, including the conversion of results from our inline XML annotation into the APF XML format.

Memory consumption during system execution is to some extent dependent on the size of the processed document, but on the ACE 2007 evaluation the variation was not great (from 116MB to 126MB). The system also required approximately 15MB of disk space to store the input corpus. As noted above, documents were not

---

[8] In the ACE 2007 TERN evaluations the weights were as follows: 1.0 for type VAL, 0.5 for ANCHOR_VAL, 0.25 for ANCHOR_DIR, 0.1 for MOD, 0.1 for SET, and 0.1 for extent (at least 0.3 overlap between matched elements, otherwise elements are not considered matched at all). The cost of a spurious TIMEX2 mention was 0.75 of the sum of the weights for the extent and for all generated attributes of the annotation.

Table 6. Execution times on the ACE 2007 eval data set

Domain	# docs	Time [s]	Av. time per doc [s]	Size [B]	Av. time/10kB [s]
Broadcast Conversations	9	8.698	0.966	48,722	1.828
Broadcast News	74	12.386	0.167	75,731	1.675
Newswire	106	36.306	0.343	209,973	1.748
Telephone Conversations	6	9.306	1.551	54,522	1.771
Usenet Newsgroups	13	9.000	0.692	48,377	1.905
Weblogs	46	23.000	0.500	137,549	1.712
Total	254	98.696	0.389	574,874	1.758

equally distributed across the domains, so we ran the system for each document source type separately in order to identify variations in performance across the different domains. On average, DANTE processed about 5.7KB of input data per second[9].

8   Conclusions and Future Work

In this paper, we have presented our approach to recognition and interpretation of temporal referring expressions in English natural language texts, and the implementation of this approach in the DANTE system. The system has been evaluated on the ACE 2007 evaluation corpus, which is a data set widely accepted by the community as a gold standard for the TERN task. The achieved results are of high enough quality use DANTE in many applications that require the interpretation of temporal expressions in text processing, such as information extraction and question answering.

Our evaluations have brought to light several areas where DANTE can be improved. Our error analysis indicates that the following steps should have the highest priority:

- First, we need to further develop the recognition grammar to cover some rarer cases. This requires both the addition of vocabulary to our existing rules, and also the development of new rules covering previously unseen structures. As the system is rule-based, this also requires careful testing to ensure that the addition or modification of rules does not introduce any incompatibilities or inconsistencies in the grammar.

- Second, we need to improve our mechanism for focus tracking in documents in order to more accurately resolve ambiguities, particularly in extended texts. Although using the document creation date as the temporal focus often works fairly well in simple news texts, it is not reliable enough for temporal expressions tagging across a broader range of text types.

Acknowledgements. We acknowledge the support of the Australian Defence Science and Technology Organisation in carrying out the work described here.

---

[9] Input data size here is the total size of the input documents including XML tags, which are ignored by the pipeline.

References

1. Ferro, L., Gerber, L., Mani, I., Sundheim, B., Wilson, G.: TIDES 2005 Standard for the Annotation of Temporal Expressions. Technical report, MITRE (2005)
2. Mikheev, A., Grover, C., Moens, M.: Description of the LTG System Used for MUC-7. In: 7th Message Understanding Conference, Fairfax, Virginia (1998)
3. Krupka, G., Hausman, K.: IsoQuest Inc.: Description of the NetOwl(TM) Extractor System as Used for MUC-7. In: 7th Message Understanding Conference, Fairfax, Virginia (1998)
4. Miller, S., Crystal, M., Fox, H., Ramshaw, L., Schwartz, R., Stone, R., Weischedel, R.: The Annotation Group: BBN: Description of the SIFT System as Used for MUC-7. In: 7th Message Understanding Conference, Fairfax, Virginia (1998)
5. Bikel, D., Schwartz, R., Weischedel, R.: An Algorithm that Learns What's in a Name. Machine Learning 34, 211–231 (1999)
6. Mani, I., Wilson, G.: Robust Temporal Processing of News. In: 38th Annual Meeting of the ACL, pp. 69–76. Assoc. for Comput. Linguistics, Morristown (2000)
7. Verhagen, M., Mani, I., Sauri, R., Littman, J., Knippen, R., Jang, S.B., Rumshisky, A., Phillips, J., Pustejovsky, J.: Automating Temporal Annotation with TARSQI. In: ACL Interactive Poster and Demonstration Sessions, pp. 81–84. Association for Computational Linguistics, Ann Arbor (2005)
8. Pustejovsky, J., Ingria, B., Sauri, R., Castano, J., Littman, J., Gaizauskas, R., Setzer, A., Katz, G., Mani, I.: The Specication Language TimeML. In: Mani, I., Pustejovsky, J., Gaizauskas, R. (eds.) The Language of Time: A Reader. Oxford University Press, Oxford (2004)
9. Negri, M., Marseglia, L.: Recognition and Normalization of Time Expressions: ITC-irst at TERN 2004. Tech. Report WP3.7, Information Society Technologies (2005) Information Soc. Technologies (2005)
10. Hacioglu, K., Chen, Y., Douglas, B.: Automatic time expression labeling for english and chinese text. In: Gelbukh, A. (ed.) CICLing 2005. LNCS, vol. 3406, pp. 548–559. Springer, Heidelberg (2005)
11. Ahn, D., van Rantwijk, J., de Rijke, M.: A cascaded machine learning approach to interpreting temporal expressions. In: Human Language Technologies: The Annual Conference of the North American Chapter of the Association for Computational Linguistics (NAACL-HLT 2007), Rochester, NY, USA (2007)
12. Schilder, F.: Extracting Meaning from Temporal Nouns and Temporal Prepositions. ACM Transactions on Asian Lang. Information Processing 3, 33–50 (2004)
13. Cunningham, H., Maynard, D., Bontcheva, K., Tablan, V.: GATE: A framework and graphical development environment for robust NLP tools and applications. In: 40th Annual Meeting of the ACL, pp. 54–62. Association for Computational Linguistics, Philadelphia (2002)
14. Mazur, P., Dale, R.: An Intermediate Representation for the Interpretation of Temporal Expressions. In: COLING/ACL 2006 Interactive Presentation Sessions, pp. 33–36. Association for Computational Linguistics, Sydney (2006)
15. Dale, R., Mazur, P.: Local Semantics in the Interpretation of Temporal Expressions. In: Workshop on Annotating and Reasoning about Time and Events (ARTE), pp. 9–16. Association for Computational Linguistics, Sydney (2006)
16. Mazur, P., Dale, R.: What's the date? High accuracy interpretation of weekday. In: 22nd International Conference on Computational Linguistics (Coling 2008), Manchester, UK, pp. 553–560 (2008)
17. Baldwin, J.: Learning Temporal Annotation of French News. Masterthesis, Department of Linguistics, Georgetown University (2002)

Hybrid Unsupervised Learning to Uncover Discourse Structure

Catherine Recanati, Nicoleta Rogovski, and Younès Bennani

LIPN - UMR7030, CNRS - Université Paris13, Avenue J-B. Clément,
F-93430 Villetaneuse, France
{Catherine.Recanati,Nicoleta.Rogovski,
Younes.Bennani}@lipn.univ-paris13.fr

Abstract. Data mining allows the exploration of sequences of phenomena, whereas one usually tends to focus on isolated phenomena or on the relation between two phenomena. It offers invaluable tools for theoretical analyses and exploration of the structure of sentences, texts, dialogues, and speech. We report here the results of an attempt at using it for inspecting sequences of verbs from French accounts of road accidents. This analysis comes from an original approach of unsupervised training allowing the discovery of the structure of sequential data. The entries of the analyzer were only made of the verbs appearing in the sentences. It provided a classification of the links between two successive verbs into four distinct clusters, allowing thus text segmentation. We give here an interpretation of these clusters by comparing the statistical distribution of independent semantic annotations.

Keywords: Discourse, Text analysis, Time, Tense, Aspect, Data mining, Unsupervised learning, Clustering, Connectionism and neural nets.

1 Introduction

Many studies emphasize the importance of tense in the narrative structure of texts (see [1] for French narratives). Much has been written about the contrast between French passé simple and imparfait. ([2] gives a good description of the opposition of these two tenses, with respect to narrative structure, focus, and aspect). Concerning aspect, it has been shown that one could not carry out the analysis of the succession of events in time using only tenses without referring to aspect (see Kamp, Vet or Vlach in [3], Kamp and Rohrer [4], Vet [5], Gosselin [6], etc.). Aspect is initially defined as the domain of temporal organization of situations. It determines their localization in time but also introduces points of view. Therefore, there are links between aspect and other semantic domains, such as intentionality or causality. Although all words of a sentence may contribute to aspectual meaning, verbs play a crucial role and lexical aspectual categories of verbs do exist. In this work, we shall attempt to detect regularities in sequences of verbs (within sentences) by focusing only on their tense and lexical aspectual category.

The French texts we analyze are short accounts of road accidents intended for the insurers. Their main purpose is to describe an accident, its causes, and to identify

Z. Vetulani and H. Uszkoreit (Eds.): LTC 2007, LNAI 5603, pp. 258–269, 2009.
© Springer-Verlag Berlin Heidelberg 2009

those who are responsible. We have considered here the sequences of verbs in these texts at a very high level of abstraction, by paying attention only at their grammatical tense and their aspectual category. We consider in fact verbs as pairs (category, tense), where category is one of the four lexical aspectual categories of a verb, and tense roughly its grammatical tense.

We sought here to isolate typical sequences of such pairs on the assumption that they could be meaningful to a certain extent, or, at the very least, for the type of account considered. Let us add that the mathematical tools used here make it possible to check the statistical validity of the resulting categories of such sequences, and that our semantic validation proceed with annotations unused by the training process.

1.1 Advantages of Our Formal Approach

One of the interests of unsupervised training is to allow the discovery of initially unknown categories. In this framework, the connectionist Self Organizing Maps of Kohonen (SOM, ([7]) provide an efficient categorization with simultaneous visualization of the results. This visualization is given by the topological map of the data (two similar data are close on the map) providing at the same time an "intelligent" coding of the data in the form of prototypes. Since these prototypes are of same nature as the data, they are interpretable, and the map thus provides a summary of the data.

From this coding, we took the Markov Models (MM) to model the dynamics of the sequences of data (here, the sequence of verbs within a sentence). The MM [8] are the best approach to treat sequences of variable length and to capture their dynamics. This is the reason why these models have been widely used in the field of voice recognition and are particularly well adapted to our objective.

To validate this hybrid approach, we used biological gene sequences and the corpus of texts presented here. See [9] for more about technical details.

1.2 Data Encoding

We encoded a hundred or so texts containing 700 occurrences of verbs. In these texts, we considered all the sequences of at least two verbs delimited by the end of a sentence. To cope with the paucity of the data, we used re-sampling techniques based on sliding windows, which increase the redundancy (redundancy ensures a better classification of the data). For coding, we combined the four aspectual categories of verbs introduced by Vendler in [10], namely state, activity, accomplishment and achievement, with the tenses of the verb to form abstract (category, tense) pairs. We based the manual indexing on tests and distinctions discussed in [11]. Table 1 below briefly summarizes our understanding of these four categories.

These accounts of road accidents mostly use the imparfait (24%) and the passé composé (34%), with a few sentences in the present. In addition, there are also some (rare) occurrences of passé simple and of plus-que-parfait. There are however a significant number of present participles (11%) and infinitives (20%).

We decided to retain all these "tenses" and carried out the training by using nine codes. (IM = imparfait ; PR = présent ; PC = passé composé ; PS = passé simple ; PQP = plus-que-parfait ; inf = infinitif ; ppr = participe présent ; pp = participe passé and pps = participe passé surcomposé).

Table 1. The Four Aspectual Categories of Verbs

STATE homogeneous, often durative, habitual or dispositional *ex: be / expect / know*	ACTIVITY durative process (usually unbounded), macro-homogeneous *ex: drive / run / zigzag*
ACCOMPLISHMENT durative process ending by a culmination point *ex: go to / park*	ACHIEVEMENT change of state (near punctual) *ex: reach / hit / break*

Example. « Le véhicule B circulait sur la voie de gauche des véhicules allant à gauche (marquage au sol par des flèches). Celui-ci s'est rabattu sur mon véhicule, me heurtant à l'arrière. Il a accroché mon pare-choc et m'a entraîné vers le mur amovible du pont de Gennevilliers que j'ai percuté violemment. »

We extracted from this text the three sequences of verbs corresponding to the three sentences: [(circulait, allant)] [(s'est rabattu, heurtant)] [(a accroché, a entraîné, ai percuté)]. Verbs are then reduced to abstract (category, tense) pairs, from their lexical entry. Here precisely: [(activity, IM) (accomplishment, pp)] [(accomplishment, PC) (achievement, pp)] [(achievement, PC) (accomplishment, PC) (achievement, PC)].

2 First Results and Comments

The first results are the percentages of tenses and aspectual categories in these texts (independently of their combined sequencing). The verbs of state account for 24% of the corpus, of activity only 10%, verbs of accomplishment 34% and of achievement 32%. The percentages of tenses by aspectual category given graphically in Fig. 1 confirm the interest of our pairings (tense, category). The nature of the aspectual categories, the aspectual specialization of grammatical tenses, and the typical structure of this kind of accounts explain these percentages rather naturally.

Verbs of States (24%). More than 70% are in the imparfait, the present, and the participe présent. This is not surprising since states are homogeneous and often durative, or characterize a disposition (habitual, or generic). We find also a significant proportion of passé composé in connection with verbs like "want" or "can" ("j'ai voulu freiner", "je n'ai pu éviter" - "I wanted to slow down", "I could not avoid").

The small proportion of present arises from the fact that the account is in the past and the historic present is a literary style not appropriate for this kind of account.

Verbs of Activities (10%). Similarly, the activities indicating unbounded processes, verbs of activity are distributed quite naturally with more than 79% in the imparfait tense (sort of progressive past in French) and in the form of present participles. That 10% of the verbs are in the infinitive can be easily explained by the fact that activities are processes which may have a beginning, and which can thus be the complement of verbs like "start", or "want" (+ infinitive in French). They can also be introduced to mention a future goal of the driver with the French preposition "pour" (+ infinitive).

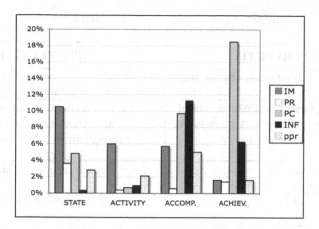

Fig. 1. Distribution of (main) Tenses by Category. (*IM*=imparfait, *PR*=présent, *PC*=passé composé, *INF*=infinitif, *ppr*= participe présent).

Accomplishments (34%) and Achievements (32%). Contrary to the two preceding categories, the telic character of these verbs explains their frequency in the passé composé. Achievements are mostly in the passé composé because denoting mainly a change of state, they are punctual (or of short time span), and take the imparfait tense only infrequently. In contrast, accomplishments often occur in the imparfait and as present participles, because they stress rather the process than its end - which brings them very close to activities. The global importance of these two categories (66%) has some connection with text typology, because an account of an accident implies a description of the sequence of the successive events that caused it.

Aspectual Specialization of Tenses. For C. Smith [12], there are three points of view in the aspectual system of French. A perfective viewpoint shows a situation as being closed. It is expressed by the passé composé and the passé simple. The imperfective and neutral viewpoints present on the contrary open situations. A neutral viewpoint is expressed by the present. An imperfective viewpoint is expressed by the imparfait, or by the locution "en train de". (As underlined by O. Ducrot in [13], it would nevertheless be a mistake to assign systematically an imperfective aspect to all imparfait).

However, the opposition perfective/imperfective will be mainly embodied in these texts by the opposition imparfait/passé composé. We borrow from Paul J. Hopper [2] Table 2, which give an excellent description of the opposition of these two modes with respect to the narrative structure, focus, and aspect.

Typical Structure of these Texts. A description of an accident generally starts with one or two sentences describing the circumstances or states of affairs before the accident. This introductive part is thus mostly in the imparfait, and contains many present participles. There are also a few verbs in the present tense, and many infinitives introduced by the preposition "pour", or occurring as complements of other verbs ("je m'apprêtais à tourner", "le feu venait de passer au rouge" - "I was on the point of turning", "The stop light had just turned red"). This first part is mainly circumstantial and contains a majority of verbs of states, but also some of activities and of accomplishments. It is characterized by an overall imperfective point of view, and the account is in background.

Table 2. The Perfective/Imperfective distinction

PERFECTIVE	IMPERFECTIVE
Strict chronological sequencing	Simultaneity or chronological overlapping
View of event as a whole, whose completion is a necessary prerequisite to a subsequent event	View of a situation or happening whose completion is not a prerequisite to a subsequent happening
Identity of subject whithin each discrete episode	Frequent changes of subject
Human topics	Variety of topics, including natural phenomena
Unmarked distribution of focus in clause, with presupposition of subject and assertion in verb	Marked distribution of focus (subject, instrument or sentence adverbial)
Dynamic, kinetic events	Static, descriptive situations
Foregrounding. Event indispensible to narrative	Backgrounding. State or situation necessary for understanding motives, attitudes, etc.

The next part of the text usually contains a description of the accident that mentions the succession of events leading to the accident and finishes with the crucial moment of the impact. This indispensable part of the text uses mostly verbs of accomplishment and achievement, generally in the passé composé. Text is in perfective mode, but since the goal is to indicate the responsibilities of the various actors, one still finds here many present participles and infinitive constructions connecting several verbs (as in "J'ai voulu freiner pour l'éviter" - "I wanted to slow down to avoid it"). At the end of the account, one occasionally finds a section with comments on the accident. That section often contains an inventory of the damage. This third part is often short and less easy to characterize. Note that the structure we indicate here is only typical. These three thematic parts can come in a different order, or some of them may be missing all together. As indicated in the next section, we have nevertheless marked each verb with at least one of these three thematic parts to provide a semantic interpretation of the categorization of verbal sequences resulting from the learning algorithm.

3   Categorization of Verbal Transitions

Our unsupervised approach provided a classification of the sequences of two consecutive verbs (within a sentence) in four groups (or *clusters*). Let us call such sequence of two verbs a *transition*. We had virtually 36 types of "verbs" (pairing 4 abstract aspectual category with 9 codes), and therefore 1296 verbal transitions (36x36), but many of them will not occur in the corpus, as explained in the preceding section.

3.1 More on Our Hybrid Algorithm

From a sequence of verbs appearing in a sentence, we consider all the transitions. A sequence of four verbs, noted (1, 2, 3, 4) gives us then three transitions: (1, 2), (2, 3), and (3, 4). Recall that our transitions are pairs of abstract types of verbs, it might be useful to take the example of section 1.2. Thus from the sentence « Il *a accroché* mon pare-choc et m'*a entraîné* vers le mur amovible du pont de Gennevilliers que j'*ai percuté* violemment », we consider the sequence

S = [(achievement, PC) (accomplishment, PC) (achievement, PC)]

From this sequence S, we extracted the two following verbal transitions:

S1= [(achievement, PC) (accomplishment, PC)]

and   S2 = [(accomplishment, PC) (achievement, PC)].

The set of data is made of all verbal transitions appearing in a sentence of these texts, considered as a whole. A first training algorithm performed a classification of these data. The output of this first step is that the profiles of the transitions (prototypes) appear on maps (SOMs) incorporating a topological notion of proximity. The matrix of the distances between the profiles of transitions provides also a distribution of the qualitative variables (tense code and aspectual category) figuring in each encoding of a verb (probabilistic SOM). This information is exploited by the next step of our hybrid algorithm.

Fig. 2 shows the first SOM obtained and the (optimized) last one. Each (squared) point of the first map represents a verbal transition, and the four clusters appear in different levels of gray.

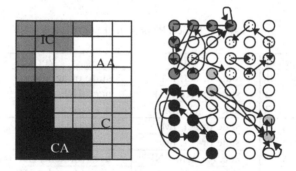

Fig. 2. The SOM of the Four Clusters

That the profiles of the verbal transitions fall into four distinct clusters accords with the Davies and Bouldin quality standard of unsupervised classification [14]. In addition, it should be pointed out that, since this number is small (only four), it is to a certain extent a confirmation of the fruitfulness of our algorithm, and of our tense/aspectual category pairing.

The next step of the algorithm exploits information concerning the distribution of each qualitative variable figuring in our particular encoding of a verb (here its aspectual category or tense) to initiate a classical learning algorithm, in charge of discovering the hidden Markov Model associated with these prototyped transitions. The output is a matrix of the probability to go from one transition (a point on the map) to another, enabling us to erase the profiles that are not significant. Fig. 3 summarizes these steps, and Table 3 gives the most typical transitions resulting from this analysis in each cluster.

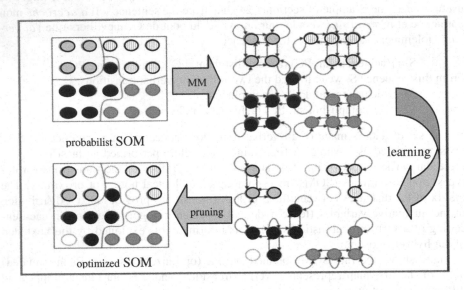

Fig. 3. Steps of our Hybrid Algorithm

Table 3. Typical Pairs in the Four Clusters

Pairs in	Verb 1	Verb 2
C 1	state or act. IM	state or act., ppr
2	state IM (or PR)	acc., INF
3	act. or ach. IM	acc. (or ach.) INF
CA 4	state or act. IM	state (or ach.), IM
5	state or act. IM	state (or ach.), PC
AA 6	acc. (or ach.) INF	acc. (or ach.) INF (or ppr)
7	ach. (or acc.) PC	acc. (or ach.) INF
8	state PC	ach. INF
IC 9	ach. (or acc.) INF	ach. PC
10	ach. or state, PC	ach. (or acc) PC

3.2 Semantic Interpretation

To provide the interpretation of these clusters, we carried out a certain number of semantic annotations. Thus, to account for the typical structure of these texts, we indexed all the verbs with a number indicating the thematic part of the text in which they occurred (1 *circumstance*, 2 *accident* and 3 *comment*).

We have also marked some of the verbs with the attributes *foreground* or *background* to indicate the type of contribution they make to the narrative structure. In order to be able to detect possible causal chains of verbs leading to the accident, we marked some verbs with the attributes *causal* and *impact* (*causal* when the verb was describing a direct cause of the accident, and *impact* when indicating the impact itself). We also marked the verbs of action according to the agent responsible for the action (A for the driver and author of the text, B for the second driver involved in the accident, and C for a third person). We also noted the presence of *negation*, and the description of objectives or possible worlds that did not occur (attribute *inertia* for goals and alternatives).

Table 4. Summary of Statistical Semantic Annotations

Cluster (IC) *Impact and Comments* Very strong causality, foregrounding, frequent impact, goals and alternatives	Cluster (AA) *Actions leading to the Accident* Strong causality, neutral foreground/background, few impacts, many goals and alternatives
Cluster (CA) *Circumstances or Appearance of an incident* Little causality, background, little impact, no goal or alternative	Cluster (C) *Circumstances* No causality, background, no impact, many goals and alternatives

The marking of negation was not really discriminating, and that of the actor (agent) not very helpful. Table 4 summarizes the main results that we obtained by doing statistical comparisons of these semantic annotations within these four clusters.

3.2 Description of the Four Clusters

Cluster (C) of Circumstances
The cluster (C) makes a clear distinction between the first and the second verb of a sequence. The first verb is 93% in the imparfait, but only 7% in the present, while the second is 63% in the infinitive and 30% in the present participle. From the point of view of aspectual categories, the first verb is a verb of state 56% of the time, and the second a verb of accomplishment 63% of the time. (The other categories divide themselves in a regular way between 12% and 16%). One can described the pairs of this group as made up of a verb of state (or activity) in the imparfait, followed by a verb of accomplishment in the infinitive or in the present participle. The analysis of the prototypes provides a finer synthesis (see Table 3).

This group favors states and activities to the detriment of achievements - accomplishments on the other hand are overwhelmingly present in the second verbal occurrence.

The cluster (C) is the one where the inertia attribute (indicating a goal or an alternative world) is the most frequent. This is explained by the many accomplishments introduced by the French preposition "pour" ("je reculais pour repartir" - "I backed up to set out again", "je sortais du parking pour me diriger" - "I left the car park to find my way"), and by the auxiliaries in the imparfait introducing an infinitive indicating the intentions of the driver ("j'allais tourner à gauche" - "I was on the point of turning left"). This is one of the reasons why we called this cluster (C) "Circumstances". Another reason is that it contains a strong majority of verbs belonging to the first part of the account (63%), and very little to the second or the third. Moreover, this cluster hardly contains verbs indicating the causes of the accident or describing the impact. Actor A is represented the most there, and the account is in narrative background.

Cluster (CA) of Circumstances or of the Appearance of an Incident

The second cluster (CA) is that of the circumstances or of the appearance of an incident. One notes here a great number of verbs of states (37.5%) and activities (17%), even more than in the preceding cluster and much higher than average. There are, on the other hand, an average number of achievements (29%), absent from the first verb but quite often present on the second. This distinguishes this cluster from the preceding one, where accomplishments played this role. Here, on the contrary, accomplishments are excluded from the second place, and are clearly under-represented (16.5%). One can synthesize the transitions of this cluster by saying that one generally has a state or an activity in the imparfait tense, followed by a state or an achievement in the imparfait or in the passé composé. (One thus connects two imperfective points of view, and sometimes, an imperfective point of view and a perfective one).

In this group 36% of verbs come from the first part of the account ("je circulais à 45 km/h environ dans une petite rue à sens unique où des voitures étaient garées des deux côtés" - "I drove at approximately 45 km/h in a small one-way street where cars were parked on each side"). There are also transitions ending by an achievement in the passé composé, coming from the second part (34%, "je roulais rue Pasteur quand une voiture surgit de la gauche" - "I drove on Pasteur street when a car emerged from the left"). This cluster contains also 25% of verbal transitions located between the two parts (providing thus half of such sequences). This is why we called it the cluster of Circumstances or of the Appearance of an incident. The account is here mainly in background. Actor A, or a third person C, are strongly indexed to the detriment of actor B. There are few allusions to the causes of the accident and to the impact, and few verbs in the foreground. The evocation of goals or alternative worlds is missing from this group (contrary to the preceding group).

Cluster (AA) of Actions Leading to the Accident

The third cluster (AA) clearly marks the account of the accident itself. It is characterized by the wealth of achievements, to the detriment of states and activities. It is in perfective mode but includes many infinitives. The detected prototypes are given in Table 3. These pairs lend themselves well to constructions of three verbs as in, "J'ai voulu m'engager pour laisser" ("I wanted to turn into to let"), or "n'ayant pas la possibilité de changer de voie et la route étant mouillée" ("not having the possibility of changing the lane and the road's being wet"). Fifty-six percents of the pairs come from the second part of the account. This is why, since this cluster also contains many accomplishments, we called it a cluster of actions leading to the accident. Nevertheless, as in cluster (C), the present participles and infinitives allow the expression of goals and alternative worlds ("désirant me rendre à" - "wishing to go to", "commençant à tourner" - "starting to turn"), so 26% of the pairs come from the first part of the account. We noted however a rather strong proportion of agent A and B, with little of C, but also little foregrounding - the account being unmarked (neither in foreground, nor in background). Many verbs describe the causal chain, but relatively few mention the impact.

Cluster (IC) of the Impact and of the Comments

The verbs of achievements (45%) appear here in a larger number than elsewhere (32% on average), to the detriment of activities (6.5%), and states (only 14.5%). This explains that this group supports the descriptive part of the accident (57%). Here also one observes an increase in infinitives and participles on the first verb to the detriment of the imparfait and of the present, and a large increase in passé composé on the second verb to the detriment of all tenses - except the present (8%, slightly higher than the average). Perhaps the occurrence of the present is related to the strong proportion of comments (29%), more important than elsewhere (18% on average). The mention of goals or alternatives is average. It is here on the other hand that foregrounding is most marked. There is an important number of references to actor B (the driver of the other vehicle) and it is here that one finds most verbs relating to the causes of the accident and the impact itself. Table 3 indicates only two typical elements in this group, which, although quite large, is more difficult to characterize. The analysis in terms of viewpoints shows nevertheless that the sequence generally finishes with a perfective viewpoint.

3.3 Comments

This categorization distinguishes quite well states and activities (groups C, CA) from telic events (groups AA, CC). In a more interesting way, accomplishments are also distinguished from achievements, justifying the distinction in opposition to a single notion of telic events. It should also be noticed that the expression of goals or alternatives often accompanies the use of verbs in the present participle or infinitive - which explains the ratio displayed by groups C and AA. However, the lexical category used influences also this expression, because the second verb in these two groups is generally an accomplishment. Moreover, the groups C and CA (unmarked for this purpose) differ precisely in the type of event appearing in second place. In the same way, elements differentiating the groups AA and CC (which contain a majority of telic events) show that the group AA (which favors accomplishments), although conveying a perfective mode, is little marked for narrative foreground. This group is also less concerned with the causes of the accident than the group CC, and it makes little allusion to the impact. Goals and intentions would thus be expressed more easily by accomplishments than by achievements - which would carry more causality. Indeed, the group CC, which favors achievements, is more strongly marked for narrative foregrounding, the impact itself, and the causal chain of events, which directly caused it. It may be that for achievements and activities, the subject has a relation of power over the direct object (or over the oblique object). One can check its existence by using adverbs of manner (gently, with caution, etc). This explains perhaps also the strong attribution of responsibility to the agent with the use of verbs of achievements.

Although the perfective/imperfective contrast emerges rather neatly (clusters AA and CC vs. C and CA), surprisingly cluster (CA) hosts both imperfective sequences and imparfait/passé composé sequences. One of the explanations is that our training algorithm did not the linking of two sentences take into account, so that the succession of several sentences in the imperfect mode, and the typical structure of these accounts (such as we perceive it) could not be detected. One thus misses a significant part of our objective. However, the results obtained in focusing only on sentences are still interesting, since the three typical parts that we have distinguished fall differently onto the four clusters, although not in a uniform way. It should also be noted, that this classification underlines the importance of infinitive turns and present participles, and the subtlety of their linking (cf. Table 3).

Technical Improvements. One built the hidden MM here by moving a window of size 2: therefore, verbs are analyzed by taking into consideration the verbs that precede and follow them, but not the N-preceding verbs and the N-following. This is not too important here, since our analysis is at the sentence level, (and in these accounts, a sentence contains rarely more than three verbs), but for an analysis taking into account the entire text, we will need to add this generalization.

In addition, we would have liked to produce typical sequences of variable length instead of simple pairs. Thus, clusters AA and CC would have provided sequences of three verbs. (This follows from the prototypes of Table 3, and is obvious on the segmentation of texts). This result could also be computed automatically (because the MM provides the probabilities of transitions between two verbs), but we have not had enough time to implement this method.

4 Conclusion

Our general project is to apply techniques of data mining to explore textual structures. For this purpose, we developed an original approach of unsupervised learning allowing the detection of sequential structures. We applied it to the analysis of sequences of verbs in sentences coming from a corpus of accounts of road accidents. We obtained a classification of pairs of two successive verbs in four groups (or clusters).

We succeeded in validating these groups satisfactorily, by basing our judgment on semantic annotations and the application of statistical analyses. This validates at the same time the power of the technique employed, and that of our coupling of the grammatical tense with the aspectual lexical category of a verb. However, this work is still in its early stages, and many points remain to elucidate. We first regret not to have been able to compare our statistical results on cross tense/category uses with those of other types of texts (and in particular, with that of simple accounts of incidents). It indeed remains to be determined what the "typological" part of the isolated sequences is. Nor did we have time to exploit the probabilities of transitions given by the MM; but this could be an interesting application of the techniques developed in this paper. The general method should also be improved in order to take into account the entire structure of a text (which is not the case here), and to make room for sequences of length higher than 2.

Acknowledgments. We warmly thank Steven Davis and Adeline Nazarenko for their help with respect to both substance and style.

References

1. Vuillaume, M.: Grammaire temporelle des récits. Minuit, Paris (1990)
2. Hopper, J.: Some observations on the typology of focus and aspect in narrative language. In: Studies in Language 3.1, pp. 37–64. J. Benjamins, Amsterdam (1979)
3. Martin, R., Nef, F. (eds.): Le temps grammatical. In: Langage n°64, Kamp, H., pp. 39–64, Vlach, F., pp. 65–79, Vet, C., pp. 109–124. Larousse, Paris (1981)
4. Kamp, H., Rohrer, C.: Tense in Texts. In: Bauerle, R., Schwarze, C., von Stechow, A. (eds.) Meaning, Use and Interpretation of Language, pp. 250–269. De Gruyter, Berlin (1983)
5. Vet, C.: Relations temporelles et progression thématique. In: Etudes Cognitives 1, Sémantique des Catégories de l'aspect et du Temps, pp. 131–149. Académie des Sciences de Pologne, Warszawa (1994)
6. Gosselin, L.: Sémantique de la temporalité en français. Duculot, Louvain-la-Neuve (1996)
7. Kohonen, T.: Self-Organizing Maps. Springer, Heidelberg (1995/2001)
8. Rabiner, L.R., Juang, B.H.: An Introduction to Hidden Markov Models. IEEE ASSP Magazine 86, 4–16 (1986)
9. Rogovschi, N., Bennani, Y., Recanati, C.: Apprentissage neuro-markovien pour la classification non supervisée de données structurées en séquences. In: Actes des 7èmes journées francophones Extraction et Gestion des Connaissances, Belgique, Namur (2007)
10. Vendler, Z.: Verbs and Times. In: Linguistics in Philosophy, pp. 9–121. Cornell University Press, Ithaca (1967)
11. Recanati, C., Recanati, F.: La classification de Vendler revue et corrigée. In: La modalité sous tous ses aspects, Cahiers Chronos 4, Amsterdam/Atlanta, GA, pp. 167–184 (1999), http://hal.archives-ouvertes.fr/hal-00085094
12. Smith, C.S.: The parameter of aspect. Studies in Linguistics and Philosophy. Kluwer Academic publishers, Dordrecht (1991)
13. Ducrot, O.: L'imparfait en français. Linguistische Berichte Braunschweig 60, 1–23 (1979)
14. Davies, D.L., Bouldin, D.W.: A Cluster Separation Measure. IEEE Transactions on Pattern Analysis and Machine Learning 1(2) (1979)

Pronoun Resolution in Turkish Using Decision Tree and Rule-Based Learning Algorithms

Savaş Yıldırım[1], Yılmaz Kılıçaslan[2], and Tuğba Yıldız[1]

[1] İstanbul Bilgi University, Department of Computer Science
Kurtuluş Deresi Cad. No:47, Dolapdere, 34440 İstanbul
[2] Trakya University, Department of Computer Engineering
Mühendislik-Mimarlık Fakültesi. Prof.Dr. Ahmet Karadeniz Yerleşkesi Merkez Edirne
{savasy,tdalyan}@cs.bilgi.edu.tr, yilmazk@trakya.edu.tr

Abstract. This paper reports on the results of some pronoun resolution experiments performed by applying a decision tree and a rule-based algorithm on an annotated Turkish text. The text has been compiled mostly from various popular child stories in a semi-automatic way. A knowledge-lean learning model has been devised using only nine most commonly employed features. An evaluation and comparison of the performances achieved with the two different algorithms is offered in terms of the recall, precision and f-measure metrics.

Keywords: Anaphora, Pronoun Resolution.

1 Introduction

Dependency relations where an expression makes reference to another constitute a challenging domain for the field of natural language processing. The dependent element in this relation is said to be an anaphor, whereas the element upon which the anaphor is referentially dependent is referred to as the antecedent. A considerable amount of work has been dedicated to the question of how to find the antecedent of an anaphor in natural language sentences or discourse fragments. The list of approaches and implementations proposed to this effect range from programs using a few heuristics for resolving anaphors [1] to approaches relying on different sources of linguistic and/or non-linguistic knowledge [2,3,4,5,6,78,9], strategies combining linguistic methods with statistical approaches [10,11] and corpus-based approaches relying hardly on linguistic knowledge [12,11,13,14,15][1].

An important contribution of this paper is in the choice of language. When compared to the abundance of work done for English, reported attempts to computationally resolve anaphora in Turkish seem to fall short of being satisfactory both in number and diversity. Two of the earliest attempts at anaphora resolution in Turkish are represented in [17,18]. The former offers a computational framework for anaphora resolution in Turkish emphasizing the role of context in this process, whereas the latter describes a

---

[1] This is certainly a non-exhaustive list of the works concerning anaphora resolution. See [16,14] for a recent survey of the major works in the field.

Z. Vetulani and H. Uszkoreit (Eds.): LTC 2007, LNAI 5603, pp. 270–278, 2009.
© Springer-Verlag Berlin Heidelberg 2009

situation-theoretic[2] approach to the problem. A reference planning system is intended to generate contextually appropriate anaphora for Turkish [21]. The system is based on Binding Theory [22] and Centering Theory [23]. Two other computational models for anaphora resolution in Turkish are proposed [24, 25]. While the former is based on Centering Theory [23], the latter is an implementation of a version of Hobbs' naïve algorithm adapted for Turkish.

Evidently, the work presented in this paper is not only new as a learning approach to anaphoric reference in Turkish but also one of the few relevant investigations concerning this language. The paper offers the design aspects of a corpus-based machine learning model intended to resolve anaphoric relations in Turkish and reports on several experiments conducted using this model with a comparative evaluation.

2 Description of the Model

2.1 Top-Level Design

Our model resolving pronouns can be defined in six stages: annotation, generating examples, filtering, partitioning into test and training sets, building a classifier, and evaluation. A schematic representation of the architectural design of the model is shown in Figure 1.

The input text is annotated with nine features that are most commonly encountered in the literature concerning anaphora resolution. This is followed by an example-generating process whereby each pronoun is paired with its candidate antecedent with appropriate positive or negative labeling. Afterwards, the negative data non-relevant to the learning task is filtered out in order to prevent negative instances from outnumbering positive ones. The balanced data is partitioned into a training set and a test set using a ten-fold cross validation technique. The training set is used to build a classifier, whereas the test set is used to evaluate the classifier. This evaluation is done using the recall, precision and f-measure metrics. What follow is a detailed description of each stage.

2.2 Data Annotation and Feature Vector

In order to carry out the annotation process semi-automatically, a tool is developed for annotating the raw text and generating feature vectors accordingly. This tool consists of the following three components which are applied in sequence to a discourse fragment:

1. A *tokenizer*, which analyzes a given discourse fragment to a list of words along with sentence boundaries.
2. A *morphological analyzer*, which uses the Zemberek library[3] in order to extract the category, case and person-number information for each word and determine the type of pronouns.

---

[2] See [19] for the original version of situation theory and [20] for a survey of changes and developments that have taken place in the theory since then.

[3] Zemberek [26] is an open source library intended to provide basic lexical operations for Turkish, such as determining roots and suffixes, spell checking and extracting syllables.

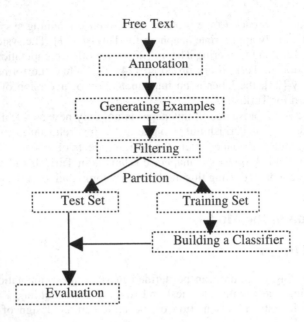

Fig. 1. Architectural Design of the Model in six stages: annotation, generating examples, filtering, partitioning into test and training sets, building a classifier, and evaluation

3. *A user interface*, which allows the annotator to correct possible errors made by the morphological analyzer, add covert pronouns to the text, specify the grammatical role, semantic type and referential status of each noun and pronoun and mark the antecedent of each pronoun.

Our corpus has been compiled from ten randomly chosen child stories. It contains more than 6000 tokens and more than 500 pronouns. A learning model requires data to be represented as a feature vector of attribute and value pairs. In our knowledge-lean model, out of 9 features used in these experiments, four relate to pronouns, three concern candidate referring expressions, and two convey information on relationships between pronouns and their candidate antecedents. The features are briefly described below:

pcase: the case of a pronoun.
pgr: the grammatical role of a pronoun
povertness: whether a pronoun is overt or not
ptype: the type of a pronoun such as personal, reflexive or locative
resemtype: the semantic class of a possible referring expression
recase: the case of a possible referring expression
regr: the grammatical role of a possible referring expression
distance: the distance between a pronoun and its possible referring expression
numberperson: The agreement in number and person. its possible values are true or false. If a pronoun and its candidate agree in number and person, the value is true, otherwise it is false.

We have selected the features by taking into consideration how often they have used in the relevant knowledge-based works. Some researchers claim that the grammatical function plays an important role for anaphora resolution. For example, The following ranking list where the grammatical functions are ordered in an increasing importance in terms of their contribution to the resolution process is suggested by [27]:

subject > object > object2 > other subcategorized object > adjunct.

On the other hand, another version of this list is proposed by [4] as follows:

subject > existential predicate nominal > object > indirect or oblique > demarcated adverbial prepositional phrase.

The significance of some case values, such as accusative and nominative, for the problem of anaphora resolution in Turkish is emphasized as in [28]. This study also underlines the effect of overtness of pronouns on this process. Therefore, case type and overtness are selected as two relevant attributes. In addition to these attributes, we also include the semantic type in our list. Many researchers have taken the semantic properties into consideration when designing their learning models [29,30,31,32,33,34,18,35,36]. Another important factor is the distance between a pronoun and a candidate. Almost all corpus-based studies take this attribute into account.

2.3 Generating Training Data

A *pair generator* pairs each pronoun with its candidate antecedents with appropriate positive or negative labeling and specifies the distance between a pronoun and a candidate antecedent. The generator outputs training and test data from the annotated text using the following algorithm:

1. Let p_list be the set of all pronouns in the discourse,
2. Let a_list be the set of antecedent candidates in the discourse. The set contains pronouns and possible referring expressions.
3. for each p in p_list:

   a) list possible antecedents from a_list, preceding p,
   b) if p explicitly or implicitly refers to an antecedent a from the list a_list preced ing p, create a positive instance containing the pair (p,a). "Implicitly" means that if any pronoun pi refers to any pronoun pj and pj refers to ax, pi refers to ax. We examine the whole of the reference chain.
   c) Create negative examples containing all combinations between p and its preceding antecedents, but previous positive examples.

4. Filter some of the negative examples according to the filtering rule. The filtering rule at hand is one based on number-person agreement, where the contradicting pairs in number and person are eliminated.

A pronoun can have more than one antecedent in a discourse fragment. However, there is a unique antecedent annotated for each pronoun in our text. But, during the generation of the training data, the chain beginning from a pronoun and ending with a noun phrase is examined as stated in step (3b) of the algorithm above. Filtering is a crucial process since most pairs in a discourse fragment are not involved in an anaphoric relation. More precisely, negative instances hugely outnumber positive ones.

Thus, the filtering process can be used to balance the class distribution. For example, before filtering our data the percentage of positive examples and negative examples were 20% and 80%, respectively. This unbalanced distribution is not appropriate especially for machine learning techniques. After the process of filtering, the ratio of positive examples turned to a desirable value, 40 %.

3 Experimental Setup and Results

Two most popular classification techniques, decision trees and two rule-based algorithms (PRISM and PART) were applied to our domain. What follows is about how those techniques are applied to our problem and what is the result of the experiment conducted.

3.1 Building a Decision Tree Classifier

All experiments were performed using Weka. This is an integrated data mining tool. First, decision tree using the Weka J48 classifier is built with the following settings:

Minimum number of instances: 2
Validation method: Cross Validation
Number of fold for validation: 10

The advantage of using a decision tree learning algorithm is that the output of the model is human-interpretable. Looking at our decision tree, we observed that the most informative features are distance and grammatical role. This finding is in line with those of other studies. Employing a cross validation technique we got an overall error rate as 17.38% and an accuracy rate as 82.61 % for the first default setting.

The recall, precision, and f-measure metrics are used in order to compare our model and some models proposed for other languages. Recall is a metric that measures the number of correctly resolved pronouns over the number of total pronouns in the text, and precision is a metric that measures the number of correctly resolved pronouns over the number of total resolved pronouns. For our model, the recall is 0.519, the precision is 0.732 and the F-measure is 0.608.

3.2 Building Rule-Based Classifiers

Quinlan, [37], states that re-expressing a classification model as production rules appears to be more intelligible than trees. This is a covering approach. Covering algorithms find a single rule that covers most instances of a class and extract these instances out. At each stage, the same process is done for each class [38,39,40]. Michalski's [41,42] AQ algorithm, Clark and Niblett's CN2 algorithm in [43] and Cendrowska's PRISM algorithm as in [44] are examples of this approach.

PRISM algorithm generates rules for each class by looking at the training data and adding rules that completely describe all tuples in that class. It generates only correct or perfect rules. PART [45] generates decision list and uses separate-and-conquer. It builds a partial C4.5 decision tree in each iteration and makes the "best" leaf into a rule. In the Weka software, PART uses J48 to generate pruned decision trees from which rules are extracted. In our experiments, two algorithms, PRISM and PART, were applied to the data set. The results are as shown in Table 1.

Table 1. Resulting of two algorithms

	Recall	Precision	F-Measure
PART	0.558	0.673	0.61
PRISM	0.893	0.384	0.537

When we examine the f-measure results, we see that the PART outperforms PRISM. Although the f-measure value, 0.61, is not an amazing result, it is still a sufficient score to create a robust model. In addition, while the time period taken to build a model with PART is 0.21 seconds, PRISM takes 2.74 second. That is, PART is quicker than PRISM as well.

3.3 Evaluation

Unfortunately, there is no corpus-based study, especially for Turkish, against which we could compare our model. For this reason, the results achieved are compared here with other studies in the area. A machine learning model with a F-measure of 57.2 is proposed [46]. A noun phrase coreference system is presented in [34]. Their best f-measure value is 70.4 on the MUC-6 coreference data set. Soon et al. (2001) [32] present a solution of noun phrase in unrestricted text with a f-measure value of 62.6 on MUC-6 data set [47]. A learning method to Japanese text is applied in [48]. Their f-measure result is 77.42. Table 2 summarizes the results including that of our model.

Table 2. Experimental results

	R %	P %	F %
For English [46]	57.2	57.2	57.2
For English [34]	75.4	73.8	74.6
For English Anaphoric NP [32]	58.6	67.3	62.6
For Japanese Text [48]	70.04	86.5	77.4
Our Decision Tree Model for Turkish Text	51.9	73.2	60.8
Our PART Model for Turkish Text	55.8	67.3	61.0
Our PRISM Model for Turkish Text	89.3	38.4	53.7

PRISM evidently yields a very unsatisfactory result. The J48 decision tree technique and the PART decision list have approximately the same f-measure results. Our scores are not very far from those of others even though not as good as them. But, it should be kept in mind that the fundamental typological differences between the languages in question does not allow one to make a reliable comparison of these scores.

4 Conclusion

Machine learning approaches have been applied successfully to the anaphora resolution problem. The model discussed in this paper employs two different albeit related techniques: a decision tree and a rule-based classification technique. It learns from a semi-automatically annotated text. This knowledge-lean model uses only 9 features in order to decrease the pre-processing time cost. We attempt to identify a unique antecedent for each pronoun. Keeping the minimum number of instances as 2 and using a cross validation method with 10 folds, we trained a decision tree model with an f-measure of 0.608 and the decision rules with an f-measure of 0.61. If the big picture which contains other studies is examined, this score seems to be an acceptable one for the task of anaphora resolution in Turkish.

Our attention in this study has been focused on anaphora. We are planning to increase the size and robustness of our text by adding new annotated discourse fragments. Adding new features to the system is also included among our future work list. Also, moving from a semi-automatic processing mode to a full-automatic one would be the essential direction in order to study in a more realistic environment.

References

1. Bobrow, D.G.: A question-answering system for high school algebra word problems. In: Proceedings of AFIPS conference, vol. 26, FJCC (1964)
2. Hobbs, J.R.: Pronoun resolution. Research Report 76-1. Department of Computer Science, City University of New York, New York (1976)
3. Hobbs, J.R.: Resolving pronoun references. Lingua 44, 339–352 (1978)
4. Lappin, S., McCord, M.: Anaphora Resolution in Slot Grammar. Computational Linguistics 16(4) (1990)
5. Carter, D.M.: A shallow processing approach to anaphor resolution. PhD thesis. University of Cambridge (1986)
6. Carter, D.M.: Interpreting anaphora in natural language texts. Ellis Horwood, Chichester (1987)
7. Rich, E., LuperFoy, S.: An architecture for anaphora resolution. In: Proceedings of the Second Conference on Applied Natural Language Processing (ANLP-2), Texas, U.S.A, pp. 18–24 (1988)
8. Carbonell, J., Brown, R.D.: Anaphora resolution: a multi-strategy approach. In: Proceedings of the 12. International Conference on Computational Linguistics (COLING 1988), Budapest, Hungary, vol. 1, pp. 96–101 (1988)
9. Lappin, S., Herbert, L.: An algorithm for pronominal anaphora resolution. Computational Linguistics 20(4), 535–561 (1994)
10. Mitkov, R.: An integrated model for anaphora resolution. In: Proceedings of the 15th International Conference on Computational Linguistics (COLING 1994), Kyoto, Japan, pp. 1170–1176 (1994)
11. Mitkov, R.: An uncertainty reasoning approach for anaphora resolution. In: Proceedings of the Natural Language Processing Pacific Rim Symposium (NLPRS 1995), pp. 149–154, Seoul, Korea (1995)

12. Kennedy, C., Branimir, B.: Anaphora for everyone: pronominal anaphora resolution without a parser. In: Proceedings of the 16th International Conference on Computational Linguistics (COLING 1996), Copenhagen, Denmark, pp. 113–118 (1996)

13. Mitkov, R.: Evaluating anaphora resolution approaches. In: Proceedings of the Discourse Anaphora and Anaphora Resolution Colloquium (DAARC'2), Lancaster, UK (1998)

14. Mitkov, R.: Anaphora Resolution. Longman (2002)

15. Baldwin, B.: CogNIAC: high precision coreference with limited knowledge and linguistic resources. In: Proceedings of the ACL 1997/EACL 1997 workshop on Operational factors in practical, robust anaphora resolution, Madrid, Spain, pp. 38–45 (1997)

16. Mitkov, R.: Anaphora resolution: the state of the art, Working paper (Based on the COLING 1998/ACL 1998 tutorial on anaphora resolution). University of Wolverhampton, Wolverhampton (1999)

17. Tin, E., Varol, A.: Computing with Causal Theories. International Journal of Pattern Recognition and Artificial Intelligence 6(4), 699–730 (1992)

18. Tin, E., Varol, A.: Situated processing of pronominal anaphora. In: Proceedings of the KONVENS 1994 Conference, Vienna, Austria, pp. 369–378 (1994)

19. Barwise, J., Perry, J.: Semantic Innocence and Uncompromising Situations. In: French, P.A., Uehling Jr., T., Wettstein, H.K. (eds.) Midwest Studies in Philosophy, vol. 6, pp. 387–403 (1981)

20. Devlin, K.: Jon Barwise's papers on natural language semantics. The Bulletin of Symbolic Logic 10(1), 54–85 (2004)

21. Yüksel, O., Bozsahin, C.: Contextually appropriate reference generation. Natural Language Engineering 8(1), 69–89 (2002)

22. Chomsky, N.: Lectures on Government and Binding. Foris, Dordrecht (1981)

23. Grosz, B., Joshi, A., Weinstein, S.: Centering: A Framework for Modeling the Local Coherence of Discourse Computational Linguistics (1995)

24. Yıldırım, S., Kılıçaslan, Y., Aykaç, R.E.: A Computational Model for Anaphora Resolution in Turkish via Centering Theory: an Initial Approach. In: International Conference on Computational Intelligence 2004, pp. 124–128 (2004)

25. Tüfekçi, P., Kılıçaslan, Y.: A Computational Model for Resolving Pronominal Anaphora in Turkish Using Hobbs' Naïve Algorithm. International Journal of Computational Intelligence 2(2), 71–75 (2005)

26. Zemberek 2 is an open source NLP library for Turkic languages, http://code.google.com/p/zemberek/

27. Brennan, S., Friedman, M.: A centering approach to pronouns. In: Proceedings of the 25th Annual Meeting of the ACL (ACL 1987), Stanford, CA, USA, pp. 155–162 (1987)

28. Turan, Ü.D.: Null Vs. Overt Subjects in Turkish Discourse: A Centering Analysis. Ph.D. Dissetation. University pf Pennysylvania, Philadelphia (1996)

29. Fisher, F., Soderland, S., Mccarthy, J., Feng, F., Lehnert, W.: Description of the umass system as used for muc-6. In: Proceedings of the Sixth Message Understanding Conference (MUC-6), pp. 127–140 (1995)

30. McCarthy, J.: A Trainable Approach to Coreference Resolution for Information Extraction. PhD thesis, Department of Computer Science, University of Massachusetts, Amherst MA (1996)

31. Cardie, C., Wagstaff, K.: Noun phrase coreference as clustering. In: Proceedings of the 1999 joint SIGDAT Conference on Empirical Methods in Natural Language Processing and Very Large Corpora, pp. 82–89 (1999)

32. Soon, W.M., Yong, D.C., Ng, H.T.: A Machine Learning Approach to Coreference Resolution of Noun Phrases. Computational Linguistics 27(4), 521–544 (2001)

33. Strube, M., Rapp, S., Müller, C.: The influence of minimum edit distance on reference resolution. In: Proceedings of the 2002 Conference on Empirical Methods in Natural Language Processing (EMNLP-2002), pp. 312–319 (2002)
34. Ng, V., Cardie, C.: Improving machine learning approaches to coreference resolution. In: Proceedings of the 40th Annual Meeting of the Association for Computational Linguistics, pp. 104–111 (2002)
35. Tüfekçi, P., Kılıçaslan, Y.: A syntax-based pronoun resolution system for Turkish. In: Proceedings of the 6th Discourse Anaphora and Anaphor Resolution Colloquium (DAARC-2007), Lisbon, Portugal (2007)
36. Yıldırım, S., Kılıçaslan, Y.: A Machine Learning Approach to Personal Pronoun Resolution in Turkish. In: Proceedings of 20th International FLAIRS Conference, FLAIRS-20, Key West, Florida (2007)
37. Quinlan, R.: C4.5: Programs for Machine Learning. Morgan Kaufmann Publishers, San Mateo (1993)
38. Cunningham, S.J., Littin, J., Witten, I.H.: Applications Of Machine Learning. Information Retrieval. Annual Review of Information Science (1997)
39. Mitchell, T.: Machine Learning. McGraw Hill, New York (1997)
40. Witten, I.H., Frank, E.: Data mining: Practical machine learning tools and techniques, 2nd edn. Morgan Kaufmann, San Francisco (2005)
41. Michalski, R.: Pattern recognition as rule-guided inductive inference. IEEE Transactions on Pattern Analysis and Machine Intelligence 2, 349–361 (1969)
42. McQueen, R.J., Garner, S.R., Nevill-Manning, C.G., Witten, I.H.: Applying machine learning to agricultural data. Computing and Electronics in Agriculture 12(4), 275–293 (1995)
43. Clark, P., Niblett, T.: The CN2 induction algorithm. Machine Learning 3, 261–284 (1989)
44. Cendrowska, J.: PRISM: An algorithm for inducing modular rules. International Journal of Man-Machine Studies 27(4), 349–370 (1987)
45. Frank, E., Witten, I.H.: Generating Accurate Rule Sets Without Global Optimization. In: Shavlik, J. (ed.) Machine Learning: Proceedings of the Fifteenth International Conference, Morgan Kaufmann Publishers, San Francisco (1998)
46. Connolly, D., Burger, J.D., Day, D.S.: A machine learning approach to anaphoric reference. New Methods in Language Processing pp. 133—144 (1997)
47. MUC-6. Coreference tast definition (v2.3, 8 Sep 95). In: Processing of the Sixth Message Understanding Conference (1995)
48. Aone, C., Bennett, S.W.: Evaluating automated and manual acquisition of anaphora resolution strategies. In: Proceedings of the 33th Annual Meeting of the Association for Computational Linguistics (1995)

LMF-QL: A Graphical Tool to Query LMF Databases for NLP and Editorial Use

Mehdi Ben Abderrahmen[1], Bilel Gargouri[2], and Mohamed Jmaiel[1]

[1] ReDCAD research unit
Ecole Nationale d'Ingénieurs de Sfax
Route de Soukra Km 3.5, B.P. W 1173, Sfax, Tunisia
mahdi.benabderrahmen@redcad.org,
mohamed.jmaiel@enis.rnu.tn
[2] MIRACL laboratory
Institut Supérieur d'Informatique et du Multimédia de Sfax
Technopole Sfax, Route de Tunis Km10, B.P. 242, 3021 Sfax, Tunisia
bilel.gargouri@fsegs.rnu.tn

Abstract. LMF is an new standard (ISO 24613) whose objective is to unify the representation of lexical resources in an XML database. LMF databases have generally complex structures which make formulating queries for extracting lexical data a hard task. Indeed, formulating a query necessitates mastering both the document structure and a query language. So in order to assist the query formulation for unskilled users and speed up this task for professional ones, we present in this paper a powerful and user-friendly graphical tool enabling automatic generation of XQuery queries for extracting lexical data from LMF databases for NLP and editorial use. To this end, we abstract database structure for specification of a query for data extraction. So, this tool accepts the query specification in term of *Input* and *Output*, where user may select only some data categories.

Keywords: LMF ISO-24613, LMF-QL, Query generation, Lexical databases, Natural Language Processing, editorial usage.

1 Introduction

Many lexical resources for the Natural Language Processing (NLP) were created. However, there is no standard format for the described structures, and the choice of data categories varies from one resource to another. So, a standard is necessary in order to allow the creation of such resources by mechanisms of fusion or exchange by simple interoperability [1]. In this context, and in order to standardize lexical databases design, the internal description format and the multilingual representation, the LMF project (Lexical Markup Framework) [2] is validated by the standardization committee ISO TC37/SC4 that deals with linguistic resources under the standard ISO 24613. This project proposes an approach for the design of XML databases starting from a single meta-model in UML for all programming languages and that allows representing multilingual

Z. Vetulani and H. Uszkoreit (Eds.): LTC 2007, LNAI 5603, pp. 279–290, 2009.

lexical data in connection with all linguistic levels (i.e. morphologic, syntactic, semantic). Some illustrations of LMF were already proposed: for instance, the Morphalou [3] database for French and ArabicLDB [4] for Arabic. However, LMF project is interesting only in lexical data representation. It does not cover the interrogation of the lexical database for the possible requirements in NLP application. Until now, two projects LEXUS [5,6] and LIRICS [7] were announced. They use the Web services in order to manage databases according to LMF standard. Nevertheless, they do not offer any assistance for accessing to these databases in order to satisfy the NLP application requirements. Indeed, to interrogate database, formulating queries is required for extracting data. This task is hard for users, even for an expert, because he needs to master the database structure which is complex. Also, formulating queries through a query language necessitate some skillfulness.

Many works such XQBE [8], VisualXQuery [9], GXQL [10], etc. have proposed languages to generate graphically queries. These languages, although they are intuitive and simple for users, they need the knowledge of the database structure. Furthermore, they require learning of new language and manipulation of many abstract symbols. So in order to simplify the query construction for unskilled users and speed up this task for professional ones, we present in this paper a powerful and a user-friendly graphical tool able to generate automatically XQuery queries to extract lexical information from any LMF database. For specifying his need, user may simply define the inputs and the outputs of the query from a list without drawing any symbol and without having any knowledge of the database structure. This tool can be used either for editorial use or NLP use after integration within NLP applications in a form of web services.

This paper first probes previous related research works. Then it presents the basis of our approach. Thereafter it shows the basic elements for specifying user requirement through the use of LMF-QL. It exposes after the transformation algorithm to XQuery syntax. The paper is completed by the description of an implementation of our tool and shows the different ways where it can be used.

2   Related Work

We present in this section a state of the art around the works related to our. It is composed of two parts. The first part concerns management tools for LMF databases. The second deals with graphical query languages.

2.1   LMF Databases Managing Tools

After the proposal of LMF standard, two great projects LEXUS and LIRICS were born around this standard. LEXUS provides an interface which helps users to define lexical databases structure. Moreover, it allows the fusion of lexical databases [11]. LEXUS aims to allow the construction of lexical databases according to LMF model and to import other structures towards LMF structure [12]. LEXUS is thus regarded as an interface of assistance to the construction of lexicons. However, it does not offer any possibility of interfacing with NLP applications. This orientation towards the interfacing with the NLP applications is now a new vision undertaken by some projects such as LIRICS which tries to provide an API for LMF which allows the exploitation of the Data Categories Registry (DCR) through an interface allowing the invocation of Web services. This API focuses on the management aspect of an LMF database by working directly on its structure.

Although the tools developed around LMF such as LEXUS and API for LMF (proposed in the LIRICS project) offer a set of services to build or to manage LMF databases, they do not offer any assistance for accessing to these databases in order to satisfy the NLP application requirements.

2.2 Graphical Query Languages

With the proliferation of XML documents, it was necessary to carry out queries on it. SQL is possible only on relational data models; that's why a new query language with similar capacities was required. After years of work, by the W3C, the specifications of XQuery made it possible to meet these needs.

Since the proposal of XQuery which is the standard of querying XML documents, several graphical query languages were proposed to allow the automatic generation of XQuery queries such as XQBE [8], GLASS [13], GXQL [14] and XML-GL [10]. Some works were made to propose interfaces in order to assist the user in the graphic interrogation providing predicates and graphic operators.

We distinguish two families of graphical query languages that query XML documents. The first family is based on XML-QL [15] language such us Miroweb Tool [16], Equix [17] and BBQ [18]. MiroWeb Tool uses a visual paradigm based on trees that implements XML-QL. Equix is a form-based query language for XML repositories, based on a tree-like representation of the documents, automatically built from their DTDs. BBQ (Blended Browsing and Querying) is a graphical user interface proposed for XMAS [19], a query language for XML based mediator systems (a simplification of XML-QL). The expressive power of BBQ is higher than Equix. For this first family of XML-QL based query languages, the support of XPATH [20] expression is limited. So, it is possible to have problems for fixing the path of some nodes in the document. Also, research by keyword can not be done. This can limit the research fields.

The second family is based on XQuery language. Many languages like XML-GL, XQBE, GXQL, GLASS and QSByE [21] were proposed. XML-GL, XQBE, GXQL and QSByE are graphic based languages. However, GLASS combines the advantages of using both graphs and texts. XML-GL and XQBE use graphs to represent document structure, GXQL uses nested windows, and QSByE uses nested tables. XML-GL does not supports neither the conditional structure (if then else) nor the disjunction. XQBE is good to express queries, but it presents some problems. It defines many abstract symbols. For example, there are two kinds of trapezoids, rhombuses and circles. It is difficult to remember which abstract symbol represents what concept. GXQL provides a powerful and easy to use environment for the non-XML users. It is also more expressive than XQBE and it has fewer symbols which are easier to remember. GLASS supports the conditional structure (if then else) opposing to XQBE and XML-GL. It integrates also XPATH expressions, logical operators (AND, OR, NOT). However, it does not offer any mechanism to control the conformity with the document structure.

Most of the above languages use two parts: the left part for specifying the input, and the right one for specifying the result. They start all from the document structure. So they use graphs, combined graphs and text, nested windows or tables to represent the document structure. This needs to have a good knowledge of the database structure which is generally not obvious. Moreover, to represent the document structure and the different relationships between nodes, these languages use many abstract symbols. This can lead to much ambiguity, and harden the task for the developers of NLP applications. These symbols must be drawn in conformity with a language that must be mastered by developers which find more and more difficulty during the task of formulating queries.

3 Proposed Approach

Our approach consists in developing a tool which generates automatically a query for the extraction of lexical data from LMF database. This tool accepts the user's requirements in term of *Input* and *Output*. The *Input* part is generally conditioned by a logical formula. The *Output* of the generation corresponds to an XQuery query meeting the expressed requirements. The facility offered by our tool is that the *Input* elements make the database structure abstract and do not refer to any particular level of the database. These levels, present generally in queries, will be determined by data categories selected in the requirements. With this intention, we propose a high-level language which we called LMF-QL. This language allows specifying the logical relation between different data categories selected in *Input* part.

The query generation is done after two steps: the first concerns the requirement specification (abstract form), and the second concerns the translation of this requirement into XQuery syntax (concrete form). In sequel, we will present respectively the requirements' specification using the LMF-QL, and the translation of these requirements to the XQuery syntax.

4 Requirements Specification

The purpose of the tool that we propose is to facilitate the task of NLP applications developers by providing an automatic generation of the XQuery queries without having necessity to know neither the database structure nor the query language.

4.1 Requirements Acquisition

A query is formally considered as a pair: $Query = (Input, Output)$
So to specify their requirements, users must first define the inputs of the query

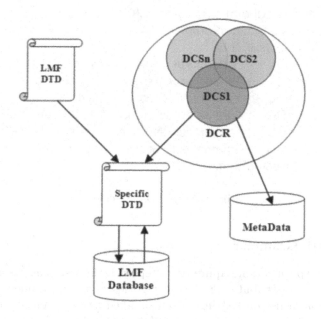

Fig. 1. Anchoring process

and then define its output which represents the required result. The proposed tool is composed of three parts (Fig. 4), the first is used to specify the *Input* of the query, the second concerns the specification of the *Output*, and the in third one the generation of the query.

For the *Input* definition, we removed all types of abstract symbols, like those used in other languages like XQBE, in order to facilitate the requirement specification. So we replaced these symbols by a selection of attributes used in the LMF database and which represent data categories (DC). In fact, the LMF DTD doesn't contain any information concerning DC. So we must use a specific DTD, which represents the structure of an LMF database enriched with data categories selection (DCS) taken from the Data Categories Registry (DCR). As revealed in the (Fig. 1), after anchoring the DCS selection into the LMF DTD, we obtain the specific DTD from which the LMF Database can be built. Also, from the DCR, we built a database of metadata, containing description of used Data Categories in order to assist the specification of the requirement.

For the definition of the query *Output*, we proceed in the same manner, with the difference that for the *Input* we are obliged to work only with attributes (leaves), and for the *Output* we can work either with attributes or elements (Internal Nodes). The query *Input* must be precise and expressed in term of attribute-value; consequently an attribute which is in an internal node (element which contains many entries) cannot belong to the *Input* of the query. For example, as shown in (Fig. 2), we cannot select *InflectedForm*, which is an element, from the *Input* list, but we can select it from the *Output* list.

```
<LemmatisedForm paradigm="asKataba">
  <DC att="wordForm" val="ذَهَبَ"/>
  <InflectedForm>
    <DC att="orthography" val="ذَهَبْتُ"/>
    <DC att="grammaticalAspect" val="accompli"/>
    <DC att="grammaticalVoix" val="actif"/>
    <DC att="grammaticalPerson" val="firstPerson"/>
    <DC att="grammaticalNumber" val="singular"/>
    <DC att="grammaticalGender" val="commun"/>
  </InflectedForm>
</LemmatisedForm>
```

Fig. 2. ArabicLDB Sample

4.2   LMF-QL Grammar

A requirement specification requires two steps. The first step as described above is the selection of attributes or data categories and their values. Values can be selected from a list or a string to put or fixed as an external variable. The second step for the requirement specification is to define relationships between the different data categories already selected. The relationship that can exist between two data categories or more is specified in the formula zone. The formula is simply a logical expression in conformity with LMF-QL grammar. We present in the Fig. 3 the LMF-QL grammar.

$$G = (\textstyle\sum, V, S, P)$$
$$\textstyle\sum = \{or, and, not, (,), E_i\}$$
$$V = \{S\}$$
$$P = \{S \rightarrow (S)|not(S)|(SorS)|(SandS)|E_i\}$$

Fig. 3. LMF-QL grammar

The LMF-QL grammar is composed of a set of terminals $\sum$, a set of non terminals V, an axiom S and a set of transformation rules P. Among the terminals, we have used logical operators which are from two types: unary operator 'not' that can be applied on one data category or on an expression and which represents disjunction, and binary operators 'or' and 'and' that can be applied on two data categories.

5   Translation

The translation is based on an algorithm that uses a generic model for concrete XQuery queries used for interrogating LMF databases. This model is inspired from the FLWR expression of XQuery. So, the algorithm takes as input a query in the abstract form (requirement specification), and produces as output its XQuery translation (concrete form), compliant to FLWR expression. The translation starts with a preprocessing of the *Inputs* and *Outputs* so as to fix for each one its path. The query is then constructed by processing the different part of the FLWR expression.

5.1 Preprocessing

During this step, the most important work is to fix for each *Input* or *Output* its path in the LMF database. These data are saved in the specific DTD. So we try after that to get the common path for all of them. This will be important for the next step. In this step also, we fix the Let part of the FLWR expression, and through which we specify the document of the LMF database. Before the processing task, one crucial step must be done and which is the control of the validity of the query. Indeed, LMQ-QL can do only a syntactic control. So possible queries can be syntactically correct but semantically they have no sense. So we provide here a control mechanism of the validity of the query and which role to reject queries semantically not correct. For example, this mechanism does not accept any specification using the logical operator 'or' between two data categories if they don't belong to same level in the database structure. So *(E1 or E2)* is forbidden in case E1 and E2 have not the same parent. The same thing if we use *not(E1 and E2)* which induces *not(E1) or not(E2)*, but *not(not(E1 and E2))* is accepted in any case.

5.2 Processing

In this step, the algorithm deals with each part of the XQuery syntax (FWR) separately, so as "For and Where" for the input part and Return for the result or the Output part. At the end of processing, it gathers all the part to build the final query. This query may have different forms which depend on the number of entries fixed in the *Input* and in the *Output* of the query.

Table 1. Different classes of requirements

Nbr Inputs	Nbr Outputs	Result Type	Requirements Class
1	0	Boolean	Existence
≥ 2	0	Boolean	Coherence
≥ 1	≥ 1	Different values	General Requirement

Each form represents a general model for a class of requirements as shown in table 1. In this table, the first class is to express existence requirement of one data categories. The second class is used for testing coherence between two data categories or more. As an example we can test the coherence of using both prefix and suffix or coherence between the triplet prefix, infix and suffix in case of Arabic language.

The construction of the Return part is very simple, but the construction of the "For and Where" part needs much effort, especially in most of cases we need imbrications. This construction starts by attributing a variable or a pointer for the common path fixed in the preprocessing stage. This pointer is used to parse the document structure forward to it, trying to reduce the visited data. For every level switch in the path of the *Inputs*, we need another pointer and consequently another "For Where Return" statement.

For the conditions applied to the *Inputs*, they can be processed differently depending on logical operator used (OR, AND) and on the path of *Inputs*. For inputs belonging to the same level (having the same parent node), conditions can be all processed in the Where part. If *Inputs* have different parents, so the use of OR operator is forbidden in the specification of the requirement, and conditions applied to *Inputs* joined by AND operator can be processed each in the "Where" part imbricated from the parent.

5.3 Example

We present now an example and we will see how to proceed for the specification. As a requirement, we want to obtain the orthography of the word "

$$ذَهَبَ$$

" verb "to go" conjugated with the first person. So the inputs of the query are wordForm which value is "

$$ذَهَبَ$$

" and grammaticalPerson which value is FirstPerson, and the ouput of the query is orthography. In the formula zone user must write (E1 AND E2) where E1 represent the first input pair (attribute, value) and E2 the second one.

5.3.1 Preprocessing Document of the LMF Database
let $x := doc("ArabicLDB.xml")$
Path of Input 1:
$//../LexicalEntry/LemmatisedForm/DC/@att$
Path of Input 2:
$//../LexicalEntry/LemmatisedForm/InflectedForm/DC/@att$
Path of Output:
$//../LexicalEntry/LemmatisedForm/InflectedForm/DC/@att$
Common path
$a = //../LexicalEntry/LemmatisedForm$

5.3.2 Processing
Condition 1 for input 1:

$$//../LexicalEntry/LemmatisedForm/DC/@att$$
$$where\ \$a/DC/@att = "wordForm"\ and\ \$a/DC/@val = "\ ذَهَبَ\ "$$

Condition 2 for input 2:
- Level Switch
- New "For Where Return" statement
- New pointer: $b Where $b/../DC/@att = "grammaticalPerson"
  and $b/../DC/@val = "firstPerson"

Result:
return < orthography > {$b/@val} < orthography >

The final query is now built by gathering

$$let\ \$x := doc("EntreeLexicale.xml")$$

$$for\ \$a\ in\ \$x//Database/Lexicon/LexicalEntry/LemmatisedForm$$

$$where\ \$a/DC/@att = "wordForm"\ and\ \$a/DC/@val = "\ ذَهَبَ\ "$$

$$return$$

$$for\ \$b\ in\ \$a/InflectedForm/DC[@att = "orthography"]$$

$$where\ \$b/../DC/@att = "grammaticalPerson"\ and\ \$b/../DC/@val = "firstPerson"$$

$$return$$

$$<\ orthography > {\$b/@val} < /orthography >$$

6   Implementation

This section briefly describes the features of our implementation of LMF-QL (a snapshot taken from the tool at work is shown in Fig. 4).

Our tool has a very simple and intuitive interface through which user can easily specify his requirement. This tool aims to be more intuitive than XQBE, Visual XQuery and GXQL by getting rid of abstract symbols and by presenting a visually obvious association between the query and its output. The most important issue in this proposal is that user does not need to control the database structure. In addition, we do not attempt to represent the entire XQuery syntax visually and support a subset of XQuery syntax only, but we try to cover XQuery syntax needed to query lexical information from LMF databases. Users can easily select attributes or elements from windows composed of two parts, corresponding to the Inputs and Output of the query. For the inputs, users can specify specific values. Through the formula zone they can identify the relations between inputs. So they can use terminals (operators and parenthesis) to express their requirements according to the grammar sketched in Section 4. Incorrect syntaxes are prevented "on line" and the queries can be generated with a single click on "Generate" button. Generated queries are shown in the right text zone, and can be saved in a file.

Also, this tool allows generating specific DTD for each LMF database. So users can change easily from one database to another and the tool generates automatically the corresponding DTD.

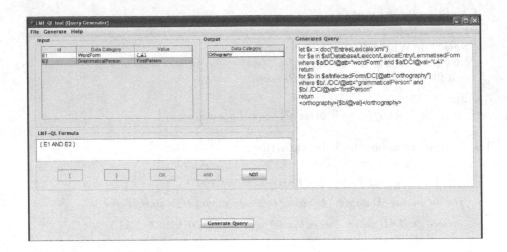

Fig. 4. LMF-QL tool (Query Generator)

7   Examples of Application

LMF-QL can extract any information stored in the LMF database and therefore can generate a large number of queries since the LMF standard (ISO 24613) supports all languages. However, all these queries can be classified into two categories depending on the complexity of the desired need. Hence, we distinguish simple needs and complex needs. For simple queries, they can be used for editorial use, while complex queries can be integrated into NLP applications to develop complete NLP systems.

7.1   Editorial Use

A large number of queries is used in an editorial context where the user asks for a simple need as the interrogation of a dictionary to find the definition of a word or a synonym. LMF-QL tool generates XQuery queries responding to the following needs:

– seeking morphological characteristics of a word,
– definitions, examples,
– synonyms and antonyms, homophones,
– female or male,
– singular or plural of a noun or an adjective,
– the list of affixes (suffixes, prefixes and infixes for Arabic etc.). ...

LMF-QL makes easy the interrogation of lexical databases. Indeed, it was useful for the ADiQTo tool [22] which was developed for the generic interrogation of standardized Arabic dictionaries.

7.2 NLP Use

Contrary to the editorial context, NLP queries are usually complicated and their results need to be more handled. For instance, the extraction of inflectional data which are not directly stored in the database. These data will be calculated through a combination between different data categories and logical operators (*and, or, not*). These results are not intended to be used directly by humans, but rather intended to be sent to NLP applications by invoking web services like presented in [23]. LMF-QL saves generated queries in a database to be reused when needed. And for each new specified need it generates a new query.

8 Conclusion and Future Works

In this paper, we presented a graphical query tool that offers a visual interface to query LMF data bases. This tool was able to simply translating a user requirement from an abstract form, using only some attributes and elements of the LMF database structure, to a concrete form compliant to the XQuery syntax. This work helps users, developing applications using LMF databases in an editorial or NLP context, to formulate in an easy way their queries.

There are several potential opportunities for future work. From a technical viewpoint, several improvements and extensions to our work are possible, and among these improvements we will give priority to take into account difficult queries accessing to intentional information.

Another opportunity is that by the LMF-QL tool, we will promote automatically a component or a service facilitating the invocation of these queries.

References

1. Francopoulo, G.: Proposition de norme des Lexiques pour le traitement automatique du langage (2003),
   http://pauillac.inria.fr/atoll/RNIL/TC37SC4-docs/N07.pdf
2. Francopoulo, G., Bel, N., George, M., Calzolari, N., Monachini, M., Pet, M., Soria, C.: Multilingual resources for NLP in the lexical markup framework (LMF). Language Resources and Evaluation (2008)
3. Romary, L., Salmon-Alt, S., Francopoulo, G.: Standards going concrete: from LMF to Morphalou. In: Proceedings of the COLING 2004 Enhancing and using electronic dictionaries, COLING, pp. 22–28 (2004)
4. Khemakhem, A., Gargouri, B., Abdelwahed, A.: Proposition d'une base lexicale pour la langue Arabe selon la future norme LMF. In: Proceedings of the Journées Scientifiques des Jeunes Chercheurs en Génie éléctrique et Informatique (2006)
5. Kemps-Snijders, M., Nederhof, M., Wittenburg, P.: LEXUS, a web-based tool for manipulating lexical resources. In: Proceedings of the fifth international conference on language resources and evaluation, pp. 1862–1865 (2006)
6. Kirsch, K.: LEXUS version 1.0. Lexus manual (2005)
7. Francopoulo, G., Nioche, J., Kemps, M.: Guidelines and tools for producing standards, test-suites and API(s). Lirics guidelines (2005)

8. Braga, D., Augurusa, A.C.S.C.E.: XQBE: XQuery By Example. Poster at ACM-WWW (in the electronic proceedings) (2003)
9. Chin, K.B.: Visual XQuery: A graphical language to represent XML XQuery language (2007), http://www.comp.hkbu.edu.hk/~bchoi/website/Introduction.html
10. Ceri, S., Comai, S., Damiani, E., Fraternali, P., Paraboschi, S., Tanca, L.: XML-GL: A Graphical Language for Querying and Restructuring XML Documents. Computer Networks 31(11–16), 1171–1187 (1999)
11. Nathan, D., Skiba, R., Uneson, M.: Language Archives Newsletter (2005), http://www.mpi.nl/LAN/lan_05.pdf
12. Vriend, F.D., Boves, L., van den Heuvel, H., van Hout, R., Kruijsen, J., Swanenberg, J.: A Unified Structure for Dutch Dialect Dictionary Data. In: Proceedings of The fifth international conference on Language Resources and Evaluation (2006)
13. Ni, W., Ling, T.W.: GLASS: A Graphical Query Language for Semi-Structured Data. In: Proceedings of the Eighth International Conference on Database Systems for Advanced Applications, pp. 363–370. IEEE Computer Society, Los Alamitos (2003)
14. Qin, Z., Yao, B.B., Liu, Y., McCool, M.D.: A graphical xQuery language using nested windows. In: Zhou, X., Su, S., Papazoglou, M.P., Orlowska, M.E., Jeffery, K. (eds.) WISE 2004. LNCS, vol. 3306, pp. 681–687. Springer, Heidelberg (2004)
15. Deutsch, A., Fernandez, M., Florescu, D., Levy, A., Suciu, D.: XML-QL: A Query Language for XML (1998), http://www.w3.org/TR/NOTE-xml-ql
16. Bouganim, L., Chan-Sine-Ying, T., Dang-Ngoc, T.T., Darroux, J.L., Gardarin, G., Sha, F.: Miro Web: Integrating Multiple Data Sources through Semistructured Data Types. In: Proceedings of 25th International Conference on Very Large Data Bases, pp. 750–753. Morgan Kaufmann, San Francisco (1999)
17. Cohen, S., Kanza, Y., Kogan, Y.A., Nutt, W., Sagiv, Y., Serebrenik, A.: Equix easy querying in xml databases. In: Proceedings of the ACM SIGMOD Workshop on The Web and Databases, pp. 43–48 (1999)
18. Comai, S., Damiani, E., Fraternali, P.: Computing graphical queries over xml data. ACM Trans. Inf. Syst. 19(4), 371–430 (2001)
19. Ludaescher, B., Papakonstantinou, Y., Velikhov, P., Vianu, V.: View definition and DTD inference for XML. In: Proceedings of the Post-IDCT Workshop (1999)
20. Clark, J., Drose, S.: Xml path language (xpath). version 1.0 (1999)
21. Filha, I.M.R.E., Laender, A.H.F., da Silva, A.S.: Querying semistructured data by example: The qsbye interface. In: Proceedings of the Workshop on Information Integration on the Web, pp. 156–163 (2001)
22. Baccar, F., Khemakhem, A., Gargouri, B., Haddar, K., Hamadou, A.B.: LMF Standardized Model for the Editorial Electronic Dictionaries of Arabic. In: Proceedings of the 5th International Workshop on Natural Language Processing and Cognitive Science, pp. 64–73. INSTICC Press (2008)
23. BenAbderrahmen, M., Chaari, F., Gargouri, B., Jmaiel, M.: Des services orientés besoin pour l'exploitation des bases lexicales normalisées. In: Proceedings of the 9th Maghrebian Conference on Software Engineering and Artificial Intelligence, pp. 451–456 (2006)

Novelty Extraction from Special and Parallel Corpora

Elżbieta Dura and Barbara Gawronska

Högskolan i Skövde, Dept. of Humanities and Informatics
Box 408
54118 Skövde, Sweden
{elzbieta.dura,barbara.gawronska}@his.se

Abstract. How can corpora assist translators in ways in which resources like translation memories or term databases cannot? Our tests on English, Polish and Swedish parts of the JRC-Acquis Multilingual Parallel show that corpora can provide support for term standardization and variation, and, most importantly, for tracing novel expressions. A corpus tool with an explicit dictionary representation is particularly suitable for the last task. Culler is a tool which allows one to select expressions with words absent from its dictionary. Even if the extracted material may be stained with some noise, it has an undeniable value for translators and lexicographers. The quality of extraction depends in a rather obvious way on the dictionary and text processing but also on the query.

Keywords: corpus, novelty, terminology, term extraction, translation, dictionary.

1 Tracing Lexical Novelties in Texts

Translators, and domain specialists alike, experience problems not only with tracing new terminology but also with setting accepted terms apart from ad hoc expressions. Term standardization is a constant battlefield. Providers of language services can state on the basis of their real every day experience that language is a process. Corpora belong to language resources which can easily follow language change and thus provide adequate assistance to translators, terminologists, lexicographers, or linguists in general. A suitable corpus tool has to supply on the fly statistics, by which the spread of a term can be judged.

1.1 Term Databases and Translation

Accurate translation equivalents are not always found in dictionaries. Properly managed translation memories can solve many terminological problems, but they require continuous and consequent updating. Translators and terminologists appreciate access to viewing several variants of potential translation equivalents in use, especially when a new term is being introduced. "Translators want to preserve flexibility, when present-day translation systems propagate rigidity, and, as a lurking consequence, poverty of style and vocabulary"[1].

Z. Vetulani and H. Uszkoreit (Eds.): LTC 2007, LNAI 5603, pp. 291–302, 2009.

Term databases result from research which is monolingual in nature. Its main concern is standardization and categorization of the relationship between concepts and terms [2]. Newly introduced terms are obviously in focus. Translation may contribute to the development of term databases in unexpected ways, particularly when gaps are discovered. When an equivalent is missing in one of the languages, new knowledge may be gained through the process of translation. For instance, there is a technique in art restoration, which was developed originally in Russia and in more recent times in Poland, and which is largely unknown in the West: "splitting of easel paintings". This term - together with the knowledge of the particular technique - has entered the English speaking world via translation.

1.2   Old vs. New Words

Shifts of terminology are unquestionably worthy of attention because they may help to discern novel paths of reasoning. Some are difficult to detect, e.g. novel use of an existing term in a given context. How can corpora provide support for term standardization and variation, and, most importantly, for tracing novel expressions?

The easy and obvious way of tracking a lexical change is in respect to some existent dictionary or ontology. The delimitation of novel terms involves necessarily a definition of "known" terms, both of general and of special language.

1.3   Extraction of Novel Terms in Culler

Culler is a corpus tool equipped with a statistics module and integrated with a dictionary [3-7]. The latter feature renders possible querying for words absent from a dictionary. A special word class variable called *&new* can be used for this purpose.

New Words. The selection of new words in Culler follows a rather clear definition. A new word is a string which:

a) is not found in the dictionary of the language in question (neither directly nor after inflectional analysis)
and
b) does not belong to such categories of non-dictionary items as: proper names, acronyms, abbreviations, symbols, numbers, foreign words, misspellings, e-mail addresses.

How precise the selection is depends thus even more on text analysis than on the dictionary itself, because all the mentioned text segments plus dictionary words need to be identified, classified and made available for searching. Setting apart true new creations from voluntary and involuntary word form distortion is one challenge. Another one is to distinguish new word formations from foreign words of almost any language. Hence. not all words classified as *&new* in Culler are genuine neologisms.

The results of the selection depend in a rather obvious way on the dictionary. Culler English and Polish dictionaries contain over 90 000 lexemes each, the Swedish dictionary counts over 70 000 lexemes. It is possible to add special glossaries to Culler dictionaries, but when none is supplied, one can actually extract the glossary of the domain using *&new*.

Table 1. The sizes of the consulted text collections

	Tokens	Types
English Prose	31 211 830	193 555
Swedish Misc	37 374 820	1 030 612
Polish Misc	51 942 817	941 075
English Acquis	52 964 940	576 021
Polish Acquis	40 834 160	506 806
Swedish Acquis	43 160 597	897 827
Cancer	63 852 283	284 861

Old Words in New Use. Novel meanings can be acquired by old word forms. This is quite common in special purpose languages [8-9]. For instance, expression in bio-medical literature means a conversion of some DNA sequence into proteins. Thanks to the statistics module such words can be selected with the help of frequency deviation calculated in relation to a reference corpus. Literary texts mixed with newspaper articles collected in the three corpora English Prose, Swedish Misc and Polish Misc act as reference corpora and provide normal frequencies from which frequency deviation is calculated.

New Multiword Terms. New multiword terms are toughest to trace [9, 10], but a good approximation may be a selection of phrases built around new words or words with high frequency deviation. When applied to special domain corpora, the query for &new words results in a glossary of the domain and not so many words that are new to domain specialists [11]. But the use of &new in a larger pattern increases the chance of selecting new multiwords even from special domain corpora, which is illustrated below.

2   The Quantitative Comparison

Our quantitative study is restricted to new words: words with new roots or new compounds or derivations. The possibility of selecting new words with &new in Culler from different text collections and in different languages allows us to compare the results. We have compared not only different genres but also texts of similar genre in three languages: English, Polish and Swedish. The questions we approach are: what portion of all word tokens and types in the text collection is constituted by new words and how this depends on the specific language and genre.

2.1 The Consulted Text Collections

The following text collections have been consulted in our study:

- mixed literary and newspaper texts:
  - English Prose
  - Polish Misc
  - Swedish Misc
- legislative texts, parallel sentence aligned corpora[1]:
  - English Acquis
  - Polish Acquis
  - Swedish Acquis
- research articles in biomedicine (English):[2]
  - Cancer.

The sizes of the consulted corpora are presented in Table 1, both in text word tokens and in text word types.

2.2 How Many Text Words are Non-dictionary Words?

The proportions of dictionary and non-dictionary words in Table 2 do not include any numeric or symbolic text tokens, only text word tokens.

Table 2. Proportions of dictionary and non-dictionary words

Corpus	Dictionary words (%)	Non-dictionary words (%)
English Prose	97,28	2,72
Swedish Misc	89,87	10,13
Polish Misc	93,92	6,08
English Acquis	93,62	6,38
Polish Acquis	91,68	8,32
Swedish Acquis	87,97	12,03
Cancer	91,24	8,76

A comparison of the selections in English, Polish, and Swedish confirms the impact of the well attested special characteristics of a given language. Swedish has the highest portion of new words due to its productive compounding and derivation, while Polish has higher portion of new words than English due to its productive derivation. In English, the share of new words grows together with the specialized

---

[1] Texts are provided by the Joint Research Center of the European Commission.
[2] Texts are special selections from PubMed, available at: www.ncbi.nlm.nih.gov/pubmed/

character of the language: it is lowest in general language (English Prose), higher in the legislative language (English Acquis), and highest in the language of biomedicine.

2.3 How Many Non-dictionary Text Words are New Words?

How many new words are there in proportion to non-dictionary text words is shown in Table 3. Numeric and symbolic strings are excluded from the number of non-dictionary words, as in Table 2. The amount of new words is reported in text word tokens and text word types.

Almost 50% of non-dictionary words in Swedish Acquis are new words. This is due to the productivity of compounding in Swedish in general combined with the excessive use of compounds in legislative language. Compounds in Swedish correspond often to regular phrases in English or Polish hence the number of text word types per text word tokens is also high.

The high percentage of new words in biomedical texts is due to special terms not present in the general dictionary. The proportion in types and tokens is similar to the proportion present in general English texts (English Prose).

Table 3. New words among non-dictionary words

	% of non-dictionary words	new words - tokens	new words - types
English Prose	10,70	90 783	34 540
Swedish Misc	30,30	1 118 863	400 792
Polish Misc	21,16	647 325	153 633
English Acquis	20,10	614 171	106 689
Polish Acquis	17,50	537 234	61 122
Swedish Acquis	49,06	2 311 725	252 924
Cancer	37,99	2 002 139	71 575

3 &new in Parallel Corpora

In Swedish Culler it is possible to distinguish new simple words from new compounds. A selection of new compounds in Swedish can thus be a gateway to selection of new multiword phrases when parallel corpora can be consulted.

Tables 4-7 present the top rows of frequency sorted selections from Swedish, English and Polish Acquis.

Table 4. Swedish Acquis

	kvalitet*=&new	
134	*kvalitetsnormer*	*(norms)*
147	*kvalitetsmål*	*(goals)*
108	*kvalitetskrav*	*(requirements)*
111	*kvalitetsvin*	*(wine)*
87	*kvalitetskontroll*	*(control)*
64	*kvalitetsförsämring*	*(depreciation)*

Table 5. English Acquis

	quality	*&noun*
224	*quality*	*standards*
170	*quality*	*objectives*
135	*quality*	*requirements*
133	*quality*	*control*
119	*quality*	*wines*
51	*quality*	*tolerances*

Table 6. Polish Acquis

	&noun	*("jakości")*	
259	*norma*	*jakości*	*(norm)*
182	*poprawa*	*jakości*	*(improvement)*
154	*kontrola*	*jakości*	*(control)*
134	*wskaźnik*	*jakości*	*(objective)*
90	*klasa*	*jakości*	*(class)*
53	*ocena*	*jakości*	*(assessment)*

The selections are obtained with the following queries:

- *kvalitet*=&new-compound*[3] selects new compounds having *kvalitet* (*quality*) as modifier (Swedish),
- *quality &noun*[4] selects nominal phrases with *quality* in modifier position (English),
- *&noun ("jakości")*[5] selects nominal phrases with *jakość* in genitive (Polish),

---

[3] The query means: any new compound beginning with *kvalitet*.
[4] The query means: any phrase beginning with *quality* followed by a noun.

- *&noun (jakościowy)*[6] selects nominal phrases with *jakościowy* as postposed modifier (Polish).

Frequency sorting applied to the selections renders the equivalents in very similar ordering.[7]

The selection from Polish diverges more from the other two, which is not surprising. Adding to differences between the language types the selection is also limited to a specific phrase form - typical of terms in Polish. The selections provide help in tracing gaps in equivalents.

For instance, *ocena jakości* (*quality assessement*) turns out to come high up because of nominal phrases used where verb phrases appear in English, such as *to assess the quality*. The lack of *quality wine* among Polish equivalents is checked in the corpus with a simple query * *wino* *[8]. It shows directly that the default Polish equivalent of *quality* is absent in this context, because there is a standard term *wino gatunkowe*, which is used instead.

Compound structure in English and Swedish disguises a variety of relations which not always can be left unstated in Polish phrasal equivalents. Therefore a selection of phrases following other possible structural patterns may be required. Table 7 shows the alternative equivalent structure with the main noun followed by the adjective *jakościowy*.

Table 7. Polish Acquis: *&noun (jakościowy)*

	&noun	*(jakościowy)*	
59	*wymagania*	*jakościowe*	(requirements)
32	*wymogi*	*jakościowe*	(requirements)
28	*normy*	*jakościowe*	(norms)
24	*cele*	*jakościowe*	(goals)
13	*kryterium*	*jakościowe*	(criteria)
12	*klasyfikacja*	*jakościowa*	(classification)

3.1 Lexical and Stylistic Variation

The apparent benefit for a translator or terminologist is that statistics can provide a good hint as to which forms dominate in each of the languages. For instance, the *quality* selection includes *kvalitetssäkring* (*quality assurance*) and *kvalitetskontroll* (*quality check*), which, dependent on the context, are used in Swedish for a more general *quality control*, dominating in English texts.

---

[5] The query means: any phrase with a noun followed by the genivite form of the noun *jakość*, the latter as a non-focal unit, i.e. disregarded in frequency sorting.

[6] The query means: any noun followed by the adjective *jakościowy*, the latter as a non-focal unit, i.e. disregarded in frequency sorting.

[7] Possibly, the similarities in frequencies should be observed even in comparable corpora.

[8] The query means: any word followed by *wino* followed by any word.

Corpora can provide insight into how phrasing may change over time. For instance, Swedish equivalents of the term *disabled persons* are first *handikappade personer*, later *funktionshindrade* or *personer med funktionshinder*.

3.2 Context Variation of Multiword Equivalents

Equivalents in term databases or translation memories are often not satisfactory because they cannot be blindly inserted in different contexts, and context is where corpora can help most.

In majority of contexts in the Polish Acquis *disabled person* is translated as *osoba niepełnosprawna* but with some modifiers it has to be rephrased, e.g. *seriously disabled persons* is rendered by the phrase *osoby o znacznej niepełnosprawności*. (lit. 'persons with considerable disability') Similar examples are easy to find in Swedish: *disabled persons* is translated as *funktionshindrade* in the majority of contexts, but not in the phrase *benefits for disabled person* where there is a special compound available: *handikappsförmåner*. (lit. disability+benefits') A similar example is the term *legal personality* which is translated into Swedish as *juridisk person* or *status som juridisk person* but not in *acquire legal personality*, where the required form is *rättskapacitet* (lit. 'legal capacity')

4 Extraction with Combined Search Parameters

A selection from a corpus system can be made as precise as the query language allows. Several parameters in the Culler system can help a translator to look for specific subsets of terminology. They are particularly effective when combined.

4.1 Using Keywords as Topic Filters

It is possible to enter words as filters for sentences or other text sections in order to narrow down the text scope of the selection. Table 8 shows a selection from the Swedish Acquis obtained with the additional word filter *+*djur** (*animal*), which means that the selection is to be performed only from the documents with words containing *djur*. The search phrase is **foder=&new-compound*[9] and frequency is chosen as the sorting key. The selection provides a glossary in the subdomain together with hints for dominating alternative forms, such as *tillskottsfoder* instead of *kompletteringsfoder*.

Polish equivalents in this subdomain can be expected in a very rigid phrasal form hence their selection does not require filtering. The two typical equivalents are: *karma dla ** or *pasza dla ** ('feedingstuffs for'; see Table 9).

4.2 Frequency Deviation and *&new*

Sorting by frequency deviation can be useful for obtaining low frequency special domain expressions, particularly if the selection is based on a precise pattern specification. Examples of such selections from a minor corpus in geology are presented below.

---

[9] The query means: any compound absent from the dictionary which ends with foder('feedingstuffs').

Table 8. Swedish Acquis: **foder=&new-compound*

	*foder=&new-compound
335	*djurfoder* (animal feedingstuffs)
34	*helfoder* (complete feedingstuffs)
18	*tillskottsfoder* (supplementary feedingstuffs)
13	*fiskfoder* feedingstuffs for fish)
9	*kompletteringsfoder* (complementary feedingstuffs)
9	*mineralfoder* (feedingstuffs composed of minerals)
6	*sällskapsdjurfoder* (petfood)
4	*tilläggsfoder* (complementary feedingstuffs)
2	*sällskapsdjursfoder* (petfood)

Table 9. Polish Acquis: *karma/pasza dla &noun*

	karma	*dla*	*&noun*
13	*karma*	*dla*	*zwierząt* (animals)
15	*karma*	*dla*	*psów* (dogs)
2	*karma*	*dla*	*ryb* (fish)
1	*karma*	*dla*	*drobiu* (poultry)
	pasza	*dla*	*&noun*
36	*pasza*	*dla*	*zwierząt* (animals)
9	*pasza*	*dla*	*ryb* (fish)
3	*pasza*	*dla*	*drobiu* (poultry)
1	*pasza*	*dla*	*indyków* (turkeys)
1	*pasza*	*dla*	*królików* (rabbits)

A glossary of a special domain includes many words of a general dictionary turned into terms having a new specific use. The selection of nouns sorted according to frequency deviation yields at the very top nouns like *ridge, mantle, crust, basin, bed, plate, pole, belt.*

Good multiword term candidates are obtained using frequency sorting and patterns with some of the nouns of the domain glossary. The list below shows the top of the selection of compounds with *bed* obtained with frequency deviation sorting:

- *drift beds,*
- *ocean bed,*
- *sea bed,*
- *clay beds,*
- *shell beds,*

- *coal beds,*
- *lignite beds.*

Frequency deviation can also help to elicit the special style of documents. For instance a query for phrases with an adjective followed by a noun in English Acquis sorted by frequency deviation has the following phrases at the top[10]:

- *agricultural protocols*
- *relevant documents*
- *important objective*
- *early notification*
- *former member*
- *transitional measures*

When *&new* is included in a search phrase and sorting by frequency deviation is applied misspelled words are selected as *&new*. For instance, the query *&noun &noun (&new)* with frequency deviation sorting yields:

- *Official Journal ot*
- *reference quantity definitively*
- *maximum force occuring*
- *tariff information issused*
- *residues limits norgestomet*
- *fishery products orginating*
- *protection measures applicab*

5   Conclusions

The quantitative study confirms the need for dictionary based selections from corpora as support for terminologists and translators. Our results show that the percentage of novel terms grows with the degree of language specialization, and most professional translators are confronted with the need of translating specialized language. Detection of novelty in texts is tough, yet there is assistance available from corpora with tools which enable querying corpora for lexical changes. A possible definition of a change is the one adopted in Culler for *&new*: a lexical word absent in a general dictionary.

Even if translators lack some types of assistance from translation memories or term databases, most of them do not turn to corpus based tools. They seem simply to be unaware of the usefulness of corpora – even if many translation theorists stress the importance of corpus based terminological work in the course of the translation process: "In specialized translation, translators also work as terminologists, as they have to make up a list of terms of a specific domain, as well as the list of their translations into the target language" [12]. Even monolingual corpora may play a role in the

---

[10] The query posed *(&stop) &adj &noun (&stop)* means: an adjective followed by a noun surrounded by some function word.

translation process if they are provided with a corpus tool including a statistics module. Hopefully our examples illustrate well the way corpora can complement other tools used by translators. Some of the example selections (section 3) are meant to show that terminologists can benefit not only from monolingual corpora but also from parallel corpora, especially with respect to context-dependent variation of translation equivalents.

References

1. Saint Robert de, M.-J.: Language Resources at the Languages Service of the United Nations Office at Geneva. In: Proceedings of LREC 2002 Workshop in Language Resources (LR) for Translation Work, Research and Training (2002)
2. Maia, B.: Corpora for terminology extraction - the differing perspectives and objectives of researchers, teachers and language service providers. In: Proceedings of LREC 2002 Workshop in Language Resources (LR) for Translation Work, Research and Training (2002)
3. Dura, E.: Concordances of Snippets. In: Coling Workshop on Using and Enhancing Electronic Dictionaries, Geneva (2004)
4. Dura, E.: Culler - a User Friendly Corpus Query System. In: Proceedings of the Fourth International Workshop on Dictionary Writing Systems. Euralex (2006)
5. Culler, http://www.nla.se/culler/, http://bergelmir.iki.his.se/culler/
6. Materials of the Workshop in Language Resources (LR) for Translation Work, Research and Training (LREC 2002), http://www.ifi.unizh.ch/cl/yuste/postworkshop
7. Proceedings of the Fourth International Workshop on Dictionary Writing Systems (Euralex (2006), http://tshwanedje.com/publications/dws2006.pdf6
8. Gawronska, B., Erlendsson, B., Olsson, B.: Tracking Biological Relations in Texts: a Referent Grammar Based Approach. In: Proceedings of the workshop Biomedical Ontologies and Text Processing, 4th European Conference on Computational Biology (ECCB 2005), Madrid, Spain, pp. 15–22 (2005)
9. Gawronska, B., Erlendsson, B.: Syntactic, Semantic and Referential Patterns in Biomedical Texts: towards in-depth text comprehension for the purpose of bioinformatics. In: Sharp, B. (ed.) Natural Language Understanding and Cognitive Science. Proceedings of the 2nd International Workshop on Natural Language Understanding and Cognitive Science NLUCS 2005, Miami, USA, pp. 68–77 (2005)
10. Fillmore, C.: Multiword Expressions: An Extremist Approach. A lecture delivered at the conference Collocations and idioms: linguistic, computational, and psycholinguistic perspectives, Berlin (Magnus-Haus) September 18-20 (2003), http://www.bbaw.de/forschung/kollokationen/documents/coll_fillmore_mwe.pdf
11. Dura, E., Erlendsson, B., Gawronska, B., Olsson, B.: Towards Information Fusion in Pathway Evaluation: Encoding Relations in Biomedical Texts. In: Proceedings of the 9th International Conference on Information Fusion, Florence, Italy, pp. 240–247 (2006)

12. Kübler, N.: Corpora and LSP Translation. In: Zanettin, F., Bernardini, S., Stewart, D. (eds.) Corpora in Tranlator Education, pp. 25–42. St. Jerome Publishing, Manchester (2003)

Construction of Text Corpus of Polish Using the Internet

Sławomir Kulików

Silesian University of Technology, Institute of Computer Science,
ul. Akademicka 16, 44-100 Gliwice, Poland
Slawomir.Kulikow@polsl.pl

Abstract. This paper describes a system, which is used to construct a corpus of Polish. It works in the same way as Internet search engines. The corpus contains Polish texts downloaded from the Internet, which are supplemented with results of linguistic analysis (morphological, syntactic and semantic). Results of statistical research based on data in the corpus are also presented. The corpus is used to test and improve linguistic analyzer developed at Silesian University of Technology.

Keywords: text corpus, linguistic analysis, Internet.

1 Introduction

Several linguistic tools are developed in the Institute of Informatics, Silesian University of Technology. The main tool is Linguistic Analysis Server – LAS, which is accessible via WWW pages or as a Web Service [1,2]. Other tools use LAS and perform some additional processing. There are among others: translating Polish texts into sign language in Thetos [3,4,5,6] and summarizing Polish texts in PolSum2 [7]. These tools have to be improved. To achieve this goal we should use as many texts as possible to test tools, find bugs and correct them. Texts can be collected from many sources but the Internet is the best choice if we would like to collect a great number of texts [8]. We can use already prepared text corpora (for example the IPI PAN Corpus of Polish [9]) or construct a new corpus by extracting texts directly from WWW pages and perform some annotation of texts. We chose to construct the new corpus and automatically annotate texts in it using linguistic analyzers implemented in LAS. This way we can also check how the analyzer works with uncleaned texts.

This paper describes a system, which is used to construct a corpus of Polish. Results of statistical research based on data in the corpus are presented.

2 Structure of the System

Construction of a corpus is realized by a system, which consists of two components: LinRobot application and LAS server (see Fig. 1). A system's structure is based on a structure of Internet search engines [10]. It consists of two main

Z. Vetulani and H. Uszkoreit (Eds.): LTC 2007, LNAI 5603, pp. 303–311, 2009.
© Springer-Verlag Berlin Heidelberg 2009

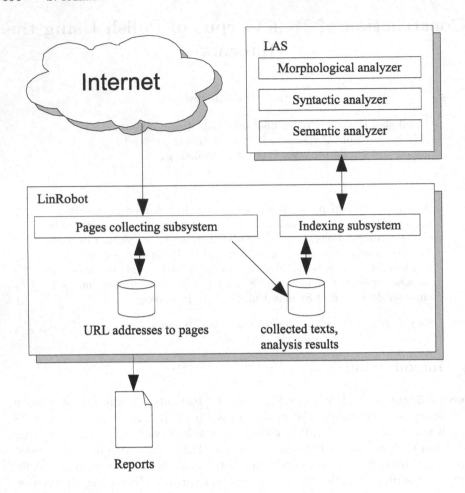

Fig. 1. Structure of the System

subsystems. The first subsystem is a pages collecting subsystem, which is used to download WWW pages from the Internet. Downloaded pages are processed by the second subsystem, indexing subsystem.

2.1 Pages Collecting Subsystem

Text–collecting subsystem executes two parallel processes. The first process downloads WWW pages and saves them to a database. Only pages permitted to download are taken into account. The administrators of Web Sites can use *robots.txt* file [11] to inform any Web Robots (including LinRobot) to not download some WWW pages. The second process extracts a list of hyperlinks from downloaded pages. Then it filters the hyperlinks using folowing rule: a hyperlink must be unvisited and must point to site in the Polish Internet domain (.pl) or similar (starting with "pl." or containing "pl" as a subdirectory).

Finally filtered hyperlinks are saved into a database. These hyperlinks are used by the first process.

2.2   Indexing Subsystem

Indexing subsystem executes three sequential actions for each downloaded WWW page: text extraction, linguistic analysis (using LAS) and statistical calculation.

In the first action it extracts a plain text from each page by removing HTML tags. Text is divided into paragraphs on the basis of appropriate HTML tags (for example $< p >$). Then paragraphs with less then three sentences are removed to avoid extraction of unimportant parts of WWW page (for example menu items). There are a lot of errors, since HTML is used to present documents, not to retrieve a text content. Since the same text content can be retrieved from different WWW pages, only unique texts are stored in the corpus (duplicates are removed).

In the second action it performs linguistic analysis for each text. Linguistic analysis is divided into three stages: morphological, syntactic and semantic analysis. The morphological analysis segments the source text into words, and determines the type and the morphological features of each word. The syntactic analysis builds a parse tree on the basis of Syntactic Group Grammar for Polish (SGGP) and finds syntactic relations between groups [12,13]. SGGP divides compound sentences into simple sentences. The semantic analysis determines the semantic roles of each syntactic group. These stages were described in our previous papers; a detailed explanation of them can be found in [4,14]. Then the indexing subsystem additionally checks if the text is Polish. I made an assumption that a text is Polish when at least 60% of words are recognized as Polish. If the text is Polish then linguistic analysis results are saved as annotations for text.

Annotation of texts is automatic, so there are also texts which have wrong annotation. This should be corrected by a human or by an improved linguistic analyzer.

In the last action statistical calculation is executed. Some of them are described in Section 4.

3   Text Corpus

The corpus was built basing on Polish texts. Nearly a half million URL addresses were checked, but only 18142 of them pointed to HTML documents containing unique Polish texts. Texts in the corpus contain from 3 to 37742 words, the whole corpus consists of approximately 11,500,000 words. The corpus size is 9 GB, where HTML documents take 518 MB (texts extracted from the documents take 33 MB) and results of linguistic analysis take 8.5 GB.

The corpus can be easily used to make research, because texts and results of linguistic analysis are stored in XML files. In addition more information is stored in MS SQL database. There are, for example, source URL address of HTML document and connections between documents (hyperlinks to base documents).

4   Experiments

4.1   Linguistic Analyzer Quality

Since we have the corpus we can check a quality of used tools. To check the quality I count number of words and analyzed words for morphological analyzer and in the similar way number of sentences for syntactic analyzer. I assumed that a word is analyzed when it is found in morphological database (I do not check if the result of analysis is correct). A sentence is analyzed when a structure of the sentence is determined (and again I do not check if the result of analysis is correct). Results are presented in Table 1.

Table 1. Quality of used linguistic analyzers

Morphological analyzer	
Number of words	11 648 659
Number of analyzed words	9 152 583 (78.57%)
Syntactic analyzer	
Number of sentences	1 459 687
Number of analyzed sentences	1 428 150 (97.84%)

In addition I counted number of texts where an effectiveness of analyzers was 100%. I found 44 texts for morphological analyzer and 2410 texts for syntactic analyzer. Number of texts for syntactic analyzer is greater than number of texts for morphological analyzer, because syntactic analyzer is prepared to work even if morphological analyzer doesn't return complete results.

Syntactic analyzer can be also used to filter results from morphological analyzer (sometimes it removes ambiguity). This feature is used in PolSum2, so I checked a quality of syntactic analyzer working as a filter. Morphological analyzer identified 123,019 unique words in the corpus. After syntactic analysis the number of unique words drops to 49,874 (40.54%). Therefore syntactic analyzer can be used as a filter.

4.2   Improving PolSum2

The main goal of the current work was to improve the automatic summarizer PolSum2 [7]. This summarizer uses five elementary techniques: text segmentation, sentence weighting, selection, substitution and joining of sentences. These techniques should be executed successively to create summary. During text segmentation a source text is divided into words and simple sentences (results of syntactic analysis are used). In the next technique each sentence is supplemented by a computed weight. The current version of summarizer uses statistical method described below. In the third technique sentences with high weight (essential sentences) are extracted from the source text. The user can determine the number of sentences that should be extracted. Usually sentences in the source text are connected with each other (for example by anaphora), but during extraction these connections can be lost. The fourth technique is used to resolve anaphora and avoid loss of information conveyed by the connections. An anaphor is replaced by an antecedent (results of semantic analysis are used, only pronouns are taken into account). The last technique is used to join extracted simple sentences into a compound sentence if they were a compound sentence in the source text.

The generator uses well known statistical method based on TF.IDF weighting to extract essential sentences from a source text. The weight of sentence is calculated as arithmetic mean of weights of words contained in the sentence. The weight of word is calculated using the following formula:

$$w = TF * IDF, \quad IDF = \log_b \frac{N}{df} \tag{1}$$

where:
w – weight of word,
TF – therm frequency (number of times a given word appears in the source text),
IDF – inverse document frequency,
b – base of logarithm (in this work equals to e),
N – number of texts in the corpus,
df – number of texts in the corpus which contains the given word.

In PolSum2 results of semantic analysis (anaphora relationships) are used during calculations. I assumed that a weight of anaphor is equal to a weight of its antecedent. The corpus should be used to compute df parameter for each word. Base morphological forms of words are used during counting, because words in Polish inflect. A fragment of table which contains df parameters calculated for each word in corpus is presented in Table 2.

The statistical method implemented here takes into account only separate words (it treats text as a bag of words). Sometimes meaning of group of words is different than meaning of each separate word, so calculated weight of sentence should be more truthful when we take into account groups of words. Groups of successive words are also known as n–grams. Common n–grams consist usually of two (bigrams) or three words (trigrams).

For each n–gram we can calculate weigh of association to determine if the n–gram is random sequence of words or the words often occur together. The weight of association is calculated using the following formula:

$$I_{n-gram} = \log_b \frac{P_{n-gram}}{\prod P_{word}} \tag{2}$$

where:
I_{n-gram} – weight of association,
b – base of logarithm (in this work equals to e),
P_{n-gram} – probability of occurring of n–gram in texts,
P_{word} – probability of occurring of word from n–gram in texts.

Table 2. Fragment of IDF table

Word	IDF
i	0.1235
do	0.1863
w	0.1939
on	0.2345
ochrona	0.2636
od	0.2975
wszystko	0.3461
cena	0.3502
pl	0.3660
s	0.3784
u	0.3819
słowo	0.3820
być	0.3850
transport	0.3871
produkt	0.3896
zobaczyć	0.4013
...	
żyłować	9.8060
żyrardowie	9.8060
żyrek	9.8060
żyrowkie	9.8060
żyrzynem	9.8060
żytko	9.8060
żytomierska	9.8060
żytomierski	9.8060
żytomierskim	9.8060
żytomierzu	9.8060
żywago	9.8060
żywczak	9.8060
żywet	9.8060
żywiecki	9.8060
żywieckie	9.8060
żywiole	9.8060
żywołowne	9.8060

The corpus consists of Polish texts from the Internet, so there is a lot of "rubbish", for example, English words or numbers, which occur only once in the corpus. This induces high weights of association for n–grams which contain such words. To avoid that I assumed that n–grams should contain only Polish words. I found 373,225 bigrams and 522,279 trigrams in the corpus. Fragments of results are shown in Table 3 and Table 4.

During calculation of sentence weight each n–gram is treated as two or three words with the same weight which is equal to a weight of n–gram. I found that

Table 3. Fragment of bigram table

Bigram	Weight of association
absolutorium abstrakt	15.9073
aklimatyzować maral	15.9073
chromolić ksenofob	15.9073
czeluść biblioteczka	15.9073
czujka ultradźwiękowy	15.9073
dogaszać pogorzelisko	15.9073
gradient adiabatyczny	15.9073
gromadnie smarkać	15.9073
guzikowy balonik	15.9073
handlara wystukiwać	15.9073
hydrografia hydrotechnik	15.9073
induktor inkubator	15.9073
jasnozielony pąsowy	15.9073
kalafiorowy mrożenie	15.9073
kloszowy pakowarka	15.9073
kontemplować rozkoszny	15.9073
konwulsyjny szamotać	15.9073
. . .	
sum u	-6.0742
u dużo	-6.1130
zobaczyć u	-6.2537
u być	-6.3218
wszystko u	-6.4366
on u	-6.5082
u z	-6.5259
u i	-6.6520
cena u	-6.6551
u na	-6.6964
od u	-6.8180
u do	-6.8425
nie u	-6.8973
z u	-6.9314
do u	-7.5356
w u	-8.2234

when n–grams are used a weight of sentence is usually lower then a weight of sentence without use of n–grams. It is true for 99.99% of n–grams. For n–grams with high weight of association change of weight of word is very low (sometimes there is no change). For n–grams with low weight of association change of weight of word is high, but these n–grams should not be taken into account. More experiments should be done to judge if n–grams should be used during automatic summarization.

Table 4. Fragment of trigram table

Trigram	Weight of association
przywdziać mniszy habit	31.8145
uzwojenie twornik indukować	31.8145
duszny pątnik nabożny	31.1214
rozkuć kajdany zwyczajność	31.1214
półautomatyczny kloszowy pakowarka	30.4282
przerywany rzewny jęk	30.4282
abiturient absolutorium abstrakt	30.0228
zalatywać krogulec krótkonogi	30.0228
żółcień alizarynowy chromowy	30.0228
balkonowy moskitiera rolować	29.7351
chodnik straganiarz rozstawiać	29.7351
sortownik odpadek dozownik	29.7351
spiżarnia duszny pątnik	29.7351
permski wymierać triasowy	29.6173
akordeon przerywany rzewny	29.5120
chromowy cynkowy kadmowy	29.5120
kawałeczek szkiełko przepłacić	29.5120
...	
nie być u	-2.1411
to być u	-2.1468
i ten i	-2.2414
na i i	-2.4266
być u on	-2.4451
on być u	-2.4451
w w w	-2.4912
w i z	-2.6235
z i w	-2.6235
z i i	-2.6616
to i u	-2.7001
z być u	-2.8682
u on w	-2.9604
i u on	-2.9984
w i w	-3.2224
w i i	-3.2604

5   Conclusion

In the paper a system of text corpus construction for Polish using Internet was presented. It is prototype, so it is under development and new features will be added (for example checking a quality of semantic analysis).

The corpus is used to test and improve linguistic analyzer developed at Silesian University of Technology. The analyzer is mainly used by summary generator

(PolSum2) and text into the sign language translator (Thetos), so quality of summarization and translation will be improved.

References

1. Linguistic Analysis Server, http://las.aei.polsl.pl/las2/
2. Kulików, S.: Implementation of Linguistic Analysis Server for Thetos – Polish Text into Sign Language Translator. Studia Informatica 24(3(55)), 171–178 (2003) (in Polish)
3. Thetos, http://thetos.polsl.pl/
4. Suszczańska, N., Szmal, P., Francik, J.: Translating Polish Texts into Sign Language in the TGT System. In: 20th IASTED International Multi–Conference Applied Informatics AI 2002, Innsbruck, Austria, pp. 282–287 (2002)
5. Szmal, P., Suszczańska, N.: Selected Problems of Translation from the Polish Written Language to the Sign Language. Archiwum Informatyki Teoretycznej i Stosowanej 13(1), 37–51 (2001)
6. Suszczanska, N., Szmal, P., Kulików, S.: Continuous Text Translation Using Text Modeling in the Thetos System. In: Okatan, A. (ed.) International Conference on Computational Intelligence. International Computational Intelligence Society, pp. 156–160 (2005)
7. Ciura, M., Grund, D., Kulików, S., Suszczańska, N.: A System to Adapt Techniques of Text Summarizing to Polish. In: Proceedings of the International Conference on Computational Intelligence, Istanbul, Turkey, pp. 117–120 (2004)
8. Kilgarriff, A.: Web as corpus. In: Proceedings of Corpus Linguistics 2001, pp. 342–344. Lancaster University (2001)
9. IPI PAN Corpus, http://korpus.pl/
10. Kłopotek, M.A.: Inteligentne wyszukiwarki internetowe. EXIT, Warszawa (2001) (in Polish)
11. The Web Robots Pages, http://www.robotstxt.org/
12. Suszczanska, N.: GS-gramatyka jezyka polskiego. In: Demenko, G., Izworski, A., Michałek, M. (eds.) Speech Analysis, Synthesis and Recognition in Technology, Linguistics and Medicine, Szczyrk 2003, Uczelniane Wydawnictwa Naukowo-Dydaktyczne AGH, Kraków (2003)
13. Suszczanska, N.: GS-model składni jezyka polskiego. In: Demenko, G., Karpinski, M., Jassem, K. (eds.) Speech and Language Technology, wolumen 7. Polskie Towarzystwo Fonetyczne, Poznan (2003)
14. Suszczańska, N., Lubiński, M.: POLMORPH, Polish Language Morphological Analysis Tool. In: 19th IASTED International Conference Applied Informatics AI 2001, Innsbruck, Austria, pp. 84–89 (2001)

A Predicate Database for Assisting the Design of a Lexicon-Grammar of Predicative Nouns

Mohamed Mahdi Malik and Jean Royauté

LIF-CNRS, Univ. de la Méditerranée
UMR 6166. F-13 288 Marseille
{malik,jean.royaute}@lif.univ-mrs.fr
http://www.lif.univ-mrs.fr

Abstract. In this paper, we present the development and the use of a database to develop a lexicon-grammar of predicative nouns in English. This data base allows to link a verbal construction to a nominal construction with an equivalent nominalization. This tool enables to assist the prediction of the structure of the correlated predicate noun phrase(s) and its dependent preposional noun phrase(s) which take an argument role: subject and possible complement(s). We also show the interest of designing a data base in order to explore, infer and register other noun phrase constructions which are not immediately correladed with verbal constructions.

Keywords: Nominalization, Predicate noun phrase, Lexicon-grammar, Argument role, Nominal and verbal constructions, Database.

1 Introduction

NLP of Predicate Noun Phrases (PNPs) is important because they appear frequently in scientific documents. For example, in the biological field, it is most common to use a PNP like *VEGF regulation by heregulin* instead of the corresponding sentence *heregulin regulates VEGF*. Generally, a PNP is defined as a noun phrase which contains a head noun mostly derived from a verb or an adjective and other nouns, not morphologically linked, but whose predicativity can be exhibited with a support verb constructions [1]. In this study, we only consider the nominalizations that are dervived from verbs. PNPs contain information which is important to examine in order to extract interesting properties such as relations between biological entities, or the involved participants. The analysis of these properties requires to define the syntactic functions of PNP arguments (subject, direct object, prepositional complements, etc.).

The observation of the syntactic forms of English PNPs was based not only on various corpora (British National Corpus [1], Web, scientific articles), but also on the use of the lexicon-grammar NOMLEX [2] and more particularly the Specialist Lexicon [3]. This lexicon has provided a basis to study the relations between verbal patterns and PNPs since it contains interesting information to be processed,

---

[1] http://www.natcorp.ox.ac.uk/

Z. Vetulani and H. Uszkoreit (Eds.): LTC 2007, LNAI 5603, pp. 312–324, 2009.

such as verbal structures and the noun complement introducers (prepositions) of the PNPs .

In this article, we propose to observe both nominal and verbal structures and determine the syntactic functions of the NP arguments by using a database of predicates (PredicateDB), a tool that is developed to handle the "Specialist Lexicon" data of verbs and their nominalizations. PredicateDB generates (section 4.1) a core lexicon-grammar of predicative nouns with more precise details on the relations between the verbs and their nominalizations and assists (section 4.2) in studying the syntactic patterns in a very flexible way to refine the core lexicon-grammar. The approach we suggest is based on the comprehension of the links that exist between the types of the verbal patterns and the way in which their PNPs are structured. This is performed by the analysis of the complementation pattern of both verbs linked to their nominalizations.

This paper is organized as follows: In section 2, we define the Predicate Noun Phrases and compare different examples of sentences and their corresponding PNPs. Section 3 describes interesting existing lexicons that can be used to analyze the links between the verbal and the nominal patterns. Section 4 details the architecture of PredicateDB, and how we use it to analyze the various syntactic patterns in order to develop the lexicon-grammar. Finally, in section 5, we show the use and interest of lexicon-grammar of nominalizations in the parsing of biological texts.

2   The Predicate Noun Phrases

A predicative noun is a noun that can be derived from a verb (*mutate*, *mutation*) or an adjectives (*capable*, *capability*) or is a noun that can occur in a support verb construction (*have an effect*) [4]. Each argument plays the role of a specific syntactic function, i.e. subject, object, prepositional complement, etc. In this study, we are only interested in these arguments in their NP form and have set aside sentential and gerundive complements. We consider as saturated a PNP when all the arguments are present, or not saturated when there is deletion of one or several arguments. Table 1 presents some examples and their corresponding PNPs. We adopt the notations of Gross in describing the verbal patterns [5], N_0 represents the subject and $N_1...N_n$ the complements. In the first example of Table 1, *abandon* and its nominalization *abandonment* are connected to the same arguments *Congress* and *WikiConstitution*. *Congress* and *WikiConstitution* respectively represent the subject and the direct object. In the corresponding

Table 1. Some sentences and their corresponding PNPs

Verbal Pattern	Sentence	Corresponding PNP
$N_0 V N_1$	*Congress abandons WikiConstitution*	*The abandonment of the WikiConstitution by the Congress*
$N_0 V N_1 Prep N_2$	*Experts attributes the painting to Picasso*	*The attribution of the painting to Picasso by experts*

PNP: *The abandonment of the WikiConstitution by the Congress*, the preposition *of* introduces the object and *by* the subject. This example highlights the existing relation between a verb employed in a transitive verbal pattern (with a direct object) and its corresponding PNP.

The second example *Experts attributes the painting to Picasso* contains: *Experts* as the subject, *the painting* as the object and *Picasso* as a prepositional complement introduced by the preposition *to*. The corresponding PNP: *The attribution of the painting to Picasso by experts* shows that all the arguments are still present. The preposition *to* still introduces the prepositional complement. The prepositions *by* and *of* introduce respectively the subject and the object. This example also shows the existing relation between a ditransitive verb (direct object followed by a prepositional complement) and its PNP.

3   Some Lexicon-Grammars

Various lexical resources provide interesting information that can be used to study the syntactico-semantic relations between the different lexical items (nouns, verbs, adjectives, etc.). Among these lexical resources, we can cite: the Specialist Lexicon [3], NOMLEX [2], WordNet [6], VerbNet which is based on the verbal classification of Levin [7], and FrameNet [8] which is founded on frame semantics of Fillmore [9].

Although all these lexicons may be interesting to use in order to study the relations between verbal patterns and their PNPs, we have chosen to use the Specialist Lexicon because it offers a wide coverage and contains useful information, such as relations between the verbs and their nominalizations, verbal structures, and noun complement introducers (prepositions) in the PNPs. Moreover, the Specialist Lexicon makes this useful information easily and directly extractable, which constitutes a real advantage, while the coverage of NOMLEX is limited and WordNet, VerbNet, and FrameNet do not treat the links that connect the verbal patterns to the nominal ones. [10] have used NOMLEX, COMLEX [11] and some morphological rules to construct NOMLEX-PLUS. NOMLEX-PLUS has a larger coverage than NOMLEX but only contains nominalizations belonging to the general language corpus Penn Treebank [12], whereas the Specialist Lexicon treats nominalizations from biomedical field.

The Specialist Lexicon: The Specialist Lexicon (SL) is an English lexicon-grammar which contains about 257,000 entries (nouns, adjectives, verbs, determiners or biomedical terms). It contains 3,847 verbs having one or more nominalizations. For each verb, the SL defines the corresponding verbal pattern.

Figure 1 shows the representation of the verb *abate* in the SL. This entry admits several fields and each field has one or several values. For example, the field `entry` represents the entry of this verb and its value is E0006436; `cat` represents the syntactic category of this entry and its value is `verb`; `variants` corresponds to information on inflectional morphology and its value `reg` means that it is a regular verb; the field `intran` that this verb is an intransitive one

```
{base=abate
entry=E0006436
cat=verb
variants=reg
intran
tran=np
nominalization=abatement|noun|E0006437}
```

```
{base=abatement
entry=E0006437
cat=noun
variants=reg
variants=uncount
compl=pphr(by,np)
compl = pphr(of,np)
nominalization_of=abate|verb|E0006436}
```

Fig. 1. Verbal entry of *abate* and its nominalization *abatement* in the SL

and **tran** means that it can also be a transitive verb with a noun phrase (**np**) as a direct object. The last field **nominalization** means this verb admits a noun as a nominalization which has the value **abatement** and where its entry number is E0006437.

The Specialist Lexicon also contains 3,957 nominalizations. Each nominalization is associated to noun complements that are introduced by different prepositions. Figure 1 also shows the representation of the nominalization **abatement**. This nominalization also admits several fields: similarly the field **cat** represents the syntactic category of the entry and its value is **noun**. The inflectional morphology field **variants** has two values: **reg** (it is a countable noun) and **uncount** (it is also an uncountable noun). This entry admits two noun complements (**compl**); the first one is a prepositional complement (**pphr**) in which the preposition **by** introduces the noun phrase **np**, and the second one is also a prepositional complement in which the preposition **of** introduces the same noun phrase. The last field means that **abatement** is derived (**nominalization_of**) from the verb **abate** which has the entry number E0006436. The "Specialist Lexicon" does not provide the syntactic function of the noun phrases which are introduced by the different prepositions.

4   PredicateDB, a Database of Predicate Nouns

PredicateDB is an Oracle Database with tools and special scripts having the capability of accomplishing several tasks such as filtering the output of the queries, upgrading the content of the tables from the "Specialist Lexicon" or other lexical resources. It deals with the verbs and their nominalizations and treats both verbal and nominal pattern properties. PredicateDB is different from LexAccess, a tool which is developed by the Lexical Systems Group [2] for providing access to information (entry identifier, base, syntactic categories) from the "Specialist Lexicon". While LexAcces does not allow the extraction of information concerning verbal and nominal patterns (syntactic pattern values, preposition values, noun complement values, etc.), PredicateDB is conceived in such a way that all information related to the verbs and their nominalizations is split. Conceiving

---

[2] http://lexsrv3.nlm.nih.gov/LexSysGroup/

PredicateDB in this way allows to access each property belonging to the verbal or nominal pattern in an independent way. This also enables the execution of SQL queries on each field (property) using more constraints in order to have relevant results. With PredicateDB, we analyse the properties of verbal and nominal patterns taken separately and cross them in order to deduce the existing links between the two patterns. The core of PredicateDB is designed around five tables (Cf. figure 2).

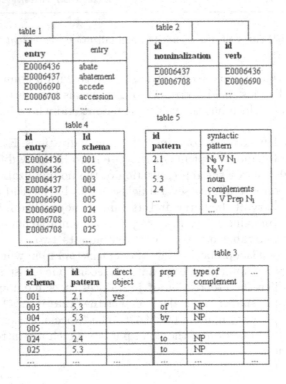

Fig. 2. The tables of PredicateDB

- In table 1, we associate each entry (verb or nominalization) with its unique identifier. It contains 12,545 entries.
- In table 2, each verb corresponds to its nominalization(s). It contains 3,993 entries.
- In table 3, we split the properties of verbal and nominal patterns. We put each property in one column. For example, the noun complement `compl = phr(to,np)` is split into 4 fields: we give this complement the unique identifier 025 (id-pattern = 025), its `id-pattern` (pattern identifier) has the value 5.3 (5 means that it is a noun complement of a nominalization and 3 means that it is a prepositional complement `pphr`), `Prep` is the preposition that introduces the noun phrase complement (`NP`) and its value is *to*. This table contains 1,026 entries.

- In table 4, we associate the entry identifiers with their pattern identifier(s). For example, if we take the verb *abate*, we associate its identifier E0006436 with its pattern identifiers 005 (intransitive pattern) and 001 (direct transitive pattern). This table contains 27,659 entries.
- In table 5, we associate each id-pattern with a syntactic pattern. For example, the id-pattern 2.4 with the syntactic pattern N_0 V $Prep$ N_1 (indirect transitive), the id-pattern 2.1 with N_0 V N_1 (direct transitive), etc. This table contains 47 entries.

For example, PredicateDB allows the extraction of all the verbs (*comply*, *commiserate*, etc.) which: (i) occur only in indirect transitive pattern, (ii) their prepositional complement is only introduced by the preposition *with* (iii) their corresponding PNPs contain noun complements that are only introduced by the prepositions *of* and *with*. This type of query helps to make interesting deductions of the links between the verbal patterns and their PNPs.

4.1   Developing a Lexicon-Grammar of Nominalizations

PredicateDB is first used to assist the development of a lexicon-grammar in which all the nominalizations with equivalent PNPs belongs to the same class. We assume that if several verbs have the same verbal pattern, their nominalizations will have equivalent PNPs. We start by putting the verbs that have the same verbal patterns in the same classes. Taking into account only the 7 patterns of Table 2, we obtain 31 disjoint classes (Cf. figure 3), where each verb only belongs to one class. For example, the following class ('ditran=np,np', 'ditran=np,pphr', 'intran', 'tran=np') brings together the following verbal patterns: N_0 V N_2 N_1, ditransitive pattern with an indirect object, without a preposition, followed by a direct object, N_0 V N_1 $Prep$ N_2, ditransitive with a direct object followed by a prepositional complement, N_0 V, intransitive, and N_0 V N_1, transitive with a direct object.

We notice in Table 2 that some verbal patterns have similar PNPs where the prepositions introduce the same arguments. For example, verbal patterns 4, 6 and 7 (N_0 V N_1 $Prep$ N_2, N_0 V $Prep$ N_2 N_1 and N_0 V N_2 N_1) have the same saturated PNP N_V of N_1 $Prep$ N_2 by N_0. We therefore put the nominalizations that correspond to these verbal patterns in the same class. If $Prep$ N_2 is deleted, the resulting non-saturated PNP N_V of N_1 by N_0 corresponds to the PNP of the second verbal pattern N_0 V N_1. Thus, we add to the previous class, the nominalizations of the second verbal pattern. The PNP's arguments of this class have the same introducers. The prepositions *of*, *by*, and *Prep* introduce, respectively, the direct object, the subject and the prepositional complement.

We apply this method to classify the 31 classes in 6 super-classes (Cf. Figure 3). For example, we bring together the nominalizations of the classes 20, 21, 22, 23, 24, 25, and 26 in the superclass 4. This superclass contains all the nominalizations having the PNP N_V of N_1 [$Prep$ N_2] by N_0 ($Prep$ N_2 is optional), where the prepositions *of*, *by*, and *Prep* introduce respectively the direct object, the subject, and the prepositional complement. For example,

Table 2. The relations between verbal patterns and the corresponding PNPs

Patterns	Examples	The corresponding PNPs
1. N_0V := intran	Marry disappeared	$N_V of N_0$ =: The disappearance of Marry
2. N_0VN_1 := tran=np	The primary ion beam ablates any surface contamination	$N_V of N_1 by N_0$ =: The ablation of any surface contamination by the primary ion beam
3. $N_0V PrepN_1$:= tran=pphr	John alluded to trends	$N_V of N_0 PrepN_1$ =: The allusion of John to trends
4. $N_0V N_1 PrepN_2$:= ditran=np,pphr	The expert attributed the painting to Picasso	$N_V of N_1 PrepN_2 by N_0$ =:The attribution of the painting to Picasso by the expert
5. $N_0V PrepN_1 PrepN_2$:= ditran=pphr,pphr	Enron competed against Total for market share	$N_V of N_0 PrepN_1 PrepN_2$ =: The competition of Enron against Total for market share
6. $N_0V PrepN_2N_1$:= ditran=pphr,np	John explained to a departmental official the matter regarding a tax liability	$N_V of N_1 PrepN_2 by N_0$ =: The explanation of the matter regarding a tax liability to a departmental official by John
7. $N_0V N_2N_1$:= ditran=np,np	The chef prepared the guests breakfast	$N_V of N_1 PrepN_2 by N_0$ =: The preparation of breakfast for the guests by the chef

admonishment, admonition, entreaty and *exchange* belong to this superclass and have in common the preposition *for* (*admonishment of Representative DeLay by the Ethics Committee for his action*). We also associate each nominalization with the prepositions that are related to it. This enables not to confuse the prepositions that introduce a prepositional complement with those that introduce an adverbial one. For example, the nominalization *admonishment* admits the prepositions *about, against and for* as a prepositional complement introducer. All the other prepositions introduce an adverbial complement. In the following example, *The admonishment of the participants on this side*, the preposition *on* introduces an adverbial complement.

The different structures of the superclasses are explained in Table 3. We give for each superclass: the syntactic pattern of its PNPs, when there is ambiguity and when not, and some examples of nominalizations belonging to this superclass. For example, the nominalizations of the superclass 1 can occur in the PNPs N_V *of* N_1 [*Prep* N_2] *by* N_0 (ditransitive or direct transitive pattern) and

```
1  ('ditran=np,np','ditran=np,pphr','tran=np','intran')---> NV of N1 [PREP N2] by N0 , NV of N0
2  ('ditran=np,np','tran=np','intran')---> NV of N1 [PREP N2] by N0 , NV of N0
3  ('ditran=np,pphr','tran=np','intran')---> NV of N1 [PREP N2] by N0 , NV of N0
4  ('ditran=pphr,np','tran=np','intran')---> NV of N1 [PREP N2] by N0 , NV of N0
5  ('ditran=np,np','intran')---> NV of N1 PREP N2 by N0 , NV of N0
6  ('ditran=np,pphr','intran')---> NV of N1 PREP N2 by N0 , NV of N0
```
Super-class 1

```
7   ('ditran=np,np','ditran=np,pphr','tran=np','tran=pphr','intran')---> NV of N1 [PREP N2] by N0 , NV of N0 [PREP N1]
8   ('ditran=np,pphr','ditran=pphr,np','tran=np','tran=pphr','intran')---> NV of N1 [PREP N2] by N0 , NV of N0 [PREP N1]
9   ('ditran=np,pphr','tran=np','tran=pphr','intran')---> NV of N1 [PREP N2] by N0 , NV of N0 [PREP N1]
10  ('ditran=np,np','tran=np','tran=pphr','intran')---> NV of N1 [PREP N2] by N0 , NV of N0 [PREP N1]
11  ('ditran=np,pphr','tran=pphr','intran')---> NV of N1 PREP N2 by N0 , NV of N0 [PREP N1]
12  ('ditran=np,pphr','tran=pphr')---> NV of N1 PREP N2 by N0 , NV of N0 PREP N1
13  ('ditran=np,pphr','tran=np','tran=pphr')---> NV of N1 [PREP N2] by N0 , NV of N0 PREP N1
14  ('ditran=np,pphr','tran=np','ditran=pphr,pphr','tran=pphr','intran')---> NV of N1 [PREP N2] by N0 , NV of N0 [PREP N1] [PREP N2]
15  ('ditran=np,pphr','ditran=pphr,pphr','tran=pphr','intran')---> NV of N1 PREP N2 by N0 , NV of N0 [PREP N1] [PREP N2]
```
Super-class 2

```
16  ('tran=np','tran=pphr','intran')---> NV of N1 by N0 , NV of N0 [PREP N1]
17  ('tran=np','tran=pphr')---> NV of N1 by N0 , NV of N0 PREP N1
18  ('tran=np','intran')---> NV of N1 by N0 , NV of N0
19  ('tran=np','ditran=pphr,pphr','tran=pphr')---> NV of N1 by N0 , NV of N0 [PREP N1] [PREP N2]
```
Super-class 3

```
20  ('ditran=np,np','ditran=np,pphr','tran=np')---> NV of N1 [PREP N2] by N0
21  ('ditran=np,np','tran=np')---> NV of N1 [PREP N2] by N0
22  ('ditran=np,pphr')---> NV of N1 PREP N2 by N0
23  ('ditran=np,pphr','ditran=pphr,np','tran=np')---> NV of N1 [PREP N2] by N0
24  ('ditran=np,pphr','tran=np')---> NV of N1 [PREP N2] by N0
25  ('ditran=pphr,np','tran=np')---> NV of N1 [PREP N2] by N0
26  ('tran=np')---> NV of N1 by N0
```
Super-class 4

```
27  ('ditran=pphr,pphr','tran=pphr','intran')---> NV of N0 [PREP N1] [PREP N2]
28  ('ditran=pphr,pphr','tran=pphr')---> NV of N0 PREP N1 [PREP N2]
```
Super-class 5

```
29  ('tran=pphr','intran')---> NV of N0 [PREP N1]
30  ('tran=pphr')---> NV of N0 PREP N1
31  ('intran')---> NV of N0
```
Super-class 6

Fig. 3. Classes classification in different superclasses

Table 3. The different Superclasses

Superclasses	Nominal patterns	Non-ambiguity cases	Ambiguity cases
Superclass1 Forgiveness, remittance, bid, remission, etc.	N_V of N_1 $[Prep N_2]$ by N_0 N_V of N_0	$Prep N_2$ OR by N_0 are present	$Prep N_2$ AND by N_0 are deleted
Superclass2 Run, running, spotting, etc.	N_V of N_1 $[Prep N_2]$ by N_0 N_V of N_0 $[Prep N_1]$	by N_0 is present	in all the other cases
Superclass3 percolation, presumption, radiation, etc.	N_V of N_1 by N_0 N_V of N_0 $[Prep N_1]$	$Prep N_1$ OR by N_0 are present	$Prep N_1$ AND by N_0 are deleted
Superclass4 excuse, respotting, allowance, etc.	N_V of N_1 $[Prep N_2]$ by N_0	All the cases	No cases
Superclass5 migration, participation, intercession, etc.	N_V of N_0 $[Prep N_1][Prep N_2]$	All the cases	No cases
Superclass6 contention, crusade, exclamation, etc.	N_V of N_0 $[Prep N_1]$	All the cases	No cases

N_V of N_0 (intransitive pattern). There is no ambiguity if $Prep\ N_2$ or $by\ N_0$ are present. In this case, the direct object and the subject are introduced respectively by the prepositions of and by. If $Prep\ N_2$ and $by\ N_0$ are deleted, there is an ambiguity between N_V of N_1 and N_V of N_0. In this case, we cannot decide if the preposition of introduces the direct object N_1 (direct transitive pattern) or the subject N_0 (intransitive pattern). To create this lexicon, we have followed several steps: (i) we used PredicateDB to understand the links which exist between the verbal patterns and their PNPs; (ii) we classified all the nominalizations which have the same corresponding verbal patterns in the same classes; (iii) we classified these classes according to the similitude of their PNPs in the same superclasses.

4.2 Refining the Lexicon-Grammar

PredicateDB also allows to process special cases, such as the verb *absorb* and its nominalization *absorption*. In the SL, *absorb* is only defined as a direct transitive verb $N_0 V N_1$. The PNPs of its nominalization *absorption* admit the prepositions *of, by, in, into*. But in the example of Table 2 (*ablation*) shows that a PNP corresponding to a direct transitive verb admits only two prepositions (*of* and *by*) to introduce respectively the direct object and subject. In this case (*absorption*), we deduce that the preposition *of* still introduces the object, but *by* (the usual introducer of the subject) can be substituted by the prepositions *in* and *into*. The general pattern is: N_0 absorb $N_1 \leftrightarrows$ *The absorption of* N_1 *by/in/into* N_0. In this example we check if *absorption* is an isolated case or if other nouns present a similar profile. This profile is thus searched in PredicateDB with a SQL request. We identify a very small number of correct nominalizations: two are variants of *absorption* (*absorbance, reasorption*) and only one is different (*alteration: alteration of [...] by/in neutral water*). This paradigm of nominalization is weakly productive.

Another class of nominalizations has interesting linguistic properties in the sublanguage of the genomics. It concerns the nominalizations of the symmetrical verbs whose principal property is to allow the permutation of two of its arguments. We give two examples of very productive classes in the sublanguage of the genomics. The first modelizes verbs with two arguments and has the following syntactic patterns.

$$- N_a\ V\ with\ N_b \leftrightarrows N_v\ of\ N_a\ with\ N_b \tag{1}$$

(*The interaction of cephaloridine with OCTN2 was...*)

$$= N_a\ and\ N_b\ V \leftrightarrows N_v\ of/between\ N_a\ and\ N_b \tag{2}$$

(*The interaction of/between cephaloridine and OCTN2 was...*)

$$= N_{plur}\ V \leftrightarrows N_v\ of/between\ N_{plur} \tag{3}$$

(*the interaction of/between these two proteins may contribute ...*)

Three verbal patterns are linked to three nominal paterns in the above examples. The first and second example are strictly equivalent. We can observe that the subject or the object can permute in the sentence and NP (*interaction of* N_a *with* N_b = *interaction of* N_b *with* N_a) this is why we have used a special notation (N_a and N_b) which means that the distinction between these two roles are not semantically suitable. The last example means that argument N_{plur} (as plural) belongs to a generic class or contains all elements of a set.

The second class has an additional argument (N_0) which is often deleted and the second and third verbal constructions are in the passive voice. As we can notice it in the example below, the permutable arguments N_a and N_b correspond to the complements of the verb:

$-\ N_0\ V\ N_a\ with\ N_b \leftrightarrows N_v\ of\ N_a\ with\ N_b\ by\ N_0$ (4)

(*the association of these two proteins with chromatin depended* ...)

$=\ N_a\ and\ N_b\ is\ Vpp\ by\ N_0 \leftrightarrows N_v\ of/between\ N_a\ and\ N_b\ by\ N_0$ (5)

(*the association of/between pol beta and DNA ligase I involves both* ...)

$=\ N_{plur}\ is\ Vpp\ by\ N_0 \leftrightarrows N_v\ of/betwenn\ N_{plur}\ by\ N_0$ (6)

(*association   of/between   DNA   sequences   by* N_0...)

It is also possible to build another sentence with this verb whose N_a and N_b are respectively subject and object (N_a *V itself with* N_b; *the cytoplasm messenger RNA associates itself with ribosomes* ...). Although this second verbal construction is numerically important, it is very difficult to distinguish it in its nominal construction compared to the first, in the event of the nonpresence of N_0. This is why we chose this first construction which maximizes the number of aguments for the analysis of the NP and of which the nominal structure is expected in both cases and can produce a correct analysis.

To identify these two subsets of nominalizations and predict the syntactic functions of its arguments linked to the equivalent verbal patterns, we proceed in two phases.

First, for all symmetrical nominalizations containing two arguments (see examples 1 to 3), we extract all the prepositional verbs with one complement introduced by the preposition *with* and cross this subset with their nominalizations whose noun phrase complements are introduced by the prepositions *of* and *with*. We identify a subset of 188 nominalizations which have the syntactic properties of these three examples.

Second, we use a similar heuristics to identify the nominalizations linked to the verbal patterns with three arguments (see examples 4 to 6). In addition, by using also an SQL request, we select all the verbs of Specialist Lexicon which have a verbal ditransitive construction with a direct object and a prepositional complement, and we cross this subset with their nominalizations which have noun-complements introduced with prepositions *of*, *by* and *with*. We obtain a new subset of predicate nouns which can appear in the syntactic patterns of these examples.

PredicateDB, by using similar heurictics, enables to identify other classes of symmetrical predicates with other prepositions like *adhesion* with two arguments (preposition *to*) or *discrimination* with three arguments (preposition *from*).

5   Lexicon-Grammar and Parsing

In this way, PredicateDB has assisted the creation of a lexicon-grammar containing all the Specialist Lexicon nominalizations and dedicated to a parser. A special module which describes the different syntactic patterns of the classes of nominalizations is added to the initial grammar of the Link Parser. These nominalizations are classified according to their behavior in the PNPs and their verbal pattern type (intransitive, direct transitive, ditransitive, symmetrical, etc.). This lexicon is applied in Information Extraction in order to identify gene interactions from Medline abstracts [13] by using the Link Parser [14]. This identification is based on a parsing of the text by using a link grammar (a variant of dependency grammars). The result of this parsing is a graph in which words are linked two by two with edges labeled by grammatical functions.

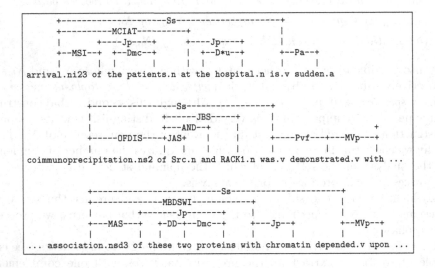

Fig. 4. Produced parsings of Predicative Noun Phrases

Figure 4 shows a produced parsing of three PNPs. The first contains the nominalization *arrival* which belongs to the superclass 6 (N_V *of* N_0 [*Prep* N_1] [*Prep* N_2]). In the resulting graph, the MSI link identifies the subject (*the patients*) which is introduced by the preposition *of*, whereas the MCIAT link marks the noun complement (*the hospital*) which is introduced by the preposition *at*. In the second, with the nominalization *coimmunoprecipitation*, we can see the parsing of an NP with a symmetrical predicate at three arguments (see section 4.2, example 2). In this example, the preposition *of* is linked to *coimmunoprecipitation* with the label OFDIS which indicates its distributive role by connecting the two arguments, N_a (*Src*) and N_b (*RACK1*), with their specific links: JAS and JBS. Lastly, the third example focuses on the analysis of an NP with a symmetrical predicate at three arguments (see section 4.2, example 4).

In this case, the nominalization *association* is connected to the preposition *of* with the link MAS and introduces the argument N_a (*these two proteins*), and to the preposition *with* with the link MBS which introduces the second argument N_b (*chromatin*).

6   Conclusion and Perspectives

In this paper, we were interested in PNPs by analyzing their structures and defining the syntactic functions of their arguments. We also described PredicateDB, a tool that exploits the Specialist Lexicon Data. We have seen how PredicateDB assisted the analysis of both verbal and nominal patterns and how we used it to deduce the existing link between arguments of verbal patterns and their corresponding PNP arguments. We have also noticed that the syntactic functions of the nominalization arguments depend strongly on the syntactic type (intransitive, direct transitive, indirect transitive, etc.) of the verbs from which the nominalizations are derived. We have used this information to classify all the nominalizations and used these classes to create a lexicon-grammar which takes into account the syntactic behavior of the different nominalizations. Finally, we show the interest of this work to create a lexicon-grammar for the parsing of biological texts where nominalizations are numerous. It is possible to parse these texts with the Link Parser and produce an identical argument representation for nominal and verbal patterns

In the future, we will consider extending this work in order to process the nominalizations which are derived from adjectives (*aberrant/aberration*). We will carry out a general study on the identification of the arguments in all the predicative forms. Furthermore, we will consider taking as a starting point the work of [15] to enrich PredicateDB with semantic information by connecting PredicateDB, VerbNet and FrameNet.

References

1. Salkoff, M.: Automatic translation of support verb constructions. In: 13th COLING, Helsinki, Finland, pp. 243-246 (1990)
2. Macleod, C., Grishman, R., Meyers, A., Barret, L., Reeves, R.: Nomlex: A Lexicon of Nominalizations. In: 8th EURALEX, Liège, Belgium, pp. 187–193 (1998)
3. Browne, A.C., Mccray, A.T., Srinivasan, S.: The SPECIALIST LEXICON Technical report, Lister Hill National Center for Biomedical Communications, National Library of Medicine, USA (2000)
4. Pasero, R., Royauté, J., Sabatier, P.: Sur la syntaxe et la sémantique des groupes nominaux à tête prédicative. Lingvisticæ Investigationes 27(1), 83–124 (2004)
5. Gross, M.: Lexicon-grammar: the representation of compound words, In: 11th Coling, Bonn, Germany, pp. 1–6 (1986)
6. Miller, G.: WordNet: A lexical database. Communication of the ACM 38(11), 39–41 (1995)
7. Levin, B.: English Verb Classes and Alternation: A preliminary Investigation. The University of Chicago Press (1993)

8. Johnson, C., Fillmore, C., Petruck, M., Baker, C., Ellsworth, M., Ruppenhofer, J., Wood, E.: FrameNet: Theory and Practice (2002), http://framenet.icsi.berkeley.edu/
9. Fillmore, C.J.: Frame semantics and the nature of language. In: Annals of the NYAS. Conference on the Origin and Development of Language and Speech, vol. 280, pp. 20–32 (1976)
10. Meyers, A., Reeves, R., Macleod, C., Szekeley, R., Zielinska, V., Young, B., Grishman, R.: The cross-Breeding of Dictionaries. In: 5th LREC, Lisbon, Portugal (2004)
11. Grishman, R., Macleod, C., Meyers, A.: Comlex Syntax: Building a Computational Lexicon. In: 15th Coling, Kyoto, Japan, vol. 1, pp. 268–272 (1994)
12. Marcus, M.P., Marcinkiewicz, M.A., Santorini, B.: Building a large annotated corpus of English: the penn treebank. Computational Linguistics 19(2), 313–330 (1993)
13. Royauté, J., Godbert, E., Malik, M.M.: Analyser les structures prédicatives pour mettre en relation des objets scientifiques. In: CIDE10, Nancy, France, pp. 51–60 (2007)
14. Sleator, D., Temperley, D.: Parsing English with a Link Grammar, Carnegie Mellon University Computer Science technical report, CMU-CS-91-196, Carnegie Mellon University, USA (1991)
15. Shi, L., Mihalcea, R.: Putting Pieces Together: Combining FrameNet, VerbNet and WordNet for Robust Semantic Parsing. In: CICLing, Mexico-city, Mexico, pp. 100–111 (2005)

A Standard Lexical-Terminological Resource for the Bio Domain

Valeria Quochi, Riccardo Del Gratta, Eva Sassolini, Roberto Bartolini,
Monica Monachini, and Nicoletta Calzolari

CNR - Istituto di Linguistica Computazionale,
Area della Ricerca CNR, Via Moruzzi 1, 56100 Pisa, Italy
{name.surname}@ilc.cnr.it
http://www.ilc.cnr.it

Abstract. The present paper describes a large-scale lexical resource for
the biology domain designed both for human and for machine use. This
lexicon aims at semantic interoperability and extendability, through the
adoption of ISO-LMF standard for lexical representation and through a
granular and distributed encoding of relevant information. The first part
of this contribution focuses on three aspects of the model that are of particular interest to the biology community: the treatment of term variants,
the representation on bio events and the alignment with a domain ontology. The second part of the paper describes the physical implementation
of the model: a relational database equipped with a set of automatic
uploading procedures. Peculiarity of the BioLexicon is that it combines
features of both terminologies and lexicons. A set verbs relevant for the
domain is also represented with full details on their syntactic and semantic argument structure.

Keywords: Lexical representation model, Lexical Database, Computational Lexicography, Special Domains, Standards.

1 Introduction

Due to the increasing production of literature in the biomedical field, intensive research is being carried out around the globe to develop language technologies to access this large body of literature and to extract knowledge from it, in order to make
it easily available esp. to researchers and students. To achieve such a goal, lexical
and ontological resources are continuously being built and/or updated, manually
or semi-automatically, (e.g. protein and gene databases like Uniprot and Entrez-
Gene), thus requiring great human effort and high costs. Most of the resources
available, moreover, are created mainly for human use, which makes them often
not particulary useful for text mining and information extraction applications.

Recently, efforts have been directed to the creation of large-scale terminological resources that merge information contained in various smaller resources:
large thesauri based on a normalized nomenclature [13], extensible lexical and
terminological databases like Termino [10] and the SPECIALIST Lexicon [19].

Z. Vetulani and H. Uszkoreit (Eds.): LTC 2007, LNAI 5603, pp. 325–335, 2009.

Access to and interoperability of biological databases, however, is still hampered, due to lack of uniformity and harmonization of both formats and information encoded. One of the current challenges in bioinformatics is to construct a comprehensive and incremental resource which integrates bio-terms encoded in existing different databases and encodes all relevant properties according to some accredited standard for the representation of lexical, terminological and conceptual information [9].

The present paper describes the design of a large-scale lexical and terminological lexicon for biology (the BioLexicon) that is currently under development within the European BOOTStrep project[1]. The lexicon we describe learns from the state-of-the-art resources (see sec. 1.1) and builds on our experience in the standardization and construction of lexical resources. The goal is to propose a standard for the representation of lexicons in the Bio domain, which could be finally interoperable with other domain lexicons.

1.1   Related Works

In this section we briefly review two advanced state-of-the-art lexicons in the bio-medical domain: the UMLS SPECIALIST Lexicon and Termino.

The UMLS SPECIALIST Lexicon has been developed by the NLM as a wide coverage lexical basis for UMLS NLP tools [19]. It encodes words gathered from texts and for each word a set of morpho-syntactic and lexical semantic information is specified (for example part-of-speech, complement pattern, etc.). The format, however, is designed to be optimal for use by specific, in-house, applications. For this reason, it may not be easily reusable nor interoperable with other resources and/or tools.

Termino, in its turn, has a more flexible structure: each type of information (e.g. POS, external sources, and others) is encoded in separate tables, so that the information can be combined in different ways according to the specific user needs [10]. The model, however, seems not to conform explicitly to any established lexical standard.

The design of the structure of our lexical-terminological resource, in sec. 2 below, aims at merging the two main features of those two resources: richness of linguistic information encoded and modularity and flexibility. The major novelty of our proposal is the adherence to the ISO standards for lexicon representation (see below) together with a detailed model suited to represent sophisticated syntactic and semantic information.

2   The BioLexicon Resource

The BioLexicon allows for the representation of morphological, syntactic and semantic properties - where applicable- of terms and their variants, and biologically relevant verbs and nominalizations.

---

[1] Bootstrapping Of Ontologies and Terminologies STrategic Project is a STREP of the FP6 IST, call 4, with six partners from four European countries (Germany, U.K., Italy, France) and one Asian partner from Singapore involved. www.bootstrep.eu

Since it aims at semantic interoperability, the Lexical Markup Framework [8] was chosen as the reference meta-model for the structure of the BioLexicon.

The Lexical Markup Framework (LMF), together with the main building blocks of lexical representation, the Data Categories, provide a common shared representation of lexical objects that allows for the encoding of rich linguistic information. Most of the Data Categories used in the BioLexicon are contained in the standardized Data Category Registry [20], which is a warranty of inter-operability.

The lexical resource model that we present here accounts for (English) biological terms and represents their morphological, syntactic and lexical semantic properties. The BioLexicon, therefore, combines both lexical items typically contained in general purpose lexicons and specific terms of the biology domain and encodes those linguistic pieces of information that domain ontologies typically lack, but which are crucial to improve text mining results (e.g. part-of-speech and subcategorization frames). The resource is designed to be flexible enough to adapt to different application needs: e.g. text mining, information extraction, information retrieval, multilingual access.

Finally, it is designed to account for automatic population and enhancement of the resource with details acquired automatically from domain corpora.

2.1 Lexical Markup Framework

The LMF defines an abstract meta-model for the construction/description of computational lexicons; it drew inspiration from the SIMPLE and ISLE/MILE [1] experiences and integrated many of their representational devices. For reasons of space, we will only briefly introduce LMF, which provides a common, shared representation of lexical objects that allows the encoding of rich linguistic information, including morphological, syntactic, and semantic aspects. LMF is organized in several different packages. The mandatory core package describes the basic hierarchy of information included in a lexical entry. This core package is then enriched by resources that are part of the definition of LMF. These resources include specific data categories used to adorn both the core model and its extensions. Data categories can be seen as the main building blocks for the representation of the entries, the actual linguistic descriptors that are used to instantiate each entry (see 2.2 below).

2.2 The Model of the Lexicon

The BioLexicon is modeled into an XML DTD according to the LMF core model (see 2.1 above) plus objects taken from the three NLP extensions for the representation of morphological, syntactic and (lexical) semantics properties of terms. The set of lexical objects and relations can be seen as the skeleton of the lexical entries. The content that allows for their actual representation is formed by the set of Data Categories, i.e. features used to decorate such objects. Data Categories are a fundamental component of lexical description, which ensure the standardization of the resource. They represent pieces of linguistic content that are not part of the model proper, but are used to describe the various instances of its objects. To do this, it will only be necessary to refer to their identifier in the the standard, or user defined, repositories.

The set of Data Categories to be used in the BioLexicon is created both by drawing them from the standard sets of the ISO Data Category Registry [20,12] and by creating specific ones for the Bio domain. In doing this, we also aim at establishing a standard set of Data Categories for this domain. Examples of ISO data categories are *partOfSpeech* (with its possible values) and *writtenForm*. *sourceDC* and *confidenceScore*, instead, are examples of DCs specifically created for the biology domain on the basis of expert requirements.

In our lexicon, most DCs have been conceived as typed feature structures, so that we can at one time distinguish them on the basis of their status, and on the other, constrain the assignment of attributes to the relevant lexical objects.

For reasons of space, in this section we focus on the main lexical objects of our model (see Fig. 1 for an overall view of the core model):

LexicalEntry, Lemma, Syntactic Behaviour and *Sense*. The last three can be viewed as the central classes of three distinct modules for morphology, syntax and semantics.

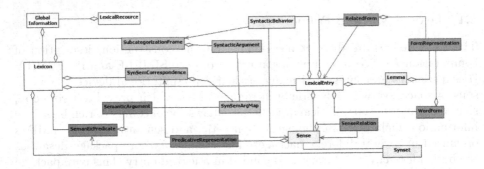

Fig. 1. The BioLexicon model

Lexical Entry represents the abstract lexical unit; it contains information about the external resources/corpora from which terms are extracted and has the main function of linking all the three main levels of description: morphology, syntax and semantics. Following the philosophy of modularity and extensibility of the LMF, in the BioLexicon we represent external references as (typed) data categories that are added as attributes of the Lexical Entry object[2].

Lemma represents the base form of the lexemes (i.e. the conventional forms of terms in the domain). The Lemma is in a one-to-one relation with the Lexical Entry, which forces homonyms to be represented as distinct lexical entries.

---

[2] For consistency, as well as for practical, reasons we represent most of the content of the lexical objects as typed Data Categories.

Syntactic Behaviour is dedicated to the representation of syntactic units, i.e. how lexical items and terms are used in context. One Syntactic Behavior describes one specific set of syntactic properties of a lexical item: syntactic features and links to subcategorization frames. The syntax module is designed in view of accommodating the subcategorization behaviors of terminological verbs, and possibly nominalizations, that are automatically extracted from texts with appropriate machine learning techniques. This means that specific Data Categories are defined to store quantitative and probability scores associated to acquired data.

Finally, **Sense** is the class used for the representation of the lexical meanings of a word/term, and it is inspired by the SIMPLE experience [17]. Sense represents lexical items as semantic units. Each Sense instance represents and describes one meaning, may contain information on the specific (sub)domain to which the term sense applies and indicate the semantic type that it instantiates. By means of the other classes of the semantic module, the BioLexicon can also represent the semantic argument structure of lexical items, where appropriate, and semantic relations between senses. In particular, the SemanticPredicate and the Syntactic- and SemanticArgument classes (see Fig. 1) are responsible for the mapping and alignment with a domain ontology (see 4 below).

3   Representing Term Variants

In a terminological lexicon for biology a key requirement is the representation of the different types of term variants. Variants, in fact, are extremely frequent and common in the literature. Nenadic et al. [15], for example, distinguish different types of variants: orthographic variants, acronyms and abbreviations, morphological variants, structural variants, semantic variants. In the BioLexicon we chose to distinguish only between two types of variants, since this is what could be classified and extracted automatically within the project: variants of form (i.e. orthographic variants, acronyms and abbreviations, and morphological variants) and variants of meaning. These two "macro-types" of variants are accounted for by means of two different representation devices: variants of form are represented in the FormRepresentation object, whereas semantic variants are represented as distinct but synonymous Lexical Entries.

FormRepresentation has the function of representing multiple orthographies of terms: orthographic variants of the same lemma. The basic DC specifying the FormRepresentation is the *writtenform*, i.e. the string identifying the form in question. Each variant is adorned with properties represented by specific DCs: the type of variants ("orthographic", "baseform", . . .), and a *confidenceScore* assigned to each variant. The latter is a fundamental Data Category for the representation of term variants extracted from texts using machine learning algorithms in that it can be used to keep track of the "goodness" of each variant.

Semantic Variants of terms are treated differently. They are represented in the Semantic module as synonymous terms. The **SenseRelation** class fulfils this purpose: semantic variants are represented as distinct lexical entries and consequently as distinct senses, but are linked together by a synonymy relation in the semantic layer. An *isSynonymOf* relation between Senses is used to keep track of all semantic variants of a term entry.

4   Representing Bio-events and Their Entities

The BioLexicon encodes verbs and nominalizations that are relevant for the specific domain it covers describing both their syntactic and semantic properties.

The importance and usefulness of representing complementation patterns and predicate-argument structures for event extraction and information extraction has been widely recognized in computational linguistics and in text mining (cfr [16], [4], [11], [14], [2], [3], [18])..

The lexical resource described here (see 1 above) allows for the representation of the syntactic and semantic combinatory properties of predicative lexical and terminological elements through the set of objects related to SyntacticBehaviour and PredicativeRepresentation.

As mentioned above, SyntacticBehaviour represents one of the possible behaviours that a lexical entry shows in context. A detailed description of the syntactic behaviour of a lexical entry is further defined by the SubcategorisationFrame object, which is the "heart" of the syntax module.

SubcategorisationFrame is used to represent one syntactic configuration and does not depend on individual syntactic units; rather, it may be shared by different units. Each SubcategorisationFrame is further described by SyntacticArguments specifying the syntactic type of phrase (i.e. NP, PP etc.), the position it occupies in the frame and its function (i.e. subject, object etc.).

The semantic module of the lexicon, on the other hand, is made of lexical objects related to the Sense class (namely PredicativeRepresentation and Sense Relation). The SemanticPredicate is independent from specific entries and represents an abstract meaning together with its associated semantic arguments. It represents a meaning that may be shared by more senses that are not necessarily considered synonymous. It is typically shared by a verb and the corresponding nominalizations, so that it can link LexicalEntries that belong to different lexical classes. The SemanticPredicate is referred to by the **PredicativeRepresentation** class, which represents the semantic behaviour of lexical entries and senses in context and encodes the link that hold between a Sense and SemanticPredicate, e.g. a verb, like *regulate* vs. nominalizations like *regulation, regulator*. As an example consider the verb *regulate*, the sense for *regulate* will point to the Semnatic Predicate *PredRegulate*, where agent and patient participants are instantiated as SemanticArguments with their selectional restrictions (Arg0 [TranscriptionFactor], Arg1 [Protein]). The predicate informs about its potential argument structure in that all lexical instances of the classes TranscriptionFactor and Protein are licensed as possible fillers of, respectively, agent and patient arguments. The PredRegulate, at the lexical level, is linked and shared by the semantic entries for "regulate" and "regulation".

4.1   Alignment with a Domain Ontology

The lexical model described here allows alignment to a domain ontology in three ways, all of which can be implemented to be used for different purposes: two are kinds of natural links, one is more indirect.

The first straightforward link is to have the Sense of a term entry point directly to the correspondent term concept in the ontology, through a DC containing the OWL URI of the concept.

The second simple link is between the event (or occurrant) concepts in the ontology and the corresponding SemanticPredicate in the lexicon, which represents an event meaning together with its associated semantic "arguments". A Semantic Predicate can be inherited from the Domain Ontology or linked to it either by automatic matching procedures or manually by a domain expert.

The indirect way of linking the lexical resource to a domain ontology is through the selection restrictions expressed in the semantic arguments of predicates. Such restriction can be expressed by means of semantic types of concepts of the reference ontology, thus allowing other kinds of inferences.

5   The BioLexicon DataBase

The software implementation of the BioLexicon consists of two modules: a relational database MySQL and a java-based loading software for the automatic population of the database. External to the DB is an XML Interchange Format (XIF hereafter) specifically tailored to the BioLexicon structure (see section 5.2).

5.1   Database Architecture

The database is structured into three logically distinct but strongly interconnected layers: Target, Dictionary and Satging layers (see Fig. 2).

The TARGET FRAME layer contains the actual BioLexicon tables, i.e. tables that directly instantiate the lexical objects and relations designed in the conceptual model. Each module of the BioLexicon structure (syntax, semantics, morphology) is independently accessible by queries and represents a self-consistent set of data. Each table has its internal identifier, but native identifiers, i.e. original source identifiers, are maintained as attributes of a given lexical entry (i.e. as DCs). The other two layers, DICTIONARY and STAGING, may be considered as operational layers: the DICTIONARY contains rules to populate target tables, the whereas STAGING is an intermediate set of hybrid tables for the storage of volatile data: staging table columns consist of attributes of the XIF and attributes of target tables. In addition, the staging frame is the level dedicated to data-cleaning and normalization. This neat separation between target tables (the BioLexicon proper) and operational tables allows for the optimization of the uploading of data into the BioLexicon DB and ensures extensibility both of the database and of the uploading procedures. Faced with the need to add a new table (i.e. a new lexical object) or a new attribute to an existing table, for example, it is sufficient to add only the definition of the new tables or attributes

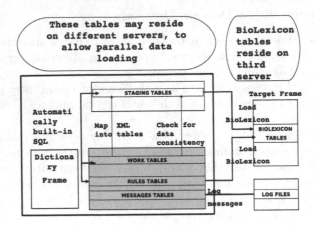

Fig. 2. BioLexicon DB Architecture

to the DB and to modify accordingly only the relevant portion of the Dictionary Frame layer to handle the new features.

5.2   The XIF and Automatic Population

The interchange format (XIF) is designed with the main purpose of automatically populating the BioLexicon with data provided by domain experts and by lexical acquisition systems. The XML Interchange Format DTD is to be considered a simplified version of the BioLexicon DTD, which accommodates the needs of data providers and facilitates the automatic uploading of the DB. Differently from other similar lexical systems (like Termino, see Harkema et al. 2004), the XIF allows for the independency of the uploading procedures from native data formats. The XIF DTD partially mirrors the way biological data are stored into domain knowledge databases and also accommodates the way these data are extracted from those resources. It is organized in clusters of terms, i.e. in sets of coherent types of information. A cluster contains one or more synonymous entries with information related to their lemmas, parts-of-speech, inflected forms, semantic relations and external references. Such an organization also permits the splitting of the input file by clusters, which in turn allows for a parallel uploading of the data into the DB.

Faced with the need to add a new table or to alter an existing one, it is sufficient to add new elements or new attributes to the XIF DTD and to add relevant instructions to the dictionary frame. The loading software interprets the XIF as usual and applies the new Dictionary instructions automatically inserting the new table or attribute. This property of the XIF together with the neat separation of the three layers of the DB mentioned above allows any agent (human or machine) to easily populate, update and create new objects and attributes.

6   Validation and General Statistics

Since we are dealing with the building of a lexical resource within an ongoing project, no proper evaluation is available yet[3]. However, some kind of content validation can be made, taking into account the input resources and the documentation so far produced. For validation of the resource we readapt templates from the ELRA Validation Manual for Lexica 2.0 [6][4].

The BioLexicon, a monolingual English lexical resource, represents Bio-terms as well as general verbs relevant to the bio-medical domain. Both nouns and verbs are represented: nouns covers a wide portion of the existing biological terminologies and come from the most used databases in the sector. Mainly, they represents terms denoting enzymes, chemical, species, genes and/or proteins. Verbs are limited in number: for the moment only around 7K relevant verb lemmas. For each entry the part-of-speech is encoded together with the written form of both its lemma and its variants. Also synonymic semantic relations are instantiated.

Finally, The BioLexicon resource is implemented as a MySQL relational database that runs both under Linux and Windows systems. The database is shaped according to the model XML DTD, and therefore easily allows for XML LMF conformant outputs. In the first uploading experiment, the DB automatically uploaded input files provided by the bio-experts within the BOOT-Strep project (EBI-Cambridge and MIB-Manchester), which gather and systematize biological terminology from the major online databases. Altogether the data amounted to 25 million records and occupies ca. 1.7G of memory space. It consists of 1,309,496 Lexical Entries; 2,047,903 orthographic variants and 1,697,804 *is_synonym_of* semantic relations. Figures about the different types of entries and information covered by the DB are reported in tables 1 and 2 below.

Table 1. Lexical Entries

POS	Sem.Type	Lexical Entries	Variants
N	Enzymes	4,016	9,379
N	Genes/Proteins	841,164	1,547856
N	Species	367,565	439,336
N	Chemicals	13437	51332

POS	Sem.Type	Lexical Entries	Infl. Forms
V		489	2435

---

[3] Within the project, evaluation tests on IE and IR are still ongoing at the moment of writing.

[4] Such validations are especially important given the automatic uploading of data provided according to the XIF by different groups.

Table 2. Semantic Relations between Senses (Entries)

Relation Type	#
is_a	464,078
is_synonym_of	847,873
is_part_of	189
is_conjugate_base_of	637

7   Concluding Remarks

With biological literature continuously developing, large-scale terminological lex-icons that can support text mining and information extraction applications can make life for biologists easier. The existence of a reusable bio-lexicon with so-phisticated linguistic information will enable the bioinformatic community to develop information extraction tools of higher quality.

The lexicon model described here is designed in such a way as to integrate both typical information provided by domain ontologies/terminologies and typi-cal linguistic information generally available in open-domain computational lex-icons: terms and variants are encoded with their semantic information as well as with typical linguistic information such as parts-of-speech and subcategoriza-tion frames. The encoding of syntactic and semantic properties of biologically relevant predicative items (verbs and nominalizations) is also precious for infor-mation extraction purposes and is a key feature of the lexicon presented in this paper.

Additionally, the possibility of linking entries and predicates in the lexicon to an external domain ontology enhances the possibility for reasoning applications.

The DB, as a reflection of the model, is a modular and flexible resource which can automatically upload new data and provide (XML) outputs by means of web services. Two of the main contributions of the resource to the biomedical field are the compliance to the most recent ISO Standard and the implementation of automatic procedures for the uploading of data provided by different sources and groups.

References

1. Calzolari, N., Bertagna, F., Lenci, A., Monachini, M. (eds.): Standards and Best Practices for Multilingual Computational Lexicons. MILE (The Multilingual ISLE Lexical Entry). ISLE CLWG Deliverable D2.2 & 3.2 Pisa (2003)
2. Carroll, J., McCarthy., D.: Word sense disambiguation using automatically ac-quired verbal preferences. Computers and the Humanities. Senseval Special Is-sue 34(1-2) (2000)
3. Cimiano, P., Hotho, A., Staab, S.: Clustering Concept Hierarchies from Text. In: Proceedings of the LREC 2004, Lisbon, Portugal (2004)

4. Faure, D., Nedellac, C.: A corpus-based conceptual clustering method for verb frames and ontology. In: Velardi, P. (ed.) Proceedings of the LREC Workshop on Adapting lexical and corpus resources to sublanguages and applications. ELRA (1998)

5. Ferrucci, D., Lally, A.: UIMA: an architectural approach to unstructured information processing in the corporate research environment. Natural Language Engeneering 10(3-4), 327–348 (2004)

6. Fersøe, H.: Validation Manual for Lexica. Technical Report. ELRA. Release 2.0 (2004)

7. Fersøe, H., Monachini, M.: ELRA Validation Methodology and Standard Promotion for Linguistic Resources. In: Proceedings of the LREC 2004, Lisbon, Portugal, pp. 941–944 (2004)

8. Francopulo, G., et al.: The relevance of standards for research infrastructure. In: Proceedings of the LREC 2006. Genoa, Italy (2006b)

9. Hahn, U., Markó, K.: Joint knowledge capture for grammars and ontologies. In: Proceedings of the 1st international conference on knowledge capture, Victoria, British Columbia, Canada (2001)

10. Harkema, H., et al.: A Large Scale Terminology Resource for Biomedical Text Processing. In: Proceedings of the BioLINK 2004, pp. 53–60. ACL (2001)

11. Hindle, D.: Noun classification from predicate argument structures. In: Proceedings of the Annual Meeting of the Association for Computational Linguistics (1990)

12. ISO-12620. Terminology and other content language resources- Data Categories- Specifications of data categories and management of a Data Category Registry for language resources. Technical Report. ISO/TC37/SC3/WG4 (2006)

13. Kors, J.A., et al.: Combination of Genetic Databases for Improving Identification of Genes and Proteins in Text. In: Proceedings of the BioLINK 2005. ACL (2005)

14. Lapata, M., Brew, C.: Using Subcategorization to Resolve Verb Class Ambiguity. In: Proceedings of the Joint SIGDAT Conference on Empirical Methods in Natural Language Processing and Very Large Corpora, College Park, MD, pp. 397–404 (1999)

15. Nenadic, G., Ananiadou, S., McNaught, J.: Enhancing Automatic Term Recognition through Term Variation. In: Proceedings of the 20th Coling, Geneve, Switzerland (2004)

16. Pereira, F., Tishby, N., Lee, L.: Distributional clustering of English Words. In: Proceedings of the 31st Annual Meeting of the Association for Computational Linguistics, pp. 183–190. ACL (1993)

17. Ruimy, N., et al.: A computational semantic lexicon of Italian: SIMPLE. Linguistica Computazionale XVIII-XIX, 821–864 (2003)

18. Spasic, I., Nenadic, G., Ananiadou, S.: Using Domain-Specific Verbs for Term Classification. In: Proceedings of the ACL 2003 Workshop on Natural Language Processing in Biomedicine, pp. 17–24 (2003)

19. SPECIALIST Lexicon and Lexical Tools. Natural Library of Medicine. UMLS Release Documentation, http://www.nlm.nih.gov/pubs/factsheets/umlslex.html

20. Wright, S.E.: A global data category registry for interoperable language resources. In: Proceedings of the LREC 2004, Lisbon, Portugal (2004)

Extracting Collocations in Contexts

Amalia Todirascu[1], Christopher Gledhill[1], and Dan Stefanescu[2]

[1] LILPA / Université Marc Bloch Strasbourg, 22, rue René Descartes, BP 80010,
67084 Strasbourg cedex, France
[2] Research Institute for Artificial Intelligence, Romanian Academy, Calea 13 Septembrie, 13,
Bucharest 050711, Romania
{todiras,gledhill}@umb.u-strasbg.fr, danstef@racai.ro

Abstract. The aim of this paper is to develop (i) a general framework for the analysis of verb-noun (VN) collocations in English and Romanian, and (ii) a system for the extraction of VN-collocations from large tagged and annotated corpora. We identify VN-collocations in two steps: (i) by calculation of the frequent lexical co-occurrences of each VN-pair, and (ii) the identification of the most typical lexico-grammatical constructions in which each VN-pair is involved in.

Keywords: collocation extraction system, systemic functional grammar, verb-noun collocations.

1 Introduction

This paper presents some of the findings established by a project supported by the *Agence universitaire pour la Francophonie* (AUF). The aim of the project was to develop a tool for the extraction of collocations from a multilingual collocation dictionary (primarily designed for German, French, Romanian, and English). However, here we limit our discussion to the specific properties of English and Romanian collocations, and to the linguistic and computational resources developed to extract them from texts.

In this paper collocation is seen from the point of view of functional approaches to language ([1], [2]) and empirical corpus linguistics ([3], [4]). According to this approach, collocation can be defined as 'a preference for all linguistic signs to be used in structurally pre-fabricated and semantically predictable sequences' ([5]:1). The correct use of collocations is a difficult problem for non-native speakers, and especially difficult for Natural Language Processing (NLP) systems. Few dictionaries, whether electronic or traditional, provide complete information about collocations [6]. For example, while some dictionaries may explain the sense of idiomatic phrases such as *cook the books* (cheat), *curry favour* (seek approval), *rue the day* (regret), they often do not give any information about the lexico-grammatical patterns that tend to arise around these expressions. However, in recent years several methods and tools for extracting collocations from texts have been developed, and the aim of this paper is to contribute to this text-based approach.

Z. Vetulani and H. Uszkoreit (Eds.): LTC 2007, LNAI 5603, pp. 336–349, 2009.
© Springer-Verlag Berlin Heidelberg 2009

It should be pointed out here that our approach to collocation is not quite the same as that adopted elsewhere. Several definitions have been proposed for by NLP researchers, linguists and corpus linguists. Summing up these different views, Gledhill [5] points out that collocations can be seen from three different perspectives: (i) 'co-occurrence', a statistical-textual view of collocation often adopted in empirical corpus linguistics ([7], [8]), (ii) 'construction', a syntactic-semantic view of collocation in terms of the privileged relationship between two lexical items such as a 'base' and its 'collocator' ([9]), and (iii) 'conventional expression', a discourse-rhetorical point of view of that emphasizes the pragmatic, 'external' function of idiomatic sequences, rather than their formal 'internal' properties ([10]). While recognizing the importance of the pragmatic dimension, in this paper we concentrate on the first two approaches to collocation, namely (i) collocation as textual co-occurrence, and (ii) collocation as lexico-grammatical construction. This combined approach thus sees collocations as sequences of two or more signs which enter into very specific lexico-grammatical relations that can be described in terms of two steps: (i) a generic pattern (such as verb + noun, noun + adjective, adverb + adjective etc.) and (ii) a specific pattern (such as 'preference for zero-article', 'preference for active voice', etc.), It is this configuration of lexico-grammatical information (what Firth called 'colligation') which we use to automatically extract collocations from texts.

The specific types of collocation that are of interest to us in this paper are verb-noun (VN) constructions, such as *make a decision* / a lua o decizie, *to make an application* / a pune în aplicare, etc. The main method we use to trawl the corpus for these sequences is simply to identify any instances of V followed by N. Of course, we refine the basic search for VN combinations by associating them with a subset of morpho-syntactic properties, such as a preference for the definite article or zero-article, for singular or plural noun, for the presence of a second complement, etc. These 'sub-regularities' are clearly important for an automatic extraction tool, since by using this contextual information, an NLP system can filter out salient collocations (i.e. VN constructions) from a larger set of candidates (i.e. VN co-occurrences).

There have been several approaches to collocation extraction. Some only use statistical methods ([11], [7]), while other approaches identify collocations by purely looking at syntactic relations ([12]) or using both syntactic and semantic properties ([13]). In this paper we adopt a hybrid approach, in that we use a statistical module to extract candidate co-occurrences and then apply a set of language-specific linguistic filters, in order to extract relevant candidates. The linguistic filters we use here were first defined as a result of comparative linguistic data, carried out on a parallel corpus, as discussed in the following section.

2 Methodology

In this paper we adopt an extraction method which has already been applied to extract collocations from German corpora ([14], [15]). This method assumes that collocations have their own morpho-syntactic properties which extend beyond the limits of a single lexical combination into the 'co-text'. This methodology has been used to analyze a large German newspaper corpus, in which any relevant morpho-syntactic information (preference for a definite article, specific prepositions, or case in German) is taken into account from the context of the expression.

We have applied a similar analysis to English, French and Romanian, in three comparable corpora. The first step of this analysis involves the identification of common morpho-syntactic properties in the three languages in order to develop configurable tools for the automatic identification of collocation candidates. The next step involves listing the extracted candidates and filtering out non-salient candidates using the morpho-syntactic information from the first step. In order to extract collocation candidates from texts, a statistical module is used to establish a complete list of candidates, using parallel, tagged corpora ([16]), for the four languages studied in the project. We are currently adapting several tools which already exist for German ([17]), French and English ([18]), and Romanian ([19]). However, this process is only semi-automatic, and a final manual check of candidates is necessary, even after filtering. We believe that the information extracted automatically from the various corpora can be used to design and to maintain a collocation dictionary.

2.1 The Corpus

In order to identify language-specific filters, we require tagged and preferably syntactically annotated corpora. We have used several corpora for comparative studies. First, a parallel corpus available in the languages of the EU was used: the *Acquis Communautaire Corpus* (ACQ) ([20]), containing all the main legal texts published by the EU member states since 1950. We selected a set of common documents from the ACQ in English, French, German and Romanian in order to have a similar-sized reference corpus (about 15 million words) for each language. It should be pointed out here that the style of the ACQ is highly impersonal, and it contains many domain-specific terms and fixed expressions which are typical of administrative texts. These factors clearly affect the types of expression which emerge from the data.

In order to compare and to select only relevant collocations, it is also necessary to compare our specialized corpora with more general text archives. For this purpose we set up various monolingual corpora (literature, newspapers and technical papers) to adjust the set of properties extracted from the ACQ. Even if the monolingual corpora do not contain the same content, we chose similar genres in every corpus. For instance, the Romanian corpus contains newspapers, the Romanian Constitution, two novels, computer science texts, and a medical corpus on human eye diseases (about 10 million words). We cleared these corpora of tables, pictures, irrelevant structural elements, and applied a uniform encoding to each. We used only texts that used diacritics properly in our corpora, since in Romanian diacritics play an important linguistic role, allowing speakers to distinguish among:

- lexical categories: peşte (*fish*) (noun) − peste (*over*) (preposition); fată (*girl*) (noun) − faţă de (*as to*) (preposition);
- grammatical categories: fata (*the girl*) − fată (*a girl*); cântă (*he/she/they sing(s)*) − cânta (*he/ she was singing*);
- semantic classes: fata (*the girl*) − faţa (*the face*).

As mentioned above, in order to identify construction-specific morpho-syntactic properties, we use a tagged and even syntactically annotated corpus. The French, English and German corpora were tagged using TreeTagger ([21]). While this tagger had previously been trained on newspaper texts, many lemmas or tags proposed for the ACQ were wrong. We trained the tagger for the new domains, after correcting manually lemmas and tags. The Romanian corpus was tagged using TTL – a complex tool for pre-processing Romanian and English texts ([22]), and the tagged data was also manually validated. Here are some examples of tags used to describe Romanian filters: NxRY – Noun (plural or singular), in direct case (Nominative or Accusative definite form); NSOY – Noun, singular, oblique case (Genitive or Dative case definite form); V3 – Verb (3rd person).

3 Linguistic Analysis

Before we set out a method of identifying VN collocations in the corpus, we need to discuss the main linguistic properties of these expressions.

3.1 VN Collocations

Verb-Noun (VN) collocations have been analyzed from various perspectives. As noted by [23], the main semantic feature of VN collocations is that in any 'complex predicate' (a construction of the type predicate + complement), the complement designates or delimits the main semantic process of the predicate. Thus in transitive VN constructions such as *make a cake, take an umbrella* the complement is simply 'affected' by a material process expressed by the verb. But in more metaphorical VN expressions such as *make fun, make a point, take the point, take stock,* the complement expresses a 'mental' process ([2], [24]) which cannot be related to a simple verb in some cases (*make fun = to fun?*), or clearly does not have the same meaning as the 'material' processes expressed by *to point, to stock,* etc. However, while we could consider these examples to be valid VN collocations, it is not clear that many formal linguists would consider them to be so. Most grammarians ([25]) and lexicologists ([26]) have usually assumed that the syntactic properties of light or 'support' verb constructions are determined by the specific type of noun in the VN construction. Thus, linguists such as [26] have proposed that the light or 'support' verbs that typically occur in VN constructions, such as `face` / *make, do,* or `lua` / *take* have little semantic role to play in the clause: they are seen as 'grammatical actualizors' of an underlying predicate expressed by the N. Notwithstanding the debate about what 'counts' as a VN construction, the main structural properties suggested by these linguists have been summarized in [23] and are set out below (with examples being given this time in English and Romanian, where appropriate):

V1. **Morphology.** Some VN constructions have a simple V equivalent (*do work = to work,* a se `face noapte` / *to become dark* = a se `înnopta`), but this is not always the case (*take a break = ?to break* and the Romanian equivalent a `face o pauză` / = *a lua o pauză`).

V2. **Arguments.** Like simple Vs, VN constructions can take direct or indirect complements: *The candidate frightened the electors / gave the electors a fright,* `Candidatul a băgat spaima în electorat`, or *He called his colleague / made a call to his colleague* / A `făcut apel la colegi`.

V3. Passivation. Some VN constructions allow active and passive forms (*The expert made a report to the Commission* / Expertul a făcut un raport vs. *A report has been made by the expert* / Raportul a fost făcut de expert), while some VN constructions do not. (for example, it is not possible to passivise a face obiectul / *make an objection*, *Obiectul a fost făcut* / *An objection was made*).

V4. Aspect. Some VN constructions express perfective aspect compared with a simple V : *She laughed / She gave a laugh / She laughed for hours / ?She gave a laugh for hours.* In Romanian, this possibility is not available.

In addition, VN constructions are characterized by some noun-specific morpho-syntactic properties:

N1. Determination. The determiner is often absent or fixed in VN constructions (*make use of* / *?make the use of*, face obiectul / *face obiect / 'is subject to'). However, when the N is modified or reformulated, the determiner is more variable for both English *make use of* / *the use made of,* and Romanian: ia o decizie / 'take a decision' / ia decizia necesară (lit. 'take decision-the necessary').

N2. Clefts. The noun in some VN constructions cannot be extracted in English (*He took flight* / *It was the flight that he took*) or in Romanian (Profesorul a luat cuvântul / 'Professor-the has taken word-the' / *The professor made a speech*, but not *Cuvântul pe care l-a luat profesorul / lit. 'The word that the professor has taken'.).

N3. Expansion. The N sometimes cannot be modified by relative clauses or other qualifiers (*He took the decision which was necessary* / *He took the flight which was necessary*; El a luat decizia care se impunea/*el a luat cuvîntul care se impunea / 'he has taken word which was imposed').

N4. Conversion. The V in some VN constructions can be converted into nominal group in which the N is introduced by a preposition: *She made a hypothesis / Her making of the hypothesis,* or in Romanian Comisia a luat măsuri/*The commission takes measures* = Luarea măsurilor de către comisie / *The taking of measures by the commission*). However, for 'locutions' this is not usually possible: *She made sense / ?Her making of sense,*

Taking into account all these different criteria, we judge that there is no one homogenous category of VN collocations. However, it appears that there are at least two basic types: (i) **complex predicate** constructions, in which the N has the syntactic function of a normal complement (examples such as *make + call, hypothesis, recommendation, a point, speech...*), and (ii) **complex predicator** constructions, or 'locutions', in which the N is integrated in the verb group, and cannot properly be considered to be an independent complement (examples such as *make + fun, haste, sense, way,* although there is no evidence these are completely 'fixed' sequences). Despite the fact that there appears to be no one formal criterion for VN collocations, the various properties discussed here (V1-V4, N1-N4) can be used to evaluate VN constructions. In the following sections we examine some of these properties, in particular the link with the process type expressed by the verb in the three languages. We also present some conclusions about the syntactic filters necessary to extract semi-automatically collocation candidates.

3.2 The Data

We focus here on two properties used to extract collocations automatically from the ACQ corpus for English and Romanian. Generally speaking, we find that there is a correlation between the type of determiner used (N1) or the voice of verb group (V3) and the type of 'semantic process' expressed by the VN construction. We distinguish three possibilities:

(A) VN constructions in which the N is determined by a definite article (*make+the+*N / *face+*N-definite article). In terms of semantic transitivity, in Romanian the use of a definite article usually corresponds to a relational process, while for English this is not the case. The most frequent VN constructions in English are material processes built around the verb *make* (examples 1 and 2, 53 occurrences), with some expressions indicating a 'communicative' process (example 3, 23 occurrences):

(1) *The competent authorities shall **make the payment** within a period of two months following receipt of the payment request.*
(2) *... the bureau to which this member belongs shall itself **make the reimbursement** in accordance with the conditions described hereunder...*
(3) *The President of the Council shall be authorized ...to **make the declaration** contained in Annex II.*

These constructions accept the passive voice (*the declaration is made, the reimbursement is made, the payment is made*). However, in Romanian, the most frequent occurrences express a 'relational' process (267 occurrences) which usually does not accept passive voice (**obiectul a fost făcut*):

(4) ...care este recunoscut pe plan internaţional şi care **face obiectul** unui audit.
'which is internationally well-known and has been subject to an audit'
(5) ...Trece peste graniţa dintre statele membre şi care **face legătura** între sistemele de transport...
'...crosses the border between member states and which joins the transportation system...'

(B) VN constructions in which the N is used with an indefinite article (*make + a/an+*N; face un/o/nişte+N). For English, most VN constructions express verbal processes (example 7, 87 occurrences), but also mental (example 6, 28 occurrences) and relational processes (example 8, 22 occurrences):

(6) *...the notifier must submit exposure data ... to enable the competent authority to **make a decision** whether to accept an RTP request or not;*
(7) *...the Commission shall **make a report** on its application, accompanied, where necessary, by appropriate proposals.*

(8) *It is necessary to* **make a distinction** *between mushrooms prepared or preserved by vinegar or acetic acid ... and mushrooms otherwise prepared ...;*

In Romanian, the presence of an indefinite article or of a quantifier is used to identify either a material process (9) or a mental one (10).

(9) Comisia poate **să facă orice modificări** la prezentul Regulament care …
'The commission should make some changes in the present rules...'
(10) Acest raportor **face o evaluare** preliminară al recursului.
'This lecturer makes a preliminary evaluation of the appeal'

Both in English and Romanian, the passive voice is possible.

(C) VN constructions without a determiner. While English VN constructions generally express material processes, the Romanian examples express relational processes:

- material process (226 occurrences):
(11) *Advice on how the consumer can* **make use** *of the manufacturer's take-back for recycling offer....*

- relational processes (321 occurrences):
(12) Pentru a putea **face față** unor situaţii de urgenţă …
'in order to deal with emergency situations'...

In Romanian, the passive form is not possible at all with this category of VN construction (it is, of course, the 'verbal locution' of traditional grammar), while English passive forms are sometimes possible.

To conclude, the determiner and the passive tests (N1 and V3) allow us to identify a broad range of VN constructions. In the following sections, we examine how these tests might be used to filter the output of the statistical module, even if manual validation is necessary.

4 Extracting Collocations

As presented in section 2, we use a hybrid extraction approach, combining statistical techniques and pattern-based matching in order to filter candidates. While the first stage is completely automated, the second one is semi-automated, since the patterns are defined on the basis of linguistic analysis. As mentioned above, since the only way to identify valid VN expressions is to establish whether the complement expresses the 'semantic range' of the predicate, such semantic properties have, in the final analysis, to be checked manually.

4.1 The Statistical Module

As mentioned above, all frequently occurring Verb-Noun pairs (even separated by one or several words) are potential VN co-occurrences. In this section we describe a statistical method for extracting VN co-occurrences inspired from [7]. In particular, we use the mean and the variance computed for the distances between pairs of words in the corpus to identify those words which appear to have a significant degree of co-occurrence. The mean is the average of the distances among the candidate words. The variance measures the deviations of the distances with respect to the mean:

$$\sigma^2 = \frac{\sum_{i=1}^{n}(d_i - \mu)^2}{n-1} \tag{1}$$

where n is the total number of distances, d_i are the distances and μ is the mean. σ^2 is the variance, while σ is the standard deviation. If two words always appear together at the same distance, the variance is 0. If the distribution of the distances is random (the case of those words which appear together by chance), then, the variance has high values.

[7] shows that candidates for collocations are those pairs of words for which the standard deviations are small. Accordingly, we computed the standard deviation for all VN co-occurrences (from the ACQ corpus) within a window of 11 content words for all the three languages involved in the project plus English. We selected all the pairs for which the standard deviation scores were smaller than 1.5 ([27]).

The next step was to further filter out some of the pairs using the Log-Likelihood (LL) score. We use the LL score to select those pairs for which the two words are not only in a fixed relation in terms of distance, but also they appear together more often than expected. The LL score works by means of finding the hypothesis that better describes the data observed by analyzing a text. We have to consider either that the two words in the text are independent, either not. Hence, the two working hypotheses:

$H_0 : P(w_2|w_1) = p = P(w_2|\neg w_1)$ (null hypothesis - independence)

$H_1 : P(w_2|w_1) = p_1 \neq p_2 = P(w_2|\neg w_1)$ (non-independence hypothesis)

$n_{12} = n_{1*} - n_{11}$
$n_{21} = n_{*1} - n_{11}$
$n_{22} = n_{**} - n_{11}$

	w_2	$\neg w_2$
w_1	n_{11}	n_{12}
$\neg w_1$	n_{21}	n_{22}

where n_{11} is the number of occurrences for the pair w_1w_2, n_{12} is the number of occurrences for the pair w_1w_i where $i \neq 2$, etc. The LL score formula is:

$$LL = 2 * \sum_{j=1}^{2}\sum_{i=1}^{2} n_{ij} * \log \frac{n_{ij} * n_{**}}{n_{i*} * n_{*j}} \tag{2}$$

If the score obtained is higher than a certain threshold, the null hypothesis (H_0) is rejected.

Thus, we computed the LL score for all the pairs obtained using the method developed by [7]. For every pair w_1w_2, the calculus took into account only those VN co-occurrences between which the distance was the same as the round of the mean computed for all distances between the w_1 and w_2. We selected the pairs for which the LL score was higher than 9. For this threshold the probability of error is less than 0.004 according to chi-square tables with one degree of freedom. Using LL filtering, we obtained lists of candidates for each language. The following table contains some of the best ones extracted for Romanian.

Table 2. Romanian candidates extracted by the statistical module

w_1 w_2	dist.	LL score	Process
Aduce atingere 'to affect/to prejudge'	1	51567.34864	Relation process
înlocui text 'replace text'	3	43992.3067	-
intra vigoare 'applied' (or literally 'placed in vigour')	2	42527.03736	
face apel la 'call for' (or lit. 'to make a call'))	3	32050.11219	Relational process
face obiectul 'be subject (to)'	1	30729.47663	Relational process
face modificări 'make changes'	4	29141.39454	Material process
modifica dată 'modify the date'	2	27658.4116	-

The statistical module can be time and memory-consuming when running on large files. At first, for a 350Mb preprocessed file, the algorithm took almost one day to complete using data bases and, when loaded everything in memory the computer ran out of it. The impact on both the improvement rate and the speed of the research process was enormous. After analyzing the problem, we noticed that the pairs counting problem can be split in separate smaller computable sub-problems that can be run either in serial or in parallel on different CPUs. Therefore we have implemented another algorithm that exploited this observation and the runtime dropped to 5 to 6 minutes for a 350Mb file. This allowed us to easily test the algorithm with different thresholds for standard deviation and LL score.

In order to distinguish valid VN expressions from other VN constructions, linguists need to analyze the contexts of the best scored pairs. These contexts are practically all the sentences (or fragments of sentences) that contain those pairs. To implement a fast method for getting contexts, we used a search engine (the Lucene Search Engine).[1] After indexing the text, the retrieval of all contexts for 10000 pairs can be done in 15 - 20 minutes.

On the basis of the analysis of these contexts, we identified some relevant morphosyntactic properties as indices to detect automatically collocation candidates. For example, the contexts for face dovada / 'make proof of' are caracterized by high fixedness, indicating a possible **complex predicator** (99,1% of noun occurrences are characterized by definite article and 100% of noun occurrences are singular).

---

[1] http://lucene.apache.org/java/docs/

Table 3. The contexts of face dovada 'make proof of'. The abbreviations used are: **nsry** – noun, singular, accusative, definite article; **vp** – past participle; **v3** – verb 3rd person; **vn**- infinitive, **vg** –gerund, **npn**-noun, plural, zero article; **npry** – noun, plural, nominative, definite article.

vlemma=face nlemma=dovadă occ=238	LL=1043.277042
face/face/v3 dovada/dovadă/nsry	92
facă/face/v3 dovada/dovadă/nsry	51
face/face/vn dovada/dovadă/nsry	43
fac/face/v3 dovada/dovadă/nsry	41
făcut/face/vp dovada/dovadă/nsry	7
făcând/face/vg dovada/dovadă/nsry	2
facă/face/v3 dovadă/dovadă/nsrn	1
face/face/v3 dovadă/dovadă/nsrn	1

In addition, the noun is much more variable if the candidate is a **complex predicate**: 58,81% definite article, plural, 37,05% of occurrences zero article, plural and the others are definite singular (4,24%).

Table 4. The contexts of lua măsură 'take measure'

vlemma=lua nlemma= măsură occ=2491	LL=19207.12849
iau/lua/v3 măsurile/măsură/npry	699
ia/lua/v3 măsurile/măsură/npry	627
ia/lua/v3 măsuri/măsură/npn	388
iau/lua/v3 măsuri/măsură/npn	271
lua/lua/vn măsuri/măsură/npn	244
lua/lua/vn măsurile/măsură/npry	148
luat/lua/vp măsuri/măsură/npn	56
luat/lua/vp măsurile/măsură/npry	37
luând/lua/vg măsurile/măsură/npry	9
luat/lua/vp măsura/măsură/nsry	6
iau/lua/v1 măsurile/măsură/npry	4
ia/lua/v3 măsura/măsură/nsry	1
luând/lua/vg măsuri/măsură/npn	1

Finally, as far as deciding whether a candidate is a VN construction or not, it is perhaps worth mentioning here that morpho-syntactic predictability might be used as a symptom for selecting possible VN constructions. However, this criterion is not sufficient to extract candidates automatically. As mentioned previously, after applying the filtering module, manual validation is still necessary.

4.2 The Filtering Module

In a previous study ([28]), we analyzed the results of the statistical module and identified several classes of 'valid' VN constructions (as presented in section 3.1), as well as 'non-valid' VN co-occurrences in English and Romanian. Some of these VN constructions or VN co-occurrences are characterized by some specific morpho-syntactic properties. For example, complex predicators are characterized by morpho-syntactic fixedness, while the properties of complex predicates are quite variable (i.e. number, gender, tense). We exploit these observations to define filtering patterns. We have defined a simple language to describe the patterns that can be observed in the corpus. A pattern is composed of tags (or lemmas) and of operators (operators meaning is similar as in any regular expression formalism):

<tag>|<lemma> (<tag>|<lemma>)$^{<op>}$

where <op> could be: {n,m} – means minimum n and maximum m tags or lemmas;+ means at least 1 tag or lemma;* means 0 or several tags or lemmas.

Based on the classification of the VN pairs, we defined several pattern classes: (i) patterns identifying valid candidates; (ii) patterns eliminating VN co-occurences; (iii) patterns eliminating mistaken identified candidates. We apply first (iii) and (ii) categories, followed by the first pattern category. We present some examples of patterns for each of these categories:

(i) Patterns selecting valid candidates on the basis of morpho-syntactic fixedness criteria. Such patterns might identify discontinuous sequences. The candidate is selected if it shows strong preferences for some morpho-syntactic properties (number, gender, mode, voice), e.g. if the pattern applies to more than 85% of its contexts. The following extraction patterns identify mostly VN constructions:

(1) a face NxRY *{1,5} NxOY
where NxRY means a definite noun (singular or plural) in direct case; NxOY means a definite noun in oblique case; {1,5} means 1 up to 5 words.
The candidates identified by this pattern express various relational processes: a face obiectul unui (*is subject to*), a face legătura cu (*relate*), a face transferul (*transfer*), but also some communicative processes (a face declarația cu privire la /*to declare*). We identify both locutions (a face obiectul) as well as complex predicates (a face legătura cu).

(2) Vfin <lemma> în NxN
 where NxN means a noun with zero article (plural or singular in nominative case) and Vfin means a finite verb.
The pattern selects candidates as a intra în vigoare (*to apply*), a pune în aplicare (*to apply*), a lua în considerare (*to take into account*), which express relational processes. These candidates are VN constructions.

(ii) Patterns filtering out invalid candidates. Some of the 'non-valid' VN co-occurrences can be classified into several classes [28]:

- predicate + intensive complement: *This Decision is **addressed** to the **Member States***
- subject + predicate combinations: acest **regulament**$_N$ va **intra**$_V$ în vigoare ("this rule will enter into force", correct: *intra*$_V$+*vigoare*$_N$);
- predicate + adjunct combinations: articolul a fost **modificat**$_V$ ultima **dată**$_N$ ("The article has been modified last time...", correct *modifica*+*articol*) *In*

*the text published$_V$ in the Official$_N$ Journal of the European Communities a material error occurred (*correct*: text+publish)*;
- noun groups: *If the measures$_N$ envisaged$_V$ are not in accordance dispoziţiile$_N$ modificate$_V$* ("the modified provisions"); correct: no extraction;

For instance, noun groups or subject + predicate constructions (in English) might be automatically eliminated, if the pattern matches more than 85% of contexts. For example, the pattern **NxN Vp** eliminates candidates as *measures engendered,* dispoziţiile modificate. The pattern **NxN V3** eliminates the Subject+Predicate constructions in English, but, while Romanian is a free order constituent language, then this pattern is not useful.

(iii) Filters eliminating noise candidates, using some extra-linguistic criteria (segmentation errors, distance between the noun and the verb). These noise candidates occur due to tagging errors, segmentation errors (absence of sentence separators), or erroneous identification of syntactic constituents (several prepositions or conjunctions occuring between the noun and the verbs). These filters eliminate only partially invalid candidates.

4.3 Evaluation

In order to evaluate the results extracted from Romanian ACQ, we manually classified the first 873 candidates. When analyzing the results of the filtering module (table 5), we noticed that complex predicators are well identified by their morpho-syntactic fixedness. For other categories, it is difficult to decide automatically the candidates. For example, complex predicates and predicate+complement have similar morpho-syntactic properties (variability in number, passive vs active forms), but only the semantic criteria helps us in distinguishing them. In Romanian, some of the non-valid candidates (Predicate+adjunct) are automatically identified by the preposition marking the case. For instance, in the absence of syntactically annotated corpus, we are not able to filter out Subject-Predicate candidates for Romanian, while this is possible in English or French. As well, the mistaken identified candidates represent an important part of the candidates (30-33%), they are eliminated by filtering patterns.

Table 5. Romanian candidates and the classes identified

Class	%
complex predicator	1,19 %
complex predicate	10,87 %
complex preposition	1,09%
construction VN + prédicator	0,29%
predicator + complement	27,74%
subject+predicate	2,6%
predicate+adjunct	35,52%
noun group	0,29%
mistaken identification	19,76%

5 Conclusion

In this paper we have presented various interesting features of VN constructions for two languages: English and Romanian. Generally speaking, Romanian shares most of the properties of VN constructions that have been identified in other Romance and Germanic languages. However, the specific configuration for each VN construction is different. It is also clear from this study that the relevant context for all of these expressions extends way beyond the basic V plus N co-occurrence: in almost every case, the expression involves a specific lexico-grammatical as well as morphosyntactic configuration: in other words, a set of contexts which are highly consistent in the corpus. Our conclusion must therefore be that the contextual features of VN constructions beyond the VN pairs themselves are crucial to the semi-automatic extraction of collocations.

Acknowledgments. This work has been funded by *Agence Universitaire pour la Francophonie* (AUF). We thank Rada Mihalcea (University of Texas, United States) for the NAACL Romanian corpus, as well as Dan Cristea (University of Iasi, Romania) for the L4TE corpus.

References

1. Firth, J.R.: Papers in linguistics 1934-1951. Oxford University Press, Oxford (1957)
2. Halliday, M.: An Introduction to Functional Grammar. Arnold, London (1985)
3. Sinclair, J.: Corpus, Concordance, Collocation. Oxford University Press, Oxford (1991)
4. Hunston, S., Francis, G.: Pattern Grammar - A Corpus-Driven Approach to the Lexical Grammar of English. John Benjamins, Amsterdam (2000)
5. Gledhill, C.: Collocations in Science Writing. Gunter Narr Verlag, Tübingen (2000)
6. Cowie, A.P.: The treatment of collocations and idioms in learner's dictionaries. Applied Linguistics 2(3), 223–235 (1981)
7. Smadja, F.A., McKeown, K.R.: Automatically extracting and representing collocations for language generation. In: Proceedings of ACL 1990, Pittsburgh, Pennsylvania, pp. 252–259 (1990)
8. Grossmann, F., Tutin, A. (eds.): Les Collocations. Analyse et traitement, coll. Travaux et Recherches en Linguistique Appliquée, Amsterdam, De Werelt (2003)
9. Hausmann, F.J.: Was sind eigentlich Kollokationnen? In: Steyer, K. (ed.) Wortverbindungen – mehr oder weniger fest, pp. 309–334 (2004)
10. Gledhill, C., Frath, P.: Collocation, phrasème, dénomination: vers une théorie de la créativité phraséologique, La Linguistique 43(1), 65–90 (2007)
11. Quasthoff, U.: Tools for Automatic Lexicon Maintenance: Acquisition, Error Correction, and the Generation of Missing Values. In: Proceedings LREC 1998, ELRA, pp. 853–856 (1998)
12. Seretan, V., Nerima, L., Wehrli, E.: A tool for multi-word collocation extraction and visualization in multilingual corpora. In: Proceedings of EURALEX 2004, Lorient, France, vol. 2, pp. 755–766 (2004)
13. Tutin, A.: Pour une modélisation dynamique des collocations dans les textes. In: Actes du congrès EURALEX 2004, Lorient, France, vol. 1, pp. 207–221 (2004)

14. Heid, U., Ritz, J.: Extracting collocations and their contexts from corpora. In: Actes de COMPLEX-2005, Budapest (2005)
15. Ritz, J., Heid, U.: Extraction tools for collocations and their morphosyntactic specificities. In: Proceedings of LREC-2006, Genova, Italia (2006)
16. Tufiş, D., Ion, R., Ceauşu, A., Stefănescu, D.: Combined Aligners. In: Proceeding of the ACL2005 Workshop on Building and Using Parallel Corpora: Data-driven Machine Translation and Beyond, pp. 107–110. Ann Arbor, Michigan (2005)
17. Kermes, H.: Off-line (and On-line) Text Analysis for Computational Lexicography. Arbeitspapiere des Instituts für Maschinelle Sprachverarbeitung (AIMS) 9(3) (2003)
18. Rousselot, F., Montessuit, N.: LIKES un environnement d'ingénierie linguistique et d'ingénierie des connaissances. In: Workshop INTEX Sofia Bulgarie (2004)
19. Stefanescu, D., Tufis, D., Irimia, E.: Extragerea colocatiilor dintr-un text. In: Atelierul, Resurse lingvistice si instrumente pentru prelucrarea limbii române, pp. 89–95. Universitatea Al.I.Cuza Iasi, Romania (2006)
20. Steinberger, R., Pouliquen, B., Widiger, A., Ignat, C., Erjavec, T., Tufiş, D., Varga, D.: The JRC-Acquis: A multilingual aligned parallel corpus with 20+ languages. In: Proceedings of the 5th LREC Conference, pp. 2142–2147 (2006)
21. Schmid, D.: Probabilistic Part-of-Speech Tagging Using Decision Trees. In: Proceedings of International Conference on New Methods in Language Processing (1994)
22. Ion, R.: TTL: A portable framework for tokenization, tagging and lemmatization of large corpora. Technical Report, Research Institute for Artificial Intelligence, Romanian Academy, Bucharest (2006) (in Romanian)
23. Gledhill, C.: Portée, Pivot, Paradigme: trois termes pour faire le point sur les expressions verbo-nominales. In: Frath, P. (ed.) Zeitschrift für Französische Sprache und Literatur Beihefte, vol. 35, pp. 59–76. Franz Steiner Verlag, Stuttgart (2008)
24. Banks, D.: The Range of Range: A transitivity problem for systemic linguistics. Anglophonia 8, 195–206 (2000)
25. Grimshaw, J., Mester, A.: Light Verbs and θ-Marking. Linguistic Inquiry 19, 205–232 (1988)
26. Gross, G.: Les constructions converses du français, Genève, Droz (1989)
27. Manning, C., Schütze, H.: Foundations of Statistical Natural Language Processing. MIT Press, Cambridge (1999)
28. Todirascu, A., Gledhill, C.: Extracting Collocations in Context: The case of Verb-Noun Constructions in English and Romanian. In: Recherches Anglaises et Nord-Américaines (RANAM), Université Marc Bloch Strasbourg (2008)

Putting Semantics into WordNet's "Morphosemantic" Links

Christiane Fellbaum[1], Anne Osherson[2], and Peter E. Clark[3]

[1] Department of Computer Science
35 Olden Street
Princeton, NJ 08540 (USA)
fellbaum@princeton.edu
[2] Oxford University
St. Hilda's College
1 Cowley Place
Oxford OX4 1DY (U. K.)
anne.osherson@st-hildas.ox.ac.uk
[3] Boeing Research and Technology
P.O. Box 3707
Seattle, WA 98124 (USA)
peter.e.clark@boeing.com

Abstract. To add to WordNet's contents, and specifically to aid automatic reasoning with WordNet, we classify and label the current relations among derivationally and semantically related noun-verb pairs. Manual inspection of thousands of pairs shows that there is no one-to-one mapping of form and meaning for derivational affixes, which exhibit far less regularity than expected. We determine a set of semantic relations found across a number of morphologically defined noun-verb pair classes.

Keywords: WordNet, semantic relations, derivational morphology.

1 Introduction

Natural Language Processing applications such as Information Retrieval and Machine Translation rely critically on lexical resources. Such resources often do not include words that are morphologically derived from base forms on the assumption that morphology is regular and that affixes carry unambiguous information both about the part of speech and the meaning of the derived word. (Many traditional paper dictionaries include derivations, but list them as run-ons without any information on their meaning.) [7] recognized the importance of morphology-based lexical nests for NLP, and created "CatVar," a large-scale database of categorial variations of English lexemes. CatVar relates lexemes belonging to different syntactic categories (part of speech) and sharing a stem, such as *hunger* (n.), *hunger* (v.) and *hungry* (adj.). CatVar is a valuable resource containing some 100,000 unique English word forms; however, no information is given on the words' meanings.

Z. Vetulani and H. Uszkoreit (Eds.): LTC 2007, LNAI 5603, pp. 350–358, 2009.

A complementary resource to CatVar is WordNet [10, [4], which focuses on semantics and expresses the meanings of some 155,000 English words in terms of semantic relations such as synonymy, antonymy, hyponymy, and meronymy. Most of WordNet's relations are paradigmatic, i.e., they link words belonging to the same syntactic category.

[11] describe the addition of "morphosemantic links" to WordNet, which connect words (synset members) that are similar in meaning and where one word is derived from the other by means of a morphological affix. For example, the verb *direct* (defined in WordNet as "guide the actors in plays and films") is linked to the noun *director* (glossed as "someone who supervises the actors and directs the action in the production of a show"). Another link was created for the verb-noun pair *direct/director*, meaning "be in charge of" and "someone who controls resources and expenditures," respectively. Most of these links connect words from different classes (noun-verb, noun-adjective, verb-adjective), though there are also noun-noun pairs like *gang-gangster*.

English derivationally morphology is generally thought to be highly regular and productive, and the addition of a given affix to a base form produces a new word whose meaning differs from that of the base word in a predictable way. For example, adding the affix *-en* to many adjectives yields a verb that denotes a change event, where an entity acquires the property denoted by the adjective:

(1) *red-redden*
   dark-darken
   sad-sadden
   fat-fatten
   etc.

English has many such affixes and associated meaning-change rules [9].

When the morphosemantic links were added to WordNet, their semantic nature was not made explicit, as it was assumed --- following conventional wisdom --- that the meanings of the affixes are highly regular and that there is a one-to-one mapping between the affix forms and their meanings.

2 Labeling Morphosemantic Links

Systems for robust textual inference make extensive use of WordNet as an informal source of knowledge (e.g., MacCartney et al. 2006). We are currently working to transform WordNet into a Knowledge Base that better supports such reasoning and inferencing [3]. WordNet's morphosemantic arcs could be valuable if the semantics of the links were spelled out. For example, while humans can easily infer that the (b,c) statements are entailed by the (a) statements, automatic systems are having trouble with this task:

(2) a. The Zoopraxiscope was invented by Mulbridge.
   b. The inventor of the Zoopraxiscope is Mulbridge.
   c. The Zoopraxiscope is an invention by Mulbridge.

(3) a. Shareholders criticized Dodge, which produces ProHeart devices.
   b. ProHeart is a product.
   c. Dodge is the producer of ProHeart.

Currently, WordNet is able to link *invented* with *inventor* and *invention* in (2) as well as *produce, product,* and *producer* in (3). But it does not tell us that *inventor* and *producer* are the Agents of the events denoted by the verbs *invent* and *produce*, respectively, or that ProHeart and the Zoopraxiscope are products. We considered examples of statements and possible inferences and noticed that in many cases, spelling out the relation between the nouns and verbs in the two sentences would facilitate the evaluation of the entailments.

We began our efforts to add explicit meaning to WordNet's morphosemantic links with those noun-verb pairs where the nouns are derived from the verbs by *-er* and *-or* suffixation (*invent-inventor, produce-producer, build-builder*). We assumed that, with rare exceptions, the nouns denote the Agents of the event referred to by the verb, as expressed by the phrases in (4):

(4) an inventor invents
    a producer produces
    a builder builds
  etc.

We will refer to pattern in (4) as the *Agentive* pattern.

We automatically extracted some 4,000 morphosemantic noun-verb pairs related via *-er* affixation from WordNet. All were manually inspected. False hits were discarded and those pairs that did not conform to the Agentive pattern were placed into a separate file. Instances where the relation between the noun and the verb were deemed too metaphorical were discarded (for example, the verb *tree* (v) "to chase (a bear) up a tree," derived from the noun *tree*, "a tall perenniel plant"). In other cases, the relation was tranpsarent but sufficiently remote to prevent us from recording a link (*crucify* (v) "kill by nailing to a cross", *crucifix* (n) "a cross representing the death of Jesus Christ").

We repeated this process with noun-verb pairs where the deverbal nouns ended in *-al* (*reverse-reversal*), *-ment* (*amaze-amazement*) and *-ion* (*infuse-infusion*). In addition, we extracted meaningfully related pairs where the verb was derived from a noun via *-ize* affixation (*alphabet-alphabetize*) or from an adjective by means of the addition of *-ify* (*beauty-beautify*).

3 How Regular Are Morphosemantics?

For the *-er* derivations, we expected to find few "exceptions" to the Agentive pattern. But surprisingly, only two thirds of the pairs could be classified as in (4). For the remaining pairs, different semantic relations were formulated and the pairs were labeled accordingly (words in parentheses identify the intended senses of polysemous nouns).

(5) Instrument
    rule- ruler (measuring stick)
    shred- shredder
    aspirate- aspirator

Instruments are distinct from Agents: an Instrument does not act alone but implies an Agent who controls it, usually intentionally. Both can co-occur as arguments of the verb: *John ruled straight lines with his ruler.* [17] distinguished "enabling" from "facilitating" instruments: the former but not the latter may appear in subject position (*the shredder shredded the paper* vs. **the ruler ruled the lines*).

   (6) Inanimate Agent/Cause
     block-blocker (drug)
     whiten-whitener
     sense-sensor
     soften-softener

Inanimate Agents or Causers are often substances and, unlike many Instruments, can act without the direct control of a human Agent, as evidenced by the fact that they can occupy the subject position: *the softener softened the clothes* vs. **the ruler ruled the lines.*

   (7) Body part
     adduct-adductor

Like Inanimate Agents/Causers, Body Parts take the place of Agents in events. The *adductor* muscle *adducts*, etc. Unlike with Agents, volition and intention are not implied.

   (8) Purpose/Function
     line-liner (coating/layer)
     read- reader (book)
     train- trainer (shoes)

The verbs express the intended purpose of function of the nouns: *trainers* are for *training*, *readers* are for *reading*, etc.

   (9) Vehicle
     commute-commuter (train)
     cruise-cruiser (boat)

The event denoted by the verb takes place in the vehicle that the noun refers to.

   (10) Location
     plant-planter(pot)
     sleep-sleeper (sofabed)
     hang-hanger
     lock- locker

The noun denotes the Location of the event or state expressed by the verb: one *plants* something in a *planter, sleeps* in a *sleeper, hangs* something on a *hanger, locks* something in a *locker*, etc.

   (11) Undergoer/Patient
     break-breaker (wave)
     broil-broiler (chicken)
     steam-steamer (clam)
     loan- loaner

The noun denotes the Undergoer of the event: the wave (*breaker*) *breaks*, the chicken (*broiler*) *broils*, a *loaner* is an item that has is *loaned*, etc.

(12) Event
    dine-dinner
    pelt-pelter

A *dining* event is a *dinner*, *pelting* rain is a *pelter*, etc.

(13) Result or Cause
    groan-groaner (bad joke)
    err-error

The event produces the entity denoted by the noun (*erring* results in an *error*), or, conversely, the noun causes the event (*groaner-groan*). We do not distinguish between eventive and product readings of the Result, though WordNet often draws this regular distinction among polysemous nouns.

Table 1 shows the number of pairs for each semantic class among all the *-er*-related pairs that were extracted from WordNet 3.0.

Table 1. Distribution of *-er* verb-noun pair relations

Agent	2,584
Instrument	482
Inanimate agent/Cause	302
Event	224
Result	97
Undergoer	62
Body part	49
Purpose	57
Vehicle	36
Location	36

4 Relations

The same relations turn up in the classification of other morphosemantically linked noun-verb pairs in WordNet that we have inspected.. The *-er/-or* pairs exhibit a particularly wide spectrum of relations; some other classes we have looked at so far include pairs that can be classified with a subset of categories only and the semantics of the affix seems to be somewhat more regular. Some affix-based classes suggest categories not found in the *-er* class.

Categories could be distinguished more or less finely (e.g., Result and Cause could be separated) or collapsed (Body Part and Inanimate Cause), and our classification is somewhat subjective, though we tried to motivate it syntactically wherever possible. For example, Purpose is different from Instrument, in that it does not allow a PP headed by *with*, a characteristic of Instruments. Similarly, Vehicles are expressed in a PP headed by a spatial proposition (*in/on*, etc.) rather than *with*, though Vehicles could be considered a subclass of Locations. Instruments presuppose an Agent who acts with intent and volition and Instrument and Agent must therefore be distinguished. Locations are where the event denoted by the verb takes place and where the Agent or Patient is located.

The labels we assigned refer to well known semantic categories and have been studied or applied in different contexts. The Cases proposed by [5], the FrameElements of FrameNet ([15]) as well the Semantic Roles that have been the target of recent automatic labeling efforts [6] all refer to sets of categories including Agents, Undergoers/Patients, Instruments, etc.

5 Polysemy

We saw that the -er suffix is polysemous; although the Agentive pattern is the default reading for deverbal nouns, there are several other patterns. For example, the verb *broil* is paired with three distinct senses of the noun *broiler* (Agent, Location, and Undergoer). Similarly, we have two pairs *plant-planter* (Agent and Location), just as in the case of *dine-diner*. Some highly polysemous noun-verb pairs enter into an even larger number of relations involving different senses of both the nouns and the verbs (*run-runner, roll-roller*).

For virtually all cases we examined, the default agentive reading of the noun is always possible, though it is not always lexicalized (and does not have an entry in WordNet or other lexicons). Speakers easily generate and process ad-hoc nouns like *planter* (gardener), but only in its (non-default) location reading ("pot") is the noun part of the lexicon, as its meaning cannot be guessed from its structure.

Examining other morphological patterns, we found that polysemy of affixes is widespread. Thus, nouns derived from verbs by -ion suffixation exhibit regular polysemy between event and result readings (*the exam lasted two hours/the exam was lying on his desk*, [14]).

We also fnd one-to-many mappings for semantic patterns and affixes: a semantic category can be expressed by means of several distinct affixes, though there seems to be a default semantics associated with a given affix. Thus, while many -er nouns denote Events, event nouns are regularly derived from verbs via -ment suffixation (*bomb-bombardment, punish-punishment*, etc.)

Patterns are partly predictable from the thematic structure of the verb. Thus, nouns derived from unergative verbs (intransitives whose subject is an Agent) are Agents, and the pattern is productive:

(14) *runner, dancer, singer, speaker, sleeper,*

Nouns derived from unaccusative verbs (intransitives whose subject is a Patient/Undergoer) are Patients:

(15) *breaker* (wave), *streamer* (banner)

This pattern is far from productive:

(16) *faller, ?arriver, ?leaver,

Many verbs have both transitive (causative) and intransitive readings (cf. [8]):

(17)a. The cook roasted the chicken
   b. The chicken was roasting

For many such verbs, there are two corresponding readings of the derived nouns: both the *host* in (17a) and the chicken in the (17b) can be referred to as a *roaster*. Other examples of Agent and Patient nouns derived from the transitive and intransitive readings of verbs are *(best)seller, (fast) developer, broiler*. But the pattern is not productive, as nouns like *cracker, stopper*, and *freezer* show.

6 Related Work

[2] examine the large number of English noun-verb pairs related by zero-affix morphology, i.e., homographic pairs of semantically related verbs and nouns (*roof, lunch, Xerox*, etc.) [2] note that this pattern of deriving verbs from nouns in English is productive and speakers readily interpret the meaning of novel verbs based on their knowledge of the nouns, even though the relations among verbs and nouns do not permit a unified semantic description.   [2] distinguish a large number of semantic noun classes that have spawned derived verbs, including Agent, Location, Instrument, Body Part, Meals, Elements, and Proper Names. [2] conclude that the meanings of the verbs depend on the time, place and circumstances of their use and are somewhat conventionalized.

In the context of the EuroWordNet project [16], [13] manually established noun-verb and adjective-verb pairs that were both morphologically and semantically related. (EuroWordNet was based on WordNet version 1.5, which lacked the morphosemantic relations added in version 2.0). Of the relations that [13] considered, the following match the ones we identified: Agent, Instrument, Location, Patient, Cause. But the methodology of [13] differed from ours. While we proceeded from the previously classified morphosemantic links and assumed a default semantic relation for pairs with a given affix, [13] selected pairs of word forms that were both morphologically related and where at least one member had only a single sense in WordNet. These were then manually disambiguated and semantically classified, regardless of regular morphosemantic patterns.

[12] automatically enrich Czech WordNet with "derivational nests," groups of morphologically and semantically related words. Czech morphology is very rich and relatively regular, allowing [12] to construct a tool that generates new word forms derived from stems by adding affixes associated with specific semantics. The noun-verb relations that the Czech team identified overlap with those reported on here for English. (Czech WordNet, and the morphological-semantic links made by [12], are linked to the Princeton WordNet.)

7 Conclusions and Future Work

Manual inspection of morphologically related verb-noun pair classes shows that, contrary to what is commonly assumed, there is no one-to-one mapping of affixes and meaning. Rather, affixes can be highly polysemous, and a given affix can be associated with several meanings, though there seems to a default reading for each affix (such as the Agentive pattern for -er deverbal nouns).When a default reading is not applicable, speakers can compute the reading from context, as suggested by [2]. Homographic derivations, like *sleeper* ("sleeping person" vs. "sleeping car"), like all cases of polysemy, require separate entries for each sense both in speakers' mental lexicon as well as in computational lexicons.

Conversely, a given semantic pattern can be associated with more than one affix. For example, both -al and -ment can denote deverbal events, as in *disbursal, disbursement* and *committal, commitment*, making the two derived nouns synonyms in each case.

Our work so far, and the independent efforts by [13] and [12] suggest that the meanings of affixes can be classified into a finite, relatively small number of semantic categories. It is important to note that the inventory of relations we presented here is somewhat arbitrary; one could certainly propose a more fine-grained or a more coarse-grained one. We expect to encode additional relations as we consider other types of morphosemantic pairs, though we anticipate a fairly small number of relations, most likely a subset of those discussed by [2]. We started to explore the encoding of these relations crosslinguistically, focusing on several Bantu languages [1]. Encoding the semantics of the relations in WordNet will make it a more useful tool for automated reasoning and inferencing.

Acknowledgments. This work was sponsored by the DTO AQUAINT program. We thank our Stanford colleagues Christopher Manning, Daniel Jurafsky, Andrew Ng and Rion Snow for valuable discussions.

References

1. Bosch, S., Fellbaum, C., Pala, K.P.: (in prep.) Derivational Morphology in Bantu, Czech, and English. To appear in the Proceedings of ALASA/HLT track
2. Clark, E., Clark, H.: When nouns surface as verbs. Language 55, 767–811 (1979)
3. Clark, P., Harrison, P., Thompson, J., Murray, W., Hobbs, J., Fellbaum, C.: On the Role of Lexical and World Knowledge in RTE3. In: ACL-PASCAL Workshop on Textual Entailment and Paraphrases, Prague, CZ (June 2007)
4. Fellbaum, C.: WordNet: An Electronic Lexical Database. MIT Press, Cambridge (1998)
5. Fillmore, C.: The Case for Case. In: Bach, E., Harms, R. (eds.) Universals in linguistic theory. Holt, NY (1968)
6. Gildea, D., Jurafksy, D.: Automatic Labeling of Semantic Roles, 512-520 (2000)
7. Habash, N., Dorr, B.: A Categorial Variation Database for English. In: Proceedings of the North American Association for Computational Linguistics, Edmonton, Canada, pp. 96–102 (2003)
8. Levin, B.: English Verb Classes and Alternations. University of Chicago Press, Chicago (1993)
9. Marchand, H.: The categories and types of present-day English word formation. Beck, Munich (1969)
10. Miller, G.A.: WordNet: a lexical database for English. Communications of the ACM 38(11), 39–41 (1995)

11. Miller, G.A., Fellbaum, C.: Morphosemantic links in WordNet. Traitement automatique de langue 44(2), 69–80 (2003)
12. Pala, K., Hlaváková, D.: Derivational Relations in Czech WordNet. In: Proceedings fo the Workshop on Balto-Slavonic, ACL, Prague, pp. 75–81 (2007)
13. Peters, W. (n.d.) The English wordnet, EWN Deliverable D032D033. University of Sheffield, England
14. Pustejovsky, J.: The Generative Lexicon. MIT Press, Cambridge (1995)
15. Ruppenhofer, B.C., Fillmore, C.J.: The FrameNet Database and Software Tools. In: Braasch, A., Povlsen, C. (eds.) Proceedings of the Tenth Euralex International Congress, Copenhagen, Denmark, vol. I, pp. 371–375 (2002)
16. Vossen, P. (ed.): EuroWordNet. Kluwer, Dordrecht (1998)
17. Wojcik, R.: Where do Instrumental NPs come From? In: Shibatani, M. (ed.) Syntax and Semantics, vol. 6, pp. 165–180 (1976)

Leveraging Parallel Corpora and Existing Wordnets for Automatic Construction of the Slovene Wordnet

Darja Fišer

Department of Translation, Faculty of Arts, University of Ljubljana, Aškerčeva 2,
1000 Ljubljana, Slovenia
darja.fiser@guest.arnes.si

Abstract. The paper reports on a series of experiments conducted in order to test the feasibility of automatically generating synsets for Slovene wordnet. The resources used were the multilingual parallel corpus of George Orwell's Nineteen Eighty-Four and wordnets for several languages. First, the corpus was word-aligned to obtain multilingual lexicons and then these lexicons were compared to the wordnets in various languages in order to disambiguate the entries and attach appropriate synset ids to Slovene entries in the lexicon. Slovene lexicon entries sharing the same attached synset id were then organized into a synset. The results obtained by the different settings in the experiment are evaluated against a manually created gold standard and also checked by hand.

Keywords: wordnet, parallel corpora, word alignment.

1 Introduction

Research teams have approached the construction of their wordnets in different ways depending on the lexical resources they had at their disposal. There is no doubt that manual construction of an independent wordnet by experts is the most reliable technique as it yields the best results in terms of both linguistic soundness and accuracy of the created database. But such an endeavor is an extremely labor-intensive and time-consuming process, which is why alternative, fully automated or semi-automatic approaches have been proposed that have tried to leverage the existing resources in order to facilitate faster and easier development of wordnets.

The lexical resources that have proved useful for such a task fall into several categories. (1) Princeton WordNet (PWN) is an indispensable resource and serves as the backbone of new wordnets in approaches following the expand model [19]. This model takes a fixed set of synsets from PWN which are then translated into the target language, preserving the structure of the original wordnet. The cost of the expand model is that the resulting wordnets are heavily biased by the PWN, which can be problematic when the source and target linguistic systems are significantly different. Nevertheless, due to its greater simplicity, the expand model has been adopted in a number of projects, such as the BalkaNet [17] and MultiWordNet [13].

(2) A very popular approach is to link English entries from machine-readable bilingual dictionaries to PWN synsets under the assumption that their counterparts in the target language correspond to the same synset [10].

Z. Vetulani and H. Uszkoreit (Eds.): LTC 2007, LNAI 5603, pp. 359–368, 2009.

A well-known problem with this approach is that bilingual dictionaries are generally not concept-based but follow traditional lexicographic principles, which is the biggest obstacle to overcome if this technique is to be useful is the disambiguation of dictionary entries.

(3) Machine-readable monolingual dictionaries have been used as a source for extracting taxonomy trees by parsing definitions to obtain genus terms and then disambiguating the genus word, resulting in a hyponymy tree [4]. Problems that are inherent to the monolingual dictionary (circularity, inconsistencies, genus omission) as well as limitations with genus term disambiguation must be borne in mind when this approach is considered.

(4) Once taxonomies in the target language are available, they can be mapped to the target wordnet, enriching it with valuable information and semantic links at relatively low cost, or they can be mapped to ontologies in other languages in order to create multilingual ontologies [5].

Our attempt in the construction of the Slovene wordnet will be to benefit from the resources we have available, which are mainly corpora. Based on the assumption that translations are a plausible source of semantics we will use a multilingual parallel corpus to extract semantically relevant information. The idea that semantic insights can be derived from the translational relation has already been explored by e.g. [14], [1] and [9]. It is our hypothesis that senses of ambiguous words in one language are often translated into distinct words in another language. We further believe that if two or more words are translated into the same word in another language, then they often share some element of meaning. This is why we assume that the multilingual-alignment based approach will convey sense distinctions of a polysemous source word or yield synonym sets. The paper is organized as follows: the next section gives a brief overview of the related work after which the methodology for our experiment is explained in detail. Sections 2.1 and 2.2 present and evaluate the results obtained in the experiment and the last section gives conclusions and future work.

1.1 Related Work

The following approaches are similar to ours in that they rely on word-aligned parallel corpora. [2] identified the different senses of a word based on corpus evidence and then grouped them in semantic fields based on overlapping translations which indicate semantic relatedness of expressions. The fields and semantic features of their members were used to construct semilattices which were then linked to PWN. [1] took a word-aligned English-Arabic corpus as input and clustered source words that were translated with the same target word. Then the appropriate sense for the words in clusters was identified on the basis of word sense proximity in PWN. Finally, the selected sense tags were propagated to the respective contexts in the parallel texts. Sense discrimination with parallel corpora has also been investigated by [9] who used the same corpus as input data as we did for this experiment but then used the extracted lexicon to cluster words into senses. Finding synonyms with word-aligned corpora was also at the core of work by [18] whose approach differs from ours in the definition of what synonyms are, which in their case is a lot more permissive than in ours.

2 Methodology

In the experiment we used the parallel corpus of George Orwell's Nineteen Eighty-Four [9] in five languages: English, Czech, Romanian, Bulgarian and Slovene. Although the corpus is a literary text, the style of writing is ordinary, modern and not overly domain-specific. Furthermore, because the 100,000 word corpus is already sentence-aligned and tagged, the preprocessing phase was not demanding. First, all but the content-words (nouns, main verbs, adjectives and adverbs) were discarded to facilitate the word-alignment process. A few formatting and encoding modifications were performed in order to conform to the required input format by the alignment tool.

The corpus was word-aligned with Uplug, a modular tool for automated corpus alignment [16]. Uplug converts text files into xml, aligns the files at sentence-level, then aligns them at word-level and generates a bilingual lexicon. Because our files had already been formatted and sentence-aligned, the first two stages were skipped and we proceeded directly to word-alignment. The advanced setting was used which first creates basic clues for word alignments, then runs GIZA++ [12] with standard settings and aligns words with the existing clues. The alignments with the highest reliability scores are learned and the last two steps are repeated three times. This is Uplug's slowest standard setting but, considering the relatively small size of the corpus, it was used because it yielded the best results. The output of the alignment process is a file with information on word link certainty between the aligned pair of words and their unique ids (see Figure 1).

Word ids were used to extract the lemmas from the corpus and to create bilingual lexicons. In order to reduce the noise in the lexicon as much as possible, only 1:1 links between words of the same part of speech were taken into account and all alignments occurring only once were discarded. The generated lexicons contain all the translations of an English word in the corpus with alignment frequency, part of speech and the corresponding word ids (see Figure 2). The size of each lexicon is about 1,500 entries.

```
<link certainty="-220" xtargets="Oen.1.1.5.6 Oen.1.1.5.7;Osl.1.2.6.6" id="SL0.35">
<wordLink certainty="0.0166666666666667" lexPair="watched;opazujejo"
xtargets="Oen.1.1.5.6.4;Osl.1.2.6.6.3" />
<wordLink certainty="0.0166666666666667" lexPair="wire;oddajnik"
xtargets="Oen.1.1.5.7.3;Osl.1.2.6.6.9" />
<wordLink certainty="0.0198634796329659" lexPair="was time;čas"
xtargets="Oen.1.1.5.6.1+Oen.1.1.5.6.5;Osl.1.2.6.6.2" />
<wordLink certainty="0.0125" lexPair="conceivable;Mogoče"
xtargets="Oen.1.1.5.6.3;Osl.1.2.6.6.1" />
<wordLink certainty="0.0214285714285715" lexPair="rate;drugače"
xtargets="Oen.1.1.5.7.1;Osl.1.2.6.6.6" /></link>
```

Fig. 1. An example of word links

The bilingual lexicons were used to create multilingual lexicons. English lemmas and their word ids were used as a cross-over and all the translations of an English word occurring more than twice were included. If an English word was translated by a single word in one language and by several words in another language, all the variants were included in the lexicon because it is assumed the difference in translation either signifies a different sense of the English word or it is a synonym to another translation variant (see the translations for the English word "army" in Figure 3 which is translated by the same words in all the languages except in Slovene). Whether the variants are synonymous or belong to different senses of a polysemous expression is to be determined in the next stage. In this way, 3 multilingual lexicons were created: En-Cs-Si (1,703 entries), En-Cs-Ro-Si (1,226 entries) and En-Cs-Ro-Bg-Si (803 entries).

```
3 0.075 age,n,doba,n oen.2.9.14.16.1.2;oen.2.9.14.16.3.2;oen.2.9.26.3.5.2;
2 0.154 age,n,obdobje,n oen.2.9.26.3.10.3;oen.2.9.26.4.6.5;
4 0.075 age,n,starost,n oen.1.4.24.1.1;oen.1.8.39.4.2;oen.2.4.55.4.3;
5 0.118 age,n,vek,n oen.1.2.38.2.1.8;oen.1.2.38.2.1.3;oen.1.2.38.2.1.1;
4 0.078 aged,a,star,a oen.1.6.4.3.12;oen.1.8.94.4.5;oen.2.1.53.12.4;
2 0.068 agree,v,strinjati,v oen.1.8.50.4.1;oen.3.4.7.1.2;
9 0.104 aim,n,cilj,n oen.1.4.24.10.6;oen.1.5.27.1.3;oen.2.8.55.6.2;
2 0.051 air,n,izraz,n oen.2.8.19.1.9;oen.2.8.52.2.3;
6 0.080 air,n,videz,n oen.2.5.2.7.12;oen.2.5.6.15.16;oen.3.1.19.6.7;
14 0.065 air,n,zrak,n oen.1.1.6.7.7;oen.1.1.7.2.12;oen.1.2.29.2.7;oen.1.3.3.7.3;
```

Fig. 2. An example of word links

The obtained multilingual lexicons were then compared against the already existing wordnets in the corresponding languages. For English, the Princeton WordNet [6] was used while for Czech, Romanian and Bulgarian wordnets from the BalkaNet project [17] were used. The decision for using BalkaNet wordnets is twofold: first, the languages included in the project correspond to the multilingual corpus we had available, and second, the wordnets were developed in parallel, they cover a common sense inventory and are also aligned to one another as well as to PWN, making the intersection easier.

2 (v)	answer	odgovoriti	odpovědět	răspunde	odgovoriti
2 (n)	argument	argument	argument	argument	argument
3 (n)	arm	roka	paže	braț	ruka
3 (n)	arm	roka	ruka	braț	ruka
2 (n)	army	armada	armáda	armată	armija
2 (n)	army	vojska	armáda	armată	armija

Fig. 3. An example of word links

If a match was found between a lexicon entry and a literal of the same part of speech in the corresponding wordnet, the synset id was remembered for that language. If after examining all the existing wordnets there was an overlap of synset ids across all the languages (except Slovene, of course) for the same lexicon entry, it was assumed that the words in question all describe the concept marked with this id. Finally, the concept was extended to the Slovene part of the multilingual lexicon entry and the synset id common to all the languages was assigned to it. All the Slovene words sharing the same synset id were treated as synonyms and were grouped into synsets (see Figure 4).

Other language-independent information (e.g. part of speech, domain, semantic relations) was inherited from the Princeton WordNet and an xml file was created.

The automatically generated Slovene wordnet was loaded into VisDic, a graphical application for viewing and editing dictionary databases stored in XML format [8]. In the experiment, four different settings were tested: SLWN1 was created from an English-Slovene lexicon compared against the English wordnet; for SLWN2 Czech was added; SLWN3 was created using these as well as Romanian, and SLWN4 was obtained by including Bulgarian as well.

```
ENG20-03500773-n luč svetilka
ENG20-04210535-n miza mizica
ENG20-05291564-n kraj mesto prostor
ENG20-05597519-n doktrina nauk
ENG20-05903215-n beseda vrsta
ENG20-06069783-n dokument papir košček
ENG20-06672930-n glas zvok
ENG20-07484626-n družba svet
ENG20-07686671-n armada vojska
ENG20-07859631-n generacija rod
ENG20-07995813-n kraj mesto prostor
ENG20-08095650-n kraj mesto prostor
ENG20-08692715-n zemlja tla svet
ENG20-09620847-n deček fant
ENG20-09793944-n jetnik ujetnik
ENG20-10733600-n luč svetloba
```

Fig. 4. An example of the created synsets for Slovene

2.1 Results

In our previous work, a version of the Slovene wordnet (SLOWN0) was created from Serbian wordnet [11] was translated into Slovene with a Serbian-Slovene dictionary [3]. The main disadvantage of that approach was the inadequate disambiguation of polysemous words, therefore requiring extensive manual editing of the results. SLOWN0 contains 4,688 synsets, all from Base Concept Sets 1 and 2. Nouns prevail (3,210) which are followed by verbs (1,442) and adjectives (36). There are no adverbs in BCS1 and 2, which is why none were translated into Slovene. Average synset length (number of literals per synset) is 5.9 and the synsets cover 119 domains (see Table 2).

In the latest approach to further extend the existing core wordnet for Slovene we attempted to take advantage of several available resources (parallel corpora and wordnets for other languages). At the same we time interested in an approach that would yield more reliable synset candidates. This is why we experimented with four different settings to induce Slovene synsets, each using more resources and including more languages in order to establish which one is the most efficient from the cost and benefit point of view.

SLOWN1: This approach, using resources for two languages, is the most similar to our previous experiment, only that this time an automatically generated lexicon was used instead of a bilingual glossary and the much larger English wordnet was used instead of the Serbian one (See Table 1). SLOWN1 contains 6,746 synsets belonging to all three Base Concept Sets and beyond. A lot more verb (2,310) and adjective synsets (1,132) were obtained, complemented by adverbs (340) as well. Average synset length is much lower (2.0), which could be a sign of a much higher precision than in the previous wordnet, while the domain space has grown (126).

Table 1. Statistics for the existing wordnets

	PWN	CSWN	ROWN	BGWN	GOLDST
synsets	115,424	28,405	18,560	21,105	1,179
avg. l/s	1.7	1.5	1.6	2.111	2.1
bcs1	1,218	1,218	1,189	1,218	320
bcs2	3,471	3,471	3,362	3,471	804
bcs3	3,827	3,823	3,593	3,827	55
other	106,908	19,893	10,416	12,589	0
domains	164	156	150	155	85
nouns	79,689	20,773	12,382	13,924	828
max l/s	28	12	17	10	8
avg. l/s	1.8	1.4	1.7	1.8	1.9
verbs	13,508	5,126	4,603	4,163	343
max l/s	24	10	12	18	10
avg. l/s	1.8	1.8	2.1	3.6	2.4
adjectives	18,563	2,128	833	3,009	8
max l/s	25	8	11	9	4
avg. l/s	1.7	1.4	1.5	1.7	1.6
adverbs	3,664	164	742	9	0
max l/s	11	4	10	2	0
avg. l/s	1.6	1.5	1.6	1.2	0

SLOWN2: Starting from the assumption that polysemous words tend to be realized differently in different languages and that translations themselves could be used to discriminate between the different senses of the words as well as to determine relations among lexemes Czech was added to the lexicon as well as in the lexicon-wordnet comparison stage. As a result, the number of obtained synsets is much lower (1,501) as is the number of domains represented by the wordnet (87). Average synset length is 1.8 and nouns still represent the largest portion of the wordnet (870).

SLOWN3: It was assumed that by adding another language recall would fall but precision would increase and we wished to test this hypothesis in a step-by-step way. In this setting, the multilingual lexicon was therefore extended with Romanian translations and the Romanian wordnet was used to obtain an intersection between lexicon entries and wordnet synsets. The number of synsets falls slightly in SLOWN3 but the average number of literals per synset increases. The domain space is virtually the same, as is the proportion of nouns, verbs and adverbs with adjectives falling the most drastically.

SLOWN4: Finally, Bulgarian was added both in the lexicon and wordnet lookup stage. The last wordnet created within this experiment only contains 549 synsets with 1.8 as average synset length. The number of noun and verb synsets is almost the same and in this case no adverbial synsets were obtained. The number of domains represented in this wordnet is 60 (see Table 2).

Table 2. Results obtained in the experiment

	SLOWN0	SLOWN1	SLOWN2	SLOWN3	SLOWN4
synsets	4,688	6,746	1,501	1,372	549
avg l/s	5.9	2.0	1.8	2.4	1.8
bcs1	1,219	588	324	293	166
bcs2	3,469	1,063	393	359	172
bcs3	0	663	230	22	99
other	0	4,432	554	496	112
domains	119	126	87	83	60
nouns	3,210	2,964	870	671	291
max l/s	40	10	7	6	4
avg l/s	4.8	1.4362	1.4	1.4	1.7
verbs	1,442	2,310	483	639	249
max l/s	96	76	15	30	26
avg l/s	8.4	3.3	2.7	3.7	2.6
adjectives	36	1,132	118	32	9
max l/s t	30	4	4	2	2
avg l/s	8.2	1.2	1.1	1.0	1.1
adverbs	0	340	30	30	0
max l/s	0	20	5	3	0
avg l/s	0	2.1	1.6	1.4	0

2.2 Evaluation and Discussion of the Results

In order to evaluate the results obtained in the experiment and to decide which setting performs best the generated synsets were evaluated against a gold standard that was created by hand. The gold standard contains 1,179 synsets from all three Base Concept Sets. This is why evaluation only takes into account the automatically generated synsets that belong to these three categories. Average synset length in the gold standard is 2.1 which is comparable to Bulgarian wordnet and to the Slovene wordnets created within this experiment. Synsets belong to 80 different domains, a major part of them are nouns (828) but there are no adverbs in the gold standard, which is why they will not be evaluated. Also, since only three adjective synsets overlapped in the gold standard and the generated wordnets, they were excluded from the evaluation as well.

Table 3 shows the results of the automatic evaluation of the wordnets obtained in the experiment. The manually created gold standard that was used for evaluation was created by hand and contains multi-word literals as well. The automatic method presented in this paper is limited to one-word translation candidates, which is why multi-word literals were disregarded in the evaluation. The most straightforward approach for evaluation of the quality of the obtained wordnets would be to compare the generated synsets with the corresponding synsets from the gold standard. But in this way we would be penalizing the automatically induced wordnets for missing literals which are not part of the vocabulary of the corpus that was used to generate the lexicons in the first place. Instead we compared literals in the gold standard and in the automatically induced wordnets with regard to which synsets they appear in.

Table 3. Automatic evaluation of the results

	SLOWN0	SLOWN1	SLOWN2	SLOWN3	SLOWN4
nouns	261	322	223	179	103
precision	50.6%	70.2%	78.4%	73.0%	84.1%
recall	89.3%	87.3%	81.7%	77.4%	78.2%
f-measure	64.6%	77.8%	80.0%	75.1%	81.1%
verbs	174	127	79	69	53
precision	43.8%	35.8%	54.2%	37.5%	46.0%
recall	74.7%	70.3%	66.2%	72.5%	59.1%
f-measure	55.3%	47.4%	59.6%	49.4%	51.7%
total	445	449	302	248	156
prec. total	48.0%	60.6%	72.3%	63.2%	71.3%
recall total	83.5%	82.6%	77.6%	76.2%	71.5%
f-m total	61.0%	69.9%	74.9%	69.1%	71.4%

This information was used to calculate precision, recall and f-measure. This seems a fairer approach because of the restricted input vocabulary. As can be seen from Table 3, the approach taken in this experiment outperforms the previous attempt in which a bilingual dictionary was used as far as precision is concerned. Also, the method works much better for nouns than for verbs, regardless of the setting used.

In general, there is a steady growth in precision and a corresponding fall in recall with a gradual growth in f-measure (see Table 3). The best results are obtained by merging resources for English, Czech and Slovene (74.89%), when adding Romanian the results fall (69.10%) and then rise again when Bulgarian is added, reaching almost the same level as setting 2 (71.34). It is interesting to see the drop in quality when Romanian is added; this might occur either because the word-alignment is worse for English-Romanian (because of a freer translation and consequently poorer quality of sentence-alignment of the corpus), or it might be due to the properties of the Romanian wordnet version we used for the experiment, which is smaller than other wordnets.

Table 4. Manual evaluation of the results

	SLOWN1	SLOWN2	SLOWN3	SLOWN4
total no. of syns	165 (100%)	165 (100%)	165 (100%)	165 (100%)
fully correct syns	96 (58.2%)	103 (62.4%)	119 (72.1%)	134 (81.2%)
no correct lit.	6 (3.6%)	5 (3.0%)	10 (6.0%)	9 (5.4%)
at least 1 corr lit.	43 (26.0%)	37 (22.4%)	20 (12.1%)	14 (8.4%)
hypernym	3 (1.8%)	3 (1.8%)	3 (1.8%)	0 (0.0%)
hyponym	6 (3.6%)	6 (3.6%)	10 (6.0%)	6 (3.6%)
sem. related lit.	2 (1.2%)	4 (2.4%)	2 (1.2%)	1 (3.6%)
more err. types	8 (4.8%)	5 (3.0%)	0 (0.0%)	0 (0.0%)

In order to gain insight into what actually goes on with the synsets in the different settings, we generated an intersection of all the induced wordnets and checked them manually. Automatic evaluation shows that the method works best for nouns, which is why we focus on them in the rest of this section. The sample we used for manual evaluation contains 165 synsets which are the same in all the generated wordnets and can therefore be directly compared. In manual evaluation we checked whether the generated synset obtains a correct literal at all. We classified errors into several categories: the wrong literal is a hypernym of the concept in question (more general), the wrong literal is a hyponym of the concept (more specific), the concept is semantically related to the concept (meronym, holonym, antonym), the literal is simply wrong. The results of manual evaluation of the small sample confirm the results obtained by automatic evaluation. However, it was interesting to see that even though SLOWN2 contains slightly more errors than SLOWN4, there is more variation (more synset members) in SLOWN2 which makes it a more useful resource and is therefore the preferred setting (see Table 4). Unsurprisingly, the least problematic synsets are those lexicalizing specific concepts (such as *"rat"*, *"army"*, *"kitchen"*) and the most difficult ones were those containing highly polysemous words and describing vague concepts (e.g. *"face"* which as a noun has 13 different senses in PWN or *"place"* which as a noun has 16 senses).

3 Conclusions and Future Work

Lexical semantics is far from being trivial for computers as well as humans. This can be seen by relatively low inter-annotator agreement scores when humans are asked to assign a sense to a word from the parallel corpus as was used in this study (approx. 75% for wn senses as reported by [9]). Comparing the size of the lexicons as well as the results obtained in the presented set of experiments they lie within these figures, showing that the method is promising for nouns (much less for other parts of speech) and should be investigated further on other, larger and more varied corpora. The next step will therefore be the application of the second setting yielding the best results in this experiment to the multilingual and much larger ACQUIS corpus [15]. Attempts have already been made to word-align the ACQUIS corpus [7] but their alignments are not useful for our method as their alignments vary greatly in length and also include function words. This is why the word-alignment phase will have to be done from scratch, a non-trivial task because a lot of preprocessing (tagging, lemmatization and sentence-alignment) is required.

The results could further be improved by using the latest versions of the wordnets. The ones that were used in this experiment are from 2004 when the BalkaNet project ended but the teams have continued developing their wordnets and they are now much larger and better resources.

References

1. Diab, M.: The Feasibility of Bootstrapping an Arabic WordNet leveraging Parallel Corpora and an English WordNet. In: Proceedings of the Arabic Language Technologies and Resources, NEMLAR, Cairo (2004)
2. Dyvik, H.: Translations as semantic mirrors: from parallel corpus to wordnet. Revised version of paper presented at the ICAME 2002 Conference in Gothenburg (2002)
3. Erjavec, T., Fišer, D.: Building Slovene WordNet. In: Proceedings of the 5th International Conference on Language Resources and Evaluation LREC 2006, Genoa, Italy, May 24-26 (2006)

4. Farreres, X., Rigau, G., Rodrguez, H.: Using WordNet for Building WordNets. In: Proceedings of COLING-ACL Workshop on Usage of WordNet in Natural Language Processing Systems, Montreal, Canada (1998)
5. Farreres, X., Gibert, K., Rodriguez, H.: Towards Binding Spanish Senses to Wordnet Senses through Taxonomy Alignment. In: Proceedings of the Second Global WordNet Conference, Brno, Czech Republic, pp. 259–264 (2004)
6. Fellbaum, C.: WordNet: An Electronic Lexical Database. MIT Press, Cambridge (1998)
7. Giguet, E., Luquet, P.-S.: Multilingual Lexical Database Generation from Parallel Texts in 20 European Languages with Endogenous Resources. In: Proceedings of the COLING/ACL 2006 Main Conference Poster Sessions (2006)
8. Horak, A., Smrž, P.: New Features of Wordnet Editor VisDic. Romanian Journal of Information Science and Technology Special Issue 7(1-2) (2000)
9. Ide, N., Erjavec, T., Tufis, D.: Sense Discrimination with Parallel Corpora. In: Proceedings of ACL 2002 Workshop on Word Sense Disambiguation: Recent Successes and Future Directions, Philadelphia, pp. 54–60 (2002)
10. Knight, K., Luk, S.: Building a Large-Scale Knowledge Base for Machine Translation. In: Proceedings of the American Association of Artificial Intelligence AAAI-1994, Seattle, WA (1994)
11. Krstev, C., Pavlović-Lažetić, G., Vitas, D., Obradović, I.: Using textual resources in developing Serbian wordnet. Romanian Journal of Information Science and Technology 7(1-2), 147–161 (2004)
12. Och, F.J., Ney, H.: A Systematic Comparison of Various Statistical Alignment Models. Computational Linguistics 29(1) (2003)
13. Pianta, E., Bentivogli, L., Girardi, C.: MultiWordNet: developing an aligned multilingual. In: Proceedings of the First International Conference on Global WordNet, Mysore, India (2002)
14. Resnik, P., Yarowsky, D.: A perspective on word sense disambiguation methods and their evaluation. In: ACL-SIGLEX Workshop Tagging Text with Lexical Semantics: Why, What, and How?, Washington, D.C, pp. 79–86 (1997)
15. Ralf, S., Pouliquen, B., Widiger, A., Ignat, C., Erjavec, T., Tufiş, D., Varga, D.: The JRC-Acquis: A multilingual aligned parallel corpus with 20+ languages. In: Proceedings of the 5th International Conference on Language Resources and Evaluation, Genoa, Italy (2006)
16. Tiedemann, J.: Recycling Translations - Extraction of Lexical Data from Parallel Corpora and their Application in Natural Language Processing, Doctoral Thesis. Studia Linguistica Upsaliensia 1 (2003)
17. Tufis, D.: BalkaNet - Design and Development of a Multilingual Balkan WordNet. Romanian Journal of Information Science and Technology Special Issue 7(1-2) (2000)
18. Van der Plas, L., Tiedemann, J.: Finding Synonyms Using Automatic Word Alignment and Measures of Distributional Similarity. In: Proceedings of ACL/COLING (2006)
19. Vossen, P. (ed.): EuroWordNet: a multilingual database with lexical semantic networks for European Languages. Kluwer, Dordrecht (1998)

An Algorithm for Building Lexical Semantic Network and Its Application to PolNet - Polish WordNet Project

Zygmunt Vetulani, Justyna Walkowska, Tomasz Obrębski, Jacek Marciniak,
Paweł Konieczka, and Przemysław Rzepecki

Adam Mickiewicz University
ul. Umultowska 87, 61-714 Poznan, Poland
{vetulani,ynka,obrebski,jacekmar,pawelk,przemekr}@amu.edu.pl

Abstract. This paper presents the PolNet - Polish WordNet project
which aims at a linguistically oriented ontology for Polish compatible
with Princeton WordNet. We present the headlines of its methodology
as well as its implementation using the DEBVisDic tool for WordNet
building. We present the results obtained so far and discuss a number of
related problems.

1 Introduction

The PolNet[1] project aims at the development of a linguistically inspired ontology useful for computer emulation of human language competence. Systems
with language competence usually process some type of knowledge about the
world, and the knowledge needs representation. Formal systems reflecting human conceptualization of the world are called ontologies (cf. [4]). Ontologies
usually extend classical logic and include a number of basic relations between
concepts, common to a given class of applications. An ontology is an extension of
logic which includes relations true in some class of "possible worlds". In the past,
ontologies were often created independently of the way concepts are represented
in language, but recent advances of language technologies are stimulating interest in linguistically motivated ontologies (like Princeton WordNet). The main
idea of those ontologies is to use language expressions (words) to construct a
formal representation of concepts. The words linked by the synonymy relations
and forming *synsets* are abstract representations of concepts. This idea corresponds to the intuition that the structure of language reflects the structure of the
world. The existance of concepts built of words substantially simplifies semantic
processing of natural language texts.

PolNet is an on-going project hosted by the department of Computer Linguistics and Artificial Intelligence of Adam Mickiewicz University (headed by Zygmunt Vetulani) and executed in close collaboration with the NLP team of the
Faculty of Informatics of the Masaryk University in Brno (headed by Karel Pala).

---

[1] The draft of this paper presented was at the LTC'07 conference [9].

Z. Vetulani and H. Uszkoreit (Eds.): LTC 2007, LNAI 5603, pp. 369–381, 2009.

The project started in December 2006. In this paper we intend to show the headlines of the methodological approach applied in the first and essential step of WordNet construction: the creation of the core set of nominal synsets with the main hierarchical relation ISA corresponding to hyponymy/hypernymy between words. This work has been done by the Polish team[2] in 3 phases. The first phase consisted in elaboration of procedures (the *algorithm*) for creating synsets and relations and in the selection of the base concepts. Phases two and three were those of the actual creation of synsets and relations. These phases appeared very efficient due to the tools provided by the Czech partners: the VisDic and DEBVisDic systems. We describe the main characteristics of these tools and present our comments, hoping that this experience may be useful to developers of WordNets for "new" languages, for which there is no real-size WordNet yet. Our algorithm (described in Section 4) allows to build WordNet from scratch on the basis of a monolingual lexicon with well-distinguished word senses and with a complete lexical and semantic coverage. It is clear that the quality of the reference dictionary will have direct impact on the quality of the output. In case of Polish, we were in good position due to the existence of highquality multimedia lexicons (cf. [2]). In the next sections we focus on the creation of synsets for nouns. Of course other categories, such as verbs and adjectives, are also considered in the PolNet project.

2   PolNet Development Guidelines

We decided to use EuroWordNet as our basic methodological reference, so in many respects we implement EWN report guidelines (cf. [11]). We divided our work into the following tasks:

- Create the core of PolNet by selecting the most important words, determining their meanings and grouping them in so-called synsets.
- Introduce hypernymy relation, possibly adding missing synsets (one level of generalization or specialization).
- Connect the synsets to PWN[3] (considered a standard and providing links between languages).
- Add other relations.

There are two recognized models of WordNet creation: the *merge* model, consisting in autonomous development of the WordNet ontology based on a list of words, and the *expand* model, consisting principally in translating an already existing WordNet (e.g. PWN). We decided to select the former model. One of the reasons was that translating directly from one language to another creates the risk of importing a conceptualisation proper to the source language, which may be different in the target language. This phenomenon may have negative impact

---

[2] The co-authors of this paper and Agnieszka Kaliska from the Department of Contrastive Linguistics of Roman Languages of the Adam Mickiewicz University.

[3] Princeton WordNet.

in some categories of applications, especially when the ontology is used to build a conceptual model of the real word for an NL-understanding system. The merge model presupposes to start WordNet construction from a rough list of words, e.g. from a corpus. (In our case, as we intend to test the WordNet in Homeland Security dedicated projects, the chosen source of words is a public security corpus; c.f. Section 1: Credits.) We decided to introduce the synonymy relations manually. Any attempt to detect synonymy without a powerful language understanding systems could lead to a large number of redundant and ambiguous synsets still requiring manual verification by human experts. Instead, we elaborated and applied an algorithm of human processing for producing a high quality WordNet. It is presented in the next section.

3   PolNet Development Algorithm

In this section we present the procedures (the algorithm) for creating synsets and hierarchical relations based on hypernymy/hyponymy relations between words. To apply the algorithm the following resources are required:

- the Visdic or DEBVisDic platform (or any functionally equivalent tool),
- on-line access to Princeton WordNet,
- a good[4]monolingual lexicon (called *reference dictionary* in the algorithm description), preferably accessible on-line (we used *Uniwersalny słownik języka polskiego PWN*[5]as basic reference lexicon [2] and *Słownik języka polskiego PWN* as a complementary one),
- a team with both language engineering and lexicographical skills.

The input consists of a list of words (lexemes). The output is a WordNet segment composed of: a) a set of synsets, b) the ISA relation between synsets represented by the hyponymy/hypernymy relation.

The general procedure consists in performing the following sequence of operations one by one for every word W from the input list. (A short example is provided in the next section).

1. For the given word W find the corresponding dictionary entry in the reference dictionary.
2. Create a list of all the word senses (literal+gloss)[6]using the dictionary definitions. If necessary, i.e. if the dictionary is not fine-grained enough, transform the dictionary definition (gloss) in order to obtain separate glosses for different word senses you wish to consider (*splitting the definition*). If you detect that the word has meanings that are not attested in the dictionary, then add the word senses to the list.

---

[4] By *good* dictionary we mean one where different word senses are distinguished explicitly.

[5] *PWN* here is the name of a Polish publishing house.

[6] By *literal* we mean the text representation of word in the dictionary; by *gloss* we mean a distinguishing description of one particular word sense.

3. Assign numerical labels to the word senses according to the order in which they appear in the reference dictionary. Word senses absent from the reference dictionary should be assigned the highest numbers. (From now on, *word sense* will mean a literal with its sense number.)

4. For each word sense Z of the given word W:

   4.1 Create a list of synonymy candidates. Perform the synonymy tests for every such candidate. The synonymy tests for nouns (cf. [11]) are: *if it is an X, then it is also a Y and if it is a Y, then it is also an X.* This means that synonymy is treated as a purely semantic relation, irrespectively of any style or dialect differences. Remove from the list those candidates that failed the test.

   4.2 Check whether Z is already present in PolNet. If so, introduce changes to the definition (if necessary) and go to 6.

   4.3 For any synonym from the list check whether it is already present in PolNet. If present: perform 4.4, if absent: perform 4.5.

   4.4 Introduce the word sense Z to the relevant synset S. If necessary, introduce changes to the definition. Introduce a usage example (if not too costly).

   4.5 Create a synset S.

   4.5.1 Introduce Z to the synset S.

   4.5.2 Introduce a usage example (if providing it is not too costly).

   4.5.3 (optional) Connect the synset to its equivalent in PWN (skip this step in case of any doubt).

   4.5.4 Provide the synset with a definition (possibly by adapting the gloss of Z) sufficient to distinguish the common meaning of all elements of the synset (in a way to distinguish it from other synsets).

   4.5.5 If the sense number of Z does not correspond (is not equal) to the dictionary number, record the dictionary number.

5. Introduce to the synset S those synonyms from the list that passed the tests. Assign a sense number to every synonym (on the basis of reference dictionary numbering).

6. Look for hypernymy candidates using the reference dictionary, the List of Suggested Relations (LSR) (cf. below), the structure of Princeton WordNet and your *language competence*. Perform hypernymy tests for all candidates.

   6.1 If the hypernym you found already exists in PolNet, introduce the relation.

   6.2 If the hypernym is not present in PolNet yet, store the information (in the Note field in DEBVisDic).

7. Look for hyponymy candidates, using your *language competence*, the dictionary, the LSR list and the structure of Princeton WordNet.

   7.1 If the hyponym you found already exists in PolNet, introduce the relation.

   7.2 If the hypernym is not present in PolNet yet, store the information (in the Note field in DEBVisDic).

The *list of suggested relations* (LSR) is compiled from notices mentioned in 6.2 and 7.2.

Notice. If for some reason the algorithm cannot be applied to a word, the word should be placed in the list of problematic words and later a new algorithm version should be applied.

3.1 A Short Example

Let us take the Polish word *zamek* as an example. The list of the word senses from step 3. would be:

- zamek-1 (zamek I-1 in the dictionary): a lock
- zamek-2 (separated from the zamek-1 meaning, where the phrase *zamek błyskawiczny* is mentioned): a zip fastener
- zamek-3 (zamek I-2): a machine blocking lock, e.g. a valve lock
- zamek-4 (zamek I-3): a gun lock
- zamek-5 (zamek II-1): a castle

Zamek-2, zamek-3 and zamek-4 will all be hyponyms of zamek-1.

Step 4.5.5 "If the sense number of Z does not correspond (is not equal) to the dictionary number record the dictionary number." In our example the sense numbers in PolNet are different from dictionary numbers. It is so because the first meaning was split into two meanings and also because Roman numbering was used in the source dictionary to distinguish the completely different meaning of zamek-5. The link between a word in a synset and its representation in the dictionary is saved in the LNote field in DEBVisDic (see Section 6). For the word senses given above the link would be noted as follows : UI1a for zamek-1, UI1b for zamek-2, UI2 for zamek-3, UI3 for zamek-4, UII1 for zamek-5 (U indicating the USJP dictionary, "a" and "b" to mark that the meaning was *split* into two sub-meanings).

3.2 Some Discussed Variants of the Algorithm

The algorithm presented in Section 4. was obtained as a result of a process of iterative approximations. In this process various variants of the algorithm were tested and evaluated regarding their potential usefulness for fast and coherent WordNet construction.

One of the discussed variants of the algorithm involved building a complete list of hyponyms and hypernyms for every new synset. All hyponymy/hypernymy links with synsets already present in PolNet would be introduced (like in the final version of the algorithm).

Additionally, in this variant, new hyponyms/hypernyms (still outside of Pol-Net at processing time) would be the next candidates for new synsets. (In the final version of the algorithm persented in Section 4. these words are only put in the "waiting list"). This variant of the algorithm assumed entering up all the hyponyms and hypernyms for any given implemented synset. In favour of this solution was the hypothesis that the knowledge about hyponyms and hypernyms of a word helps to identify meaning variants. However, implementing WordNet in such way would inevitably lead to uncontrolled increase of the number of synsets unrelated to the original list of words. We intend to add this kind of words at a later stage.

Another discussed variant of the algorithm assumed that extraction of word senses from dictionary definition would also take into account the words used in idiomatic expressions. For example, building up a synset containing the word *krew* (blood) would inevitably imply consideration of idioms such as *błękitna krew* (blue blood). This approach would contribute to a good coverage of the semantic field of all considered words and it would help avoid omitting word senses, but it would significantly slow down the process of WordNet extension. Our decision not to consider the idiomatic parts of dictionary entries at this stage means that we are postponing considering some meanings, but we are not ignoring them.

4 Application of the Algorithm

The above-decribed algorithm allowed for the creation of the first part of PolNet. Over 10000 synsets were obtained by the algorithm application. We achieved such a good result thanks to the appropriate software tools that assisted the lexicographers.

Initially, we used the VisDic system, a desktop application created at Brno University. As VisDic does not support parallel, distributed work, the team later (at mid-term of the first WordNet task) migrated to DEBVisDic[7][6].

The creation of synsets and identification of hypernymy/hyponymy relations was done by 4 lexicographers (PhD students with lexicographical training). One more person (experienced senior researcher) was responsible for merging the separate pieces of WordNet developed while working in VisDic, and also for assignment of words to the four lexicographers (each of them using their own input list of words).

The first 6700 synsets were created at effort of env. 5 man-months during 3 months. The input list contained together over 3000 units (words). The words were extracted from:

1. the Generative Lexicon of Polish Verbs [7]. We considered the set of semantic descriptors (761 entry words) used in the Lexicon [8],
2. corpora of text for the chosen domain: homeland security terminology (1360), emergency situations dialogue corpus (630).

3900 more synsets were created as a result of additional 4.5 man-month at a later stage, from a list of 3600 words.

The initial phases of the PolNet project has been completed with very satisfactory results: 10612 synsets at the cost of 9.5 man-months for the application of the algorithm.

---

[7] The DEBVisDic was not available at the project start.

The everage size of a synset is 1.78 word senses (total number of word senses is 18644). Number of different words is 10983.

10675 hypernimy and 117 holo-part relations were created. There are 1390 synsets with no hypernym indicated and 1189 synsets with more than one hypernym. The average depth of a synset in hypernymy relation hierarchy is 5.1. 1800 synsets are of depth 10 or more.

4.1 Merging-Related Problems

In the process of merging synsets created during the second phase of the project (VisDic) it turned out that a significant number of synsets were repeated (introduced into PolNet by more than one coder) despite the fact that the input lists were disjoint.

The result of the second phase were four independently created WordNet parts. The parts' sizes were 633, 697, 1480, and 952 synsets what gave the total of 3762 synsets.

We assumed that each part was internally consistent, but across the parts we expected inconsistence of two kinds:

a) synsets describing the same concept appearing in two or more different parts,
b) inconsistent sense numbering for a word across parts.

In the total of 2478 synsets there were no nonempty intersections with synsets from other parts. In the remaining set of 1284 "suspected" synsets, we found 253 synsets with two or more elements (word senses) repeated in another synset, 458 synsets with one element repeated in another synset, and 573 synsets with no elements repeated in any other synset, but containing a word common with a synset from another part.

These "suspected" synsets were submitted to a manual verification procedure to discover duplicated concepts. As the result 240 synsets were removed or joined with other synsets. Word sense numbering appeared to be consistent across all the four parts: there were only a few cases where different lexicographers assigned different numerical labels to the identical word senses. The information provided for each word sense (linking it to the sense description in the reference dictionary) was very helpful for disambiguation.

It has been observed that the overlap of WordNets created independently starting with disjoint word lists was quite significant and that the merging procedure was time-consuming.

The use of the DEBVisDic platform during the next phase of PolNet building resulted with substantial reduction of processing effort (which may be estimated as over 20% of production time).

4.2 Problems Not Considered in the Algorithm

One of the distinctive features of Slavonic languages (Polish, Czech, Russian,...) is the possibility of creating augmentative and diminutive forms. The algorithm does not determine the way of handling this phenomenon. In practice, in some cases the lexicographers decided to introduce those forms into the very synset containing the basic form, in others they created new synsets and connected them to the basic form by the hypernymy relation. There are more problems of this kind to be noted. Often it is possible to create multi-storey constructions of augmentative and diminutive forms. Also, the diminutive form of a word may carry two different meanings: it may mean that the object is physically smaller, but it can also indicate the speaker's contemptuous attitude. In CzechWordNet the augmentative/diminutive form problem was solved by a special derivative relation between the synsets, but this solutions was not applied for Polish (further studies concerning these issues seem necessary).

Another interesting issue is the one related to the existence of female forms of nouns denoting people. In PolNet, due to the lack of suitable instructions in the algorithm, the coders face a certain dilemma. Let us suppose that there is a synset describing the concept *księgowy* (accountant) and another synset representing *pracownik* (employee) which is the former's hypernym. Given that, should the word *księgowa* (female accountant) be a hyponym of *księgowy* (accountant) or *pracowniczka* (female employee)? The authors of CzechWordNet addressed this problem by introducing a special relation to inform that a synset contains the female forms of words from another one.

A difficult problem was the one of proper processing of vulgarisms and colloquial forms. Linguistic descriptions of these categories are far from being satisfactory and dictionaries are very incomplete in this respect. It was often unclear whether a vulgar term and its neutral "synonym" should be placed in the same synset. In the case of the strongest vulgarisms, we decided to use the solution found in Princeton WordNet: create a separate synset with the vulgar terms and describe it as a hyponym of the basic one.

One more situation not anticipated by the algorithm is the possible difference in word meanings depending on whether the considered words are capitalized or not (*waga* meaning a scale and *Waga* as the zodiac sign Libra). DEBVisDic, the tool used by the team, is case sensitive, so the entities *Waga*:1 and *waga*:1 would not be considered equal (and thus conflicting). Regardless of that, the team decided to procede as in the Princeton WordNet: all meanings of one word have common numbering, no matter whether they are capitalized or not. As a result, it is not possible to have two literals that have the same number and only differ in the case of the first letter.

Another class of problems reported by the lexicographers were those related with the hypernymy for relatively general concepts. It was often difficult to find appropriate hypernyms other than those belonging to the Top Ontology.

4.3   Faults Caused by Departures from the Algorithm

Even though there were a few cases in which the algorithm turned out not to be fully sufficient, it worked very well for most words. Still, in the WordNet produced by the Polish team some recurring mistakes have been found that result from the bad routine of the lexicographers.

Faults of this kind were often caused by too much trust in the dictionary. The dictionary used by the team, *Uniwersalny słownik języka polskiego*, contains some pieces of a semantic network. A number of words are linked with their synonyms, hypernyms etc.

However, those relations are by no means complete and they are often incorrect. According to the algorithm, the lexicographers should look for relations in a number of sources (not only the dictionary) and should not hesitate using their *language competence*. Practice has shown that, due to mechanical-routine work, some synsets lacked basic synonyms only because the relation was not found in the dictionary, even though the dictionary contained synonymical entries and the relation could have easily been inferred from the dictionary definition.

Another common mistake of similar nature was duplicating synsets when the first one introduced was incomplete. Let us imagine a concept that can be described by 10 synonyms. If one person, starting from a word, created a synset with only 4 synonyms, the other lexicographers (who reached the concept through a different word) should find the existing synset, looking for it through all the words it should contain. Unfortunately, often the lexicographers, while checking whether synsets already existed, did not consider all possible synonyms, but only some arbitrary selected subsets. This resulted with the creation of a number of synsets describing the same concept and partly containing the same literals. Fortunately, the recent version of DEBVisDic reports attempts to save literals that already exist in the WordNet being developed.

4.4   Additional Comments

There are some additional costs related to the merge model of WordNet creation from word lists. As the algorithm refers to some reference dictionary, all the word senses are systematically introduced into PolNet, even those most archaic or highly technical. One could argue that their existence in PolNet is unnecessary. If so, criterion to omit word senses should be proposed.

Some doubts arose while connecting PolNet with Princeton WordNet. The Princeton WordNet is very fine-grained; the words have been divided into a lot of narrow meanings. Sometimes it is hard to find an English equivalent, because the Polish synset appears to be the hypernym of a number of English synsets rather than a translation equivalent of one of them. This issue has been reported by a number of teams working on WordNets. Some of them address the problem by introducing inter-language relations of *weak synonymy* (like EQ_NEAR_SYNONYM proposed by the Piek Vossen team of the Amsterdam University) instead of simply translating synsets. For example, the Polish word *pączek* has the meaning similar to the English word *doughnut*, but there is an important difference in shape: *doughnuts* normally have a hole (are ringshaped), while Polish *pączek* is full and round. *Near synonymy* would be the most correct relation for them.

5   Tools for WordNet Creation

As it has been mentioned above, during Polish WordNet creation we used tools developed at the Faculty of Informatics at Masaryk University.

The first of the tools, VisDic [13] is a desktop application designed to browse and edit any lexical data can be stored in the XML format. The authors of the programme defined XML-based formats for WordNet data. The application, working both under Linux and Windows, allows work with a number of dictionaries at the same time and provides an easy way to introduce inter- and intra-language relations. Thanks to its high level of configurationality and its data consistency verification mechanisms, VisDic made it possible for the Pol-Net coders to work effectively in a distributed manner (see 4.2).

During the course of the project we decided to switch to a newly released tool called DEBVisDic (cf. [6]). As both systems used the same XML-based formats the migration appeared an easy task. The main advantage of the new application was its client-server architecture. Thanks to it, several lexicographers were able to access the shared database at the same time, with the data being integrated systematically by the application. DEBVisDic has all the important VisDic features. It works in Mozilla Development environment, thus it is accessible from all popular platforms. We observed considerable increase in the work effectiveness after installing DEBVisDic onto a server located in a fast local network.

6   Conclusions

The list of problems considered and discussed in this paper is far from reflecting the totality of methodological and technical problems we were confronted with. In this presentation we focus on the processing algorithm. We conclude that the methodology presented here supported with new generation tools (DEBVisDic), opens very promising perspectives for building new high-quality WordNets in a fast and efficient manner even with limited human resources.

Acknowledgements. This work has been partly supported by Polish Ministry of Science and Higher Education, grant R00 028 02 (within the Polish Platform for Homeland Security)[8]. We also benefited from the generous assistance of Karel Pala and his team from Masaryk University in Brno, who provided us with the DEBVisDic tool.

References

1. Chaudhri, A.B., Rashid, A., Zicari, R. (eds.): XML Data Management: NativeXML and XML-Enabled Database Systems. Addison Wesley Professional, Reading (2003)

---

[8] PolNet is one of the projects realized within the Polish Platform for Homeland Security (PPBW).

2. Dubisz, S.: Uniwersalny słownik języka polskiego PWN, 2nd edn. Wydawnictwo Naukowe PWN, Warszawa (2006)
3. Feldt, K.: Programming Firefox: Building Rich Internet Applications with Xul. O'Reilly, Sebastopol (2007)
4. Gruber, T.R.: Towards principles for the design of ontologies used for knowledge sharing. Technical Report KSL 93-04, Stanford University, Knowledge Systems Laboratory (1993)
5. Horák, A., Pala, K., Rambousek, A., Povolný, M.: First version of new client-server wordnet browsing and editing tool. In: Proceedings of the Third International WordNet Conference – GWC 2006, Jeju, South Korea, Masaryk University, Brno, pp. 325–328 (2006)
6. Horák, A., Pala, K., Obrębski, T., Rzepecki, P., Konieczka, P., Marciniak, J., Rambousek, A., Vetulani, Z., Walkowska, J.: DEB Platform tools for effective development of WordNets in application to PolNet. In: Vetulani, Z. (ed.) Proceedings of the 3rd Language and Technology Conference, October 5-7, 2007, pp. 514–518. Wydawnictwo Poznańskie Sp. z o.o., Poznań (2007)
7. Polański, K. (ed.): Słownik syntaktyczno-generatywny czasowników polskich (Generative Syntactic Lexicon of Polish Verbs). vol. I-IV. Ossolineum, Wrocław, vol. V, Instytut Języka Polskiego PAN, Kraków (1980-1992)
8. Vetulani, Z.: Linguistically Motivated Ontological Systems. In: Callaos, N., Lesso, W., Schewe, K.-D., Atlam, E. (eds.) Proceedings of the SCI 2003, Orlando, USA. Int. Inst. of Informatics and Systemics, vol. XII, pp. 395–400 (2003)
9. Vetulani, Z., Walkowska, J., Obrębski, T., Rzepecki, P., Marciniak, J.: PolNet – Polish WordNet project algorithm. In: Vetulani, Z. (ed.) Proceedings of the 3rd Language and Technology Conference, October 5-7, 2007, pp. 172–176. Wydawnictwo Poznańskie Sp. z o.o., Poznań (2007)
10. American Psychological Association: Publications Manual. American Psychological Association, Washington, DC (1983)
11. Vossen, P.: EuroWordNet General Document, Version 3. University of Amsterdam (2003)
12. Vossen, P.: The Cornetto project web site (2007), http://www.let.vu.nl/onderzoek/projectsites/cornetto/start.htm
13. Horak, A., Smrz, P.: VisDic - Wordnet Browsing and Editing Tool. In: Proceedings of the Second International WordNet Conference - GWC 2004, Brno, Czech Republic, Masaryk University, pp. 136–141 (2004)

Appendix: A PolNet Sample

A sample of PolNet in XML format: entries corresponding to the word *zamek*.

```
<SYNSET>
  <ID>ADD_ENG20-03545154-n</ID>
  <POS>n</POS>
  <DEF>
    USJP: "urządzenie do zamykania drzwi, szuflad, walizek itp., którego główną częścią jest mechanizm sterujący
    przesuwaniem zasuwki"
  </DEF>
  <SYNONYM>
    <WORD>zamek</WORD>
    <LITERAL lnote="UI1" sense="1">zamek</LITERAL>
    <WORD>zamek</WORD>
  </SYNONYM>
  <USAGE>Zamek kodowy, szyfrowy, cyfrowy.</USAGE>
  <ILR type="hypernym" link="POL-2141575741">zamknięcie:2</ILR>
  <BCS/>
  <NL>false</NL>
  <STAMP>agav 2007-07-25 10:31:24</STAMP>
```

```
<CREATED>agav 2007-07-25 10:31:24</CREATED>
<RILR type="hypernym" link="POL-2141703211">zasuwa:1, zapora:3</RILR>
<RILR type="hypernym" link="POL-2141703214">zatrzask:2</RILR>
<RILR type="hypernym" link="1">zamek:2, suwak:1, zamek błyskawiczny:1, ekler:1</RILR>
</SYNSET>
<SYNSET>
<STAMP>ynka 2009-01-21 09:34:59</STAMP>
<ILR type="hypernym" link="ADD_ENG20-03545154-n">zamek:1</ILR>
<DEF>
Wikipedia: zapięcie służące do czasowego łączenia dwóch kawałków tkaniny
</DEF>
<SYNONYM>
<WORD>zamek</WORD>
<WORD>suwak</WORD>
<WORD>zamek</WORD>
<WORD>błyskawiczny</WORD>
<WORD>ekler</WORD>
<LITERAL lnote="UI1b" sense="2">zamek</LITERAL>
<LITERAL lnote="UI1" sense="1">suwak</LITERAL>
<LITERAL lnote="UI1" sense="1">zamek błyskawiczny</LITERAL>
<LITERAL lnote="UI1" sense="1">ekler</LITERAL>
</SYNONYM>
<ID>1</ID>
<BCS/>
<NL>false</NL>
<CREATED>ynka 2009-01-21 09:34:59</CREATED>
<POS>n</POS>
</SYNSET>
<SYNSET>
<STAMP>ynka 2009-01-21 09:29:49</STAMP>
<ILR type="hypernym" link="Prz-743964851">urządzenie:2, aparat:1, ustrojstwo:1</ILR>
<ID>POL-2141601305</ID>
<DEF>
USJP: "(techn.) urządzenie do łączenia lub zabezpieczania w ustalonym położeniu elementów maszyny"
</DEF>
<SYNONYM>
<WORD>zamek</WORD>
<LITERAL lnote="UI2" sense="3">zamek</LITERAL>
</SYNONYM>
<USAGE>Zamek zaworowy, łopatkowy.</USAGE>
<BCS/>
<CREATED>ynka 2007-03-20 22:09:40</CREATED>
<NL>false</NL>
<POS>n</POS>
<RILR type="hypernym" link="POL-2141574984">blok:5</RILR>
</SYNSET>
<SYNSET>
<STAMP>ynka 2009-01-21 09:29:33</STAMP>
<ILR type="hypernym" link="ENG20-03598777-n">mechanizm:1, maszyneria:1</ILR>
<ID>POL-2141601306</ID>
<DEF>
USJP: "mechanizm broni palnej służący do zamykania na czas wystrzału i otwierania po strzale tylnej części lufy"
</DEF>
<SYNONYM>
<WORD>zamek</WORD>
<LITERAL lnote="UI3" sense="4">zamek</LITERAL>
</SYNONYM>
<BCS/>
<CREATED>ynka 2007-03-20 22:10:21</CREATED>
<NL>false</NL>
<POS>n</POS>
</SYNSET>
<SYNSET>
<STAMP>ynka 2009-01-21 09:29:04</STAMP>
<ILR type="hypernym" link="POL-2141574379">budowla obronna:1</ILR>
<ID>ENG20-02874319-n</ID>
<DEF>
USJP: "warowna budowla mieszkalna otoczona pierścieniem murów z basztami, wieżami, często z barbakanem i zwodzonym mostem
nad fosą; w średniowieczu: siedziba pana feudalnego, później rezydencja królewska, książęca lub magnacka"
</DEF>
<SYNONYM>
<WORD>zamek</WORD>
<WORD>zamczysko</WORD>
<LITERAL lnote="UII1" sense="5">zamek</LITERAL>
<LITERAL lnote="UI1" sense="1">zamczysko</LITERAL>
</SYNONYM>
<USAGE>
Zamek feudalny, gotycki, romański, rycerski, królewski.
</USAGE>
<SNOTE>--zameczek</SNOTE>
<SNOTE>--bastylia</SNOTE>
<SNOTE>--kasztel</SNOTE>
<SNOTE>--palatium</SNOTE>
<BCS/>
<CREATED>pique 2007-03-21 13:11:29</CREATED>
<NL>false</NL>
<POS>n</POS>
</SYNSET>
<SYNSET>
<ID>POL-2141700734</ID>
```

```
<POS>n</POS>
<DEF>
  USJP: "zawiązek pędu liścia lub kwiatu, zwykle ochraniany przez łuski"
</DEF>
<SYNONYM>
  <WORD>pączek</WORD>
  <WORD>pąk</WORD>
  <LITERAL lnote="" sense="1">pączek</LITERAL>
  <WORD>pączek</WORD>
  <LITERAL lnote="" sense="1">pąk</LITERAL>
  <WORD>pąk</WORD>
</SYNONYM>
<ILR type="hypernym" link="ENG20-10924345-n">kwiat:1, kwiatek:1, kwiatuszek:1</ILR>
<ILR type="hypernym" link="ENG20-12399907-n">liść:1</ILR>
<ILR type="hypernym" link="POL-2141704368">zawiązek:1</ILR>
<BCS/>
<NL>false</NL>
<STAMP>krzyzang 2007-07-30 14:51:01</STAMP>
<CREATED>krzyzang 2007-07-30 14:51:01</CREATED>
<RILR type="hypernym" link="POL-1404118086">oczko:15</RILR>
<RILR type="hypernym" link="POL-439158303">oczko:14</RILR>
</SYNSET>
<SYNSET>
  <ID>POL-2141700736</ID>
  <POS>n</POS>
  <DEF>
    USJP: "ciastko o kształcie kulistym, nadziewane, smażone w tłuszczu"
  </DEF>
  <SYNONYM>
    <WORD>pączek</WORD>
    <LITERAL lnote="" sense="2">pączek</LITERAL>
    <WORD>pączek</WORD>
  </SYNONYM>
  <USAGE>objadać się pączkami</USAGE>
  <ILR type="hypernym" link="POL-2141704084">ciastko:1, ciacho:1</ILR>
  <BCS/>
  <NL>false</NL>
  <STAMP>krzyzang 2007-07-28 13:36:43</STAMP>
  <CREATED>krzyzang 2007-07-28 13:36:43</CREATED>
</SYNSET>
<SYNSET>
  <ID>POL-2141700737</ID>
  <POS>n</POS>
  <DEF>
    USJP: "przy rozmnażaniu się wegetatywnym u roślin i zwierząt niższych: wyodrębniona część organizmu macierzystego
    w postaci komórki, kompleksu komórek lub tkanek, rozwijająca się w organizm potomny"
  </DEF>
  <SYNONYM>
    <WORD>pączek</WORD>
    <LITERAL lnote="" sense="3">pączek</LITERAL>
    <WORD>pączek</WORD>
  </SYNONYM>
  <USAGE/>
  <ILR type="hypernym" link="POL-2141574505">część ciała:1, część organizmu:1</ILR>
  <BCS/>
  <NL>false</NL>
  <STAMP>przemekr 2007-07-05 16:53:05</STAMP>
  <CREATED>przemekr 2007-07-05 16:53:05</CREATED>
</SYNSET>
```

ECODE: A Definition Extraction System

Rodrigo Alarcón[1], Gerardo Sierra[1], and Carme Bach[2]

[1] Grupo de Ingeniería Lingüística, Universidad Nacional Autónoma de Mexico,
Ciudad Universitaria, Torre de Ingeniería, Basamento 3, 04510, Mexico City, Mexico
{ralarconm,gsierram}@iingen.unam.mx
[2] Instituto Universitario de Lingüística Aplicada, Universidad Pompeu Fabra,
Pl. de la Mercè 10-12, 08002, Barcelona, Spain
carme.bach@upf.edu

Abstract. Terminological work aims to identify knowledge about terms in specialised texts in order to compile dictionaries, glossaries or ontologies. Searching for definitions about the terms that terminographers intend to define is therefore an essential task. This search can be done in specialised corpus, where they usually appear in definitional contexts, i.e. text fragments where an author explicitly defines a term. We present a research focused on the automatic extraction of those definitional contexts. The methodology includes three different processes: the extraction of definitional patterns, the automatic filtering of non-relevant contexts, and the automatic identification of constitutive elements, i.e., terms and definitions.

Keywords: Definition extraction, definitional knowledge, definitional contexts, information extraction, computational terminography.

1 Introduction

A common need in terminological work is the extraction of knowledge about terms in specialised texts. Some efforts in the field of NLP have been done in order to develop tools that help in this need, such as corpora, where a large quantity of technical documents are digitally stored, as well as term extraction systems, which automatically identify relevant terms in corpora.

Nowadays there is a growing interest on developing systems for the automatic extraction of useful information to describe the meaning of terms. This information commonly appears in structures called *definitional contexts* (DCs), which are structured by a series of lexical and metalinguistic patterns that can be automatically recognised [1], [2]. Following this idea, our work is focused on developing a system for the automatic extraction of definitional contexts on Spanish language specialised texts. Such system includes the extraction of definitional pattern's occurrences, the filtering of non-relevant contexts, and the identification of DCs constitutive elements, i.e., terms and definitions.

This system has been developing for Spanish language and it will be helpful in the elaboration of ontologies, databases of lexical knowledge, glossaries or specialised dictionaries.

Z. Vetulani and H. Uszkoreit (Eds.): LTC 2007, LNAI 5603, pp. 382–391, 2009.

In this paper we will describe the structure of DCs; we will make a short review of related works; we will present the methodology we have followed for the automatic extraction of DCs, in addition with a methodology's evaluation; and finally we will describe the future work.

2 Definitional Contexts

A definitional context is a textual fragment from a specialised text where a definition of a term is given. It is basically structured by a term (T) and its definition (D), being both elements connected by typographic or syntactic patterns. Mainly, typographic patterns are punctuation marks (comas, parenthesis), while syntactic patterns include definitional verbs –such as *definir* (to define) or *significar* (to signify)– as well as discursive markers –such as *es decir* (that is, lit. (it) is to say), or *o sea* (that is, lit. or be-subjunctive)–. Besides, DCs can include pragmatic patterns (PP), which provide conditions for the use of the term or clarify its meaning, like *en términos generales* (in general terms) or *en este sentido* (in this sense).

The next is an example of a definitional context:

"Desde un punto de vista práctico, los opioides se definen como compuestos de acción directa, cuyos efectos se ven antagonizados estereoespecíficamente por la naloxona."

In this case, the term *opioides* is connected to its definition (*compuestos de acción directa [...]*) by the verbal pattern *se definen como* (are defined as), while the general sense of the context is modified by the pragmatic pattern *desde un punto de vista práctico* (from a practical point of view).

2.1 Related Work

The study of automatic extraction of definitional knowledge has been approached from both theoretical-descriptive and applied perspectives.

One of the first theoretical-descriptive works is Pearson's [1], in which the behaviour of the contexts where terms appear is described. Pearson mentions that, when authors define a term, they usually employ typographic patterns to visually bring out the presence of terms and/or definitions, as well as lexical and metalinguistic patterns to connect DCs elements by means of syntactic structures.

Meyer [2] reinforced this idea and also states that definitional patterns can provide keys that allow the identification of the definition type occurring in DCs, which is a helpful task in the elaboration of ontologies. Other theoretical-descriptive works can be found in [3] and [4].

Applied investigations, on the other hand, leave from theoretical-descriptive studies with the objective of elaborate methodologies for the automatic extractions of DCs, more specifically for the extraction of definitions in medical texts [5], for the extraction of definitions for question answering systems [6], for the automatic elaboration of ontologies [7], for the extraction of semantic relations from specialised texts [8], as well as for the extraction of relevant information for eLearning purposes [9], [10].

In general words, those studies employ definitional patterns as a common start point for the extraction of knowledge about terms. In order to developing our methodology we start from the analysis and integration of theoretical-descriptive and applied studies.

3   Definitional Contexts Extraction

As we have mentioned before, the main purpose of a definitional context extractor would be to simplify the search of relevant information about terms, by means of searching occurrences of definitional patterns.

An extractor that only retrieves those occurrences of definitional patterns would be a useful system for terminographical work. Nevertheless, the manual analysis of the occurrences would still suppose an effort that could be simplified by an extractor, which also includes an automatic processing of the information obtained.

Therefore, we propose a methodology that includes not only the extraction of occurrences of definitional patterns, but also a filtering of non-relevant contexts (i.e. non definitional contexts) and the automatic identification of the possible constitutive elements of a DC: terms, definitions and pragmatic patterns. In the next sections we explain each step of our methodology.

3.1   Corpus

We took as reference the IULA´s Technical Corpus and its search engine bwanaNet[1], developed on the Instituto Universitario de Lingüística Aplicada (IULA, UPF). The corpus is conformed by specialised documents in Law, Genome, Economy, Environment, Medicine, Informatics and General Language. It counts with a total of 1,378 documents in Spanish (December 2008). For the experiments we use all the areas except General Language, and the number of treated documents was 959 with a total number of 11,569,729 words.

3.2   Extracting Definitional Patterns

For the experiments we searched for definitional verbal patterns (DVPs). We worked with 15 patterns that include *simple definitional verbal patterns* (SDVP) and *compound definitional verbal patterns* (CDVP). As we can see in table 1, patterns of the simple forms include only the definitional verb, while patterns of the compound forms include the definitional verb plus a grammatical particle such as a preposition or an adverb.

Each pattern was searched in the Technical IULA's corpus through the *complex search* option, which allows users to obtain the occurrences with POS tags. We also delimitate the search to no more of 300 occurrences for each verbal pattern, using the random (and representative) recovery option.

The verbal patterns were searched taking into account the next restrictions:

Verbal forms: infinitive, participle and conjugate forms.

Verbal tenses: present and past for the simple forms, any verbal time for the compounds forms.

---

[1] http://bwananet.iula.upf.edu/indexes.htm

Table 1. Simple & compound Definitional Verbal Patterns

Type	Verbs
Simple	concebir (to conceive), definir (to define), entender (to understand), identificar (to identify), significar (to signify)
Compound	consistir de (to consist of), consistir en (to consist in), constar de (to comprise), denominar también (also denominated), llamar también (also called), servir para (to serve for), usar como (to use as), usar para (to use for), utilizar como (to utilise as), utilizar para (to utilise for)

Person: 3rd singular and plural for the simple forms, any for the compound forms.

The obtained occurrences were automatically annotated with *contextual tags*. The function of these simple tags is to work as borders in the next automatic process. For each occurrence, the definitional verbal pattern were annotated with "<dvp></dvp>"; everything after the pattern with "<left></left>"; everything before the pattern with "<right></right>"; and finally, in those cases where the verbal pattern includes a nexus, like the adverb *como* (as), everything between the verbal pattern and the nexus were annotated with <nexus></nexus>.

Here is an example of a DC with contextual tags:

<left>El metabolismo</left> <dvp>puede definir se </dvp> <nexus>en términos generales como</nexus> <right>la suma de todos los procesos químicos (y físicos) implicados.</right>

It is important to mention that from this contextual annotation process, all the automatic process was done with scripts in Perl. We choose this programming language mainly by its inherent effectiveness to process regular expressions.

3.3 Filtering Non-relevant Contexts

Once we have extracted and annotated the occurrences with DVPs, the next process was the filtering of non-relevant contexts. We apply this step based on the fact that definitional patterns are not used only in definitional sentences. In the case of DVPs some verbs trend to have a high metalinguistic meaning rather than others. That is the case of *definir* (to define) or *denominar* (to denominate), vs. *concebir* (to conceive) or *identificar* (to identify), where the last two ones could be used in a wide variety of different sentences. Moreover, the verbs with a high metalinguistic meaning are not used only for defining terms.

In a previous work an analysis was done in order to determine which kind of grammatical particles or syntactic sequences could appear in those cases when a DVP is not used to define a term.

Those particles and sequences were found in some specific positions, for example: some negation particles like *no* (not) or *tampoco* (either) were found in the first position before or after the DVP; adverbs like *tan* (so), *poco* (few) as well as sequences like *poco más* (not more than) were found between the definitional verb and the nexus *como*; also, syntactic sequences like adjective + verb were found in the first position after the definitional verb.

Thus, considering this and other frequently combinations and helped by contextual tags previously annotated, we developed a script in order to filtering non-relevant contexts. The script could recognise contexts like the following examples:

Rule: **NO <left>**
<left>En segundo lugar, tras el tratamiento eficaz de los cambios patológicos en un órgano pueden surgir problemas inesperados en tejidos que previamente **no </left>** <dvp>se identificaron</dvp> <nexus> como </nexus> <right> implicados clínicamente, ya que los pacientes no sobreviven lo suficiente.</right>

Rule: **<nexus> CONJUGATED VERB**
<left>Ciertamente esta observación tiene una mayor fuerza cuando el número de categorías </left> <dvp> definidas</dvp> **<nexus> es** pequeño como</nexus> <der>en nuestro análisis.</der>

3.4 Identifying DCs Elements

Once the non-relevant contexts were filtered, the next process in the methodology is the identification of main terms, definitions and pragmatic patterns. In Spanish's DCs, and depending on each DVP, the terms and definitions can appear in some specific positions. For example, in DCs with the verb *definir* (to define), the term could appear in left, nexus or right position (T *se define como* D; *se define* T *como* D; *se define como* T D), while in DCs with the verb *significar* (to signify), terms can appear only in left position (T *significa* D). Therefore, in this phase the automatic process is highly related to deciding in which positions could appear the constitutive elements.

We decided to use a decision tree [11] to solve this problem, i.e., to detect by means of logic inferences the probable positions of terms, definitions and pragmatic patterns. We established some simple regular expressions to represent each constitutive element[2]:

T = BRD (Det) + N + Adj. {0,2} .* BRD
PP = BRD (sign) (Prep | Adv) .* (sign) BRD

As well as in the filtering process, the contextual tags have functioned as borders to demarcate decision tree's instructions. In addition, each regular expression could function as a border. In a first level, the branches of the tree are the different positions in which constitutive elements can appear (left, nexus or right). In a second level, the branches are the regular expressions of each DC element. The nodes (branches conjunctions) corresponds to decisions taken from the attributes of each branch and are also horizontally related by *If* or *If Not* inferences, and vertically through *Then* inferences. Finally, the leaves are the assigned position for a constitutive element.

Hence, in figure 1 we present an example of the decision tree inferences to identify left constitutive elements[3]:

---

[2] Where: Det= determiner, N= name, Adj= adjective, Prep= preposition, Adv= adverb, BRD= border and ".*"= any word or group of words.

[3] TRE = term regular expression | PPRE = pragmatic pattern regular expression | DRE = definition regular expression.

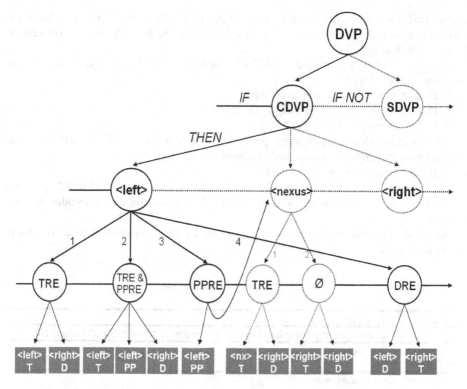

Fig. 1. Example of the identification of DCs elements

This tree should be interpreted in the next way:
Given a series of DVPs occurrences:
D   = BRD Det. + N .* BRD
If verbal pattern = compound definitional verbal pattern, *then*:
1. *If* left position corresponds *only* to a term regular expression, *then*:
<left> = term | <right> = definition.
If Not:
2. *If* left position corresponds to a term regular expression and a pragmatic pattern regular expression, *then*:
<left> = term & pragmatic pattern | <right> = definition.
If Not:
3. *If* left position *only* corresponds to a pragmatic pattern regular expression, *then*[4]:
<left> = pragmatic pattern | *If* nexus corresponds *only* to a term regular expression, *then* <nexus> = term & <right> = definition; *If Not* <right> = term & definition.
4. *If* left position corresponds only to a definition regular expression, *then*:
<left> = definition | <right> = term.
To exemplify we can observe the next context:

---

[4] In some cases the tree must resort to other position inferences to find terms and definitions.

"<left>En sus comienzos</left> <dvp>se definió</dvp> <nexus>la psicología como </nexus><right>"la descripción y la explicación de los estados de conciencia" (Ladd, 1887).</right>"

Once the DVP was identified as a CDVP – *definir como* (to define as) – the tree infers that left position:

1. Does not correspond only to a TRE.
2. Does not correspond to a TRE and a PPRE.
3. It does correspond only to a PPRE.

Then: left position is a pragmatic pattern (*En sus comienzos*). To identify the term and definition the tree goes to nexus's inferences and finds that:

1. It does correspond only to a TRE.

Then: nexus's position corresponds to the term (*la psicología*) and right's position corresponds to the definition ("la descripción y la explicación de los estados de conciencia […]").

As result, the processed context was reorganised into terminological entries as in the next example:

Table 2. Example of the results

Term	psicología
Definition	"la descripción y la explicación de los estados de la conciencia" (Ladd, 1887).
Verbal Pattern	se define
Pragmatic Pattern	En sus comienzos

To conclude this part we have to mention that the algorithms implement non-complex regular expressions as well as simple logic inferences to find, analyse and organise definitional knowledge. Furthermore, the design of the algorithms allows the implementation in other languages by replacing the correspondent regular expressions as well as the logical inferences.

4 Evaluation

The evaluation of the methodology consists in two parts:

1. We evaluate the extraction of DVPs and the filtering of no relevant contexts using Precision & Recall. In general words, Precision measures how many information extracted is *relevant*, while Recall measures how many *relevant* information was extracted from the input.
2. For the identification of constitutive elements, we manually assigned values that helped us to statistically evaluate the exactitude of the decisions tree.

4.1 Evaluation of DVP's Extraction and Non-relevant Contexts Filtering

We determine Precision & Recall by means of the following formulas:

P = the number of filtered DCs automatically extracted, over the number of contexts automatically extracted.

R = the number of filtered DCs automatically extracted, over the number of *non-filtered* DCs automatically extracted.

The results for each verbal pattern can be seen in table 3. In the case of Precision, there is a divergence on verbs that usually appear in metalinguistic sentences. The best results were obtained with verbs like *denominar* (to denominate) or *definir* (to define), while verbs like *entender* (to understand) or *significar* (to signify) recover low Precision values. Those verbs with lower results can be used in a wide assortment of sentences, (i.e., not necessarily definitional contexts), and they trend to recover a big quantity of noise. In the case of Recall, low results indicate that valid DCs were filtered as non-relevant contexts. The wrong classification is related to the non-filtering rules, but also in some cases a wrong classification was due to a POS tagging errors in the input corpus.

Table 3. Precision & Recall results

Verbal Patten		Precision	Recall
Concebir (como)	To conceive (as)	0.67	0.98
Definir (como)	To define (as)	0.84	0.99
Entender (como)	To understand (as)	0.34	0.94
Identificar (como)	To identify (as)	0.31	0.90
Consistir de	To consist of	0.62	1
Consistir en	To consist in	0.60	1
Constar de	To comprise	0.94	0.99
Denominar también	Also denominated	1	0.87
LLamar también	Also called	0.90	1
Servir para	To serve for	0.55	1
Significar	To signify	0.29	0.98
Usar como	To use as	0.41	0.95
Usar para	To use for	0.67	1
Utilzar como	To utilise as	0.45	0.92
Utilizar para	To utilise for	0.53	1

The challenge we faced in this stage is directly related to the elimination of noise. We have noticed that the more precise the verbal pattern is, the better results (in terms of less noise) can be obtained. Nevertheless, a specification of verbal patterns means a probable lost of recall. Although, a revision of filtering rules must be done in order to improve the non-relevant contexts identification and avoid the cases when some DC where incorrect filtered.

4.2   Evaluation of DVP's Extraction and Non-relevant Contexts Filtering

To evaluate the DCs elements identification, we manually assign the next values to each DC processed by the decisions tree:

3 for those contexts where the constitutive elements were correct classified;
2 for those contexts where the constitutive elements were correct classified, but

some extra information were also classified (for example extra words or punctuation marks in term position);

1 for those contexts where the constitutive elements were *not* correct classified, (for example when terms were classified as definitions or vice versa).

Ø for those contexts the system could not classify.

In table 4 we present the results of the evaluation of DCs elements identification. The values are expressed as percentages, and the amount of all of them represent the total number of DCs founded with each verbal pattern. From DCs evaluation we highlight the following facts:

The average percentage of the correct classified elements (group "3") is over the 50 percent of the global classification. In these cases, the classified elements correspond exactly with a term or a definition.

In a low percentage (group "2"), the classified elements include extra information or noise. Nevertheless, in these cases the elements where also good classified as in group "3".

The incorrect classification of terms and definitions (group "1"), as well as the unclassified elements (group "Ø") correspond to a low percentage of the global classification.

Table 4. Evaluation of DCs elements identification

Verbal Patten		3	2	1	Ø
Concebir (como)	To conceive (as)	68.57	15.71	11.42	04.28
Definir (como)	To define (as)	65.10	18.22	10.41	06.25
Entender (como)	To understand (as)	54.16	20.83	8.33	16.66
Identificar (como)	To identify (as)	51.72	5.17	34.48	08.62
Consistir de	To consist of	60	0	20	20
Consistir en	To consist in	60.81	8.10	15.54	15.54
Constar de	To comprise	58.29	22.97	2.97	15.74
Denominar también	Also denominated	21.42	28.57	7.14	42.85
LLamar también	Also called	30	40	0	30
Servir para	To serve for	53.78	27.27	0.007	18.18
Significar	To signify	41.26	44.44	3.17	11.11
Usar como	To use as	63.41	14.63	17.07	4.87
Usar para	To use for	36.26	32.96	4.39	26.37
Utilzar como	To utilise as	55.10	28.57	10.20	6.12
Utilizar para	To utilise for	51.51	19.69	10.60	18.18

Since the purpose of this process was the identification of DCs elements, we can argue that results are generally satisfactory. However, there is a lot of work to do in order to improve the performance of decision's tree inferences. This work is related to the way the tree analyses the different DCs elements of each verbal pattern.

5   Conclusions and Future Work

We have presented the process of developing a definitional knowledge extraction system. The aim of this system is the simplification of the terminological practice related to the search of term's definitions in specialised texts.

The methodology we have presented includes the search of definitional patterns, the filtering of non-relevant contexts and the identification of DCs constitutive elements: terms, definitions, and pragmatic patterns.

At this moment we have worked with definitional verbs and we know that there is a lot of work to do, which basically consists of the following points:

a) To explore other kind of definitional patterns (mainly typographical patterns and reformulation markers) that are capable to recover definitional contexts.
b) To include those definitional patterns mentioned above in each step of the methodology.
c) To improve the rules for the non-relevant contexts filtering process, as well as the algorithm for the automatic identification of constitutive elements process.

Acknowledgments. This research has been developed by the sponsorship of the Mexican National Council of Science and Technology (CONACYT), the DGAPA UNAM, as well as the Macro Project *Tecnologías para la Universidad de la Información y la Computación*, UNAM. We also acknowledge the help of Bertha Lecumberri in the translation of this paper.

References

1. Pearson, J.: Terms in Context. John Benjamin's, Amsterdam (1998)
2. Meyer, I.: Extracting Knowledge-rich Contexts for Terminography. In: Bourigault, D., Jacquemin, C., L'Homme, M.C. (eds.), pp. 278–302. John Benjamin's, Amsterdam (2001)
3. Péry-Woodley, M.-P., Rebeyrolle, J.: Domain and Genre in Sublanguage Text: Definitional Microtexts in Three Corpora. In: First International Conference on Language Resources and Evaluation, Grenade, pp. 987–992 (1998)
4. Bach, C.: Los marcadores de reformulación como localizadores de zonas discursivas relevantes en el discurso especializado. Debate Terminológico, Electronic Journal 1 (2005)
5. Klavans, J., Muresan, S.: Evaluation of the DEFINDER System for Fully Automatic Glossary Construction. In: Proceedings of the American Medical Informatics Association Symposium, pp. 252–262. ACM Press, New York (2001)
6. Saggion, H.: Identifying Definitions in Text Collections for Question Answering. In: Proceedings of the 4th International Conference on Language Resources and Evaluation, Lisbon, pp. 1927–1930 (2004)
7. Malaisé, V.: Méthodologie linguistique et terminologique pour la structuration d'ontologies différentielles á partir de corpus textuels. PhD Thesis. UFR de Linguistique, Université Paris 7 – Denis Diderot, Paris (2005)
8. Sierra, G., Alarcón, R., Aguilar, C., Bach, C.: Definitional Verbal Patterns for Semantic Relation Extraction. Terminology 14(1), 74–98 (2008)
9. Del-Gaudio, R., Branco, A.: Automatic Extraction of Definitions in Portuguese: A Rule-Based Approach. In: Proceedings of the 2nd Workshop on Text Mining and Applications, Guimarães (2007)
10. Degórski, L., Marcinczuk, M., Przepiórkowski, A.: Definition Extraction Using a Sequential Combination of Baseline Grammars and Machine Learning Classifiers. In: Proceedings of the 6th International Conference on Language Resources and Evaluation, Forth-Coming, Marrakech (2008)
11. Alarcón, R., Bach, C., Sierra, G.: Extracción de contextos definitorios en corpus especializados. Hacia la elaboración de una herramienta de ayuda terminográfica. In: Revista de la Sociedad Española de Lingüística 37, pp. 247–278. Madrid (2007)

Using Graph-Based Indexing to Identify Subject-Shift in Topic Tracking

Fumiyo Fukumoto and Yoshimi Suzuki

Interdisciplinary Graduate School of Medicine and Engineering,
University of Yamanashi, Kofu 400-8511, Japan
{fukumoto,ysuzuki}@yamanashi.ac.jp

Abstract. This paper focuses on *subject shift* in chronologically ordered news story streams, and presents a method for topic tracking which makes use of the subject-shift. For finding the discussion of a topic (we call it subject term), we applied *keygraph* method to each story. Similar to tf*idf method, keygraph is a term weighting method which is based on co-occurrence graphs consisting high frequency terms and their co-occurrence terms. Subject-shifts are identified based on the difference between two types of subject terms: one is extracted from a test story itself, and another is extracted from the test story by using topic terms (terms related to a topic) of initial positive training stories. The method was tested on the TDT English corpus, and the results showed that the system is competitive to other sites, even for a small number of initial positive training stories.

Keywords: Topic tracking, Term weighting, Topic, Subject, Subject shift.

1 Introduction

With the exponential growth of information on the Internet, it is becoming increasingly difficult to find and organize *relevant* materials. Topic tracking, *i.e.*, it starts from a few sample stories and finds all subsequent stories that discuss the target topic, is a research to attack the problem [2]. Here, a topic is the same as TDT project: something that occurs at a specific place and time associated with some specific actions.

A wide range of statistical and machine learning (ML) techniques have been applied to topic tracking, including k-Nearest Neighbor classification, Decision Tree induction [5], relevance feedback method of IR [17], [6], unsupervised and supervised clustering [10], and a variety of Language Modeling [15], [14]. The main task of these techniques is to tune the parameters or the threshold for binary decisions to produce optimal results. In the TDT context, however, parameter tuning is a tricky issue for tracking because only a small number of labeled positive stories is available for training. Moreover, empirical results in the TDT evaluations by CMU and other research sites have shown that optimal parameter settings for early and later stories are often very different, and it is

Z. Vetulani and H. Uszkoreit (Eds.): LTC 2007, LNAI 5603, pp. 392–404, 2009.

overly optimistic to expect optimal parameter settings to generalize to new topics [3], [20]. This may be because of the fact that the discussion of a topic, *i.e.*, the subject changes over time, since the data for tracking is collected over an extended period of time.

In this paper, we propose a method for topic tracking on broadcast news stories to recognize and handle subject-shifts. We identify the subject of a topic for each story by applying an automatic indexing method, *keygraph* to each story. Keygraph is a term weighting method based on co-occurrence graphs consisting high frequency terms and their co-occurrence terms. The basic assumption of a topic and subject by using keygraph is as follows: terms related to a topic (we call these topic terms) are the same as Luhn's keyword extraction, *i.e.*, a topic frequently appeared in a story [16]. Terms related to a subject (we call these subject terms), the discussion of a topic, is located around the topic terms. We hypothesized that subject terms co-occurred in the topic terms. Let s_1 be positive training story of the target topic. Let also s_2 be related story of the target topic, and the subject of s_1 be shifted to the subject of s_2. This can be interpreted as subject terms of s_2 and subject terms (we call these subject-shift terms) which are extracted from s_2 by using the topic terms of s_1 are similar with each other. This is because s_1 and s_2 are the same topic. We identified subject-shifts using this feature of a topic and a subject.

The rest of the article is organized as follows. The next section provides an overview of existing techniques, which are accommodated the fact that the subject of stories changes over time. Section 3 explains why we need to detect subject shift by providing notions of a *topic*, and a *subject* which are properties that identify subject-shift. After describing keygraph, we explain a tracking method. Finally, we report some experiments using the TDT English corpus and end with a discussion of evaluation.

2 Related Work

Topic tracking is similar to information filtering task [4] of Information Retrieval (IR), since both handle shift, *i.e.*, topic tracking handles subject-shift and information filtering handles a change of user's interest. Allan proposed a method of incremental relevance feedback for information filtering which is based on weighting stories [1]. The result of the method which was tested on the data from the TREC routing experiments [11] has shown satisfactory performance. However, TREC data provides a large amount of training data with queries and relevance judgments. For the TDT conditions, on the other hand, the number of labeled positive training examples which are allowed is very small (one to four).

More recently, Elsayed [7], Connell [6], and Allan's group [6] explored on-line adaptive filtering approaches based on the threshold strategy. The basic idea behind their work is that stories closer together in the stream are more likely to discuss related topics than stories further apart. The method presented by Allan's group at UMass is based on adaptation, the traditional vector space model with tf*idf weighting, and relevance models [6]. Adaptation allows the addition of the incoming story to the topic representation and recomputes the topic centroid. Adaptation uses an additional threshold which determines whether a new story is similar enough to the centroid to be added to the topic. A new centroid is computed from the story vectors each time a new story is added to the topic. The method proposed in this paper is similar to Allan's group which uses term weighting and adaptation, while the term weighting method we used is to identify subject-shifts.

As well as information retrieval, an increasing number of ML techniques have been applied to the topic tracking task [2], [20]. Zhang's group at CMU combined Rocchio and logistic regression for bias variance trade off [21]. They reported that the performance was 449.17 utility using the TDT4 corpus which was the best among all submitted supervised adaptation topic tracking results, while they mentioned that parameter tuning is a tricky issue for robustness of the tracking system. Klinkenberg et al. presented a method to handle concept changes with SVMs [13]. They use $\xi\alpha$-estimates [12] to select the window size so that the estimated generalization error on new examples is minimized. The result which was tested on a subset of 2,608 stories of the data set of the TREC shows that the algorithm achieves a low error rate and selects appropriate window sizes. $\xi\alpha$-estimates have also been applied to model selection for text classification [12], since it can estimate the generalization performance of SVMs without any computation-intensive re-sampling. Much of these work on $\xi\alpha$-estimates use a large number of training data, while the number of initial positive training stories is very small in the TDT condition. Therefore, the system needs to estimate whether the test stories are the same topic with few information about the topic.

3   A Topic and a Subject

The tracking task is one of the five different tasks: story link detection, clustering topic detection, new event detection, story segmentation and topic tracking, defined by the TDT project. As illustrated in Fig 1, it starts from a few training stories and classifying all subsequent stories as to whether or not they discuss the target topic. For topic tracking where data is collected over an extended period of time, the discussion of a topic *i.e.*, the subject changes over time.

Here, a subject refers to a *theme* of the story itself, i.e. something a writer wishes to express. It appears across stories with related theme, but does not appear in other stories [16]. A topic, on the other hand, is something that occurs at a specific place and time associated with some specific actions, and it appears across stories about the target topic. Let us take a look at the following three stories concerning the Kobe Japan quake from the TDT1.

The underlined words in Fig. 2 denote a subject term in each story. Terms marked with "{}" refer to a topic term. Words such as "Kobe" and "Japan" are associated with a topic, since all of these stories concern the Kobe Japan quake. The first story says that emergency work continues after the earthquake in Japan. Underlined words such as "rescue", "crews", "people", and "injuries" denote the

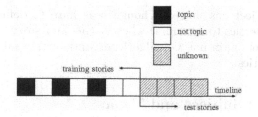

Fig. 1. The Tracking Task defined by the TDT

---

1. Emergency work continues after earthquake in Japan

1-1. Casualties are mounting in {Japan}, where a strong {earthquake} eight hours ago struck {Kobe}. Up to 400 people related deaths are confirmed, thousands of injuries, and rescue crews are searching
. . . .

---

2. Quake Collapses Buildings in Central Japan

2-1. At least two people died and dozens injuries when a powerful {earthquake} rolled through central {Japan} Tuesday morning, collapsing buildings and setting off fires in the cities of {Kobe} and Osaka.

2-2. The {Japan} Meteorological Agency said the {earthquake}, which measured 7.2 on the open-ended Richter scale, rumbled across Honshu Island from the Pacific Ocean to the {Japan} Sea.

2-3. The worst hit areas were the port city of {Kobe} and the nearby island of Awajishima where in both places dozens of fires broke out and up to 50 buildings, including several apartment blocks,
. . . .

---

3. US forces to fly blankets to Japan quake survivors

3-1. United States forces based in {Kobe} {Japan} will take blankets to help {earthquake} survivors Thursday, in the U.S. military's first disaster relief operation in {Japan} since it set up bases here.

3-2. A military transporter was scheduled to take off in the afternoon from Yokota air base on the outskirts of Tokyo and fly to Osaka with 37,000 blankets.

3-3. Following the {earthquake} Tuesday, President Clinton offered the assistance of U.S. military forces in {Japan}, and Washington provided the Japanese
. . . .

Fig. 2. Documents concerning the Kobe Japan Quake

subject of the story. The second story states that the quake collapsed buildings in central Japan. These two stories mention the same thing: A powerful earthquake rolled through central Japan, and many people were injured. Therefore, the subject has not changed.

The third story, on the other hand, states that the US military will fly blankets to Japan quake survivors. The subject of the story is different from the earlier ones, i.e., the subject has shifted. Though it is hard to define a subject, it is easier to find properties to determine whether the later story discusses the same subject as an earlier one or not. Our algorithm for detecting subject-shift exploits this feature of stories.

4   Identifying Subject and Topic

The goal of this article is to recognize subject-shift for topic tracking. Let s_1 be positive training story of the target topic. Let also s_2 be related story of the target topic, and the subject of s_1 be shifted to the subject of s_2. This can be interpreted as subject terms of s_2 and subject terms which are extracted from the story s_2 by using topic terms of s_1 are similar. This is because s_1 and s_2 are the same topic. We identified subject-shifts using this feature of a topic and a subject.

For finding the discussion of a topic in each story, the system identifies subject and topic terms in each story. To this end, we used *keygraph*. Keygraph is an automatic indexing which is based on a co-occurrence graph [18]. The basic idea is that terms which refer to the author's point in the story co-occur with terms which frequently appeared in a story. More detail about keygraph can be found in [18]. We applied their technique to identify subject-shift.

The basic assumption of the topic and subject using keygraph is as follows: terms related to a topic (we call them topic terms) are the same as Luhn's keyword extraction, *i.e.*, the topic frequently appeared in a story [16]. We extracted terms with high frequency, *i.e.*, we chose the topmost 10 terms according the frequency and regarded them as topic terms. Terms related to a subject, the author's point (we call them subject terms), are located around the topic terms. We thus assume that the subject terms co-occur with the topic terms.

Let S be a story which consists of $t_1, \cdots, t_{n-1}, t_n$, and $r_1, \cdots r_{m-1}$ and r_m. Here, $t_1, \cdots, t_{n-1}$ and t_n are nodes (terms) in the graph G with high frequency, and $r_1, \cdots r_{m-1}$ and r_m are not. In Fig. 3 (1), black and white circle denotes a node with and without high frequency in a document, respectively. For each $t_1, \cdots t_n$, if t_i and t_j co-occurred within the document, we connect them by an edge. (Fig. 3 (2)) Next, we delete an edge which is not a constituent of maximal connected sub-graph. Here, a graph is a maximal connected sub-graph when there are no nodes and edges in the graph that could be added to the sub-graph and still leave it connected. After eliminating edges (Fig. 3 (3)), we extract nodes as topic terms. Next, for each extracted topic term $tt_1, \cdots tt_{n'}$, if tt_i and r_j co-occurred in the document, we connect them by an edge. (Fig. 3 (4)). We extract terms whose co-occurrence is larger than 3 as subject terms[1] Double circles in Fig. 3 (5) denotes the extracted terms as a subject of the document[2].

---

[1] The value is empirically determined, *i.e.*, different numbers of co-occurrence were tested, and the number that optimized F score for tracking was chosen.

[2] As shown in Fig. 3 (5), some terms are both subject and topic terms.

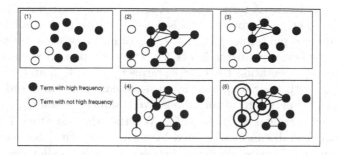

Fig. 3. Identifying Subjects and Topics

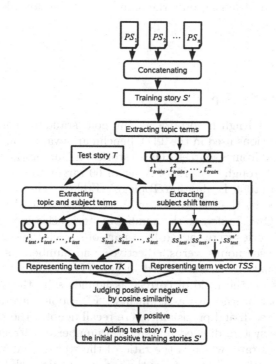

Fig. 4. Tracking based on the Subject-Shift

5 Tracking Based on the Subject-Shift

The tracking task, finding stories that discuss the target topic from incoming stories is done by identifying subject-shift.

Fig. 4 illustrates tracking based on subject-shifts. Let $PS_1, \ldots, PS_n$ be initial positive training stories. We concatenate these into one story S', and extract topic terms $t^1_{train}, \cdots, t^m_{train}$ from the story S'. Suppose we determined whether a test story T is positive. We apply keygraph method, and extract topic terms

$t_{test}^1, \cdots, t_{test}^l$ and subject terms $s_{test}^1, \cdots, s_{test}^{l'}$. Next, we extract subject-shifts terms, $ss_{test}^1, \cdots, ss_{test}^{m'}$ of story T. This is done by not using the topic terms of T, but instead using topic terms $t_{train}^1, \cdots, t_{train}^m$ of initial positive training stories extracted by the keygraph method. The test story is represented as two vectors: one is a vector representation TK of topic terms $t_{test}^1, \cdots, t_{test}^l$ and subject terms $s_{test}^1, \cdots, s_{test}^{l'}$, with their frequency in an n-dimensional space, and another is a vector TSS of topic terms of initial positive training stories, $t_{train}^1, \cdots, t_{train}^m$ and subject-shift terms, $ss_{test}^1, \cdots, ss_{test}^{m'}$. Whether the test story T is positive is judged using the distance (measured by cosine similarity) between TK and TSS. If the value of cosine similarity between them is smaller than a certain threshold value, the test story is regarded as positive, and added to the initial positive training stories, S'. This procedure is repeated until the last test story is assigned. Similar to Allan's group, the number of stories for adaptation is less than 100 [1], [14], [6].

6 Experiments

6.1 Experiments Set Up

We chose the TDT3 English corpora as our gold standard corpora, and set the evaluation conditions used in the TDT benchmark evaluation. The stories of TDT3 were collected from 8 sources (34,600 stories) including the ABC News for the period of Oct. through Dec. 1998. A set of 60 target topics were manually identified as topics (1999 Evaluation Topics).[3] Table 1 illustrates examples of target topics defined by the TDT. "ID" in Table 1 shows the id number defined by the TDT, and "OnT." refers to the number of stories classified into the target topic. All English stories were tagged by a part-of-speech tagger [19], and stop word removal. We used nouns, verbs, adjectives, and numbers as terms.

We set the evaluation measures used in the TDT benchmark evaluations. "Precision" stands for the ratio of correct assignments by the system divided by the total number of system's assignments. "F" (pooled average) is a measure that balances recall and precision, where recall denotes the ratio of correct assignments by the system divided by the total number of correct assignments. "Miss" denotes Miss rate, which is the ratio of the stories that were judged as YES but were not evaluated as such for the run in question. "F/A" shows false alarm rate, which is the ratio of the stories judged as NO but were evaluated as YES. The DET curve plots misses and false alarms, and better performance is indicated by curves more to the lower left of the graph. The detection cost function (C_{Det}) is defined by Eq (1).

$$C_{Det} = (C_{Miss} * P_{Miss} * P_{Target} + C_{Fa} * P_{Fa} * (1 - P_{Target}))$$
$$P_{Miss} = \#Misses/\#Targets$$
$$P_{Fa} = \#FalseAlarms/\#NonTargets \tag{1}$$

---

[3] http://projects.ldc.upenn.edu/TDT3/

Table 1. Examples of Topic Name

ID	Topic name	OnT.	ID	Topic	OnT.
30001	Cambodian government coalition	34	30003	Pinochet trial	312
30006	NBA labor disputes	221	30012	Princess Diana crash investigation	12
30017	North Korean food shortages	24	30018	Tony Blair visits China in Oct.	8
30022	Chinese dissidents sentenced	48	30030	Taipei mayoral elections	10
30031	Shuttle Endeavour mission for space station	158	30033	Euro introduced	126
30034	Indonesia-east Timor conflict	28	30038	Olympic bribery scandal	53
30041	Jiang's historic visit to Japan	22	30042	PanAm lockerbie bombing trial	108
30047	Space station module Zarya launched	77	30048	IMF bailout of Brazil	104
30049	North Korean nuclear facility?	55	30050	U.S. mid-term elections	502
30053	Clinton's Gaza trip	182	30055	D'Alema's new Italian government	35
30057	India train derailment	17	30060	Hyndai Aids N. Korean Economy	14

C_{Miss}, C_{Fa}, and P_{Target} are the costs of a missed detection, false alarm, and priori probability of finding a target, respectively. C_{Miss}, C_{Fa}, and P_{Target} are usually set to 10, 1, and 0.02, respectively. The normalized cost function is defined by Eq (2), and lower cost scores indicate better performance. More information about these measures can be found in [9]

$$(C_{Det})_{Norm} = C_{Det}/MIN(C_{Miss} * P_{Target}, C_{Fa} * (1 - P_{Target})) \qquad (2)$$

6.2 Basic Results

Table 2 summaries the tracking results, and Fig. 5 shows DET curves varying the number of initial positive training stories. The threshold of cosine similarity is set to 0.4. "N_t" denotes the number of initial positive training stories. "Miss" denotes Miss rate, and "F/A" shows false alarm rate. "Prec" stands for precision, and "F" (pooled avg) is a measure that balances recall and precision. MIN denotes $MIN(C_{Det})_{Norm}$ which is the value of $(C_{Det})_{Norm}$ at the best possible threshold. We can see from Table 2 and Fig. 5 that the method correctly extracted stories related to the target topic even for a small number of positive training stories, as the value of $MIN(C_{Det})_{Norm}$ is at most .116.

To examine how the threshold of cosine similarity affects the overall performance of our method, we tested by varying the threshold values. The results are shown in Fig. 6. Fig. 6 shows the impact by our method that varying thresholds has on the effectiveness for tracking at every N_t values.

Table 2. Basic Results

				TDT3 (60 topics)		
N_t	Miss	F/A	Recall	Precision	F	MIN
1	58%	.08%	42%	31%	.35	.116
2	48%	.07%	52%	41%	.46	.087
4	43%	.08%	52%	58%	.55	.087

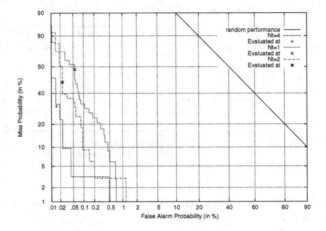

Fig. 5. Tracking Result against # of N_t Values

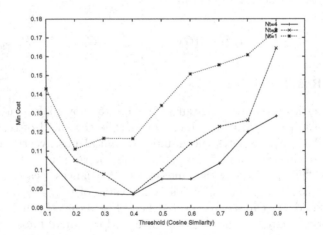

Fig. 6. Min Cost against Threshold Values

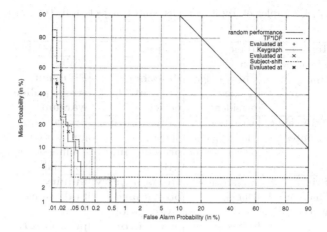

Fig. 7. The Efficacy of Subject-Shifts based on Keygraph

6.3 The Efficacy of Subject-Shifts Based on Keygraph

We identified the subject of a topic for each story by applying an automatic indexing method, keygraph to each story in order to handle subject-shifts. The contribution of the subject-shift based on keygraph is best explained by looking at two results: the traditional vector space model with (i) tf*idf weighting, and (ii) keygraph. In the method (ii), keygraph indexing method is applied to each training and test story, and topic and subject terms are extracted. In each method, the top 100 terms are used as a vector representation of each story, and cosine similarity between training and each test story is calculated. Like our method, if the value of cosine similarity between them is smaller than a certain threshold value, the test story is regarded as positive. Fig. 7 illustrates DET curves by three methods including our method. To make some comparison possible, only the $N_t = 4$ is given for each. The threshold value of cosine similarity for (i) tf*idf was 0.5, and that for (ii) keygraph was 0.3, each of which was the best results. We can see from Fig. 7 that our method, *i.e.*, subject-shift curve is better (lower) than other two curves.

Table 3 shows examples of topic and subject terms (top five) extracted by our method ($N_t = 4$). "ID" denotes topic number defined by the TDT. "Topic" shows topic terms extracted from the initial positive training stories. "Subject" and "Subject-shift" refer to subject terms, and subject-shift terms from the first story which should be judged as positive, respectively. As can be clearly seen from Table 3, each extracted term is related to the *content* of each topic, *i.e.*, "Topic name" in Table 3 which is provided by the TDT project. Moreover, the extracted subject and subject-shift terms is almost the same. This shows that the method successfully captures the feature of subject-shifts.

Table 3. Examples of Topic, Subject, and Subject-shift Terms (Top 5)

Topic name	Topic	Subject	Subject-shift
Pinochet trial	Pinochet Chile, judge, London president	**Chile Pinochet warrant**, data, **police**	**Chile Pinochet**, arrest, **police**, **warrant**
NBA labor disputes	exception player, game owner, season	**game, team** player, **pre-season**, NBA	**pre-season**, **game, team** commissioner, national
Princess Diana crash investigation	investigator Diana, Mercedes, princess, Uno	**Diana inquiry, bodyguard**, investigation, **prosecutor**	**inquiry, bodyguard, Diana, prosecutor**, Paris

Table 4. Results by Our Method and Other Sites(N_t=1)

TDT3 (30 topics, N_t=1)			
Site	MIN	Site	MIN
LIMSI	**.1203**	RMIT3	.3636
Ulowa1	.1857	UMASSI	**.1468**
Keygraph(adaptation)	**.1446**		

6.4 The Efficacy of the Incremental Approach

We recall that Allan's group explored adaptation method with relevance models and reported that incremental approach is effective for the tracking task[1], [14], [6]. We thus used adaptation in our method. In the tracking task, if a test story is regarded as positive, the test story is added to the initial positive training stories, and keygraph is re-applied. This procedure is repeated until the last test story is judged. Similar to Allan's group, the number of stories for adaptation is less than 100. Fig. 8 shows result. The result by adaptation is slightly better than the result obtained by not using adaptation, especially the DET curve obtained by adaptation shows an emphasis on low false alarm rates.

6.5 Comparison with Related Works

Table 4 illustrates the performance of our method compared to the other research sites which tested on the 2001 training topics, *i.e.*, 60 topics in all, and 30 each drawn from the 1999 and 2000 evaluation sets (withheld topics). Table 4 shows the result when N_t is set to 1. Each site in Table 4 was reported by Fiscus [8][4].

---

[4] http://www.nist.gov/speech/tests/tdt/tdt2001/PaperPres/Nist-pres/ NIST-presentation-v6_files/frame.htm

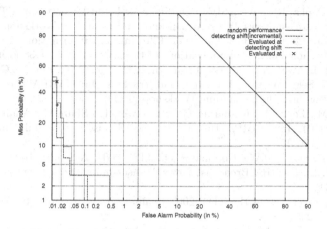

Fig. 8. The Efficacy for Incremental Approach

The threshold of cosine similarity used in our method is 0.4 which was learned from 2000 evaluation topics. We can see that the performance by our method is competitive to other sites, since the top site is LIMSI(.1203), and the result by our method(.1446) is very similar to Ulowa1(.1857).

7   Conclusion

We proposed a method for topic tracking to identify subject-shift based on key-graph. The purpose of this study was to investigate whether using subject-shift is effective to track the target topic. While much of the previous work rely on statistics such as tf*idf weighting, some language modelings such as relevance model, or ML techniques to produce optimal results, we tried to make a clear distinction between a topic and a subject of a story to identify subject-shifts. The empirical results are very encouraging and show that the method is effective even for a small number of positive training stories. Future work includes (i) extending the method to utilize a large number of labeled negative training stories to obtain further advantages in effectiveness in the tracking, (ii) applying the method to the TDT4 corpora for quantitative evaluation, and (iii) extending the method to multilingual topic tracking.

References

1. Allan, J.: Incremental Relevance Feedback for Information Filtering. In: 19th Annual International ACM SIGIR Conference on Research and Development in Information Retrieval, pp. 270–278 (1996)
2. Allan, J., Carbonell, J., Doddington, G., Yamron, J., Yang, Y.: Topic Detection and Tracking Pilot Study Final Report. In: DARPA Broadcast News Transcription and Understanding Workshop (1998)

3. Allan, J., Papka, R., Lavrenko, V.: On-line New Event Detection and Tracking. In: DARPA Broadcast News Transcription and Understanding Workshop (1998)
4. Belkin, N.J., Croft, W.B.: Information Filtering and Information Retrieval: Two sides of the same coin? Communications of the ACM 35(2), 29–38 (1992)
5. Carbonell, J., Yang, Y., Lafferty, J., Brown, R.D., Pierce, T., Liu, X.: CMU Report on TDT-2: Segmentation, Detection and Tracking. In: DARPA Broadcast News Transcription and Understanding Workshop (1999)
6. Connell, M., Feng, A., Kumaran, G., Raghavan, H., Shah, C., Allan, J.: UMass at TDT 2004. In: DARPA Broadcast News Transcription and Understanding Workshop (2004)
7. Elsayed, T., Oard, D.W., Doermann, D.: TDT-2004: Adaptive Topic Tracking at Maryland. In: DARPA Broadcast News Transcription and Understanding Workshop (2004)
8. Fiscus, J.: Overview of the TDT 2001 Evaluation and Results. In: Workshop on TDT 2001 (2001)
9. Fiscus, J.G., Doddington, G.R.: Topic Detection and Tracking Evaluation Overview. In: Allan, J. (ed.) Topic Detection and Tracking. Kluwer Academic Publisher, Dordrecht (2002)
10. Franz, M., McCarley, J.S.: Unsupervised and Supervised Clustering for Topic Tracking. In: 24th Annual International ACM SIGIR Conference on Research and Development in Information Retrieval, pp. 310–317 (2001)
11. Harman, D.: Overview of the fourth Text REtrieval Conference (TREC4). In: 4th Text REtrieval Conference, TREC-4 (1996)
12. Joachims, T.: Estimating the Generalization Performance of an SVM Efficiently. In: 17th International Conference on Machine Learning, pp. 431–438 (2000)
13. Klinkenberg, R., Joachims, T.: Detecting Concept Drift with Support Vector Machines. In: 17th International Conference on Machine Learning, pp. 487–494 (2000)
14. Larkey, L.S., Feng, F., Connell, M., Lavernko, V.: Language-specific Model in Multilingual Topic Tracking. In: 27th Annual International ACM SIGIR Conference on Research and Development in Information Retrieval, pp. 402–409 (2004)
15. Lowe, S.A.: The Beta-binomial Mixture Model and its Application to TDT Tracking and Detection. In: DARPA Broadcast News Transcription and Understanding Workshop (1999)
16. Luhn, H.P.: The Automatic Creation of Literature Abstracts. IBM journal 2(1), 159–165 (1958)
17. Oard, D.W.: Topic Tracking with the PRISE Information Retrieval System. In: DARPA Broadcast News Transcription and Understanding Workshop, pp. 94–101 (1999)
18. Ohsawa, Y., Benson, N.E., Yachida, M.: KeyGraph: Automatic Indexing by Co-occurrence Graph Based on Building Construction Metaphor. In: Advances in Digital Libraries Conference, pp. 12–18 (1998)
19. Schmid, H.: Improvements in Part-of-Speech Tagging with an Application to German. In: EACL SIGDAT Workshop (1995)
20. Yang, Y., Ault, T., Pierce, T., Lattimer, C.W.: Improving Text Categorization Methods for Event Tracking. In: 23rd Annual International ACM SIGIR Conference on Research and Development in Information Retrieval, pp. 65–72 (2000)
21. Zhang, Y., Callan, J.: CMU DIR Supervised Tracking Report. In: DARPA Broadcast News Transcription and Understanding Workshop (2004)

Result Aggregation for Knowledge-Intensive Multicultural Name Matching

Keith J. Miller and Mark Arehart

MITRE Corporation, 7515 Colshire Dr., McLean VA 22102, USA
{keith,marehart}@mitre.org

Abstract. In this paper, we describe a metasearch tool resulting from experiments in aggregating the results of different name matching algorithms on a knowledge-intensive multicultural name matching task. Three retrieval engines that match romanized names were tested on a noisy and predominantly Arabic dataset. One is based on a generic string matching algorithm; another is designed specifically for Arabic names; and the third makes use of culturally-specific matching strategies for multiple cultures. We show that even a relatively naïve method for aggregating results significantly increased effectiveness over each of the individual algorithms, resulting in nearly tripling the F-score of the worst-performing algorithm included in the aggregate, and in a 6-point improvement in F-score over the single best-performing algorithm included.

Keywords: Information Retrieval, Name Matching, System Combination.

1 Introduction

Matching multicultural romanized names is a difficult problem due to variation in transliteration, database fielding and segmentation, the presence of incomplete names, titles, initials, abbreviations, and nicknames, and various forms of data corruption such as typos, OCR errors, and truncation. These difficulties are particularly acute for Arabic names. In addition to substantial transliteration variation, Arabic names are structurally complex and may contain several more segments than a typical Anglo name. These name segments carry varying information value, and a single individual may use varying subsets of the name segments in his or her full name in a given context.

Commercial and open source algorithms for name matching include name compression techniques, generic string matching, culture-specific name matching, and multicultural name matching. For many name matching tasks, particularly those with noisy and multicultural data, a single matching algorithm may be inadequate.

We describe a metasearch tool resulting from experiments in aggregating the results of different name matching algorithms on a particularly knowledge-intensive multicultural name matching task. Three retrieval engines that match

Z. Vetulani and H. Uszkoreit (Eds.): LTC 2007, LNAI 5603, pp. 405–412, 2009.
© Springer-Verlag Berlin Heidelberg 2009

romanized names were tested on a noisy dataset composed predominantly of names of Arabic origin. One engine is based on a generic string matching algorithm; another is designed specifically for Arabic names; the third makes use of culturally-specific matching strategies for multiple cultures. We show that even a relatively naïve method for aggregating results can significantly increase effectiveness over results from each of the individual algorithms taken in isolation.

2   Method

2.1   Training/Test Corpus

Our matching task is modeled as running a set of name queries against a larger name data list. Based on a small survey of real-world data sources containing name data, the underlying data model for the name element in both our query list and our data list contains fields for surname and given name. Furthermore, the test data was designed to include the types of noise that were observed in the name data we surveyed (e.g. given name and surname data in incorrect fields, deleted name segments, misspellings and typos, initials in place of full names, etc.).

The data list contains 313,557 (unique) names. Of these, 10,852 (3.5%) are partial names, meaning the surname or given name is either empty or a token such as FNU (first name unknown) or LNU (last name unknown). The partial names, though marginally useful as identifiers of individuals, were included because search algorithms must nevertheless process and score them in real-life situations. The data list is approximately 75% Arabic (according to an automatic classification tool using broad criteria that may also classify a certain percentage of Persian names as Arabic), with most of the remaining names being Anglo and Hispanic.

Although the exact number is not known, there are far fewer unique individuals in the data set than there are unique names. A given individual may be represented by several aliases and name variants. The types of name variation observed can be divided into element-level variation (affecting individual name segments) and structural variation (involving more than one segment). After examining samples of the data list, we have broken down these types of variation into the categories below:

1. Element variations
   (a) Data errors
       i. Optical Character Recognition errors
       ii. Typos
       iii. Truncations
   (b) Name particles
       i. Segmentation, e.g. *Abd Al Rahman = Abdal Rahman, De Los Angeles = Delosangeles*
       ii. Omission, e.g. of *bin* in Arabic names or *de* in Hispanic names.
   (c) Short forms
       i. Abbreviations, e.g. *Muhammad = Mhd*

      ii. Initials, e.g. *John Smith = J Smith*
  (d) Spelling variations
      i. Alternate spellings, e.g. *Jennifer = Jenifer*
      ii. Transliteration, e.g. *Husayn = Husein*
  (e) Nicknames and diminutives, e.g. *Robert = Bob*
  (f) Translation variants, e.g. *Joseph = Giuseppe*
2. Structural variations
  (a) Additions/deletions, e.g. *John Smith = John Charles Smith*
  (b) Fielding variation: division of full name into surname and given name, or swapping given name and surname
  (c) Permutations, e.g. *Clara Lucia Garcia = Lucia Clara Garcia*
  (d) Placeholders: non-name tokens like FNU, LNU, UNK
  (e) Element segmentation, e.g. *Mohamed Amin = Mohammedamin*

Because these types of variation, which may occur singly or in combination, go beyond superficial spelling differences, we would expect searches based on generic string matching algorithms to perform relatively poorly.

The query list contains 621 names. About 20% were created to be near matches to data list names. About 13% were taken directly from the data list, and were exact matches to a record in the data list. Finding an exact match is of course trivial, but many data sources contain clusters of similar or near duplicate names. The task for the search engines is to match all the other members of the cluster, which may display variations in spellings and structural representation. The rest of the queries come from a variety of sources. Mirroring the composition of the data list, the majority of the query names are Arabic, and the rest are primarily Anglo and Hispanic.

The 621 query names were randomly partitioned into 421 training queries and 200 held-out test queries.

2.2   Ground Truth Data

To compile ground truth data for name matches, we adapted the methodology used for the National Institute for Standards in Technology (NIST) Text REtrieval Conference (TREC) [1] [2]. As in the TREC methodology, adjudication pools were generated and then judged manually.

Given that it is impossible to adjudicate every possible query-list/data-list name pair—the 621 queries and 313,557 names would yield 194,718,897 combinations, only a tiny portion of which are good matches—it is necessary to construct adjudication pools in order to be able to estimate system performance in terms of recall. In order to maximize the likelihood that the pools contain all the true matches, they are generated by combining the returns of all the available algorithms using lower-than-normal matching thresholds as cutoff values for inclusion in the pools. The algorithms used included five commercial-off-the-shelf tools and one open-source string matching algorithm. These searches resulted in pools containing an average of 124 returns to be adjudicated per query. These

pools were adjudicated by a team of individual adjudicators, following guidelines
that were iteratively developed and refined in consultation with the research
team.

In adjudicating the results, the definition of a "match", i.e. the question asked
of adjudicators, cannot be determined devoid of context, but must reflect a
certain use case. The scenario envisioned here is one in which a system presents
name search results to an end user who has access to additional identifying
attributes in order to make a decision about an overall identity match. We assume
a "high risk" environment where there is a low tolerance for false negatives, and
a correspondent higher tolerance for false positives. That is, the end user is
relatively willing to sift through a fair number of spurious matches in order to
ensure that she does not miss a potentially good identity match between a query
and a name in the data list.

We therefore developed a set of guidelines using an intentionally "loose" truth
criterion, according to which two names should be considered a match despite
significant variation beyond superficial spelling differences, as long as there exists
some plausible relationship between the names. Matching record pairs in the
resulting ground truth set therefore exist along a wide continuum, from exact
matches at one extreme to pairs for which the similarity is much more distant at
the other. For instance, the name records below, in which the data contained in
the surname field appears in all capital letters, would be considered a possible
match.

$$\text{Mohamed BIN AHMED HAMMADI} \tag{1}$$

$$\text{Haji Muhammad Hamadi AL MASRI} \tag{2}$$

Note that only two of the four tokens in (1) are matched in (2), and two of the five
tokens in (2) are matched to (1). Furthermore, there are no matching elements
between the surname fields. Because of the structure of Arabic names however,
the apparently mismatching elements do not necessarily conflict. Bin Ahmed is
an optional name element meaning "son of Ahmed", Haji is an honorific title
used by someone who has made the pilgrimage to Mecca, and Al Masri means
"the Egyptian". It is therefore possible that these two names could belong to a
single person whose full name is Haji Mohamed Bin Ahmed Hammadi Al Masri.
It is worth noting that different use cases may call for different adjudication
criteria, which could result in a different composition of the ground truth set.

Names not in the adjudication pools—and thus not in the ground truth set—
are assumed to be false matches for purposes of evaluation. To the extent that
this is not the case, the evaluation metric will overestimate recall. However, the
relative scores are still fair, so long as each algorithm is allowed to contribute
equally to the adjudication pools.

2.3   Name Matchers and Aggregation Strategy

The algorithms available for this study include the open source Jaro-Winkler
string similarity metric [3] [4], a commercial tool that is based on generic string

similarity measures, a commercial tool specialized for Arabic names, and a commercial tool that does culturally-sensitive name matching for names from a variety of cultural origins. Each tool was evaluated individually for precision and recall. Then, experimentation continued to determine a method for augmenting recall while maintaining precision. The resulting system was an aggregation of the three commercial tools.

Aggregation Strategy. The simplest method of aggregation would be simply to return a union of all results from the three tools in question. A cursory consideration of the shortcomings of such a result set reveals a set of desiderata for our result aggregation module. A simple union of tools' results would:

1. contain all of the good *and* all of the bad result records from each tool,
2. contain duplicate result records from the data list,
3. result in an unordered set of results, leaving the end user to guess whether any particular result record is better than any other, and
4. (if scores were retained) contain scores from separate tools that are on different scales and thus cannot be compared. Such information in the result set would be at best uninformative, and at worst misleading.

In order to deal with these shortcomings, we would ideally like to have a) a way of choosing an optimal threshold for each tool, such that precision and recall for that tool are maximized, b) a normalization function such that scores between systems can be compared, c) a method for combining those scores, such that we arrive at a single score for each record in the result set, with that score preferably being influenced more by the more effective tool, and d) a final filter, such that records that do not pass this filter are not included in the aggregate result set. This final filter serves to maintain or enhance precision, whereas the initial union of the tools' outputs serves to increase recall.

Threshold Determination. Thresholds for the individual algorithms were determined using an exhaustive search to find the combination of thresholds that yields the best set of combined results according to the F-measure. In practice, an exhaustive search of thresholds is only feasible with a limited number (i.e. two or three) algorithms because the combinatorial explosion of possibilities would prevent exhaustive search as this number grows larger. This approach was deemed acceptable for our purposes insofar as most practical metasearch systems combining strategies would be limited to two or three base algorithms.

Score Normalization (Rescaling). Aggregation of scores was achieved using a weighted average of normalized scores of the three base searches. The returns from each search are rescored using simple linear rescaling, to meet the following criteria:

$$0 \leq score_{norm} \leq 1 \text{ and} \tag{3}$$

$$score_{norm} = \frac{(score_{raw} - score_{min})}{(score_{max} - score_{min})} \tag{4}$$

where $score_{max}$ is the highest score an algorithm can return, and $score_{min}$ is the cutoff threshold used for that algorithm.

Score Combination. In order to produce a ranked list of returns rather than a set, the individual scores need to be combined. Aggregation of scores was accomplished by using a weighted average, with the weights determined using the linear regression function from the WEKA machine learning package [5]. We created a training set from the base runs consisting of match pairs scoring above their individual thresholds. Matching name pairs were assigned a value of 1 and non-matches 0.

These weights were then rescaled to sum to one in order to produce a weighed average over the range 0 to 1. The final equation for aggregation of scores from the three commercial tools is:

$$s(x, y) = \sum_{i=1}^{n} w_i s(x, y)_i \tag{5}$$

where $s(x, y)$ indicates the rescaled score resulting from the comparison of names x and y by an algorithm, the index i indicates a base algorithm, and w a weight.

Other models, such as logistic regression, decision trees, and Bayesian networks were considered, but initial experiments did not yield better results, so these additional experiments were left as future work.

Final Result Set Production and Presentation. Once the results were ranked using the weighted average, a final threshold was chosen that yielded the best F-score on the training data. Finally, it was necessary to perform a final rescaling of the score for each record returned. This was based on requirements from two fronts: the first reason was largely psychological. Preliminary discussions with potential end-users indicated that they were accustomed to scores for record pairs that they considered to be "good matches" to be in the range of roughly 0.80–1.00, not in the 0.20 range (which was the range in which we had been able to set the final threshold for our aggregated metasearch system). They indicated that they were less inclined to consider a record a good match if its score were in this lower range. Secondly, developers of other systems who were considering integration of our module into larger systems indicated that it would be easier for them to integrate our scores if they underwent a final rescaling. Thus, in order to make the result set scores more palatable to end users and to allow for combination of our name similarity scores with those from other identity attributes, we incorporated this final rescaling into our design.

3   Results

Precision, recall, and F-scores on the held-out test data are shown in Table 1. All of the algorithms are configurable by threshold. The results shown are for the threshold that yielded the highest F-score. The commercial tools allow for varying amounts of customization, but for purposes of this evaluation we used out-of-the-box configuration options. It is possible that performance could be improved by manipulating various parameter settings, but that is a nontrivial effort beyond the scope of this paper.

Table 1. Name Matching Performance

Algorithm	Precision	Recall	F
Open Source	0.08	0.07	0.08
Commercial 1	0.35	0.18	0.24
Commercial 2	0.53	0.31	0.39
Commercial 3	0.71	0.44	0.55
Combination	0.62	0.60	0.61

4   Related Work

Aslam and Montague [6] provide an overview of aggregation strategies (which they term metasearch) in the Information Retrieval field. Based on the results of experiments on TREC data, they suggest that aggregation using rank-based normalization performs as well as or better than strategies based on score combination.

A rank-based approach was initially appealing in that it provided a relatively simple yet effective aggregation strategy. Unlike the similarity metrics produced by different algorithms, ranks are directly comparable. Ranks can be converted into scores using the Borda count, in which the top-ranked candidate receives c points, the second $c - 1$, etc., where c is a parameter that determines how many candidates each system can consider. Scores can be summed across searches, and if training data is available, weighted based on a system's average precision.

However, a key difference between our problem and the one modeled by TREC precluded our using this approach. In the TREC task, it is known *a priori* that every query will have true matches in the test database. For any given query there is a relatively consistent and high base rate of matches. Thus it is likely, for instance, that the top-ranked result of any reasonable search algorithm will be relevant. Where there are large pools of relevant results, the information loss in converting scores into ranks is not great.

In our task, however, there is high variability in the number of true matches per query. Indeed, for some queries there are no true matches in the database at all. The closest match for one name query may be an exact match, and for another it may be a match on one third of the name parts, which may not be an acceptable degree of similarity for the application at hand. In a rank-based approach, such matches would receive the same score, e.g. a Borda score of c. The information loss of transforming scores into ranks was judged too great for this domain.

5   Conclusion and Future Work

We have shown that a relatively simple aggregation model can significantly improve name search results on a noisy and difficult data set. As mentioned in the previous section, this dataset has different properties in terms of the level and variation in the base rate of matches compared to the traditional TREC-style information retrieval task.

Future work will focus on selection of an optimal group of search engines from among those available to us as well as on different aggregation strategies. Linear regression is not the best model for this data, because the ground truth is a binary category denoting match or nonmatch. Casting these categories into the values 0 and 1 in order to perform linear regression is statistically improper, strictly speaking, but we found the results to be superior to an unweighted average or to a max of the three base searches. The use of more sophisticated models will require finer-grained control over and more extensive experimentation with the training parameters, such as the proportion of matches and non-matches in the training data and selection of score ranges for training instances.

References

1. Voorhees, E.M., Harman, D.K.: Overview of the Eighth Text REtrieval Conference (TREC-8). In: Voorhees, E.M., Harman, D.K. (eds.) The Eighth Text REtrieval Conference (TREC-8). U.S. Government Printing Office, Washington (2000)
2. Voorhees, E.M.: The philosophy of information retrieval evaluation. In: Peters, C., Braschler, M., Gonzalo, J., Kluck, M. (eds.) CLEF 2001. LNCS, vol. 2406, pp. 355–370. Springer, Heidelberg (2002)
3. Jaro, M.A.: Advances in Record-linkage Methodology a Applied to Matching the 1985 Census of Tampa, Florida. Journal of the American Statistical Association 89, 414–420 (1989)
4. Winkler, W.E.: String Comparator Metrics and Enhanced Decision Rules in the Fellegi-Sunter Model of Record Linkage. In: Proceedings of the Section on Survey Research Methods, pp. 354–359. American Statistical Association (1990)
5. Witten, I.H., Frank, E.: Data Mining: Practical Machine Learning Tools and Techniques, 2nd edn. Morgan Kaufmann, San Francisco (2005)
6. Aslam, J.A., Montague, M.: Models for Metasearch. In: Proceedings of the 24th Annual International ACM SIGIR conference on Research and Development in Information Retrieval, pp. 276–284. ACM Press, New York (2001)

Comparison of String Distance Metrics for Lemmatisation of Named Entities in Polish

Jakub Piskorski[1], Marcin Sydow[2], and Karol Wieloch[3]

[1] Joint Research Centre of the European Commission,Web Mining and Intelligence of IPSC,T.P. 267, Via Fermi 2749, 21027 Ispra (VA), Italy
Jakub.Piskorski@jrc.it

[2] Polish-Japanese Institute of Information Technology,Web Mining Lab, Intelligent Systems Dept.,Koszykowa 86, 02-008 Warsaw, Poland
msyd@pjwstk.edu.pl

[3] Poznań Univeristy of Economics,Department of Information Systems,Al. Niepodległośći 10, 60-967 Poznań, Poland
K.Wieloch@kie.ae.poznan.pl

Abstract. This paper presents the results of recent experiments on application of string distance metrics to the problem of named entity lemmatisation in Polish. It extends of our work in [1] by introducing new results for organisation names. Furthermore, the results presented here and in [2,3] centering around the same topic were used to make a comparative study of the average usefulness of the numerous examined string distance metrics to lemmatisation of Polish named-entities of various types. In particular, we focus on lemmatisation of country names, organisation names and person names.

Keywords: named entities, lemmatisation, string distance metrics, highly inflective languages.

1 Introduction

A frequently appearing problem in the context of text processing technologies involves making a decision whether two distinct names refer to the same real-world object. Name matching has been thoroughly studied in the past and approaches ranging from linguistically oriented ones [4] to very lightweight approximate-string matching techniques [5,6,7] have been proposed.

While the research in this area mainly focused on major languages, e.g., English, tackling the problem for highly inflectional languages like Slavonic has been almost neglected. An intuitive solution to the problem would be to first lemmatise names and then to deploy any techniques, which perform well for inflection-poor languages. However, it is known that lemmatisation of names in Slavonic languages is an extremely hard task, which has been exemplified in [8][1].

---

[1] For instance, lemmatisation of compound person names in Polish depends on several factors, e.g. (a) the gender of the first name, (b) the part-of-speech information and gender of the word which constitutes the surname, (c) origin/pronunciation of the name.

Z. Vetulani and H. Uszkoreit (Eds.): LTC 2007, LNAI 5603, pp. 413–427, 2009.

This paper reports on numerous experiments on utilisation of well-established string distance metrics and some modifications thereof for lemmatising named-entities in Polish, a Western Slavonic language[2]. In particular, we study their performance when applied to various types of names, including countries, organisations, and person names. Furthermore, a comparative study of the overall usefulness of the examined string distance metrics is given, i.e., we measured their average performance across different named-entity types.

1.1   Related Work

Application of string distance metrics for name matching tasks in inflection-poor languages was studied before in [5,6,7,9]. However, for Polish, which is an example of highly-inflective language, the problem was not explored until recently.

Up to the authors' knowledge, the first experiments on using string distance metrics for lemmatisation of names and name matching in Polish are reported in [3]. The paper formulates the problem and proposes some evaluation metrics. The experiments concerned first names of persons, and names of countries. A couple of well-known edit distance metrics, the soundex metric and the recursive Monge-Elkan metric were tested. The paper also introduces some common-prefix-based metrics which outperform all the other metrics for the first-name matching problem and are among the best for other tasks.

The problem is further studied in [1] where the set of tested metrics is substantially enhanced by 2 other recursive metrics and positional n-grams and the domain of the datasets additionally includes compound person names.

In [2] we focus on the sub-problem of lemmatisation of person names, where we also report on a linguistically sophisticated approach to person name lemmatisation for Polish, which turned to perform worse than the knowledge-poor methods based on string distance metrics. Finally, in [10], which continues the work presented in [2], we extensively explore various ways of combining string distance metrics and application of suffix-based patterns for lemmatisation of person names and for the more general task of person name matching in text. The accuracy evaluation metrics have been redefined appropriately for the latter task. Furthermore, the aforementioned work encompasses also experiments on extending the algorithms through utilisation of the local context, in which person names appear.

1.2   Contributions

This paper is an extension of [1] and includes the very recent results of experimenting with new datasets consisting of over 300 multi-token names of Polish organisations. In addition, the experiments are repeated and reported for the case of purposely enlarged search space to study the robustness of the approach.

Next, we propose some ranking methods and present novel results aiming at objective identification of the best string distance metrics independently on

---

[2] This work has been partially supported by the MEI grant no. 3 T11C 007 27.

the lemmatisation task or dataset. Finally, we propose a simple method for comparing the relative hardness of each lemmatisation task.

The rest of the paper is organized as follows. Section 2 introduces string distance metrics used in our study. Next, in section 4 the evaluation methodology and experiment set-up are described. Subsequently, section 4 presents the results of the experiments. Main results: comparison of the metrics and problem hardness are presented in section 5. Finally, we end with a summary in section 6.

2   String Distance Metrics

In this paper, we consider the set of 23 different basic string distance metrics and 3 recursive "meta-metrics". Thus, the set of considered metrics is larger than that studied in [1][3], which potentially gives $23 + 3 \times 23 = 92$ different metrics. Most of these metrics are typically used for record linkage in databases.

The first group of metrics explored in our experiments are extensions of the well-known *Levenshtein* (*LV*) metric, which computes the minimum number of character-level insertion, deletion or substitution operations needed to transform one string to another [11]. The *Needleman-Wunsch* (*NW*) [12] metric modifies the *Levenshtein* metric in that it allows for variable cost adjustment to the cost of a gap, i.e., insert/deletion operation and variable cost of substitutions. Another variant, namely the *Smith-Waterman* (*SW*) metric [13], additionally uses an alphabet mapping to costs. Two settings for this metric were tested: (a) one which normalizes the *Smith-Waterman* score with the length of the shorter string, and (b) one which uses for the same purpose the *Dice coefficient*, i.e., the average length of strings compared (*SWD*). A further extension (denoted as *SWAG*) of the *Smith-Waterman* metric introduces two extra edit operations, *open gap* and *end gap*. The cost of extending the gap is usually smaller than the cost of opening a gap, and this results in small cost penalties for gap mismatches than the equivalent cost under the standard edit distance metrics. Finally, we created a variant thereof, which uses a character substitution cost function adapted to Polish name declension[4] (*SWAG-PL*). In general, the computation of most edit-distance metrics requires $O(|s| \cdot |t|)$. We have also considered the *bag distance* metric [14] which is a good approximation of the more complex edit distance metrics, and is calculated (in linear time) as $bag_{dist}(s, t) = \max(|M(s) \backslash M(t)|, |M(t) \backslash M(s)|)$, where $M(x)$ denotes the multiset of the characters in x.

Good results for name-matching tasks [5] have been reported using variants of the *Jaro* (*J*) metric [15], which is not based on the edit-distance model. It considers the number and the order of the common characters between two strings. Given two strings $s = a_1 \ldots a_K$ and $t = b_1 \ldots b_L$, we say that a_i in s is *common* with t if there is a $b_j = a_i$ in t such that $i - R \leq j \leq i + R$,

---

[3] Where 18 different metrics were studied.

[4] There are three different scores for substitution operation: (a) exact match between characters (score +5), (b) approximate match between similar characters (+3), where for Polish two characters are considered similar if they both appear in one of the sets: {a,e,i,o,u,y,ą,ę,ó},{c,ć},{s,ś},{n,ń},{l,ł},{k,c},{t,c}, (c) mismatch of characters (-5).

where $R = \lfloor \max(|s|, |t|)/2 \rfloor - 1$. Further, let $s' = a'_1 \ldots a'_{K'}$ be the characters in s which are common with t (with preserved order of appearance in s) and let $t' = b'_1 \ldots b'_{L'}$ be defined analogously. A *transposition* for s' and t' is defined as the position i such that $a'_i \neq b'_i$. Let us denote the number of transposition for s' and t' as $T_{s',t'}$. The *Jaro* similarity is then calculated as: $J(s,t) = 1/3 \cdot (|s'|/|s| + |t'|/|t| + (|s'| - \lfloor T_{s',t'}/2 \rfloor)/|s'|)$

A *Jaro-Winkler* (*JW*) variant boosts the *Jaro* similarity for strings with agreeing initial characters and is calculated as: $JW(s,t) = J(s,t) + \delta \cdot boost_p(s,t) \cdot (1 - J(s,t))$, where δ denotes the common prefix adjustment factor (default: 0.1) and $boost_p(s,t) = \min(|lcp(s,t)|, p)$. Here $lcp(s,t)$ denotes the longest common prefix between s and t. Further, p stands for the upper bound of $|lcp(s,t)|$, i.e., up from a certain length of $lcp(s,t)$ the boost value' remains the same. For multi-token strings we extended JW to JWM by replacing $boost_p$ with $boost_p^*$. Let $s = s_1 \ldots s_K$ and $t = t_1 \ldots t_L$, where s_i (t_i) represent i-th token of s and t respectively, and let without loss of generality $L \leq K$. $boost_p^*$ is calculated as:

$$boost_p^*(s,t) = \frac{1}{L} \cdot \left(\sum_{i=1}^{L-1} boost_p(s_i, t_i) + \frac{boost_p(s_L, t_L..t_K)}{L} \right)$$

The time complexity of 'Jaro' metrics is $O(|s| \cdot |t|)$.

The *q-gram* (*QG*) metric [16] is based on the intuition that two strings are similar if they share a large number of character-level q-grams. Let $G_q(s)$ denote the multiset of all q-grams of a string s.[5] The q-gram metric is calculated as: $q-grams(s,t) = |G_q(s) \cap G_q(t)| / \max(|G_q(s)|, |G_q(t)|)$. An extension to this metric is to add positional information, and to match only common q-grams that occur within a maximum distance to each other (*positional q-grams - QGP*) [17]. Further, [18] introduced *skip-gram* (*SG*) metric. It is based on the idea that in addition to forming bigrams of adjacent characters, bigrams that skip characters are considered. *Gram classes* are defined that specify what kind of skip-grams are created, e.g. $\{0,1\}$ class means that normal bigrams are formed, and bigrams that skip one character. The q-gram type metrics can be computed in $O(\max\{|s|, |t|\})$.

Considering the declension paradigm of Polish we also considered a basic and time efficient metric based on the longest common prefix information, which would intuitively perform well in the case of single-token names. It is calculated as: $CP_\delta(s,t) = ((|lcp(s,t)| + \delta(s,t))^2)/|s| \cdot |t|$. The parameter $\delta(s,t)$ favours certain suffix pairs in s (t). We have experimented with two variants, CP_{δ_1} (denoted as CPD) and CP_{δ_2} ($CPD2$). In CP_{δ_1} the value of $\delta(s,t)$ is set to 0 for all s and t. In CP_{δ_2}, as a result of empirical study of the data and the declension paradigm $\delta(s,t)$ has been set to 1 if s ends in: o,y,q,e, and t ends in an a. Otherwise $\delta(s,t) = 0$. For coping with multi-token strings, we tested a similar metric called *longest common substrings* distance (*LCS*). Let $lcs(s,t)$ denote the 'first'

---

[5] Since q-grams at the beginning and the end of the string can have fewer than q characters, the strings are extended by adding $q-1$ unique initial and trailing characters.

longest common substring for s and t and let s_{-p} denote a string obtained by removing from s the first occurrence of p in s. The LCS metric is calculated as:

$$LCS(s,t) = \begin{cases} 0 & \text{if } |lcs(s,t)| \leq \phi \\ |lcs(s,t)| + LCS(s_{-lcs(s,t)}, t_{-lcs(s,t)}) & \text{otherwise} \end{cases}$$

The value of ϕ is usually set to 2 or 3. The time complexity of LCS is $O(|s| \cdot |t|)$. We extended LCS to $WLCS$ by additional weighting of the $|lcs(s,t)|$. The main idea is to penalize longest common substrings which do not match the beginning of a token in at least one of the compared strings. Let α be the maximum number of non-whitespace characters, which precede the first occurrence of $lcs(s,t)$ in s or t. Then, $lcs(s,t)$ is assigned the weight: $w_{lcs(s,t)} = (|lcs(s,t)| + \alpha - \max(\alpha, p))/(|lcs(s,t)| + \alpha)$ with p set to 4 experimentally.

For multi-token strings, we also tested 3 recursive schemas. Each of them uses some basic string distance metric as the secondary (or internal) metric. The first is known as *Monge-Elkan* (ME) distance [19]. Let us assume that the strings s and t are broken into substrings (tokens), i.e., $s = s_1 \ldots s_K$ and $t = t_1 \ldots t_L$. The intuition behind *Monge-Elkan* measure is the assumption that s_i in s corresponds to a t_j with which it has highest similarity. The similarity between s and t equals the mean of these maximum scores, i.e., the *Monge-Elkan* metric is calculated as:

$$Monge\text{-}Elkan(s,t) = \frac{1}{K} \cdot \sum_{i=1}^{K} \max_{j=1\ldots L} sim(s_i, t_j),$$

where sim denotes some secondary similarity function. Inspired by the multi-token variants of the JW metric presented in [7] we applied two additional metrics, which are similar in spirit to the *Monge-Elkan* metric. The first one, *Sorted-Tokens* (ST) is computed in two steps: (a) firstly the tokens constituting the full strings are sorted alphabetically, and (b) an arbitrary metric is applied to compute the similarity of the 'sorted' strings. The second metric, *Permuted-Tokens* (PT) compares all possible permutations of tokens constituting the full strings and returns the maximum calculated similarity value.

3   Setup of Experiments

We define the problem as follows. Let A, B and C, $B \subseteq C$, be three sets of strings over some alphabet Σ representing the inflected forms of some names, base forms of these names and the search space, respectively. Further, let $f : A \to B$ be the (ground-truth) function that maps inflected forms into their base forms. Given, A and C, the task is to approximate f, with $\widehat{f} : A \to C$. If $\widehat{f}(a) = f(a)$ for $a \in A$, we say that $\widehat{f}$ returns a correct answer for a, otherwise, $\widehat{f}$ is said to return an incorrect answer. Secondly, we consider a relaxed form of the task, namely finding a function $f^* : A \to 2^C$, where f^* is said to return a correct answer for $a \in A$ if $f(a) \in f^*(a)$. The idea is as follows: for each inflected form $a \in A$ and all possible candidate strings $c \in C$ from the search space, a string distance metric

d is applied for any pair (a, c) and the set $b^*(a) = \{c \in C : c = argmin_C\, d(a, c)\}$ is computed as the approximation of the correct base form $f(a)$ of b.

The experiments reported here concern 8 different lemmatisation tasks: country names, organisation names (2 variants of search space), full names (3 variants of search space), first names (2 variants of search space), all for the Polish language. We study 23 different string distance metrics in 4 different modes: basic, *Monge-Elkan*, *Sorted Tokens* and *Permuted Tokens*, where in the last 3 recursive modes one of 23 basic metrics is used as the internal metric see sections 2 and 4. First names are single tokens so only the basic mode is applied for them.

3.1 Datasets

For the experiments we have used four lexicons, each consisting of pairs $(in, base)$, where in is an inflected form and $base$ stands for the corresponding base form of the name. The first one contains the most frequent Polish first names (PL-F-NAM). The second one contains forms of country names (PL-CTR). The third lexicon consists of compound person names (first name + surname) (PL-FULL-NAM). It was created semi-automatically as follows. We have automatically extracted a list of 22485 compound person-name candidates from a corpus of 15,724 on-line news articles from *Rzeczpospolita*, one of the leading Polish newspapers, via using PL-F-NAM lexicon and an additional list of 58038 uninfected foreign first names. Subsequently, we have selected an excerpt of about 1900 entries (inflected forms) from this list. 1/3 of this excerpt are the most frequent names appearing in the corpus, 1/3 are the most rare names, and finally 1/3 of the entries were chosen randomly. The last resource contains organization names (PL-ORG), which encompasses names of companies actively present on Polish market, banks, holdings, schools and governmental institutions. It includes a large number of multi-token names (similarly to PL-CTR but to a higher extent). 28% of the names in PL-ORG consist of two or more (33%) tokens. Moreover, PL-ORG lexicon also contains pairs where a common variant of the name is used instead of an inflected form. Typical variants have a part of the name abbreviated or missing, which makes them difficult to lemmatise.

In the basic experiments solely the base forms were used as the search space, however variants of PL-F-NAM, PL-FULL-NAM and PL-ORG with extended search space were created, e.g., through enriching the search space by adding base forms of foreign first names (PL-F-NAM-2) and adding a complete list of full names extracted from the *Rzeczpospolita* corpus (PL-FULL-NAM-3). Table 1 gives an overview of our test datasets[6].

3.2 Evaluation Metrics

Since for a given string more than one answer can be returned, we measured the accuracy in three ways. Firstly, we calculated the accuracy with the assumption that a multi-result answer is not correct and we defined (*all-answer accuracy*)

---

[6] Pairs, where inflected form is identical with the base form have been excluded from the experiments since in such a case finding an answer is straightforward.

Table 1. Datasets used for the experiments

Dataset	#inflected	#base	search space	Dataset	#inflected	#base	search space
PL-F-NAM	5941	1457	1457	PL-FULL-NAM-2	1900	1219	2351
PL-F-NAM-2	5941	1457	25490	PL-FULL-NAM-3	1900	1219	20000
PL-CTR	1765	220	220	PL-ORG	1000	336	336
PL-FULL-NAM	1900	1219	1219	PL-ORG-2	1000	336	1322

(AA) measure which penalizes the accuracy for multi-result answers. Secondly, we measured the accuracy of single-result answers (*single-result accuracy* (SR)) disregarding the multiple-result answers. Finally, we used a somewhat weaker measure which treats a multi-result answer as correct if one of the results in the answer is correct (*relaxed-all-answer accuracy* (RAA)).

Let s (m) denote the number of strings, for which a single result (multiple result) was returned. Further, let s_c and m_c denote the number of correct single-result answers returned and the number of multi-result answers containing at least one correct result resp. The accuracy metrics are computed as: $AA = s_c/(s+m)$, $SR = s_c/s$, and $RAA = (s_c + m_c)/(s+m)$. For assessing multiple-result answers we computed the average number (AV) of results in such answers.

4   Experimental Results on Lemmatising Names

4.1   Country Names

The first test was carried out on the PL-CTR, which contains many multi-token strings, where the number of tokens varies from 1 to 7. We also considered *Monge-Elkan* metric, *Sorted-Tokens* and *Permuted-Tokens* to better cope with multi-token strings. The aforementioned metrics were tested with different 'internal' metrics. The results are given in table 2.

The best results were achieved by the *Smith-Waterman* metrics. On the contrary, *Monge-Elkan* performed rather badly (probably due to the varying number of tokens the names consist of – on average the number of tokens in a country name is 1.87). Using CP_{δ_1} as internal metric yielded the best results. The results for *Sorted-Tokens* and *Permuted-Tokens* were significantly better, with *Smith-Waterman* as the best internal metric.

4.2   Organization Names

For the PL-ORG resources were basically followed the same scheme of experiments used for country names. The notable difference lies mainly in the higher diversity of organization name variants as mentioned in previous section. The complete results are given in Table 3.

The *JWM* based metrics performed best for AA and RAA evaluation (0.906 for both AA and RAA) while *Smith-Waterman* performed best for SR evaluation (0.920) among all non-recursive metrics. If recursive metrics are considered *Monge-Elkan* is the worst choice (similarly to PL-CTR experiment). The

Table 2. Results for PL-CTR for 4 different modes (left to right): 'basic', *Monge-Elkan*, *Sorted-Tokens* and *Permuted-Tokens*. The unit for 3-digit numbers is 1/1000. The names of the string distance metrics in this table and all other tables are abbreviated according to the definitions in 2. In case of q-gram based metrics the value of q is attached to metric's acronym.

Metric	AA	SR	RAA	AV	AA	SR	RAA	AV	AA	SR	RAA	AV	AA	SR	RAA	AV
BAG	369	461	402	2.60	461	602	526	3.05	370	461	402	2.60	370	461	402	2.60
LEV	564	590	586	2.94	573	639	593	2.79	614	656	640	2.56	543	603	566	2.30
NW	720	779	763	2.95	532	663	577	3.08	483	527	518	3.25	618	663	650	2.71
SW	**904**	**936**	**928**	3.34	205	494	291	4.94	**898**	**931**	**919**	2.84	**895**	**921**	**916**	2.93
SWD	849	858	858	2.00	620	672	627	2.94	835	891	838	2.01	798	803	801	2.00
SWAG	799	805	802	2.45	607	633	615	3.02	801	826	802	2.06	760	766	763	2.50
SWAGpl	793	797	797	2.22	584	605	591	3.00	784	800	786	2.06	749	754	752	2.20
J	432	437	436	2.00	552	624	563	3.02	757	767	768	2.19	786	800	793	2.21
JW	452	457	452	2.06	557	623	563	3.07	769	774	772	2.44	790	803	793	2.00
JWM	453	458	453	2.06	556	621	562	3.07	770	774	773	2.44	866	872	866	2.00
QG2	665	693	689	2.72	607	696	635	2.98	711	767	736	2.10	724	757	751	2.37
QG3	633	650	649	3.02	620	781	657	3.09	760	801	774	2.12	768	793	787	2.58
QG4	594	610	608	2.63	625	813	665	3.11	768	821	789	2.51	767	793	782	2.92
QGP2	425	470	440	4.08	619	794	653	3.09	723	787	745	2.57	756	783	771	2.36
QGP3	425	491	445	9.49	627	830	664	3.08	730	797	755	9.32	767	791	783	2.55
QGP4	427	491	443	124	629	838	668	3.12	742	804	765	9.48	769	796	785	2.90
SG01	662	681	672	2.13	619	664	637	2.94	709	729	722	2.02	693	718	707	2.09
SG02	613	635	627	2.19	618	662	636	2.94	709	729	722	2.02	698	723	713	2.09
SG012	603	623	616	2.06	610	691	630	2.94	709	729	722	2.02	698	723	713	2.09
LCS	749	781	783	54.61	620	813	672	4.59	738	829	768	5.32	710	732	732	14.93
WLCS	530	545	550	816	636	837	688	4.55	741	817	750	5.86	781	801	801	16.64
CPD	416	421	420	2.35	**694**	**868**	**716**	3.08	765	776	769	2.00	885	889	889	2.00
CPD2	419	423	422	2.35	632	846	670	3.13	767	778	771	2.00	887	891	891	2.00

Table 3. Results for PL-ORG for 4 different modes (left to right:) basic, *Monge-Elkan*, *Sorted-Tokens* and *Permuted-Tokens*. The unit for 3-digit numbers is 1/1000.

Metric	AA	SR	RAA	AV	AA	SR	RAA	AV	AA	SR	RAA	AV	AA	SR	RAA	AV
BAG	739	797	774	2.48	718	822	800	5.48	739	798	774	2.47	739	798	774	2.47
LEV	833	834	833	2.00	799	843	834	2.50	831	832	831	2.00	836	837	836	2.00
NW	738	794	771	3.34	742	**864**	812	4.55	771	816	792	3.04	817	861	845	2.53
SW	874	**920**	895	8.94	326	656	606	8.00	868	**920**	897	7.86	871	**926**	895	7.59
SWD	877	879	877	2.00	813	859	**848**	2.89	864	867	865	2.33	879	881	879	2.00
SWAG	875	877	876	3.00	811	861	843	2.62	865	868	867	3.00	877	879	878	3.00
SWAGpl	877	880	878	2.67	**815**	862	847	2.76	866	869	868	2.75	879	882	880	2.67
J	900	904	900	2.66	792	841	828	2.66	**882**	894	883	2.54	904	910	904	2.29
JW	901	905	901	2.50	802	844	834	2.62	**882**	892	883	2.64	909	913	909	2.75
JWM	**906**	910	**906**	2.50	802	844	834	2.62	**882**	892	883	2.64	**915**	919	**915**	2.75
QG2	795	796	795	3.00	781	817	812	2.34	796	797	796	2.00	799	800	799	3.00
QG3	733	733	733	1.00	740	770	770	2.41	735	735	735	1.00	741	741	741	1.00
QG4	654	654	654	1.00	688	715	717	2.42	659	660	659	2.00	669	669	669	1.00
QGP2	580	582	583	4.00	778	805	804	2.48	489	491	490	2.20	764	770	771	2.25
QGP3	519	519	519	1.00	735	761	761	2.47	435	436	435	2.50	707	711	712	2.00
QGP4	443	443	443	1.00	684	707	709	2.48	372	373	372	2.50	625	628	629	2.00
SG01	800	801	800	3.00	787	822	819	2.57	805	806	805	2.00	807	808	807	3.00
SG02	800	801	800	3.00	787	822	819	2.57	805	806	805	2.00	807	808	807	3.00
SG012	776	776	776	1.00	778	814	810	2.68	783	784	783	2.00	789	789	789	1.00
LCS	823	825	824	3.00	783	811	814	2.62	823	825	824	3.00	825	827	826	2.67
WLCS	811	815	812	3.60	781	805	808	2.53	768	770	769	2.00	819	821	820	3.00
CPD	410	410	410	1.00	770	792	795	2.57	342	342	342	1.00	613	613	613	1.00
CPD2	410	410	410	1.00	771	792	795	2.59	342	342	342	1.00	613	613	613	1.00

best performing metric is *Permuted-Tokens* with *JWM* as internal metric for AA (0.915) and RAA (0.915) evaluation and with *Smith-Waterman* as internal metric in case of SR (0.926) indicator. *Sorted-Tokens* variants performed worse than its non-recursive counterparts, which indicates that the order of tokens in multi-token names in comparing them is important.

The results for PL-ORG-2 are given in Table 4. The application of *Smith-Waterman* metrics, either alone or as internal metrics, yields top results.

Table 4. Results for PL-ORG-2 for 4 different modes (left to right:) basic, *Monge-Elkan, Sorted-Tokens* and *Permuted-Tokens*. The unit for 3-digit numbers is 1/1000.

Metric	AA	SR	RAA	AV	AA	SR	RAA	AV	AA	SR	RAA	AV	AA	SR	RAA	AV
BAG	169	239	300	2.67	205	292	343	4.88	169	239	300	2.67	169	239	300	2.67
LEV	229	360	456	2.73	212	344	449	3.52	225	355	454	2.73	225	359	457	2.73
NW	154	206	233	2.60	199	270	301	5.48	207	273	287	2.63	230	297	312	2.44
SW	247	438	439	5.42	152	**569**	507	19.02	248	405	430	5.78	248	464	489	5.35
SWD	**398**	**462**	**491**	2.22	307	419	496	3.31	**396**	**460**	**491**	2.25	397	**471**	492	2.23
SWAG	288	340	375	2.10	251	323	382	3.40	290	340	375	2.12	n.a.	n.a.	n.a.	n.a.
SWAGpl	275	331	372	2.17	246	318	377	3.52	276	331	373	2.19	n.a.	n.a.	n.a.	n.a.
J	366	443	466	2.19	290	408	485	3.43	330	412	441	2.20	366	459	487	2.21
JW	363	434	466	2.17	291	410	493	3.29	321	397	436	2.17	363	452	487	2.18
JWM	378	449	479	2.18	291	410	493	3.29	322	400	440	2.17	376	462	**496**	2.16
QG2	221	330	441	2.79	213	320	454	3.56	222	337	450	2.78	226	340	449	2.78
QG3	211	304	420	2.71	211	311	437	3.51	212	307	425	2.73	218	314	426	2.73
QG4	201	276	385	2.72	207	293	401	3.45	198	273	386	2.74	204	281	388	2.72
QGP2	216	315	401	2.69	211	321	448	3.59	082	123	283	2.74	214	324	449	2.81
QGP3	204	287	373	2.62	209	309	430	3.56	076	110	258	2.66	204	298	421	2.73
QGP4	193	258	333	2.58	207	294	397	3.51	072	098	226	2.64	193	267	380	2.73
SG01	245	322	404	2.47	221	306	402	3.21	249	327	410	2.50	245	325	410	2.49
SG02	245	322	404	2.47	221	306	402	3.21	249	327	410	2.50	245	325	410	2.49
SG012	233	289	362	2.41	216	291	378	3.31	237	297	372	2.41	n.a.	n.a.	n.a.	n.a.
LCS	219	342	465	2.82	214	319	454	3.49	220	343	468	2.84	218	343	453	2.78
WLCS	220	341	470	2.84	213	316	455	3.41	166	259	417	2.85	221	345	467	2.81
CPD	286	316	346	2.29	320	426	503	2.95	185	206	254	2.32	359	413	442	2.27
CPD2	315	335	346	2.45	**344**	447	**518**	2.95	219	233	254	2.52	**402**	436	444	2.44

Table 5. Results for PL-FULL-NAM with basic metrics (top) and AA accuracy for PL-FULL-NAM-2 with recursive metrics (bottom)

Metric	AA	SR	RAA	AV	Metric	AA	SR	RAA	AV
Bag Distance	891	966	966	3.13	Jaro	957	970	964	3.54
Levenshtein	951	978	970	4.59	JW	952	964	958	3.74
Smith-Waterman	965	980	975	3.5	JWM	962	974	968	3.74
Smith-Waterman-D	972	985	980	3.62	2-grams	957	988	987	3.915
Smith-Waterman-AG	970	982	975	3.75	pos 3-grams	941	974	966	4.32
Smith-Waterman-AG-PL	970	982	978	3.75	skip-grams	973	991	990	5.14
Needleman-Wunsh	896	956	935	2.88	LCS	971	992	990	5.7
					WLCS	**975**	**993**	**992**	6.29

Internal M.	Monge Elkan	Sorted Tokens	Permuted Tokens	Internal M.	Monge Elkan	Sorted Tokens	Permuted Tokens
Bag Distance	868	745	745	3-grams	848	930	911
Jaro	974	961	968	pos 3-grams	855	928	913
JWM	**976**	**976**	975	skip-grams	951	967	961
SmithWaterman	902	972	967	LCS	941	960	951
Smith-Waterman-D	**976**	**976**	**976**	WLCS	962	967	967
Smith-Waterman-AG	958	966	955	CP_{δ_1}	969	n.a.	n.a.
Smith-Waterman-AG-PL	965	971	961	CP_{δ_2}	974	n.a.	n.a.
Needleman-Wunsch	808	903	857				

However, the accuracy figures are significantly worse than in the case of PL-ORG, which indicates that utilisation of string distance metrics for lemmatisation of organisation names might not be the best choice in general.

4.3 Person Names

Finally, we have carried out experiments for compound person names, each represented as two tokens[7]. Noteworthy, in fraction of the entries in the test data the order of the first name and the surname is swapped, which complicates the task since some surnames may also function as first names. Nevertheless, the results of the experiment on PL-FULL-NAM given in table 5 are nearly optimal.

---

[7] The results for first names are given in [1].

Table 6. Results for PL-FULL-NAM-3. Top: with basic metrics. Bottom: AA and SR accuracy with recursive metrics. The unit for 3-digit numbers is 1/1000.

Metrics	AA	SR	RAA	AV	Metrics	AA	SR	RAA	AV
Levenshtein	791	896	897	2.20	JW	791	807	802	2.11
Smith-Waterman	869	892	889	2.35	JWM	892	900	901	2.11
Smith-Waterman-D	899	911	910	2.08	skip-grams	852	906	912	2.04
Smith-Waterman-AG	840	850	850	2.04	LCS	827	925	930	2.48
Smith-Waterman-AG-PL	842	857	854	2.09	WLCS	876	**955**	**958**	2.47

Metric	AA	Metric	SR
ME & CP_{δ_2}	**937**	ST & WLCS	949
ME & JWM	923	PT & WLCS	948
ME & CP_{δ_1}	921	ME & CP_{δ_2}	947
PT & JWM	914	ME & WLCS	939
ST & Smith-Waterman-D	911	ME & JWM	936
ME & Smith-Waterman-D	908	ME & CP_{δ_1}	935
ST & JWM	904	PT & JWM	927
PT & Smith-Waterman-D	899	ST & Smith-Waterman-D	924

JWM, WLCS, LCS, skip grams and *Smith-Waterman* were among the 'best' metrics. The recursive metrics scored in general only slightly better. The best results oscillating around 0.97, 0.99, and 0.99 for AA, SR and RAA were obtained with *LCS, WLCS, JWM, CP_δ* and *Smith-Waterman* as internal metrics.

We have further compared the performance of the aforementioned 'recursive' metrics on PL-FULL-NAM-2, which has a larger search space. The most significant results for the AA accuracy are depicted in Table 5 (bottom). The *JWM* and *Smith-Waterman-D* metric seem to be the best choice as an internal metric, whereas *WLCS, CP_{δ_2}* and *Jaro* perform slightly worse.

In our last experiment, we selected the 'best' metrics so far and tested them against PL-FULL-NAM-3 (largest search space). The top results for non-recursive metrics are given in Table 6. *SWD* and *JWM* turned out to achieve the best scores in the AA accuracy, whereas *WLCS* is far the best metric w.r.t. SR accuracy. The top scores achieved for the recursive metrics on PL-FULL-NAM-3 (see Table 6) were somewhat better. In particular, *Monge-Elkan* performed best with CP_{δ_2} as internal metric (0.937 AA and 0.947 SR) and slightly worse results were obtained with *JWM* and *WLCS*. *Sorted-Tokens* scored best in AA and SR accuracy with *SWD* (0.904) and *WLCS* (0.949), resp. For *Permuted-Tokens* using *JWM* and *WLCS* yielded the best results, namely 0.912 (AA) and 0.948 (SR), resp. Interestingly, the *Smith-Waterman* metrics used as internal metric resulted in lower values of SR accuracy than *WLCS* and *JWM*. Comparing all the results for PL-FULL-NAM-3 reveals that a further improvement could be achieved via combining of *WLCS* and *Monge-Elkan* with CP_{δ_2}, i.e., if *WLCS* returns a single answer, return it, otherwise return the answer of *Monge-Elkan* with CP_{δ_2}. We explore such combinations in [10].

5   Aggregated Analysis of the Results

In previous section, we presented the detailed experimental results concerning usability of particular string distance metrics for lemmatisation of named-entities of various types. This section presents various aggregations of these results aiming at identifying the string distance metrics which are most robust and perform best across all the named-entity types and datasets used.

First, we compare the basic 23 metrics across the 6 datasets[8] used either in the stand-alone (basic) mode or as an internal metric in some recursive scheme and the 2 variants concerning first name lemmatisation (basic mode only). For each of these $6 \times 4 + 2 = 26$ combinations we computed how many times a particular basic metric was the top-1 or among the top-3 results in terms of the value of the evaluation measures (Table 7, rows 1-4)[9].

Table 7. The best of the 23 compared metrics across all the datasets, the numbers count how many times a metric was top-1 or among the top-3. The last 2 rows present the top-ranking metrics in terms of average AA.

metric:	JWM	CPD2	SWD	SW	WLCS	CPD	J	SWAGPL	
top-1 AA:	9	6	5	4	2	1	1	1	
metric:	JWM	SWD	CPD2	SW	J/JW	CPD	WLCS	SWAG	SG*
top-3 AA:	16	14	9	8	7	6	5	4	2 or 1
metric:	JWM	SWD	SWAG	J	SWAGPL	SG01	JW	WLCS	LCS
aver. AA:	0.783	0.785	0.762	0.761	0.759	0.737	0.731	0.720	0.718

Top-1 and top-3 count rankings infer very similar top lists of the metrics. In particular, both identify JWM as the most frequently winning distance metric and both identify $CPD2$, SWD and SW as being the top-4 most frequently winning ones. The top-3 ranking scheme is introduced to make the ranking more robust and it generally confirms the results of the top-1 ranking count scheme. More generally speaking, both rankings in Table 7 identify metrics derived from *Jaro*, *Smith-Waterman* and common-prefix-based metrics as the best.

For each of 23 distance metrics, we also computed their AA values averaged over all combinations of datasets and basic/recursive modes. The top metrics are presented in the last 2 rows of Table 7. This ranking is different than top-1 and top-3 rankings. The best averages are obtained with JWM, SWD and similar metrics, also $SG01$ has very high average, which is along the lines of the previous rankings. Very interestingly, however, CPD and $CPD2$ are completely absent in this list, they obtained average AA of 0.547 and 0.569, respectively, which are *the worst figures* among the 23 metrics.

5.1   Grouping the String Distance Metrics

The results presented up to now treat each metric separately which exhibits some noise in rankings or evaluation figures. However, looking at Table 7 we can observe that different variants of the same metrics are always high in rankings.

---

[8] Countries, full-names (3 variants of dataset), organisations (2 variants of dataset).

[9] The first row sums up to 29 instead of 26 because some metrics obtained the same top-1 results (ex-equo).

Thus, grouping the metrics according to their similarity of definition could reduce the noise. This approach would be also further supported by the observation that metrics defined in similar ways perform similarly in terms of the evaluation measures presented in the tables in section 4. Taking this into account we group all of the 23 metrics tested in this paper as follows:

1. **(SW)** Smith-Waterman alike (4 members: *SW, SWD, SWAG, SWAGPL*)
2. **(J)** Jaro alike (3 members: *J, JW, JWM*)
3. **(nGr)** n-gram (3 members: *QG2, QG3, QG4*)
4. **(pGr)** positional n-gram (3 members)
5. **(sGr)** skip-grams (3 members: {0,1},{0,2} and {0,1,2} *skip-grams*)
6. **(LCS)** longest common substring alike (2 members: *LCS, WLCS*)
7. **(CP)** longest common prefix alike (2 members: *CPD, CPD2*)
8. each other metric constituted its own 1-element group (**LEV,BAG,NW**)

The next experiments aim at identifying the best groups of metrics. Table 8 presents the results analogous to those in Table 7, however on the level of the groups of metrics. We say a group is a top-1 if it contains the metric which obtained the best result and the group is among the top-k, $k > 1$, iff it contains the top metric after removing all the top-j, $0 < j < k$, groups from consideration. Notice, that, according to this definition, top-3 group ranking is not exactly the same as the one obtained by simply summing the counts for the top-3 metrics from Table 7. The latter one is presented as a separate (third) row in Table 8. We also computed the average AA values for each group (the last row in Table 8).

Table 8. The top metric groups compared across all the datasets. The numbers count how many times a group was top-1 or among the top-3. The last 2 rows present the groups ranked wrt average AA. Notice the worst rank of CP here.

group:	J	SW	CP	LCS	SGR	LEV	NW	NGR	PGR	BAG
top-1 group AA:	12	10	7	2	0	0	0	0	0	0
top-3 group AA:	22	20	10	10	7	5	2	1	1	0
aggr. top-3 AA:	30	28	15	5	5	na	na	na	na	0
top-1 group SR:	0	10	2	12	0	1	1	0	0	0
top-1 group RAA:	3	9	3	11	0	0	0	0	0	0
top-3 group SR:	18	13	8	16	8	5	4	3	3	0
top-3 group RAA:	19	12	6	17	8	5	3	3	2	0

group:	J	SW	LCS	SGR	LEV	NGR	NW	PGR	BAG	**CP**
aver. AA:	0.758	0.752	0.719	0.700	0.659	0.640	0.622	0.597	0.582	**0.558**

Most importantly, introducing the group level resulted in a quite stable and clear ranking of the metrics. For the most important (and restrictive) AA evaluation measure, either top-1 group or more robust top-3 group or aggregated top-3 statistic rank the string metric groups in *the same order*. The top-4 ranking is (starting with the best group): **J, SW, CP, LCS** and this groups accompanied by **SGR** and **LEV** seem to perform best (the columns of Table 8 are sorted according to this order). A bit more noisy results are obtained with SR and RAA evaluation measures, but still **J**, **SW**, **LCS** and **CP** groups are among the top ones. To the contrary, the ranking generated by average AA presents the CP group as the very interesting case: it obtained the *worst* rank here, despite the fact that *CPD2* performs the best for some particular tasks.

This result leads to the conclusion that *CPD2*, should be definitely considered for lemmatisation of named-entities of particular type, but for the choice of a single 'all-rounder' metric, which performs across various named-entity types, *JWM* or *SWD* seem to be the best ones. Also *WLCS* is an option here.

5.2   Comparison of Recursive Metrics

Next experiment aims at comparing the general usability of recursive metrics (see Table 9). The comparison techniques based on identifying the top-k winners used in the previous subsections cannot be applied here since the different recursive metrics did not compete with each other in our experiments. Instead, in order to compare the recursive schema, we computed average values of all 4 evaluation metrics on all $23 \times 6 = 138$ combinations of basic distance metric and datasets, which included multi-token names.

Table 9. The evaluation metrics averaged over 6 datasets and 23 basic distance metrics

mode:	stand-alone	Monge-Elkan	Sorted Tokens	Permuted Tokens
average AA:	0.651	0.670	0.680	**0.717**
average SR:	0.723	0.736	0.716	**0.758**
average RAA:	0.725	0.729	0.725	**0.768**
average AV :	5.694	4.506	**2.804**	**2.894**

All the evaluation measures quite consistently indicate that *Permuted Tokens* is definitely better than any other recursive schema, and *Sorted Tokens* is the worst one as well as application of any recursive scheme performs better than bare basic metrics in a stand-alone mode.

5.3   Comparison of Hardness of the Problems

Finally, we compare the hardness of the lemmatisation problem for the case of the 6 datasets containing multi-token names (see 3.1). For each of the 6 problems (datasets) and each of the 4 settings (basic, *Monge-Elkan*, *Permuted* and *Sorted Tokens*) we computed the mean and median value across all of the 23 string distance metrics. Next we computed medians of these 4 means and medians. We report only the results for medians, because they were more stable (Table 10). The results for means were similar but more noisy, due to outliers.

One can easily observe that all the evaluation metrics unequivocally sort the 6 lemmatisation problems in the same order (the columns in the table are presented in the order of increasing hardness): full-names are easier than organisation

Table 10. Global statistics comparing the relative hardness of the lemmatisation task

	FULL	FULL 2	FULL 3	ORG	COUNTRIES	ORG 2
AA	0.97	0.96	0.83	0.8	0.68	0.23
RAA	0.98	0.97	0.88	0.81	0.71	0.43
SR	0.98	0.97	0.88	0.81	0.73	0.33

names which are easier than countries (except the very hard case of the extended ORG-2 dataset). Despite the fact that these results depend somehow on the datasets used, the 'unequivocal' ordering is interesting.

6   Summary and Further Work

We have carried out numerous experiments on deploying various string distance metrics for tackling the lemmatisation of Polish named entities. More precisely, the experiments concern *a few thousand different combinations* of named-entity type, distance metric, evaluation measure or other settings. The large amount of collected information, after aggregation, can serve as a valuable tool for robust identification of the techniques that perform best. Our analyses indicate that the string distance metrics derived from *Jaro, Smith-Waterman, Common-Prefix* or *Longest Common Substring* generally outperform all the other studied metrics for Polish, independently of the named entity type being concerned. Additionally, our experiments revealed that recursive schema improve the performance, especially *Monge-Elkan*, whose complexity is lower than that of *Permuted-Tokens* (actually the best schema but prohibitively complex) and performs very well.

Although our study was focused on Polish, we believe that the results presented in this paper constitute a handy guideline for developing a fully-fledged name lemmatisation component for other highly inflective languages. To our knowledge the presented work together with various extensions, e.g., combining different strategies [10] constitute the first comprehensive comparison of lightweight methods applied to the task of lemmatising Polish names.

References

1. Piskorski, J., Sydow, M.: Usability of String Distance Metrics for Name Matching Tasks in Polish. In: Proceedings of LTC 2007, Poznań, Poland (2007)
2. Piskorski, J., Sydow, M., Kupść, A.: Lemmatization of Polish Person Names. In: Proceedings of the ACL 2007 Workshop on Balto-Slavonic Natural Language Processing 2007 (BSNLP 2007), Prague, Czech Republic (2007)
3. Piskorski, J., Sydow, M.: String distance metrics for reference matching and search query correction. In: Abramowicz, W. (ed.) BIS 2007. LNCS, vol. 4439, pp. 353–365. Springer, Heidelberg (2007)
4. Morton, T.: Coreference for NLP Applications. In: Proceedings of ACL (1997)
5. Cohen, W., Ravikumar, P., Fienberg, S.: A Comparison of String Distance Metrics for Name-Matching Tasks. In: Proceedings of IJCAI-2003 Workshop on Information Integration on the Web (IIWeb-2003), Acapulco, Mexico, pp. 73–78 (2003)

6. Cohen, E., Ravikumar, P., Fienberg, S.: A Comparison of String Metrics for Matching Names and Records. KDD Work. on Data Cleaning, Object Consolid (2003)
7. Christen, P.: A Comparison of Personal Name Matching: Techniques and Practical Issues. Technical report, TR-CS-06-02, Computer Science Laboratory, The Australian National University, Canberra, Australia (2006)
8. Piskorski, J.: Named-entity recognition for polish with sProUT. In: Bolc, L., Michalewicz, Z., Nishida, T. (eds.) IMTCI 2004. LNCS (LNAI), vol. 3490, pp. 122–133. Springer, Heidelberg (2005)
9. Elmagaramid, A., Ipeirotis, P., Verykios, V.: Duplicate Record Detection: A Survey. IEEE Transactions on Knowledge and Data Engineering 19(1) (2007)
10. Piskorski, J., Wieloch, K., Sydow, M.: On Knowledge-poor Methods for Person Name Matching and Lemmatization for Highly Inflectional Languages. Information Retrieval: Special Issue on non-English Web Search (to appear, 2009)
11. Levenshtein, V.: Binary Codes for Correcting Deletions, Insertions, and Reversals. Doklady Akademii Nauk SSSR 163(4), 845–848 (1965)
12. Needleman, S., Wunsch, C.: A General Method Applicable to Search for Similarities in the Amino Acid Sequence of Two Proteins. Molec. Biol. J. 48(3), 443–453 (1970)
13. Smith, T.F., Waterman, M.S.: Identification of Common Molecular Subsequences. J. Mol. Biol. 147, 195–197 (1981)
14. Bartolini, I., Ciaccia, P., Patella, M.: String matching with metric trees using an approximate distance. In: Laender, A.H.F., Oliveira, A.L. (eds.) SPIRE 2002. LNCS, vol. 2476, pp. 271–283. Springer, Heidelberg (2002)
15. Winkler, W.: The State of Record Linkage and Current Research Problems. Technical report, U.S. Bureau of the Census, Washington, DC (1999)
16. Ukkonen, E.: Approximate String Matching with q-grams and Maximal Matches. Theoretical Computer Science 92(1), 191–211 (1992)
17. Gravano, L., Ipeirotis, P., Jagadish, H., Koudas, N., Muthukrishnan, S., Pietarinen, L., Srivastava, D.: Using q-grams in a DBMS for Approximate String Processing. IEEE Data Engineering Bulletin 24(4), 28–34 (2001)
18. Keskustalo, H., Pirkola, A., Visala, K., Leppänen, E., Järvelin, K.: Non-adjacent digrams improve matching of cross-lingual spelling variants. In: Nascimento, M.A., de Moura, E.S., Oliveira, A.L. (eds.) SPIRE 2003. LNCS, vol. 2857, pp. 252–265. Springer, Heidelberg (2003)
19. Monge, A., Elkan, C.: The Field Matching Problem: Algorithms and Applications. In: Proceedings of Knowledge Discovery and Data Mining 1996, pp. 267–270 (1996)

An Iterative Model for Discovering
Person Coreferences
Using Name Frequency Estimates

Octavian Popescu and Bernardo Magnini

FBK-Irst (Trento, Italy)
{popescu,magnini}@fbk.eu

Abstract. In this paper we present an approach to person coreference in a large collection of news, based on two main hypothesis: first, coreference is an iterative process, where the easy cases are addressed first and are then made available as an incrementally enriched resource for resolving more difficult cases. Second, at each iteration coreference among two person names is established according to a probabilistic model, where a number of features (e.g. frequency of first and last names) are taken into account. The approach does not assume any prior knowledge about persons mentioned in the collection and requires basic linguistic processing (named entity recognition) and resources (a dictionary of person names). The system parameters have been estimated on a Italian news corpus of 5K and then experimented on a collection containing more than 7 millions person names. Evaluation, over a sample of four days news, shows that the error rate of the system (1.4%) is above a baseline (5.4%) for the task. Finally, we discuss open issues for evaluation[1].

Keywords: Cross Document Coreference, Name Frequency, Dynamic Cascade Clustering, Random Interval Coverage.

1 Introduction

Finding information about people is likely to be one of the principal interests of someone reading a newspaper. In the web space, person search is a very popular task and, as a person is primarily identified by her/his name, usually such name is the key of the search. However, as names are very ambiguous (Artiles et al. 2007), it is a big challenge for automatic systems to cluster name occurrences in a corpus according to the persons they refer to.

Person cross-document coreference is the task of clustering the names appearing in a collection of documents, such as news or web pages, according to the persons they refer to (Grishman 1994). We consider the input of a coreference system a document collection where person names are already identified; the output is a set of clusters of person names, where each cluster represents a different person.

---

[1] This paper has been partially supported by the Ontotext project (http://tcc.itc.it/projects/ ontotext/) under the FUP-2004 research program of the Autonomous Province of Trento.

Z. Vetulani and H. Uszkoreit (Eds.): LTC 2007, LNAI 5603, pp. 428–439, 2009.

The task is sometimes referred as *name discrimination*, since a name may refer ambiguously to different persons. However, in contrast to other ambiguity tasks, such as Part of Speech Tagging and Word Sense Disambiguation, the list of possible options for a name is not known apriori, which makes not feasible to address cross-document coreference as a classification problem and, as a consequence, to use supervised approaches.

Person coreference has been addressed in previous work (e.g. Baga and Baldwin 1998, Pederson et *al.* 2006) building vector-based representations (i.e. the *association set*) of persons' names using lists of named entities (e.g. persons, locations, organizations) associated with person names candidate for coreference. The underlying idea is that a person can be identified by the events he/she is associated with, and that such events can be conveniently represented by the list of the named entities mentioned in a particular document.

Pederson et *al.* 2006 also noticed the connection between the probability of occurrences of pairs of named entities and unique descriptions of a person. However, all person names have been assumed to behave equally.

The approach we propose is based on two main working hypotheses. The first one is that establishing coreference is an iterative process, where at each cycle the system attempts at establishing new coreferences, taking advantage of the coreferences established in previous cycles. The iterative design of the system has a relevant impact. Firstly, we do not need to specify an apriori number of clusters, and, secondly, we can resolve more difficult cases, i.e. when evidences are spread among instances, only after the coreference of easier cases become available. At each step of iteration, the association set of a person is merged with the association sets derived from other coreferences and therefore new evidences are obtained. When no new coreferences are realized, the algorithm stops.

The second consideration that has motivated our work is that the full potential of person names has not been exploited yet. First, it is useful to distinguish between first and last names. They behave differently with respect to coreference (three times less perplexity for last names than for first names) and, as there are items that could be both first and last names, making the distinction helps in reducing false coreference. Secondly, we can identify rare names for which the probability of different persons carrying them is very low and therefore their coreference may be realized loosening the conditions on the number of named entities in common.

According with the two hypotheses above, in this paper we present a general system for person cross-document coreference that combines name frequency estimates with association sets in an iterative model. A number of experiments have been carried out on a large-scale corpus of Italian news collection, where some 5M person names have been clustered into some 6K different persons. The evaluation has been driven over a sample of about 500 news manually annotated. Results show a significant improvement over a baseline algorithm, which indicates an accurate output of our approach. A second, somehow indirect evaluation comes from the fact that a variant of the present algorithm has been successfully applied to the Web People Search task in the Semeval 2007 competition, achieving the second position out of sixteen participant systems.

The paper is organized as follows. In section 2 we present the general characteristics of our system. Sections 3, 4 and 5 are dedicated to the description of the main modules of the system, respectively first and second name identification, local coreference and global coreference. Finally, in Section 6 we present the evaluation of our system on the I-CAB benchmark.

2 System Architecture

The system has three main modules, depicted in Figure 1: a Person Name Splitter, a Local Coreference module and a Global Coreference module, corresponding to three main steps of the process. The first step is the identification, for each token of a Named Entity (NE), referred as person name (PN), of its type, either first_name or last_name . This information is used at the second step, local coreference, where the coreference among the names in the same document is established. The output of the Local Coreference module is a list of names, which represents the input of the third module, Global Coreference. Two names from different documents corefer if their contexts are similar (where context is considered a bag of words with no linguistics processing). The cluster of globally coreferred names represents the names of a unique person. These three steps are repeated till no new coreferences are established. In Figure 1 we present schematically the system architecture.

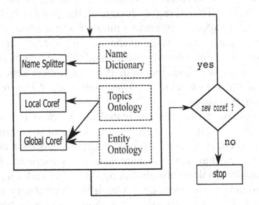

Fig. 1. Coreference System Architecture

During the process the system may consult three resources. A *Name Dictionary,* where first and last names of persons are reported. In our experiments the *Name Dictionary* initially covered only 49% of the names present in corpus and more than a third of the first names were also recorded as last names. The first module of the system, the Person Name splitter, dynamically enriches this resource.

We also consider a *Topic Ontology*, which is a resource specific for the news domain, where each document of the collection is classified under a limited number of topics. In our case we used the thirteen newspaper's sections of our document collection as topics.

The last resource, the *Entity Ontology,* contains the identified persons (and their PN mentions). The entity ontology is initially empty (i.e. no person is identified) and it is dynamically enriched at each iteration.

The *Name Splitter* module is executed mainly off line. It gathers the information regarding the frequency of each name token detected in the corpus and it creates the database required for making decisions regarding the name topology. Very often PNs of just one token corefer. However, their coreference is conditioned by their complementary distribution – a first name corefers with a last name, but the coreference of two last names is an exception.

The *Local Coref* module is applied to each piece of news independently. The name references to each person are clustered together using a specific algorithm. These clusters represent document entities (as opposed to global entities found in the *Entity Ontology*). Names in a local coref clusters are merged so to create the most complete form considering all the PN variants found inside the respective news.

The *Global coref* module is applied only to the most complete names determined at the Local Coref step. It implements a clustering algorithm based on a vectorial similarity measure. As pointed out in Section 1 the data variation in the cross document coreference task is very high and a unique similarity formula is unlikely to appropriately cluster the majority of PNs. We show that there is an algorithmic statistical procedure to partition the data into clusters of meaningful disjunctive sets.

3   Name Splitter

This module determines a token of a PN instance is either a first or a second name (we refer to them as "categories"). For example, the PN "Bertolucci Anna Maria" is decomposable into a last name (i.e. "Bertolucci") and two first names (i.e. "Anna" ad "Maria"). We classify tokens in a PN by means of a multi layer perceptron, which assigns a score to each token in a PN. The token in a PN with the highest weight above a threshold is selected as last_name. We used a feed forward Neural Network (Figure 2) and have trained it on a set of unambiguous names existing in the Name Dictionary.

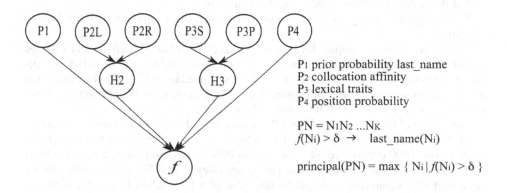

P_1 prior probability last_name
P_2 collocation affinity
P_3 lexical traits
P_4 position probability

$PN = N_1 N_2 ... N_K$
$f(N_i) > \delta \rightarrow last\_name(N_i)$

$principal(PN) = \max \{ N_i | f(N_i) > \delta \}$

Fig. 2. Feed Forward Name Splitter Neural Network

We use five parameters P_1, P_2, P_3, P_4, and P_5 to compute the probability of being a last name for each token. The first four parameters are encoded into the neural network, while the fifth is used as a supervisor.

- The first parameter, P_1, estimates the prior probability of a token to function as a last name. It is the probability of a token to be a last name regardless of the categories of the other tokens it combines with.
- The second parameter, P_2, measures the collocational affinity of a token. We actually distinguish two distinct parameters, P_{2L} and P_{2R}, which are the probabilities for a token to collocate on the lef, or on the right of a last name. The probability to collocate with a first name is the difference to 1.
- The third parameter, P_3, computes a lexical probability. Very often the lexical characteristics of a token are a powerful indicator of its category. We compute a list of suffixes/prefixes which, with a certain probability, are specific to last names. Therefore, this parameter is made up of two distinct parameters, let's call them P_{3suf} and P_{3pref}.
- The fourth parameter, P_4, represents the probability of a position within a name to be the position of a last name. This parameter is related to the names usage in language. In many languages, either the first or the last position in a name is the last name preferred position.
- The fifth parameter, P_5, is the probability that a name has a certain composition. In many languages the most frequent form is "First name Last name". However, the frequencies of a name may be highly variable from language to language. For example "First name Last name Last name" could be quite common in Spanish, but in Romanian it is almost inexistent.

For estimating P_1 we have used the Web. First, we extracted from the corpus the names that collocate with known names (i.e. existing in the Name Dictionary), from which we obtained a list of some15,000 unknown names. From a public webpage we extracted the list of the top twenty frequent first and last names respectively. We use the Google API interface to see how many times each unknown name appears with one of the twenty last names and compute the average.

P_2 is computed using the corpus itself, counting the frequencies of the known bigrams.

The value of P_3, is computed by taking into account a list of prefixes and suffixes which discriminate first names from last names (e.g. the suffix "*ni*" in Italian is typical of surnames). We consider all the suffixes and prefixes which are discriminative in more than 90% of cases, with more than 100 occurrences. In this way we have obtained a short list of 312 prefixes and 255 suffixes.

The values of the parameters P_4 and P_5 are determined buy counting using the corpus itself. On our type of corpus – Italian newspaper – we have notice that, based on the distribution of 200 occurrences of unambiguous PNs of two tokens the preferred order is "first name last name". However this rule is not obeyed in 8.5% of the cases and we computed a 95% confidence interval for this value (8.5-1.15, 8.5+1.15)=(7.35, 9.20).

4 Local Coreference

This module addresses coreference among person names within a single document. The input of the module are the PNs of the document, as resulting from the application of the Name Splitter. The local coreference algorithm assumes the *"one entity per document"* hypothesis, according to which within a news the same name always refers to the same person.

However, a major issue in establishing local coreferences is that a high proportion of PNs in a corpus are not complete, i.e. they are composed by either just the first_name (e.g. *"Silvio"*) or just the last_name (e.g. *"Berlusconi"*), which makes it hard applying the one entity per document assumption. We call such PNs *partial PNs* (as opposed to *complete PNs*), and distinguish between *free_first_name* (i.e. only the first_name is present in a PN) and *free_last_name* (i.e. only the last_name is present). Then, the local coreference can be formulated as the task of finding the most probable last_name for a given free_first_name in the document. All the other cases (e.g. two free_last_names) are all solved straightforwardly according to the one entity per document assumption.

Given a partial PN, we describe the completion task as a probabilistic event, modelled by the following random variables: the first name (l), the last name (L), first_last name (l_L) and the topic (t). Finding the most probable last_name for a free_first_name is to find the value of L which maximizes the following joint probability:

$$max_L \, p(l, L, l\_L, t) \quad = max_L \, p(t) \, p(L \mid t) \, p(l \mid L, t) \, p(l\_L \mid l, L, t) \qquad (1)$$

where:

- $p(t)$, is an independent constant, which does not count in the computation of (1).

- $p(L \mid t)$, the probability that a last_name is in a news of a certain topic, shows the connection between a topic and a last_name and may be computed in two ways: (i) by let it to take values in $\{60/100, 29/100, 10/100, 1/100\}$ corresponding to "very frequent", "frequent", "little frequent" and "no clue" respectively. (ii) By using Bayes theorem, and keeping in mind that p(t) does not count, we have $p(L \mid t) = p(t \mid L) \, p(L)$. Let $p(L)$, which represents the probability that a certain last_name is in the newspapers, may be computed as a raport. The probability $p(t \mid L)$ is normalized as above.

- $p(l \mid L, t)$ is the probability that a certain person is referred by a first_name in a news. If nothing is known we consider it 1/2. Otherwise, corpus examples already seen, we compute a yes/no function, considering whether it is more probable for that person of being called by first_name than not, and consequently, a quantity is added/subtracted from 1/2.

- $p(l\_L \mid l, L, t)$ is the probability that a person's name is made out of first_name and a last_name. We approximate it as $\{80/100, 20/100, 0\}$ considering the probability that the_last name is indeed a last_name. "0" value means that we have unmatched abbreviations.

All the above probabilities have been calculated over the whole document collection. We chose to normalize each probability and the reason is twofold. First, such probabilities can be very low and we are unable to correctly set a probabilistic space (the sum of marginal probabilities to be 1). Second, the number of occurrences of a collocation, such as last_name and topic, or first_name and last_name, is relevant once a certain threshold is passed. We cannot say that one person is more a politician than another once we know that both are, or that a legal name is more legal than another.

To each cluster of coreferred PNs we associate a name (i.e. the largest PN of the cluster without abbreviation) and call such name the *local head* of the cluster. As the local coreference module may coreference a free_first_name with a (free) last name, the resulting local head could be a name which is not a PN in the text. For example, in a news in which we find "*G.W.B.*", "*George Bush*" and "*Bush*" we create the local head "*George W. Bush*", a name which is not found as such in the respective news.

The local coreference procedure works as follows. At the first step, the procedure declares local heads all different PNs which have both a first and a last name and are not included in others PNs. A complete name is coreferred with the local head that contains it (according to the "one entity per document" hypothesis). At the second step, for each free_name a completion is searched, such as to form a local entity with a complete name. The list of candidates is restricted to the PNs which are present in the respective news. For example, consider a news within we have "*Bush*", "*Berlusconi*", "*Silvio*", "*Michelangelo*", "*G.W.*". Using (1) one may decide that "*Silvio*" is coreferred with "*Berlusconi*", "*Michelangelo*" with no one, and "*G.W.*" with "*Bush*".

5 Global Coreference

Once the intra document entities have been clustered, the relevant context of PNs (i.e. the association set) is considered. We use three different types of contextual information: (i) Named Entities (NEs), (ii) special words denoting professions and (iii) statistically relevant common words. NEs are determined using a Named Entity Recognizer based on SVM. The special words are selected according to a preexisting resource; in particular we used SUMO, a general ontology aligned to WordNet, which in turn is already available in many languages, including Italian (Pianta et al.).

In Section 1 we intuitively sketched the role of name frequency estimations: the rarer the name the more probable is that its instances are coreferred. We address this matter in a formal way here.

Apparently there is no correlation between the number of occurrences of a particular PN and the number of entities it refers too. However, the number of occurrences of a PN in newspaper corpus is determined mainly by two factors: (a) the commonness – how many different persons happen to have the same name and (b) the celebrity – the number of news related to a certain person. In Table 1 we list the number of occurrences of PNs from the seven years "Adige" newspaper corpus we used in the experiments reported in this paper.

Table 1. The distribution of PNs in the "Adige" news corpus

interval	different val(PNM)	# PNM
1	317,245	317,245
2 - 5	166,029	467,560
6 - 20	61,570	634,309
21 - 100	25,651	1,090,836
101 - 1000	7,750	2,053,994
1001 - 2000	4,25	569,627
2001 - 4000	157	422,585
4001 - 5000	17	73,860
5001 - 31091	22	190,373

By looking at the number of occurrences of a certain name we have to consider the relation between the commonness of a name and the fame of one person carrying that name. An example of this situation is the following: both "Carlo" and "Azeglio", two Italian first names, have had a big number of occurrences. We can deduce from this that the perplexity of "Carlo" and "Azeglio" is the same, therefore their coreference conditions should be the same, or close to one another. However, this is not a valid inference. The fact that "Azeglio" has a relatively high number of occurrences is due to the fact that the person named "Carlo Azeglio Ciampi" is mentioned very often. In fact, understanding the class of commonness for each name gives us a very important piece of information and a direct way to provide the relationship between the commonness class of a name and the number of different entities it refers to. For example, a very uncommon name like "Azeglio" can confidently be linked to just one person, while a very common name like "Carlo" to many.

The distribution of the commonness is not uniform and most probably it has not close analytical expression. We propose a distributional free method for estimating the probability that a certain PN belongs to a certain commonness class.

Suppose that we have a sample from the corpus population of PNs. The pth quantile, ζ_p, which the real value for which p% behave alike – in our settings the value for which p% from the population has less than a given number of different person can be estimated as follow: let $k = [p(n+1)]$ where n is the sample size. And [] represents the closest integer. Then Y_k is an unbiased estimator of ζ_p where Y_k is the kth ordered random sample.

By itself the number ζ_p may not be of great help because from the point of view of the coreference system two PNs are or not corefered. However we can estimate a confidence interval using the formula:

$$P(Yi < \zeta_p < Yj) = \sum_t C(p,w)p^t (1-p)^t , t \text{ in } [i,j] \qquad (2)$$

We can compute (1) by considering a partition of the data generated by the perplexity of one token PN. For a first name the perplexity is the size of the set of all last names with which that particular first name appear in the corpus and vice versa. We have used five categories; "very rare", "rare", "common", "frequent" and "very frequent" and we found that heir distribution in the population is unbalanced (see Table 2 and 3).

Finally we can compute the figure we are most interested in, namely the tolerance interval for ζ_p, which gives the percentage of the population within a certain confidence interval.

$$\gamma = P(F(Yj) - F(Yi) < p) = 1 - \int_0^p \Gamma(n+1)/(\Gamma(i-j)) \Gamma(n-j++i+1)x^{j-i-1}(1-x)^{n-j+i}dx \qquad (3)$$

The probability γ is the probability that p% from the interval computed with formula (2) is in the interval $[Y_i, Y_j]$. For example in the category "very rare", p = .95, $\zeta_p = 1$, $(Y_i, Y_j) = (1,2)$ with $\gamma = 99,6\%$. That it a "very rare" name stands for a single person with 95% probability and, most important, 99,6% of all "very rare" names stand for one or maximum two different persons.

Table 2. First name commonness

Commonness	Percentage
very frequent	5.3%
Frequent	8.7%
Common	20.9%
Rare	28%
very rare	40%

Table 3. Last name commonness

commonness	percentage
very frequent	0.11%
Frequent	3.48%
Common	17.52%
Rare	20.41%
very rare	59.02%

The name frequency class determines the value of a dynamic threshold used by the similarity measure during the global coreference process. For each name frequency, this dynamic threshold shows the degree of similarity we are willing to consider in order to realize the coreference of two PNs.

6 Evaluation

We run the three modules of the system described in Sections 3, 4 and 5 on a corpus made out of news appeared in the Italian newspaper "L'Adige" in a seven years period. First, all named entities (persons, locations and organizations) in the corpus where detected using TextPro (Zanoli & Pianta, 2006). As a result, there are 5,559,314 PNs in the corpus, out of which 558,352 are distinct.

For evaluation purposes we used a small portion of the corpus (four days distributed in a one year period), called Italian Content Annotation Bank (I-CAB), which was manually annotated at several semantic levels, including coreference (Magnini et al, 2006) . Table 4 shows the I-CAB figures relevant for our evaluation. We distinguish first, middle and last names and for each we report: the number of occurrences (second column) with, within parentheses, the proportion of mentions containing a certain attribute; the number of distinct names (third column); the number of distinct persons carrying them (fourth column). Additional details on the I-CAB corpus, relevant for estimating the difficulty of coreference task, are reported in (Popescu et *al.* 2006, Magnini et *al.* 2006b).

Table 4. I-CAB parameters for coreference tasks

PNs	#occ I-CAB	#distinct	#persons
first	2299(31%)	676	1592
middle	110(1%)	67	74
last	4173(57%)	1906	2191

As a baseline for cross document coreference we used the "all for one" baseline: all equal PNs stand for the same person. Partial_names are completed with the most frequent complete name that includes them (for instance, the free_first_name "*Carlo Arzeglio*" is completed with "*Carlo Arzeglio Ciampi*"). The right most token in a PM is considered the last name.

Evaluation of the Name Splitter

The *Name Dictionary* we used for the Name Splitter module (see Section 3) covers 87.3% of first names and 91,8% of last names occurring in the I-CAB corpus. There are 245 ambiguous names, out of which 9 are actually ambiguously used in ICAB, and there are 13 ambiguous abbreviations.

The Name Splitter Module performs quite well. We report a 96,73% precision for first_name and 98,17% precision for last name. In total the module has 97,45% accuracy. The errors most likely do not influence the coreference results as they occur just one time. The baseline goes at 89,13%.

Evaluation of Local Coreference

The baseline for local coreference is very high: only 29 errors. That is, there are only 29 cases in which the coreference is not trivial, or the most frequent collocation is not the correct answer. Our algorithm scores better: it saves 11 cases out of these 29 cases. It is relevant to discuss performance in terms of ratios. There are 6633 PNs in ICAB and 2976 local coreferences, which means an average of 2.22 PNs per local coreferred persons. Our algorithm, which for the first run behaves like the baseline algorithm, has found 1,039,203 local coreferences out of 5,559,314 PNs, which means a 5,34 average, which is almost twice. At the end, the local coreference module outputs 1,748,212 local coreferred PNs, with an average of 3.17, which is probably closer to the true value.

Evaluation of Global Coreference

The Global Coreference module is evaluated for those cases where the name appears at least two times in I-CAB. For all complete names the baseline goes wrong in 24 cases. It means that there are 24 cases in four days where the same complete name does not refer to the same person. Our algorithm performs a little better, since it keeps them correctly separated in 17 cases. However, there are 10 coreferred names which our algorithm does not realize. As far as partial names are concerned, there are 91 last_names which do not have a first name and refer to different persons. The system scores 87 while the baseline scores 0. (i.e. it always finds a first name). There are 45 first names referring to different persons, yet without having the last name mentioned. Our algorithm realizes correctly in 34 cases that the respective names should remain free and distinct.

In Table 5 we summarize the above information specifying on the second and third column the performances of both the system and the baseline.

Table 5. Performance evaluation (error rate)

module	#system errors	#baseline errors
Name Splitter	151(2.6%)	603(10.97%)
Local Coref	11(0.4%)	29(0.8%)
Global Coref	31(1.4%)	150(5.49%)

Before ending this section we would like to have a broader view on the evaluation. The baseline we choose is a naïve one. However, in spite of its limitations, it is not entirely clear how bad it performs and how much better a different algorithm may perform. If we set H_0 to be the "all for one" baseline we have the highest significance level of the test possible. It follows that the power test is zero (second type of error is 1). The baseline algorithm goes wrong every time it has the chance to do so. Exactly the same holds with H_0 "one for one": for each distinct PN there is exactly one person. The distribution of PNs shows that for each of these two hypotheses there is a great amount of data that verifies it. A possibility to alleviate, and to raise, the power test of the baseline, would be to consider special cases only, especially those with relatively few occurrences and high frequency of their names.

7 Conclusion and Further Research

We have presented a cross document coreference system that takes into account differences that exist between person names. The system combines probabilistic information of the names behavior with the contextual information. Our finding is that probabilistic information brings a certain amount of certainty in establishing the coreference.

One of the main problems that must be addressed is that association sets may contain little information is some cases. We have estimated that for some frequent names, from 10 to 15% of the whole names, the association sets do not contain enough evidence for coreference. Under the same name, probably many times referring to just one person, we have an average of 4 different persons. The problem is how to decide whether the merging is appropriate in those cases. Our belief is that cross document coreference can benefit from the information contained outside the text. One advantage of the system we have proposed is the capacity to identify the cases lacking sufficient information, which means that we can design specific solution for them, which is our immediate goal for future work.

We have started working on a solution for sparse association sets. The main idea is to identify key words within already coreferred clusters and to use them further for coreference. A first result shows that using a td/idf strategy combined with a score for the distance between the PN and the key word considerably increases the number of coreference among PNs. We would also like to develop an evaluation procedure for these new coreferences.

Additional information for coreference may come from world knowledge among entities in the association set, such as for instance ontological relationships among a certain PN and LOCATIONs in the association set, or PNs and ORGs. It is generally difficult to extract and manipulate ontological information. In our opinion a realistic goal is to identify useful connection between a determinator, such as profession or place, and a person name. Once such connections are correctly identified, we can use an Ontology to infer whether to different determinators function the same in respect with the name of interest. This goal requests minimal linguistics processing, a shallow parser should suffice, and minimal ontological inferences.

References

Artiles, J., Gonzalo, J., Sekine, S.: Establishing a benchmark for the Web People Search Task: The Semeval 2007 WePS Track. In: Proceedings of Semeval 2007, Association for Computational Linguistics (2007)

Bagga, A., Baldwin., B.: Entity-based cross-document co-referencing using the vector space model. In: Proceedings of the 17th international conference on Computational Linguistics, pp. 75–85 (1998)

Grishman, R.: Whither Written Language Evaluation. In: Human Language Technology Workshop, pp. 120–125. San Mateor Morgan Kaufmann (1994)

Magnini, B., Pianta, E., Girardi, C., Negri, M., Romano, L., Speranza, M., Bartalesi Lenzi, V., Sprugnoli, R.: I-CAB: the Italian Content Annotation Bank. In: Proceedings of LREC-2006, Genova, Italy (2006)

Magnini, B., Pianta, E., Popescu, O., Speranza, M.: Ontology Population from Textual Mentions: Task Definition and Benchmark. In: Proceedings of the OLP2 workshop on Ontology Population and Learning, Sidney, Australia. Joint with ACL/Coling (2006)

Pedersen, T., Purandare, A.: Name Discrimination by Clustering Similar Contexts. In: Proceedings of the World Wide Web Conference (2006)

Popescu, O., Magnini, B., Pianta, E., Serafini, L., Speranza, M., Tamilin, A.: From Mentions to Ontology: A Pilot Study. In: Proceedings SWAP 2006, Pisa, Italy (2006)

Zanoli, R., Pianta, E.: Intelligenza Artificiale. Associazione Italiana per l'Intelligenza Artificiale 4(2) (2007)

Hapax Legomena: Their Contribution in Number and Efficiency to Word Alignment

Adrien Lardilleux and Yves Lepage

GREYC, University of Caen Basse-Normandie, France
{Adrien.Lardilleux,Yves.Lepage}@info.unicaen.fr
http://users.info.unicaen.fr/~{alardill,ylepage}

Abstract. Current techniques in word alignment disregard words with a low frequency because they would not be useful. Against this belief, this paper shows that, in particular, the notion of *hapax legomena* may contribute to word alignment to a large extent. In an experiment, we show that pairs of *corpus hapaxes* contribute to the majority of the best word alignments. In addition, we show that the notion of *sentence hapax* justifies a practical and common simplification of standard alignment methods.

Keywords: word alignment, low frequency term, hapax.

1 Introduction

Alignment is an important task in natural language processing for a variety of purposes like the constitution of lexical resources, machine translation or cross-lingual information retrieval.

The purpose of this paper is to contribute to the domain of alignment between two languages. Our work focuses on the impact of *hapax legomena*[1]. Contrary to common knowledge in the field, we show that hapaxes contribute to a considerable extent to word alignment. In addition, we show that the distribution of words in our corpus logically leads to a justification of a practically fast implementation of a standard alignment method.

The paper is organised as follows. Section 2 briefly recalls main results about hapaxes in corpora. Section 3 introduces the cosine method to compute word alignments and gives some theoretical insights. Section 4 describes the data used in our experiments and details experimental results: hapaxes are useful for alignment as they contribute to up to 86% of the best word alignments. Section 5 shows how the notion of hapax in a sentence leads to an efficient simplification of the cosine method.

---

[1] From the Greek *hapax legomenon* 'what has been uttered once.' In the following we shall use the plural *hapaxes* for convenience.

Z. Vetulani and H. Uszkoreit (Eds.): LTC 2007, LNAI 5603, pp. 440–450, 2009.

2   Hapaxes

2.1   Common Negative Attitude towards Hapaxes

A hapax is a word that occurs only once in a single text or corpus. A general belief in the field holds that:

> *Hapax legomenon* and other so-called rare events present an interesting problem for corpus-based applications: due to their low frequency, they fail to provide enough statistical data for applications like word alignment or statistical machine translation [1].

As a matter of fact, by definition, hapaxes are discarded from the data in those approaches which filter out any word with a low frequency. This is usually the case in statistical machine translation or word alignment. For example, Cromières [2] sets a lower bound on frequencies to consider a word for alignement. Giguet and Luquet [3] define a threshold proportional to the inverse term length.

In addition to their infrequency, a presumed drawback of hapaxes is that they often include newly coined words (neologisms) and misspelled words [1]. Neologisms should be considered words on their own right. As for misspelled words, their number depends mostly on the quality of the corpus. According to Nishimoto [4], who interprets the results of Evert and Lüdeling [5], each error in a corpus occurs only once in average. Misspelled words are thus typically hapaxes, but their proportion remains relatively low.

2.2   Positive Aspects of Hapaxes

Various experiments have been conducted so far on hapaxes. Cartoni [6] reports that hapaxes generally represent about 40% of words of a corpus. This number may vary according to the following aspects:

- the *richness of the vocabulary*: the proportion of hapaxes reflects the quantity of different words used in the text. Counts on Shakespeare's most read plays yield up to 58% hapaxes;[2]
- the *degree of synthesis* of the language: isolating, synthetic or polysynthetic. The more synthetic a language, the more inflected words, and consequently, the more different words. The proportion of hapaxes increases accordingly. On a corpus of Inuktitut, a highly synthetic language of Canada, Langlais et al. [7] report more than 80% of hapaxes. In such a case, rejecting hapaxes is tantamount to consider only 20% of the data, which may obviously hinder the relevance of any subsequent processing.

In addition to account for a large proportion of word tokens, the relation of hapaxes to unknown words has already been demonstrated [6,8]. This aspect makes

---

[2] Word frequencies available at Mt. Hararat High School web site:
http://www.mta75.org/curriculum/English/Shakes/index.html

them useful to estimate the behaviour of unseen words, in machine translation for example.

In accordance to these facts, the purpose of this article is to show that hapaxes are useful in word alignment.

3   Alignment Method

Ideally, word alignments consist of translation pairs (*source word, target word*). Practically, alignment methods deliver scores that reflect the probability of *target word* being an accurate translation of *source word*. Various methods have been developed to compute word alignments. They are generally based on statistics on words [9,10,11,12,13,14], distribution similarities [2,3], linguistic heuristics [15], or oppositions between sentences [16].

We propose to use the cosine method in order to calculate word alignments. It is a standard technique for the computation of similarities or distances between distributions. It has been widely used in various domains, from Named Entity discovery [17] to conceptual vectors for semantic tasks [18,19].

In the case of word alignment between two parallel corpora, the basic steps are the following:

- start with an aligned bicorpus of n lines, *i.e.*, n sentences in a source language with their corresponding translations in a target language. Each line becomes a dimension in a vectorial field;
- for a given word w, build its associated vector $\boldsymbol{w}$ in this vectorial field by taking the number of occurrences of w on the ith line as the value of the ith component of vector $\boldsymbol{w}$;
- do this for each word in the source language and each word in the target language;
- for each pair of words w_s and w_t in the source and the target languages, compute the angle between their associated vectors $\boldsymbol{w_s}$ and $\boldsymbol{w_t}$:

$$(\widehat{\boldsymbol{w_s}, \boldsymbol{w_t}}) = acos \left(\frac{\boldsymbol{w_s} \cdot \boldsymbol{w_t}}{\| \boldsymbol{w_s} \| \times \| \boldsymbol{w_t} \|} \right) \qquad (1)$$

where $\boldsymbol{u} \cdot \boldsymbol{v}$ is the scalar product of vectors $\boldsymbol{u}$ and $\boldsymbol{v}$ and $\| \boldsymbol{v} \|$ is the norm of vector $\boldsymbol{v}$. This value is the score of the alignment (w_s, w_t).

Since all components of $\boldsymbol{w_s}$ and $\boldsymbol{w_t}$ are positive, the previous computation yields only positive values in the range of 0 to $\pi/2 \simeq 1.57$, inclusive.

Intuitively, we would like the cosine measure to correspond to the idea that the lesser the angle, the better the quality of the word alignment. In other words, we would like to interpret the cosine measure as a kind of translation distance. Thus, the word alignments in which we are interested are those with a measure close to zero.

Theoretically, an angle of 0 means that $\boldsymbol{w_s}$ and $\boldsymbol{w_t}$ are parallel, i.e., the two words appear exclusively on the same lines and their number of occurences on these lines is proportional: $w_s = \lambda w_t$. In practice, on our data λ equals 1 most of the time. The desired interpretation of an angle of zero is that both words would be perfect translations of one another (lexical equivalence), but this may not be true all the time (see Sec. 4.2 for examples).

An angle of $\pi/2$ implies that the cosine equals 0. This happens when each component of the scalar product is zero, *i.e.*, when the intersection of the lines on which the source and target words appear together is empty. This happens almost all the time when we consider all possible pairs of words. Consequently, efficient implementations of the cosine method do not compute angles between all possible pairs of vectors. Instead, they restrict the computation to those pairs of vectors associated with words that appear at least once on the same line. This narrows vectors down to the dimensions that are relevant for the computation. Suffix arrays [20,21] are an efficient data structure to implement this.

4   Hapaxes in Word Alignments

4.1   The Data

We used the training corpus from the IWSLT 2007 machine translation evaluation campaign [22] to conduct our experiments. It consists in roughly 40,000 pairs of aligned utterances in Japanese and English (average sentence length in English: 9.1 words) from the BTEC [23]. Japanese sentences are segmented into words using ChaSen [24]. Sentences in the corpus are independent. A sample of aligned sentences is shown on Fig. 1.

この 切符 を キャンセル し たい の です が 。
/kono kippu o kyanseru si tai no desu ga ./   ↔   I'd like to cancel this ticket .

どんな 映画 が あり ます か 。
/donna eiga ga ari masu ka ./   ↔   What kind of movies are there ?

コーヒー を 下さい 。
/kôhî o kudasai ./   ↔   Could I have coffee , please ?

先方 が 通話 を 拒否 なさい まし た 。
/senpou ga tuuwa o kyohi nasai masi ta ./   ↔   Your party refused the call .

二人 です 。 ツイン を 希望 し ます 。
/hutari desu . tuin o kibou si masu ./   ↔   Two . I want a twin .

Fig. 1. Excerpt of the data used to conduct the experiment. Each line is a pair of aligned utterances. Transliterations are not part of the original corpus.

The proportion of hapaxes in this corpus is 44% for the Japanese part and 43% for the English part, figures which are conform to other figures reported in the litterature (see above, Sec. 2.2).

4.2   Results with the Cosine Method

Tables 1 and 2 give samples of word alignments obtained using the cosine method.

Table 1. Examples of word pairs ordered by angles in increasing order, obtained by sampling. The sample meets intuition: the pair with a lower angle is a better translation. The sample also reflects the distribution of the angles between 0 and $\pi/2$ (see Fig. 2).

Japanese	freq.	English	freq.	angle $(0 \sim \pi/2)$
鬘 /katura/ 'wig'	1	wig	1	0.00
閉まる /simaru/ 'to close'	8	Close	2	1.32
毛布 /môhu/ 'blanket'	42	blankets	1	1.42
に対する /nitaisuru/ 'in (in dollars)'	13	dollar	112	1.48
指定 /sitei/ 'assignment'	25	seat	468	1.49
、 /,/ ','	8,569	them	300	1.50
大体 /daitai/ 'about'	22	hundred	377	1.51
こんな /konna/ 'such'	38	happens	7	1.51
今 /ima/ 'now'	442	Would	703	1.56
気分 /kibun/ 'feeling'	54	Okay	268	1.56

Table 2. Sample of pairs of words with angle 0

Japanese	freq.	English	freq.
クリントン /kurinton/ 'Clinton'	3	Clinton	3
レターヘッド /retâheddo/ 'letterhead'	2	letterhead	2
ミズカワ /mizukawa/ 'Mizukawa (firstname)'	2	Toshiki	2
大陸 /tairiku/ 'continent'	1	continent	1
ちり紙 /tirigami/ 'tissue'	1	tissue	1
埼玉 /saitama/ 'Saitama'	1	Saitama	1
交響曲 /kôkyôkyoku/ 'symphony'	1	symphonies	1
ケネー /kenê/ 'Quesnay (lastname)'	1	Quesnay	1
フェニックス /fenikkusu/ 'phoenix'	1	phoenix	1
最高裁判所 /saikôsaibansyo/ 'supreme court'	1	supreme	1

The method can lead to apparently surprising results. For instance, the alignment between "ミズカワ" /mizukawa/ 'Mizukawa' and "Toshiki" illustrates the fact that even a "perfect" alignment (angle of zero) does not mean that the words are translations of each other. It only depicts the reciprocal presence of the two words on any line. In this corpus, the person named "Toshiki Mizukawa" always utters his full name: the words "Toshiki" and "Mizukawa" are collocations.

These examples show that word alignments with a score of one are just a quite safe subset of all possible word pairs. The purpose of the next section is to show that hapaxes contribute to this safe subset for a good part.

4.3   Distribution of Alignments

The distribution of pairs of words according to their angle on our data is shown by the graph on Fig. 2. Alignments are divided according to their scores into three populations.

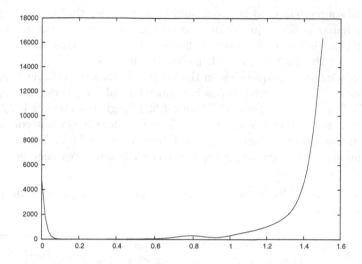

Fig. 2. Smoothed distribution of pairs of words. On the x-axis, the angle of alignments. On the y-axis, the number of alignments.

The first and largest one (not plotted) is a set of pairs with angle $\pi/2$ (141,367, 221 pairs). It consists only of pairs of words which never appear on the same line. Such alignments are to be rejected.

The second population starts around $\pi/4$ and extends to $\pi/2$. It consists of pairs of words which are *a priori* no translations because of their bad scores (see last lines of Table 1). For clarity, pairs with an angle greater than 1.5 are not plotted (700,828 pairs).

The third population is the pairs with angle near 0. There are 4,833 such pairs, 4,156 (86%) of which contain hapaxes in *both* languages, with an angle of 0. Rejecting hapaxes would thus reduce this population to almost nothing: the efficiency of the method in good candidates for translation pairs would be of roughly 600 pairs for 40,000 sentences involving more than ten thousand words in each language!

Hapaxes are responsible for such a large proportion of the best alignments because, two *corpus hapaxes* appearing respectively in a source and a target sentence of a same line are, by definition, aligned with an angle of 0.

4.4 Distribution of Hapaxes

As illustrated previously (Table 2), some alignments with an angle of 0, which are mainly obtained by hapaxes, are not valid word-to-word alignments. This happens because, when a sentence contains more than one *corpus hapax*, every source hapax gets aligned with every target hapax with an angle of 0. On the other hand, if there is only one source hapax and only one target hapax on a line, the resulting alignment is guaranteed to be correct. More generally, if there is only one source hapax and several target hapaxes on a line, (resp. one target hapax and several source hapaxes) it is reasonable to consider that the translation of the source hapax is the sequence of target hapaxes (resp. the translation of the target hapax is the sequence of source hapaxes). To study this phenomenon, we further inspect the distribution of hapaxes in our data.

The average hapax frequencies on the corpus is shown on Table 3. Although the number of hapaxes in the corpus is almost half of the words, they appear in only 3,975 Japanese sentences (10%) and 4,691 English sentences (12%). More importantly, the sentences containing a hapax generally do not contain more than one hapax: most of them (90% in Japanese and 86% in English) contain exactly one hapax, the average being less than 1.2 hapax per sentence.

Table 3. Japanese and English average hapax frequencies, computed on the sentences hapaxes appear in

Language	Number of sentences containing a hapax	Number of sentences containing exactly 1 hapax	Avg.±std. dev.
Japanese	3,975	3,559 (90%)	1.19±0.54
English	4,691	4,025 (86%)	1.18±0.54

Among the alignments based only on hapaxes, 2,129 (44%) are actually obtained by aligning a single hapax with a sequence of hapaxes (this produces as many alignments with an angle of 0 as there are hapaxes in the sequence), and 1,437 (30%) are "single-to-single" hapax alignments, i.e., alignments of hapaxes from lines that contained exactly one hapax in both languages.

Note that the 4,156 hapax-based alignments cover 2,828 Japanese words (23% of the total number of Japanese words) and 2,769 English words (24% of English words). Consequently, the 1,437 "single-to-single" alignments actually cover the vocabulary implied in hapax-based alignments up to 51% for Japanese and 52% for English. In other words, one can rely on these few alignments only (which are most certainly among the best alignments, see Table 4) to cover respectively 11% and 13% of the total vocabulary of our data.

4.5   Alignments of Sequences of Hapaxes

From the above results, one could draw the hypothesis that alignments of *sequences of hapaxes* would be safe. Further studies confirmed the well-foundedness and the reliability of such an hypothesis. Consequently, in [16] we were able to propose a simple yet efficient multilingual alignment method that solely relies on this evidence. It consists in reducing all words frequencies by sampling the initial corpus. By doing so, sequences of words with identical distributions (i.e., their associated vectors are parallel) emerge and are aligned. In this setting, almost all alignments output by the method are *sequences of hapaxes*. The quality of the alignment has been shown to be competitive to state-of-the-art techniques (see [16] for details).

Table 4. Sample of pairs of aligned "single hapaxes" (hapaxes from sentences with one hapax only). In this sample, only one alignment is wrong ("Olympics").

Japanese	English
キール /*kîru*/ 'kir'	kir
龍 /*tatu*/ 'dragon'	Dragon
司会 /*sikai*/ 'chairman'	moderator
同情 /*dôjô*/ 'sympathy'	sympathy
くらげ /*kurage*/ 'jellyfish'	jellyfish
ポタージュ /*potâju*/ 'potage'	Potage
ポマード /*pomâdo*/ 'pomade'	pomade
バンコック /*bankokku*/ 'Bangkok'	Bangkok
開催 /*kaisai*/ 'open an exhibition'	Olympics
メリークリスマス /*merîkurisumasu*/ 'Merry Christmas'	Merry

5 Simplifying Common Alignment Methods with Hapaxes

5.1 *Sentence Hapaxes* vs. *Corpus Hapaxes*

We will now show that the distribution of words in sentences, and specifically, the notion of hapaxes in sentences, can lead to a simplification of the cosine method. To our knowledge, this common simplification is never justified.

In a first step, we determine how frequent a word is in the sentences it appears in, i.e., we compute the total number of occurences of a word in the corpus divided by the number of sentences it appears in. Since a hapax in a corpus is necessarily a hapax in the sentence it appears in, the number of *sentence hapaxes* in a sentence is greater than or equal to the number of *corpus hapaxes* in this sentence.

Table 5 summarizes the results. In average, 94% of the words have a frequency of 1 on the sentences they appear in. Those include hapaxes in the corpus. On the whole, the average frequency is 1.005, very close to 1: almost all words are hapaxes in the sentences they appear in.

Consequently, instead of considering the actual number of times a word appears in a sentence, counting its presence or absence suffices. This reduces to see each word of the corpus as a *sentence hapax* (caution: not necessarily a *corpus hapax*). By doing so, the components in the vectors w_s and w_t now take their value in the set $\{0, 1\}$, and (1) thus simplifies to:

$$(\widehat{w_s, w_t}) = acos \left(\frac{\mid S_s \cap S_t \mid}{\sqrt{\mid S_s \mid \times \mid S_t \mid}} \right) \qquad (2)$$

where S_s is the set of lines in the source corpus on which w_s appears (same for S_t)[3].

---

[3] Note that the argument of *acos* is different from the Jaccard coefficient:
$\mid S_s \cap S_t \mid / \mid S_s \cup S_t \mid$.

Table 5. Japanese and English average word frequencies

	Total number of words	Number of words such that nbr. occ./sentence=1	Avg.±std. dev.
Japanese	12,535	11,882 (95%)	1.006±0.055
English	11,342	10,704 (94%)	1.005±0.055

The next section shows that this simplification does not alter the quality of the alignments obtained.

5.2 Comparison between the Original and the Simplified Methods

Comparison in Scores. In order to show that the previous simplification can be used as a substitute for the original method, we conducted a systematic comparison between the alignments obtained by the two methods, the original one serving as a baseline.

First, it is worth noticing that the simplification theoretically does not produce any new alignment within the two populations of alignments with an angle different from $\pi/2$ in comparison with the original method. This is verified in practice. Its effect reduces to a modification of the angle for pairs of words where one of the words is not a *sentence hapax* for any definite sentence (the angle of a pair (*corpus hapax, corpus hapax*) will not change).

Among the 804,749 alignment angles from the above mentioned populations, 25% (201,191) appear to be strictly identical, up to 10 decimals. For the remaining 75%, the relative variation between the original angle and the one in the simplified method amounts to 0.29% (average) ± 1.53% (standard deviation)[4]. Clearly, the difference in angles between the original cosine method and the simplified version should not affect the quality of any subsequent processing task. This simplification successfully applies in the method presented in [16].

The distribution of pairs of words according to their angle, obtained with the simplified cosine method, is shown on Fig. 2, along with the original graph. No difference is visible.

Comparison in Runtime. The main advantage of the simplified method lies in its speed. It is much faster than the original one, because it is possible to use binary operations[5] On several machines with different architectures, the observed speed-up was around 10 to 15 times (from the minute to few seconds on our data).

6   Conclusion

This paper addressed the impact of hapaxes on word alignment using the cosine method.

---

[4] 0.21% ± 1.31% on the whole.

[5] An intersection is computed using a logical AND and the number of set bits in a machine-word can be computed in $O(\log n)$.

We first showed that *corpus hapaxes* contribute to up to 86% of the best alignments obtained by the cosine method. Such pairs of *corpus hapaxes* align almost 25% of the entire vocabulary on our data. These best alignments correspond to one of the three main populations of alignments we obtained by the cosine method, the two remaining and largest ones covering alignments that turn out to be no translation at all. In addition, word alignments with a mitigated score are almost inexistent. These results clearly demonstrate that the common attitude of rejecting hapaxes may lead to an important loss in efficiency.

We also showed, at least on our data, that the notion of *sentence hapax* justifies in a logical manner a practical and common simplification of the cosine method. This simplification appears to be very reliable since it yields an average difference of only 0.21% in scores when compared with the original method, 25% of the scores remaining unchanged. An improvement of 10 to 15 times in speed is observed.

The basic results presented in this article are the basis for the design and the implementation of a new alignment method presented in [16]. A free implementation is available at http://users.info.unicaen.fr/~alardill/malign/

References

1. Schrader, B.: How does morphological complexity translate? A cross-linguistic case study for word alignment, Tübingen, Germany (February 2006)
2. Cromières, F.: Sub-sentential alignment using substring co-occurrence counts. In: Proceedings of the COLING/ACL 2006 Student Research Workshop, Sydney, Australia, July 2006, pp. 13–18 (2006)
3. Giguet, E., Luquet, P.S.: Multilingual lexical database generation from parallel texts in 20 european languages with endogenous resources. In: Proceedings of the COLING/ACL 2006 Main Conference Poster Sessions, Sydney, Australia, July 2006, pp. 271–278 (2006)
4. Nishimoto, E.: Defining new words in corpus data: Productivity of English suffixes in the British National Corpus. In: 26th Annual Meeting of the Cognitive Science Society (CogSci 2004), Chicago, USA (August 2004)
5. Evert, S., Lüdeling, A.: Measuring morphological productivity: Is automatic preprocessing sufficient? In: Proceedings of Corpus Linguistics 2001 (CL2001), Lancaster, UK (April 2001)
6. Cartoni, B.: Constance et variabilité de l'incomplétude lexicale. In: Proceedings of TALN/RECITAL 2006, Leuven, Belgium, April 2006, pp. 661–669 (2006)
7. Langlais, P., Gotti, F., Cao, G.: English-Inuktitut word alignment system description, Ann Arbor, Michigan, USA, pp. 75–78 (2005)
8. Baayen, H., Sproat, R.: Estimating lexical priors for low-frequency morphologically ambiguous forms. Computational Linguistics 22, 155–166 (1996)
9. Brown, P., Pietra, S.D., Pietra, V.D., Mercer, R.: The mathematic of statistical machine translation: Parameter estimation. Computational Linguistics 19, 263–311 (1993)
10. Marcu, D., Wong, W.: A phrase-based, joint probability model for statistical machine translation. In: Proceedings of the Conference on Empirical Methods in Natural Language Processing (EMNLP 2002), Philadelphia, Pennsylvania, USA (July 2002)

11. Och, F., Ney, H.: A systematic comparison of various statistical alignment models. Computational Linguistics 29, 19–51 (2003)
12. Matusov, E., Zens, R., Ney, H.: Symmetric word alignments for statistical machine translation. In: Proceedings of the 20th International Conference on Computational Linguistics (Coling 2004), Geneva, Switzerland, August 2004, pp. 219–225 (2004)
13. Zhang, Y., Vogel, S.: An efficient phrase-to-phrase alignment model for arbitrarily long phrase and large corpora. In: Proceedings of the Tenth Conference of the European Association for Machine Translation (EAMT-2005), Budapest, Hungary (May 2005)
14. Moore, R., tau Yih, W., Bode, A.: Improved discriminative bilingual word alignment. In: Proceedings of the 21st International Conference on Computational Linguistics and 44th Annual Meeting of the Association for Computational Linguistics, Sydney, Australia, July 2006, pp. 513–520 (2006)
15. Melamed, I.D.: Automatic evaluation and uniform filter cascades for inducing n-best translation lexicons. In: Proceedings of the Third Workshop on Very Large Corpora, Boston, Massachusetts, USA, June 1995, pp. 184–198 (1995)
16. Lardilleux, A., Lepage, Y.: A truly multilingual, high coverage, accurate, yet simple, sub-sentential alignment method. In: Proceedings of the 8th Conference of the Association for Machine Translation in the Americas (AMTA 2008), Waikiki, Hawai'i, USA, October 2008, pp. 125–132 (2008)
17. Shinyama, Y., Sekine, S.: Named entity discovery using comparable news articles. In: Proceedings of the 20th International Conference on Computational Linguistics (Coling 2004), Geneva, Switzerland, August 2004, pp. 848–853 (2004)
18. Lafourcade, M., Boitet, C.: UNL lexical selection with conceptual vectors. In: Proceedings of the Third International Conference on Language Resources and Evaluation (LREC), Las Palmas de Gran Canaria, Spain, 1958–1964 (2002)
19. Turney, P., Littman, M.: Corpus-based learning of analogies and semantic relations. Machine Learning 60, 251–278 (2005)
20. Manber, U., Myers, G.: Suffix array: A new method for on-line string searches. SIAM Journal on Computing 22, 935–948 (1993)
21. Nagao, M., Mori, S.: A new method of n-gram statistics for large number of n and automatic extraction of words and phrases from large text data of Japanese. In: Proceedings of the 15th International Conference on Computational Linguistics (COLING 1994), Kyoto, Japan (August 1994)
22. Fordyce, C.S.: Overview of the IWSLT 2007 evaluation campaign. In: Proceedings of the 4th International Workshop on Spoken Language Translation (IWSLT 2007), Trento, Italy, October 2007, pp. 1–12 (2007)
23. Takezawa, T., Sumita, E., Sugaya, F., Yamamoto, H., Yamamoto, S.: Toward a broad-coverage bilingual corpus for speech translation of travel conversation in the real world. In: Proceedings of the third International Conference on Language Resources and Evaluation (LREC) Las Palmas de Gran Canaria, Spain, pp. 147–152 (2002)
24. Matsumoto, Y.: Japanese morphological analyser ChaSen. Journal of Information Processing Society of Japan 41, 1208–1214 (2000)

Statistical Machine Translation from Slovenian to English Using Reduced Morphology

Mirjam Sepesy Maučec and Janez Brest

Faculty for Electrical Engineering and Computer Science
University of Maribor
Smetanova 17, 2000 Maribor, Slovenia
mirjam.sepesy@uni-mb.si, janez.brest@uni-mb.si

Abstract. This paper describes the study of word-based statistical machine translation to language pair Slovenian - English. The problem when dealing with Slovenian language is data sparsity and consequently, error-full translations. The aim of the work is to define the approach to reduce the inflectional morphology of the Slovenian language for translation into less inflected language. The reduction is performed by a Differential Evolution algorithm, which belongs to Evolutionary Algorithms, and is widely used for global optimization problems. The experiments were carried out using a freely-available parallel English-Slovenian SVEZ-IJS corpus, which is lemmatised and annotated with morpho-syntactic description (MSD) tags. A set of baseline experiments is described and compared with experiments done on reduced MSD tags. The paper reports an improvement in translation results when compared to using words, lemmas and fully morpho-syntactically annotated words.

Keywords: statistical machine translation, morphology, data sparsity, optimization.

1 Introduction

Machine translation from one human language to another is a longstanding goal of computer science. The growing availability of bilingual, machine-readable text has stimulated interest in statistical methods. The use of statistical methods was first published by IBM in the early nineties [2]. The statistical machine translation (SMT) system acquires specific rules automatically from bilingual and monolingual text corpora. A number of SMT systems have been presented over recent years [15,7,13,21]. Some of them use word-based translation models. More sophisticates use complex phrase structures. In present research, word-based models are under consideration.

The historical enlargement of the EU has brought many new and challenging language pairings for machine translation. Slovenian - English is one of them [11,20].

Z. Vetulani and H. Uszkoreit (Eds.): LTC 2007, LNAI 5603, pp. 451–460, 2009.

2   Related Work

Many researchers have studied the effects of morphological features in highly inflected language on machine translation. Niessen and Ney explore morpho-syntactic restructuring to improve English-German alignment [13]. Their experiments show significant improvement in translation quality. They introduce the idea of hierarchical lexicon, where a word is represented at various levels of inflectional specificity, starting with the base form. Their models were able to infer translations of word forms from translation of other word forms of the same lemma. Their technique yielded a reduction in subjective semantic error rate. Popović and Ney [16] built on the concept of the hierarchical lexicon. They use a modified EM alignment algorithm to treat each of these representations as a hierarchy, with alignment possible at any of three levels. They evaluated the effects on a variety of baseline systems, producing at least modest improvements in every case. Use of the specific source language's knowledge to remove inflectional morphemes or function words that are not translatable, leads to a significantly reduced lexicon, and improved translations. Goldwater and Mc-Closky [6] set up a variety of experiments in Czech-English machine translation. They found that certain morphological tags were more useful when treating them as discrete input words, while others provided a greater benefit when attached directly to their lemmas. The phrase-based statistical machine translation was applied to Estonian-English language pair [8]. No morphological information was used. They concluded that some techniques for reducing the data sparsity are needed. Using morphs instead of words was examined on Finnish language, being the most difficult language to translate from or to. They did not obtain better results, but the proportion of untranslated words was reduced. The impact of morphology-based data transformation was evaluated in Spanish-English translation [9]. Word alignment error rate was remarkably reduced. The advantages of using lemmas in two-stage translation from Spanich tp English were reported [14]. State of the art and related work show that morphological information can be useful. Using all the morphological information available results in increased data sparsity and, consequently, error-full translations [10]. Morphology of highly inflected languages has been studied also in other applications [12]. The aim of this paper is to extract a useful subset of morphological features in source language automatically, by means of an evolutionary algorithm.

3   Statistical Machine Translation

The goal of statistical machine translation is to translate a source string of words $f = f_1 f_2 ... f_j ... f_J$ into a target string of words $e = e_1 e_2 ... e_i ... e_I$. The string with the highest probability is chosen from among all possible target strings, as given by the Bayes decision rule:

$$\hat{e} = \arg\max_e P(e|f) = \arg\max_e P(e)P(f|e) \ . \tag{1}$$

$P(e)$ is the language model of the target language, whereas $P(f|e)$ is the translation model. The arg max operation denotes the search for an output string in the target language. This paper concentrates on the translation model.

The translation model can be rewritten to

$$P(f|e) = \sum_a P(f, a|e),$$
(2)

where a is called alignment and represents mapping from the source words to target words. It is composed of different types of probability estimates. We expose just two of them, namely translation probability, and distortion probability.

Translation probability $t(f_j|e_i)$ is the probability of source word f_j being a translation of target word e_i.

Distortion probability $d(\Delta|\mathcal{A}(e_i), \mathcal{B}(f_j))$ is used to model word reordering. In general, words in the target language are not in the same order as in the source language. Words are mapped into classes before the training of the distortion probabilities is performed. There are two independent mappings, $\mathcal{A}$ for English words and $\mathcal{B}$ for Slovenian words. The mapping of words into classes is based on the assumption, that word displacement depends on certain features, which are common to many words.

In standard implementations f_i represents full word form and does not have any information about the fact that some different word forms are derivations of the same lemma and that some others share similar morphosyntactic features.

We are translating from a more inflected language to a less inflected one. The idea is to reduce word forms in the source language to a representation more suitable for training the translation and distortion probabilities.

4 Lemma-Tag Representation

The following information is available in the Slovenian part of the corpus:

- word form, i.e. the word as it appears in the sentence,
- lemma, i.e. a word in its canonical form, e.g., infinitive for verbs, nominative singular for regular nouns, etc.,
- part of speech (POS), e.g. noun, verb, adjective, adverb, etc.,
- additional morphosyntactic tags, i.e. gender (masculine, feminine or neuter), number (singular, plural or dual), etc.

In lemma-tag representation, the last two types of information are joined into a Morpho-Syntactic Description (MSD) of a word. We have lemma and MSD attached to it. The first letter of MSD encodes the POS. The letters following the POS give the values of the morphosyntactic features. For example, the MSD Ncfsa expands to POS Noun, type:common, Gender:feminine, Number:singular, Case:accusative. Figure 1 shows an example of an annotated sentence. The attribute ana contains the MSD. MSD tags are described in details in [3].

```
<seg lang="sl">
 <w ana="Ncnsn" lemma="meso">Meso</w>
 <c>,</c>
 <w ana="Afpnsa" lemma="namenjen">namenjeno</w>
 <w ana="Spsa">za</w>
 <w ana="Ncfsa" lemma="proizvodnja">proizvodnjo</w>
 <w ana="Afpfsg" lemma="konzerviran">konzervirane</w>
 <w ana="Ncfsg" lemma="hrana">hrane</w>
 <c>.</c>
</seg>
```

Fig. 1. Annotated sentence (No. 8005) from the Slovenian part of the SVEZ corpus. Translation into English: *Meat intended for the manufacture of preserved food.*

Following the lemma-tag representation, the word form f_j is replaced by its lemma and MSD tag. For example the word form proizvodnjo is replaced by proizvodnja[Ncfsa] (see Fig. 1). Replacing words with lemma-tag representations does not yet tackle the problem of data sparsity. Just the opposite, we have made it more evident, because of homographs. For example, in our experimental corpus, the word form je is most often replaced by biti[Vcip3s--n], but also by jesti[Vcip3s--n] and on[Pp3fsg--y-n]. Lemma-tag representation is a starting point for the reduction of MSDs.

5   Data Driven Optimization

The idea is to eliminate those features in MSD tag, which are unimportant for translation, by using a data-driven approach. We chose an evolutionary algorithm, named Differential Evolution (DE), which is a simple, yet powerful, algorithm for global optimization [17,18]. Differential evolution is so universal that it can be applied to practically any optimization problems, whether it is linear/nonlinear, continuous or combinatorial, or else a mixed-variable one [17,5]. Recently some improvements have been proposed [1].

DE is a population-based algorithm. DE creates new candidate solutions by combining the parent individual and several other individuals of the same population. A candidate replaces the parent only if it has better fitness value. During one generation for each individual, DE employs mutation and crossover operations to produce a trial individual. Then a selection operation is used to choose individuals for the next generation. There are many original DE strategies [5]. In this paper we used the strategy, named 'rand/1/bin' [17].

A DE algorithm is used to reduce the MSD tag. An individual is a translation system, trained on "somehow" reduced MSD tags. The reduction is done by DE mutation. Mutation uses two operations: addition and subtraction, based on the length of the MSD tag. The length of the MSD tag (denoted with *len*) equals the number of MSD features. The strategy 'rand/1/bin' works as follows:

$$len_{i,k} := len_{r_1,k} + F(len_{r_2,k} - len_{r_2,k}) \tag{3}$$

where k is the index of the MSD under consideration. r_1, r_2 and r_3 are three distinct indexes of individuals taken randomly. They are also different from the current i. F is a scaling factor, which is usually taken from interval $(0, 1]$. The value of len should be between 1 and max_{len} (the length of MSD with all tags). If it is under the lower bound, it is set to be 0. If it is over the upper bound, it is set to be max_{len}.

The reduction of MSD tags is restricted to be performed from right to left. The interdependence of morpho-syntactic features is more complex, but with some simplification it can be asserted that more-significant features are positioned before less-significant ones.

A common choice for automatic evaluation of machine translation is Bleu metric. We decided to use it as fitness function of DE. Bleu is calculated on held-out data (development set), which is neither part of the train set nor the test set. The advantage of a population-based algorithm is its robustness. It is less probable that it get trapped into local optima. Individuals of the initial population (i.e. trial translation systems) are spread over the whole search space.

6   Experiments

The experiments were performed on the SVEZ-IJS parallel English-Slovenian corpus [4]. It contains $2\times$ 5 million words of EU legal text. The corpus was lemmatised and tagged with MSDs. The inflectional nature of the Slovenian language is evident from Table 1.

Table 1. Statistics of the training set

	Slovenian	English
Sentences	98,291	98,291
Words (tokens)	614,997	694,585
Word forms (types)	63,575	39,189
-singletons	31,517	20,013
Lemmas	44,916	–
-singletons	24,839	–
MSDs	1,024	–

The corpus was split into training, development and test sets in the ratio 8:1:1. The test and development sets (each 12,847 sentences long) were taken at regular intervals from the corpus. In the training set we only used sentences shorter than 16 words because of computational complexity. No limit regarding sentence length was set for sentences in the development and test sets.

Translation model training was performed using the program GIZA++ [15] with 10 iterations for each of five models. The models are indexed according to their increasing complexity in training. The parameters are transferred from one model to an other, for example from Model 2 to Model 3. It means that the final parameter values of Model 2 are the initial parameter values of Model 3. Models 4 and 5 are the most sophisticated.

Both vocabularies (English and Slovenian) contained all the words of the training corpus. English words were mapped into 100 automatically built classes (see mapping $\mathcal{A}$ in Section 3). Slovenian words were mapped into classes, based on MSDs, when possible (see mapping $\mathcal{B}$ in Section 3). Each MSD defined it's own class. When MSD tags were absent (in the first and second experiments), Slovenian words were clustered automatically into 1,000 classes.

The language model for the English language was a word-based back-off trigram model. The perplexity on the test set was 198.

Table 2. Data sparsity reduction in the Slovenian part of the corpus

Modelling unit	Types	MSDs
Word	63,575	0
Lemma	44,916	0
Lemma+POS	47,800	12
Lemma+full MSD	83,237	1,042
Lemma+reduced MSD	53,565	105

Table 3. Translation results

Modelling unit	WER [%]	Bleu [%]
Word	52.3	34.44
Lemma	52.6	34.21
Lemma+POS	53.2	34.23
Lemma+full MSD	53.7	33.83
Lemma+reduced MSD	51.0	35.77

Table 4. Translation results with only one POS reduced

POS	full length of MSD	reduced MSD length	Bleu [%]
N	8	4	34.95
V	15	3	34.41
A	9	3	35.42
S	4	4	33.83
P	13	4	34.27
M	9	3	34.22

Five experiments were performed. During the set-ups of each experiment we counted the number of different units (i.e. types), and the number of different MSDs (see Table 2). The results of five experiments are presented in Table 3. In each experiment word error rate (WER) and the Bleu score on the test set were computed. The first row reports those result obtained using words (full word forms) as modelling units. 55% of word forms were only seen once in the training corpus (see Table 1), and it is obvious that learning the correct translations is difficult for many words.

Words are often derived from a much smaller set of lemmas. In the second and third experiments lemmas were used instead of full-word forms (only in the Slovenian part of the corpus). In these experiments different word forms, derived from the same lemma are considered equivalent. The number of types decreased considerably (see Table 2). When using lemmas, we also have less than half as many singletons as in the first experiment (see Table 1). Because data sparsity was reduced to a great extent, we expected improved translation results. Surprisingly, the results (in terms of WER and Bleu) become slightly worse (see second row in Table 3). We reduced data sparsity, but we also lost some information relevant for translation.

In the third experiment, POS tags were attached to lemmas. The results did not improve, when compared with lemma-based models. Using only POS tags is insufficient for determining the information relevant for translation.

In the next experiment, lemmas with full MSDs were used. The worst results were then obtained. In this experiment the corpus was the scarcest. A full MSD adds some for translation redundant information.

The above experiments confirm the hypothesis, that only some MSD tags are relevant for translation. In the last experiment the subset of MSD tags, considered relevant for translation, was determined by a DE algorithm.

DE is a population based algorithm. The initial population was generated uniformly at random. The population contained 50 individuals. The fitness value was a Bleu score on the development set. Thirty generations were evaluated. Figure 2 shows Bleu scores (on test and development sets) for all individuals in the initial and final population. It can be seen that the population moves (slowly) to the upper right-hand corner.

The last row in Table 3 contains the best Bleu test set score from among all individuals in the final population. The results show that it outperformed all previous experiments. The relative improvement in Bleu score is 3.86%. We should keep in mind that differences in Bleu scores between all experiments are relatively small. The number of different MSDs reduced, approx., to tenth the original set. If the translation expert were to look at the reduced tag set, he/she will probably disagree that these features are the most relevant for translation. We have extracted them using the data-driven approach without expert knowledge about the language pair under consideration. The aim was to improve translation quality. Table 4 shows the influence of reduced MSD tags for each POS separately. In each experiment we reduced only the MSDs for selected POS. The remaining units got full MSDs. The results of most important POS are presented: Noun (N), Verb (V), Adjective (A), Adposition (S), Pronoun (P), and Numeral (M). We can see that the biggest contribution was obtained by the reduction of Adjective (A).

Table 5. Example of translations obtained by using different modelling units

---

Sentence No. 444
f (input sentence): KER SO BILI V ALBANIJI ZABELEŽENI PRIMERI KOLERE
e (ref. transl.): WHEREAS CASES OF CHOLERA HAVE BEEN RECORDED IN ALBANIA

Modelling unit: **word**
f: KER SO BILI V ALBANIJI ZABELEŽENI PRIMERI KOLERE
e: WHEREAS ESTABLISHED TO EXAMPLES OF CHOLERA ACUTELY WITHDRAWN

Modelling unit: **lemma**
f: KER BITI BITI V ALBANIJA ZABELEŽEN PRIMER KOLERA
e: WHEREAS IN ALBANIA BE REPORTED EXAMPLES OF CHOLERA

Modelling unit: **lemma +POS**
f: KER[C] BITI[V] BITI[V] V[S] ALBANIJA[N] ZABELEŽEN[A] PRIMER[N]
KOLERA[N]
e: WHEREAS IN ALBANIA REPORTED EXAMPLES OF CHOLERA

Modelling unit: **lemma +full MSD**
f: KER[CSS] BITI[VCIP3P--N] BITI[VCPS-PMA] V[SPSL] ALBANIJA[NPFSL]
ZABELEŽEN[AFPFDA] PRIMER[NCFDA] KOLERA[NCFSG-]
e: WHEREAS THEY HAVE BEEN ACUTELY IN ACKNOWLEDGMENT OF CHOLERA UNKNOWN

Modelling unit: **lemma + reduced MSD (by DE)**
f: KER[CS] BITI[VCIP3] BITI[VCP] V[SPS] ALBANIJA[N] ZABELEŽEN[A]
PRIMER[NCFD] KOLERA[NCFS]
e: WHEREAS IT HAS BEEN REPORTED EXAMPLES OF CHOLERA IN ALBANIA

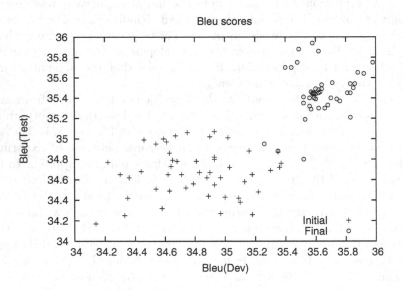

Fig. 2. Initial and final populations

An example of translations obtained in different experiments is given in Table 5. It can be seen, that we obtained comprehensible translations using lemmas, lemmas+POS, and lemmas+reduced MSD.

7 Conclusion

In this work we studied translation from the more-inflected Slovenian language to the less-inflected English language. We have presented an approach for the data-driven reduction of MSD tags, with the aim of improving statistical translation (by data-sparsity reduction). The reduction of MSDs was performed by an evolutionary algorithm. No language specific rules were used. The same approach could be used for other pairs of languages with the proviso that we translate from more-inflected language to less-inflected language.

The results of our experiments show the existence of an optimal subset of MSDs. Perhaps we did not discovered the most optimal one yet, but we believe we are approaching it. This approach is time-consuming, because we used the program code of SMT as a whole. Future work should focus on the use of parallel computing systems.

References

1. Brest, J., Mauèec, M.S.: Population Size Reduction for the Differential Evolution Algorithm. Applied Intelligence 29(3), 228–247 (2008)
2. Brown, P.F., Pietra, S.A.D., Pietra, V.J.D., Mercer, R.L.: The Mathematics of Statistical Machine Translation: Parameter Estimation. Computa Linguistics 19(2), 263–311 (1993)
3. Erjavec, T. (ed.): Specifications and Notation for MULTEXT-East Laxicon Encoding. Tech. rep., Institute Jožef Stefan, Ljubljana (2001)
4. Erjavec, T.: The English-Slovene ACQUIS corpus. In: Proceedings of LREC (2006)
5. Feoktistov, V.: Differential Evolution. In: Search of Solutions, Springer, New York (2006)
6. Goldwater, S., McClosky, D.: Improving Statistical MT through Morphological Analysis. In: Proceedings of the Conference on EMNLP, Vancouver, Canada (2005)
7. Čerjek, M., Cuřin, J., Havelka, J.: Czech-English dependency-based machine translation. In: Proceedings of the European Chapter of the ACL, vol. 29 (2003)
8. Fishel, M., Kaalep, H.-L., Muischnek, K.: Estonian-English Statistical Machine translation: the First Results. In: Proceedings of the NODALIDA, pp. 278–283 (2007)
9. Popović, M., de Gispert, A., Deepa Gupta, A., Lambert, P., Ney, H., Marino, J.B., Federico, M., Banchs, R.: Morpho-syntactic information for automatic error analysis of statistical machine translation output. Proceedings of the Workshop on Statistical Machine Translation, HLT-NAACL, New York, NY, USA, pp. 1–6 (2006)
10. Mauèec, M.S., Brest, J., Kaèiè, Z.: Statistical machine translation from Slovenian to English. CIT. J. Comput. Inf. Technol. 15(1), 47–59 (2007)
11. Mauèec, M.S., Brest, J., Kaèiè, Z.: Statistical Alignment Models in Machine Translation from Slovenian to English. Electrotechnical Review 73(5) (2006)
12. Mauèec, M.S., Brest, J., Rotovnik, T., Kaèiè, Z.: Using Data-Driven Sub-Word Units In Language Model Of Highly Inflective Slovenian Language. International Journal of Pattern Recognition and Artificial Intelligence (accepted)
13. Niessen, S., Ney, H.: Improving SMT Quality with Morpho-Syntactic Analysis. In: Proceedings of the 20th International Conference on Computational Linguistics, Saarbrucken, German (2000)

14. Pérez, A., Torres, I., Casacuberta, F.: Towards the improvement of statistical translation models using linguistic features. In: Salakoski, T., Ginter, F., Pyysalo, S., Pahikkala, T. (eds.) FinTAL 2006. LNCS (LNAI), vol. 4139, pp. 716–725. Springer, Heidelberg (2006)
15. Och, F.J., Ney, H.: Statistical Alignment Models. Computational Linguistics 29(1) (2003)
16. Popović, M., Ney, H.: Improving Word Alignment Quality using Morpho-syntactic Information. In: Proceedings of 20th International Conference on Computational Linguistics (CoLing), Geneva, Switzerland (2004)
17. Price, K.V., Storn, R.L., Lampinen, J.: Differential Evolution, A Practical Approach to Global Optimization. Springer, Heidelberg (2005)
18. Storn, R., Price, K.: Differential Evolution – A Simple and Efficient Heuristic for Global Optimization over Continuous Spaces. Journal of Global Optimization 11, 341–359 (1997)
19. Virpioja, S., Väyrynen, J.J., Creutz, M., Sadeniemi, M.: Morphology-aware statistical machine translation based on morphs induced in an unsupervised manner. In: Proceedings of the MT Summit XI, Copenhagen, Denmark, pp. 491–498 (2007)
20. Vičič, J., Erjavec, T.: The beginning is always hard: training of machine translation from Slovene to English (in Slovenian lang.). In: Proceedings of the Language Technologies Conference (2002)
21. Vogel, S., Zhang, Y., Huang, F., Tribble, A., Venugopal, A., Zhao, B., Waibel, A.: The CMU Statistical Machine Translation System. In: Proceedings of the Machine Translation Summit IX, New Orleans, Louisiana, USA, vol. 29 (2003)

Semi-automatic Creation of a Dictionary of Nominal Compounds

Tomasz Stępień and Bartosz Podlejski

Wrocław University
tpj@poczta.onet.pl,
bartosz.podlejski@gmail.com

Abstract. This paper presents a method of semi-automatic creation of a dictionary of nominal compounds. For each English expression, several possible Polish translations are generated and the number of occurrences on the Internet is checked for each of them separately. The most frequent form is supposed to be the right one, which is proved by analysis of ca. 500 phrases.

Keywords: machine translation, dictionary creation, nominal compounds, noun chains.

1 Introduction

In this paper we present a method of semi-automatic creation of dictionary of nominal compounds, which can be used in machine translation systems. The quality of translation provided by transfer-based systems relies heavily on the size and correctness (coverage) of dictionaries used. Especially, the coverage of phrase dictionary is important since the process of coining new multiword terms (of various degree of idiomaticity) from already existing words is extremely productive. Creating and developing a dictionary of phrases that would follow constant changes occurring in language with little, if any, human contribution seems therefore to be a desirable goal.

This paper is organised as follows. First, we make some theoretical insight into English nominal compounds and their Polish counterparts. In section 3 we present the developed method in some detail and in section 4 we describe the experiment in which the method was tested. Finally, we make concluding remarks and discuss prospects of further research.

2 English Nominal Compounds in Translation into Polish

The terms in focus here are nominal compounds or noun chains (NC, henceforth). They occur in English very often, presenting the whole range of idiomaticity: from unstable and generally compositional in meaning to fixed and usually conventional[1]. Translating the latter automatically is obviously much more difficult (if at all possible)

---

[1] These terms should be understood as in [3] and [4].

Z. Vetulani and H. Uszkoreit (Eds.): LTC 2007, LNAI 5603, pp. 461–469, 2009.

but even the former pose some difficulty when the target language is highly inflectional. The meaning of such a phrase remains compositional but its components can be combined morphologically in more than one way. Moreover, the components usually have many translations, which leads to a potentially great number of candidate expressions.

In this paper we focus on unmodified two-word noun chains, which are the most frequent type of nominal compounds[2]. A two-word English NC consists of a head and a modifier [2]; as a rule the head comes second. In Polish expressions equivalent to NCs, the head receives the nominative case (in the canonical form) and undergoes declension when used in texts; the modifier may come before or after the head and may have different forms, including that of denominal adjective. The possible structures are as follows:

1. the head + the modifier in the genitive case, e.g. *rada miasta* 'city council'
2. the head + denominal adjective of the modifier, e.g. *komitet obywatelski* 'citizens committee'
3. denominal adjective of the modifier + the head, e.g. *nocny pociąg* 'night train'
4. the head + preposition + the modifier, e.g. *raport z autopsji* 'autopsy report'.

Although no relevant frequency study is known to us, we claim that the first three patterns are most common. However, it is not possible to predict the proper form and, obviously, the correct translation of the components of a given NC. In spite of this, most of the MT systems produced today deal with translating unrecognised NCs with the use of one, arbitrarily adopted, procedure: they combine the first translations of the components according to the pattern (1) listed above. (It is a common practice to create a dictionary in such a way that the first translation of a source word should be appropriate in most of contexts, which is obviously not necessarily true.) However, as we know, a wrongly chosen expression sounds strange and may result in a low evaluation of the translation by the user. We therefore believe that it is plausible to make an attempt at translating NCs more correctly. Below we present a system that generates possible Polish translations of English NCs and evaluates them returning the most likely target expression(s).

3   Translation and Evaluation Procedure

Our method of phrase dictionary creation requires using specially designed software whose task is to analyse large volumes of texts in a source language (here, English), detect noun chains and translate them correctly into a target language (here, Polish) adopting the proper morphological form. Obviously, it may only succeed when the source expressions are compositional in meaning and when their components are already stored in a bilingual dictionary accessible to the system. The choice of the translation is done solely on the basis of estimated number of its occurrences in a corpus of the target language. Theoretically, it could be any corpus but since the frequency is the only criterion applied, the worldwide web must be used for the sake of statistical accuracy.

---

[2] In a sample of over 28,000 NCs extracted from the Penn Treebank corpus, ca. 89% are two-word phrases.